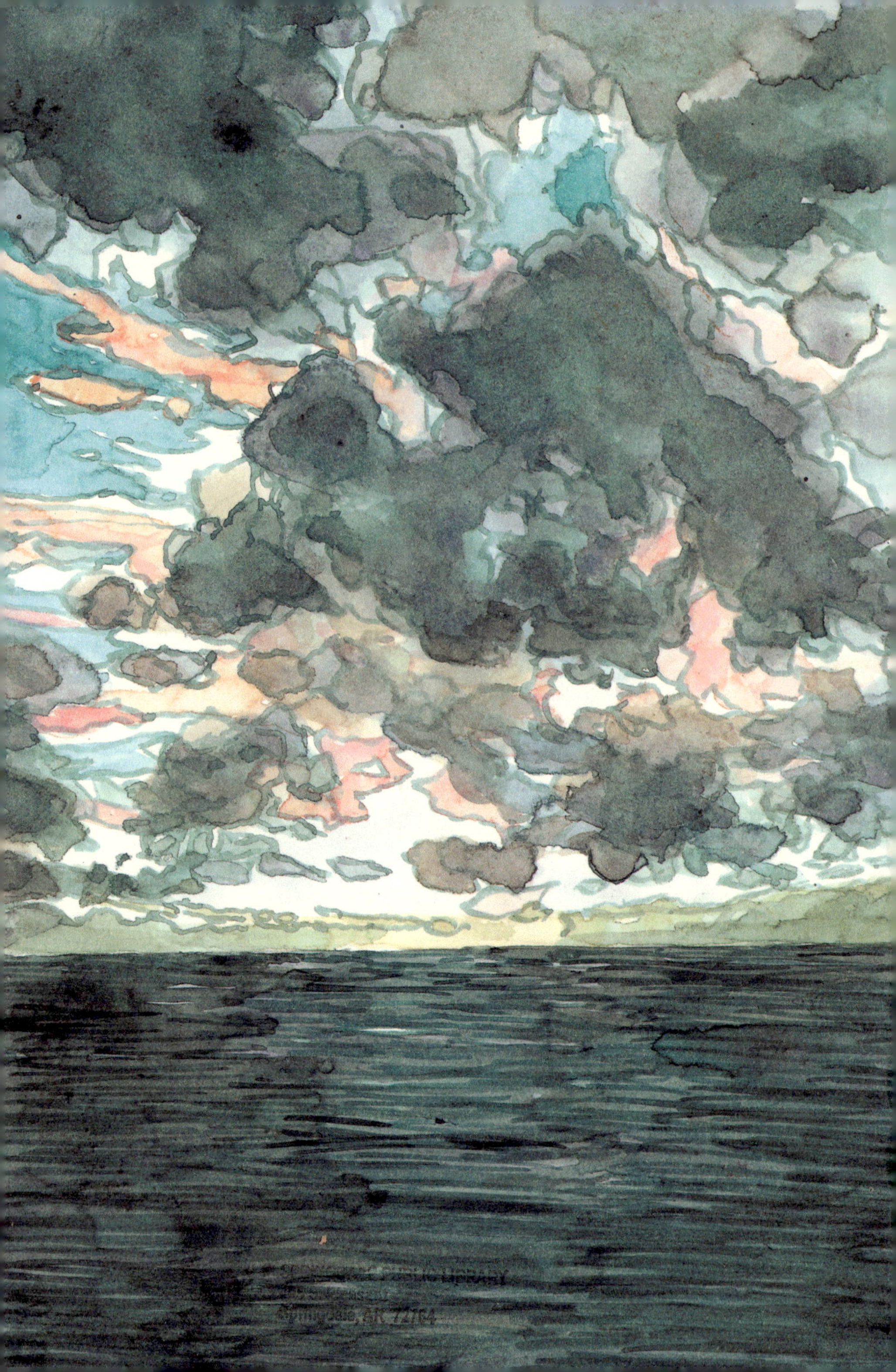

CHILDREN OF THE SEA

DAISUKE IGARASHI

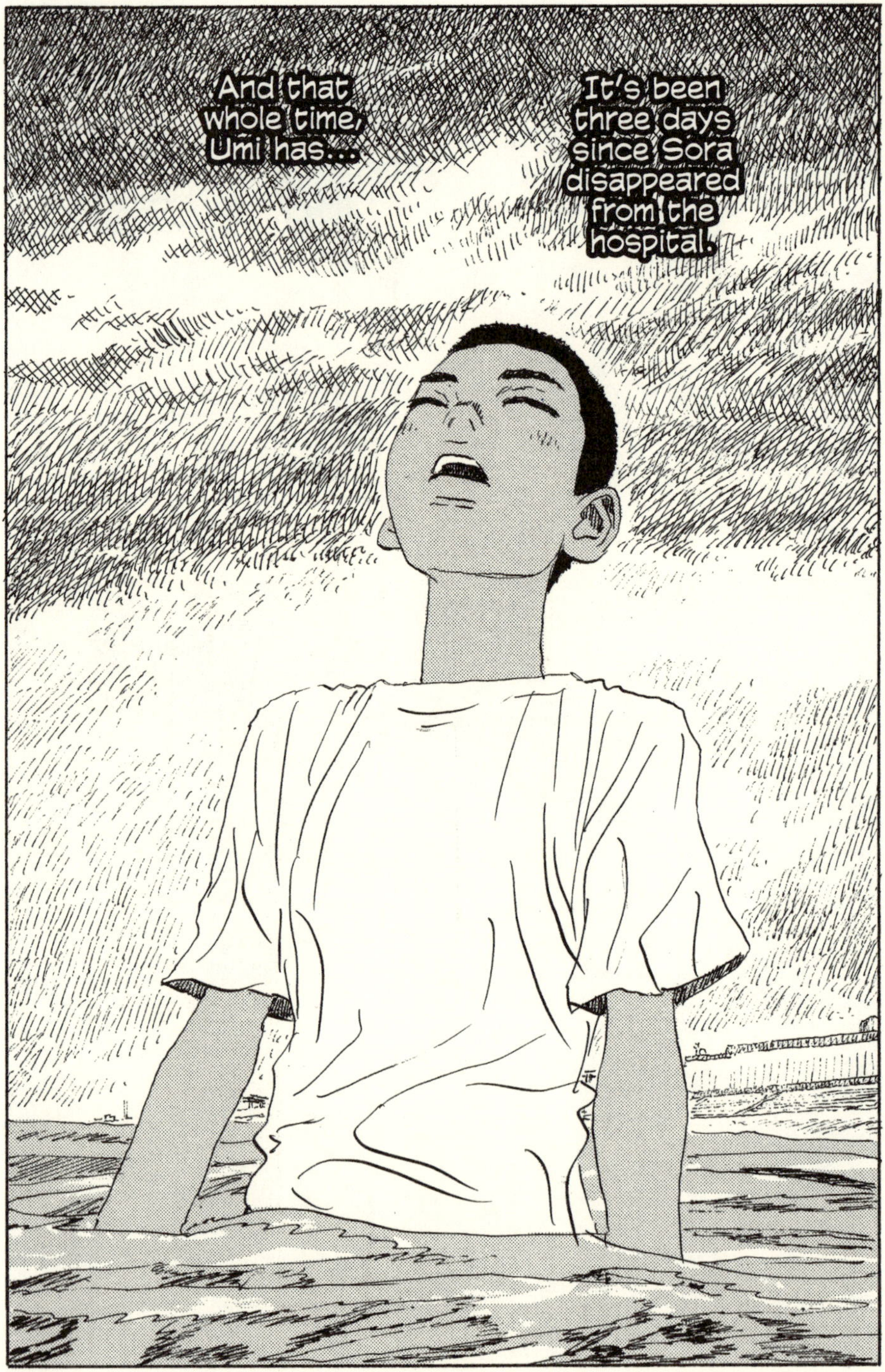
It's been three days since Sora disappeared from the hospital.
And that whole time, Umi has...

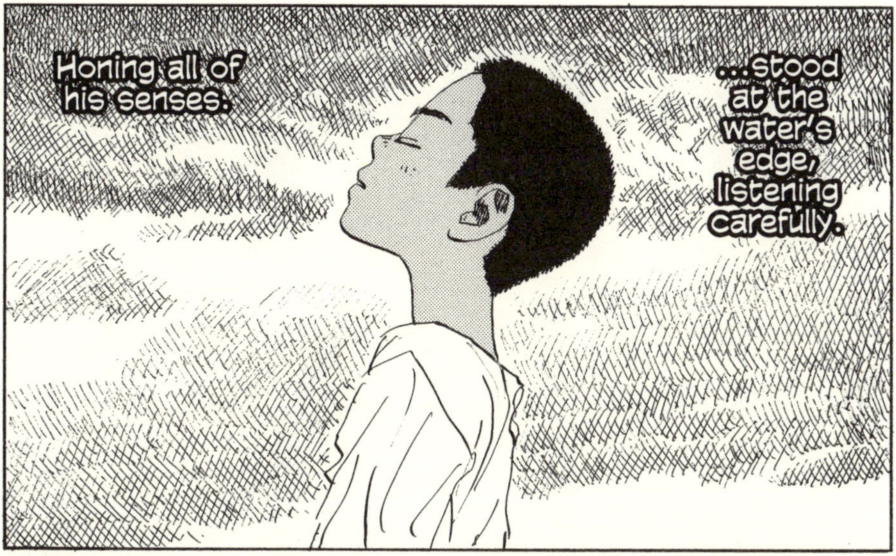
...stood at the water's edge, listening carefully.
Honing all of his senses.
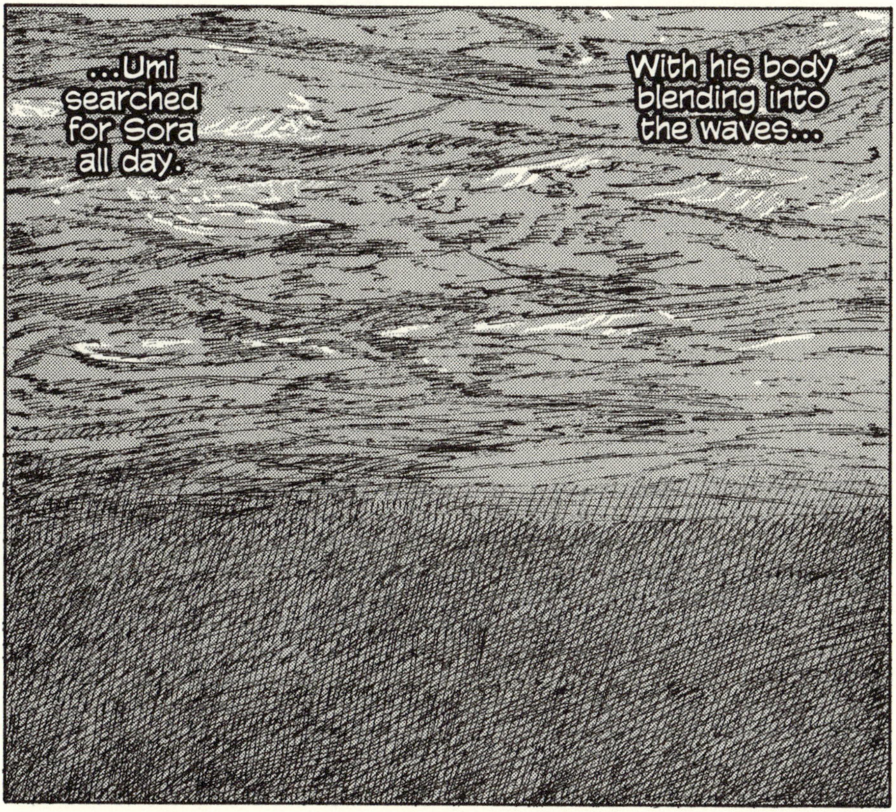
With his body blending into the waves...
...Umi searched for Sora all day.

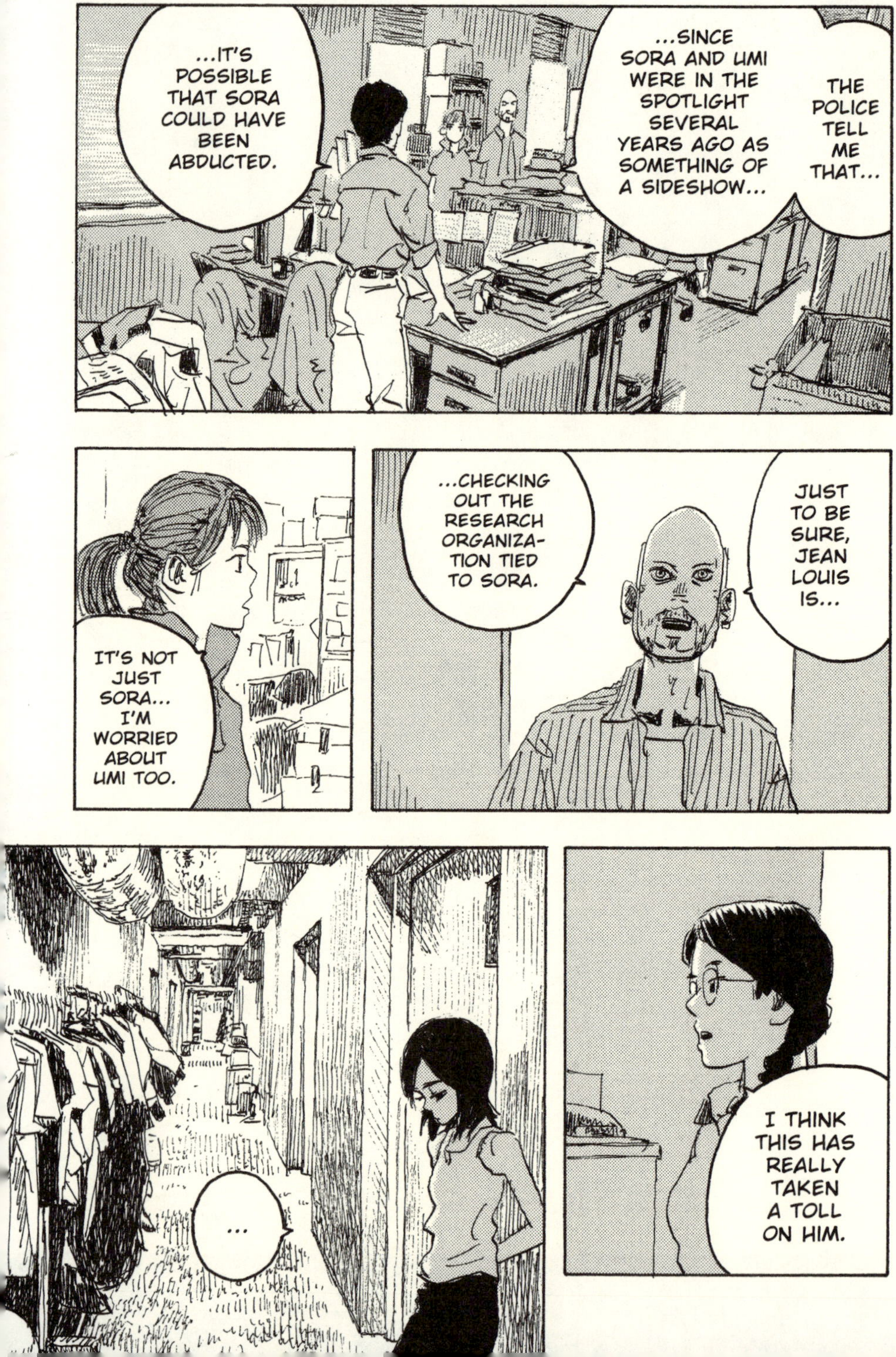
THE POLICE TELL ME THAT...
...SINCE SORA AND UMI WERE IN THE SPOTLIGHT SEVERAL YEARS AGO AS SOMETHING OF A SIDESHOW...
...IT'S POSSIBLE THAT SORA COULD HAVE BEEN ABDUCTED.
JUST TO BE SURE, JEAN LOUIS IS...
...CHECKING OUT THE RESEARCH ORGANIZATION TIED TO SORA.
IT'S NOT JUST SORA... I'M WORRIED ABOUT UMI TOO.
I THINK THIS HAS REALLY TAKEN A TOLL ON HIM.
...

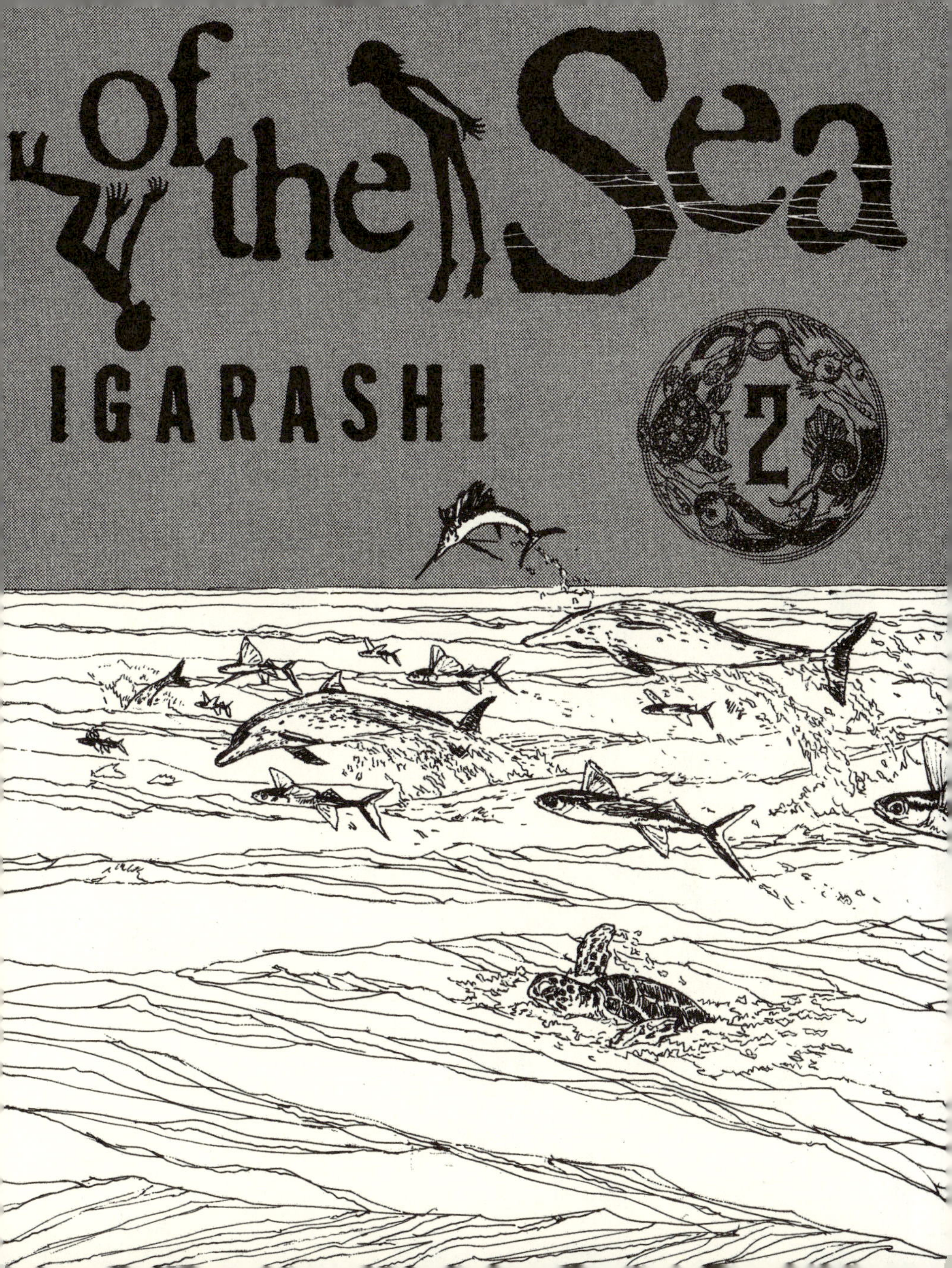
of the Sea
IGARASHI
2

Children

DAISUKE

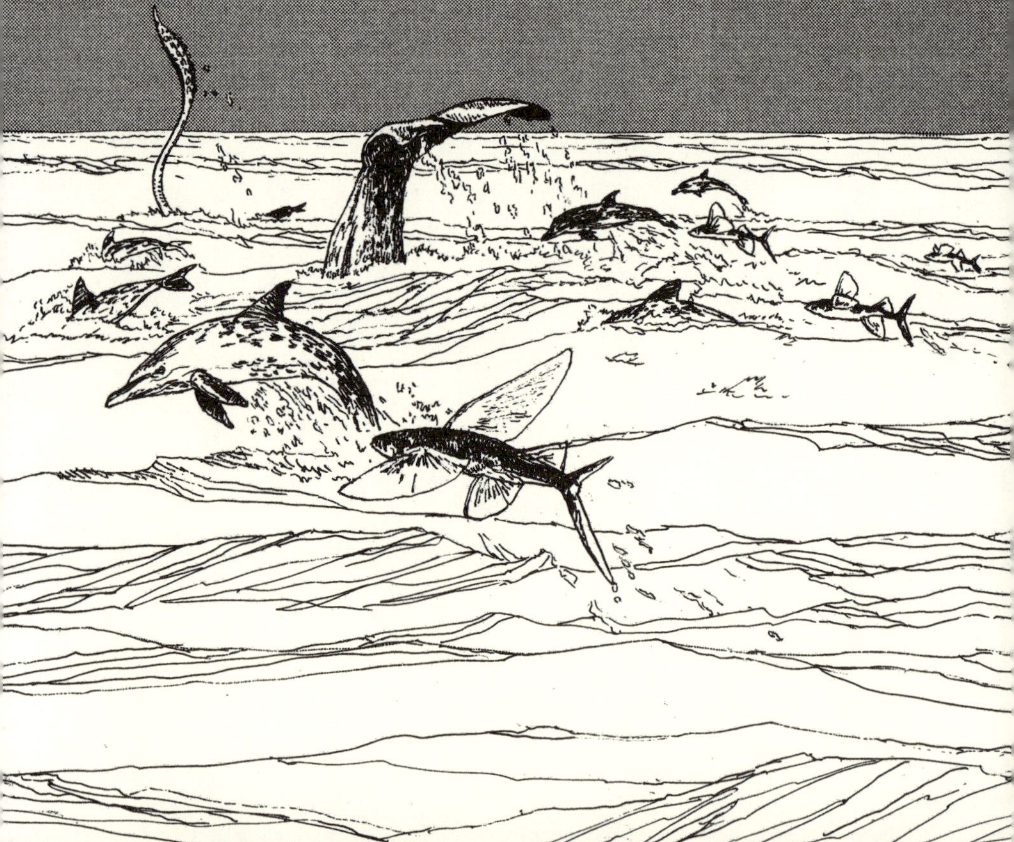

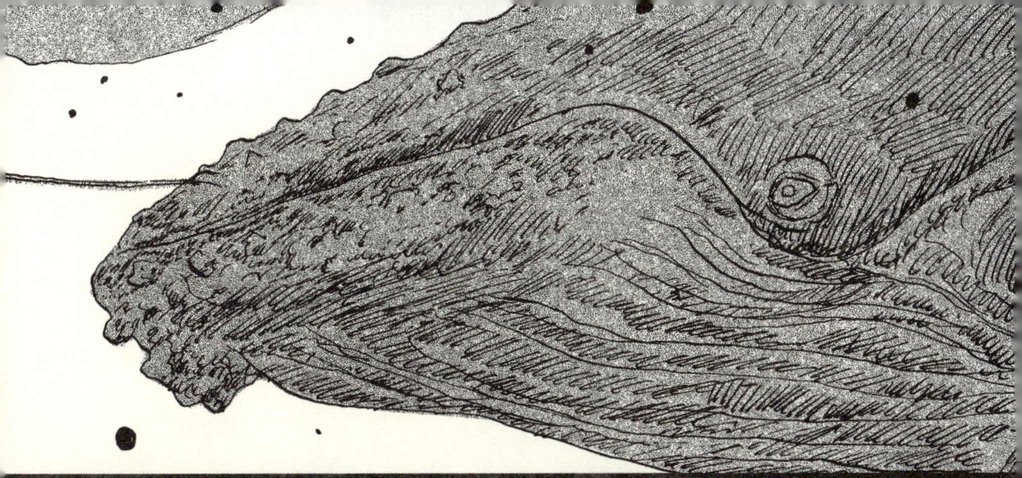

(to eat...?) Umi and Sora.

Children of the Sea

THE STORY THUS FAR

On the first day of summer vacation, Ruka gets in trouble for fighting with a classmate. She's feeling alone with nowhere to go when she meets a boy named Umi. Captivated by his swimming ability, she learns that Umi, along with another boy named Sora, were raised by dugongs.

Now that Ruka has met the boys, strange things start to happen. A mysterious shooting star, the feeling that there's something unknown out there...

The three of them witness a whale shark turn into light and disappear in the ocean. Right after that, Sora's body also starts to glow and fish gather around him. After the incident, Sora is hospitalized but suddenly vanishes from his room. Meanwhile, there are reports from around the world of fish disappearing from the oceans.

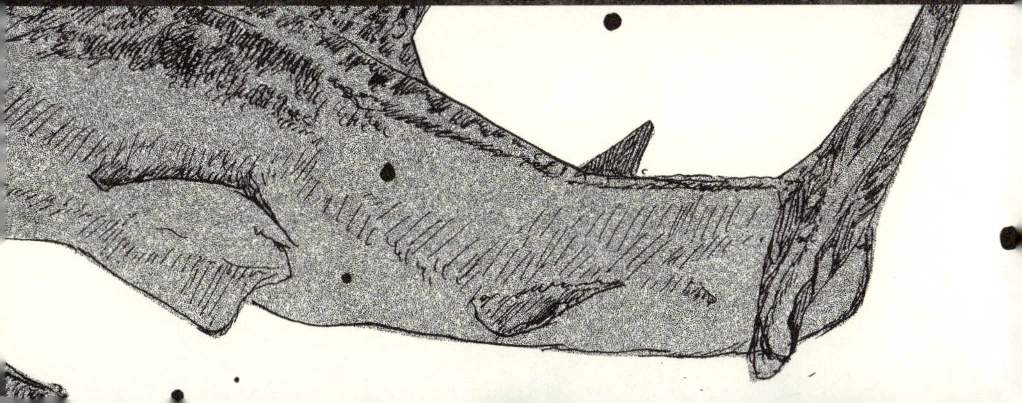

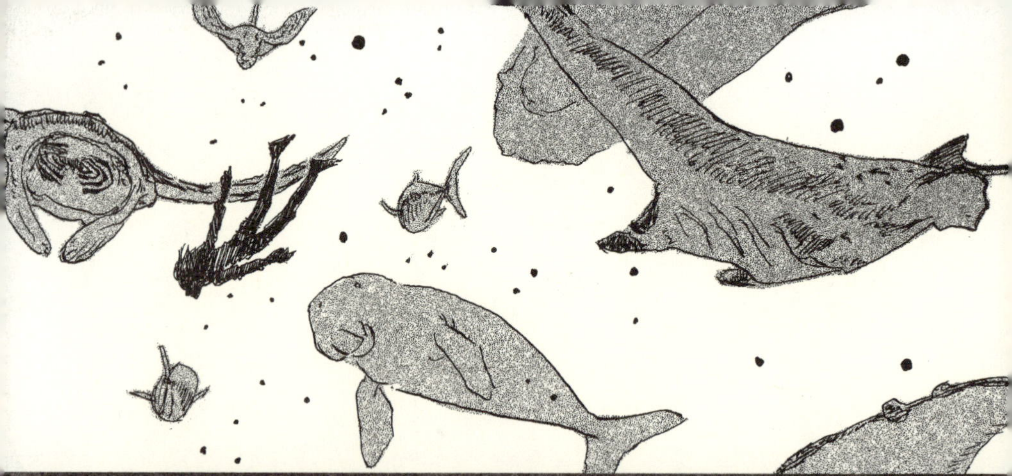

They gather around to see

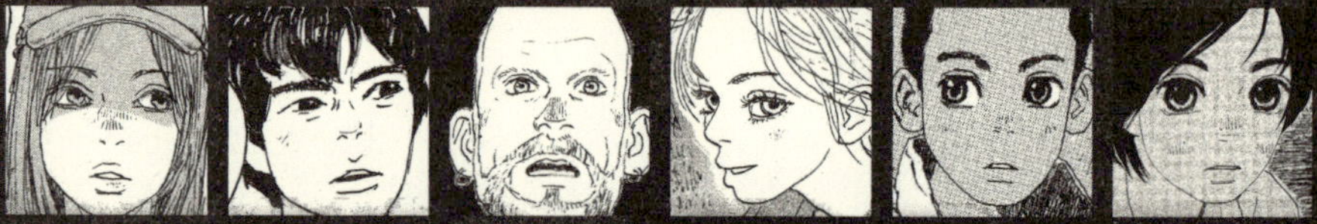

KANAKO AZUMI

Ruka's mother. She used to work at the aquarium.

MASA-AKI AZUMI

Ruka's father. He works at the aquarium.

JIM CUSACK

A marine biologist. He acts as Sora and Umi's guardian.

SORA

Raised as Umi's older brother. He is physically weak and is often in the hospital.

UMI

A boy found off the Philippine coast over ten years ago. The aquarium has been taking care of him and Sora. His skin is susceptible to dryness.

RUKA AZUMI

A middle school student who has a hard time articulating her feelings and tends to use her fists and not her words. Her parents are separated and she lives with her mother.

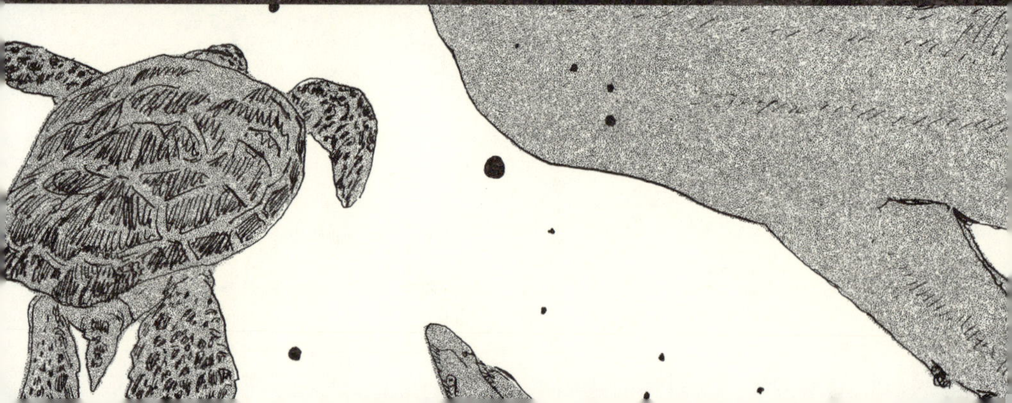

UNKNOWN OCEANS

Children of the Sea

TABLE of CONTENTS

2

Chapter 9: Isana

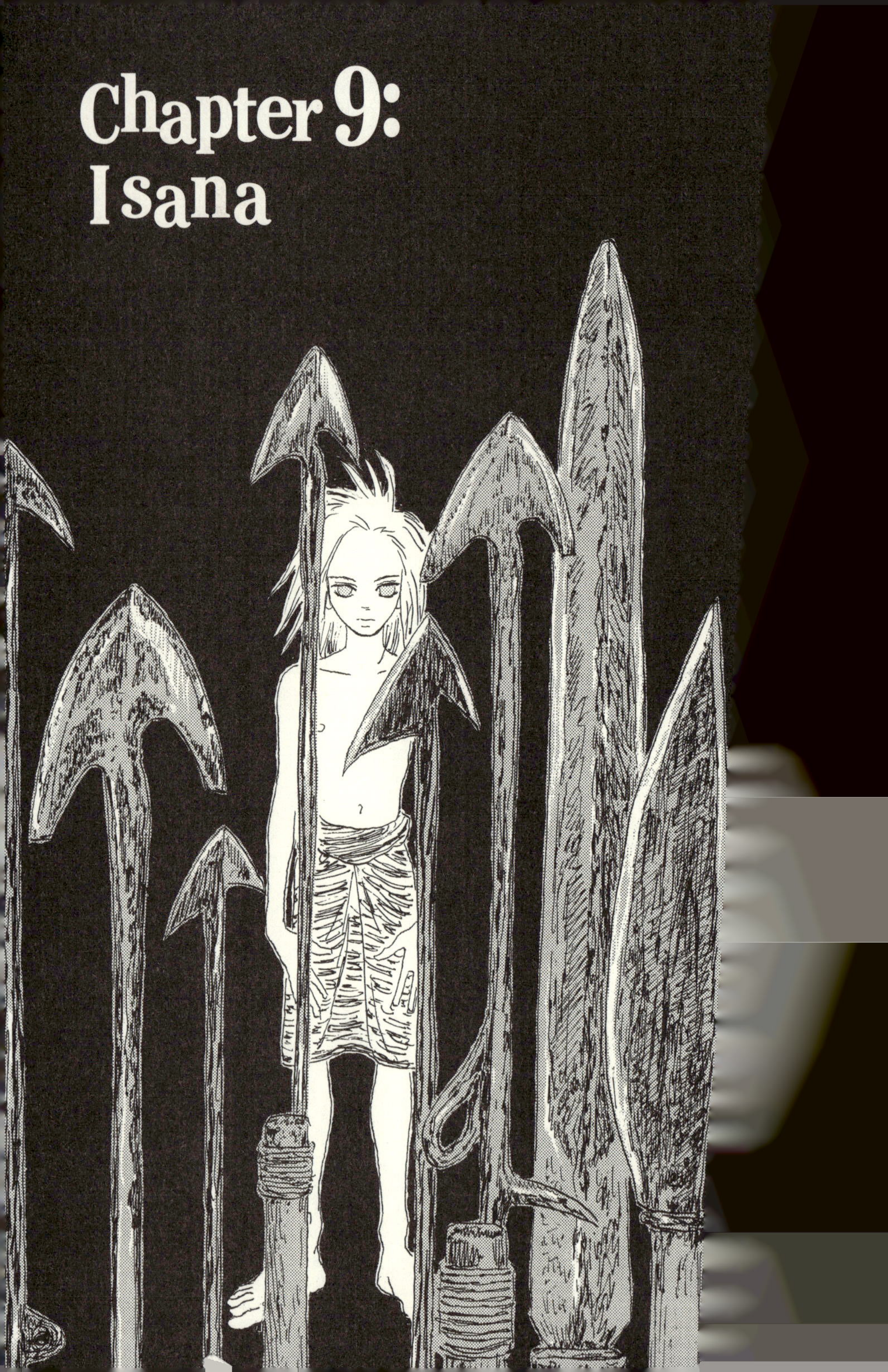

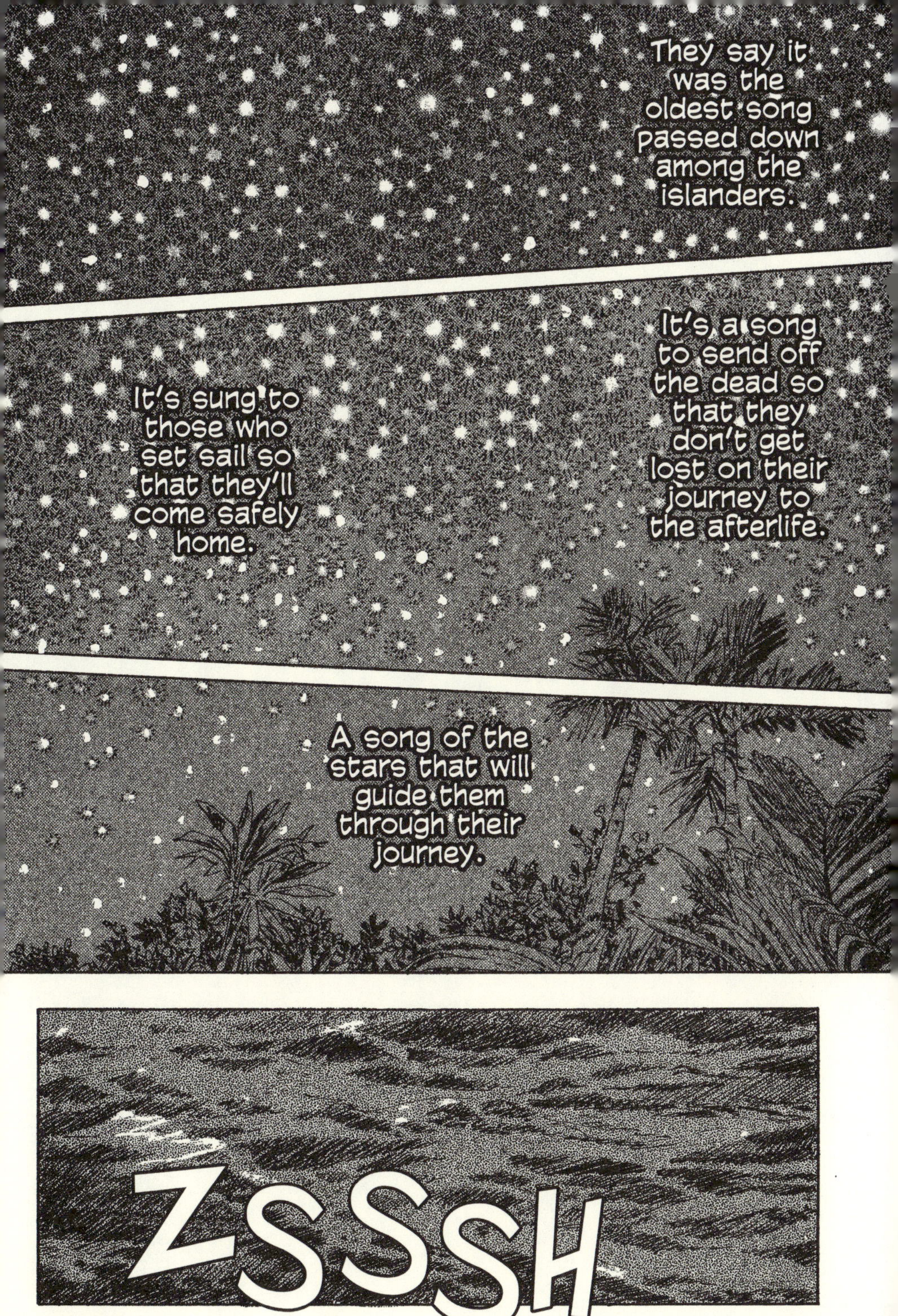
They say it was the oldest song passed down among the islanders.
It's a song to send off the dead so that they don't get lost on their journey to the afterlife.
It's sung to those who set sail so that they'll come safely home.
A song of the stars that will guide them through their journey.
ZSSSH

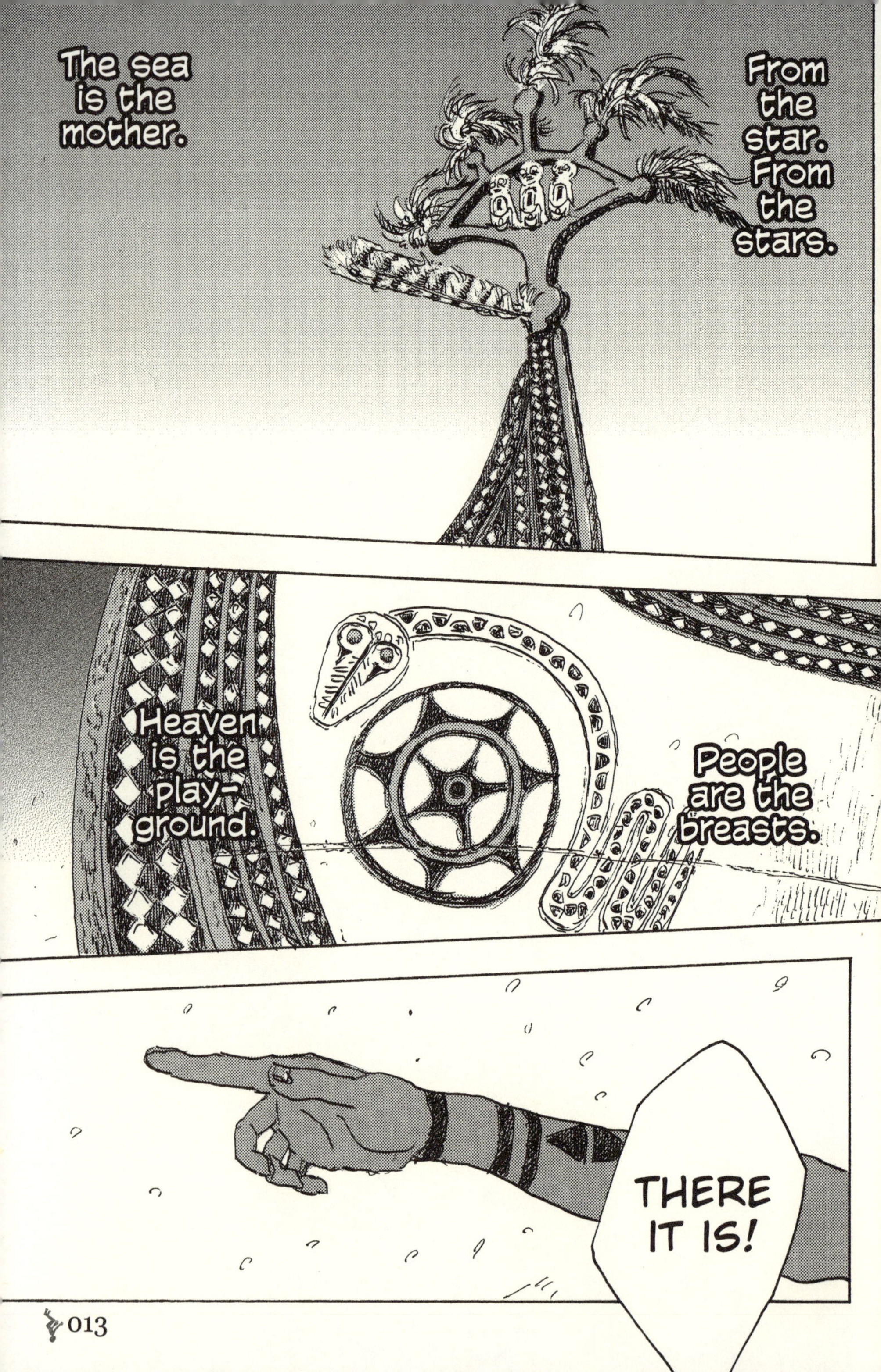
From the star. From the stars.
The sea is the mother.
People are the breasts.
Heaven is the play-ground.
THERE IT IS!

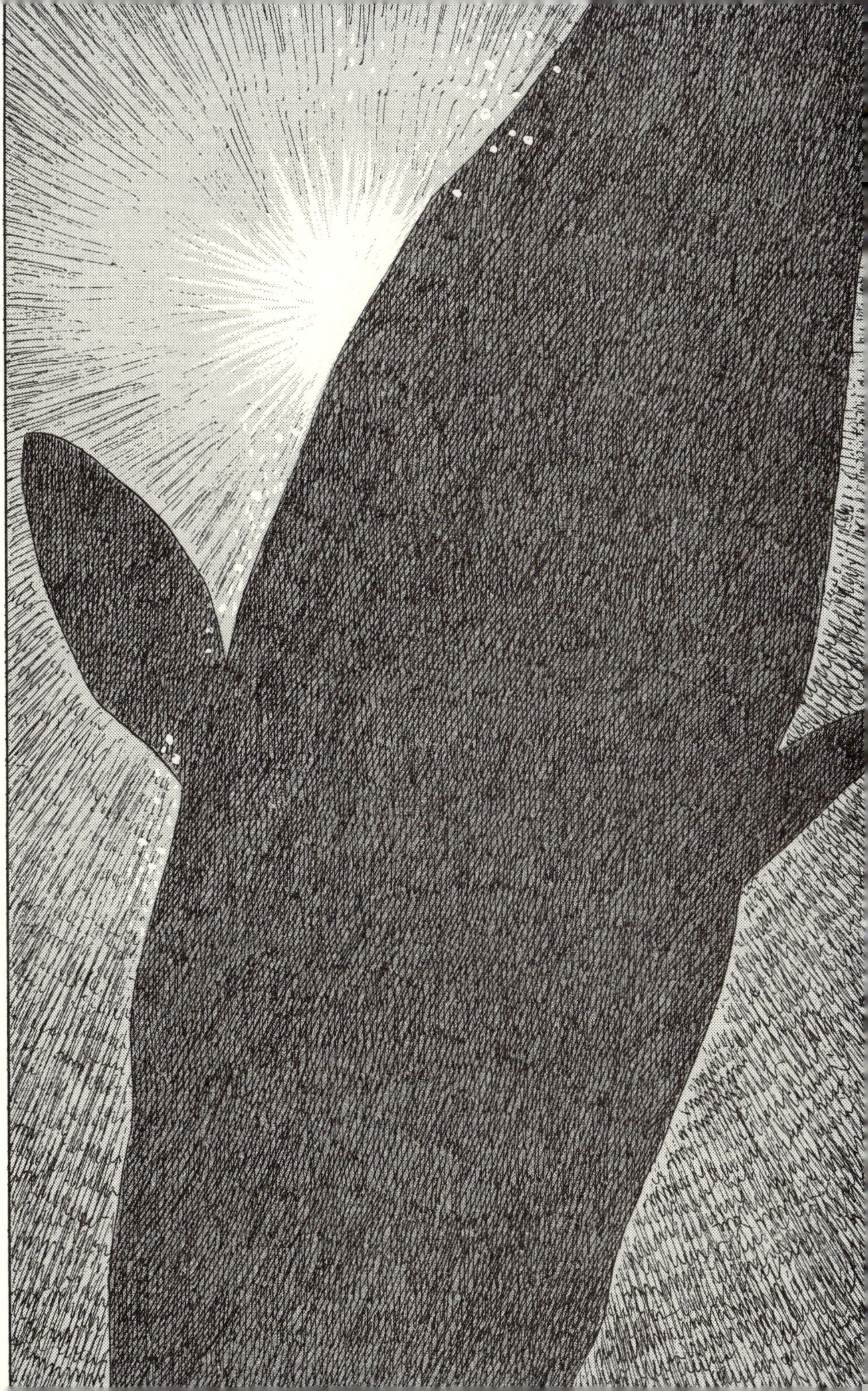

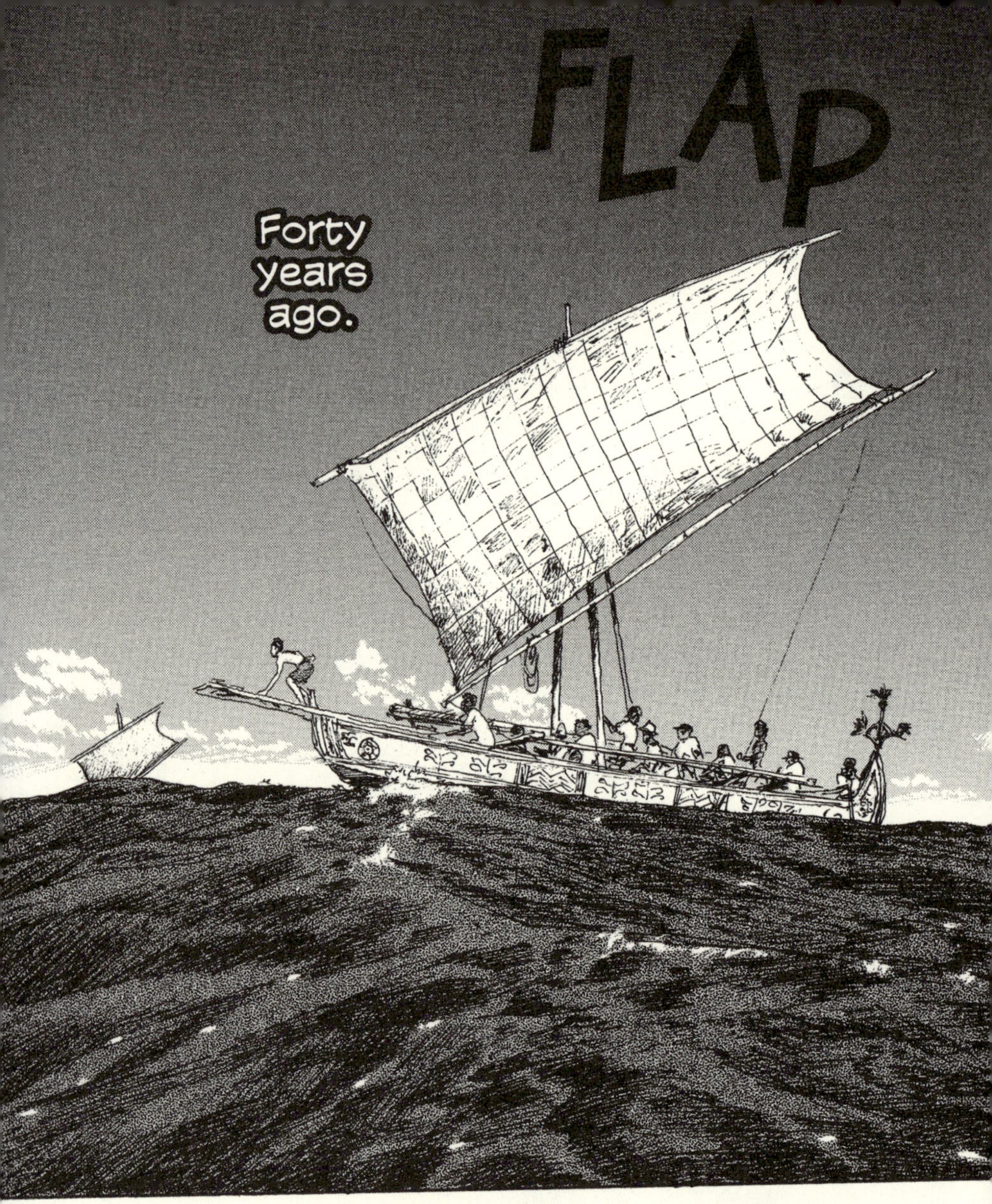
FLAP
Forty years ago.
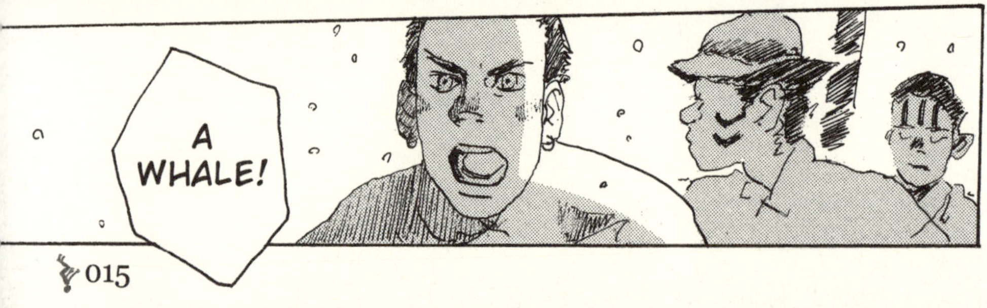
A WHALE!

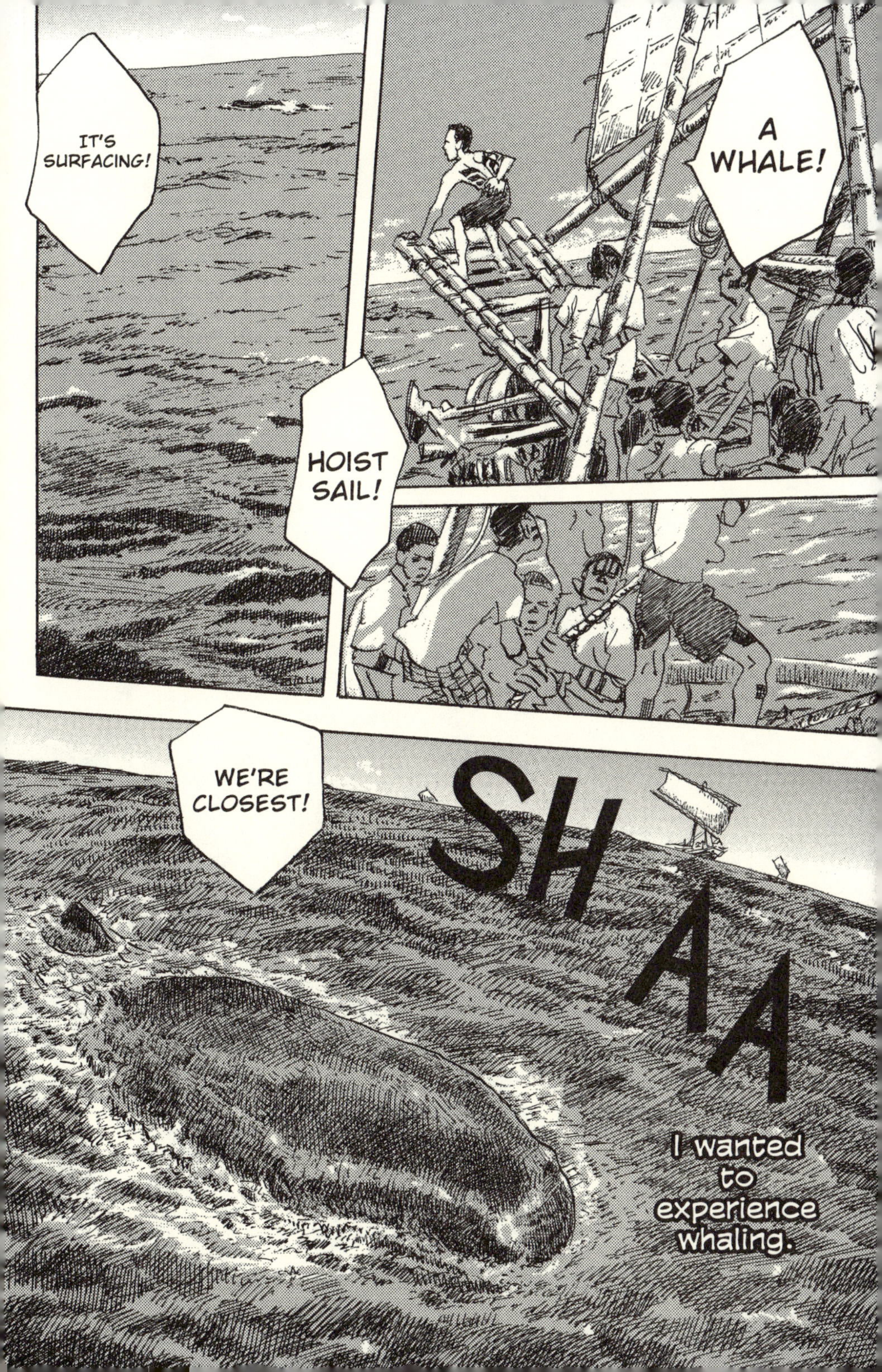
A WHALE!
HOIST SAIL!
IT'S SURFACING!
WE'RE CLOSEST!
SHAA
I wanted to experience whaling.

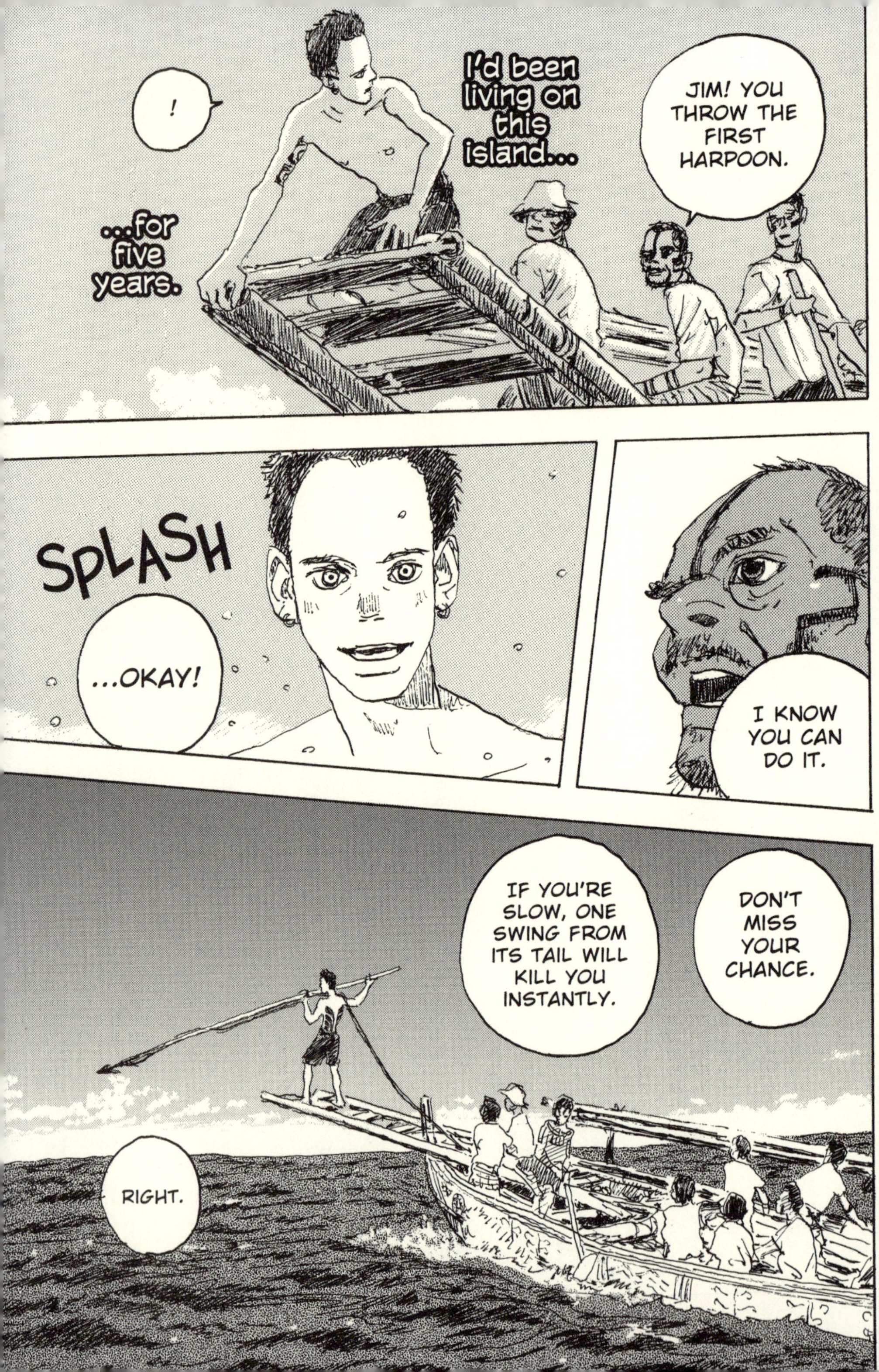
JIM! YOU THROW THE FIRST HARPOON.
I'd been living on this island...
!
...for five years.
I KNOW YOU CAN DO IT.
SPLASH
...OKAY!
DON'T MISS YOUR CHANCE.
IF YOU'RE SLOW, ONE SWING FROM ITS TAIL WILL KILL YOU INSTANTLY.
RIGHT.

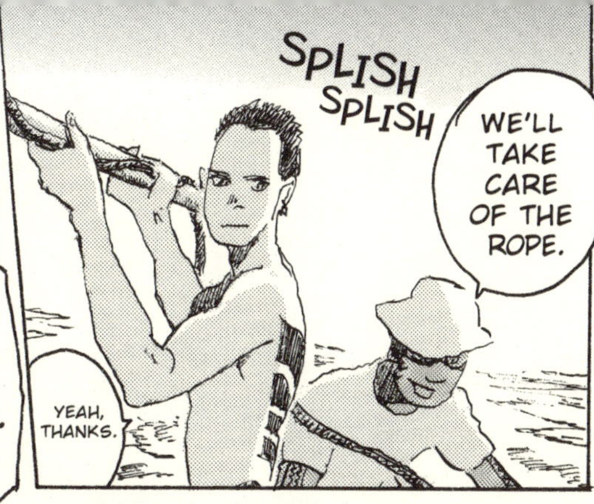
WE'LL TAKE CARE OF THE ROPE.
SPLISH SPLISH
YEAH, THANKS.
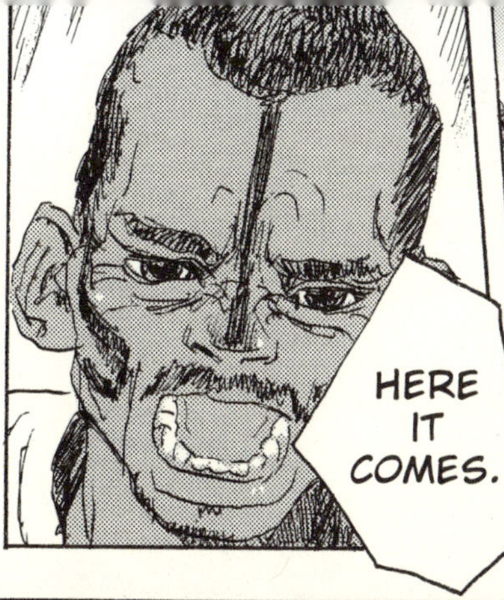
HERE IT COMES.
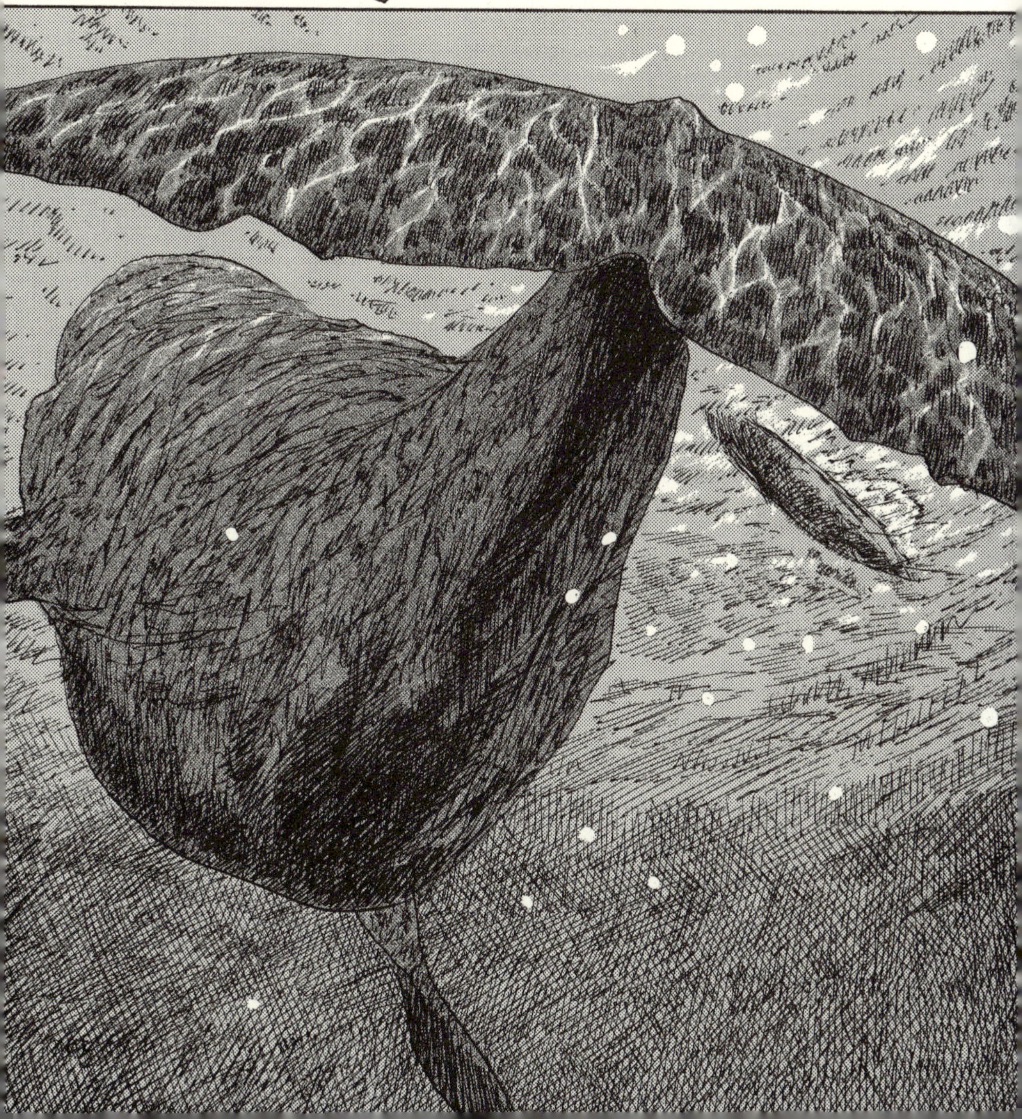

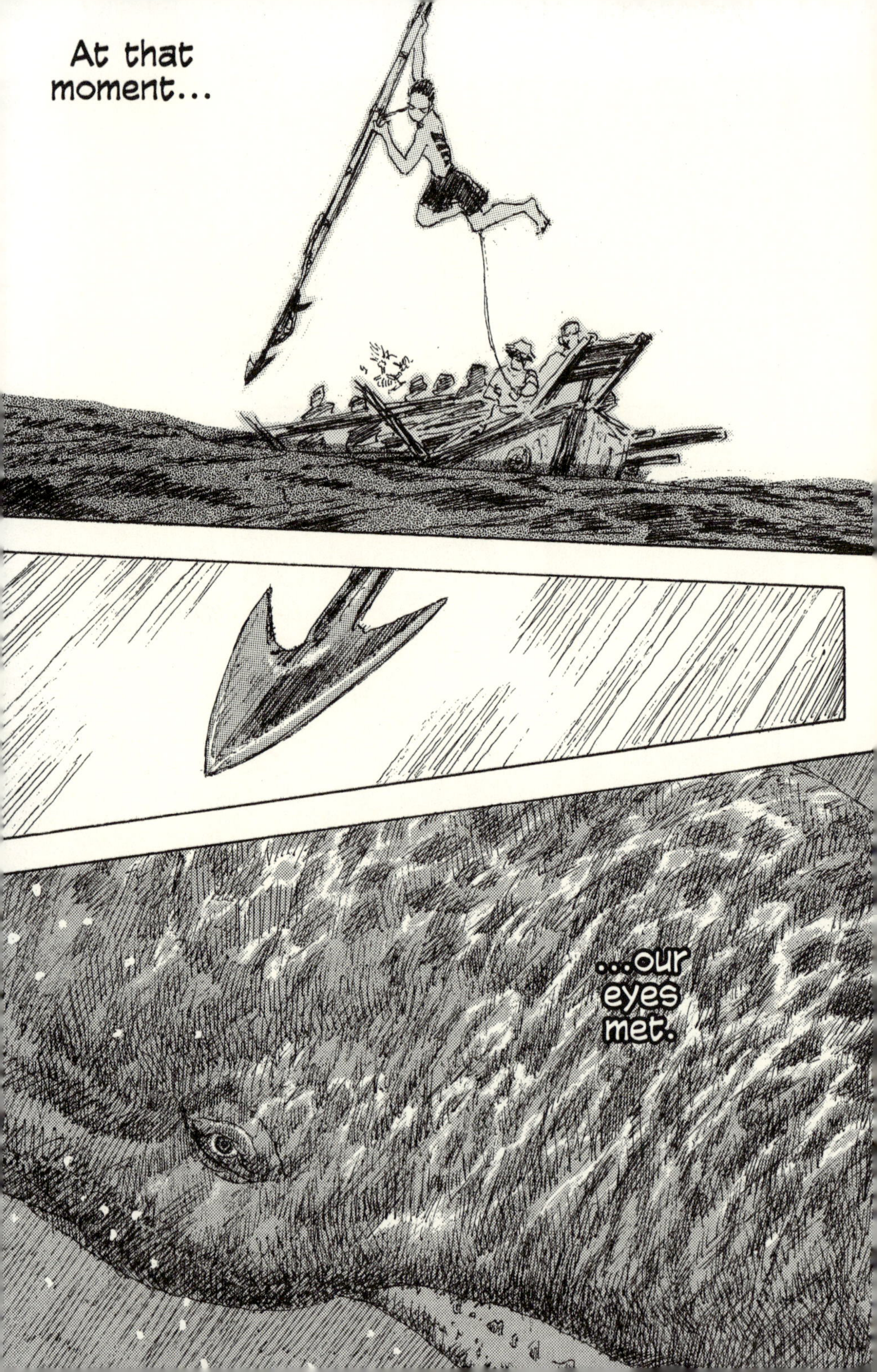
At that moment...
...our eyes met.

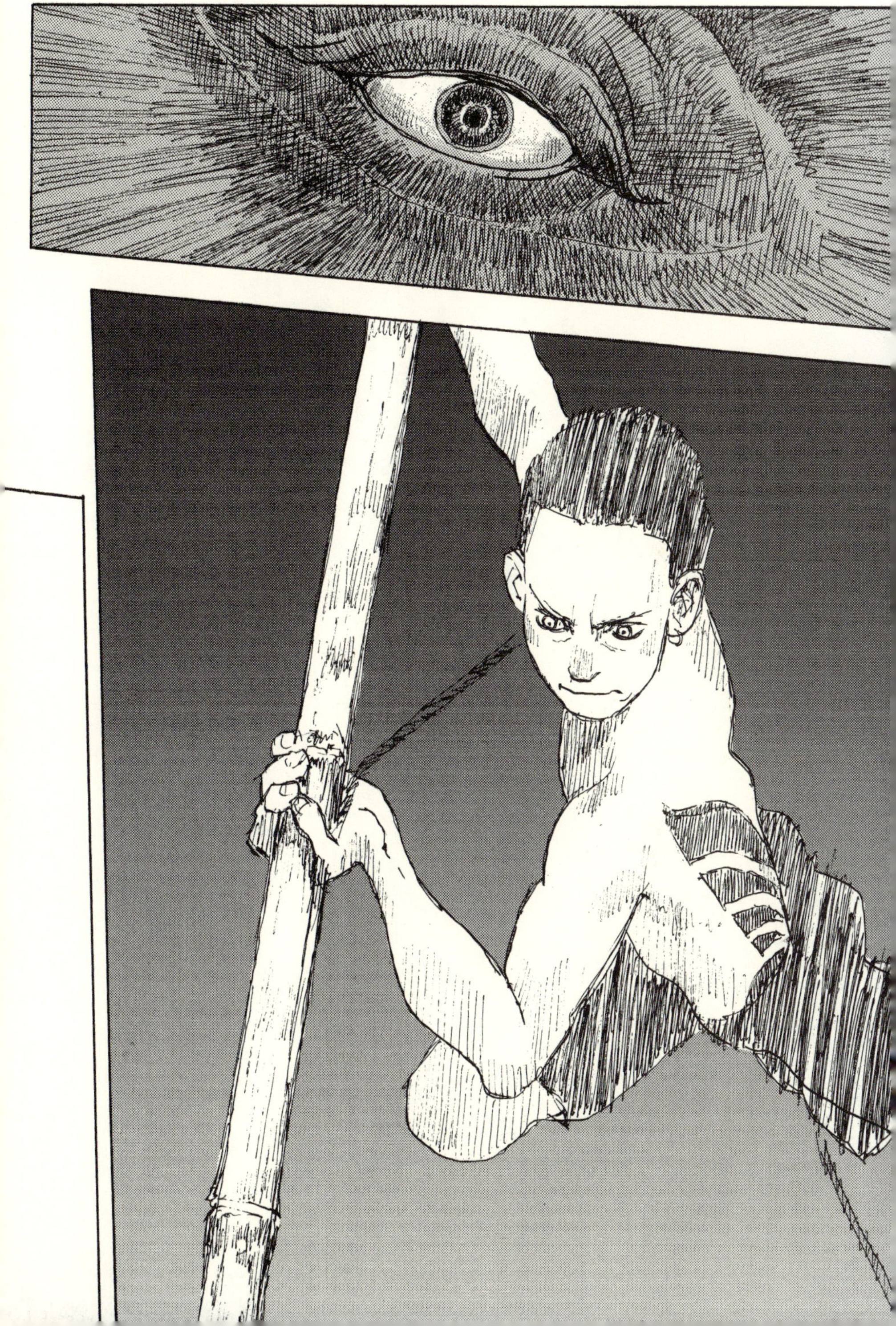

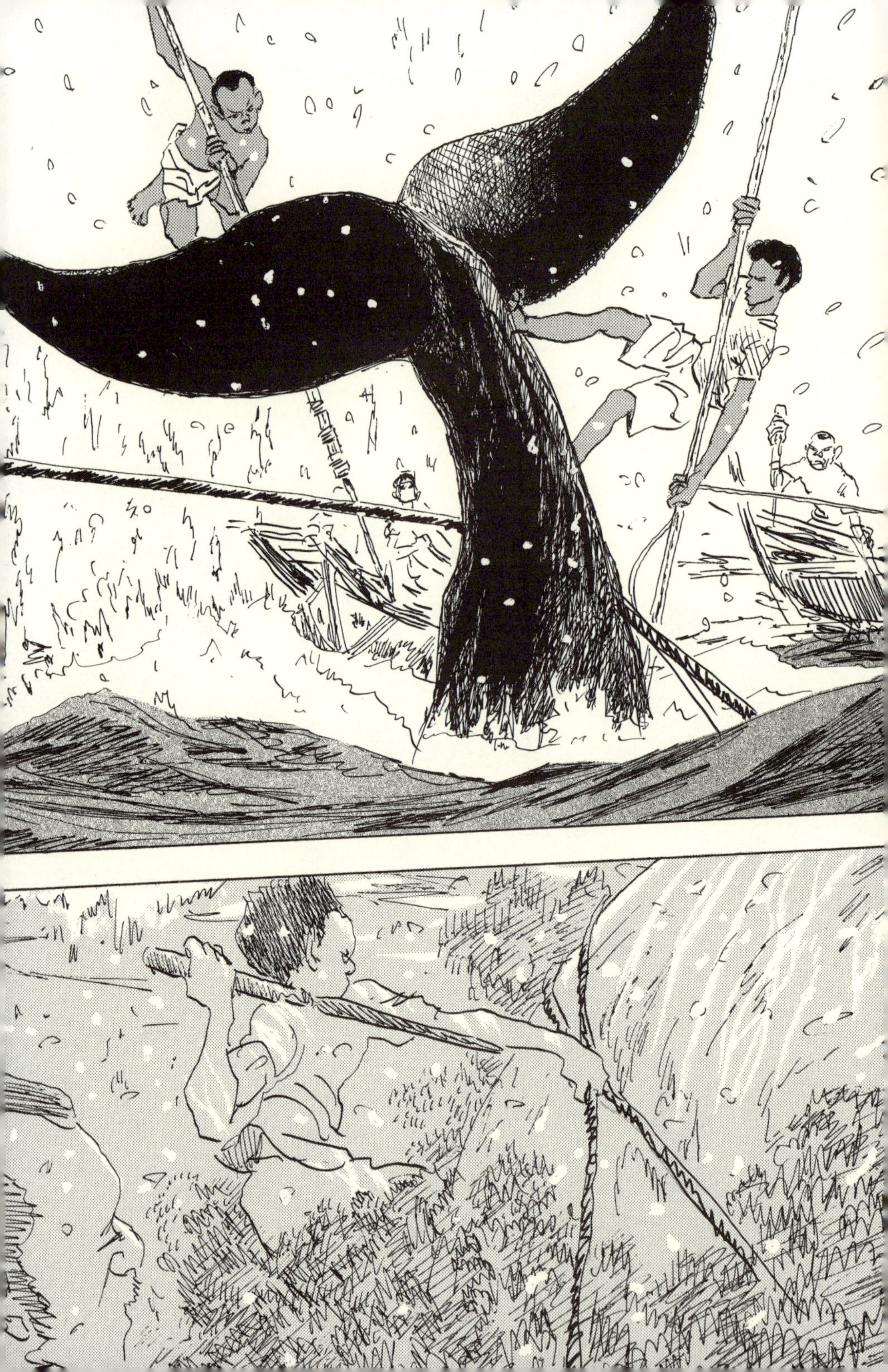

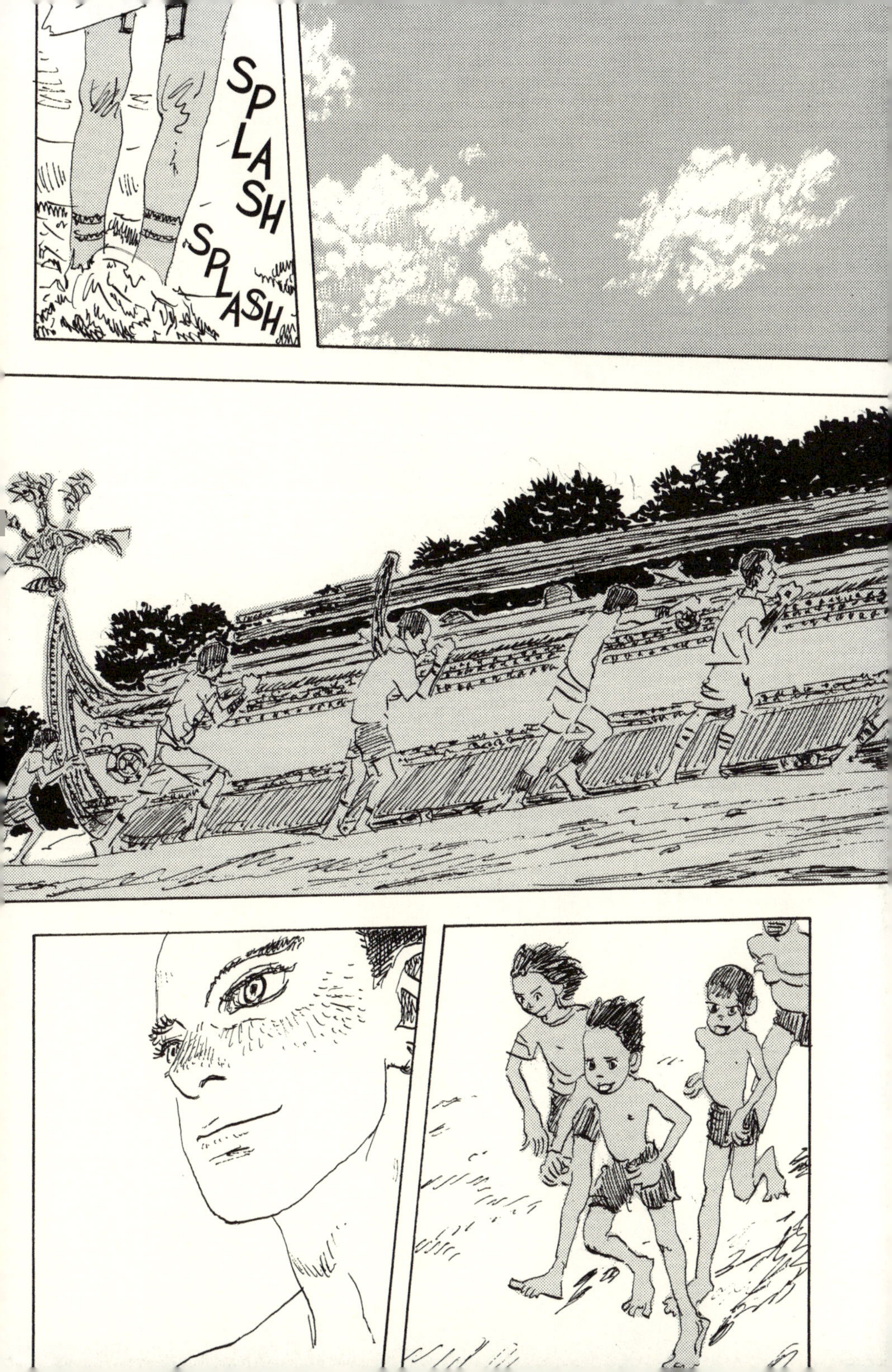
SPLASH
SPLASH

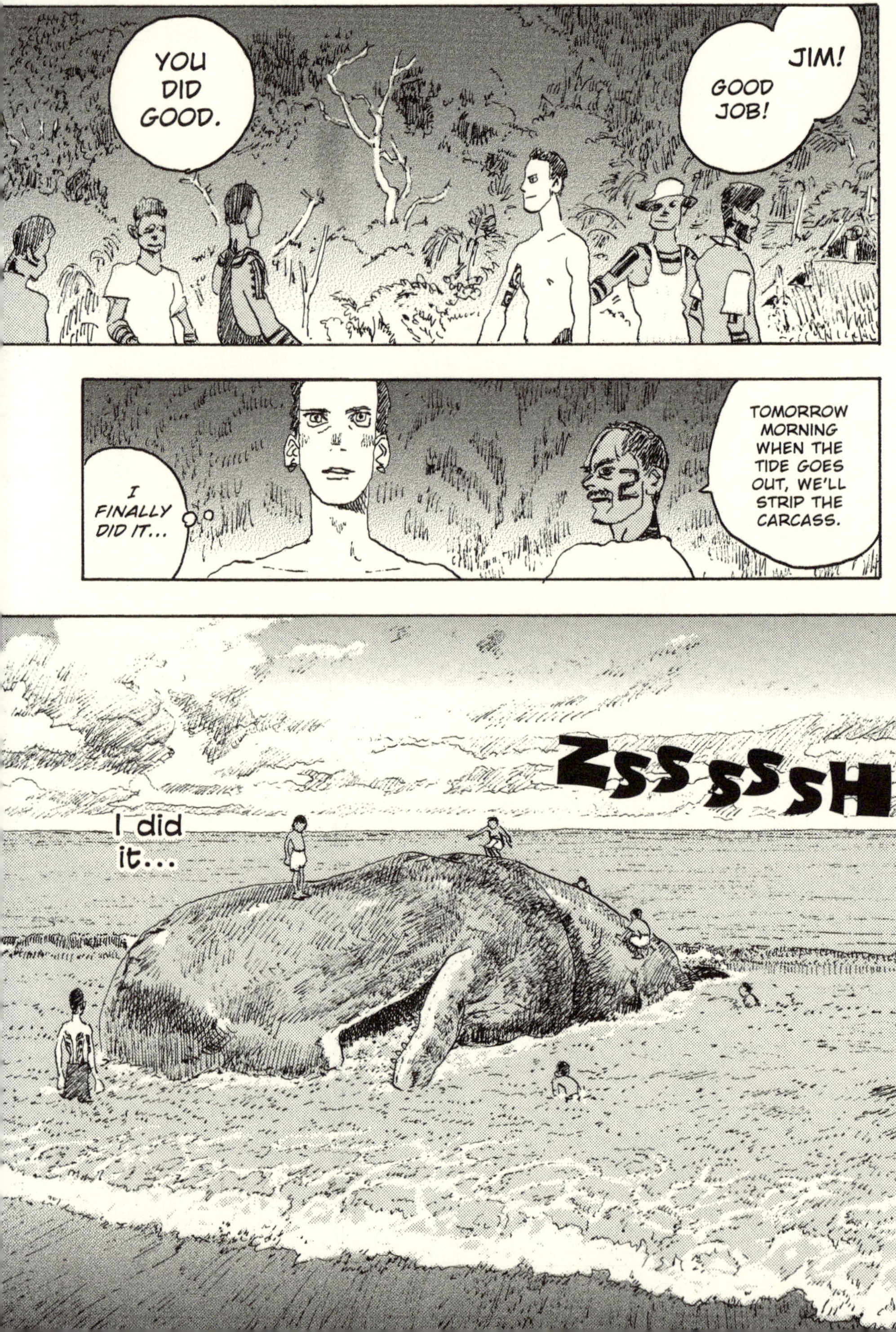
JIM! GOOD JOB!
YOU DID GOOD.
TOMORROW MORNING WHEN THE TIDE GOES OUT, WE'LL STRIP THE CARCASS.
I FINALLY DID IT...
ZSSSSSH
I did it...

ZSSSSSH

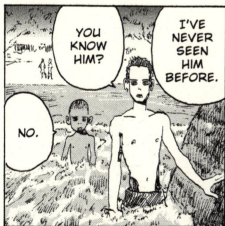

YOU KNOW HIM?

I'VE NEVER SEEN HIM BEFORE.

NO.

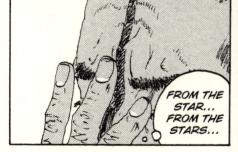

FROM THE STAR... FROM THE STARS...

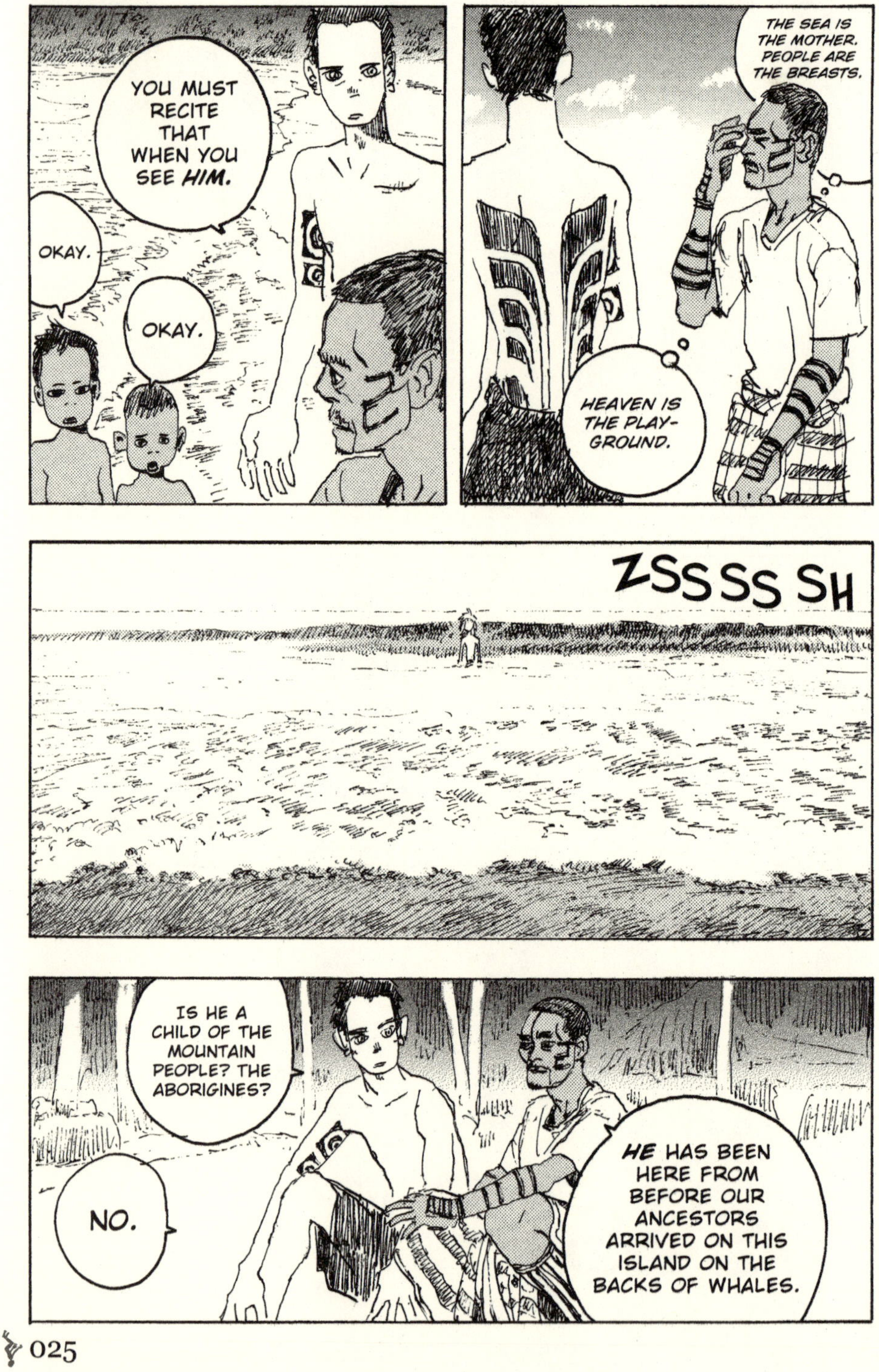
THE SEA IS THE MOTHER. PEOPLE ARE THE BREASTS.
HEAVEN IS THE PLAY-GROUND.
YOU MUST RECITE THAT WHEN YOU SEE *HIM.*
OKAY.
OKAY.
ZSSSSSH
IS HE A CHILD OF THE MOUNTAIN PEOPLE? THE ABORIGINES?
NO.
HE HAS BEEN HERE FROM BEFORE OUR ANCESTORS ARRIVED ON THIS ISLAND ON THE BACKS OF WHALES.

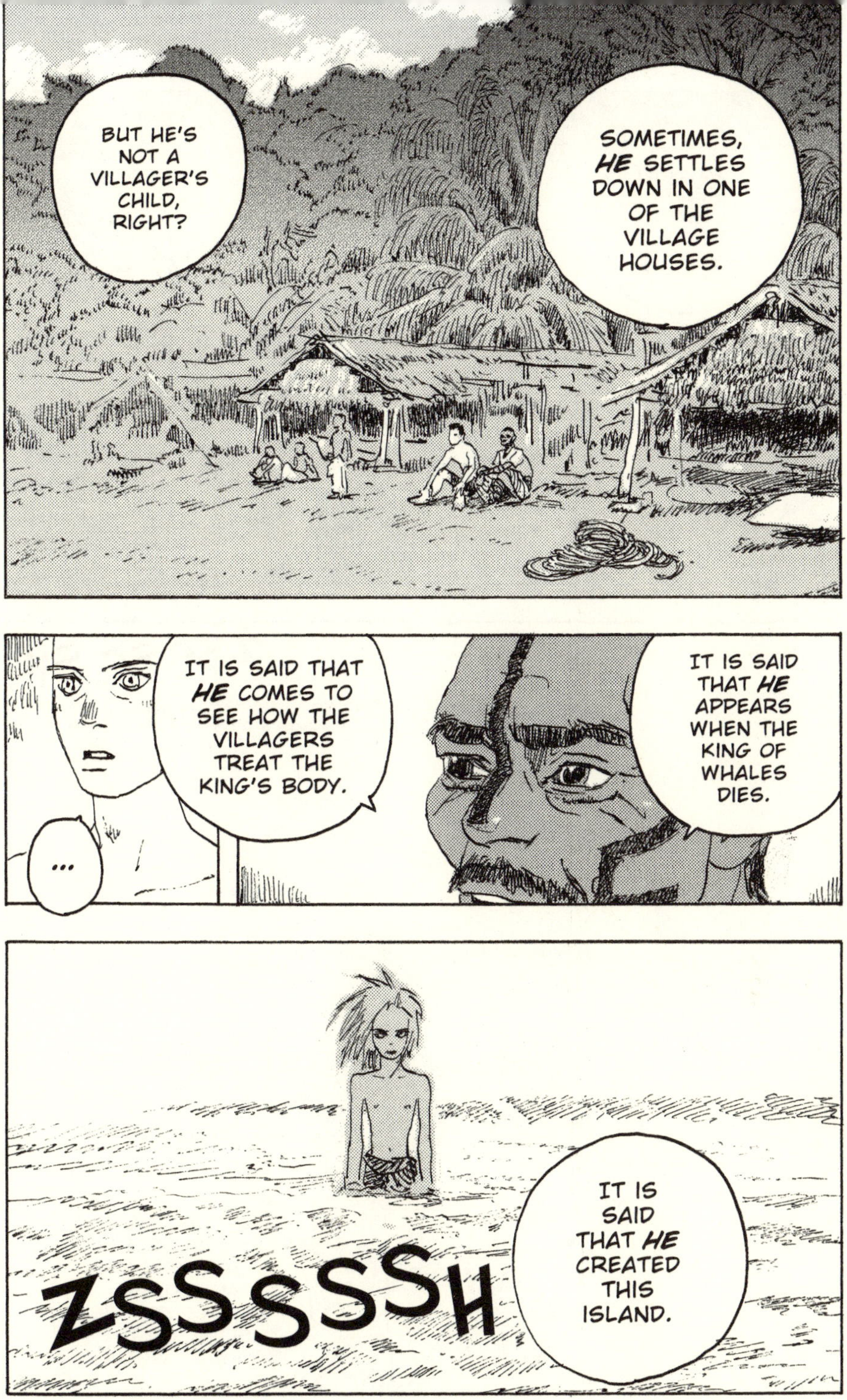
SOMETIMES, *HE* SETTLES DOWN IN ONE OF THE VILLAGE HOUSES.
BUT HE'S NOT A VILLAGER'S CHILD, RIGHT?
IT IS SAID THAT *HE* APPEARS WHEN THE KING OF WHALES DIES.
IT IS SAID THAT *HE* COMES TO SEE HOW THE VILLAGERS TREAT THE KING'S BODY.
...
IT IS SAID THAT *HE* CREATED THIS ISLAND.
ZSSSSSH

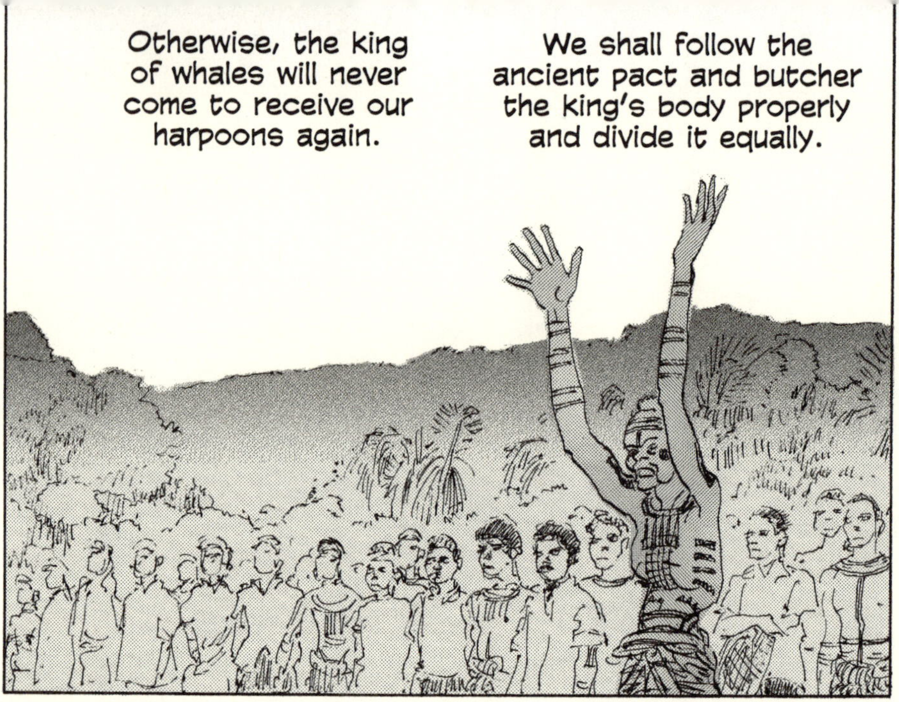
We shall follow the ancient pact and butcher the king's body properly and divide it equally.
Otherwise, the king of whales will never come to receive our harpoons again.

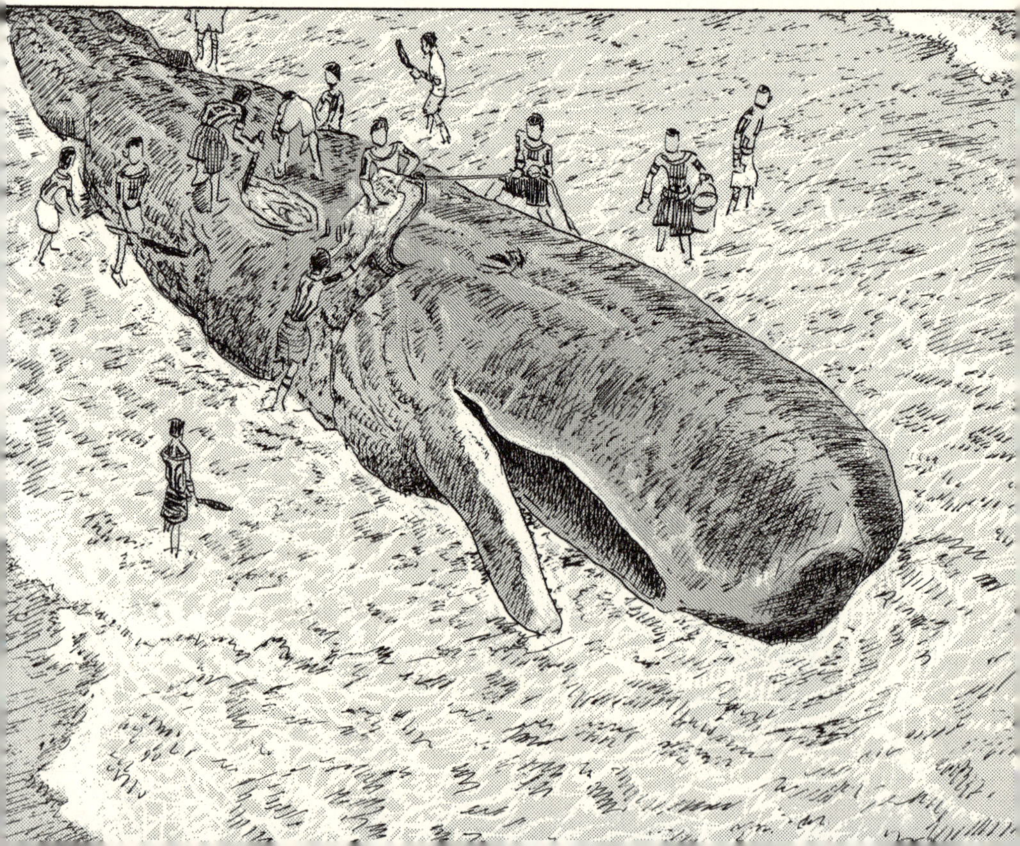

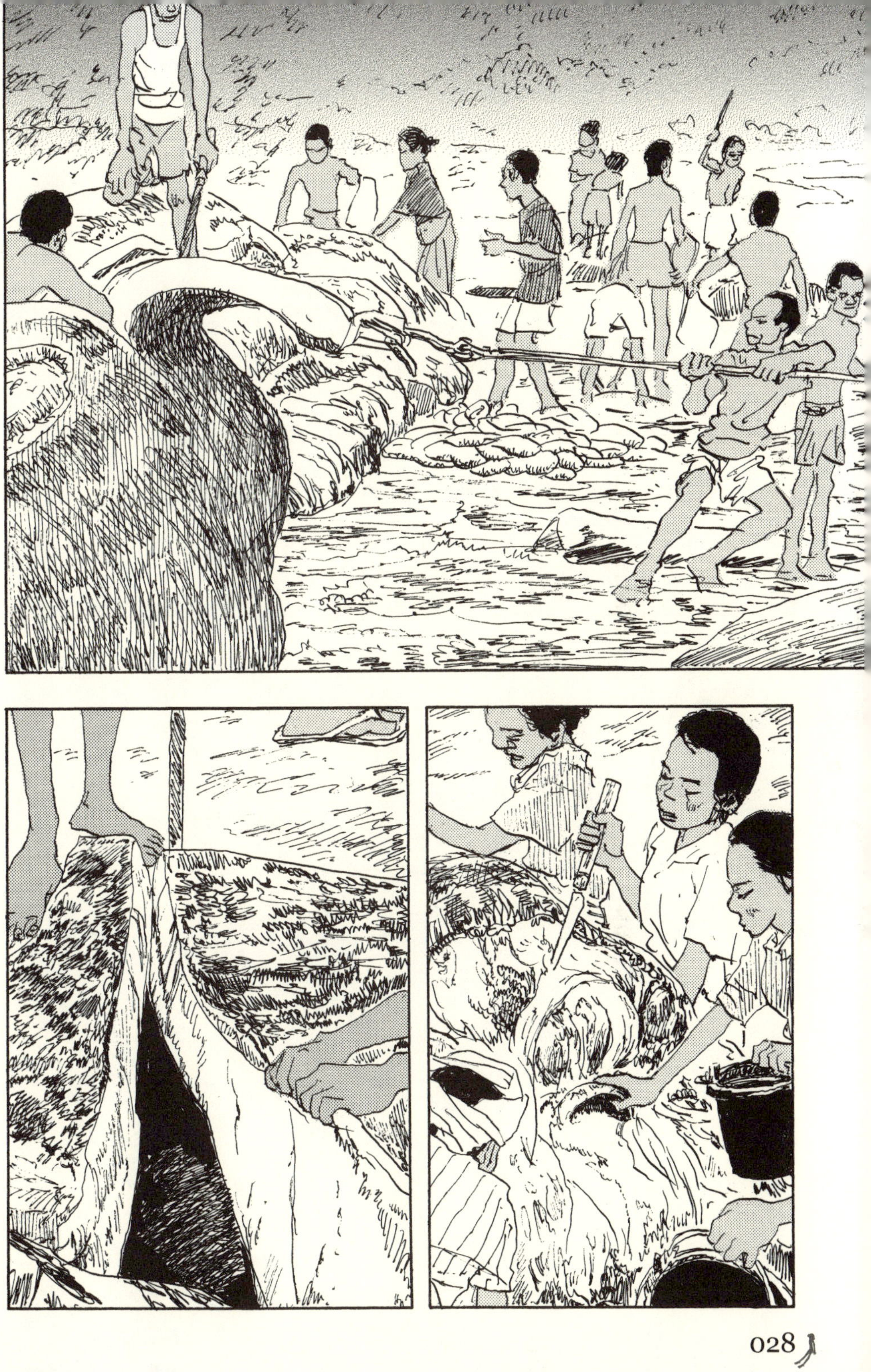

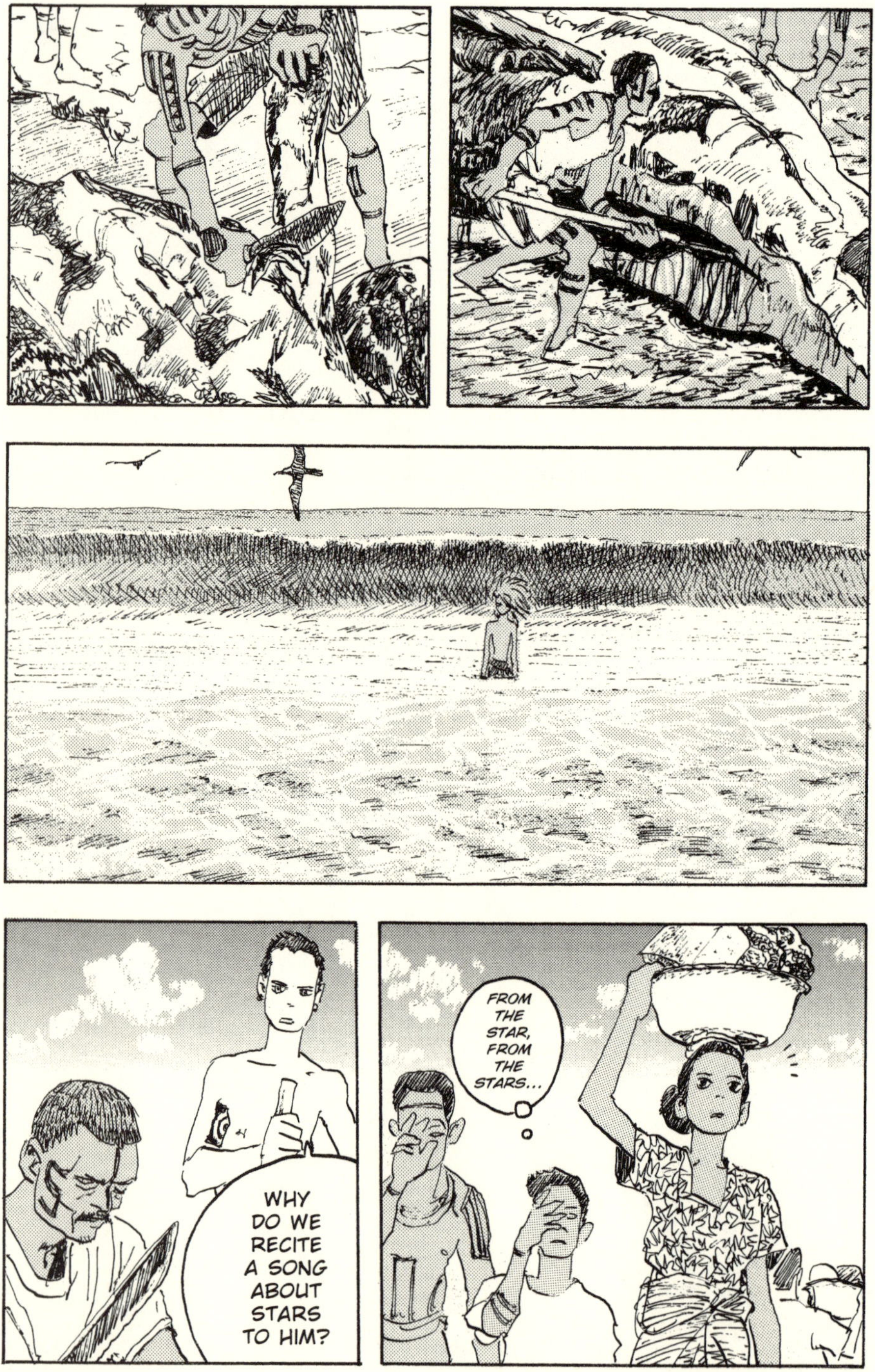
FROM THE STAR, FROM THE STARS...
WHY DO WE RECITE A SONG ABOUT STARS TO HIM?

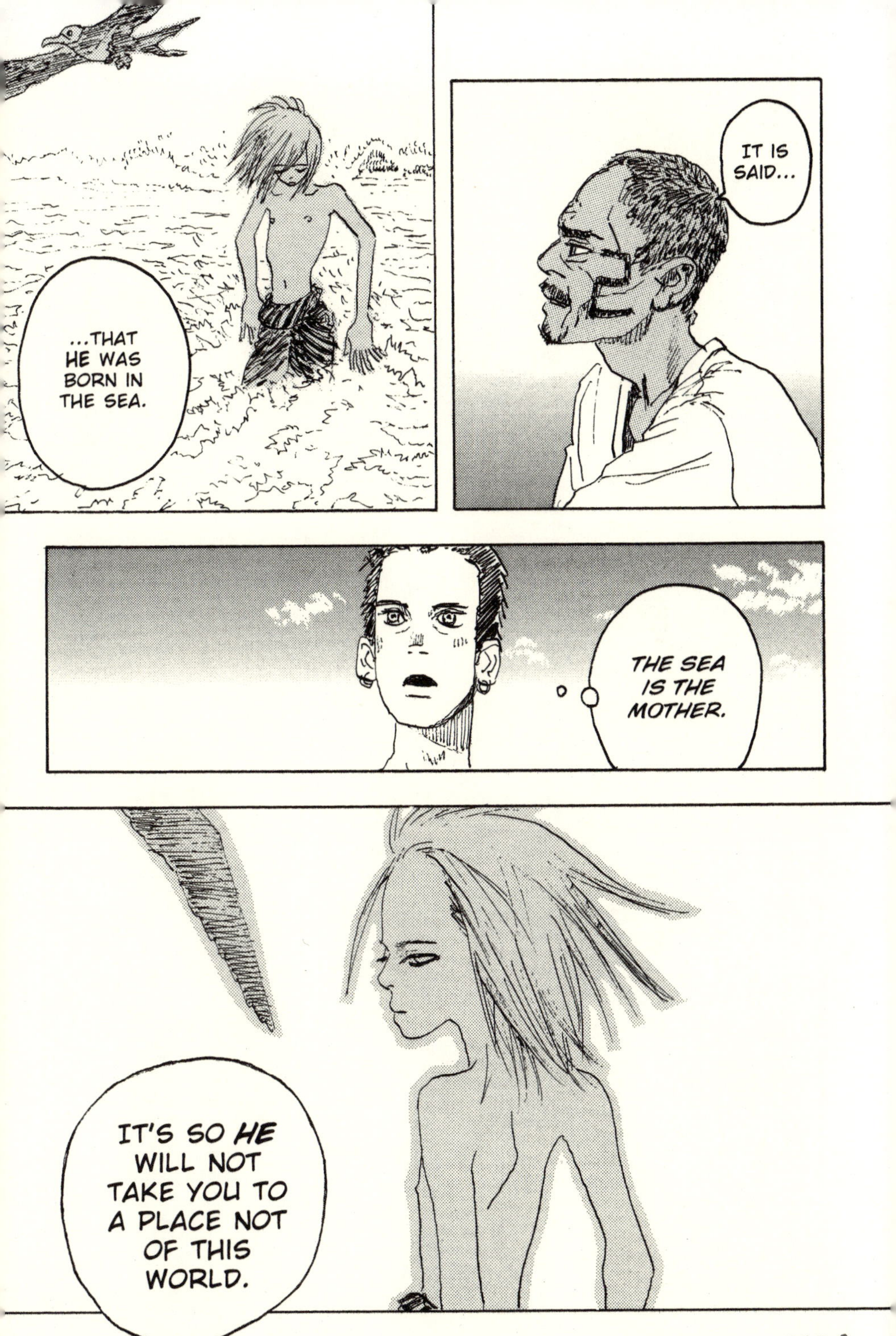
IT IS SAID...
...THAT HE WAS BORN IN THE SEA.
THE SEA IS THE MOTHER.
IT'S SO *HE* WILL NOT TAKE YOU TO A PLACE NOT OF THIS WORLD.

AND SO WE DO NOT LOSE OUR WAY.

...

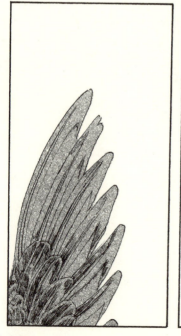

What a beautiful child...

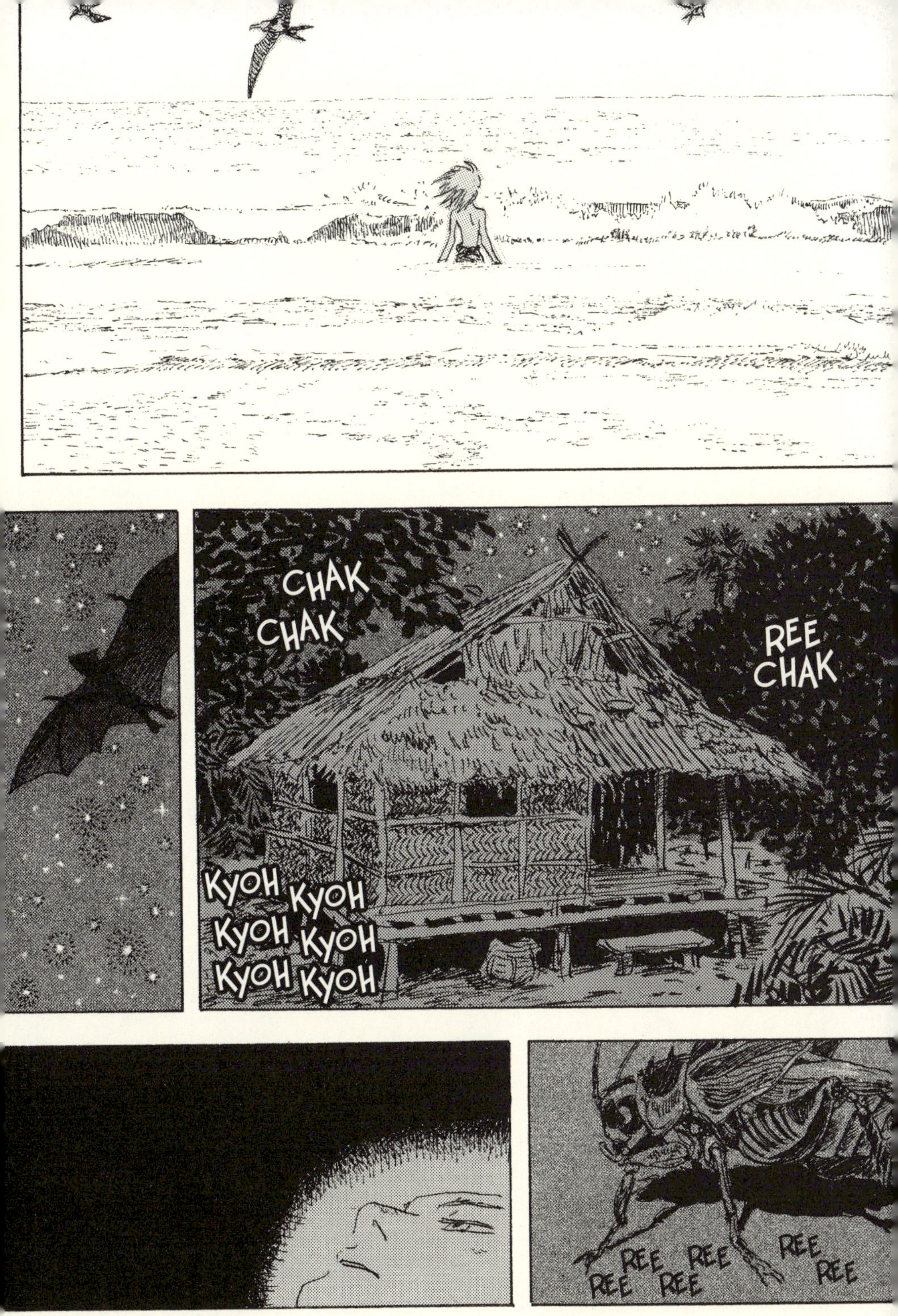
REE CHAK
CHAK CHAK
KYOH KYOH KYOH KYOH KYOH KYOH
REE REE REE REE REE REE

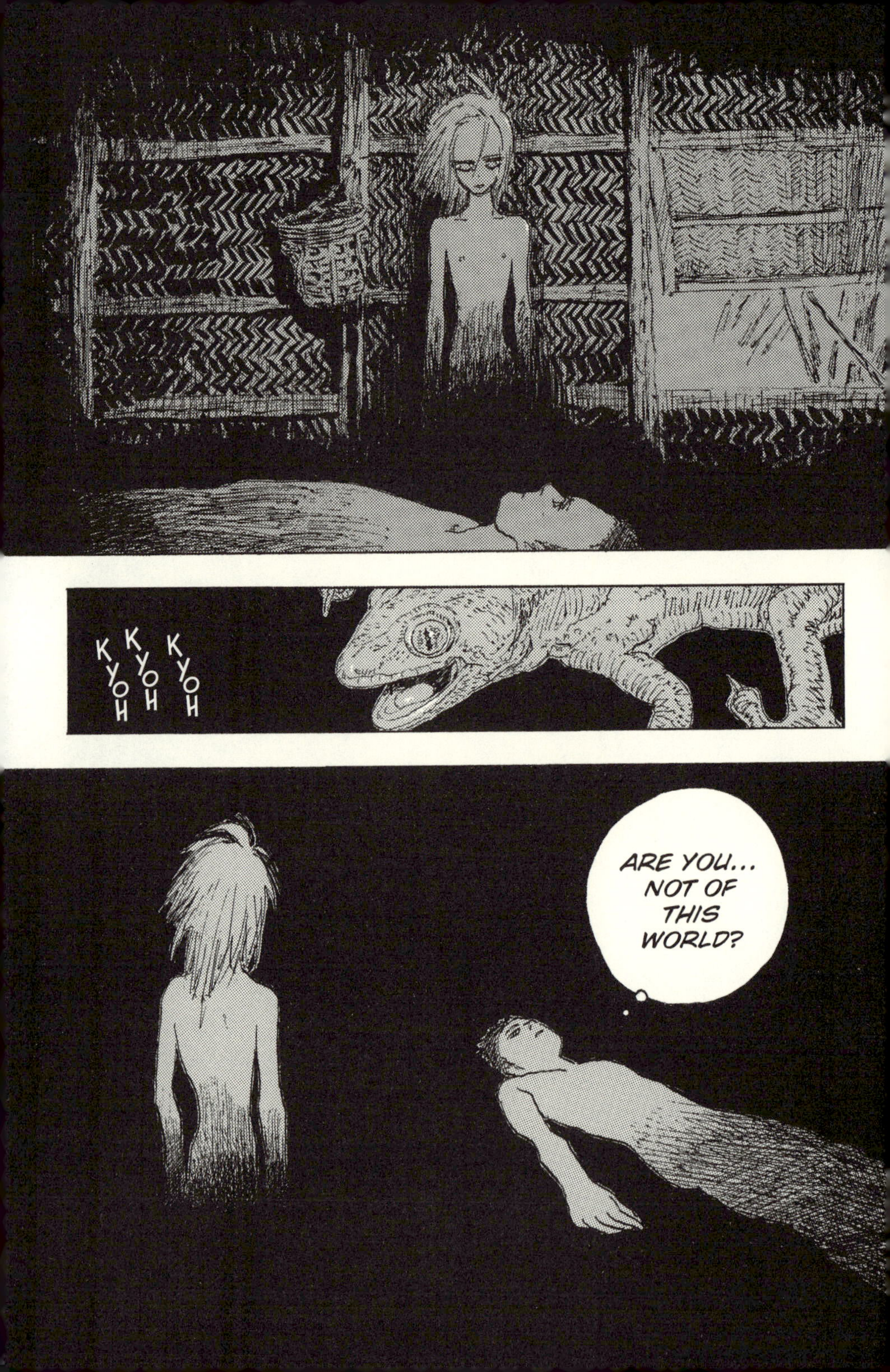
KYOH KYOH KYOH
ARE YOU... NOT OF THIS WORLD?

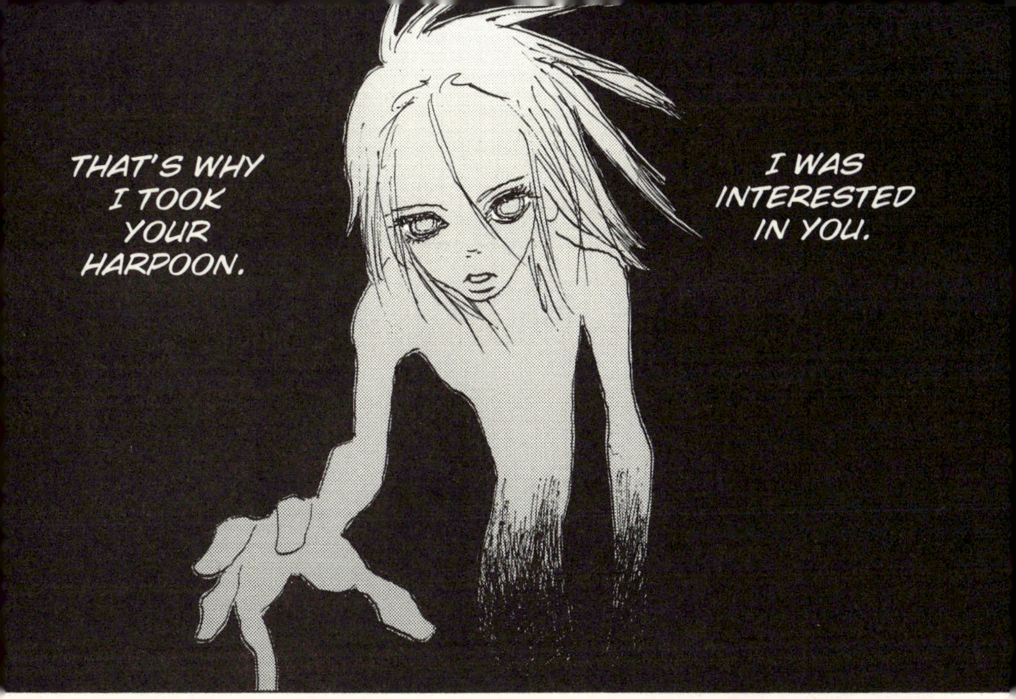
I WAS INTERESTED IN YOU.
THAT'S WHY I TOOK YOUR HARPOON.
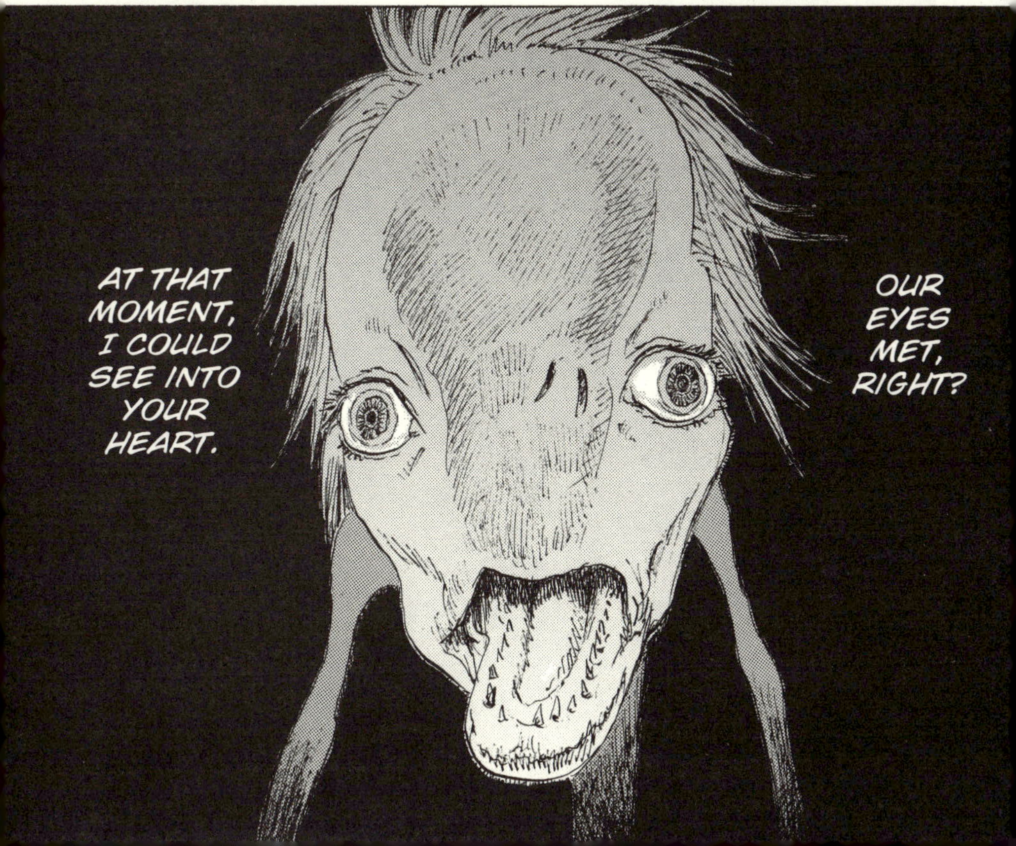
OUR EYES MET, RIGHT?
AT THAT MOMENT, I COULD SEE INTO YOUR HEART.

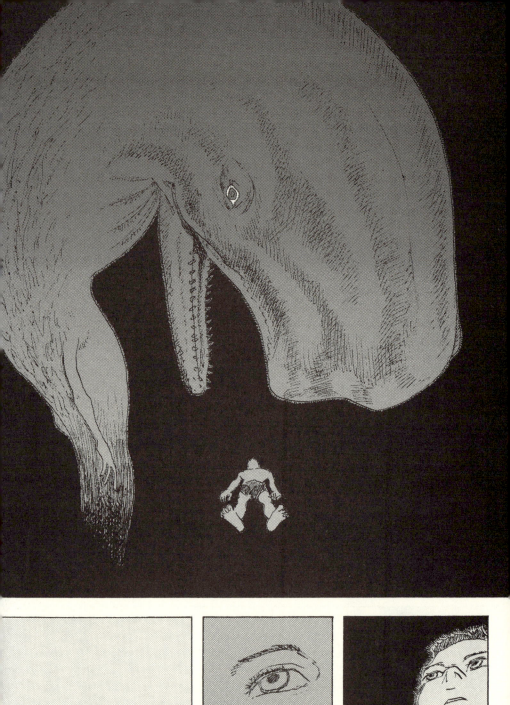
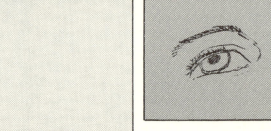

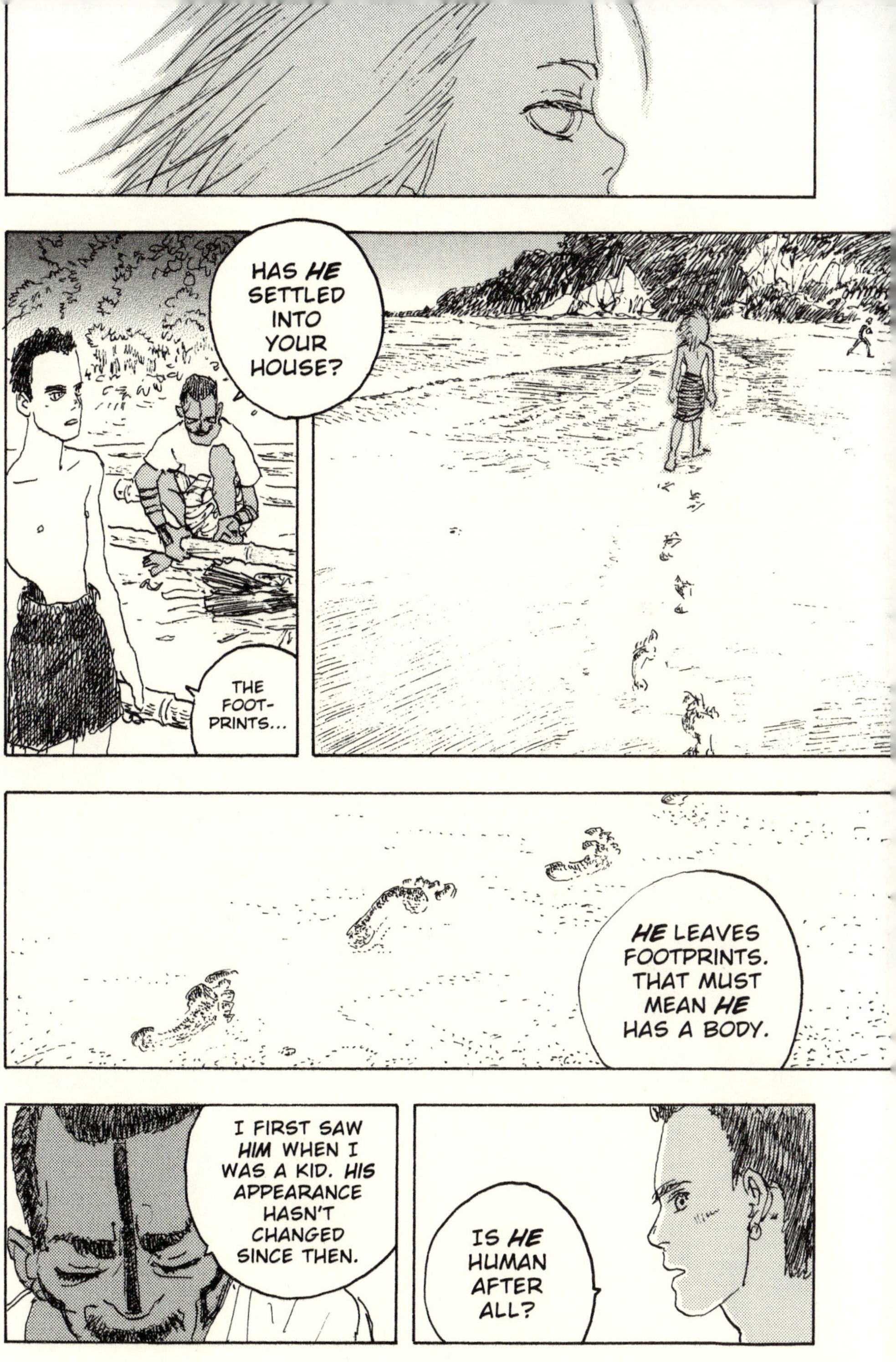
HAS HE SETTLED INTO YOUR HOUSE?
THE FOOTPRINTS...
HE LEAVES FOOTPRINTS. THAT MUST MEAN HE HAS A BODY.
IS HE HUMAN AFTER ALL?
I FIRST SAW HIM WHEN I WAS A KID. HIS APPEARANCE HASN'T CHANGED SINCE THEN.

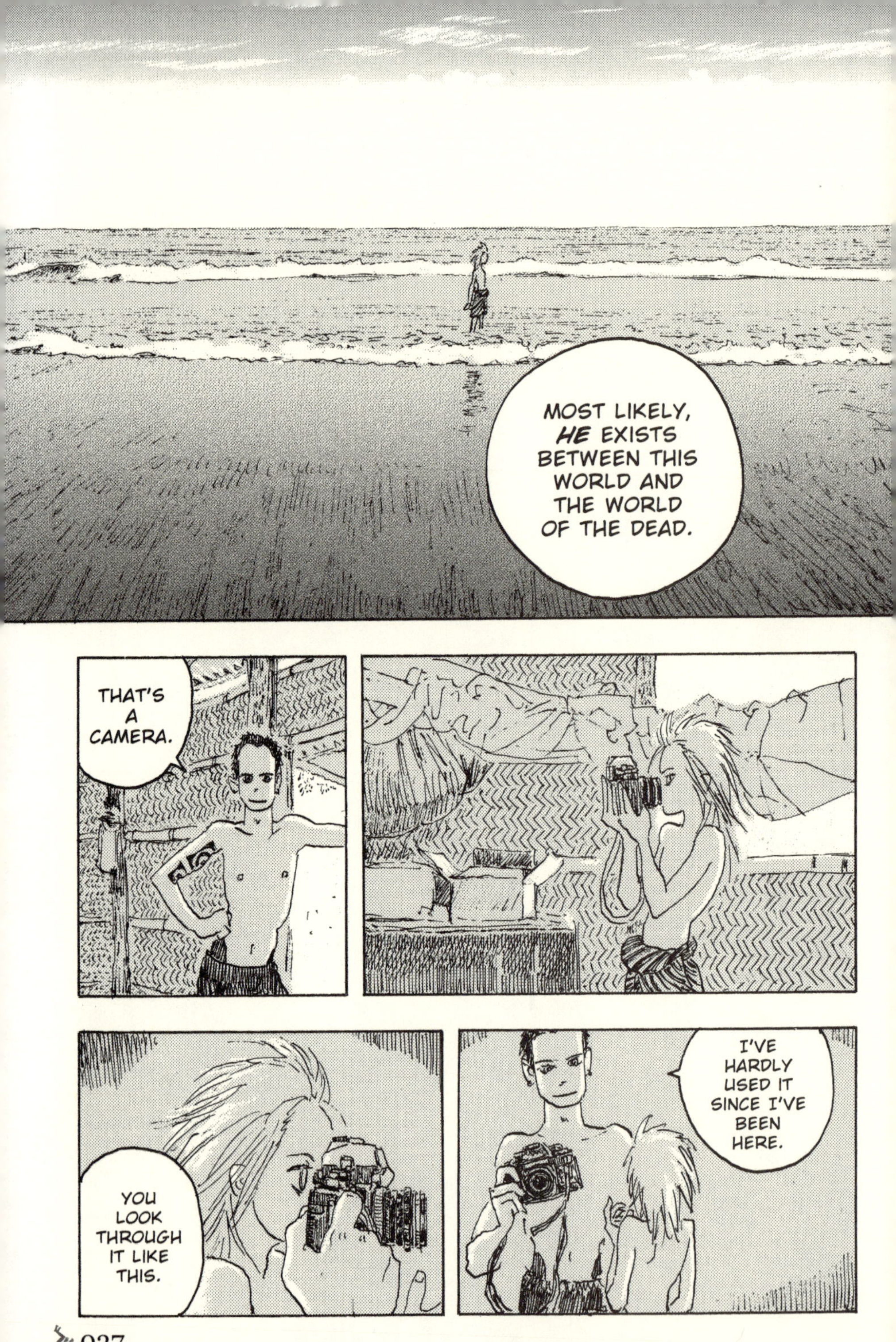
MOST LIKELY, ***HE*** EXISTS BETWEEN THIS WORLD AND THE WORLD OF THE DEAD.
THAT'S A CAMERA.
I'VE HARDLY USED IT SINCE I'VE BEEN HERE.
YOU LOOK THROUGH IT LIKE THIS.

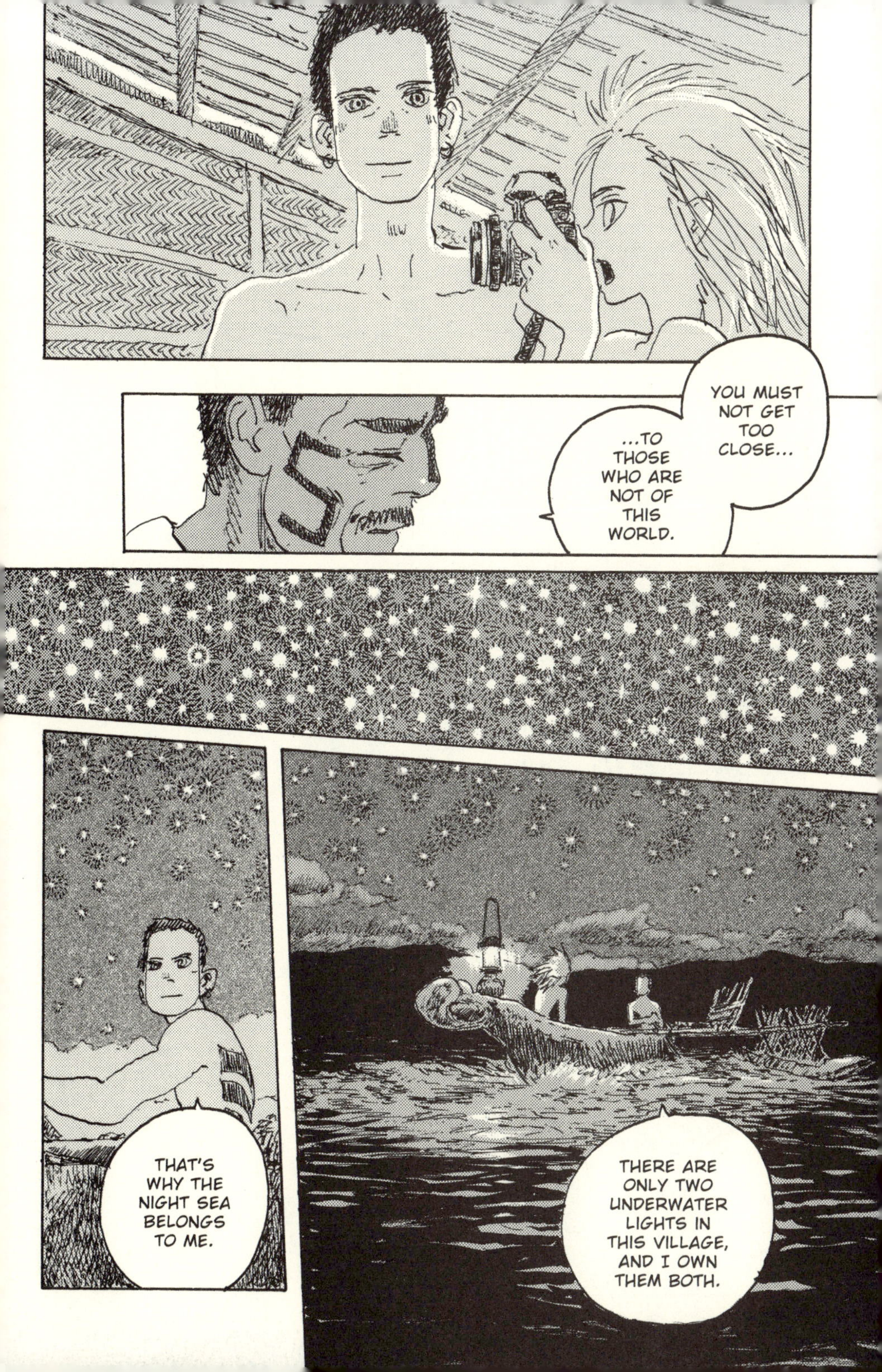
YOU MUST NOT GET TOO CLOSE...
...TO THOSE WHO ARE NOT OF THIS WORLD.
THERE ARE ONLY TWO UNDERWATER LIGHTS IN THIS VILLAGE, AND I OWN THEM BOTH.
THAT'S WHY THE NIGHT SEA BELONGS TO ME.

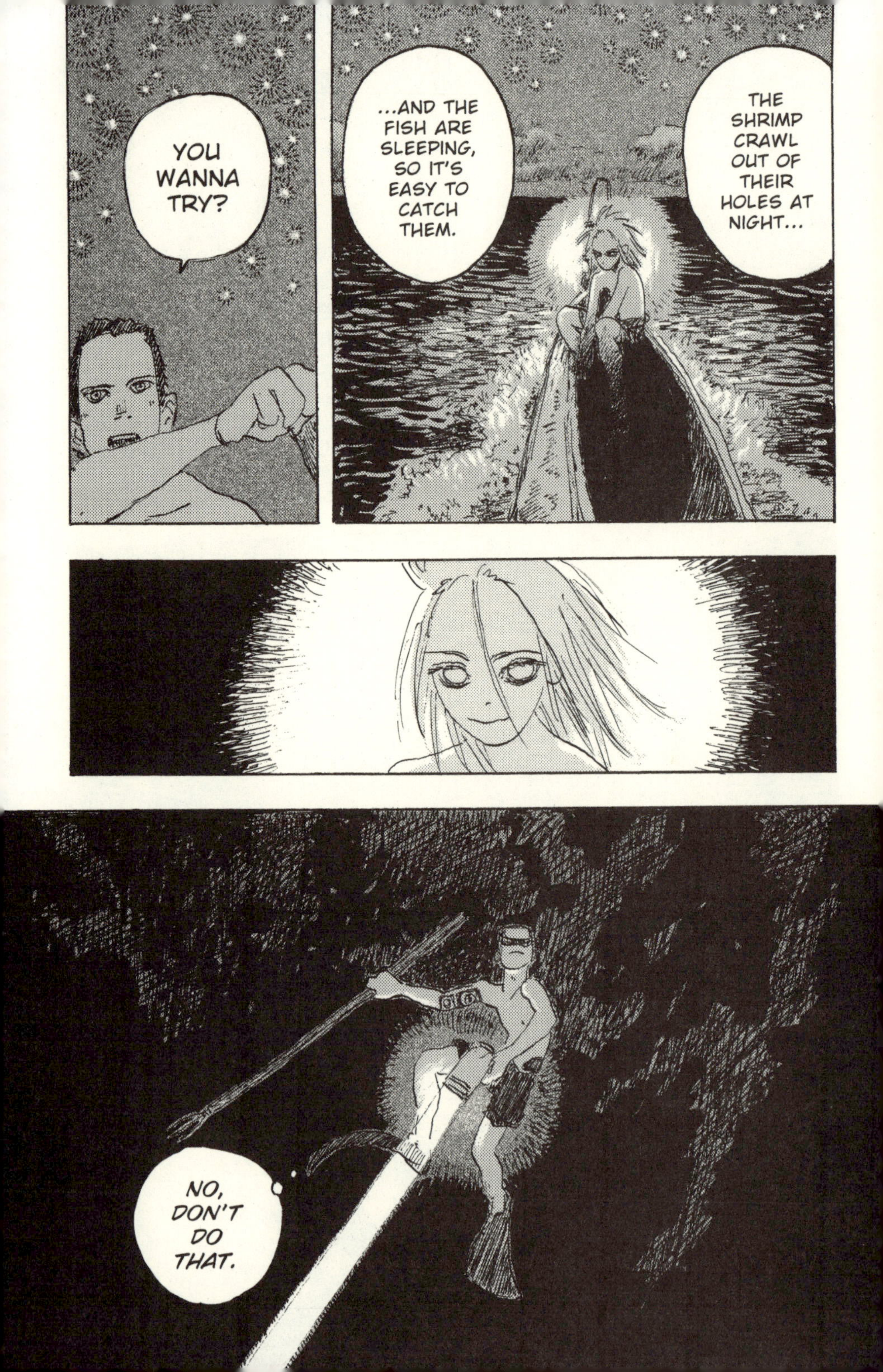
THE SHRIMP CRAWL OUT OF THEIR HOLES AT NIGHT...
...AND THE FISH ARE SLEEPING, SO IT'S EASY TO CATCH THEM.
YOU WANNA TRY?
NO, DON'T DO THAT.

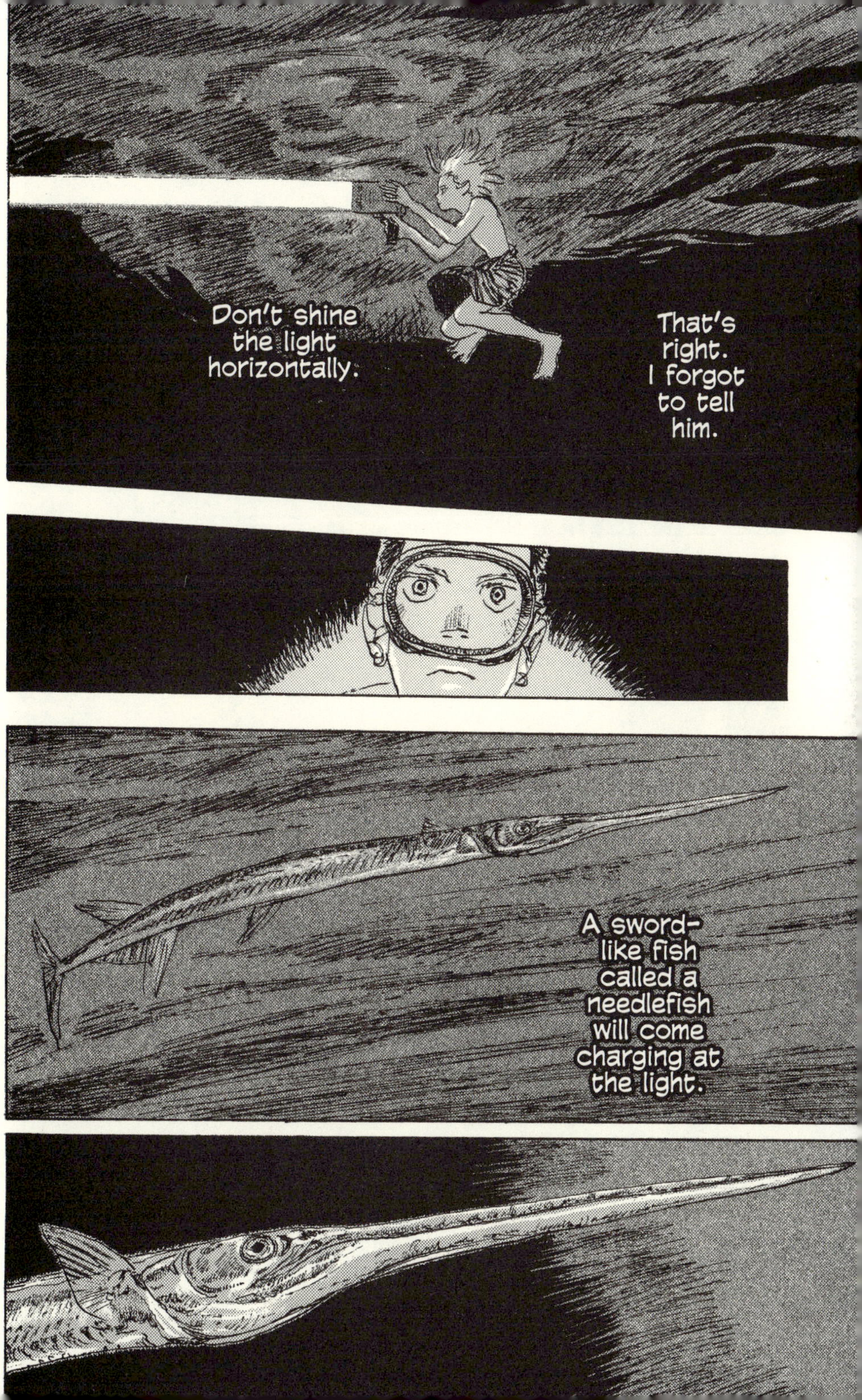
That's right. I forgot to tell him.
Don't shine the light horizontally.
A sword-like fish called a needlefish will come charging at the light.

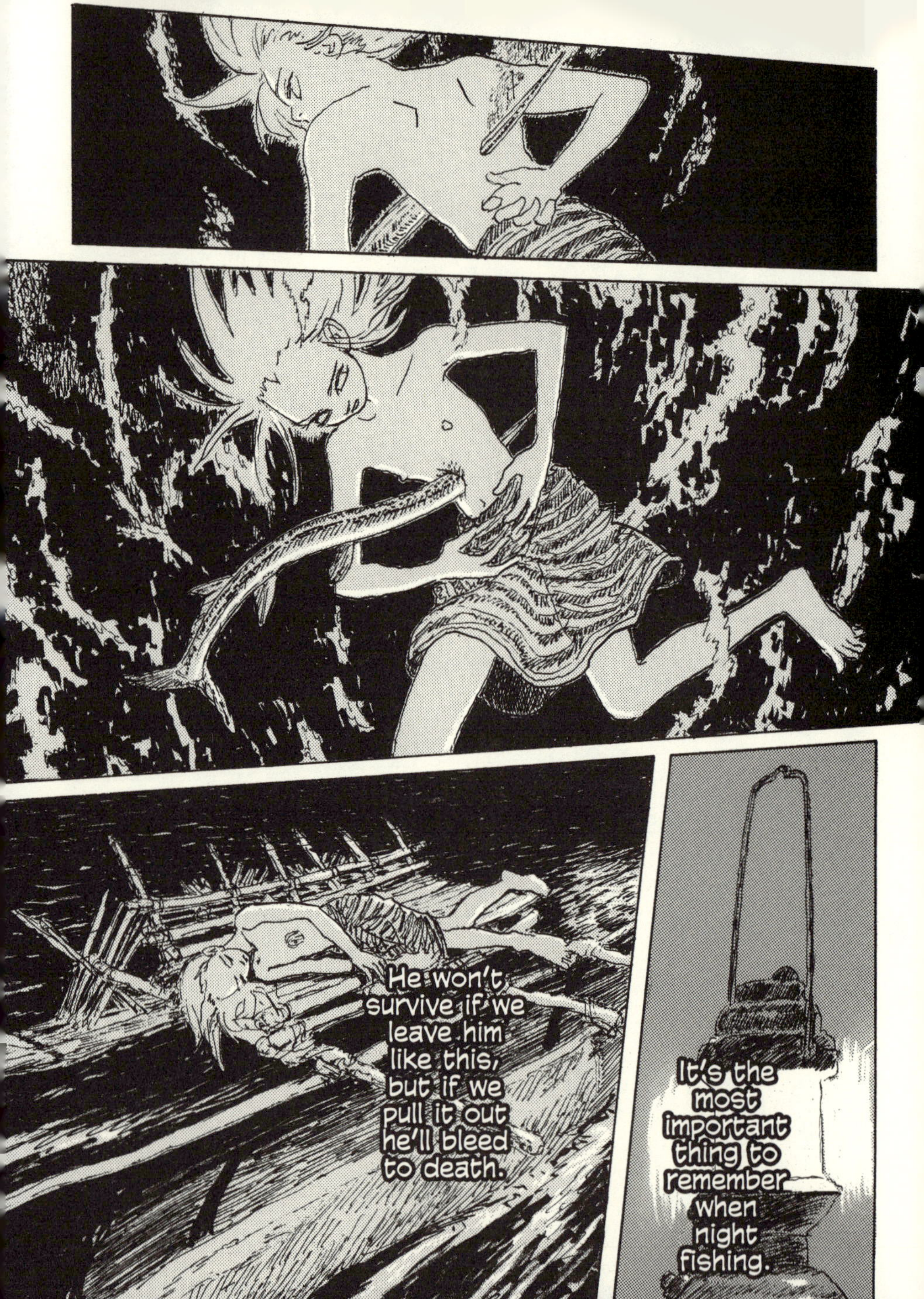
It's the most important thing to remember when night fishing.
He won't survive if we leave him like this, but if we pull it out he'll bleed to death.

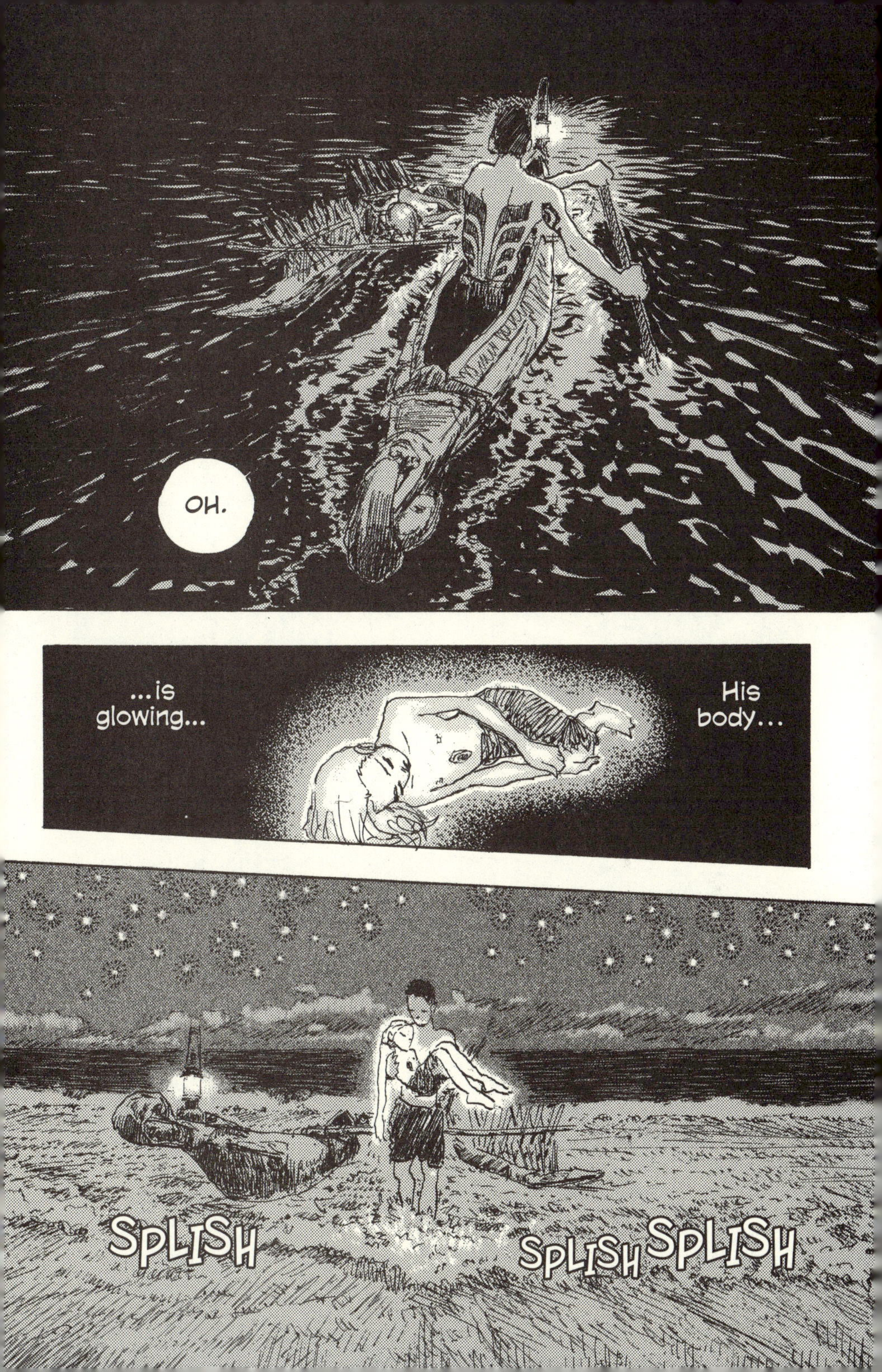
OH.
His body...
...is glowing...
SPLISH
SPLISH
SPLISH

WHAT HAPPENED?
SHHH

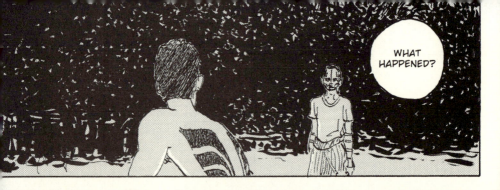

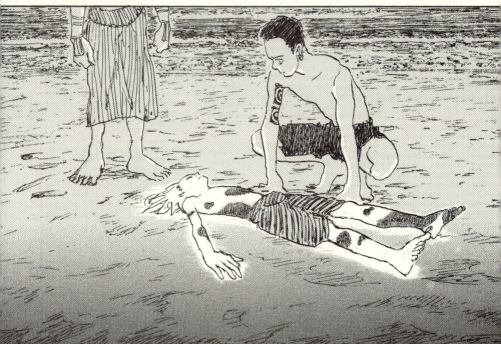

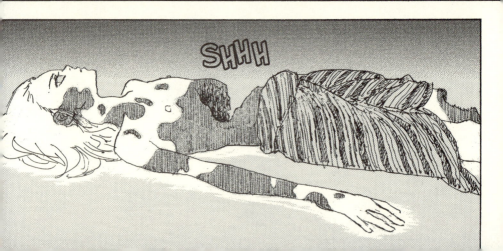

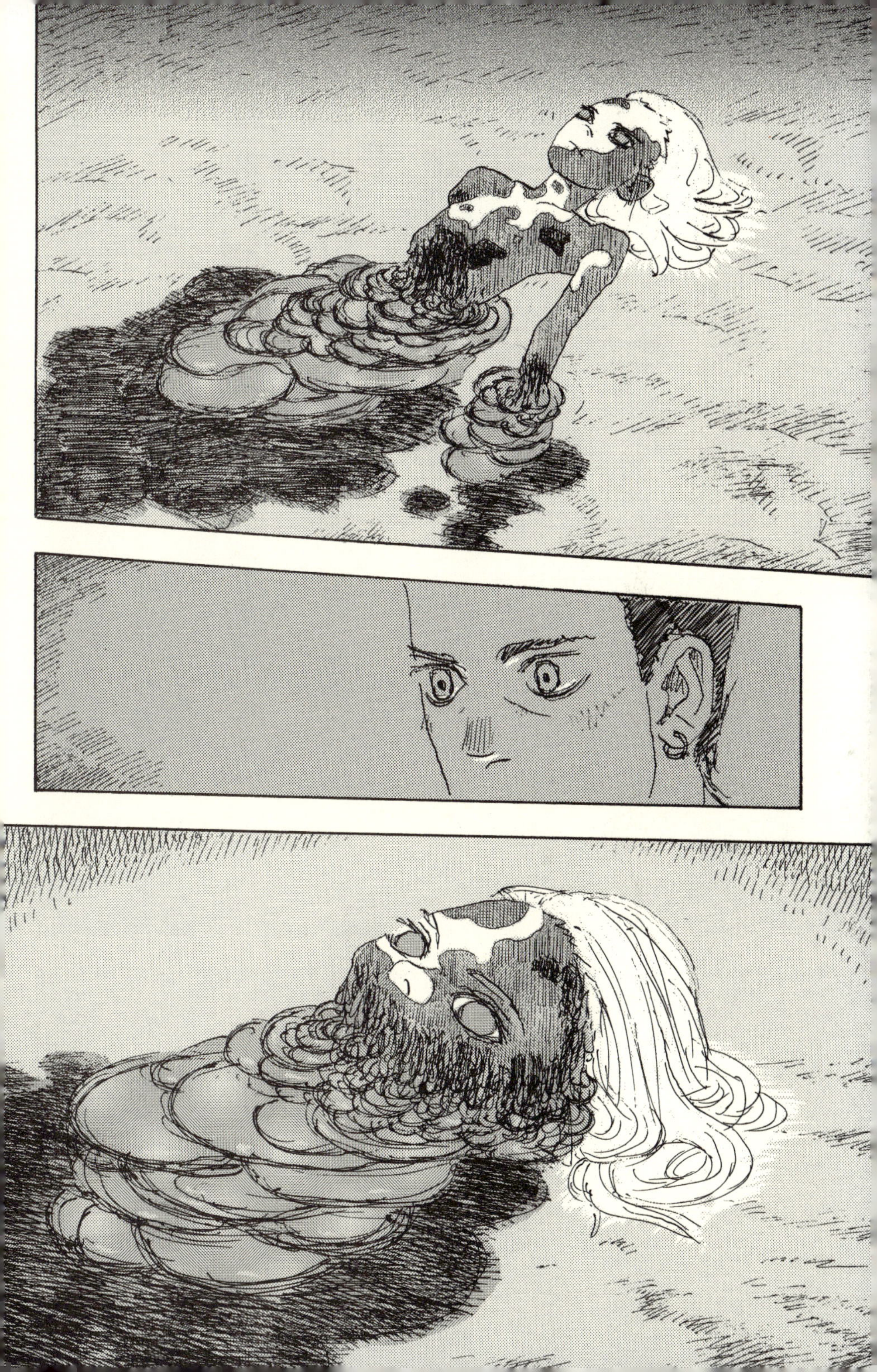

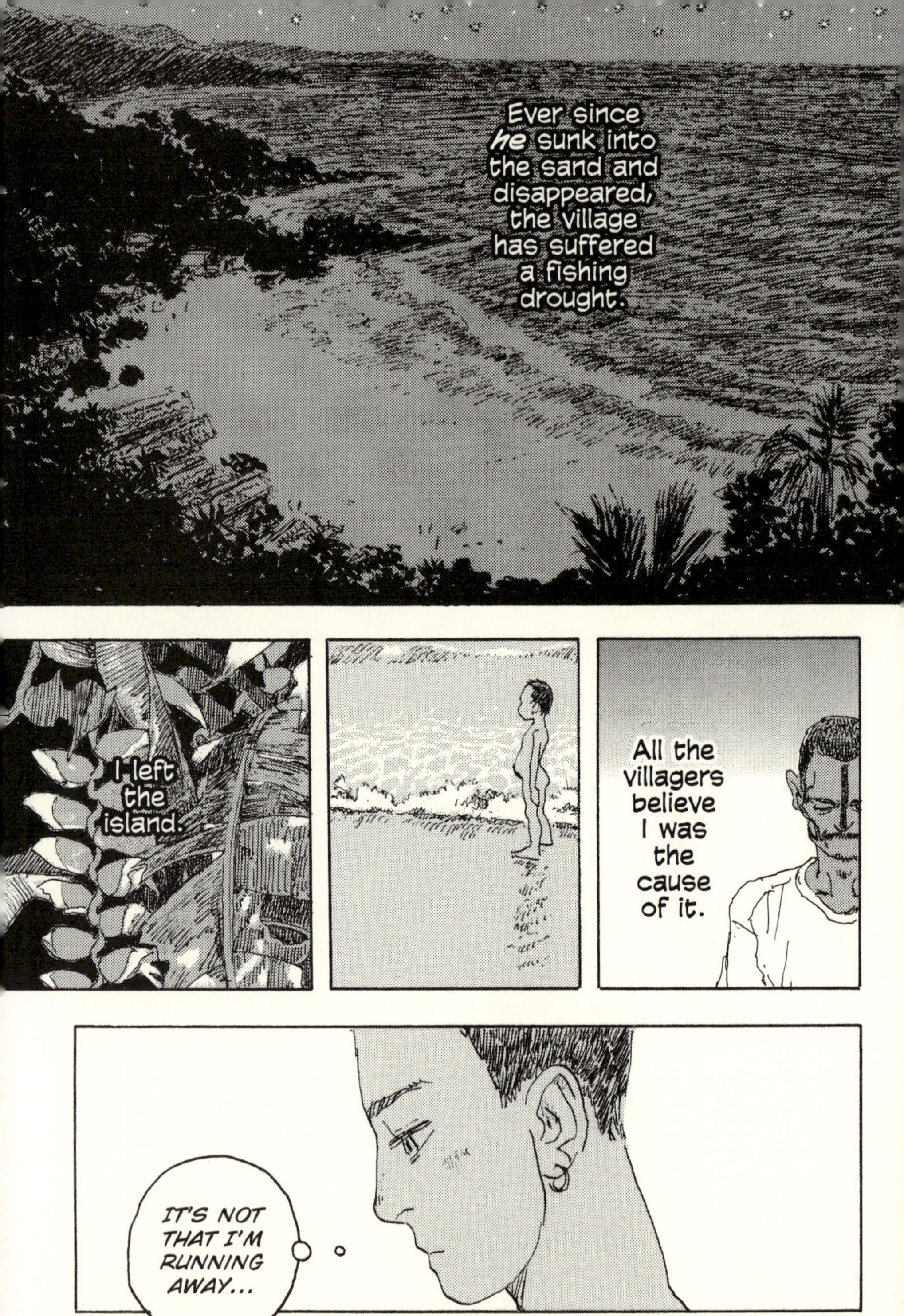
Ever since he sunk into the sand and disappeared, the village has suffered a fishing drought.
All the villagers believe I was the cause of it.
I left the island.
IT'S NOT THAT I'M RUNNING AWAY...

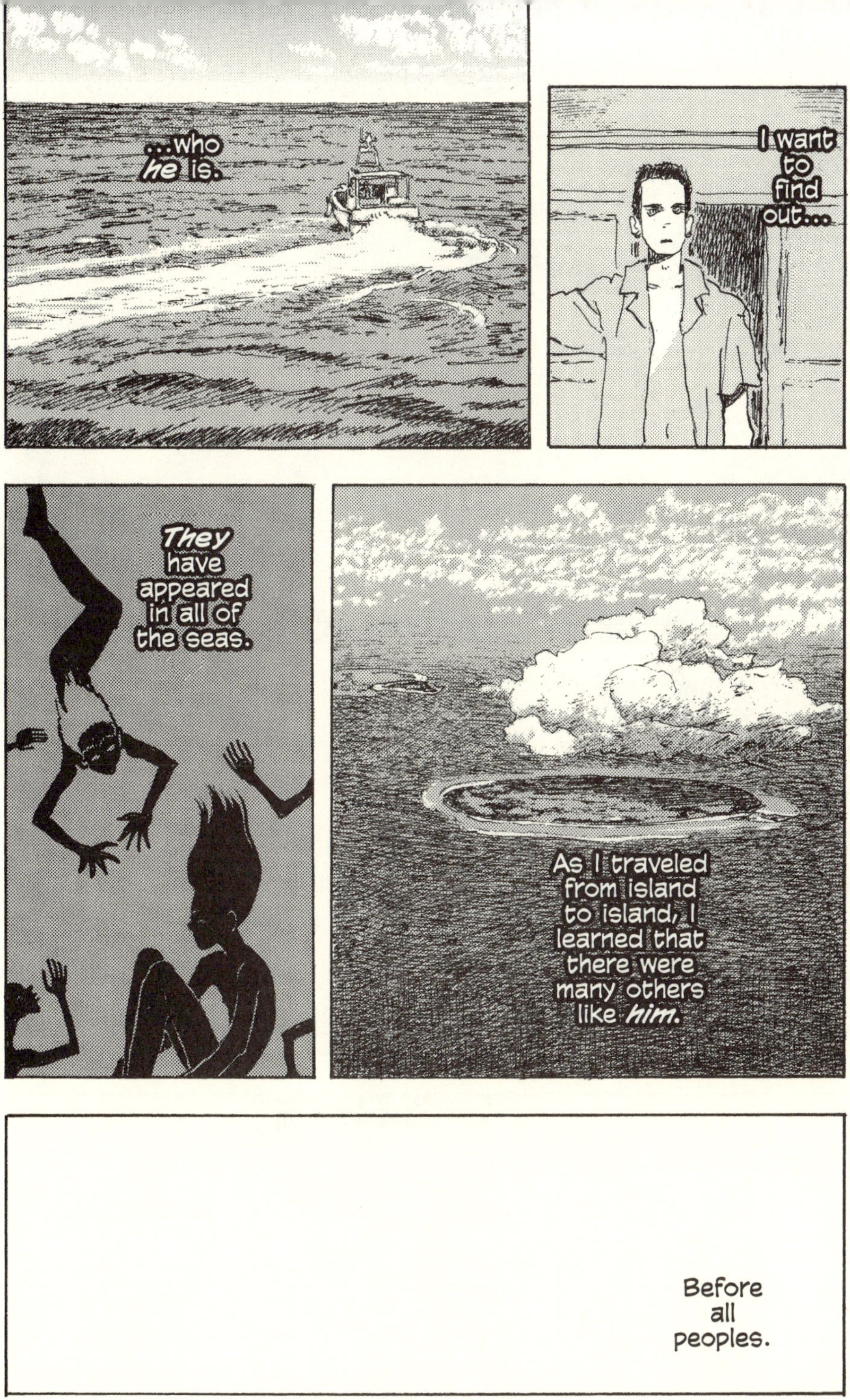
I want to find out...
...who *he* is.
As I traveled from island to island, I learned that there were many others like *him*.
They have appeared in all of the seas.
Before all peoples.

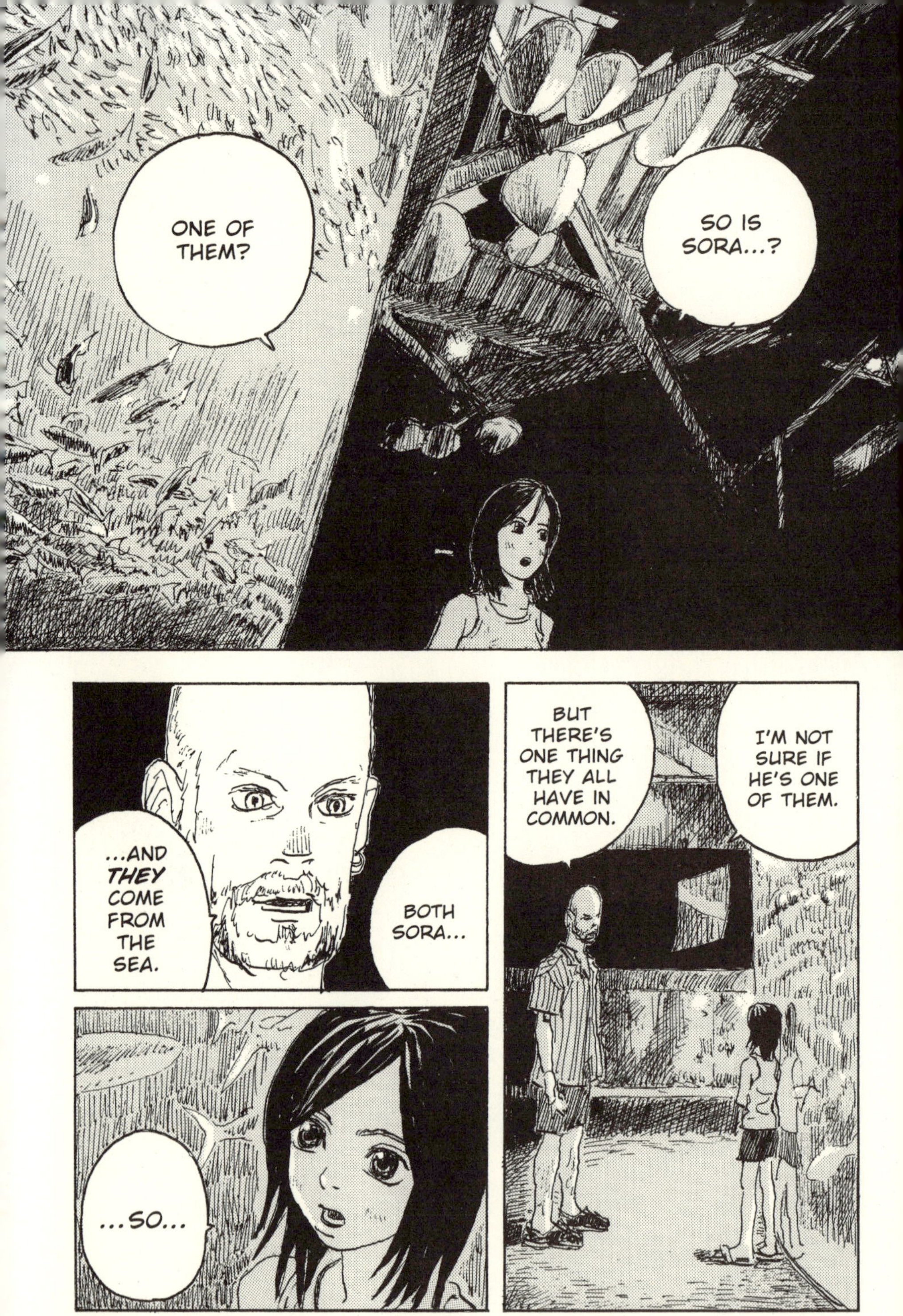
SO IS SORA...?
ONE OF THEM?
I'M NOT SURE IF HE'S ONE OF THEM.
BUT THERE'S ONE THING THEY ALL HAVE IN COMMON.
BOTH SORA...
...AND *THEY* COME FROM THE SEA.
...SO...

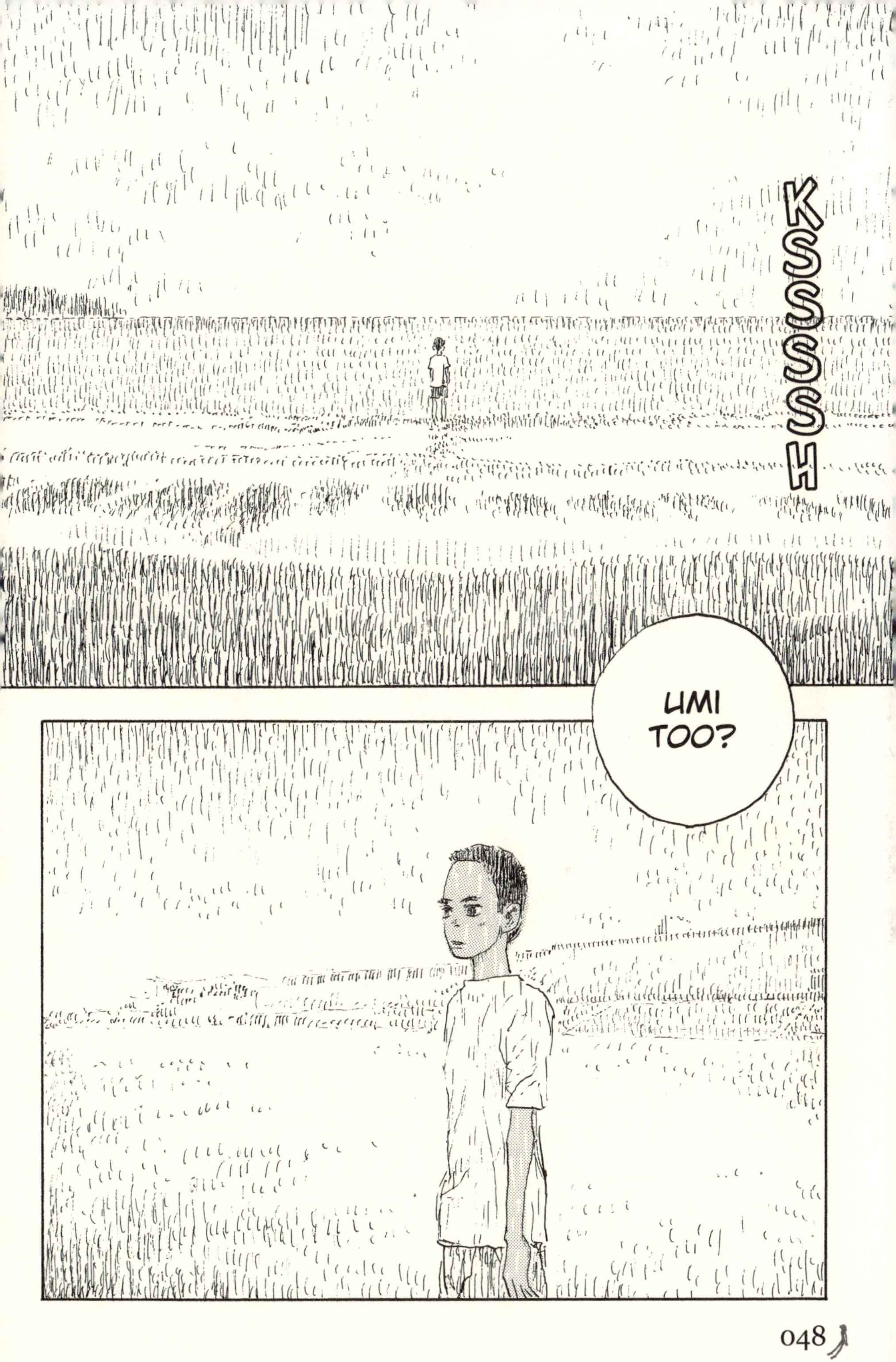
KSSSSH
UMI TOO?

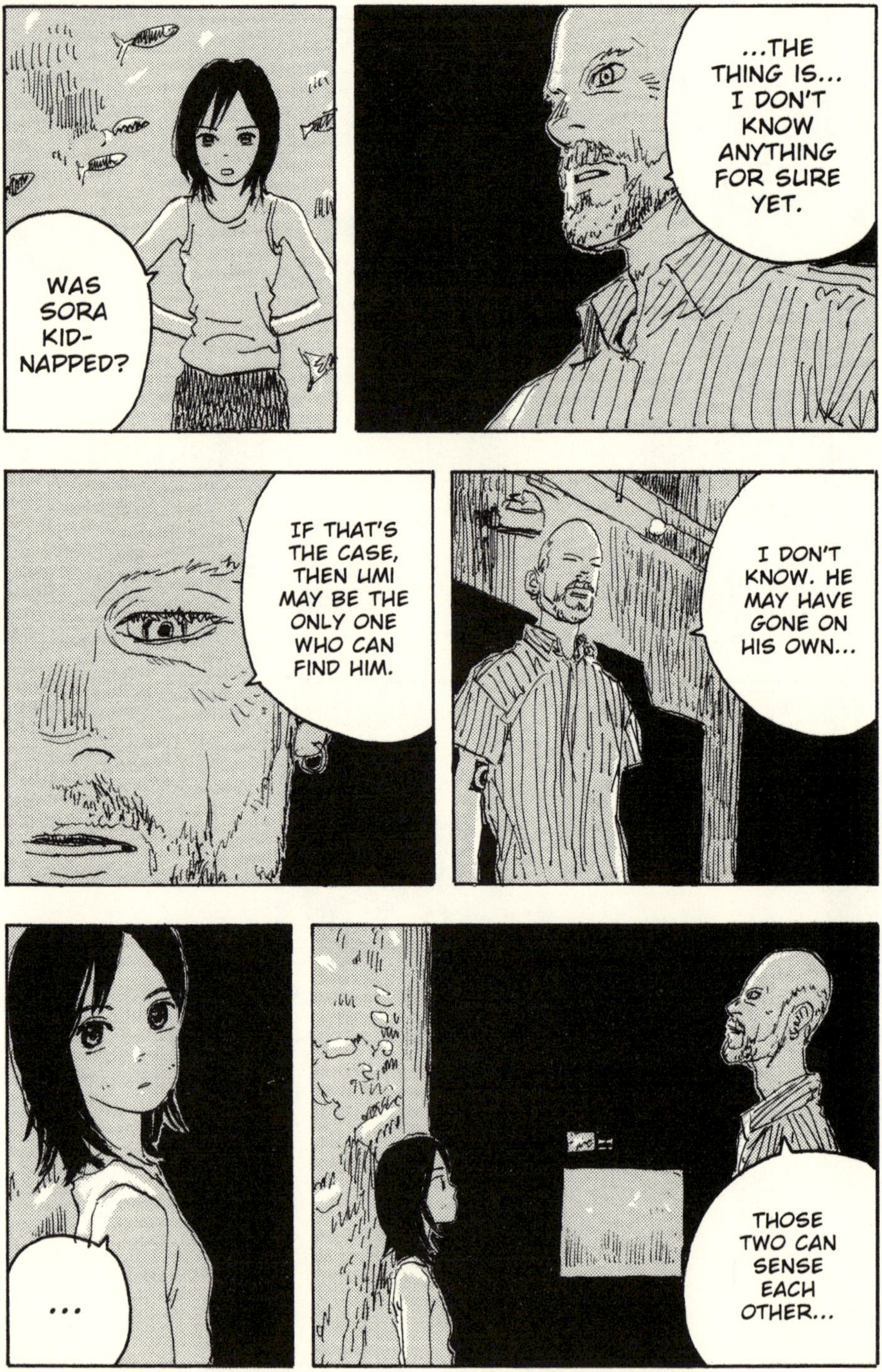
...THE THING IS... I DON'T KNOW ANYTHING FOR SURE YET.
WAS SORA KID-NAPPED?
I DON'T KNOW. HE MAY HAVE GONE ON HIS OWN...
IF THAT'S THE CASE, THEN UMI MAY BE THE ONLY ONE WHO CAN FIND HIM.
THOSE TWO CAN SENSE EACH OTHER...
...

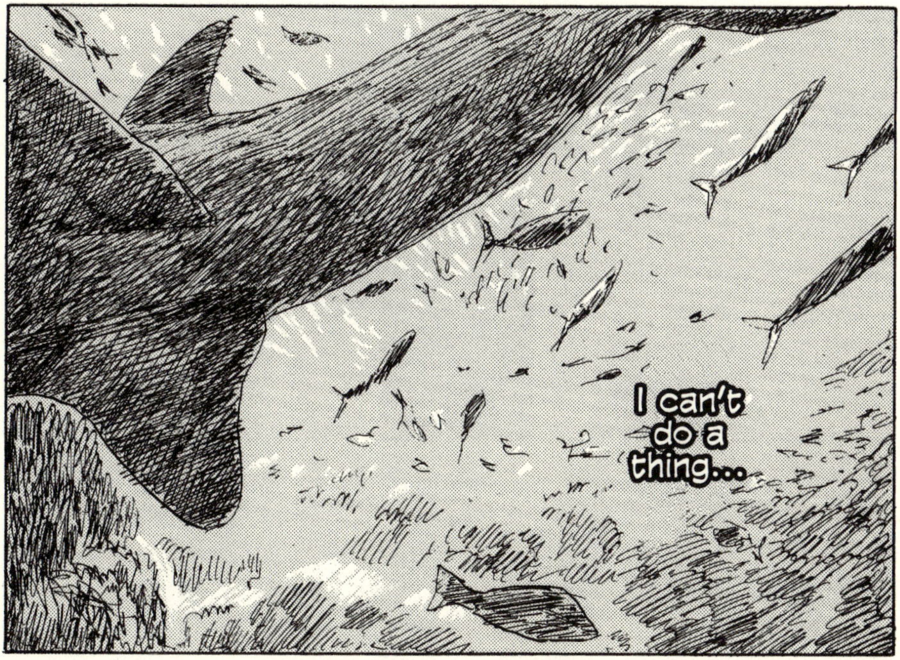
I can't do a thing...
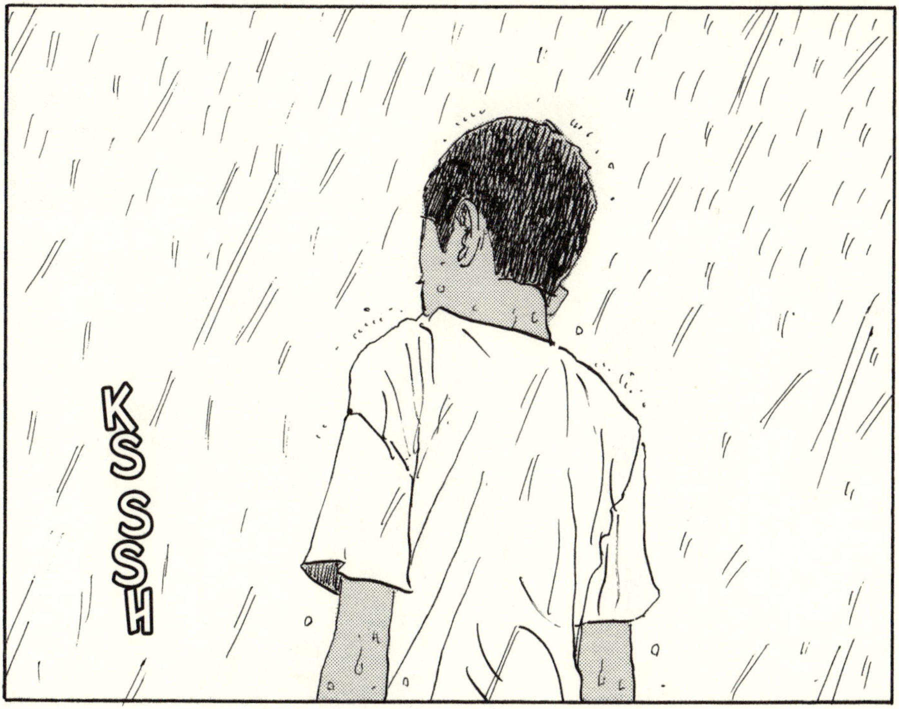
KSSSH

Chapter 10: A Strong Wind at Sea

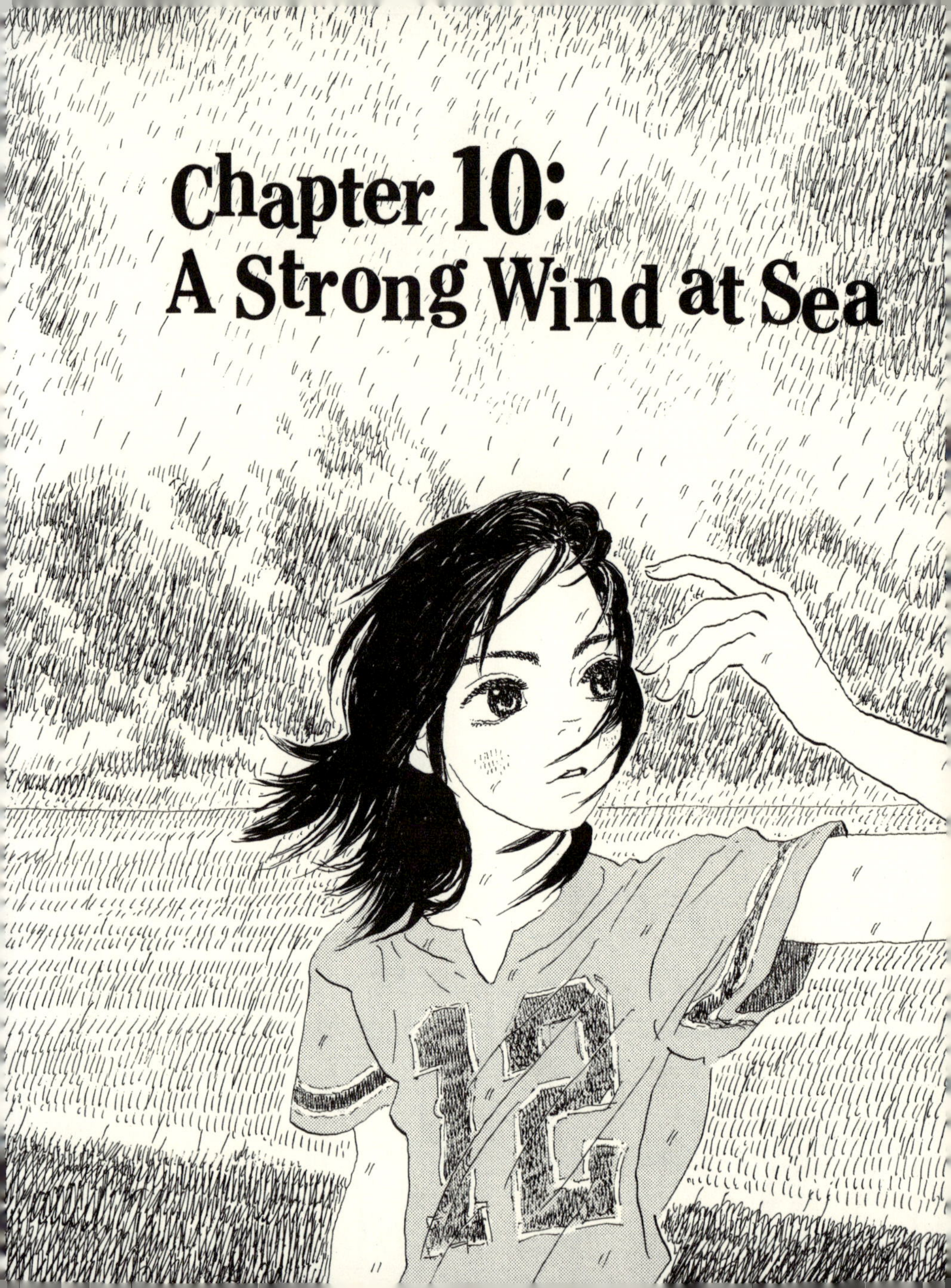

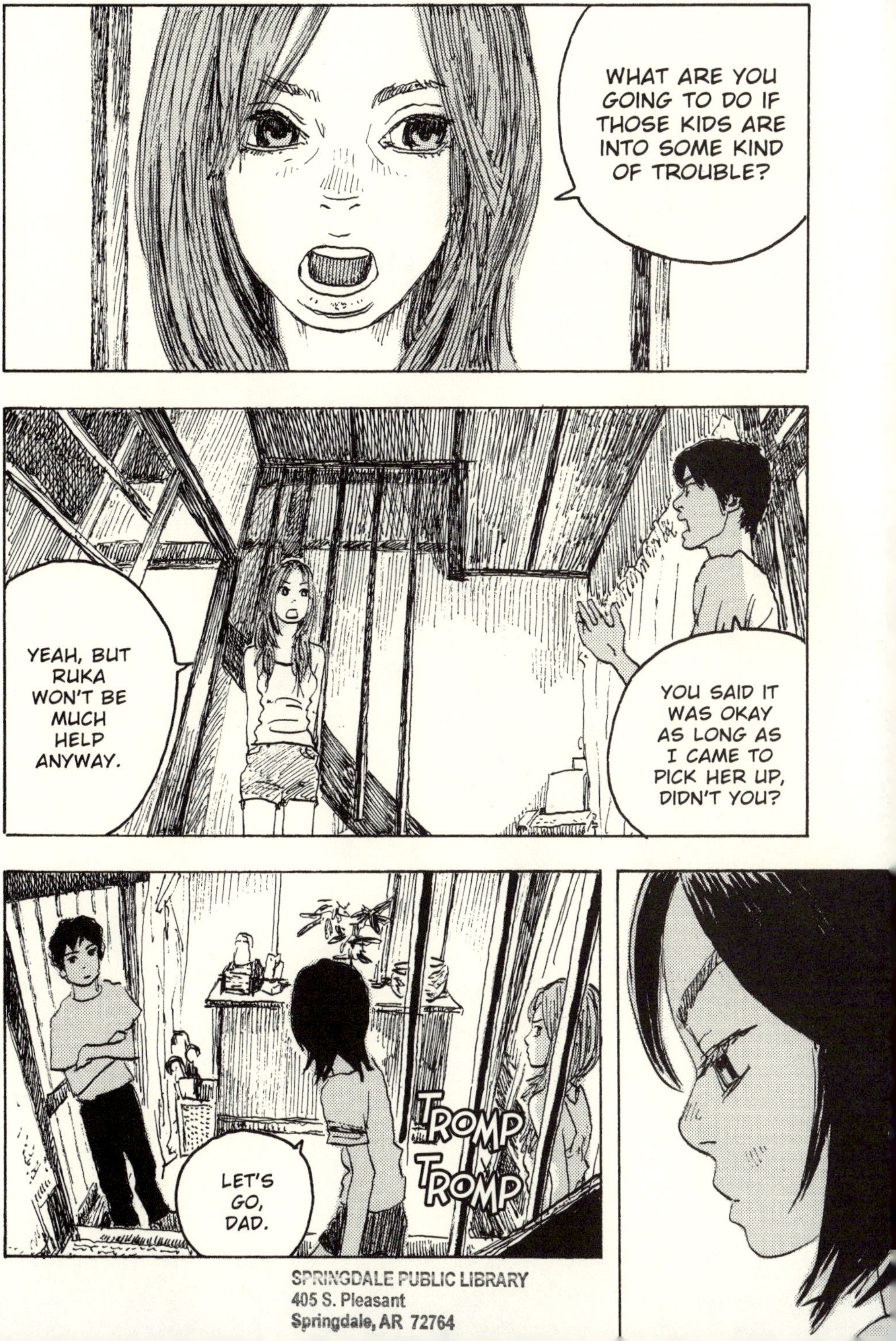
WHAT ARE YOU GOING TO DO IF THOSE KIDS ARE INTO SOME KIND OF TROUBLE?
YOU SAID IT WAS OKAY AS LONG AS I CAME TO PICK HER UP, DIDN'T YOU?
YEAH, BUT RUKA WON'T BE MUCH HELP ANYWAY.
TROMP
TROMP
LET'S GO, DAD.

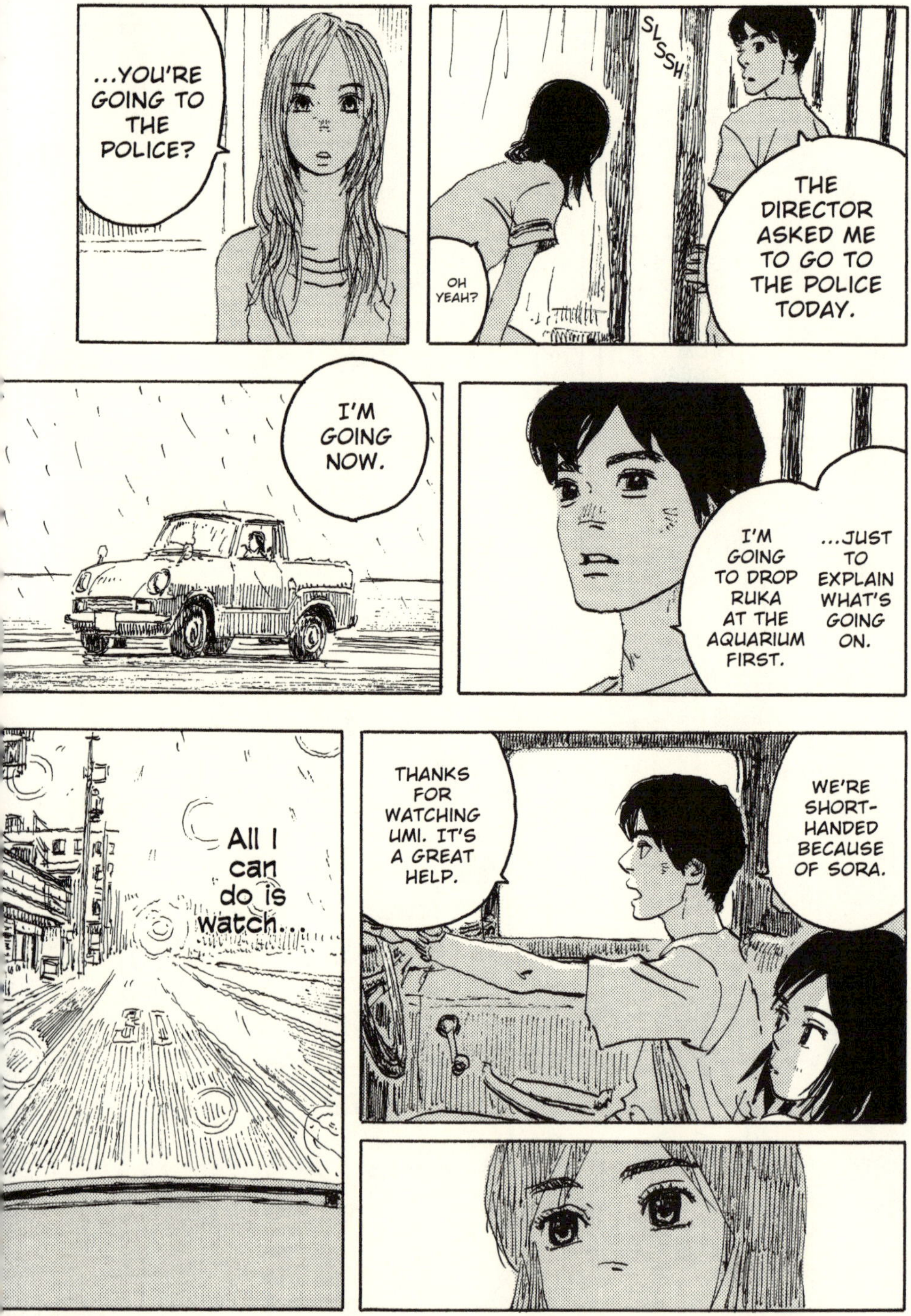
SLSSH
THE DIRECTOR ASKED ME TO GO TO THE POLICE TODAY.
OH YEAH?
...YOU'RE GOING TO THE POLICE?
I'M GOING TO DROP RUKA AT THE AQUARIUM FIRST. ...JUST TO EXPLAIN WHAT'S GOING ON.
I'M GOING NOW.
WE'RE SHORT-HANDED BECAUSE OF SORA.
THANKS FOR WATCHING UMI. IT'S A GREAT HELP.
All I can do is watch...

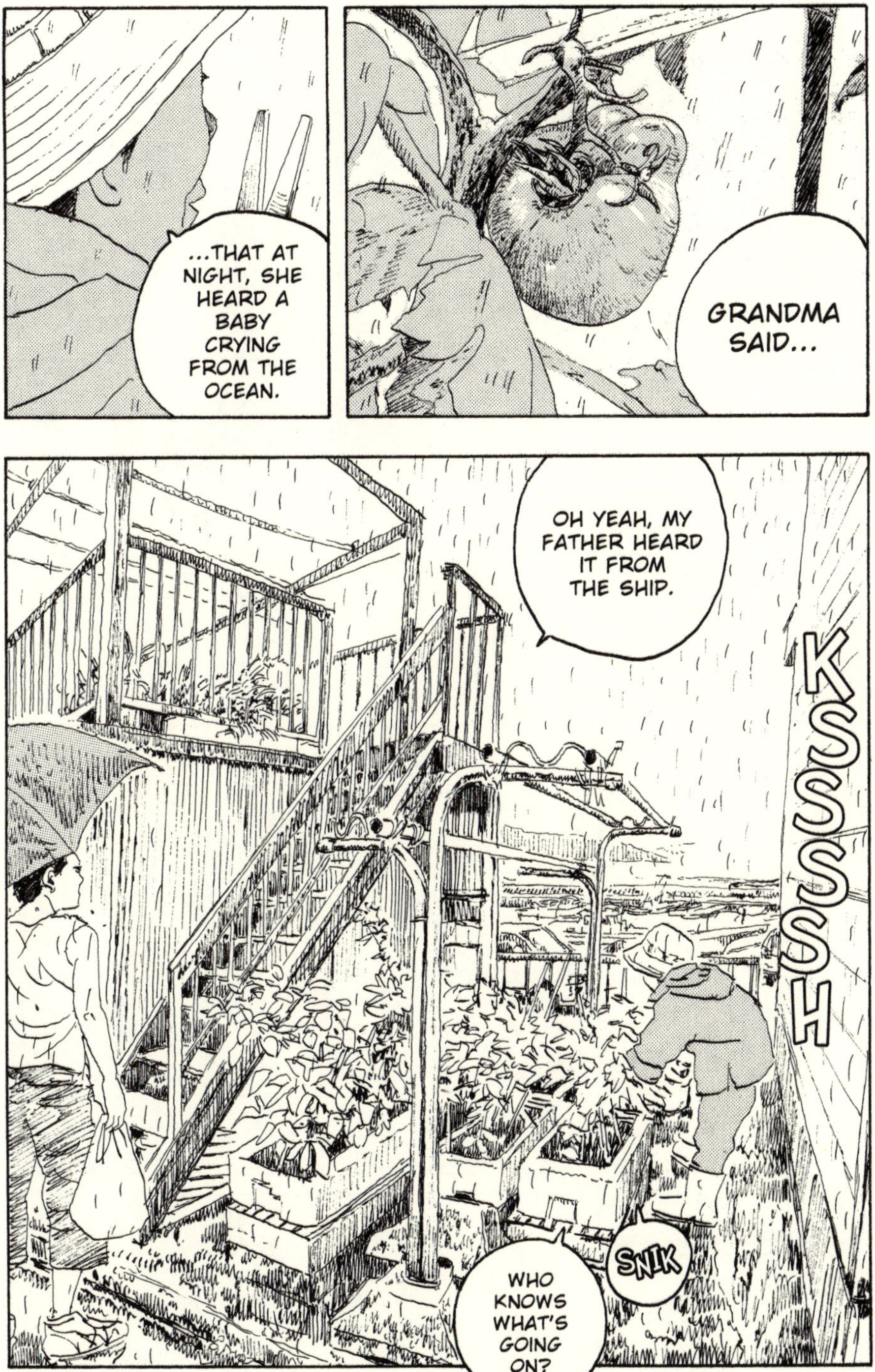
GRANDMA SAID...
...THAT AT NIGHT, SHE HEARD A BABY CRYING FROM THE OCEAN.
OH YEAH, MY FATHER HEARD IT FROM THE SHIP.
KSSSSSH
SNIK
WHO KNOWS WHAT'S GOING ON?

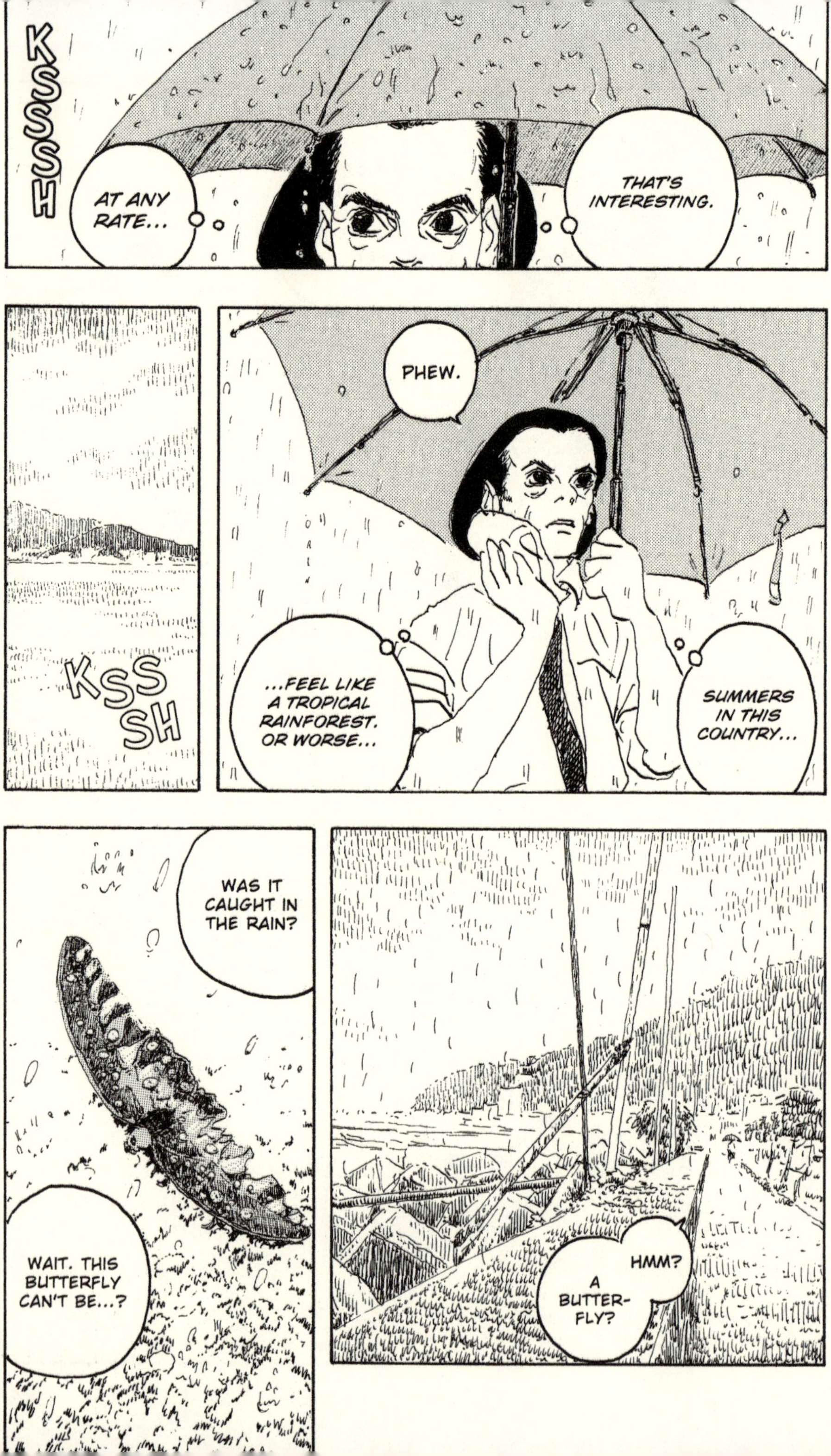
THAT'S INTERESTING.
AT ANY RATE...
KSSSH
PHEW.
SUMMERS IN THIS COUNTRY...
...FEEL LIKE A TROPICAL RAINFOREST. OR WORSE...
KSSSH
HMM?
A BUTTERFLY?
WAS IT CAUGHT IN THE RAIN?
WAIT. THIS BUTTERFLY CAN'T BE...?

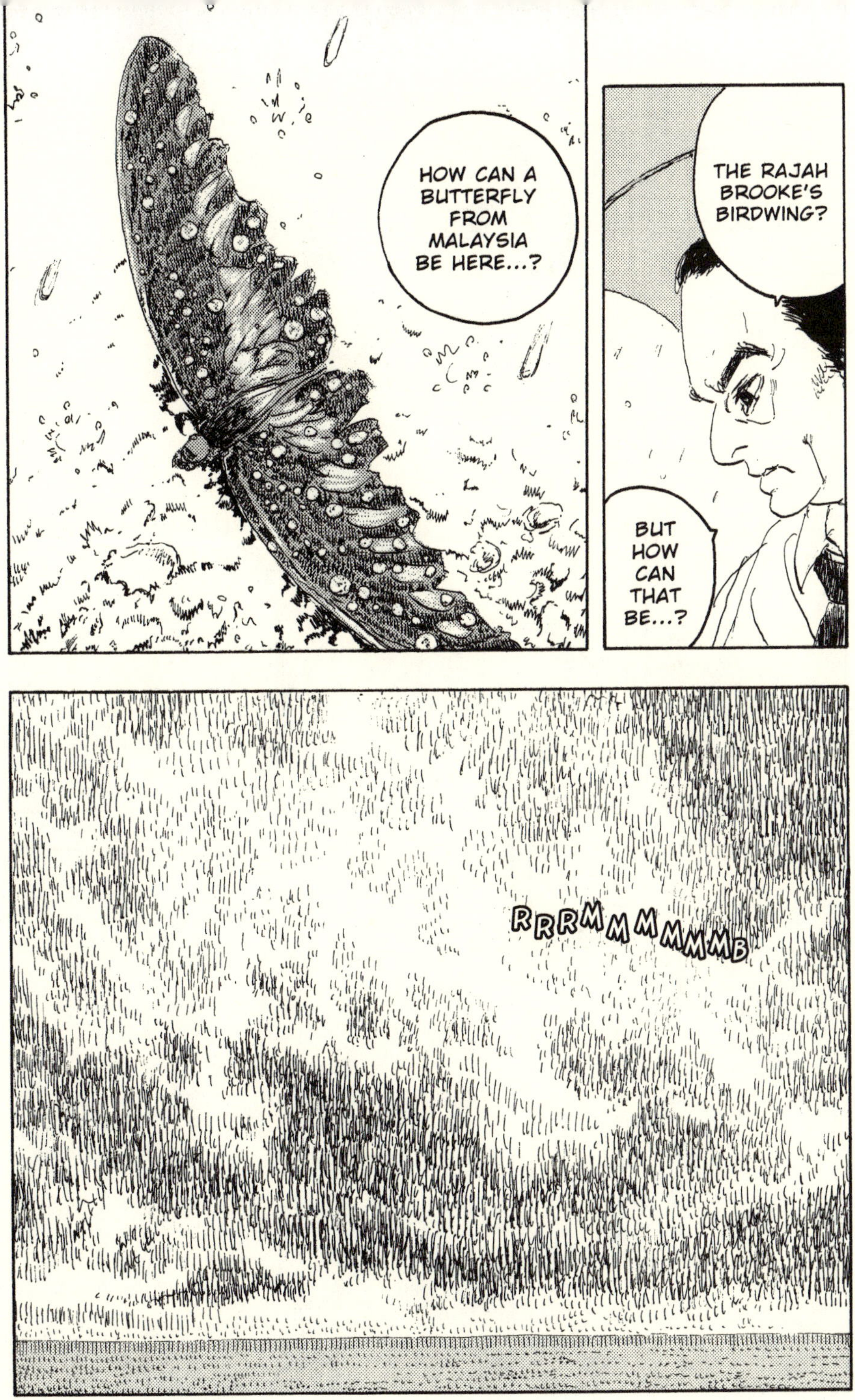
THE RAJAH BROOKE'S BIRDWING?
BUT HOW CAN THAT BE...?
HOW CAN A BUTTERFLY FROM MALAYSIA BE HERE...?
RRRMMMMMMMB

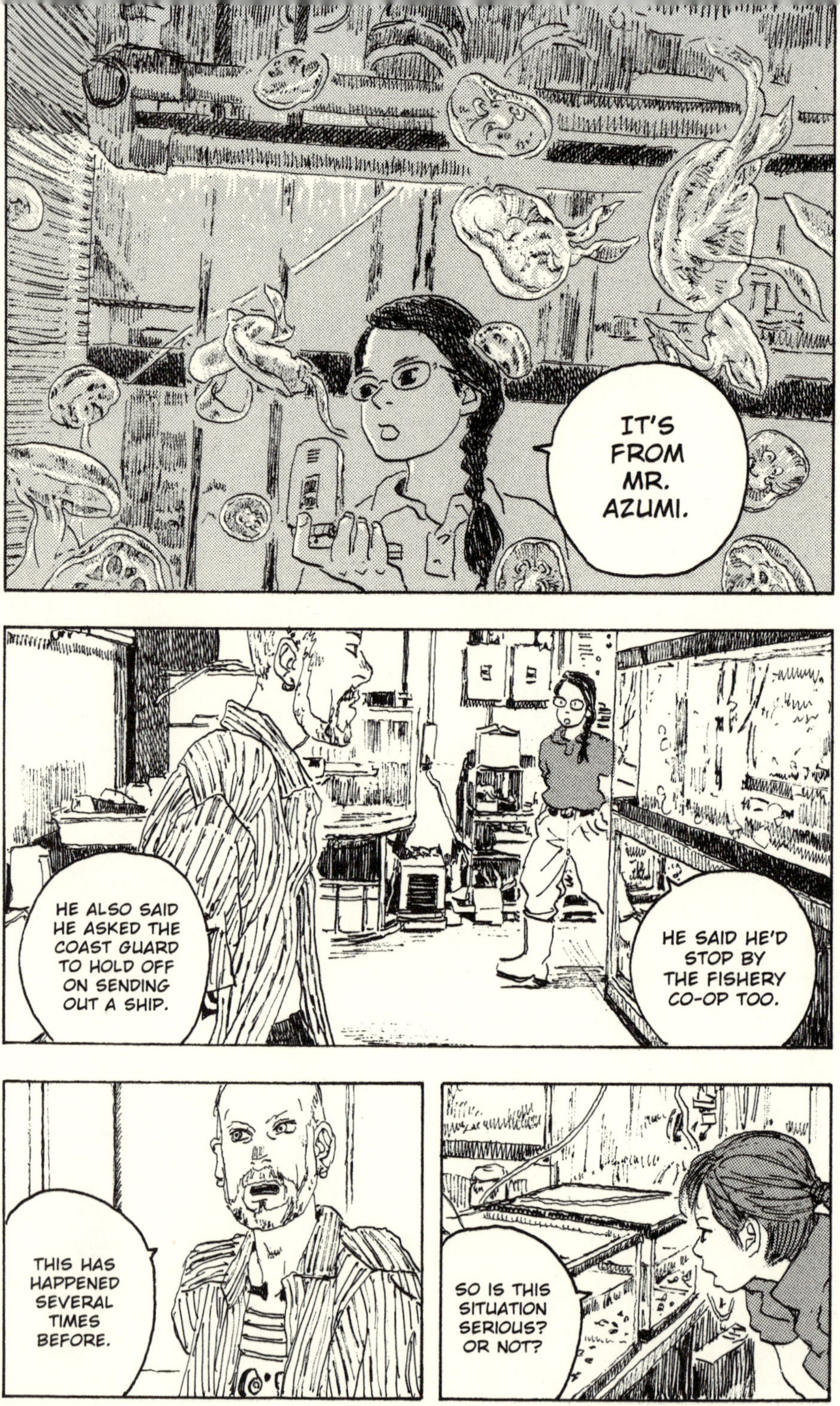
IT'S FROM MR. AZUMI.
HE SAID HE'D STOP BY THE FISHERY CO-OP TOO.
HE ALSO SAID HE ASKED THE COAST GUARD TO HOLD OFF ON SENDING OUT A SHIP.
SO IS THIS SITUATION SERIOUS? OR NOT?
THIS HAS HAPPENED SEVERAL TIMES BEFORE.

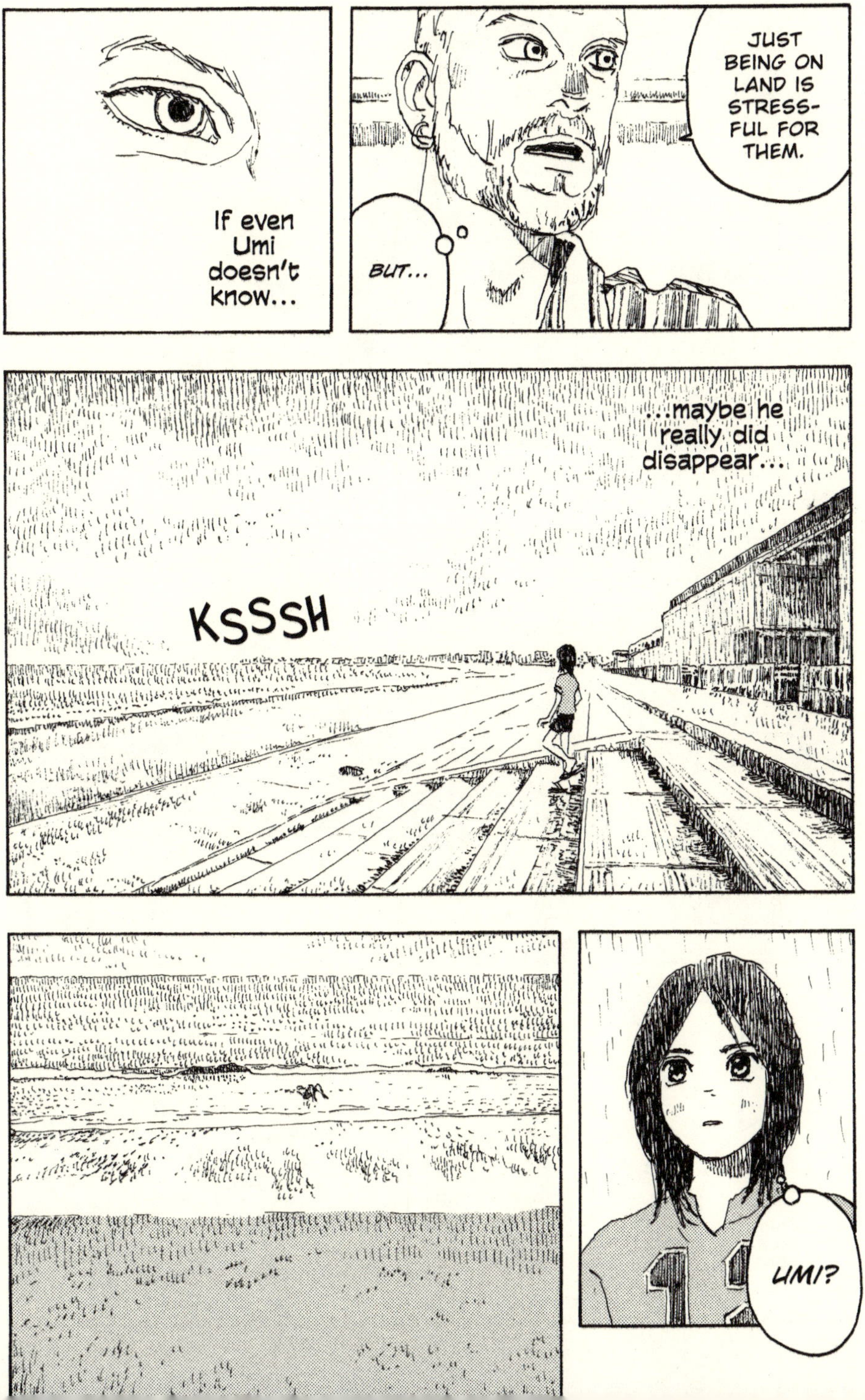
JUST BEING ON LAND IS STRESS-FUL FOR THEM.
BUT...
If even Umi doesn't know...
...maybe he really did disappear...
KSSSH
UMI?

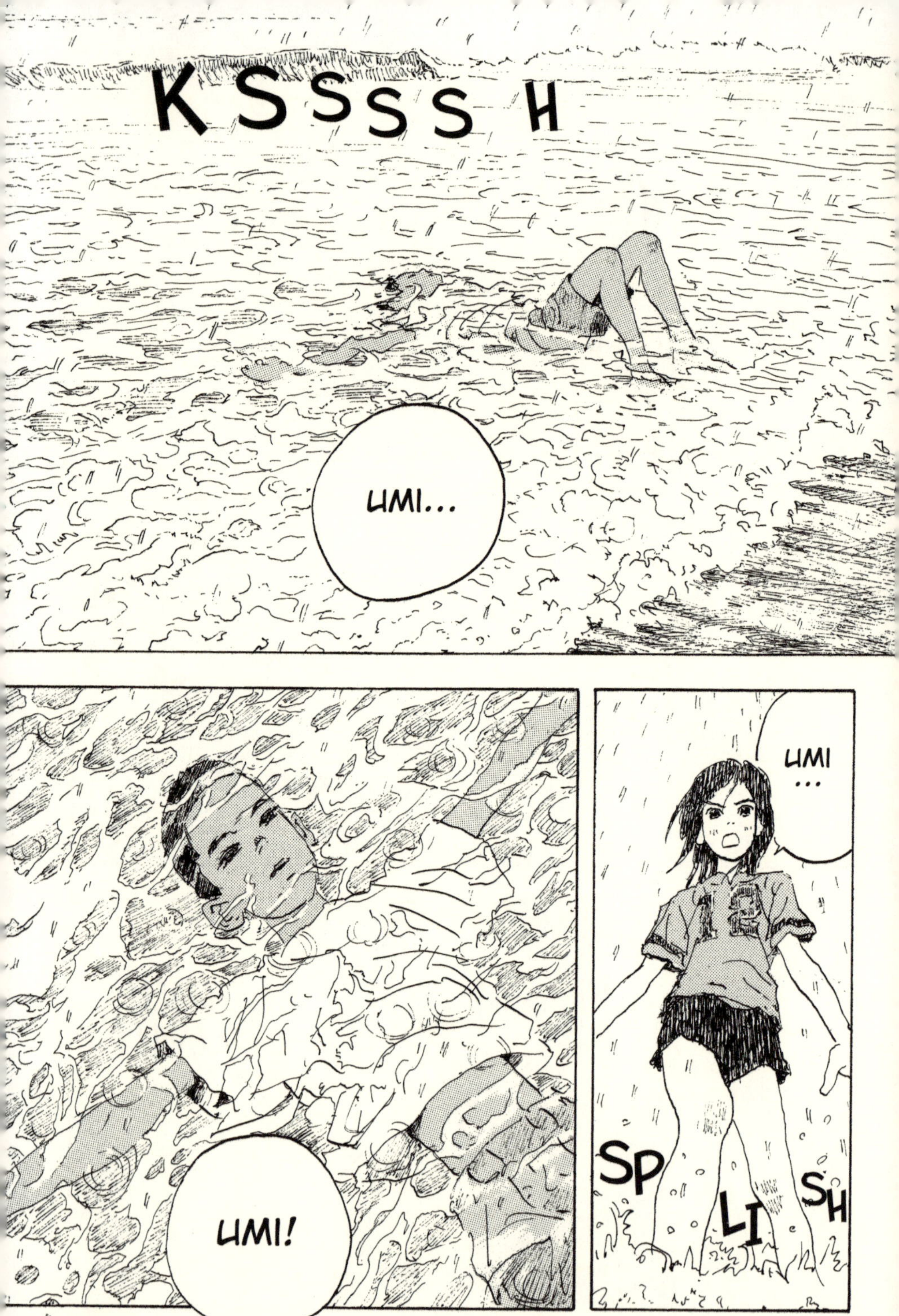
KSSSSH
UMI...
UMI ...
SPLISH
UMI!

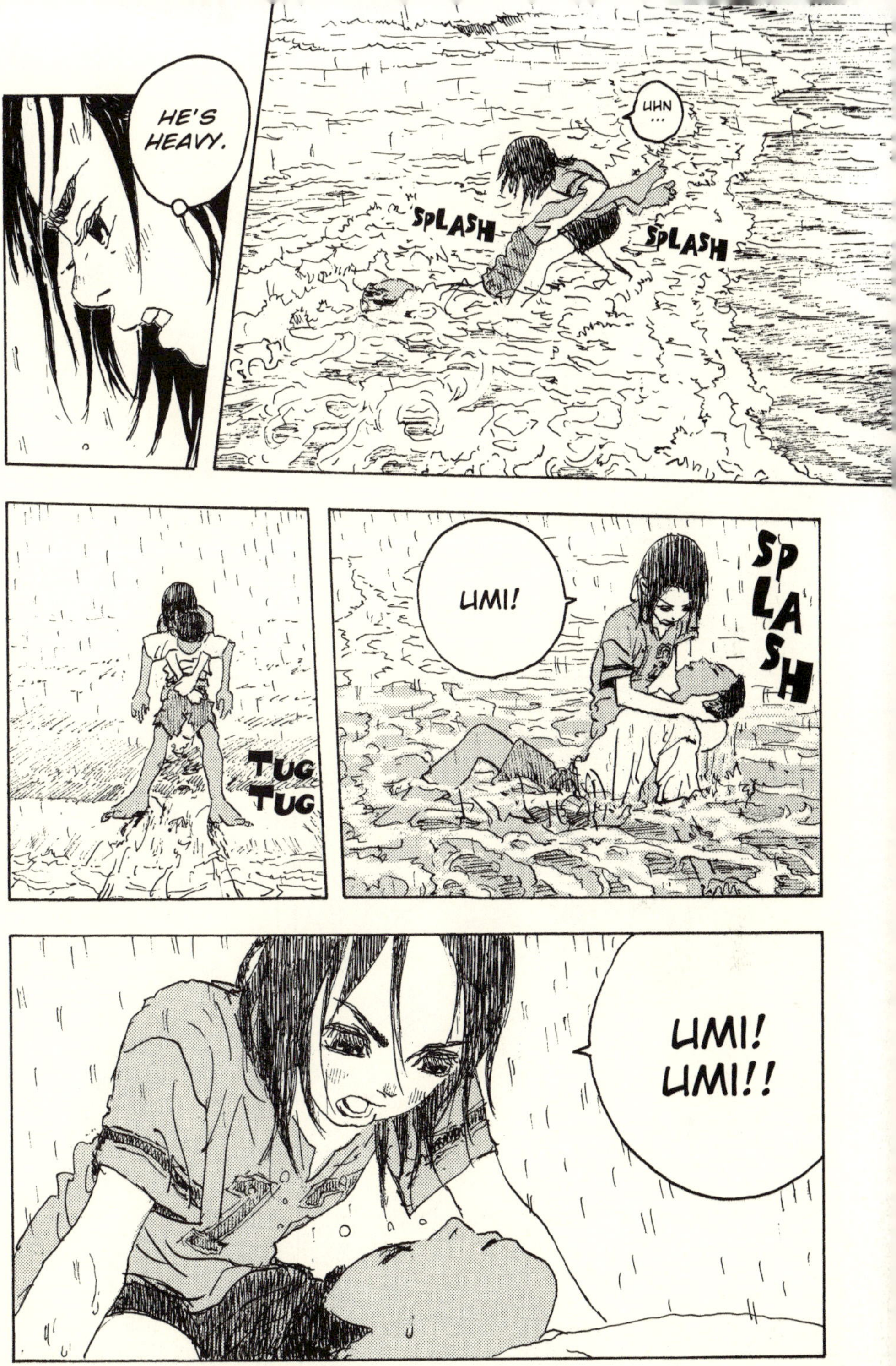
UHN ...
SPLASH
SPLASH
HE'S HEAVY.
UMI!
SPLASH
TUG TUG
UMI! UMI!!

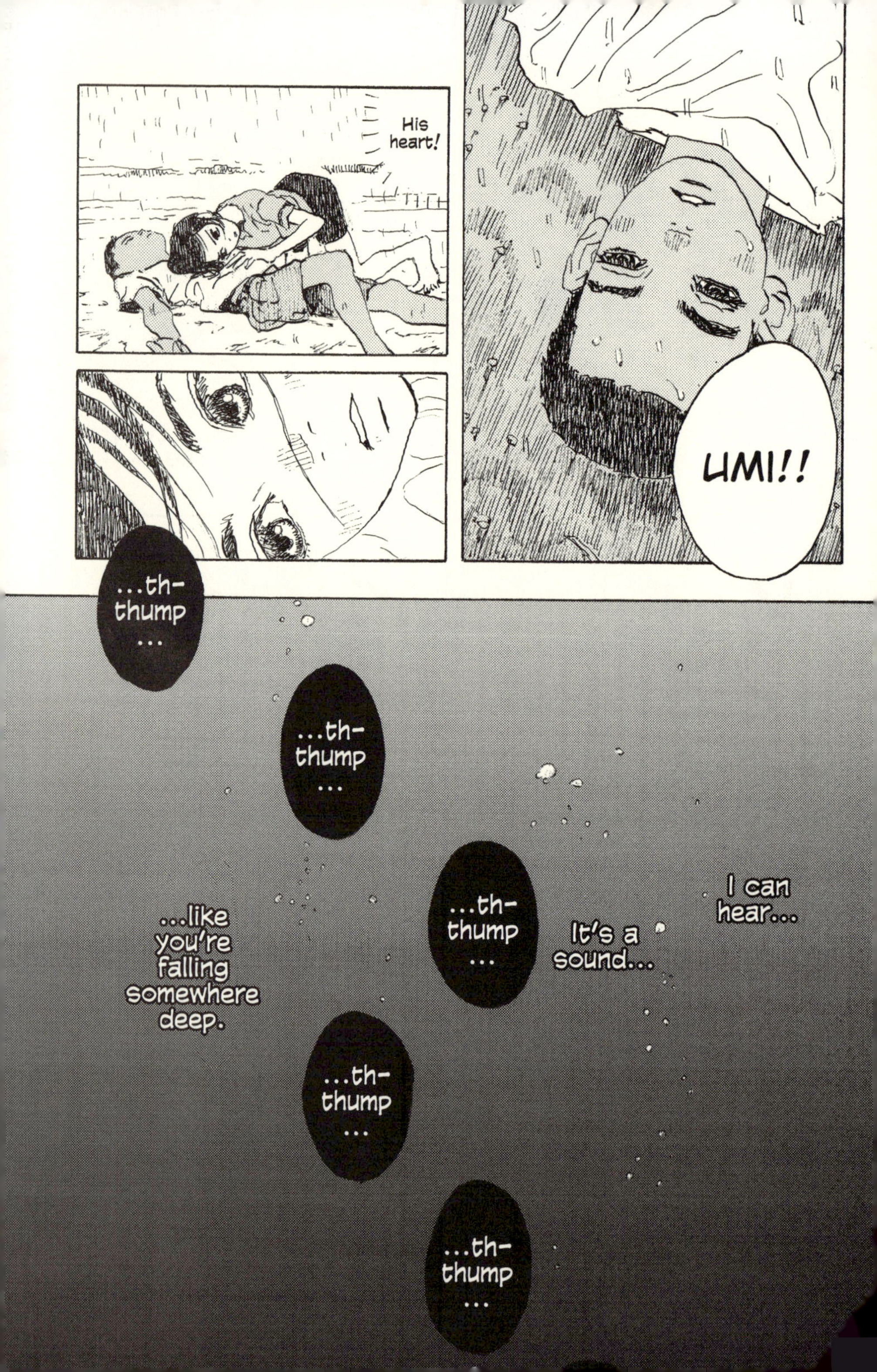
UMI!!
His heart!
...th-thump...
...th-thump...
I can hear...
It's a sound...
...th-thump...
...like you're falling somewhere deep.
...th-thump...
...th-thump...

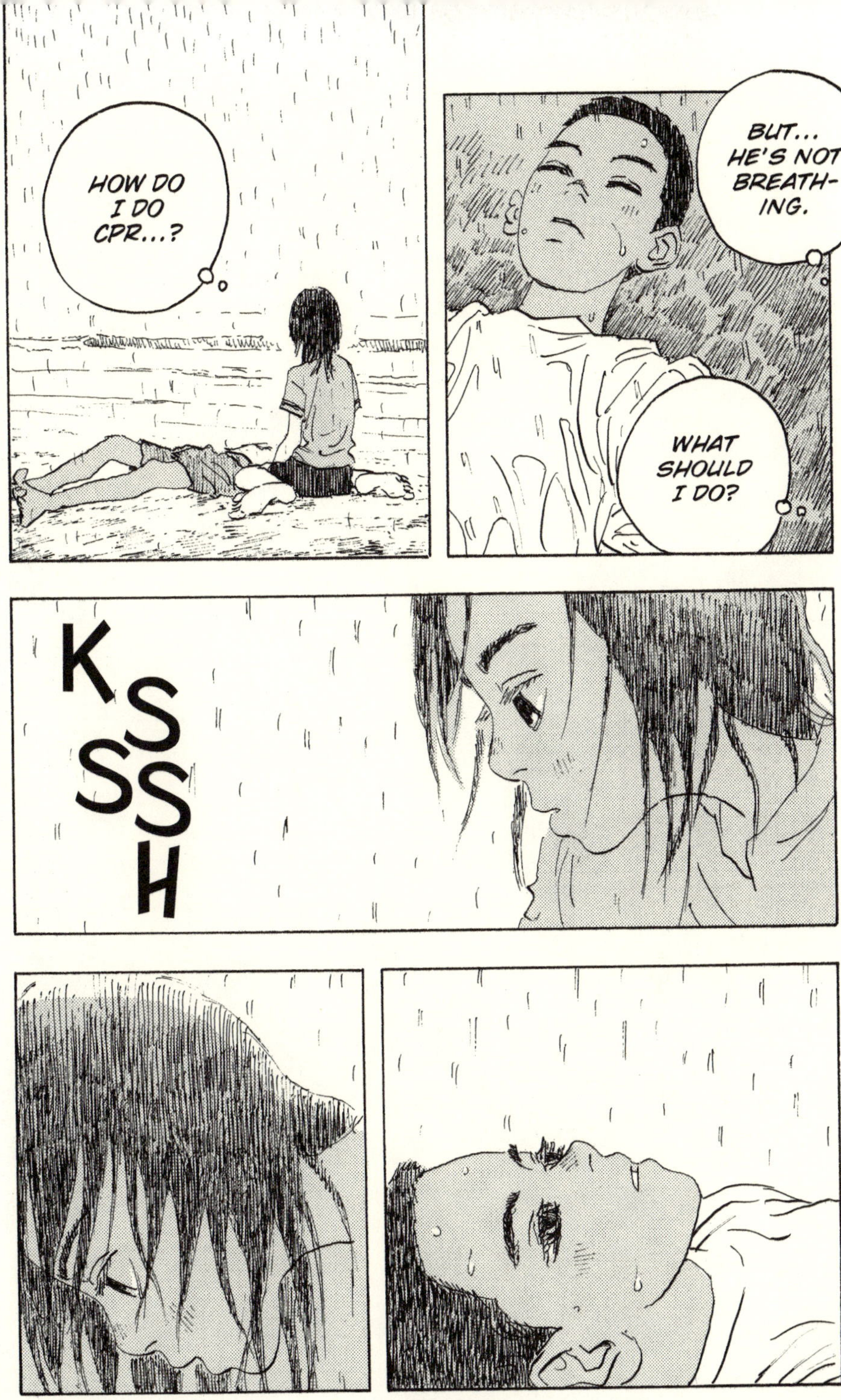
BUT... HE'S NOT BREATHING.
WHAT SHOULD I DO?
HOW DO I DO CPR...?
KSSSH

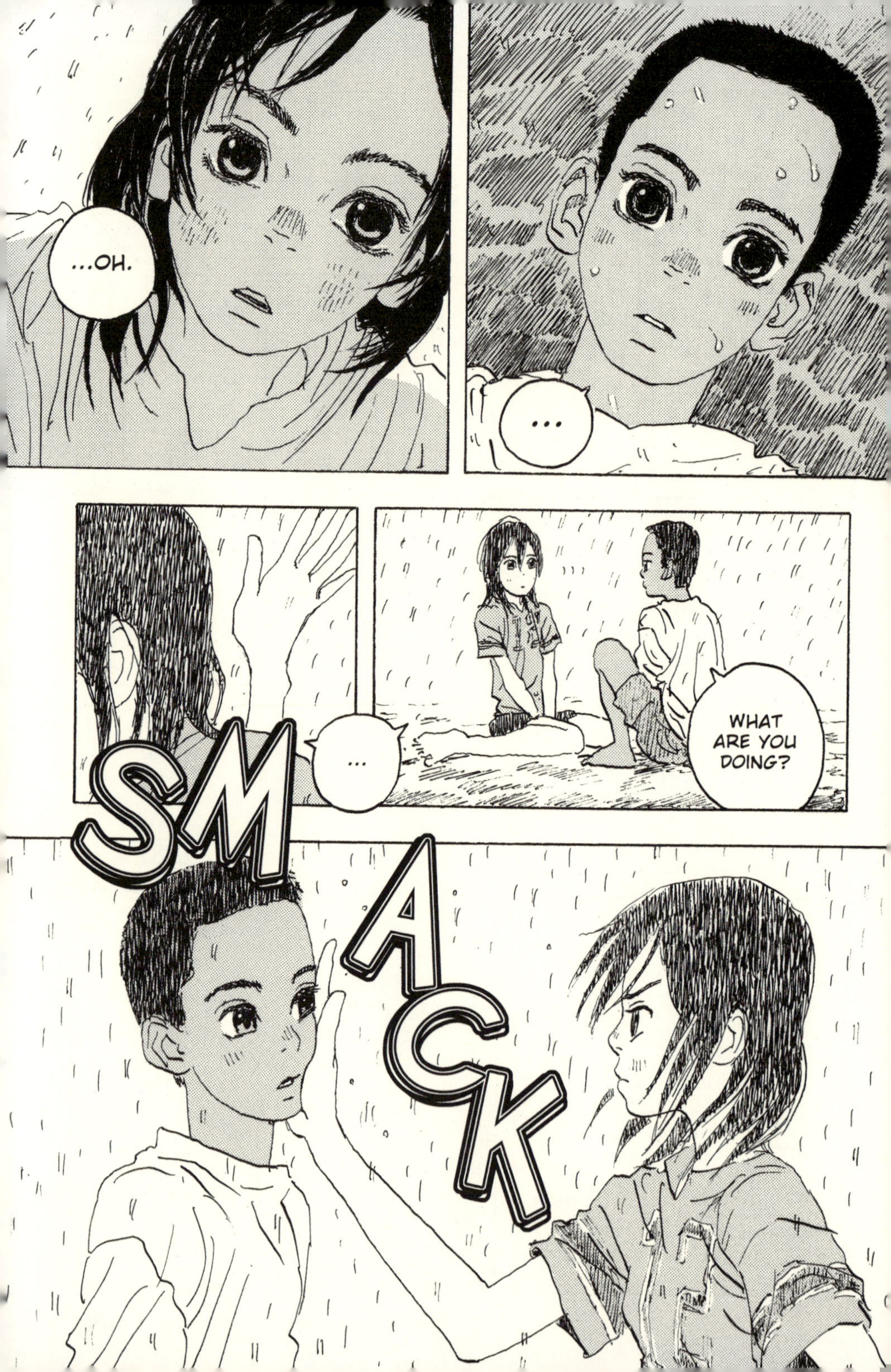
...
...OH.
WHAT ARE YOU DOING?
...
SMACK

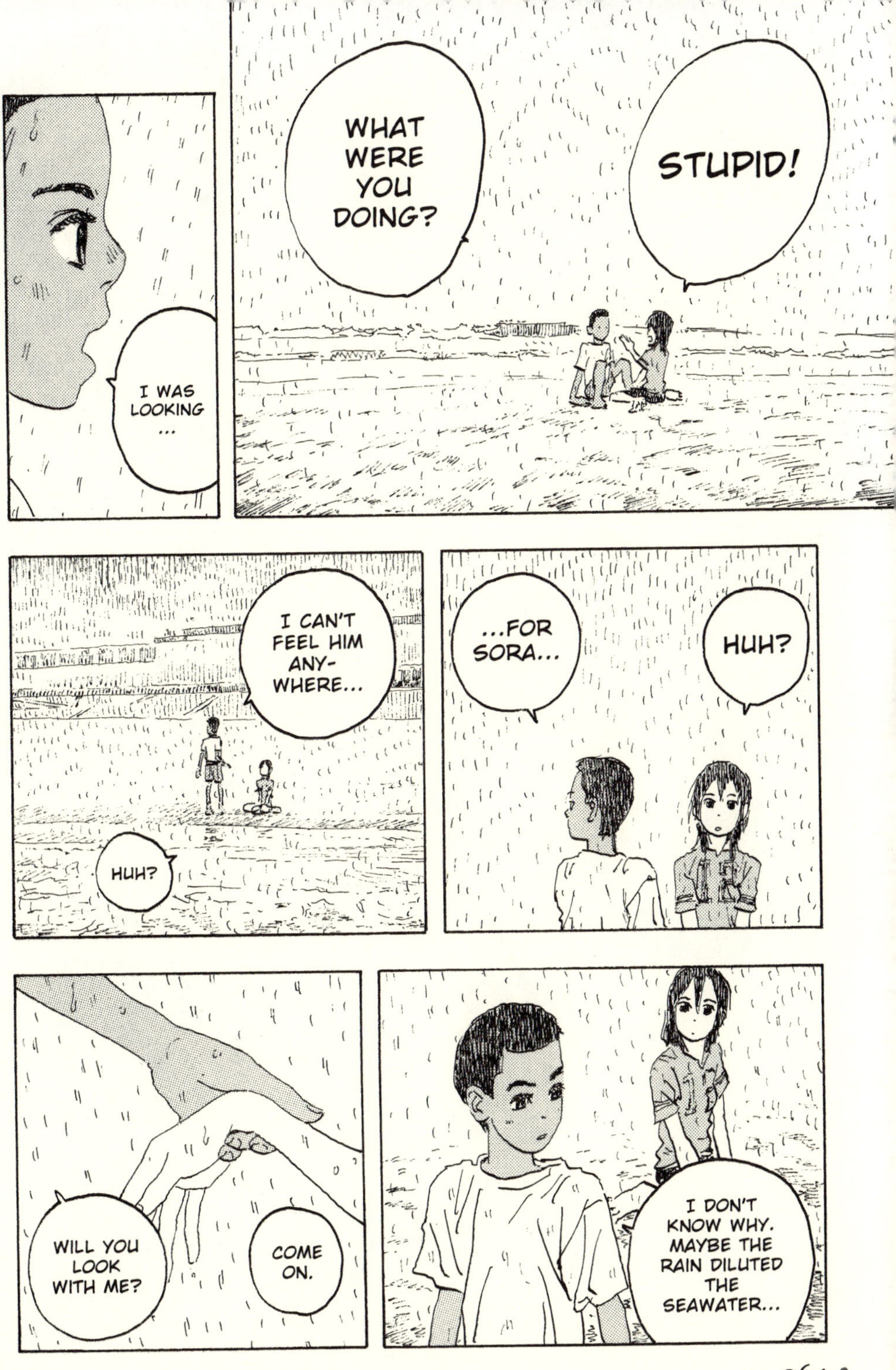
STUPID!
WHAT WERE YOU DOING?
I WAS LOOKING ...
HUH?
...FOR SORA...
I CAN'T FEEL HIM ANY-WHERE...
HUH?
I DON'T KNOW WHY. MAYBE THE RAIN DILUTED THE SEAWATER...
COME ON.
WILL YOU LOOK WITH ME?

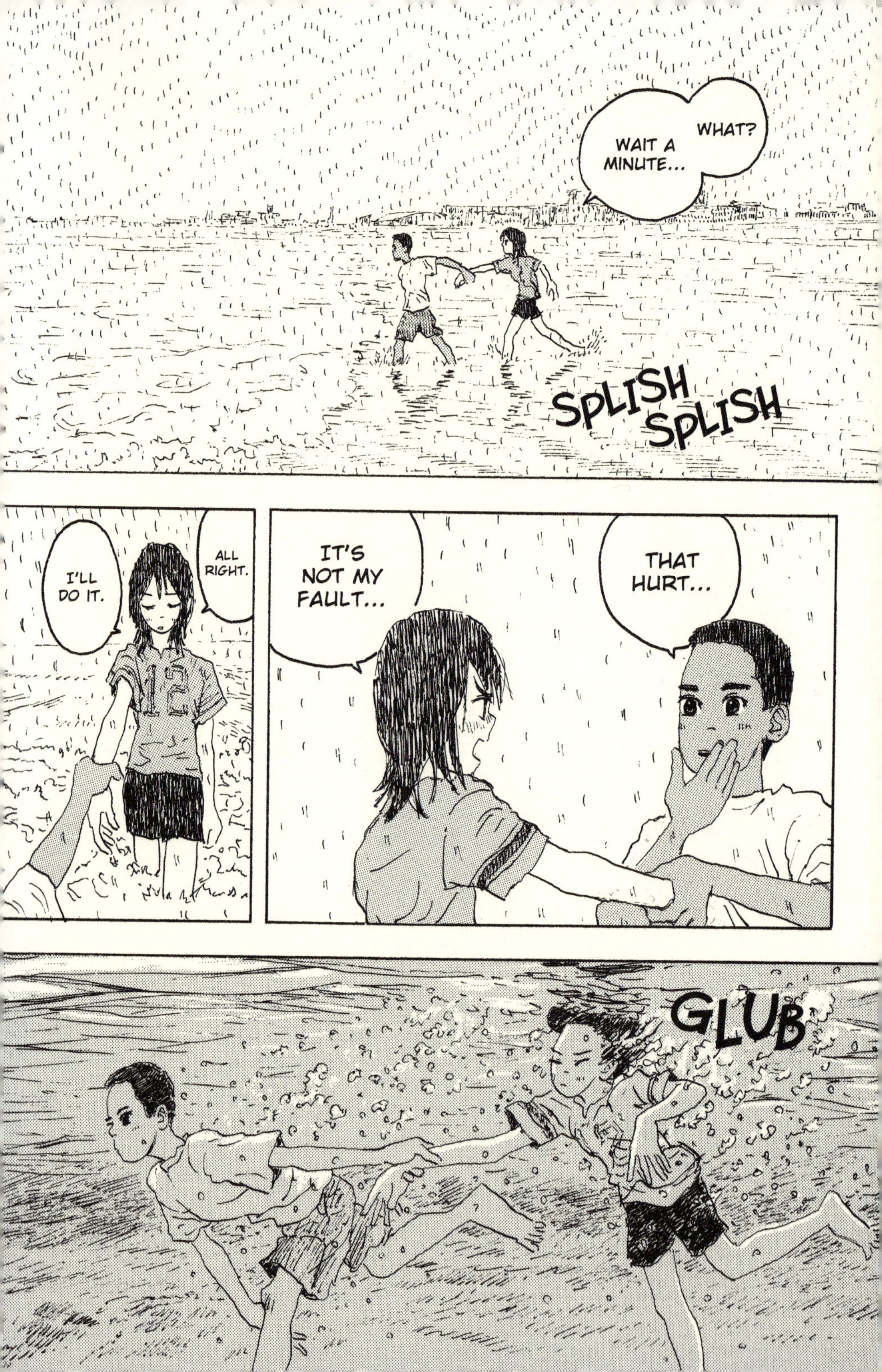
WHAT?
WAIT A MINUTE...
SPLISH SPLISH
THAT HURT...
IT'S NOT MY FAULT...
ALL RIGHT.
I'LL DO IT.
GLUB

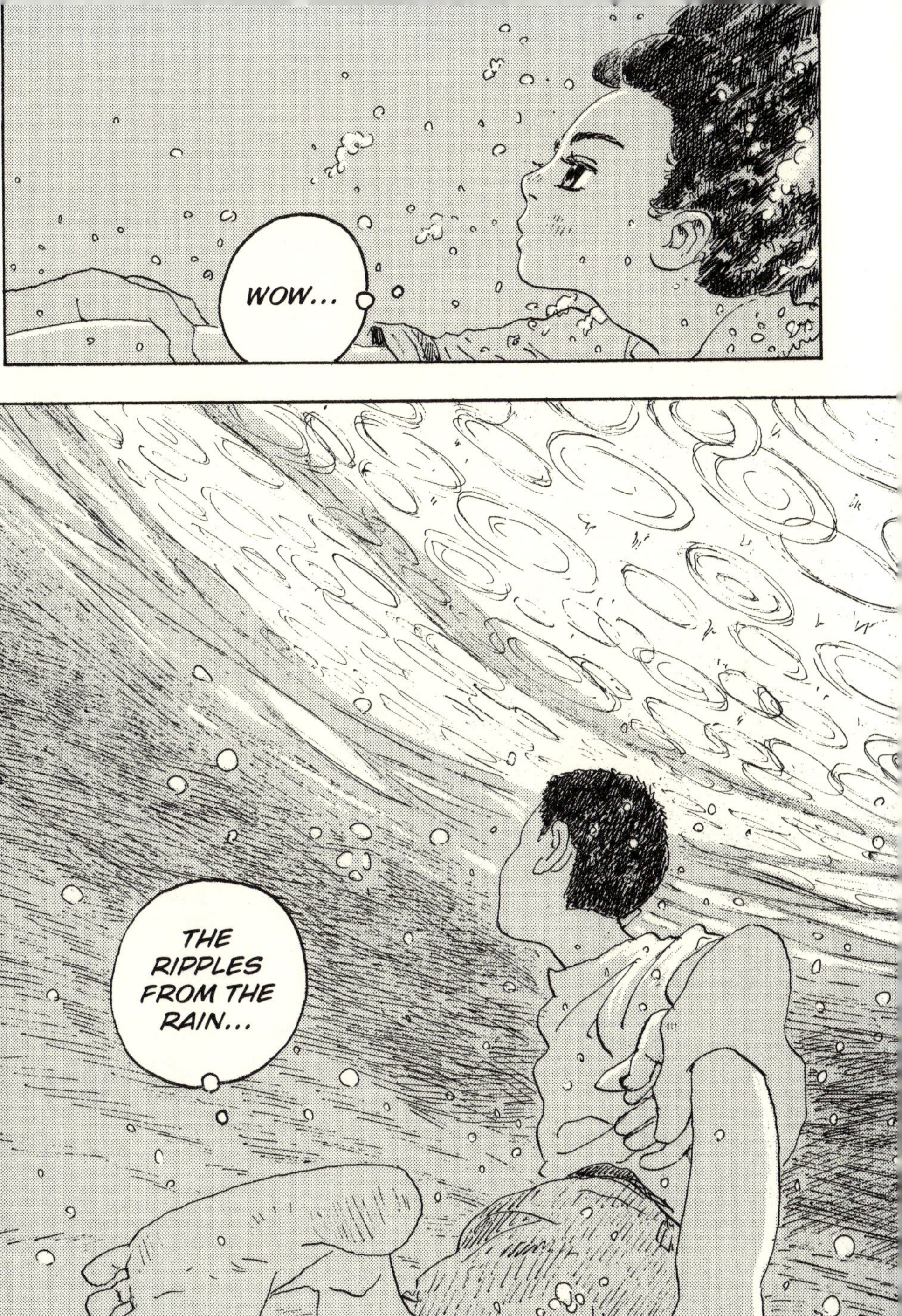
WOW...
THE RIPPLES FROM THE RAIN...

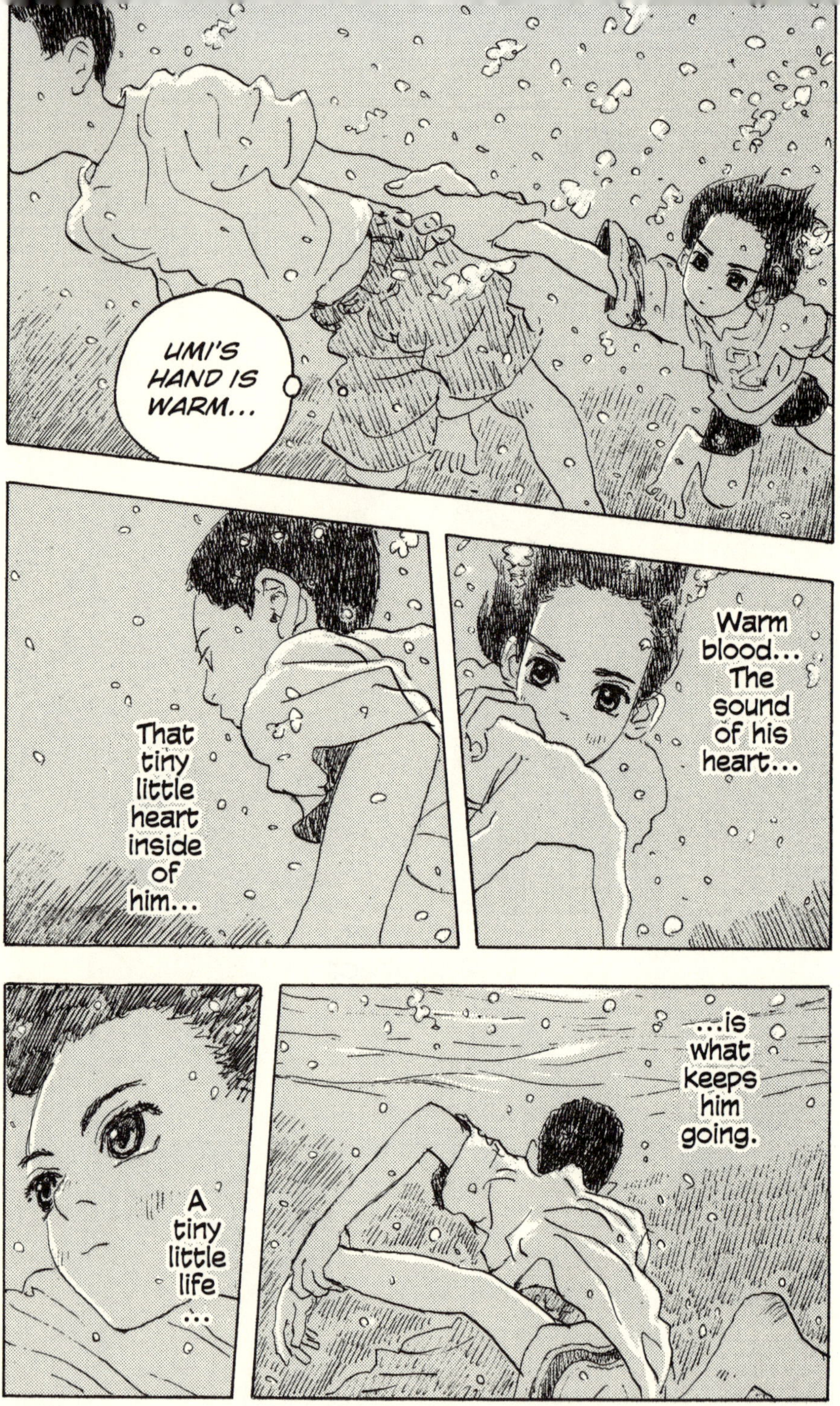
UMI'S HAND IS WARM...
Warm blood... The sound of his heart...
That tiny little heart inside of him...
...is what keeps him going.
A tiny little life ...

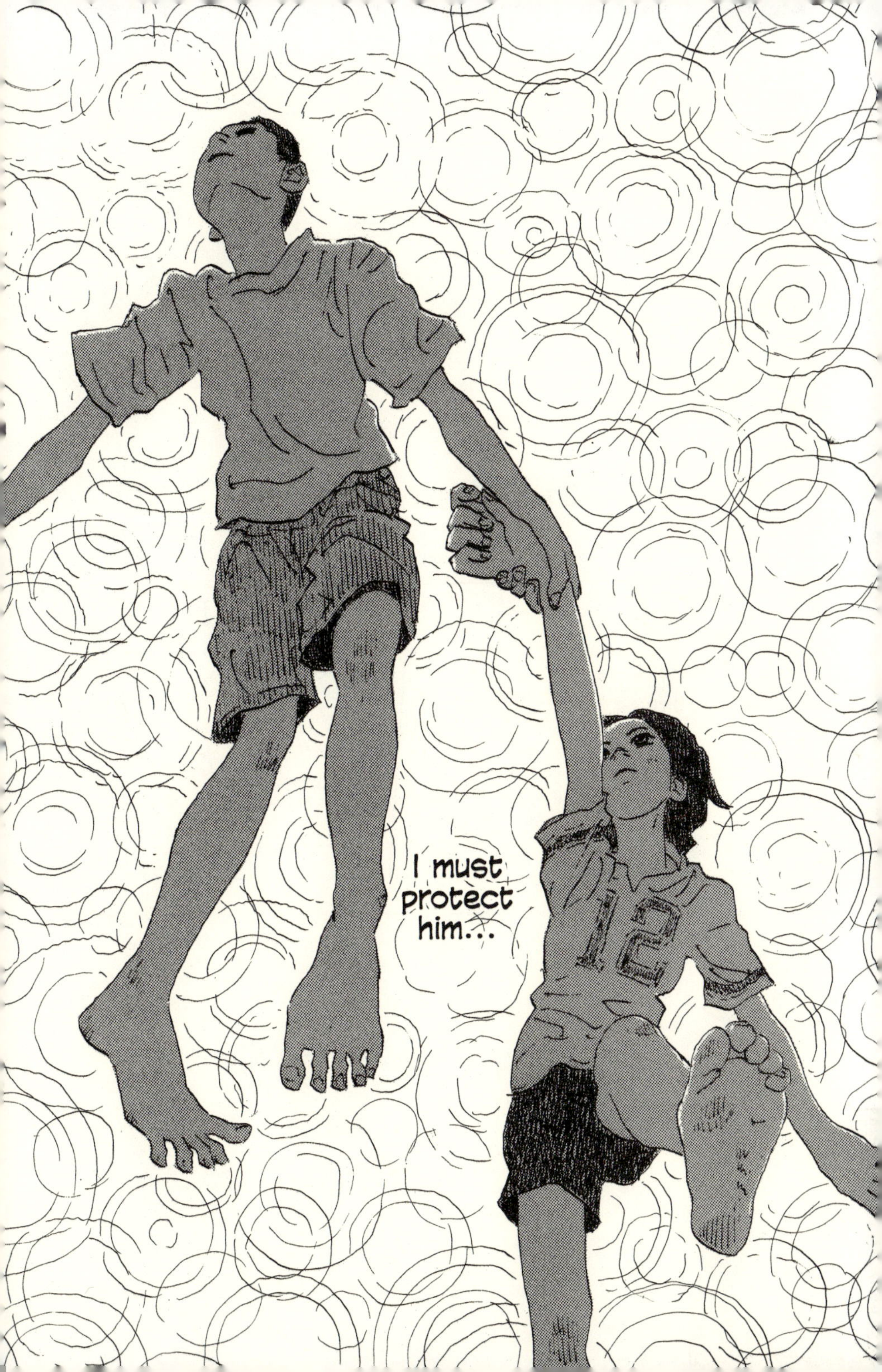
I must protect him...

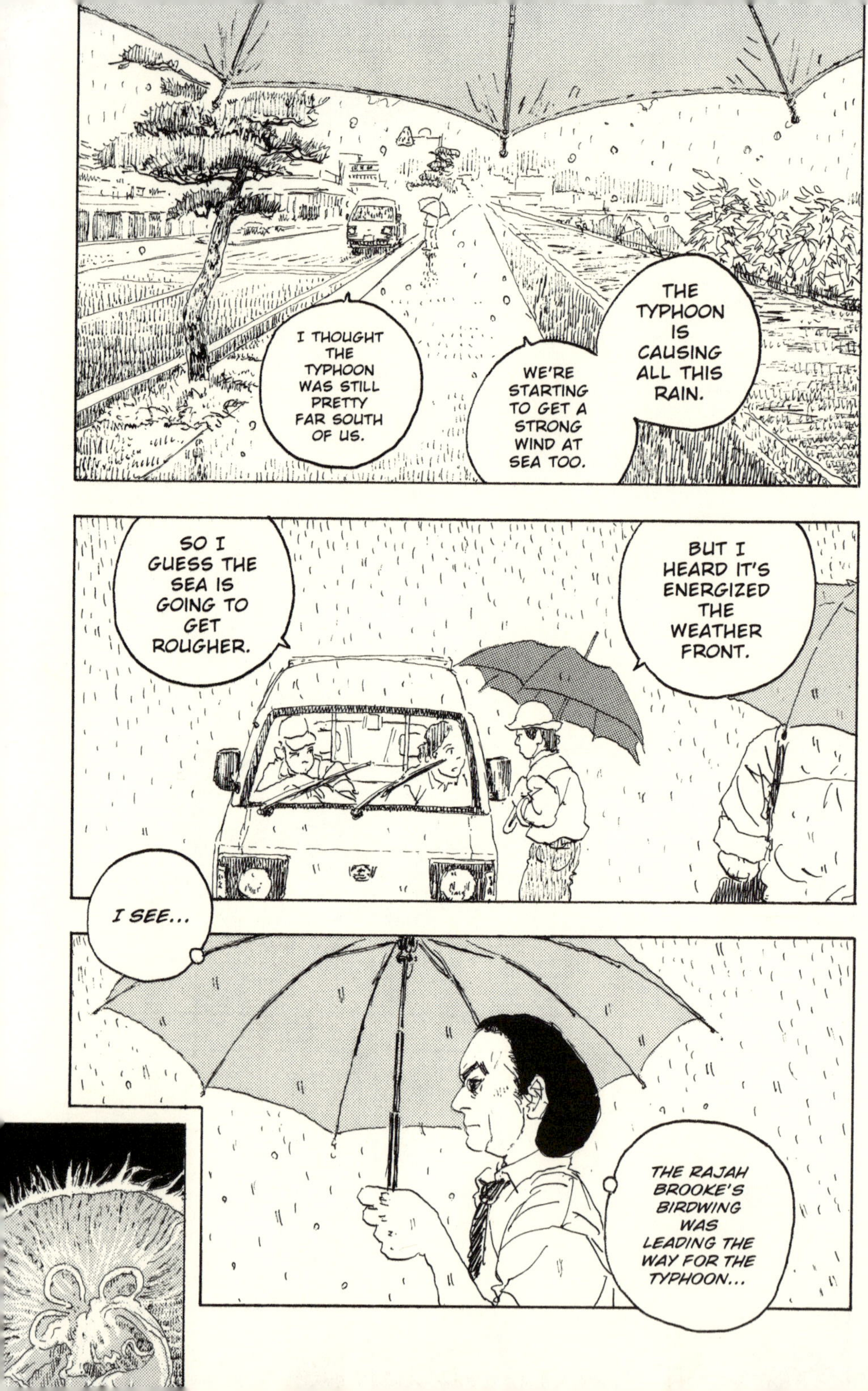
THE TYPHOON IS CAUSING ALL THIS RAIN.
WE'RE STARTING TO GET A STRONG WIND AT SEA TOO.
I THOUGHT THE TYPHOON WAS STILL PRETTY FAR SOUTH OF US.
BUT I HEARD IT'S ENERGIZED THE WEATHER FRONT.
SO I GUESS THE SEA IS GOING TO GET ROUGHER.
I SEE...
THE RAJAH BROOKE'S BIRDWING WAS LEADING THE WAY FOR THE TYPHOON...

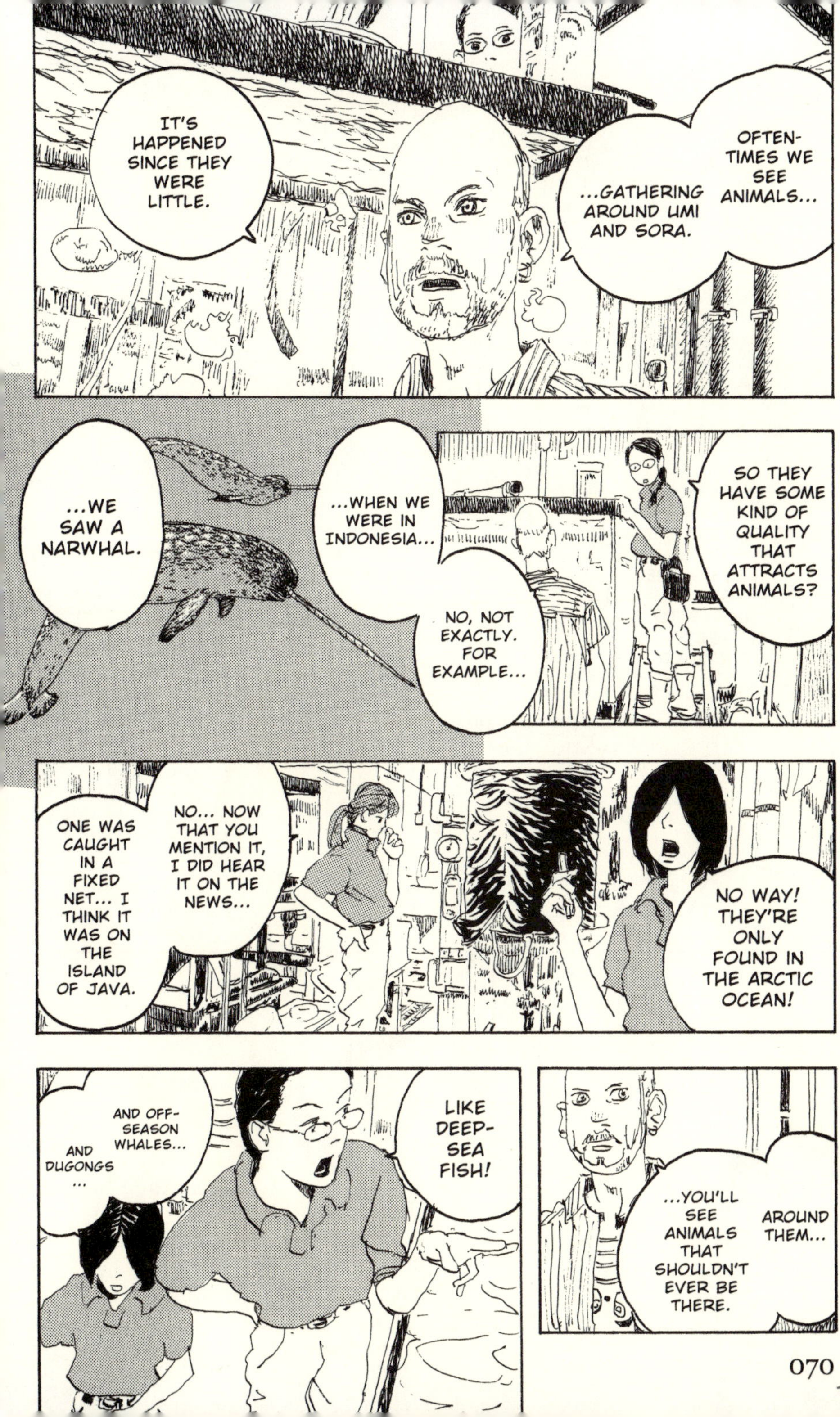
OFTEN-TIMES WE SEE ANIMALS...
...GATHERING AROUND UMI AND SORA.
IT'S HAPPENED SINCE THEY WERE LITTLE.
SO THEY HAVE SOME KIND OF QUALITY THAT ATTRACTS ANIMALS?
NO, NOT EXACTLY. FOR EXAMPLE...
...WHEN WE WERE IN INDONESIA...
...WE SAW A NARWHAL.
NO WAY! THEY'RE ONLY FOUND IN THE ARCTIC OCEAN!
NO... NOW THAT YOU MENTION IT, I DID HEAR IT ON THE NEWS...
ONE WAS CAUGHT IN A FIXED NET... I THINK IT WAS ON THE ISLAND OF JAVA.
AROUND THEM...
...YOU'LL SEE ANIMALS THAT SHOULDN'T EVER BE THERE.
LIKE DEEP-SEA FISH!
AND OFF-SEASON WHALES...
AND DUGONGS...

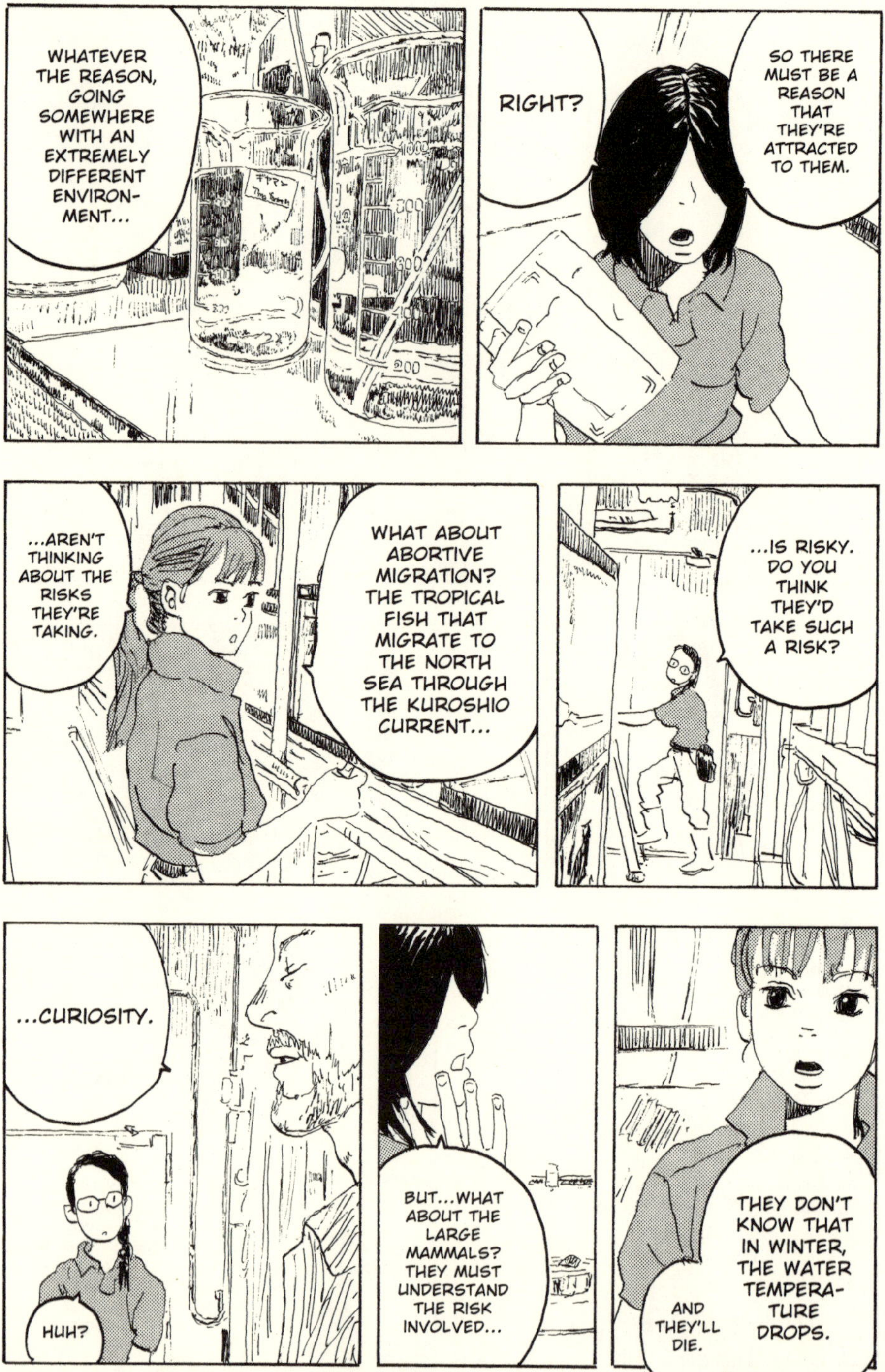
SO THERE MUST BE A REASON THAT THEY'RE ATTRACTED TO THEM.
RIGHT?
WHATEVER THE REASON, GOING SOMEWHERE WITH AN EXTREMELY DIFFERENT ENVIRON-MENT...
...IS RISKY. DO YOU THINK THEY'D TAKE SUCH A RISK?
WHAT ABOUT ABORTIVE MIGRATION? THE TROPICAL FISH THAT MIGRATE TO THE NORTH SEA THROUGH THE KUROSHIO CURRENT...
...AREN'T THINKING ABOUT THE RISKS THEY'RE TAKING.
THEY DON'T KNOW THAT IN WINTER, THE WATER TEMPERA-TURE DROPS.
AND THEY'LL DIE.
BUT...WHAT ABOUT THE LARGE MAMMALS? THEY MUST UNDERSTAND THE RISK INVOLVED...
...CURIOSITY.
HUH?

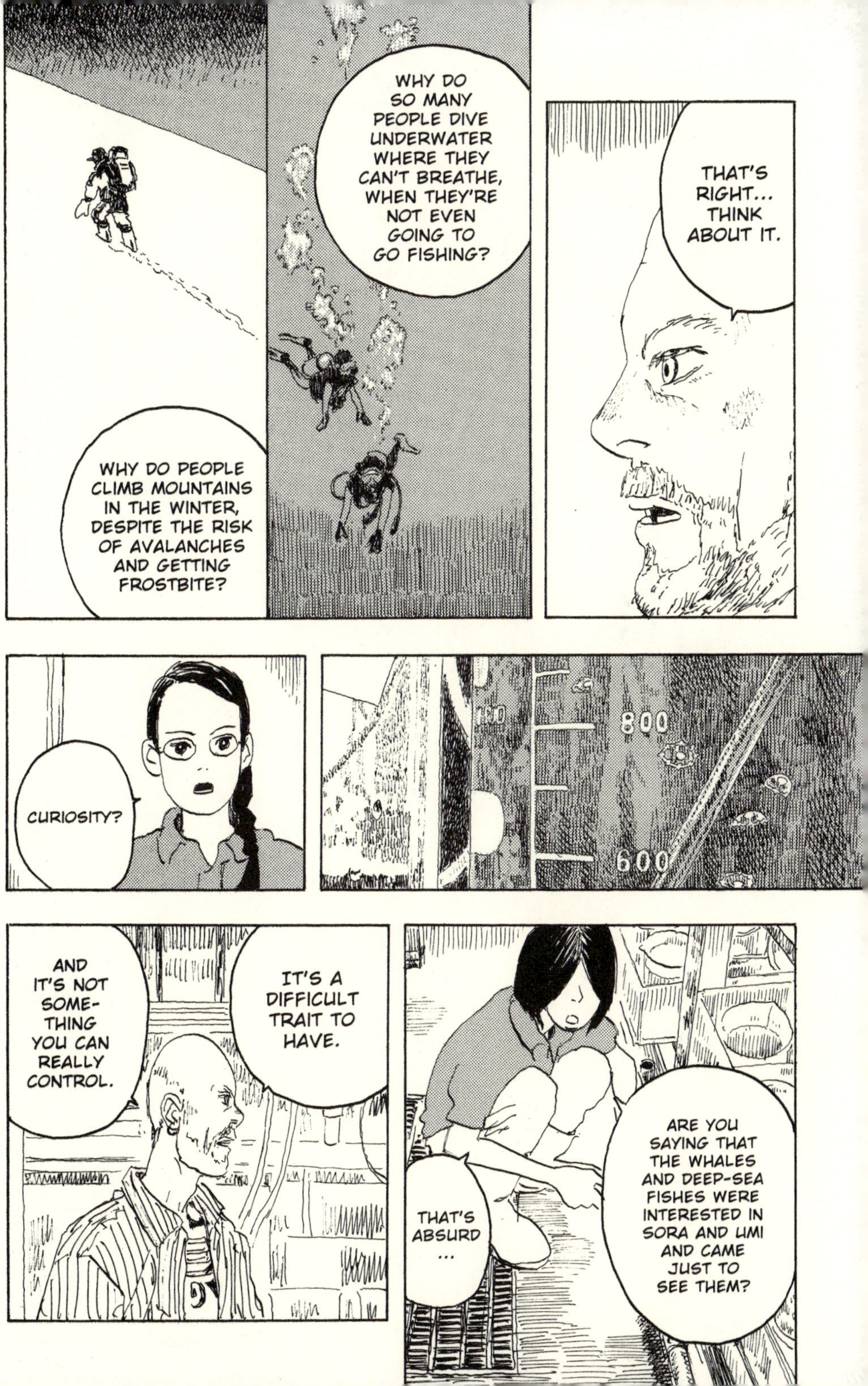
THAT'S RIGHT... THINK ABOUT IT.
WHY DO SO MANY PEOPLE DIVE UNDERWATER WHERE THEY CAN'T BREATHE, WHEN THEY'RE NOT EVEN GOING TO GO FISHING?
WHY DO PEOPLE CLIMB MOUNTAINS IN THE WINTER, DESPITE THE RISK OF AVALANCHES AND GETTING FROSTBITE?
800
600
CURIOSITY?
ARE YOU SAYING THAT THE WHALES AND DEEP-SEA FISHES WERE INTERESTED IN SORA AND UMI AND CAME JUST TO SEE THEM?
THAT'S ABSURD ...
IT'S A DIFFICULT TRAIT TO HAVE.
AND IT'S NOT SOME-THING YOU CAN REALLY CONTROL.

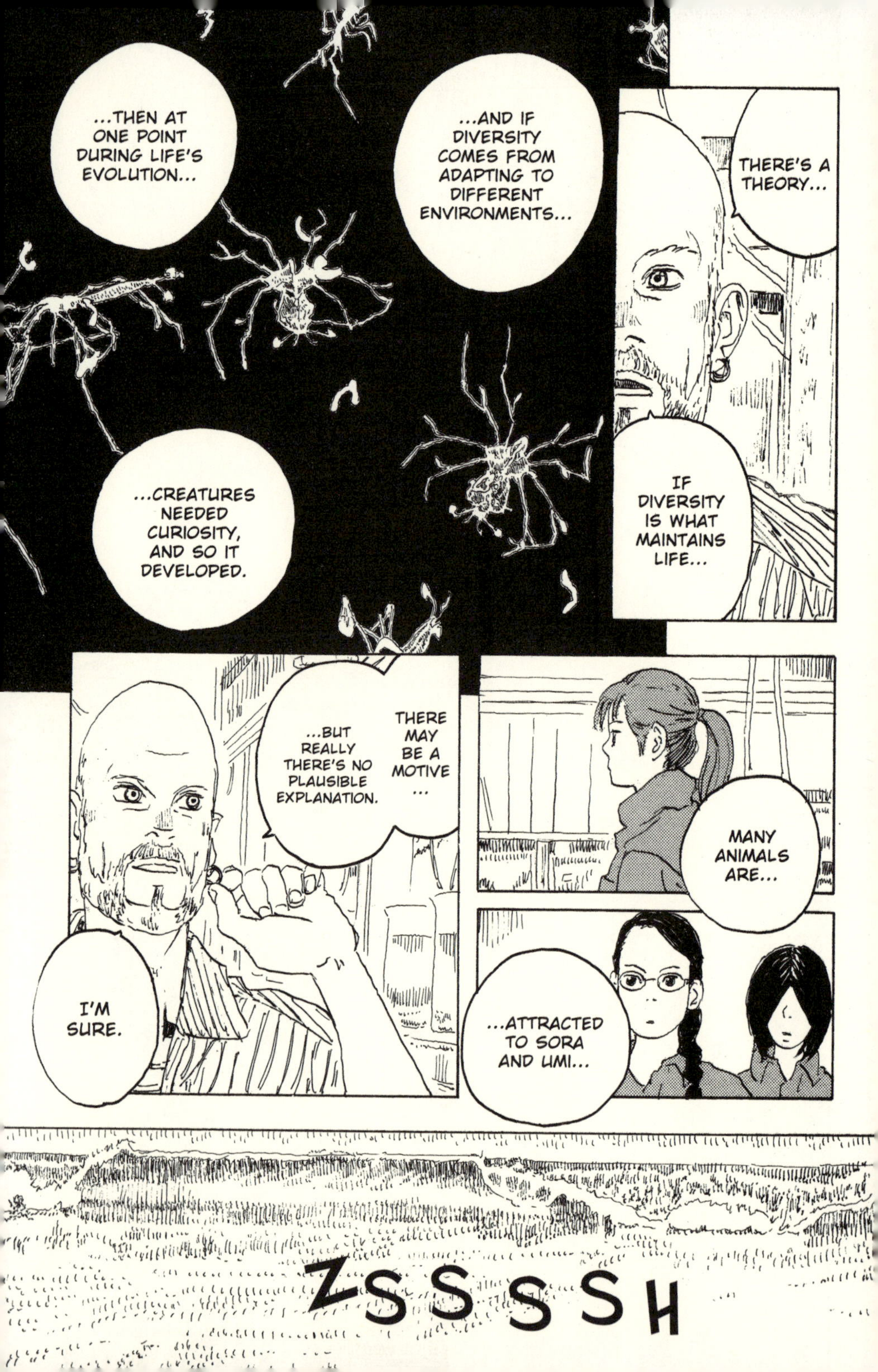
THERE'S A THEORY...
IF DIVERSITY IS WHAT MAINTAINS LIFE...
...AND IF DIVERSITY COMES FROM ADAPTING TO DIFFERENT ENVIRONMENTS...
...THEN AT ONE POINT DURING LIFE'S EVOLUTION...
...CREATURES NEEDED CURIOSITY, AND SO IT DEVELOPED.
MANY ANIMALS ARE...
...ATTRACTED TO SORA AND UMI...
THERE MAY BE A MOTIVE ...
...BUT REALLY THERE'S NO PLAUSIBLE EXPLANATION.
I'M SURE.
ZSSSSH

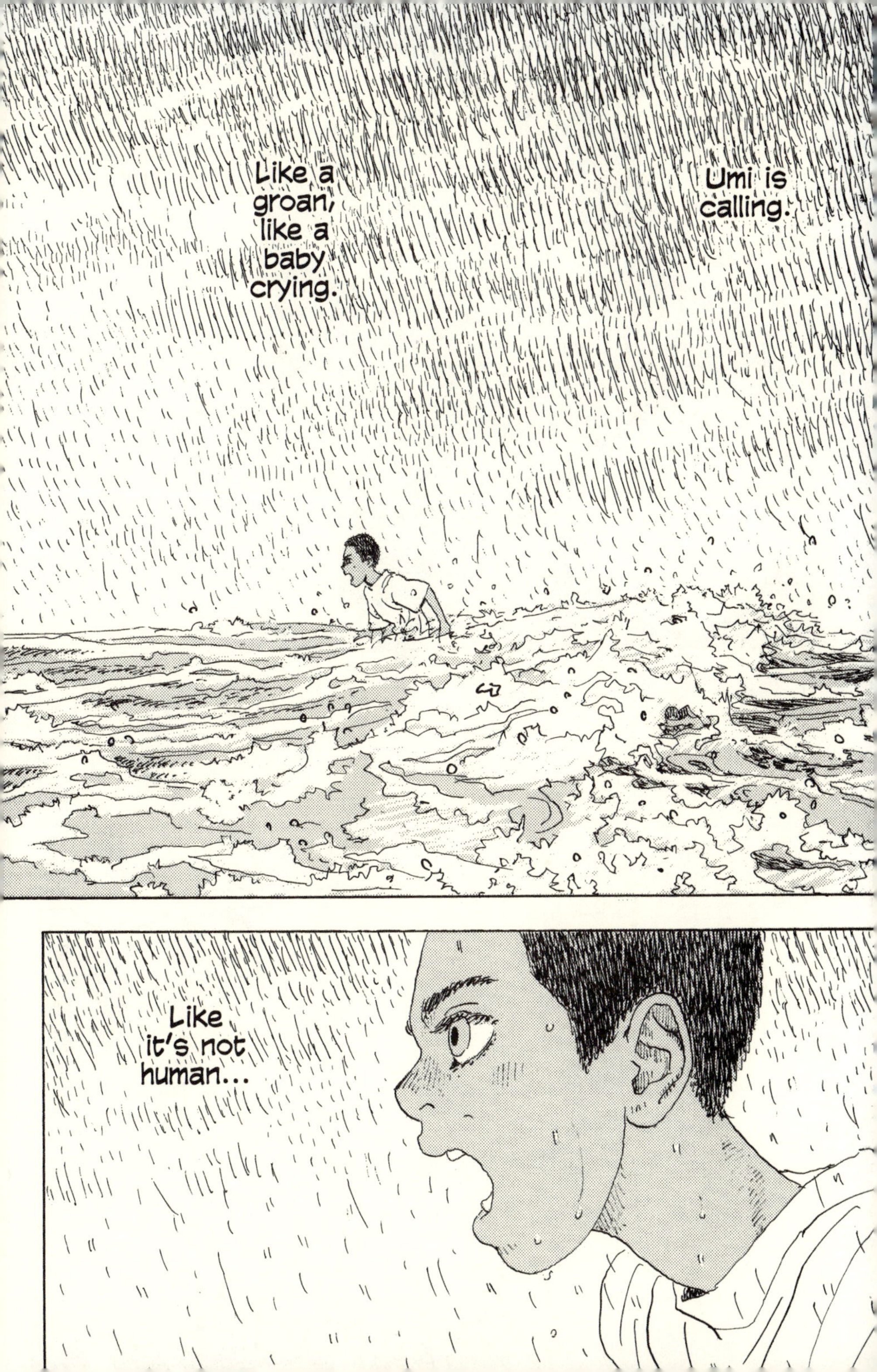
Umi is calling.
Like a groan, like a baby crying.
Like it's not human...

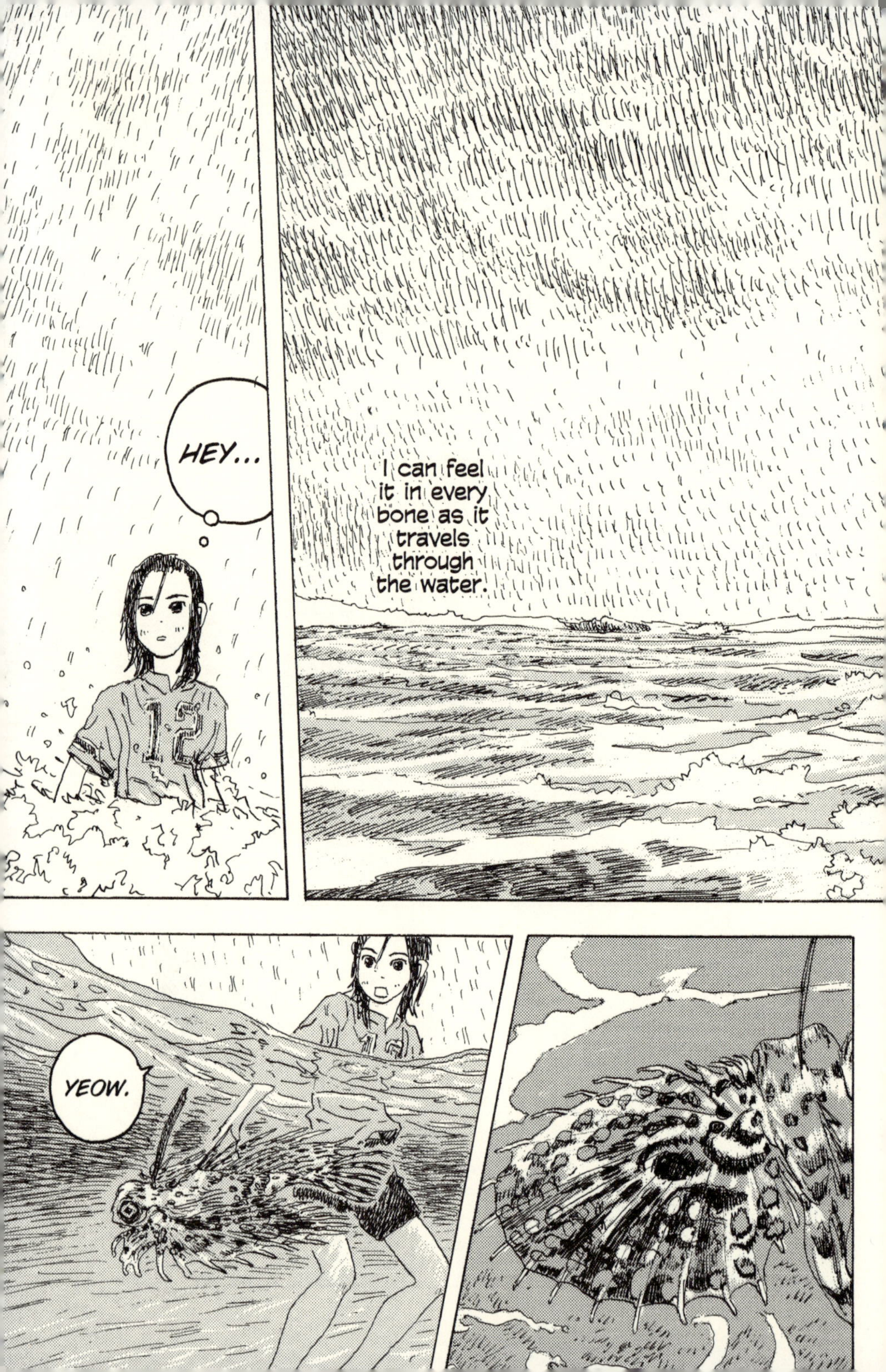
I can feel it in every bone as it travels through the water.
HEY...
YEOW.

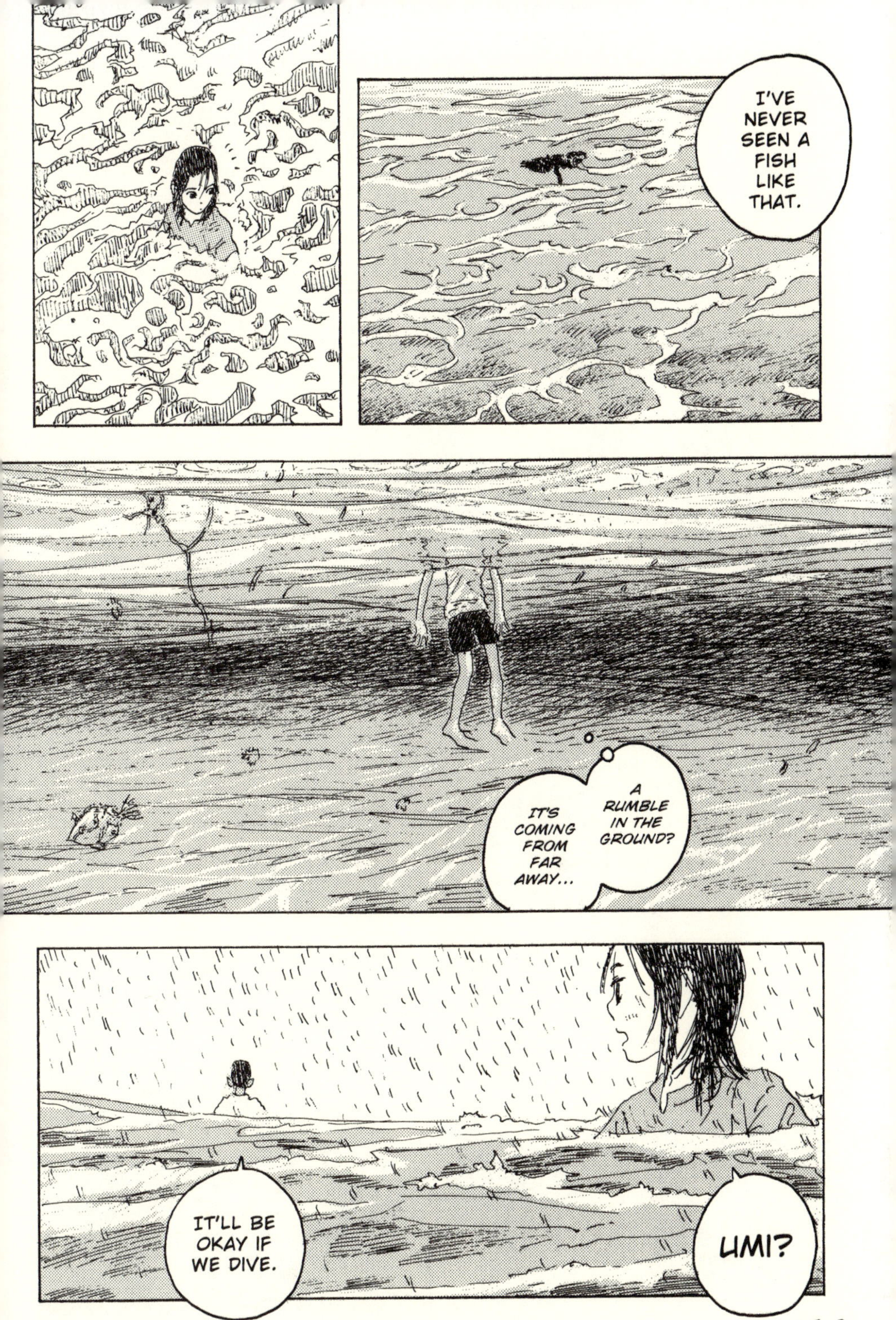
I'VE NEVER SEEN A FISH LIKE THAT.
A RUMBLE IN THE GROUND?
IT'S COMING FROM FAR AWAY...
UMI?
IT'LL BE OKAY IF WE DIVE.

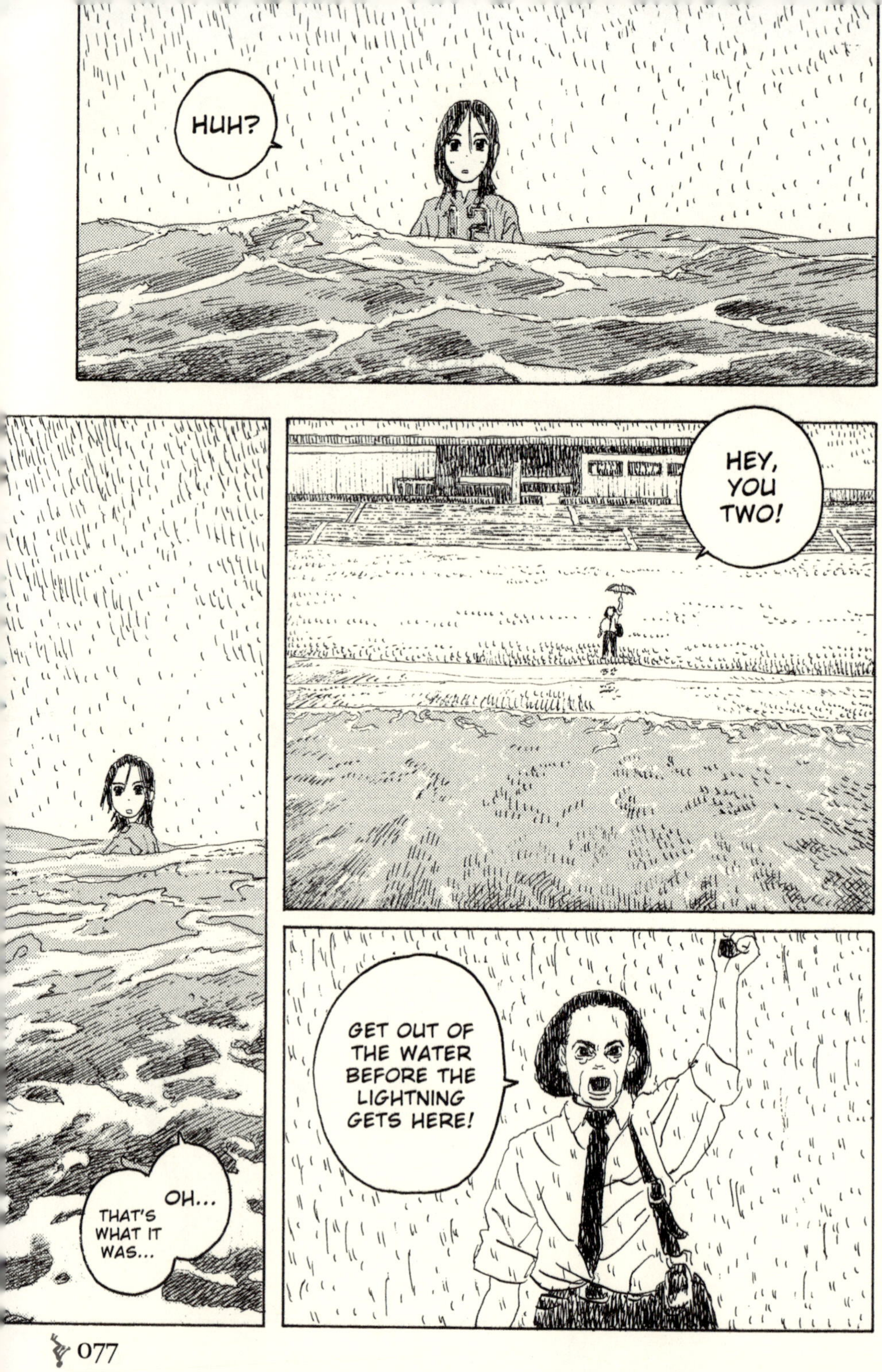
HUH?
HEY, YOU TWO!
GET OUT OF THE WATER BEFORE THE LIGHTNING GETS HERE!
OH...
THAT'S WHAT IT WAS...

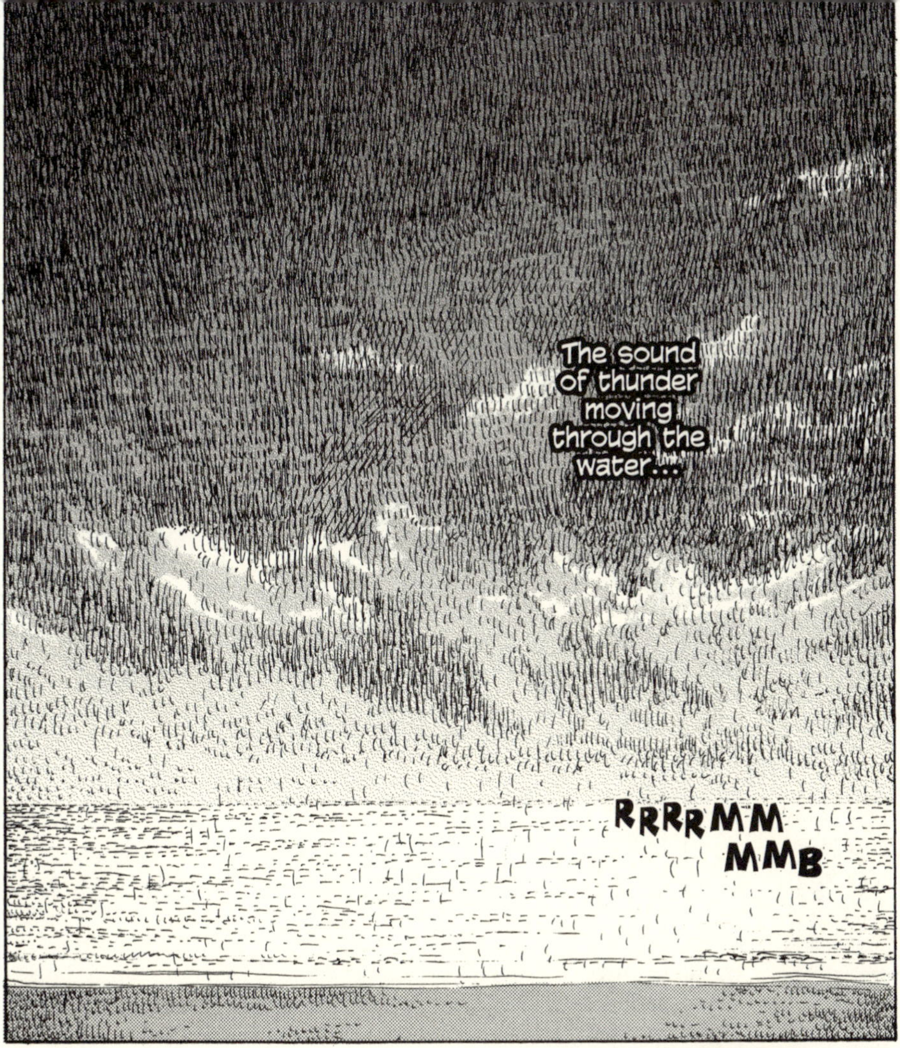
The sound of thunder moving through the water...
RRRRMM MMB
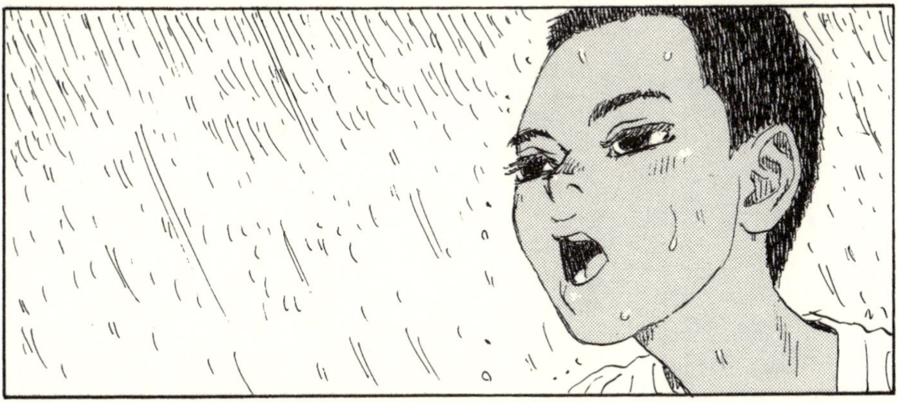

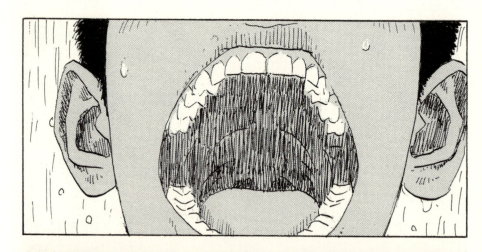

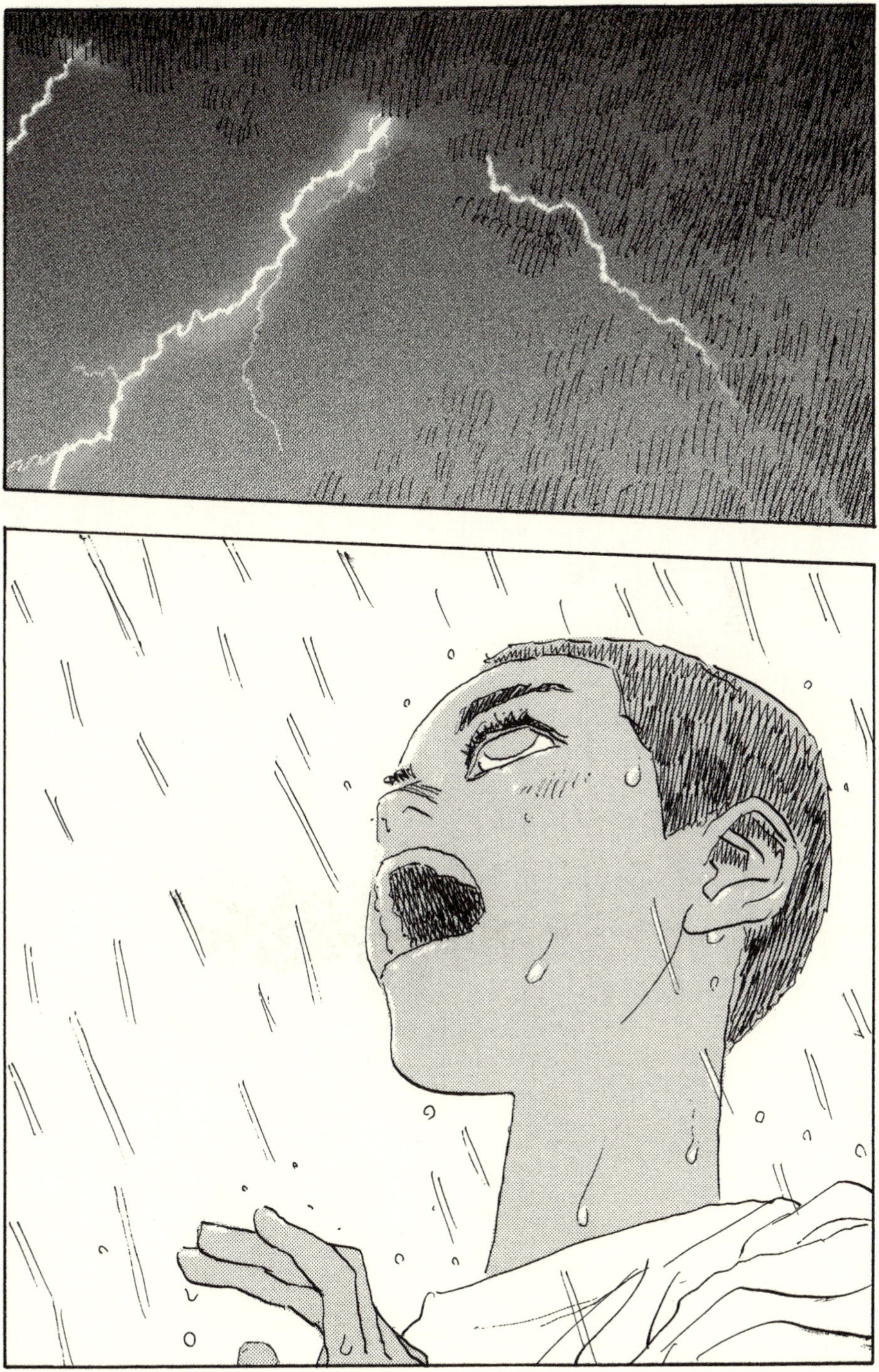

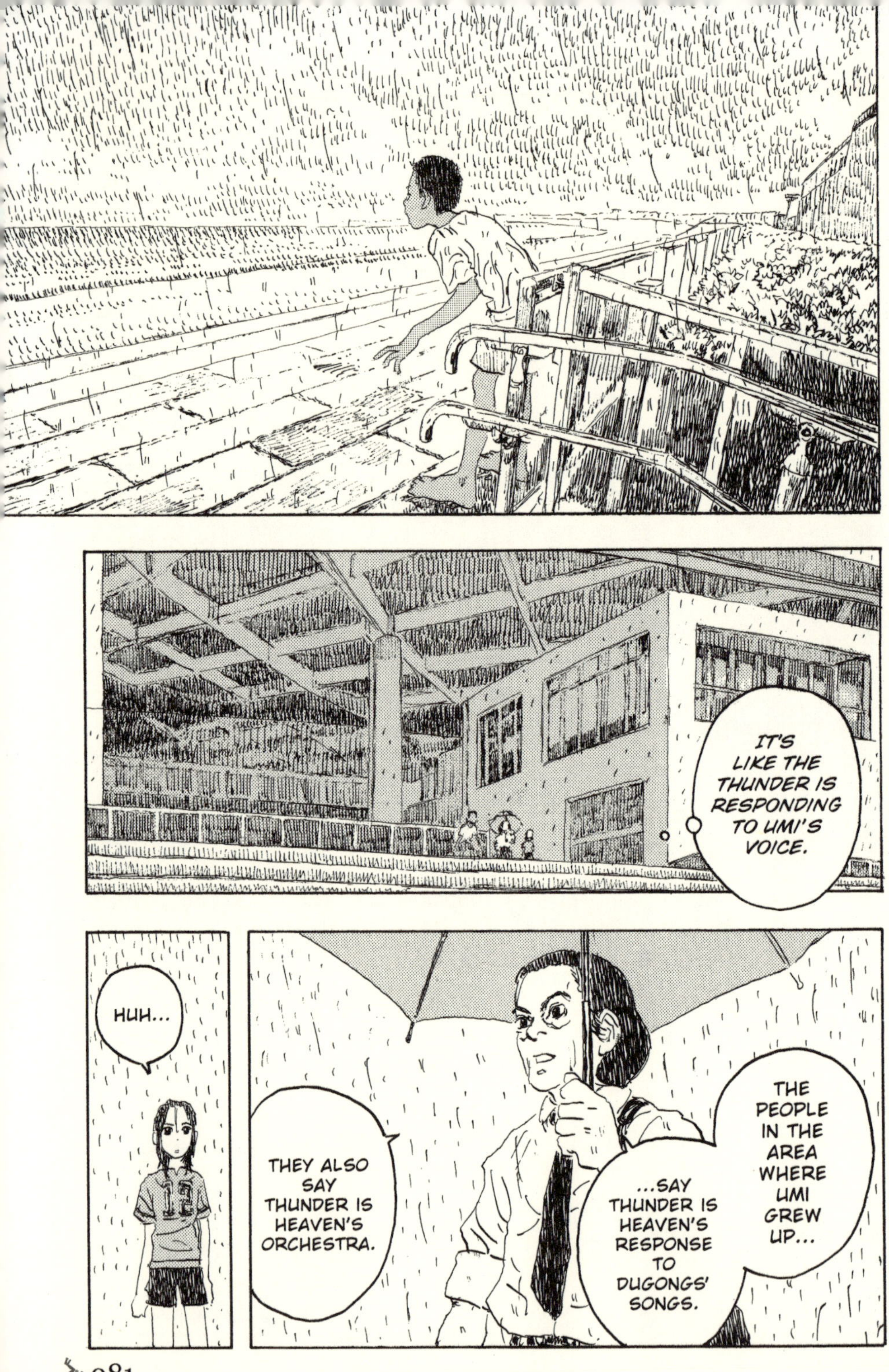
IT'S LIKE THE THUNDER IS RESPONDING TO UMI'S VOICE.
THE PEOPLE IN THE AREA WHERE UMI GREW UP...
...SAY THUNDER IS HEAVEN'S RESPONSE TO DUGONGS' SONGS.
THEY ALSO SAY THUNDER IS HEAVEN'S ORCHESTRA.
HUH...

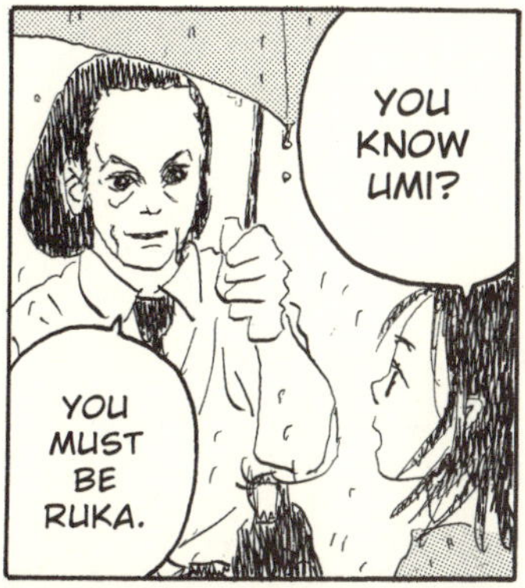
YOU KNOW UMI?
YOU MUST BE RUKA.
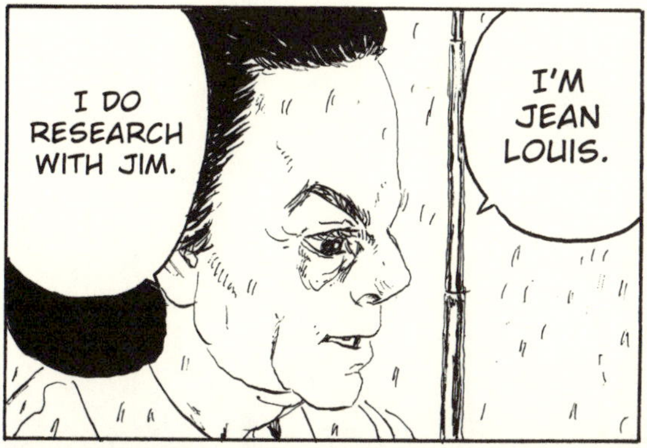
I'M JEAN LOUIS.
I DO RESEARCH WITH JIM.
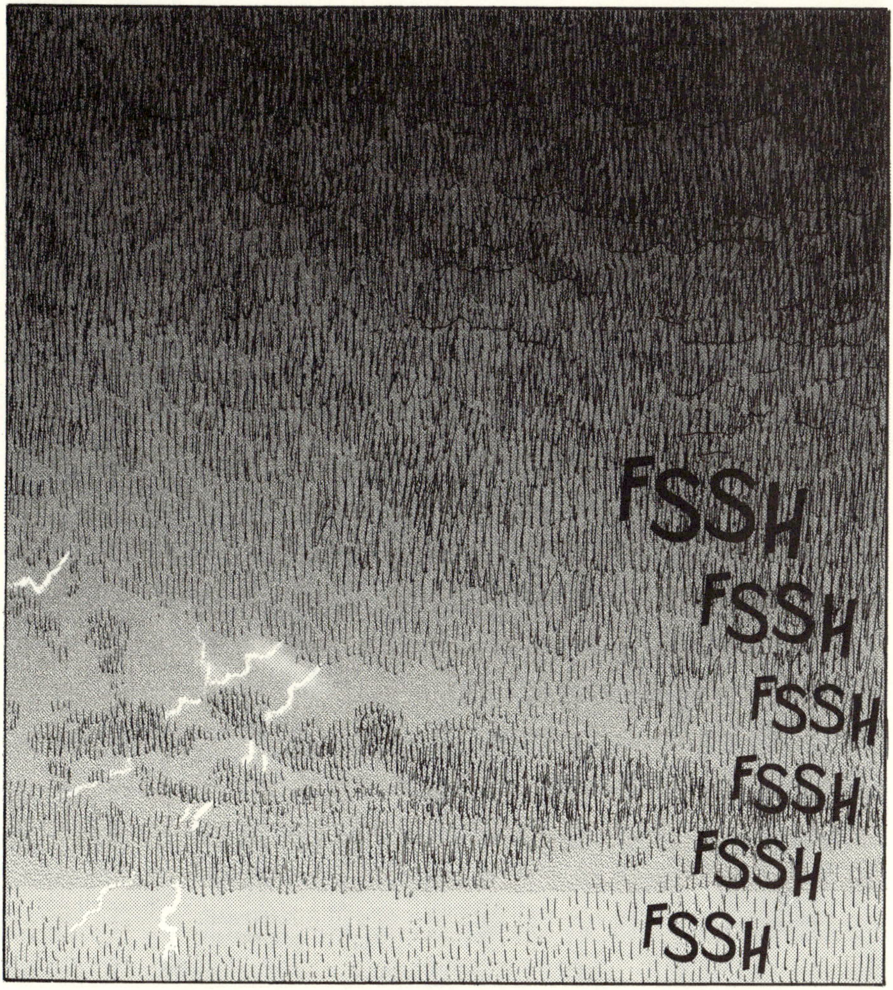
FSSH
FSSH
FSSH
FSSH
FSSH
FSSH

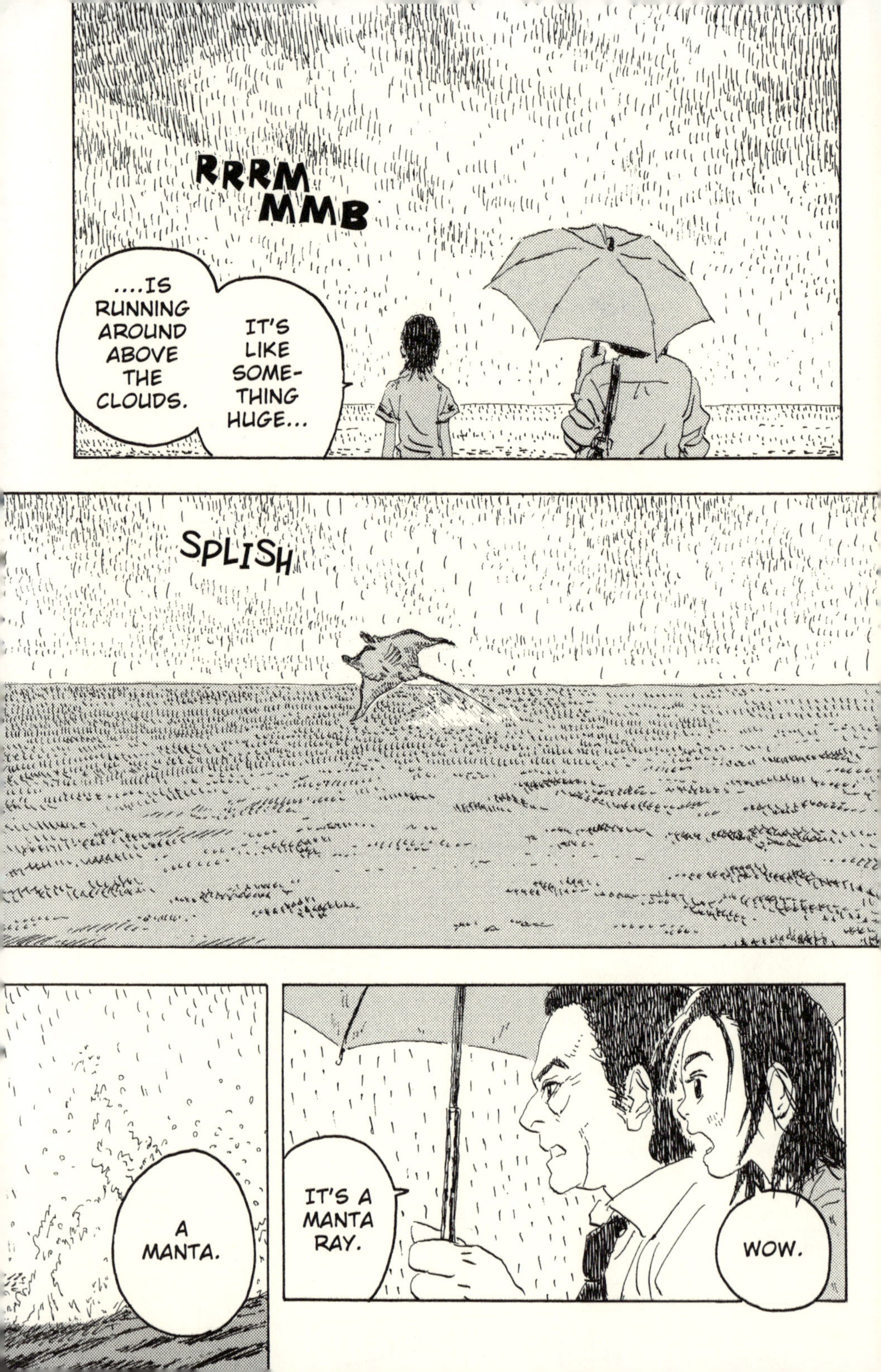
RRRM MMB
IT'S LIKE SOME-THING HUGE...
....IS RUNNING AROUND ABOVE THE CLOUDS.
SPLISH
WOW.
IT'S A MANTA RAY.
A MANTA.

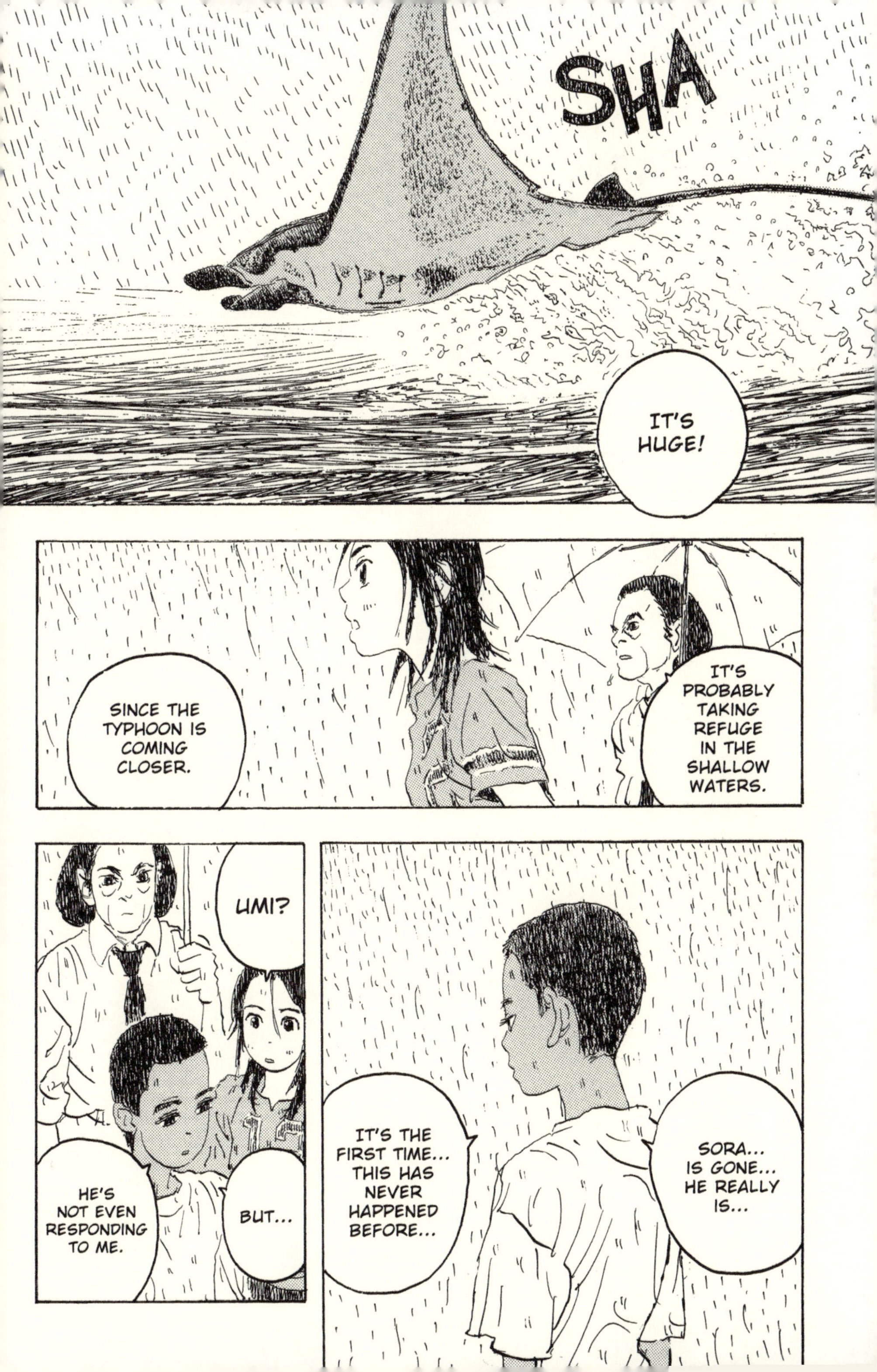
SHA
IT'S HUGE!
IT'S PROBABLY TAKING REFUGE IN THE SHALLOW WATERS.
SINCE THE TYPHOON IS COMING CLOSER.
SORA... IS GONE... HE REALLY IS...
IT'S THE FIRST TIME... THIS HAS NEVER HAPPENED BEFORE...
UMI?
BUT...
HE'S NOT EVEN RESPONDING TO ME.

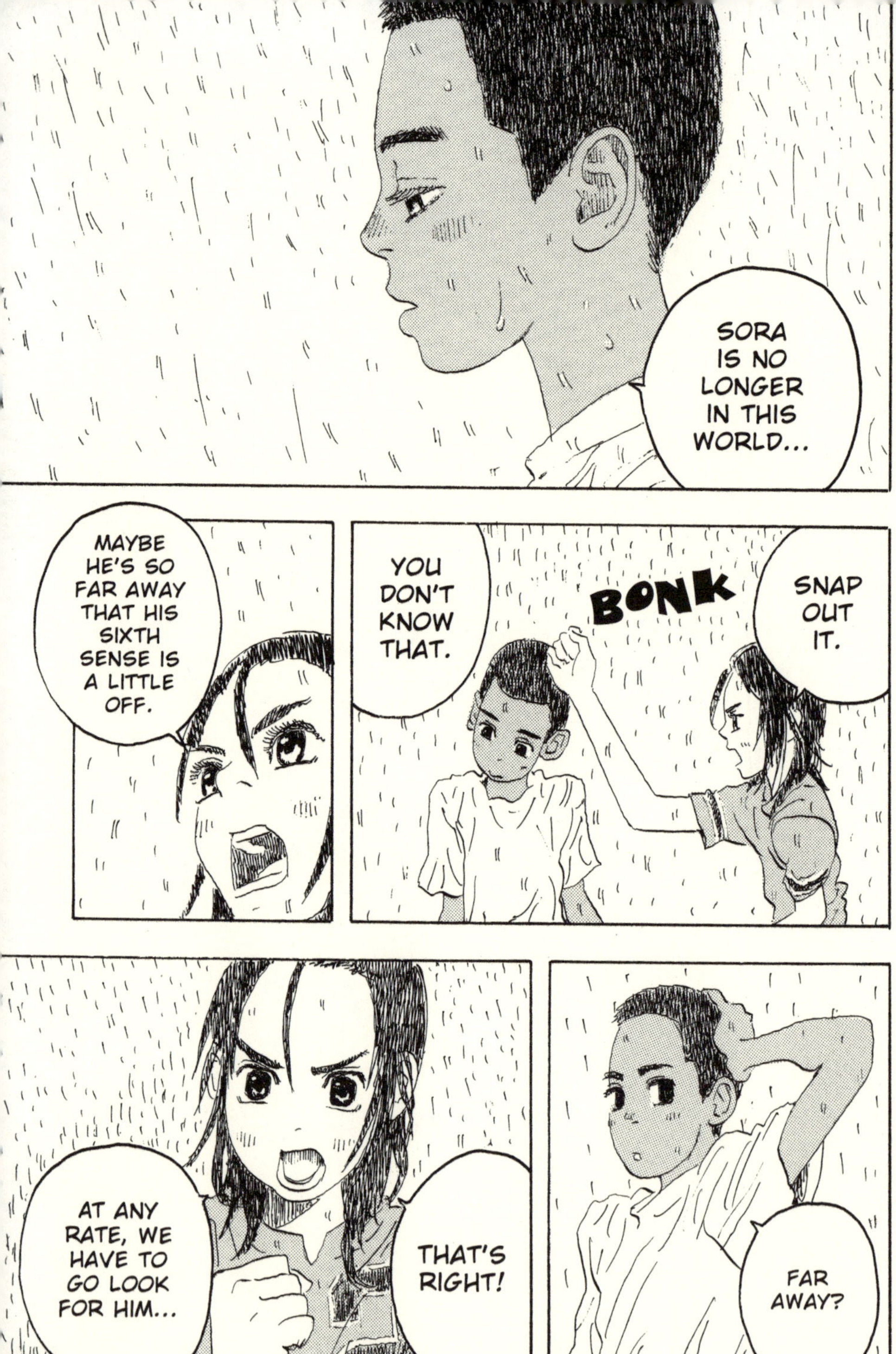
SORA IS NO LONGER IN THIS WORLD...
SNAP OUT IT.
BONK
YOU DON'T KNOW THAT.
MAYBE HE'S SO FAR AWAY THAT HIS SIXTH SENSE IS A LITTLE OFF.
FAR AWAY?
THAT'S RIGHT!
AT ANY RATE, WE HAVE TO GO LOOK FOR HIM...

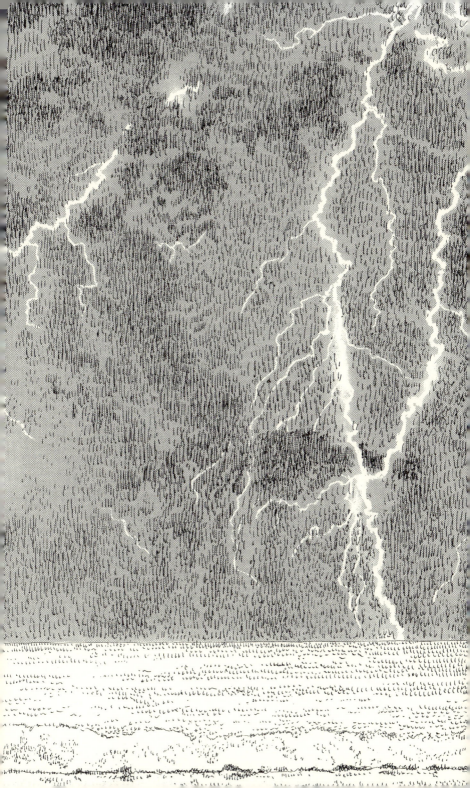

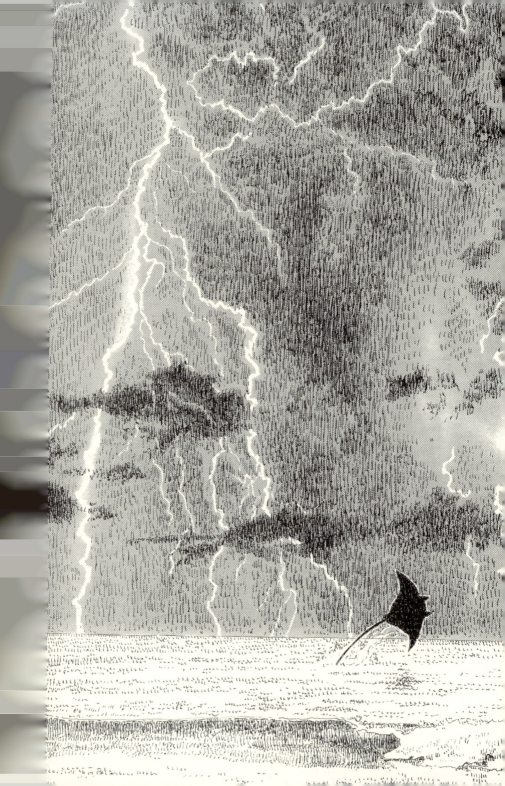

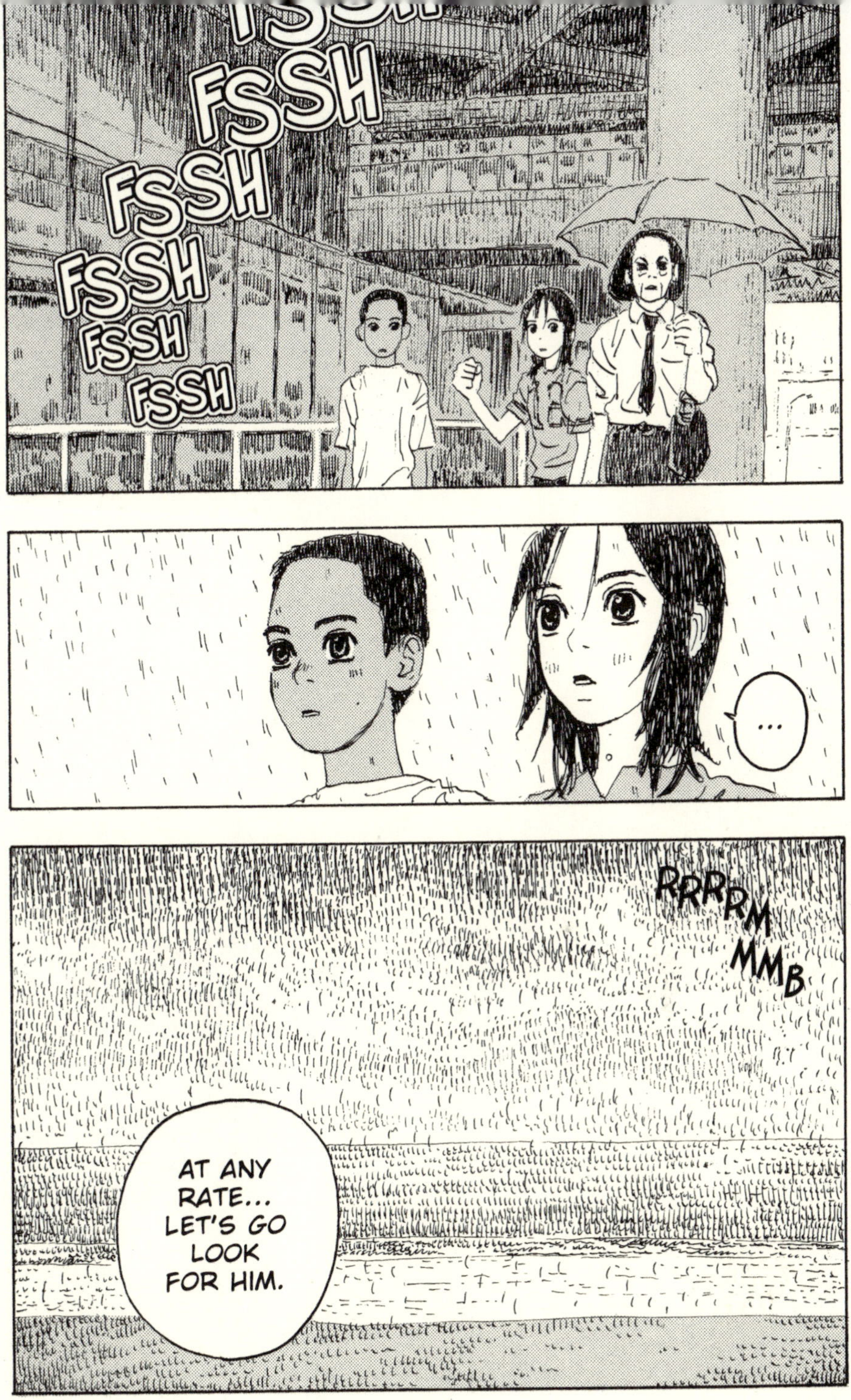
FSSH
FSSH
FSSH
FSSH
FSSH
...
RRRRM MMMB
AT ANY RATE... LET'S GO LOOK FOR HIM.

Chapter 11: Beyond the Tide

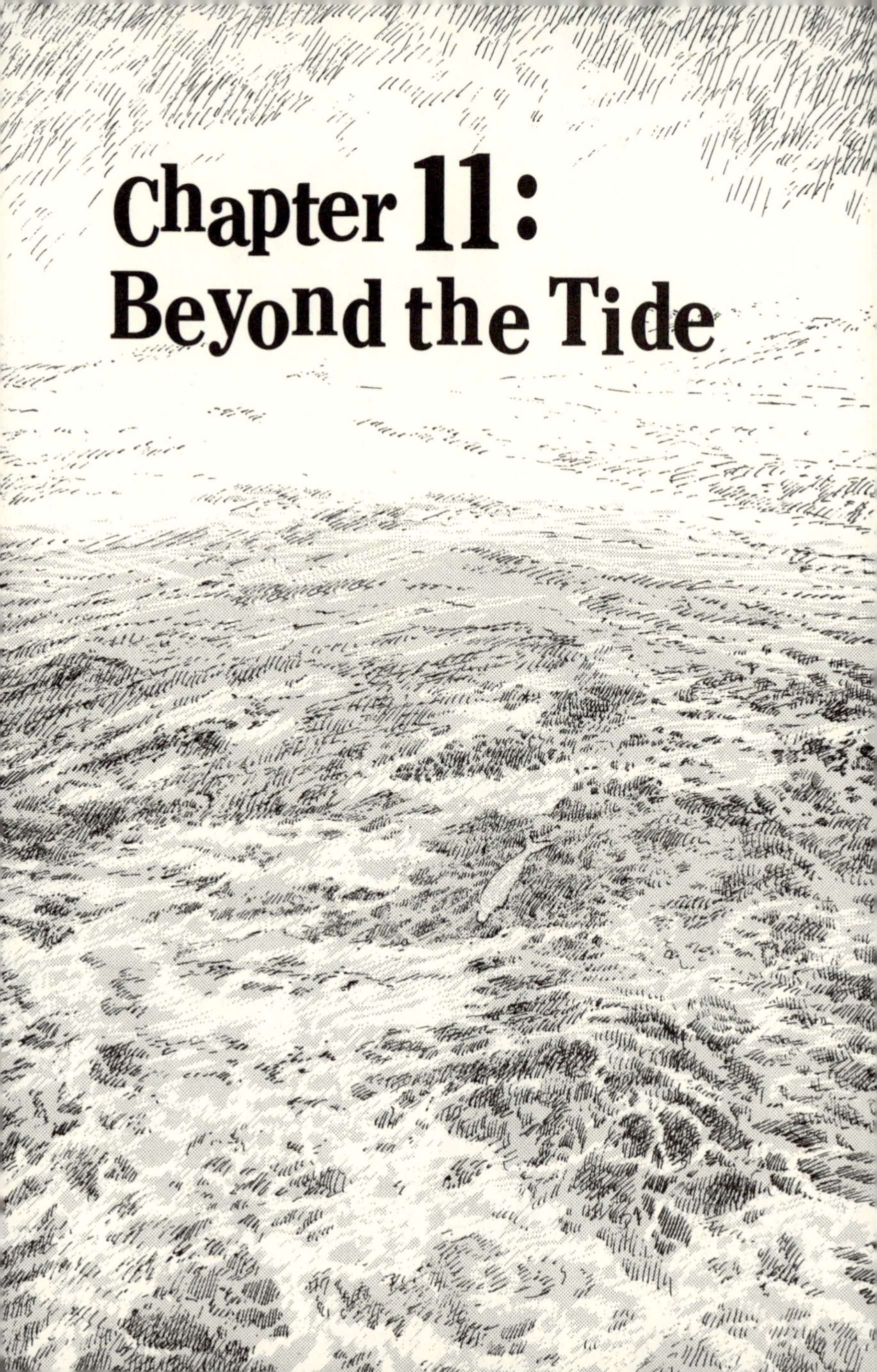

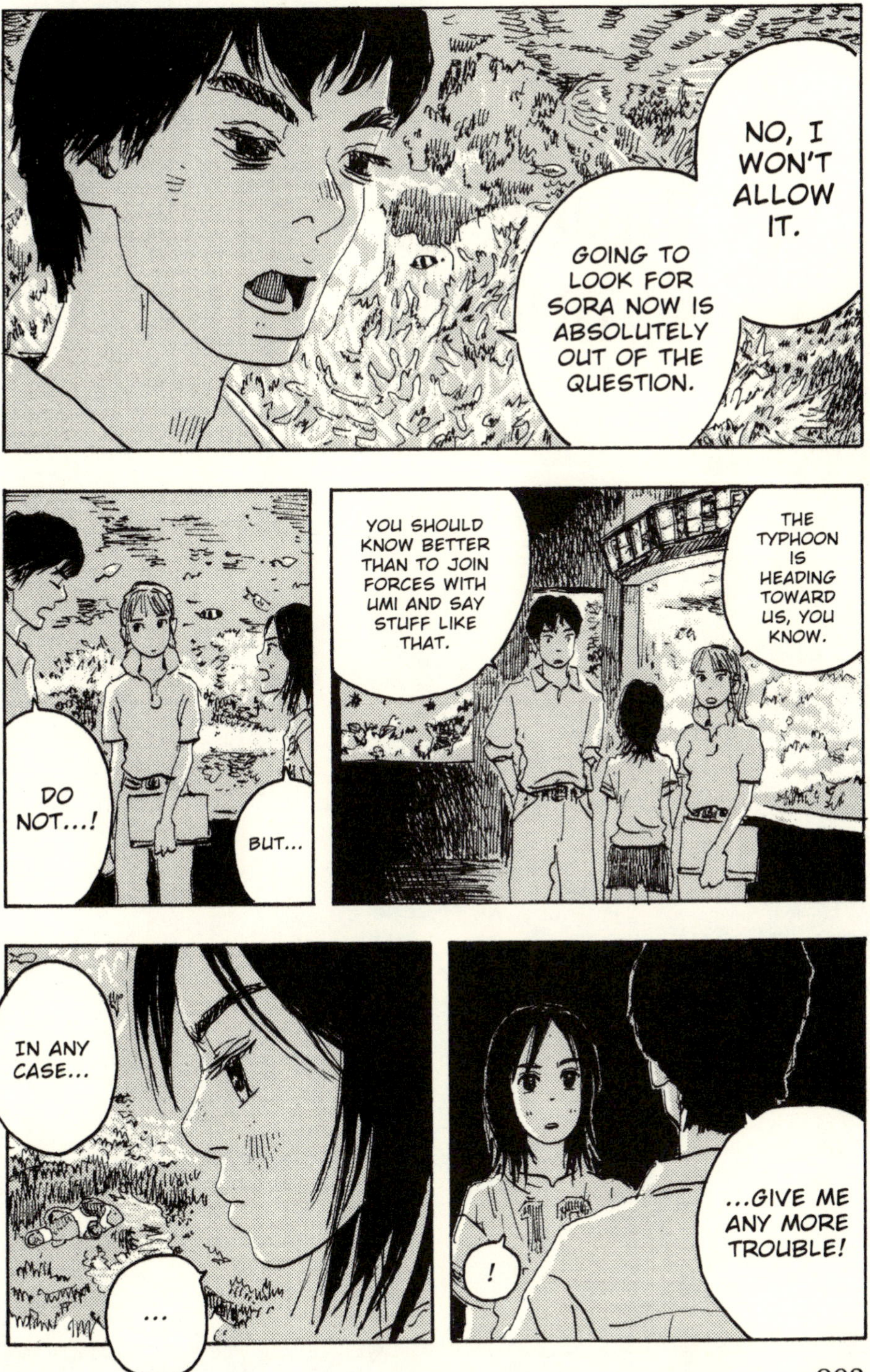
NO, I WON'T ALLOW IT.
GOING TO LOOK FOR SORA NOW IS ABSOLUTELY OUT OF THE QUESTION.
THE TYPHOON IS HEADING TOWARD US, YOU KNOW.
YOU SHOULD KNOW BETTER THAN TO JOIN FORCES WITH UMI AND SAY STUFF LIKE THAT.
BUT...
DO NOT...!
...GIVE ME ANY MORE TROUBLE!
!
IN ANY CASE...
...

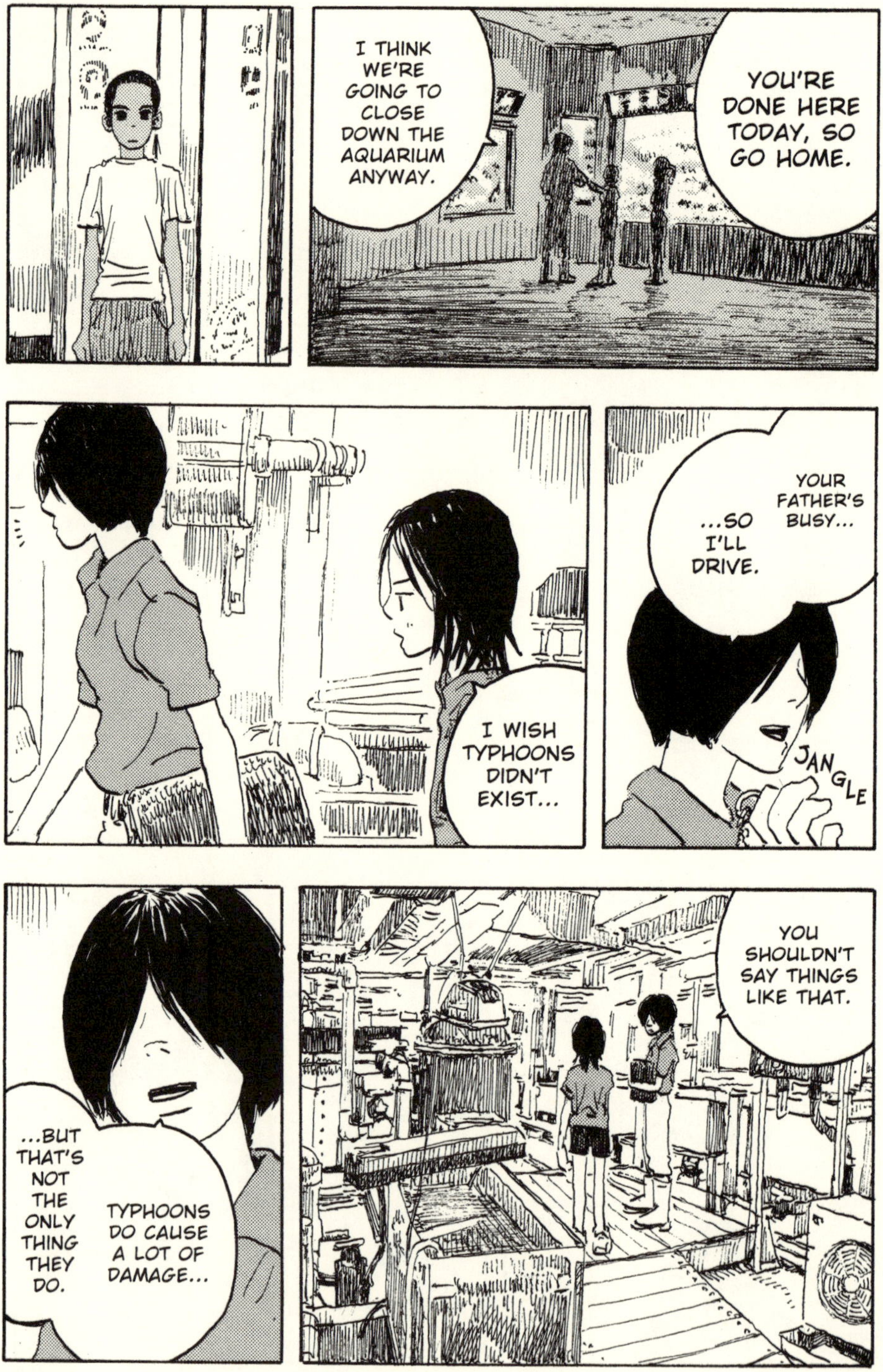

YOU'RE DONE HERE TODAY, SO GO HOME.
I THINK WE'RE GOING TO CLOSE DOWN THE AQUARIUM ANYWAY.
YOUR FATHER'S BUSY...
...SO I'LL DRIVE.
JANGLE
I WISH TYPHOONS DIDN'T EXIST...
YOU SHOULDN'T SAY THINGS LIKE THAT.
TYPHOONS DO CAUSE A LOT OF DAMAGE...
...BUT THAT'S NOT THE ONLY THING THEY DO.

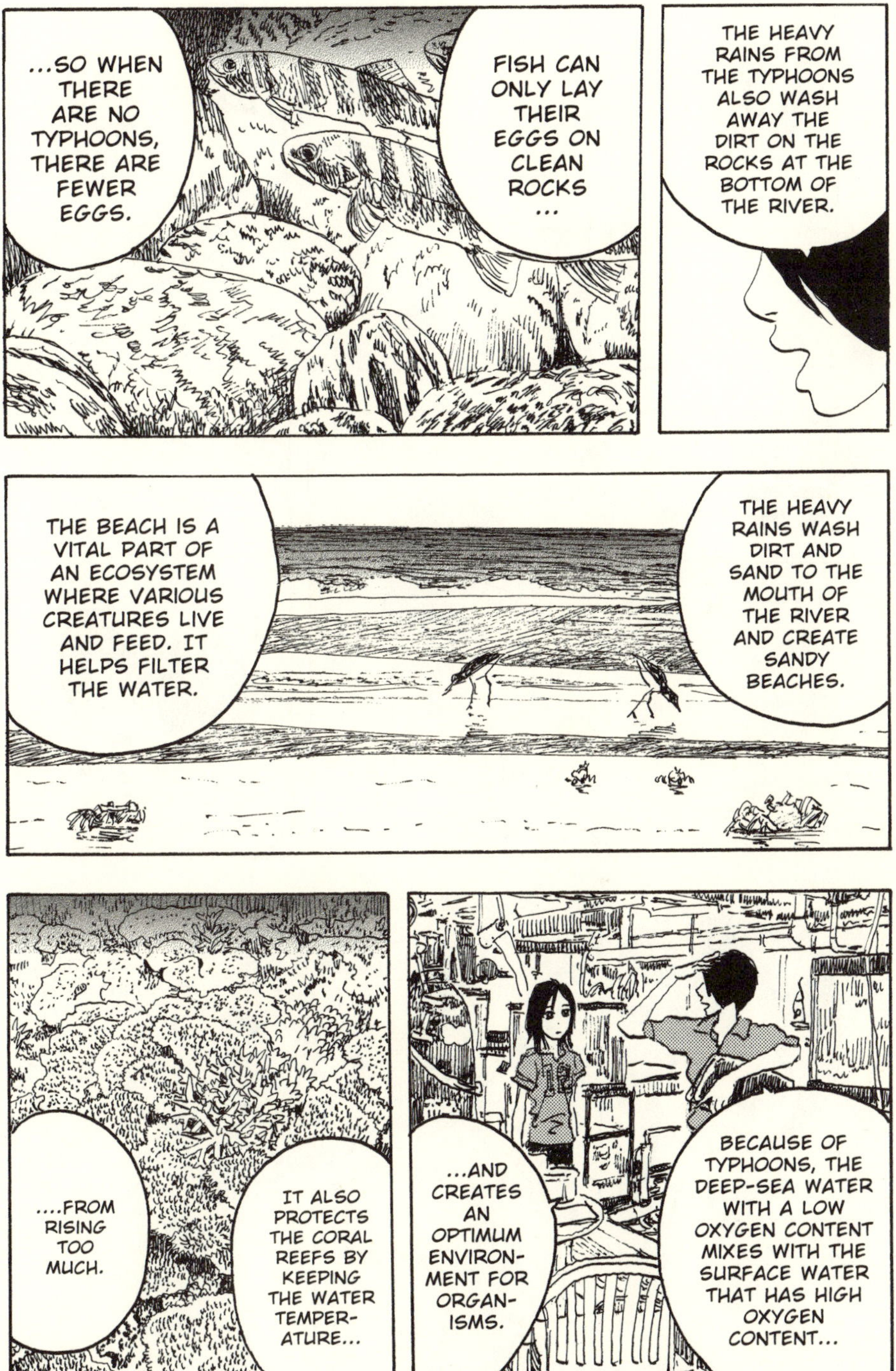
THE HEAVY RAINS FROM THE TYPHOONS ALSO WASH AWAY THE DIRT ON THE ROCKS AT THE BOTTOM OF THE RIVER.
FISH CAN ONLY LAY THEIR EGGS ON CLEAN ROCKS ...
...SO WHEN THERE ARE NO TYPHOONS, THERE ARE FEWER EGGS.
THE HEAVY RAINS WASH DIRT AND SAND TO THE MOUTH OF THE RIVER AND CREATE SANDY BEACHES.
THE BEACH IS A VITAL PART OF AN ECOSYSTEM WHERE VARIOUS CREATURES LIVE AND FEED. IT HELPS FILTER THE WATER.
BECAUSE OF TYPHOONS, THE DEEP-SEA WATER WITH A LOW OXYGEN CONTENT MIXES WITH THE SURFACE WATER THAT HAS HIGH OXYGEN CONTENT...
...AND CREATES AN OPTIMUM ENVIRON-MENT FOR ORGAN-ISMS.
IT ALSO PROTECTS THE CORAL REEFS BY KEEPING THE WATER TEMPER-ATURE...
....FROM RISING TOO MUCH.

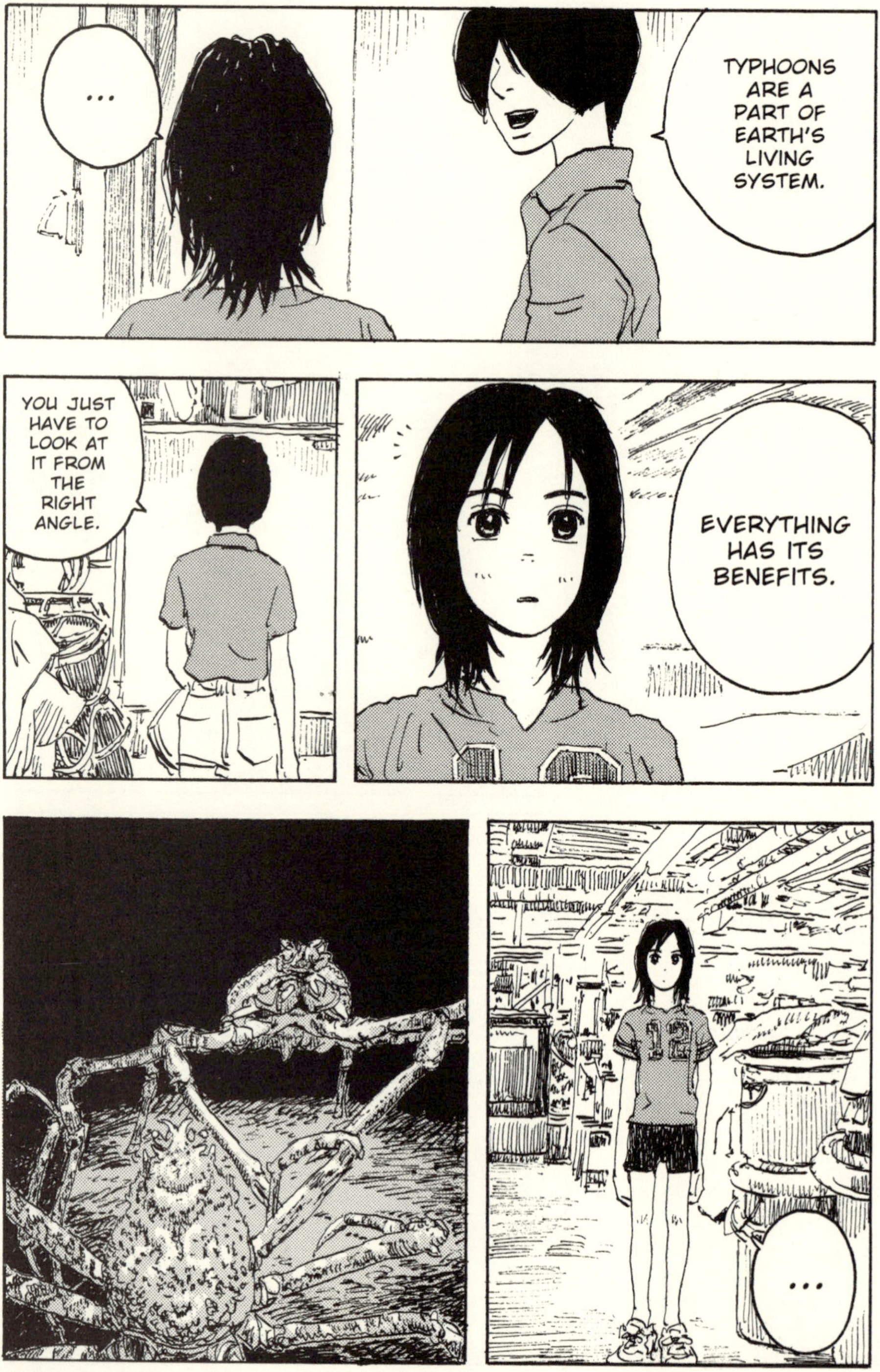
TYPHOONS ARE A PART OF EARTH'S LIVING SYSTEM.
...
EVERYTHING HAS ITS BENEFITS.
YOU JUST HAVE TO LOOK AT IT FROM THE RIGHT ANGLE.
...

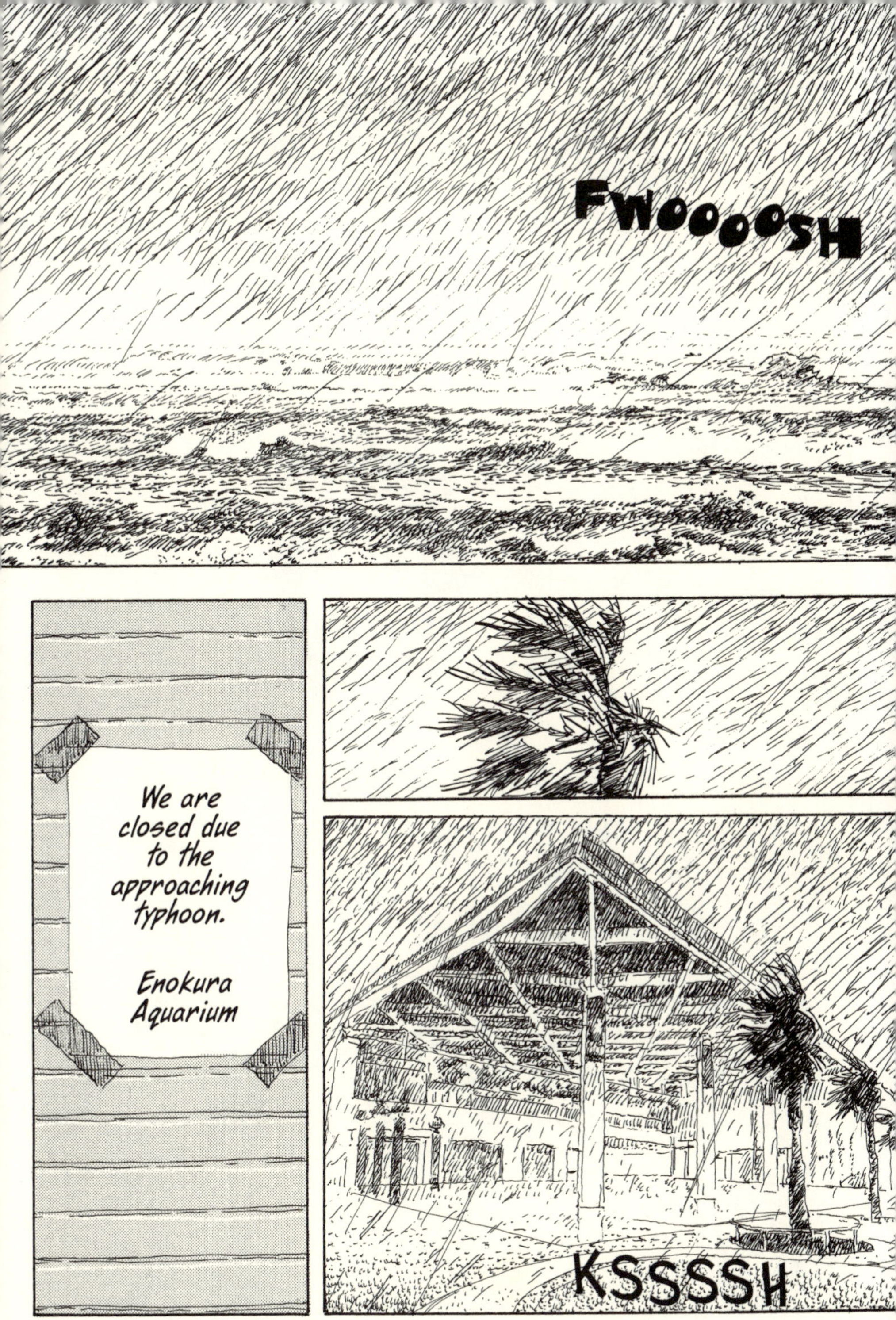
FWOOOOSH
KSSSSH
We are closed due to the approaching typhoon.
Enokura Aquarium

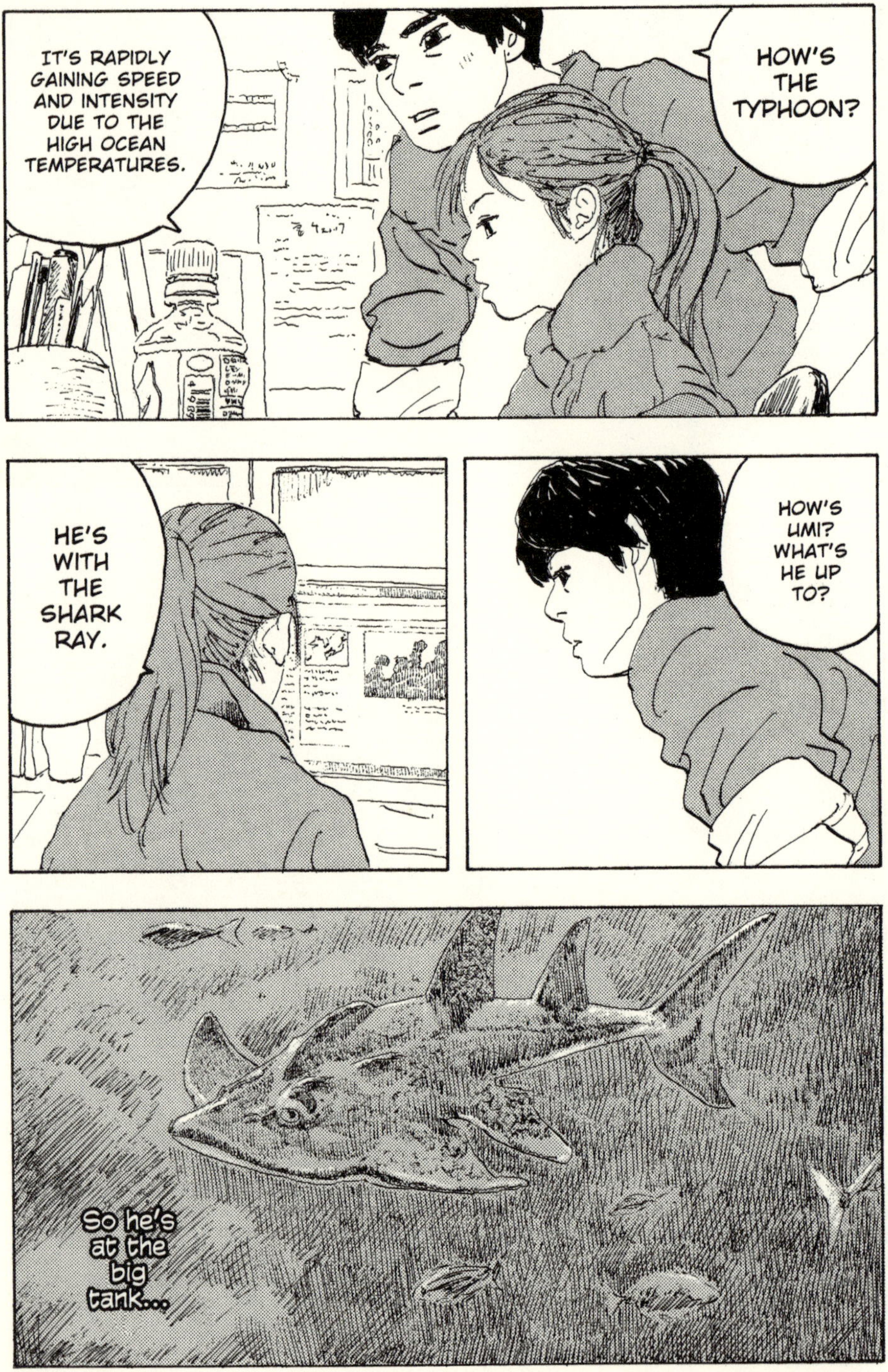
HOW'S THE TYPHOON?
IT'S RAPIDLY GAINING SPEED AND INTENSITY DUE TO THE HIGH OCEAN TEMPERATURES.
HOW'S UMI? WHAT'S HE UP TO?
HE'S WITH THE SHARK RAY.
So he's at the big tank...

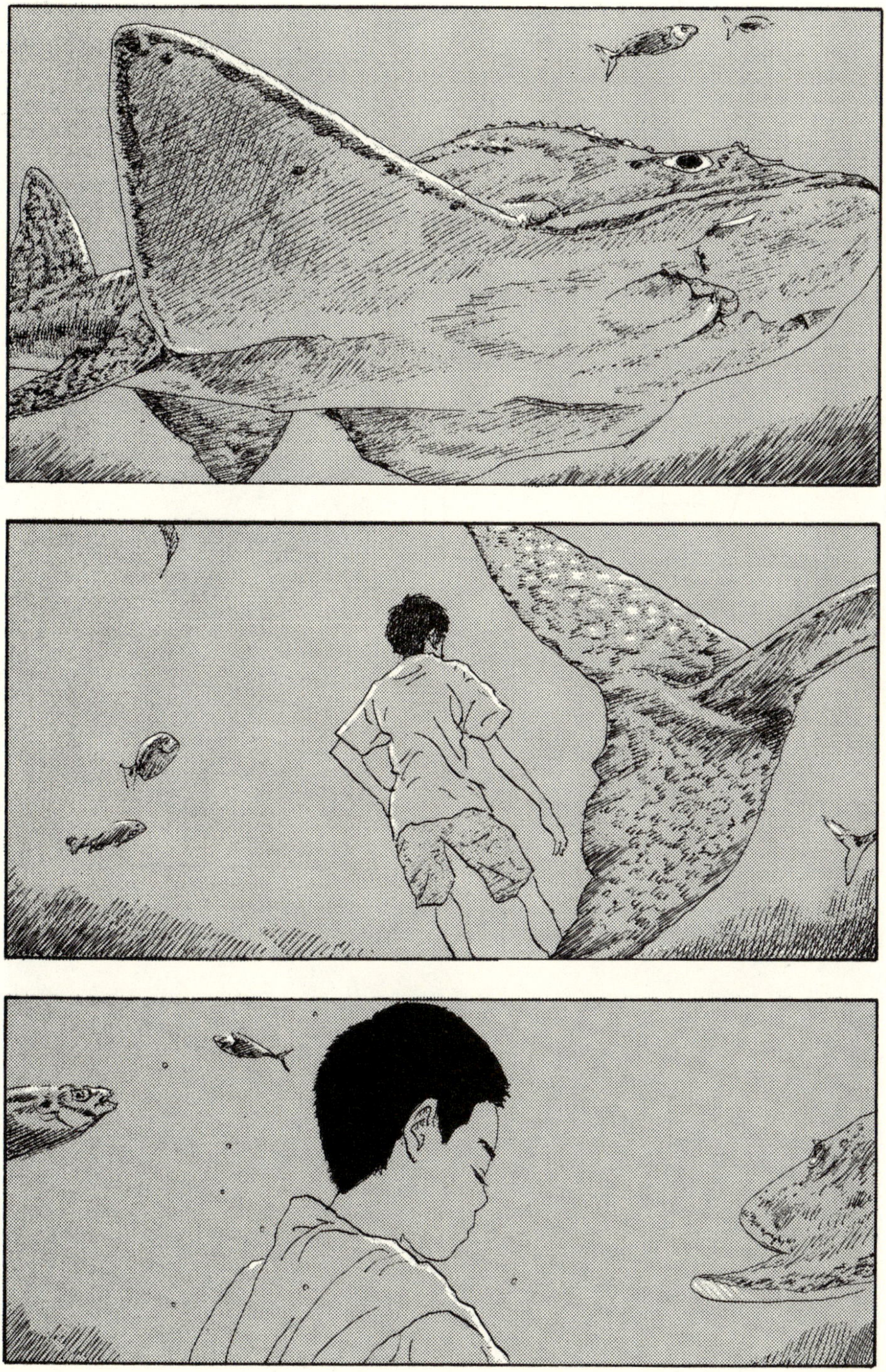

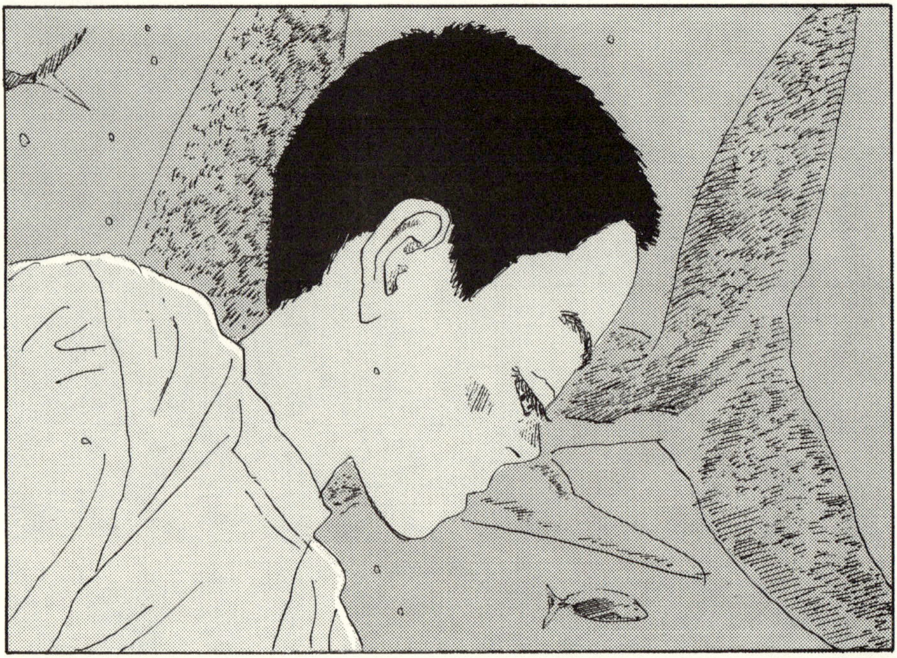
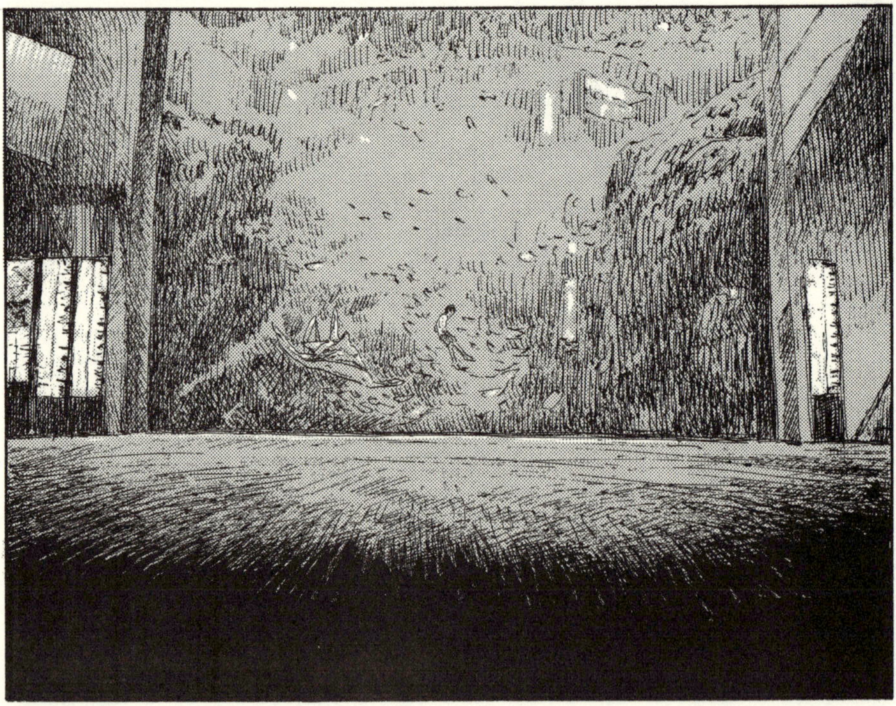

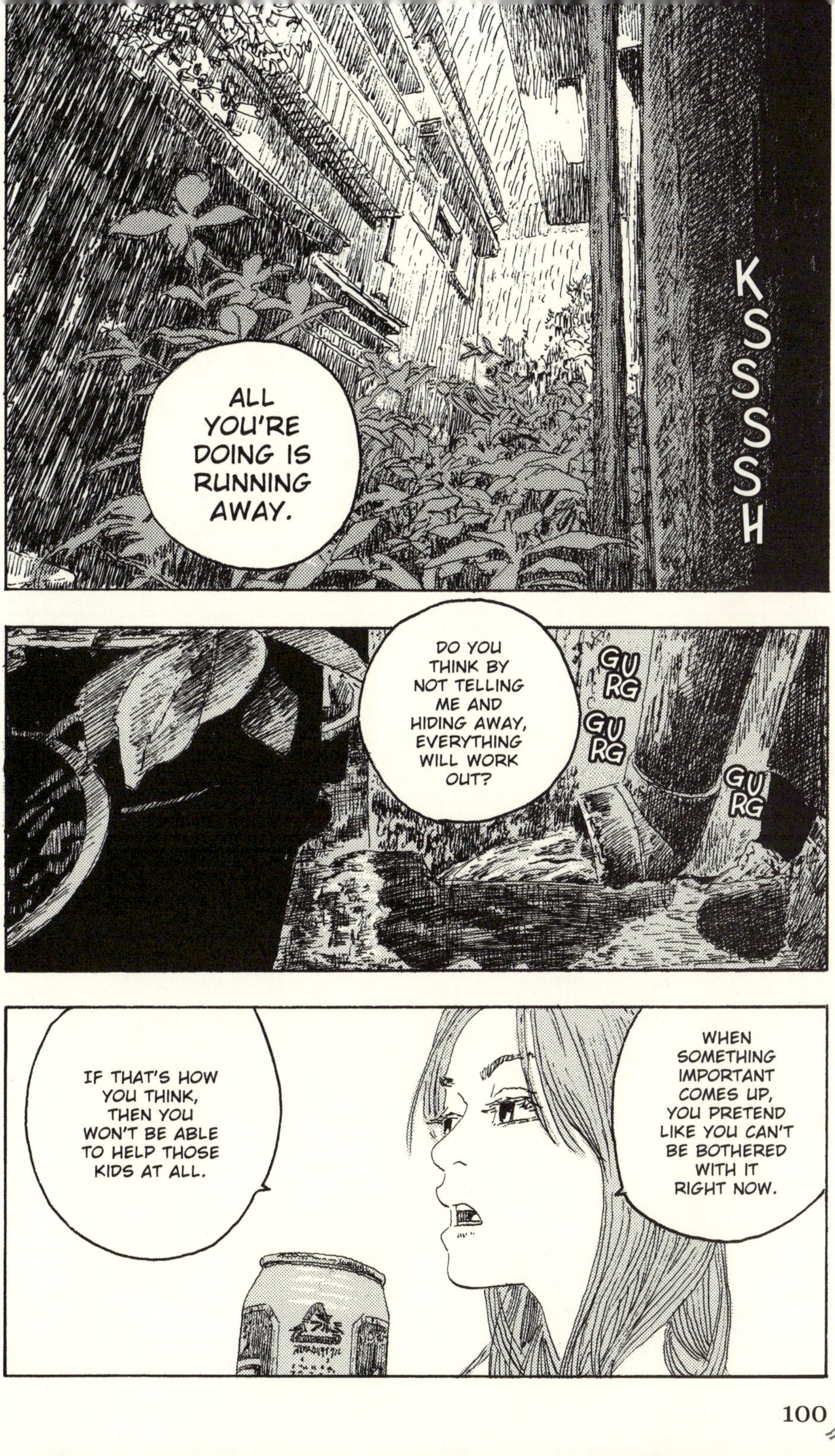
ALL YOU'RE DOING IS RUNNING AWAY.
KSSSSH
DO YOU THINK BY NOT TELLING ME AND HIDING AWAY, EVERYTHING WILL WORK OUT?
GURG
GURG
GURG
WHEN SOMETHING IMPORTANT COMES UP, YOU PRETEND LIKE YOU CAN'T BE BOTHERED WITH IT RIGHT NOW.
IF THAT'S HOW YOU THINK, THEN YOU WON'T BE ABLE TO HELP THOSE KIDS AT ALL.

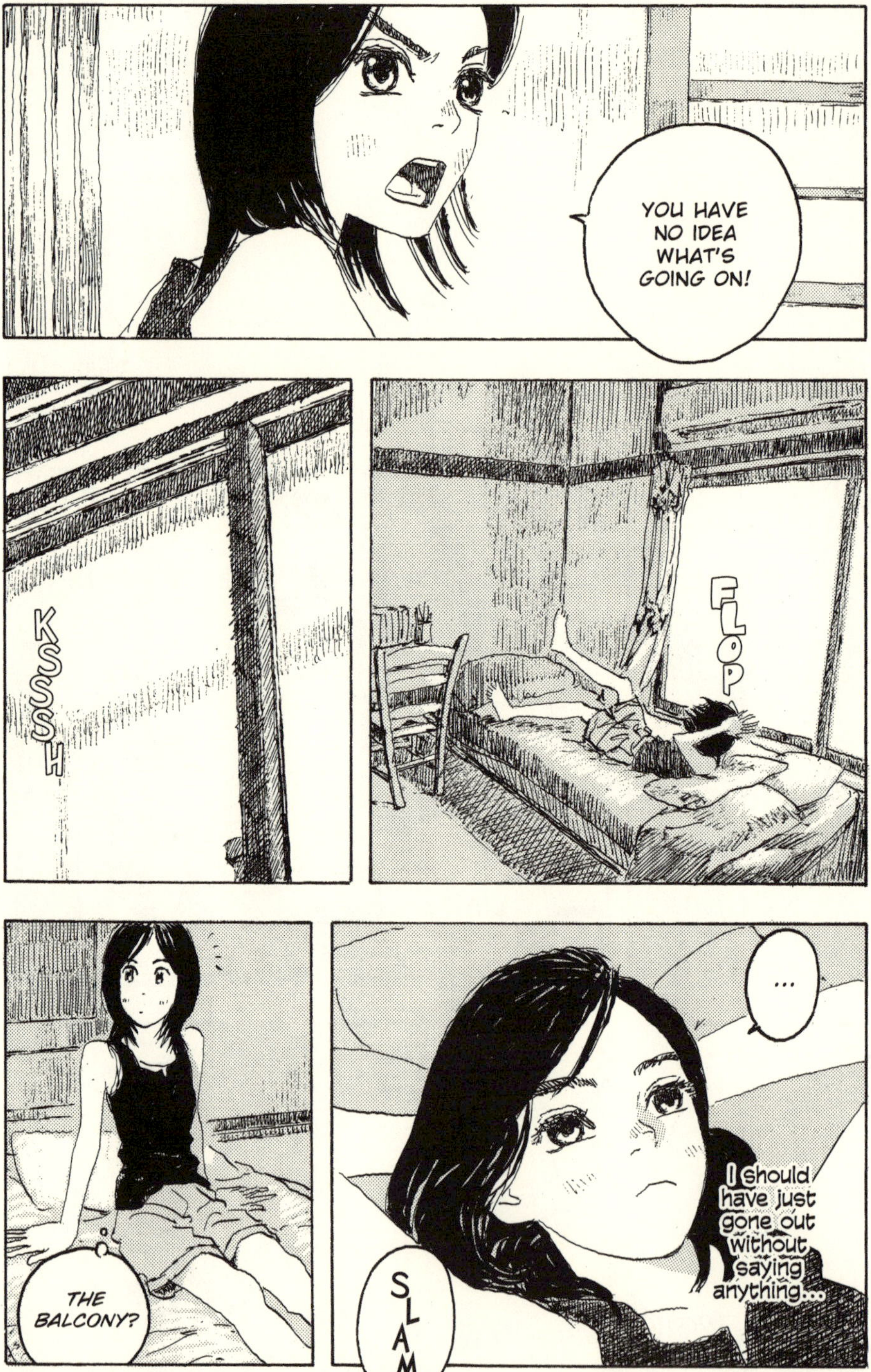
YOU HAVE NO IDEA WHAT'S GOING ON!
FLOP
KSSSH
...
I should have just gone out without saying anything...
SLAM
THE BALCONY?

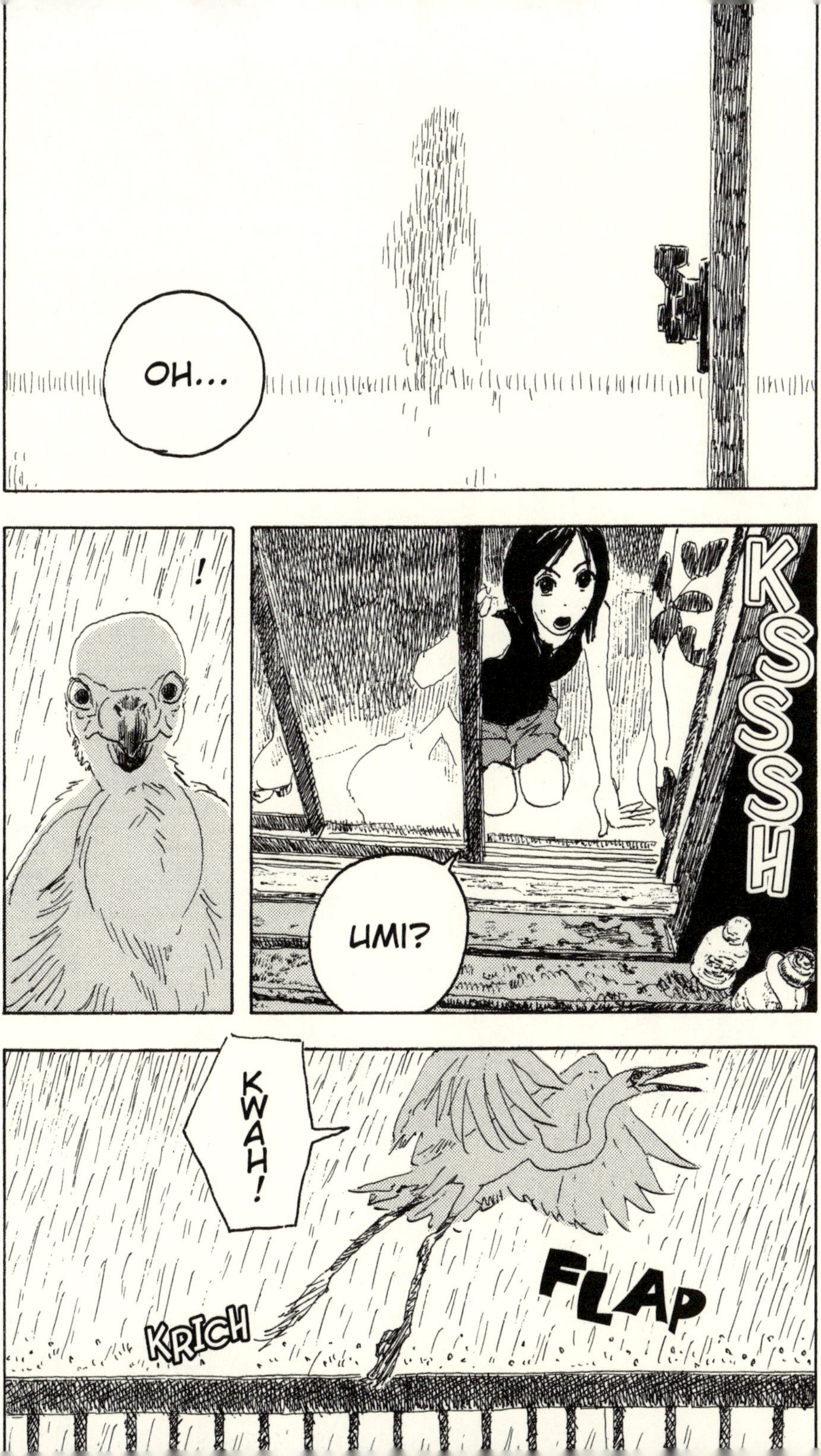
OH...
KSSSH
UMI?
!
KWAH!
FLAP
KRICH

FLAP

KSSSSH

HEY! WHERE ARE YOU GOING?

TROMP

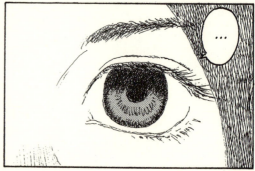

...

KSSSSH

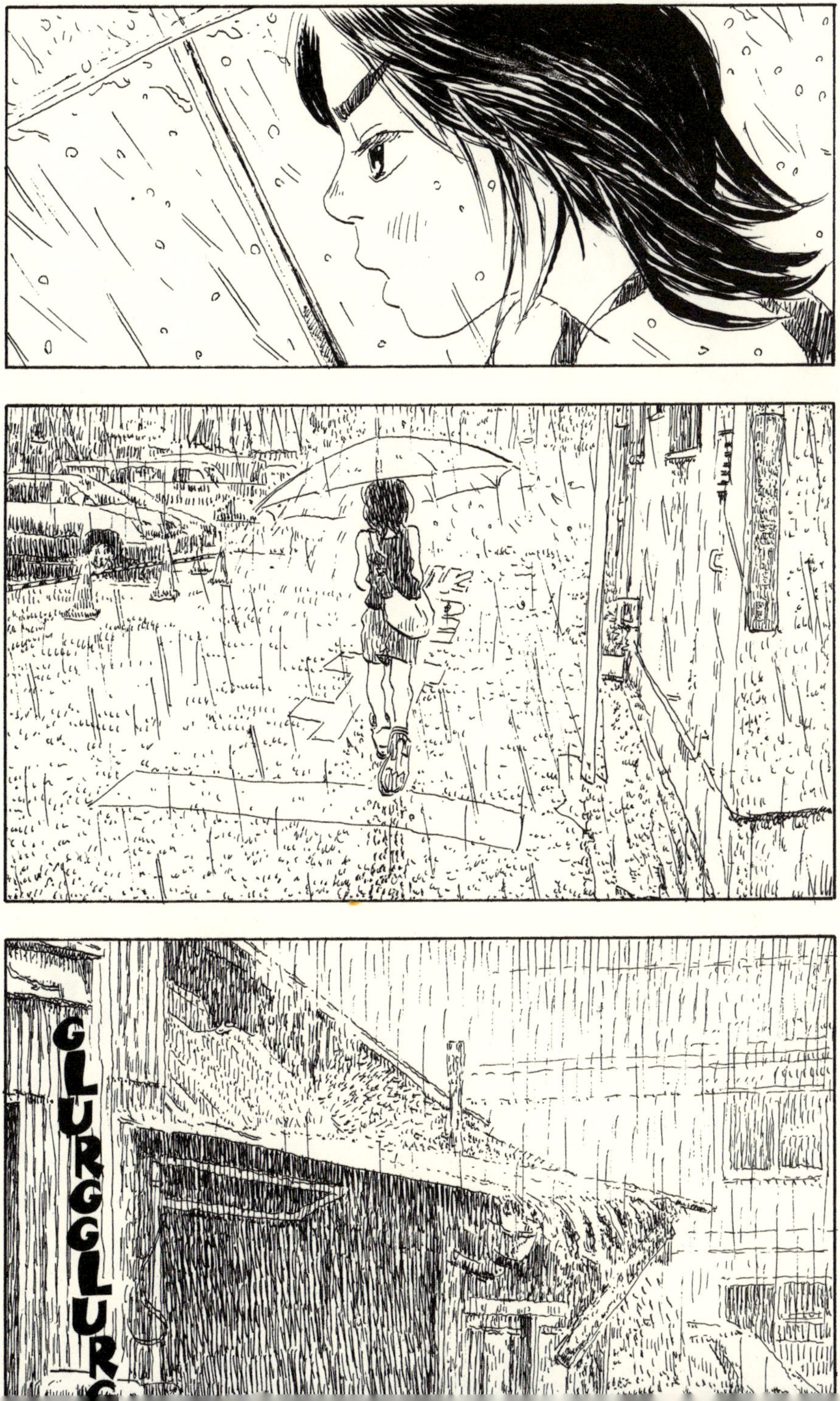
GLURGGLUR

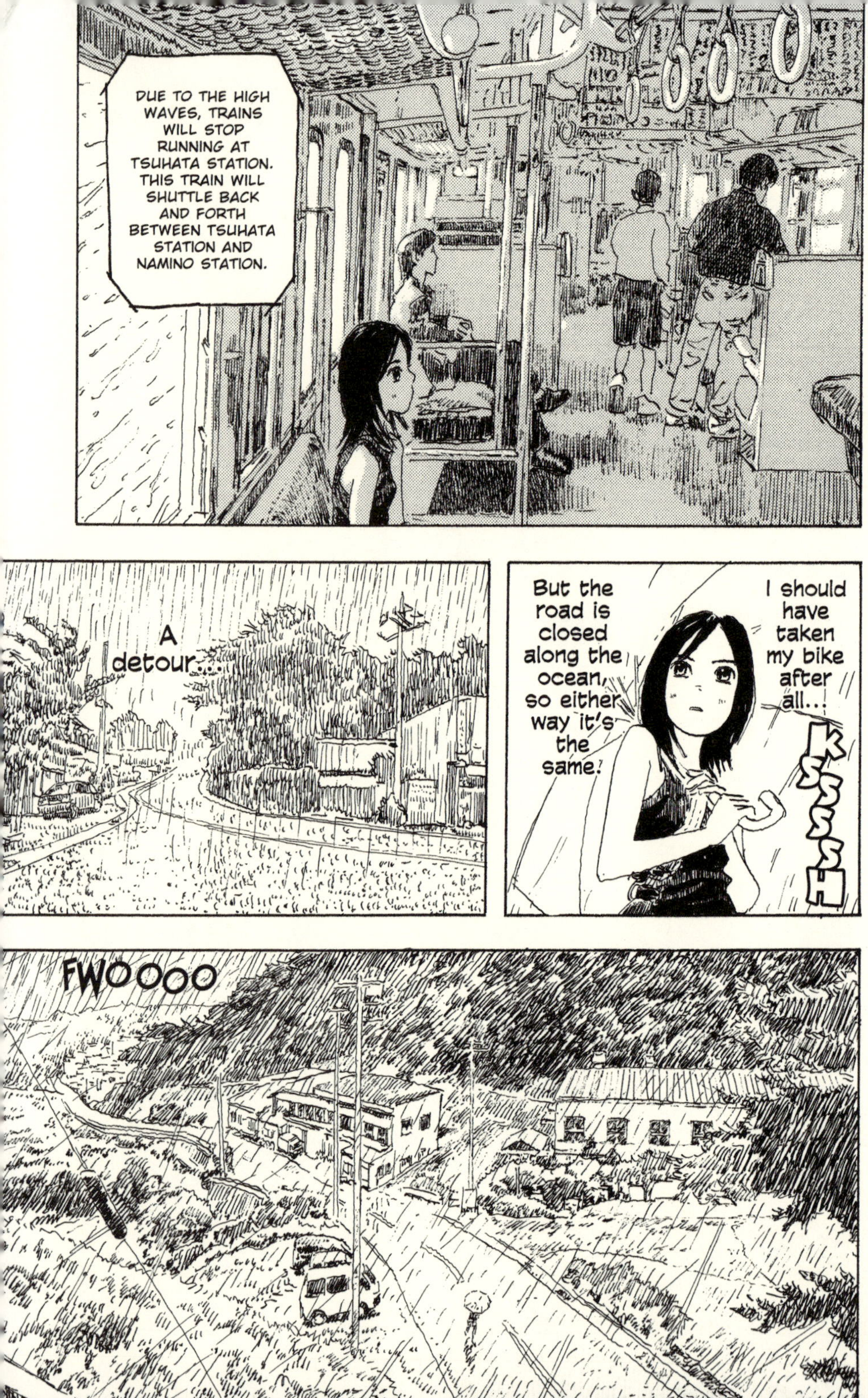
DUE TO THE HIGH WAVES, TRAINS WILL STOP RUNNING AT TSUHATA STATION. THIS TRAIN WILL SHUTTLE BACK AND FORTH BETWEEN TSUHATA STATION AND NAMINO STATION.
I should have taken my bike after all...
But the road is closed along the ocean, so either way it's the same.
KSSSH
A detour...
FWOOOO

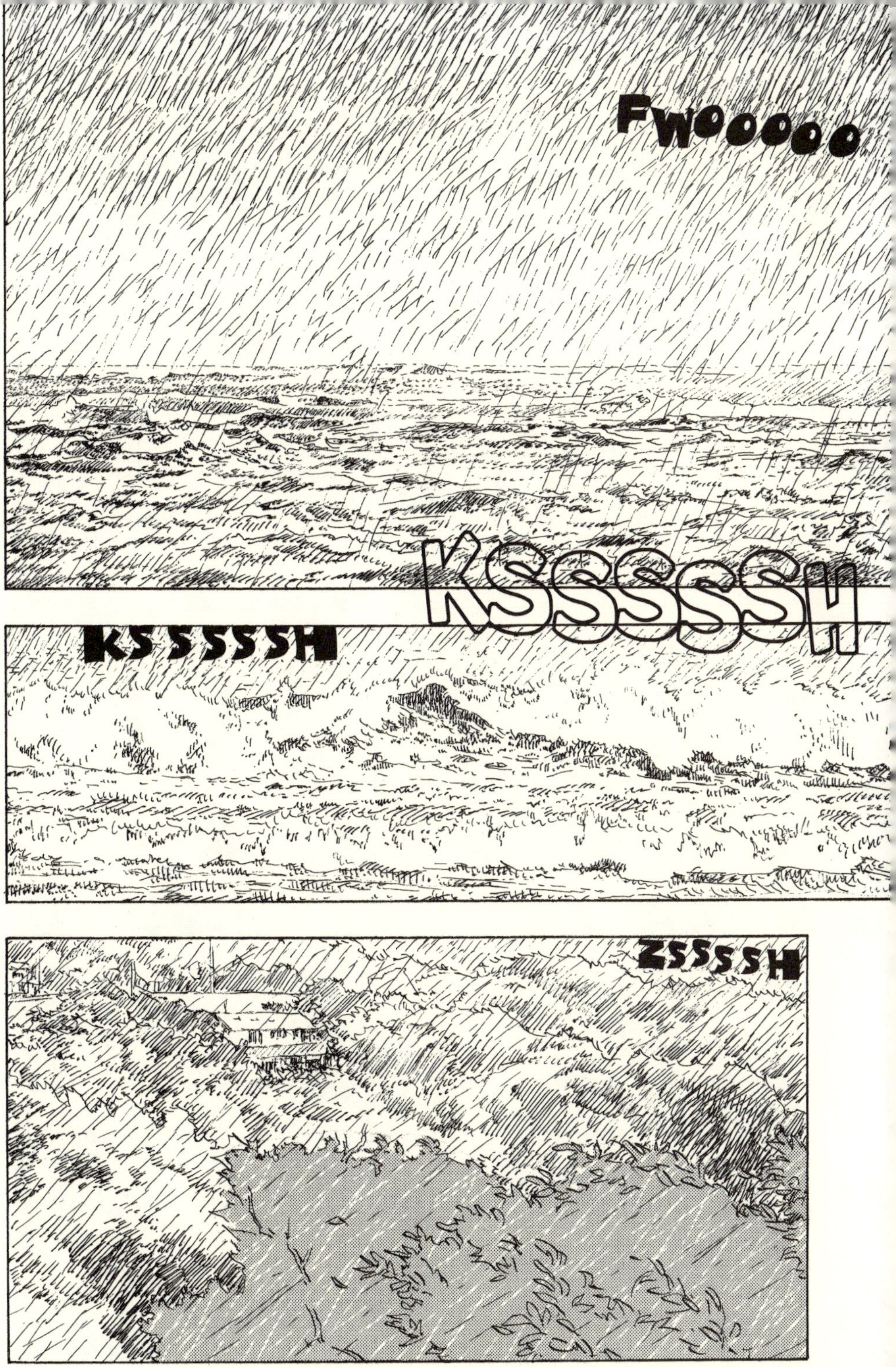
FWOOOOO
KSSSSSH
KSSSSSH
ZSSSSH

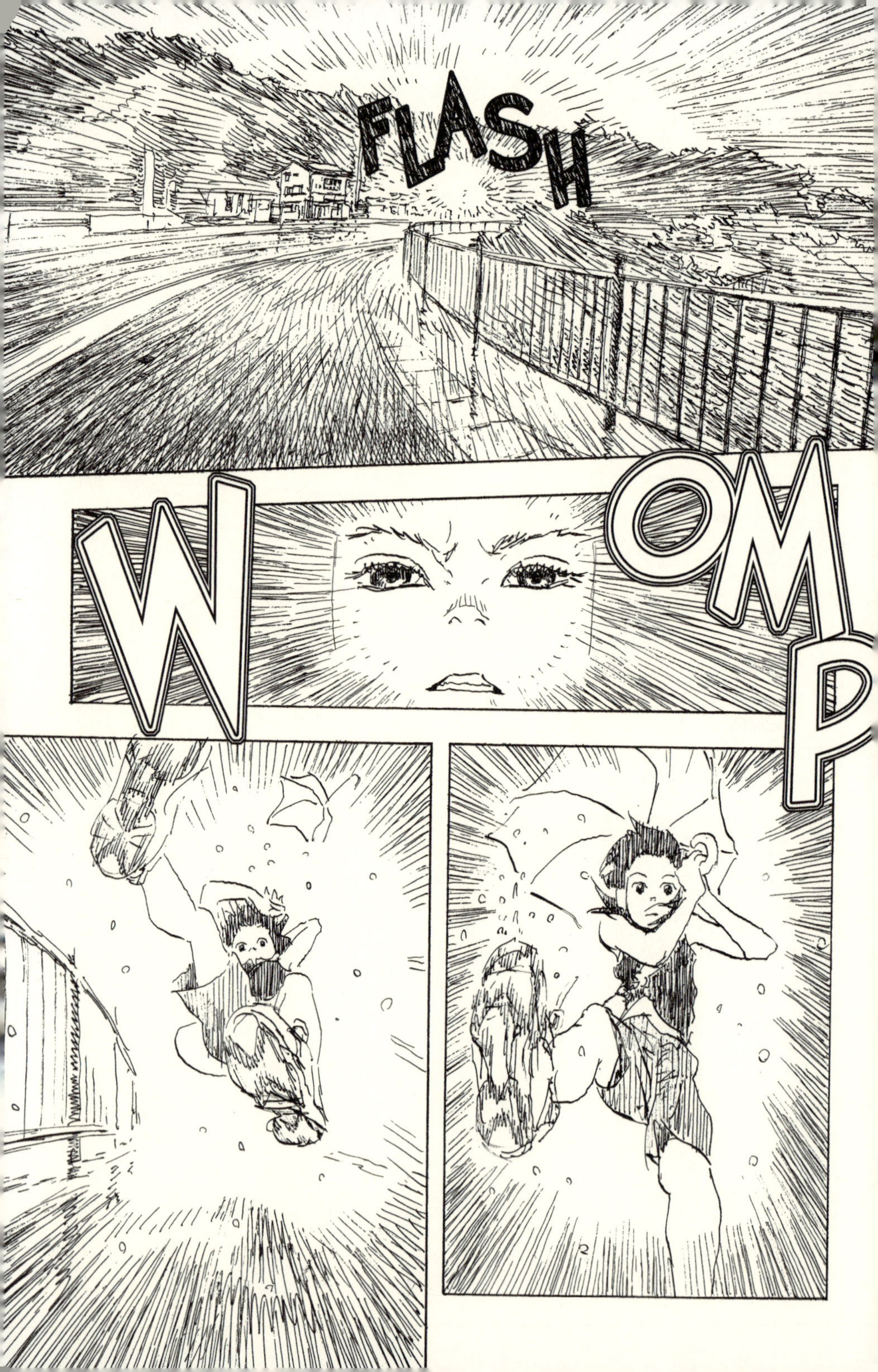
FLASH
WOMP

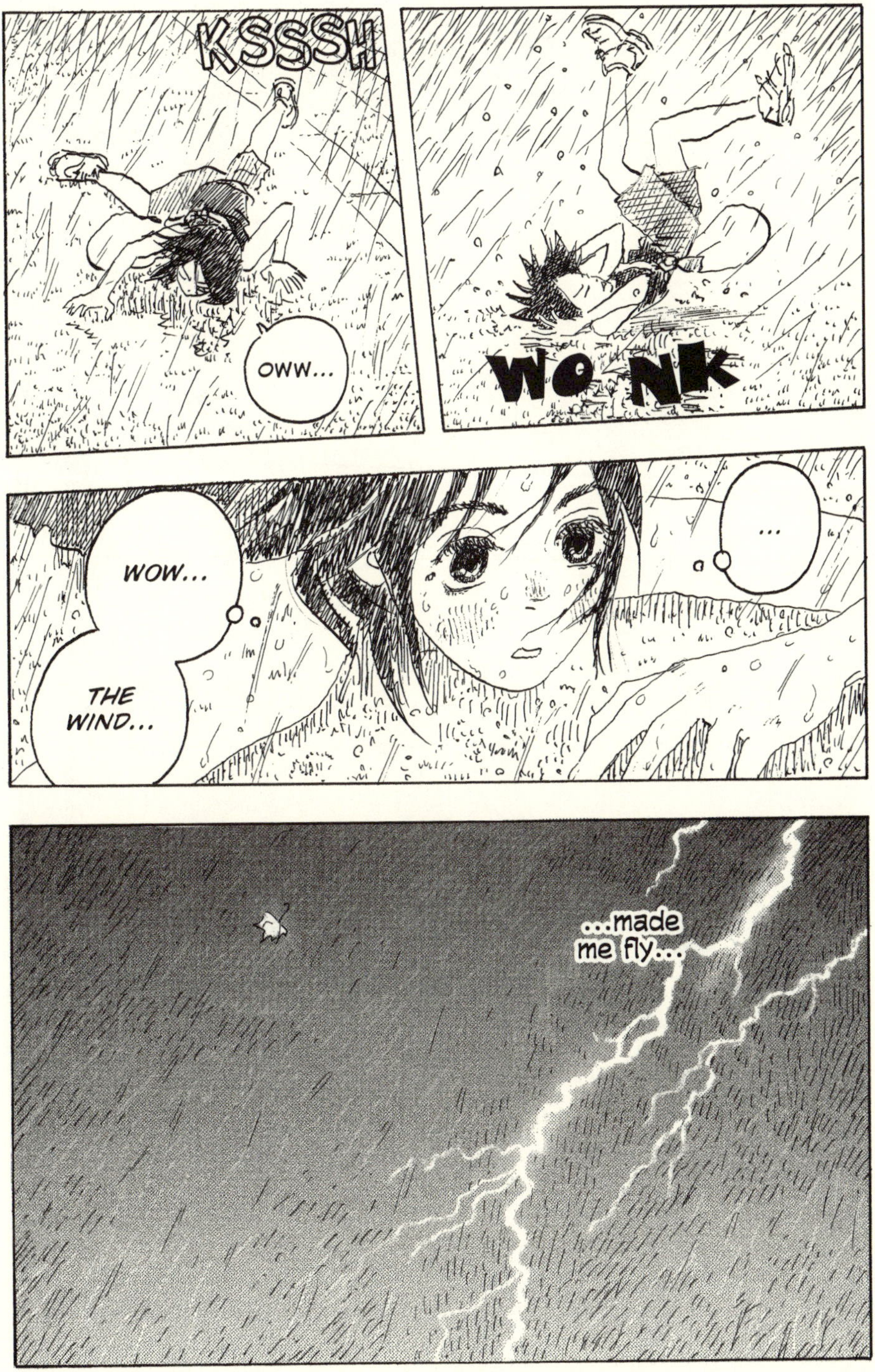
WONK
KSSSH
OWW...
...
WOW...
THE WIND...
...made me fly...

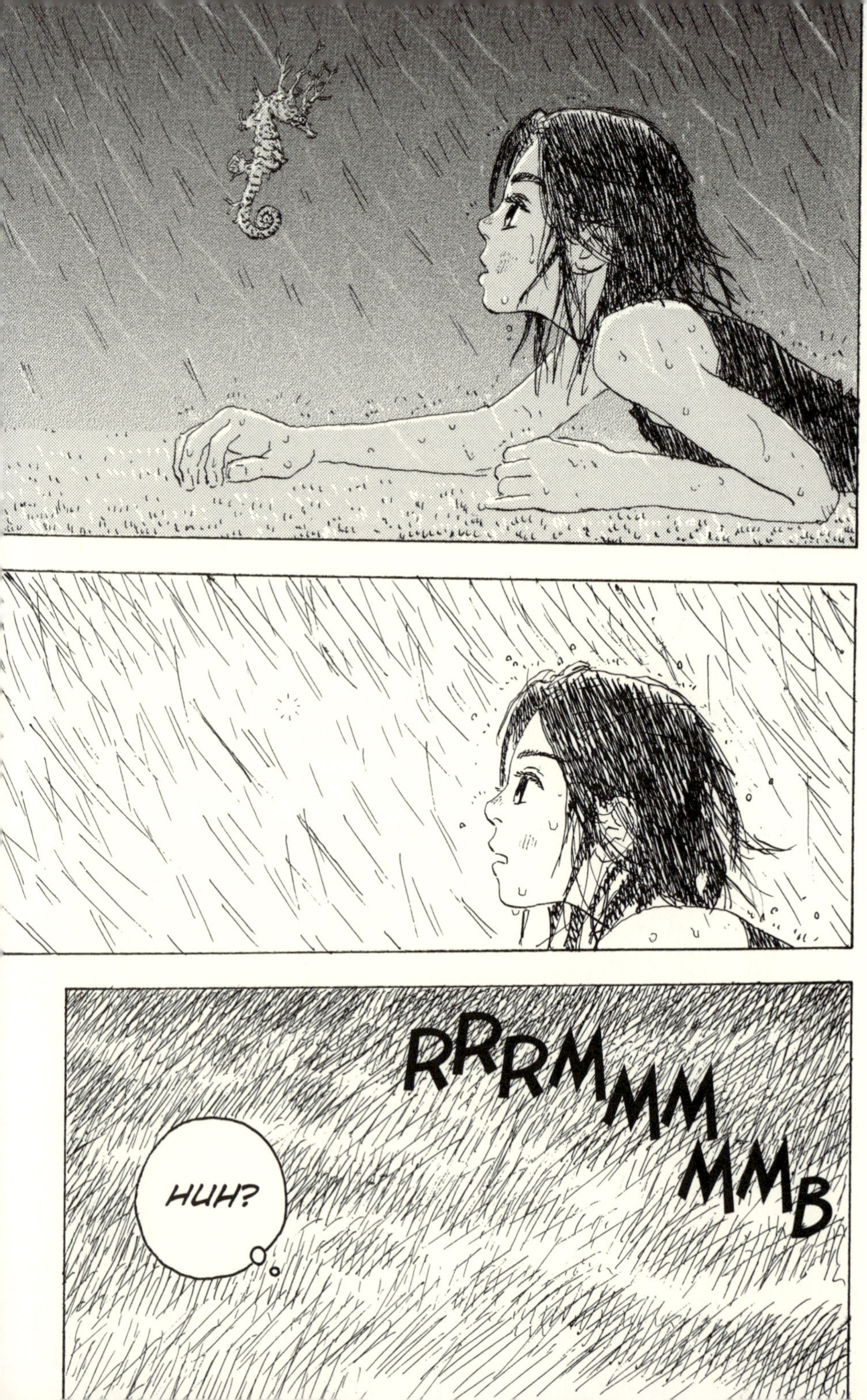
RRRMMMMMB
HUH?

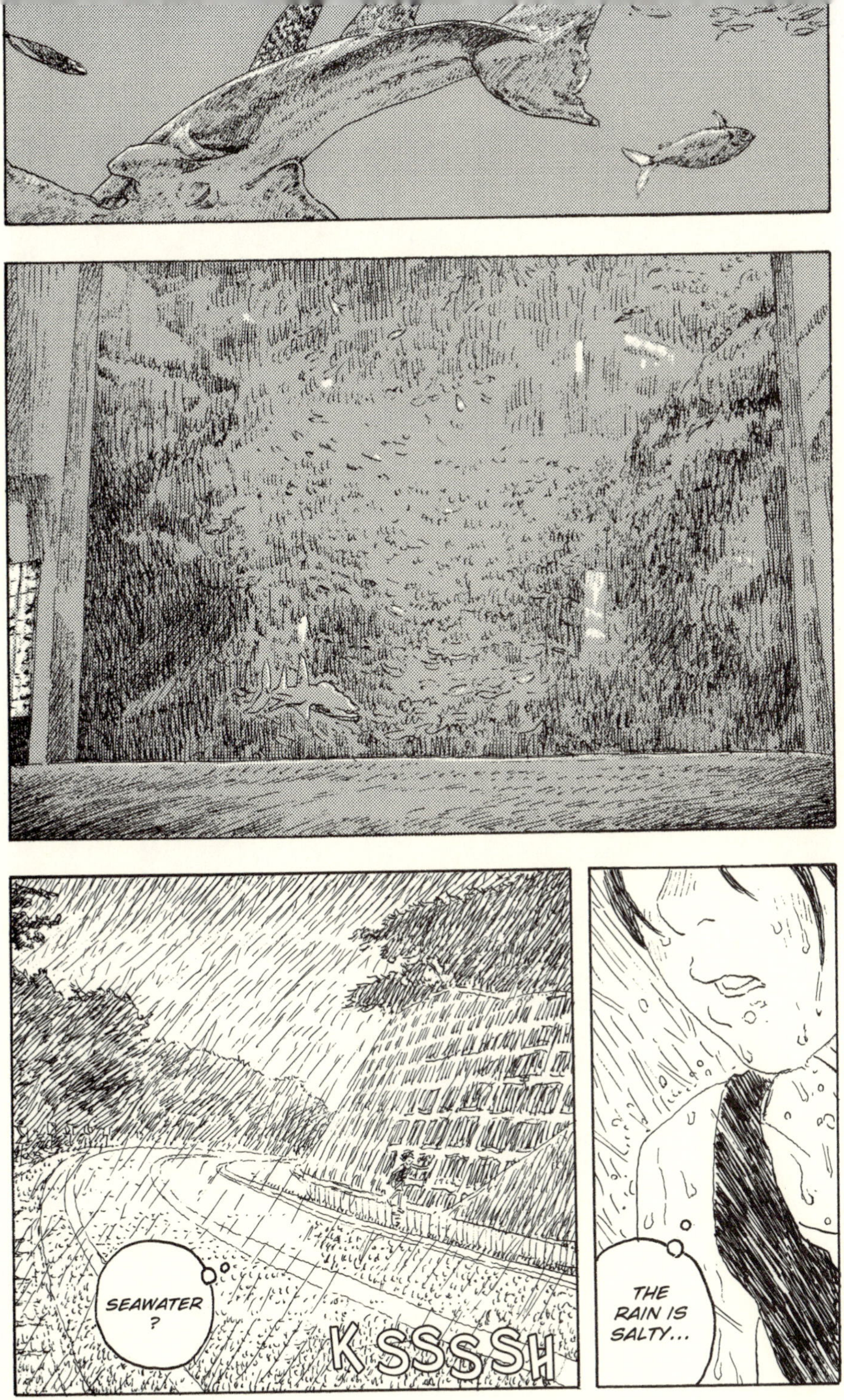
THE RAIN IS SALTY...
SEAWATER ?
KSSSSH

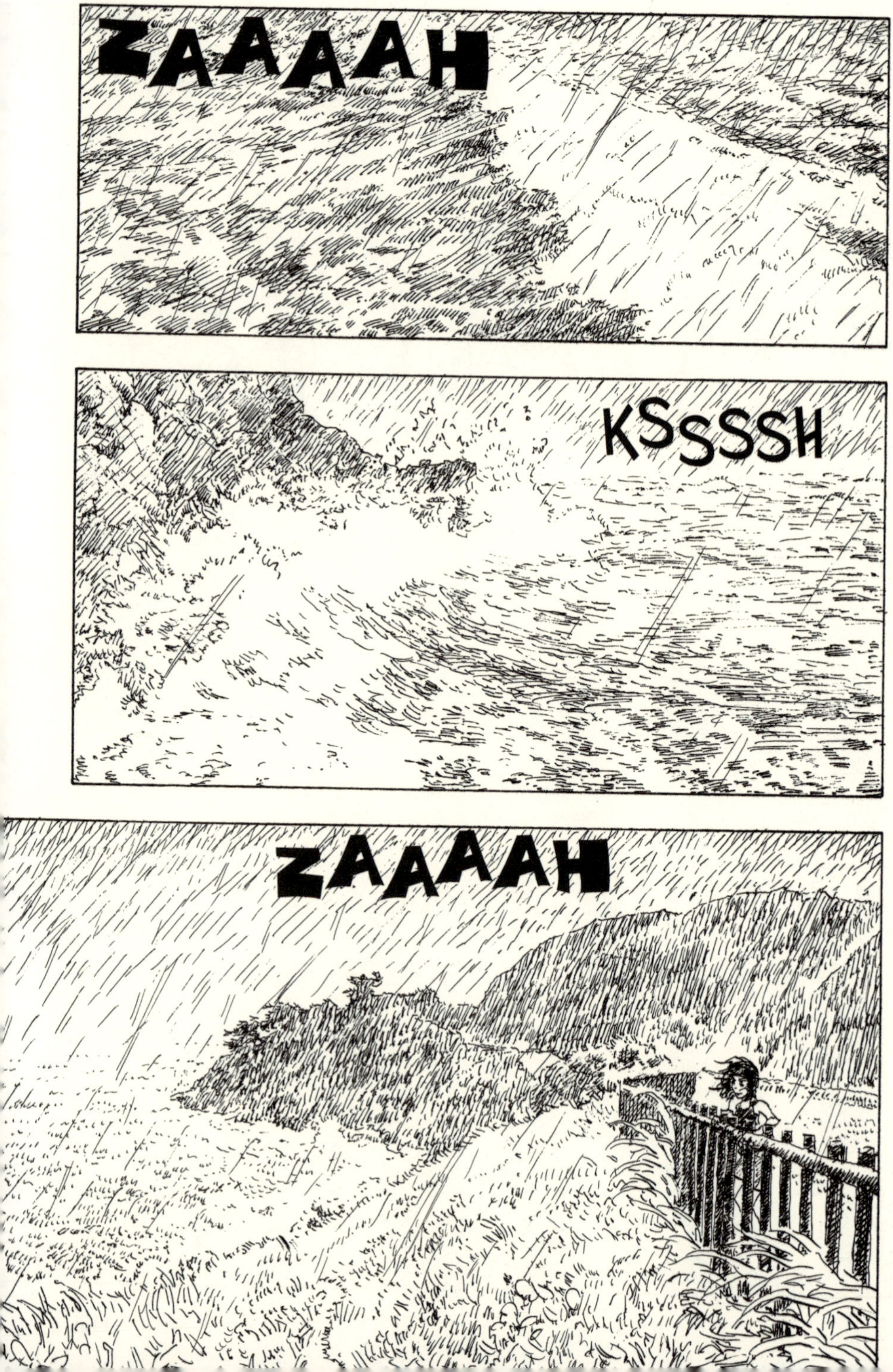
ZAAAAH
KSSSSH
ZAAAAH

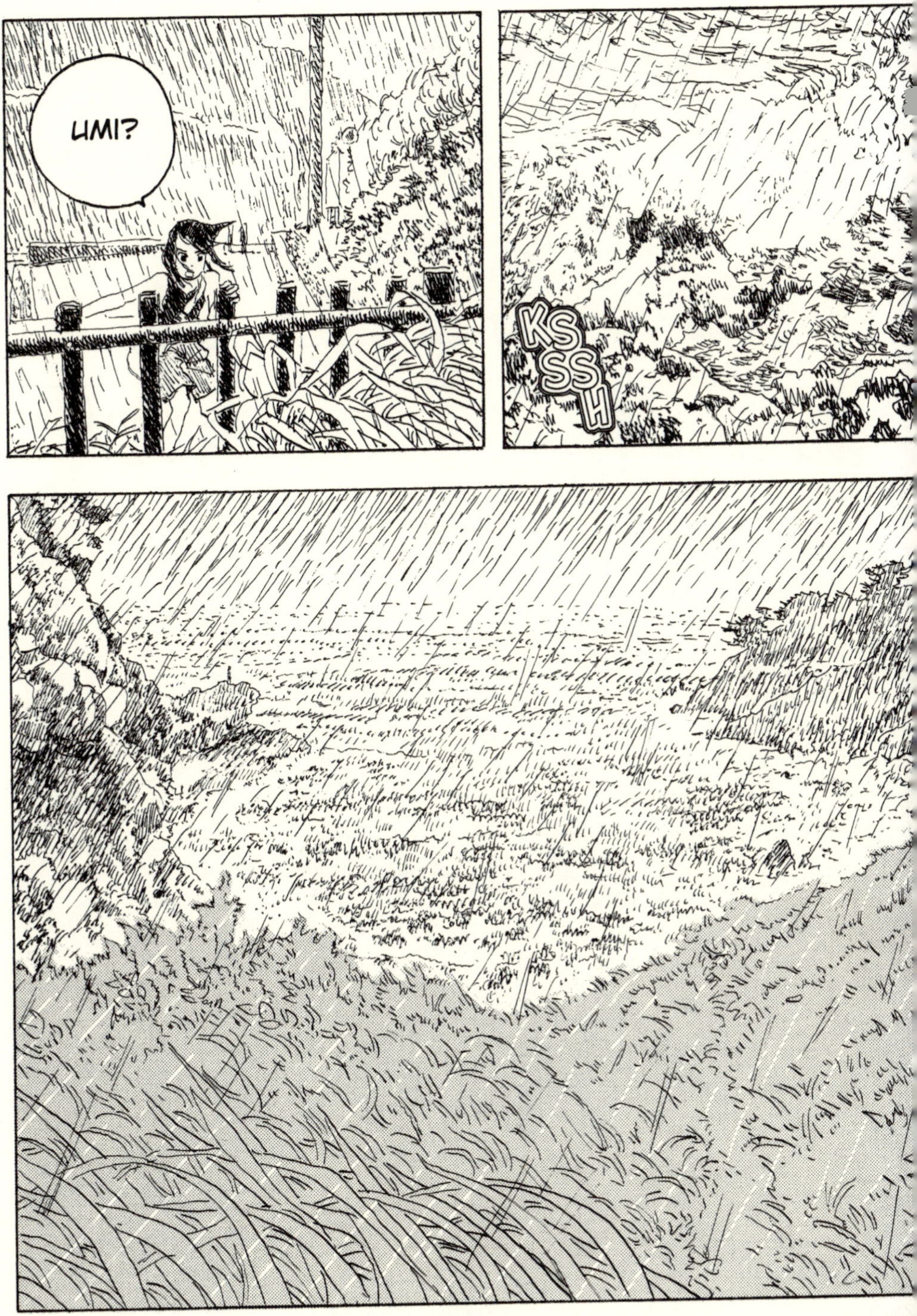
KSSSH
UMI?

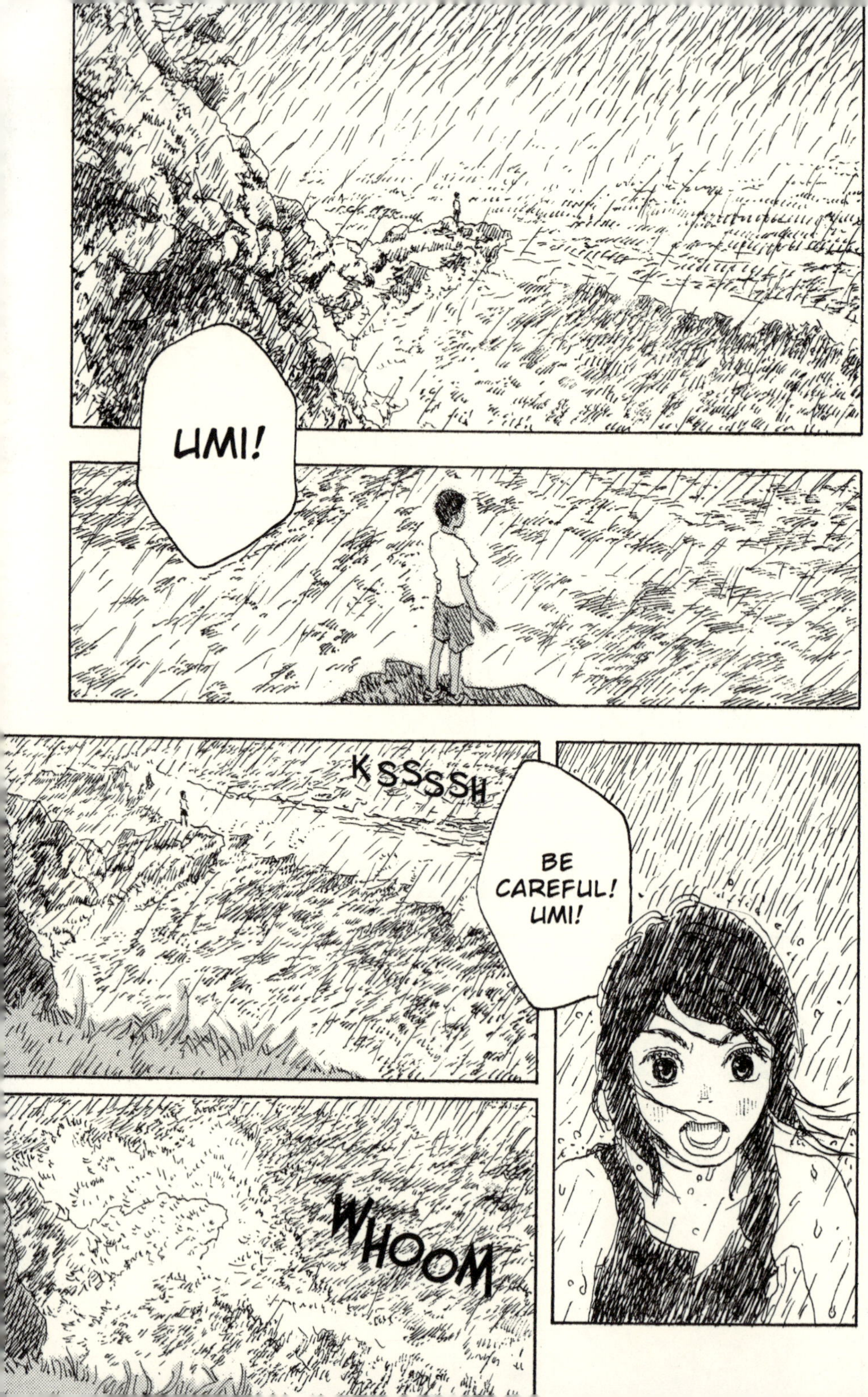
UMI!
BE CAREFUL! UMI!
KSSSSH
WHOOM

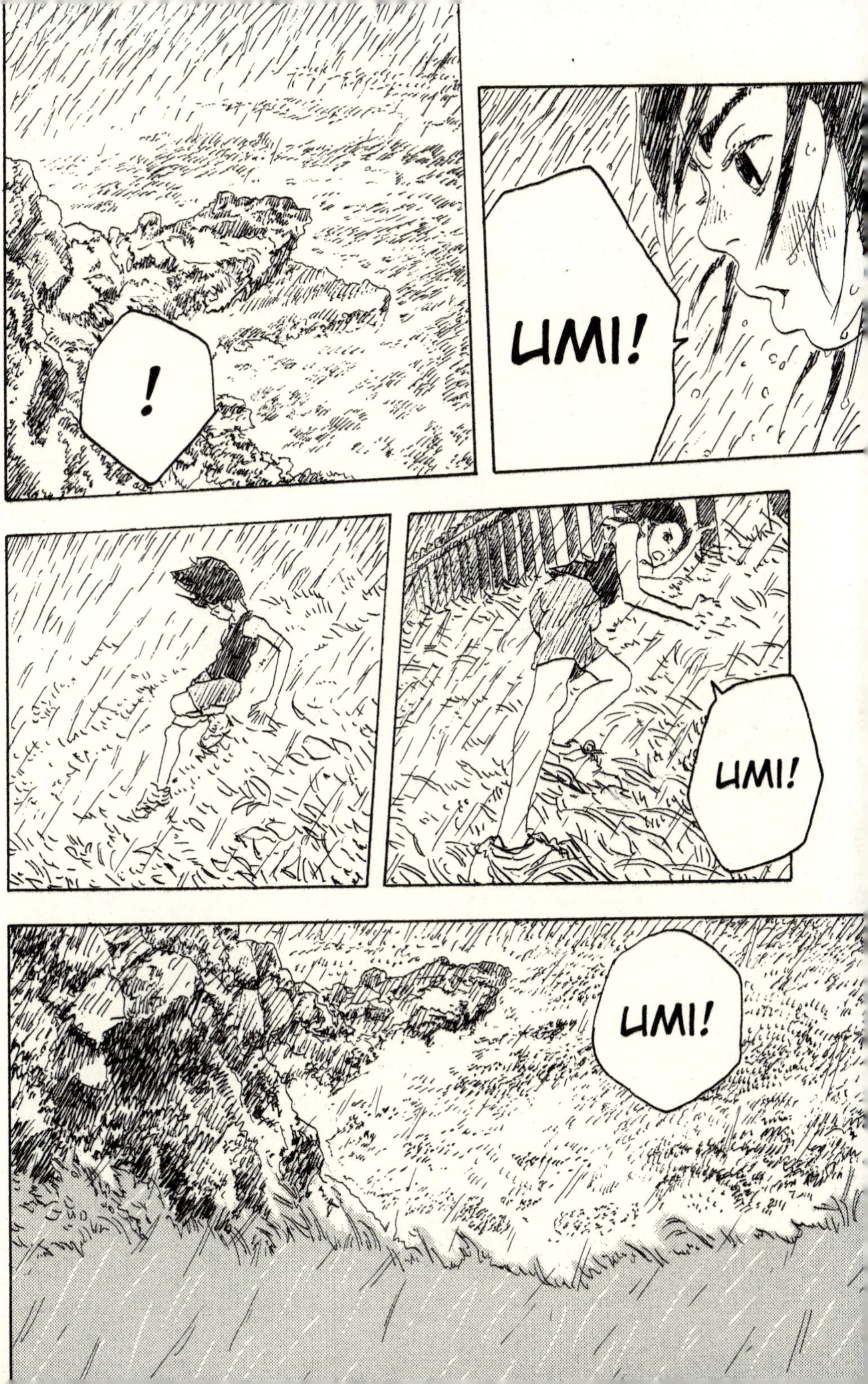
UMI!
!
UMI!
UMI!

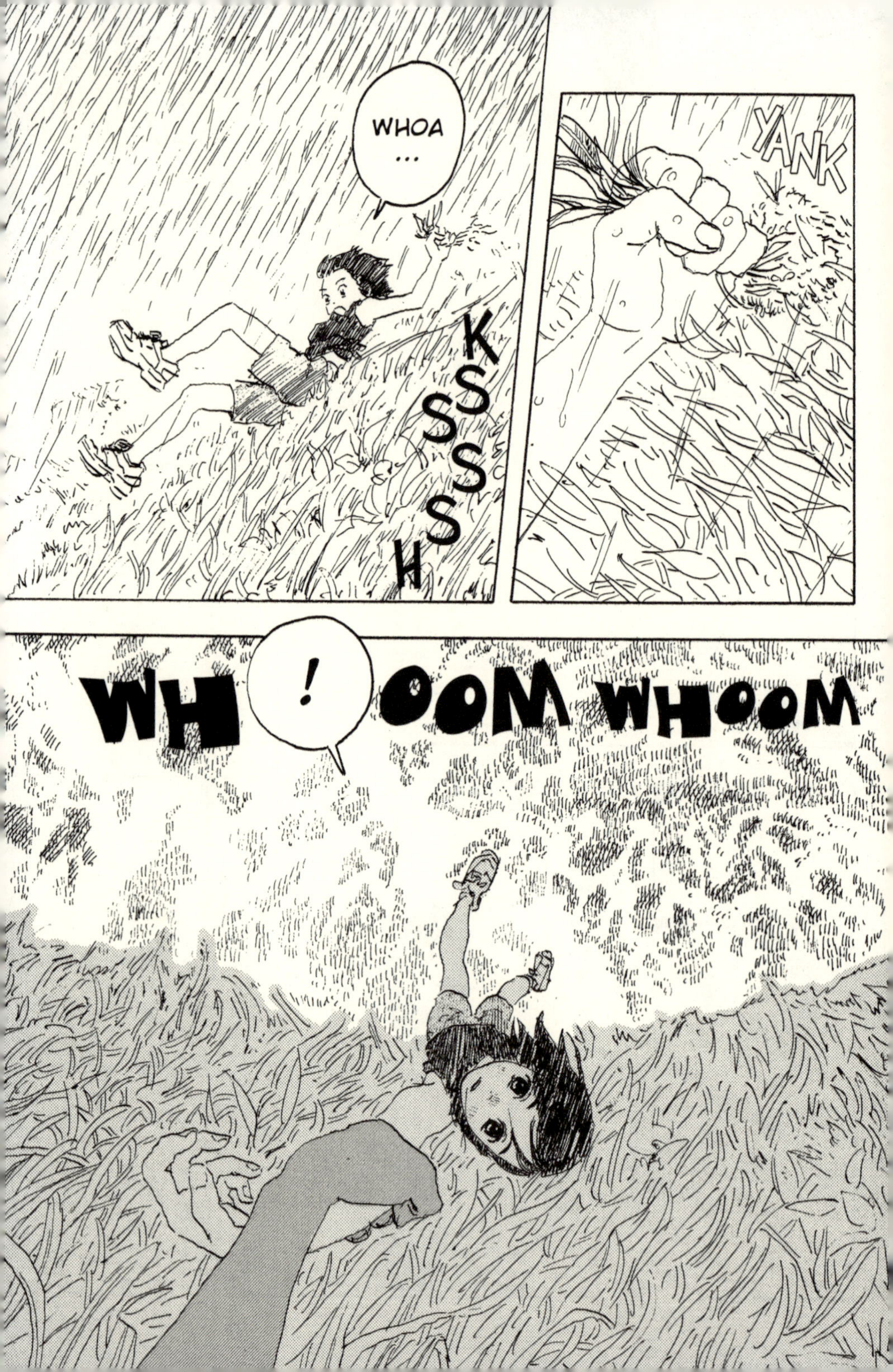
YANK
WHOA
...
KSSSSH
WHOOM WHOOM
!

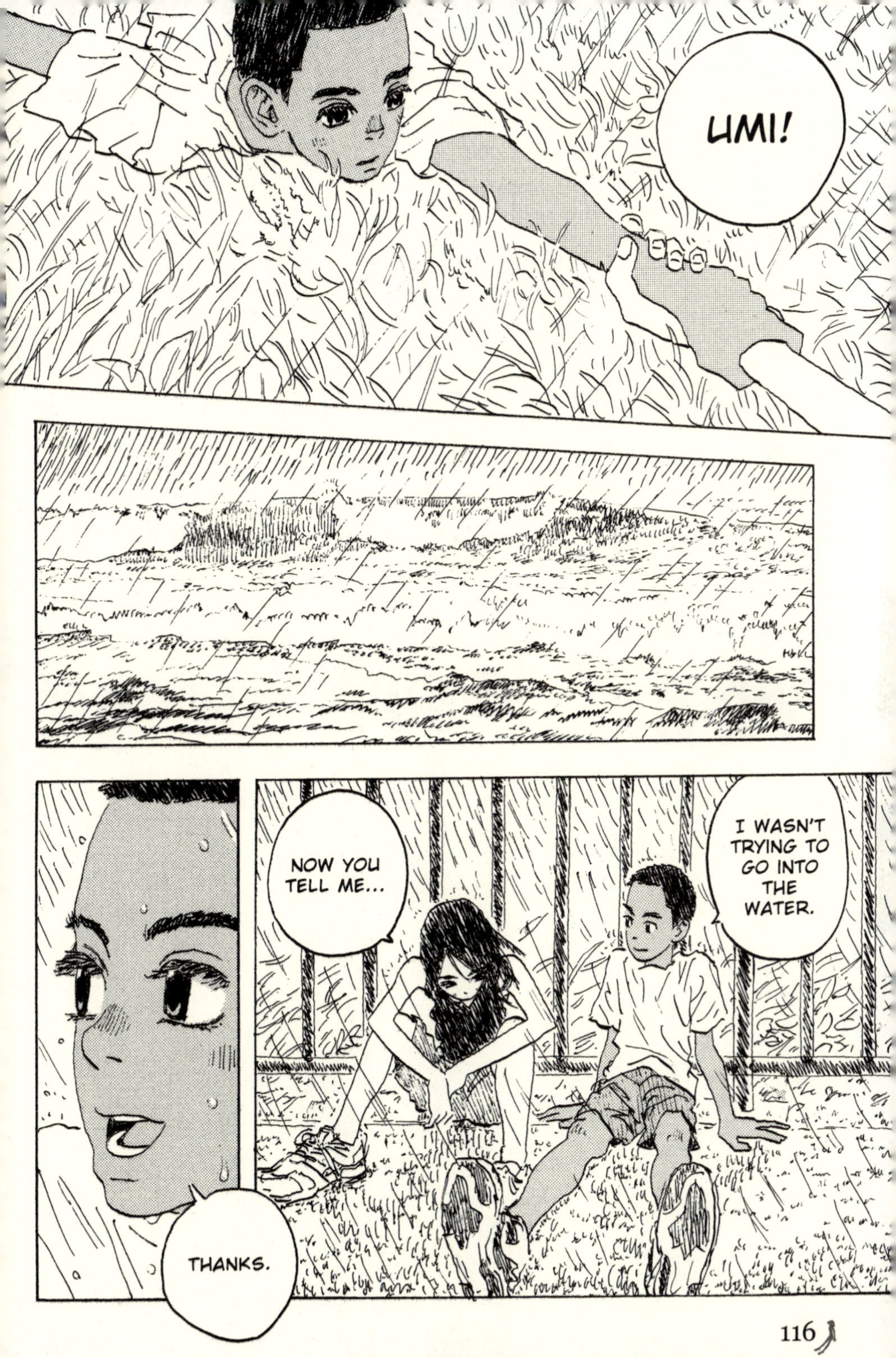
UMI!
I WASN'T TRYING TO GO INTO THE WATER.
NOW YOU TELL ME...
THANKS.

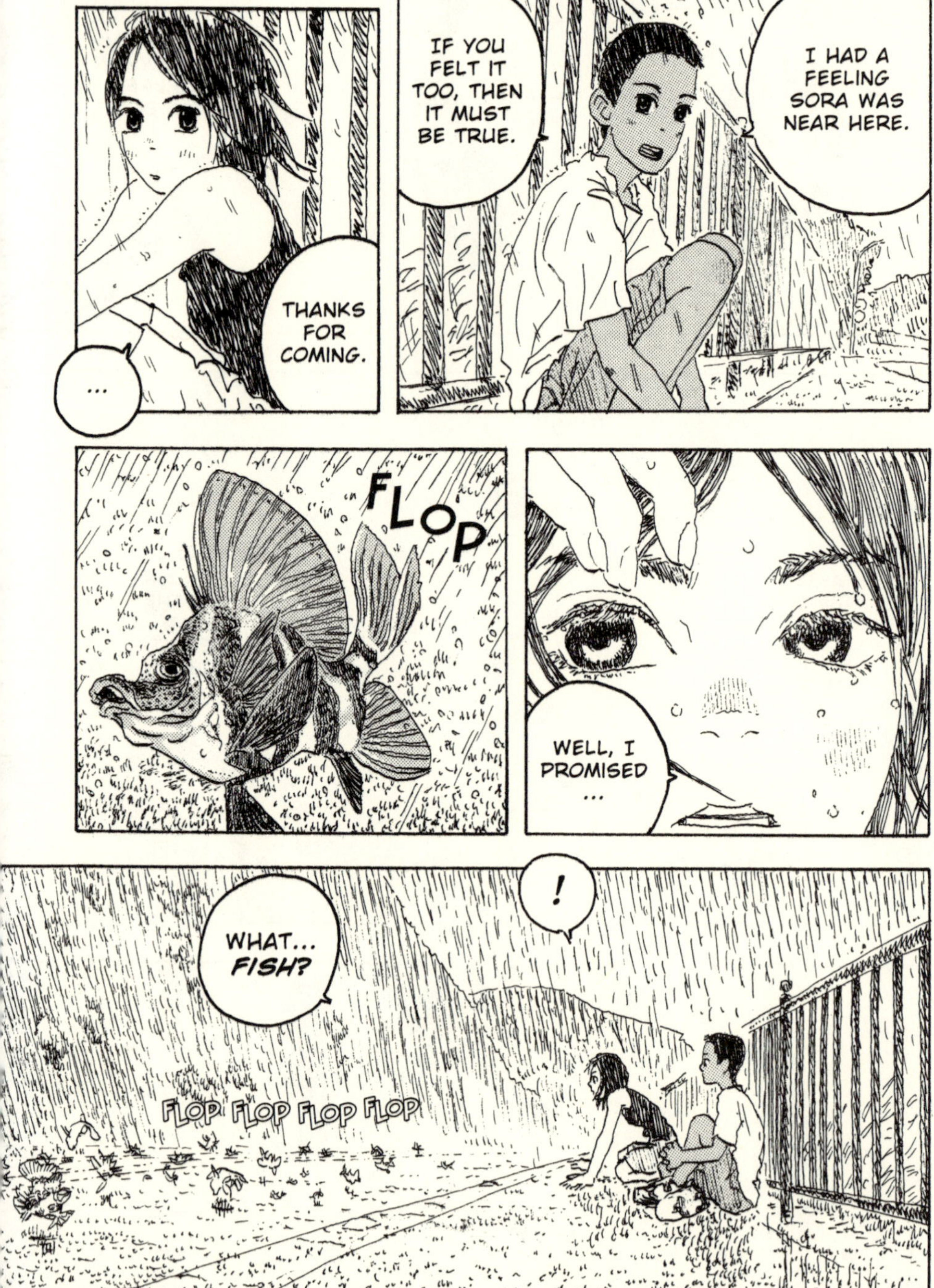
I HAD A FEELING SORA WAS NEAR HERE.
IF YOU FELT IT TOO, THEN IT MUST BE TRUE.
THANKS FOR COMING.
...
WELL, I PROMISED ...
FLOP
!
WHAT... *FISH?*
FLOP FLOP FLOP FLOP

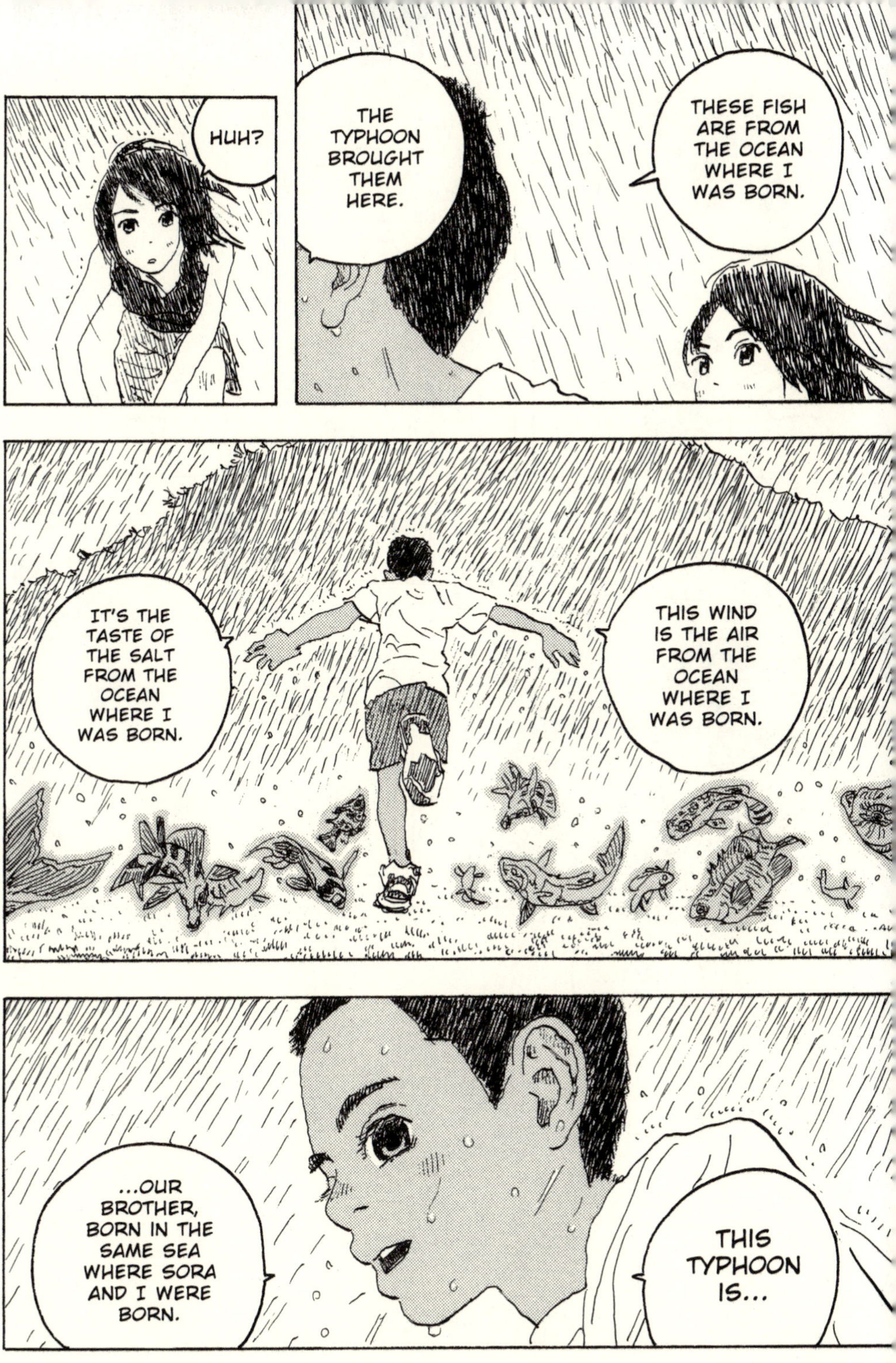
THESE FISH ARE FROM THE OCEAN WHERE I WAS BORN.
THE TYPHOON BROUGHT THEM HERE.
HUH?
THIS WIND IS THE AIR FROM THE OCEAN WHERE I WAS BORN.
IT'S THE TASTE OF THE SALT FROM THE OCEAN WHERE I WAS BORN.
THIS TYPHOON IS...
...OUR BROTHER, BORN IN THE SAME SEA WHERE SORA AND I WERE BORN.

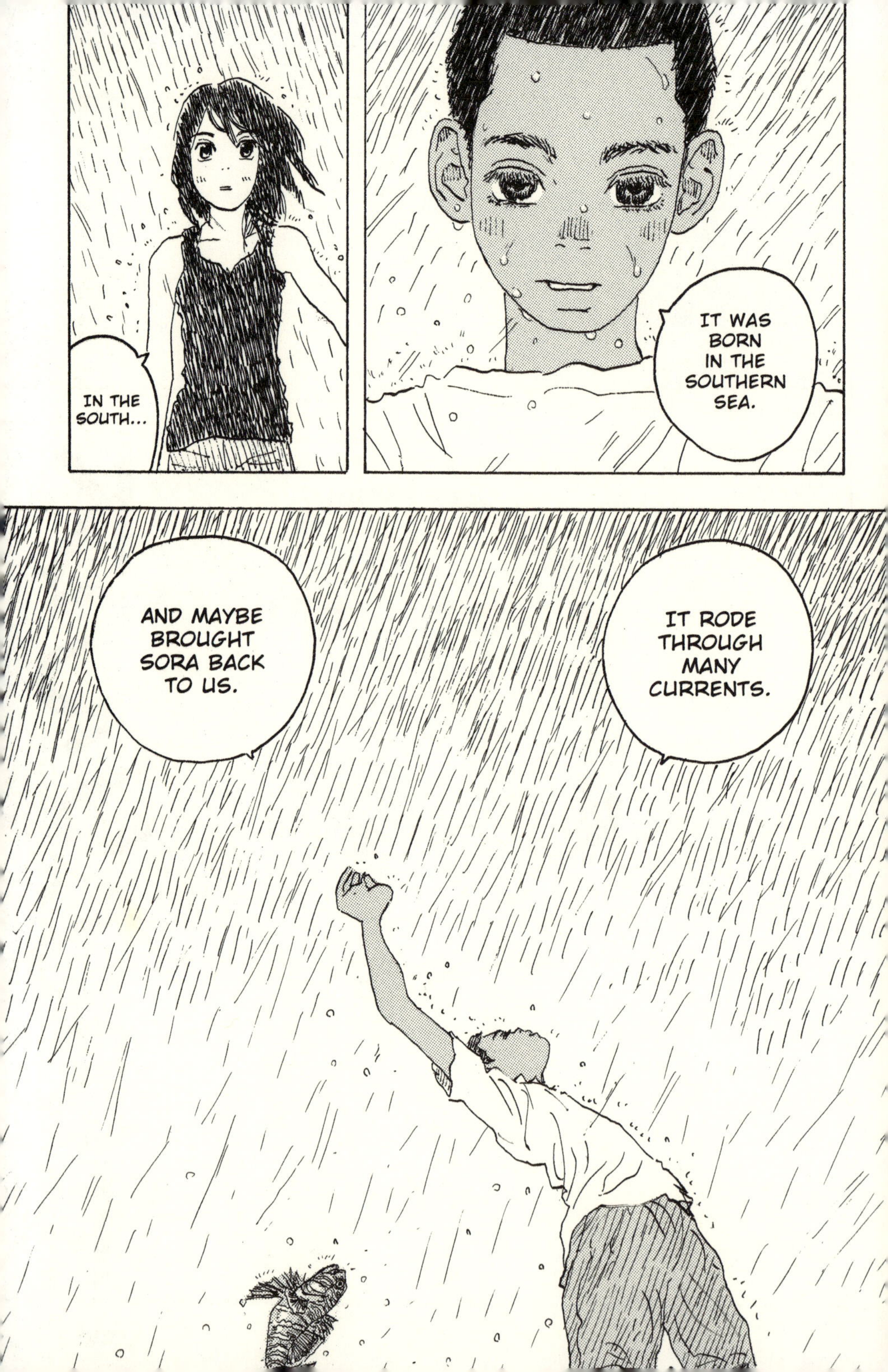
IT WAS BORN IN THE SOUTHERN SEA.
IN THE SOUTH...
IT RODE THROUGH MANY CURRENTS.
AND MAYBE BROUGHT SORA BACK TO US.

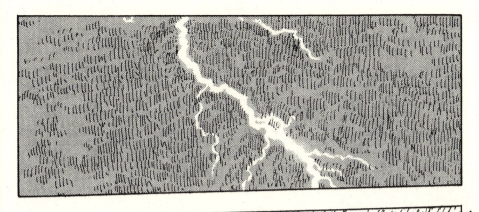

KSSSSH

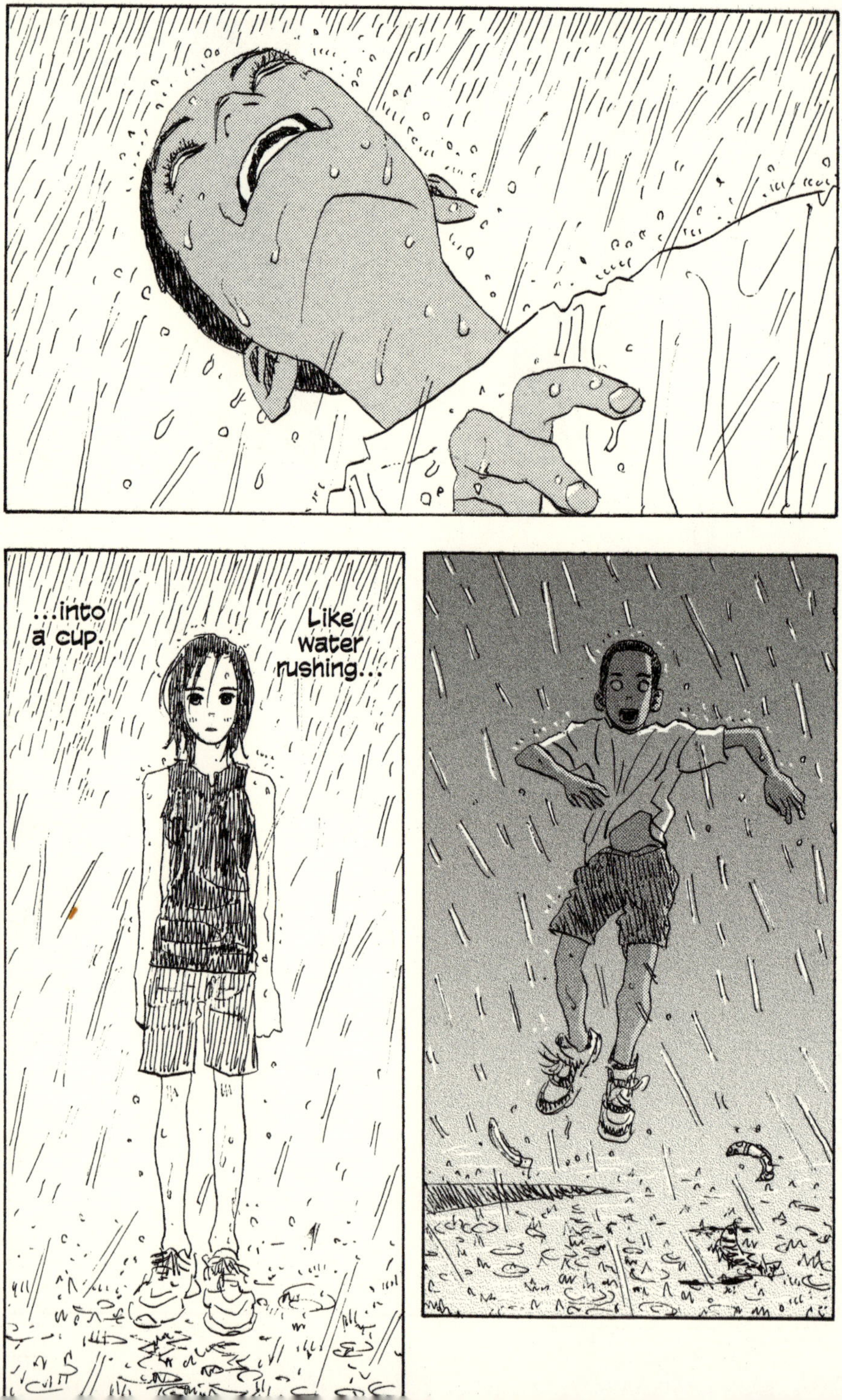
Like water rushing...
...into a cup.

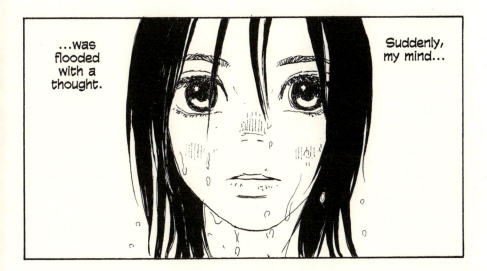

Suddenly, my mind...
...was flooded with a thought.
"There's something I must do."

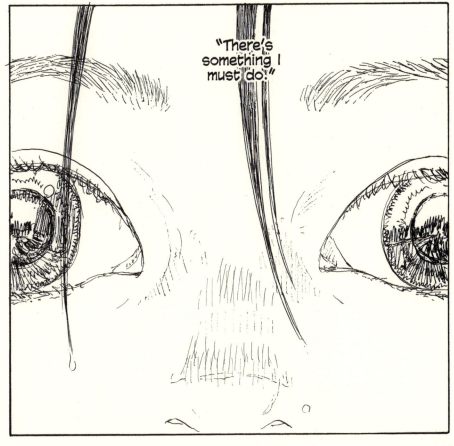

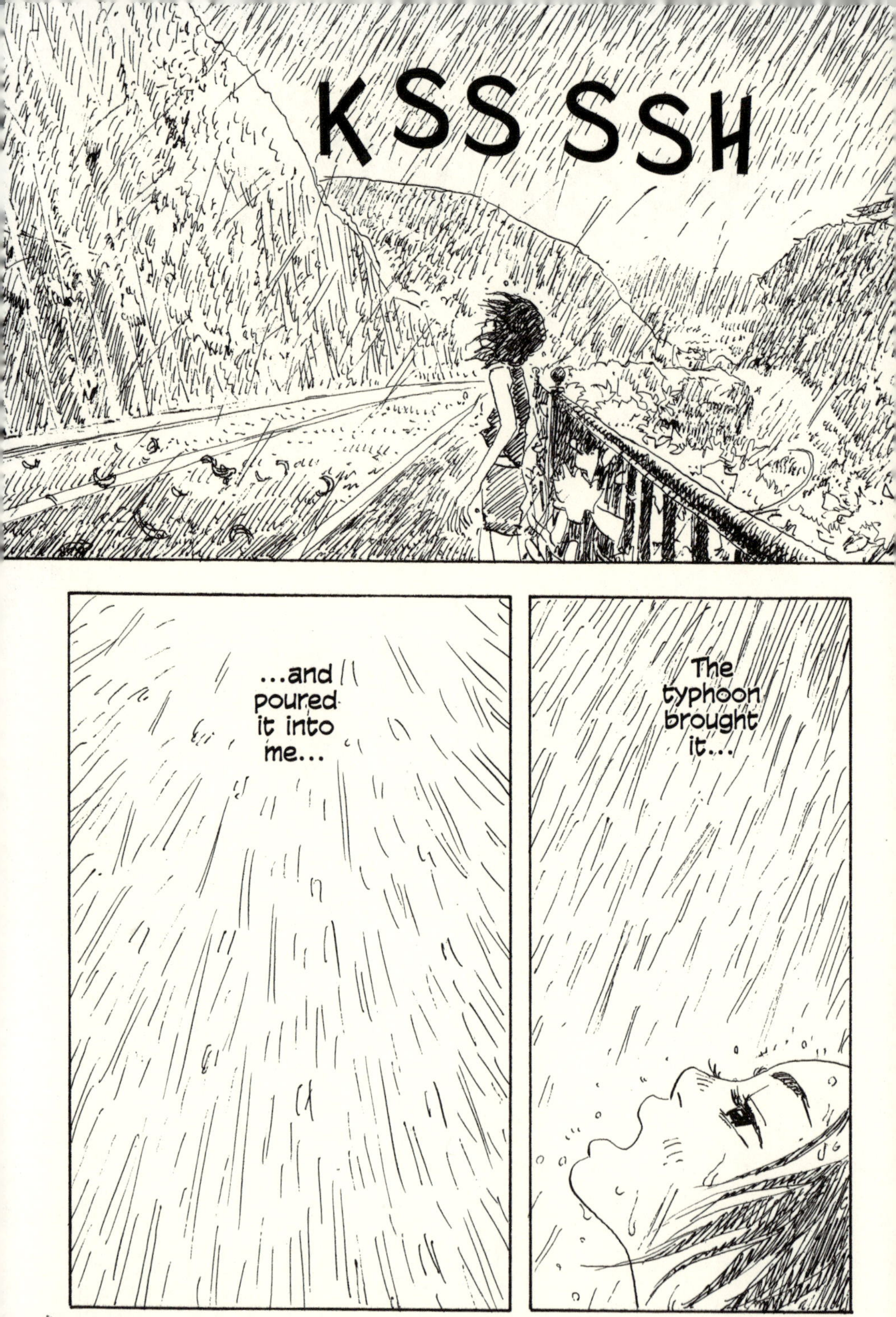
KSSSSH
The typhoon brought it...
...and poured it into me...

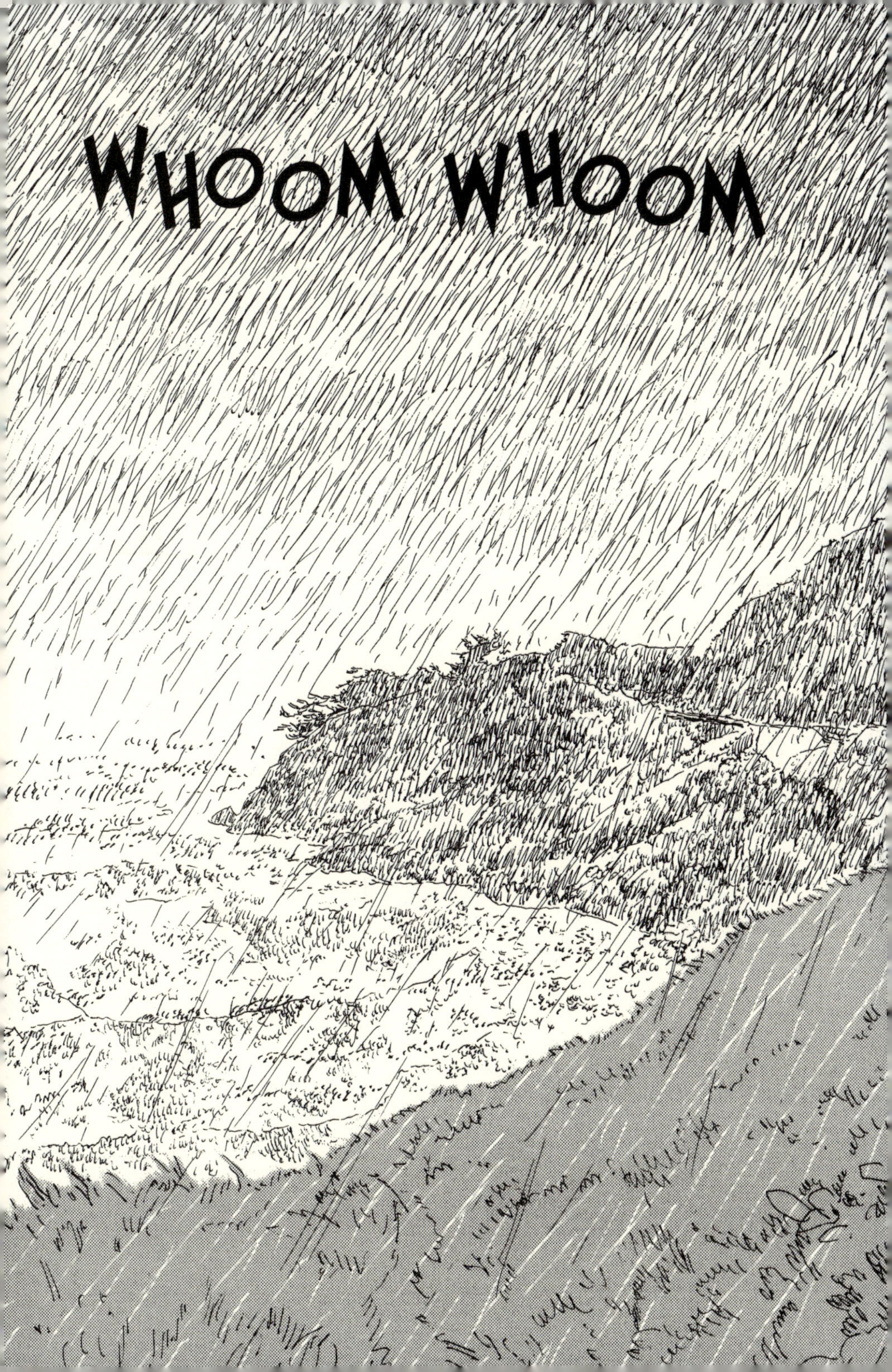
WHOOM WHOOM

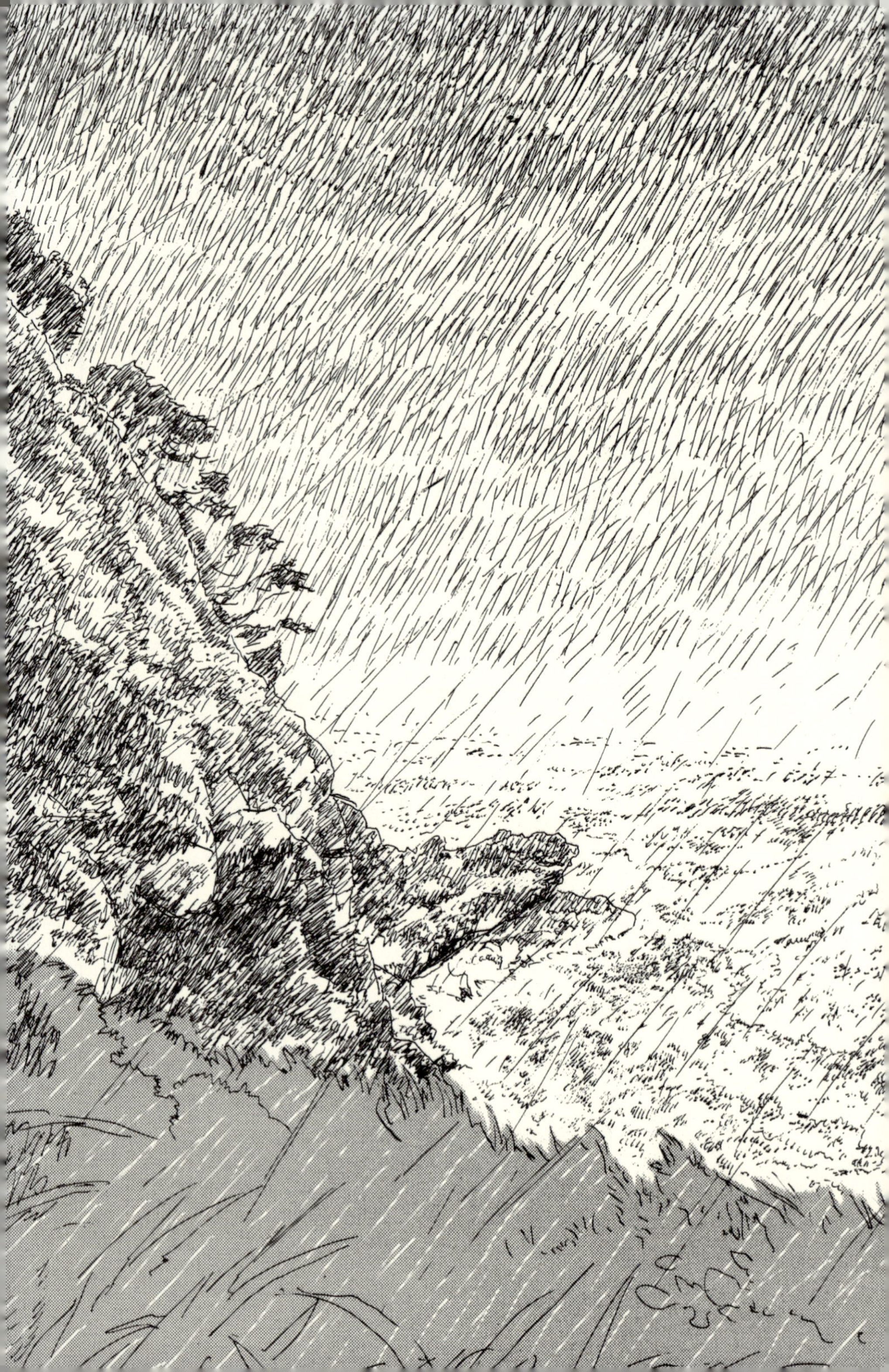

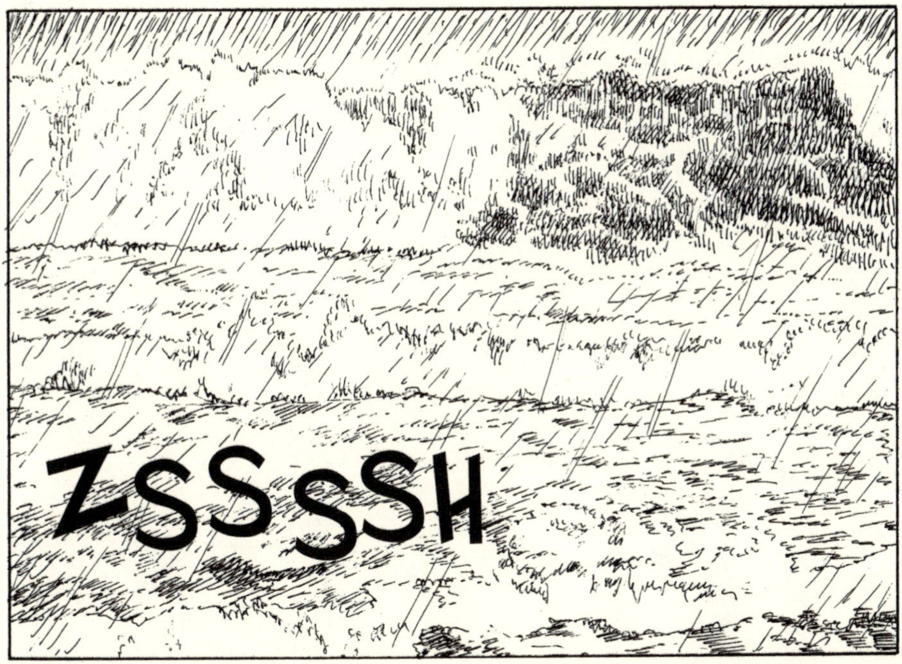
ZSSSSH

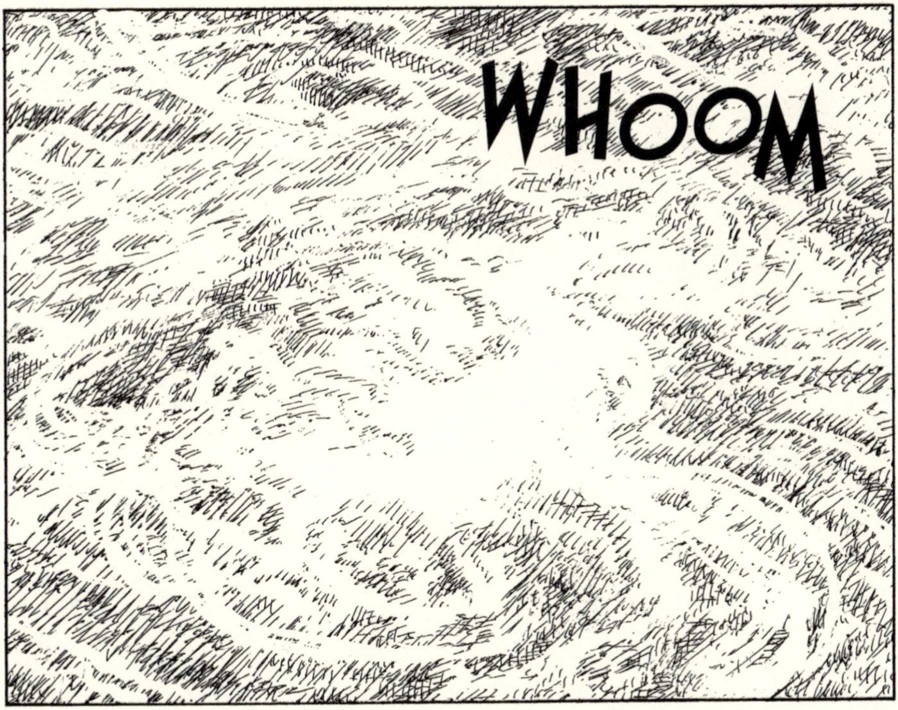
WHOOM

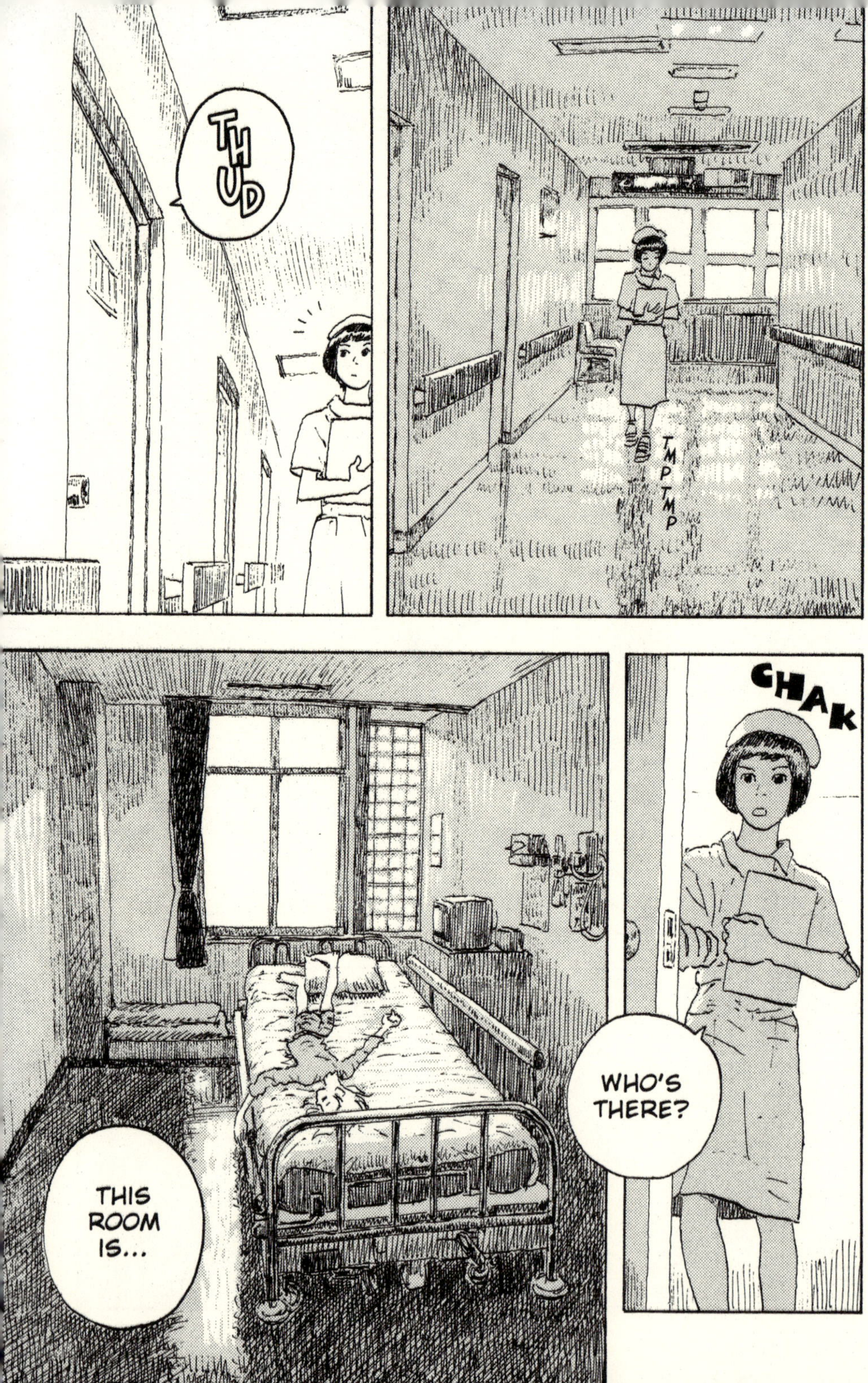
TMP TMP
THUD
CHAK
WHO'S THERE?
THIS ROOM IS...

SORA?!

OH...

FLOP
FLOP

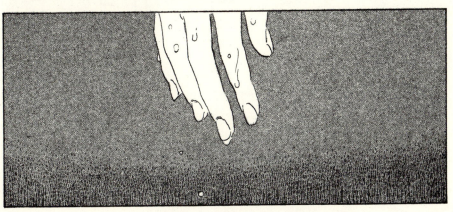

Chapter 12:
Falling Rain Collecting in Pools

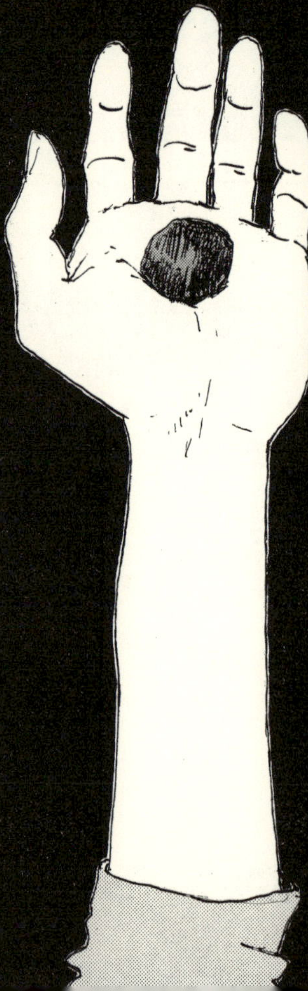

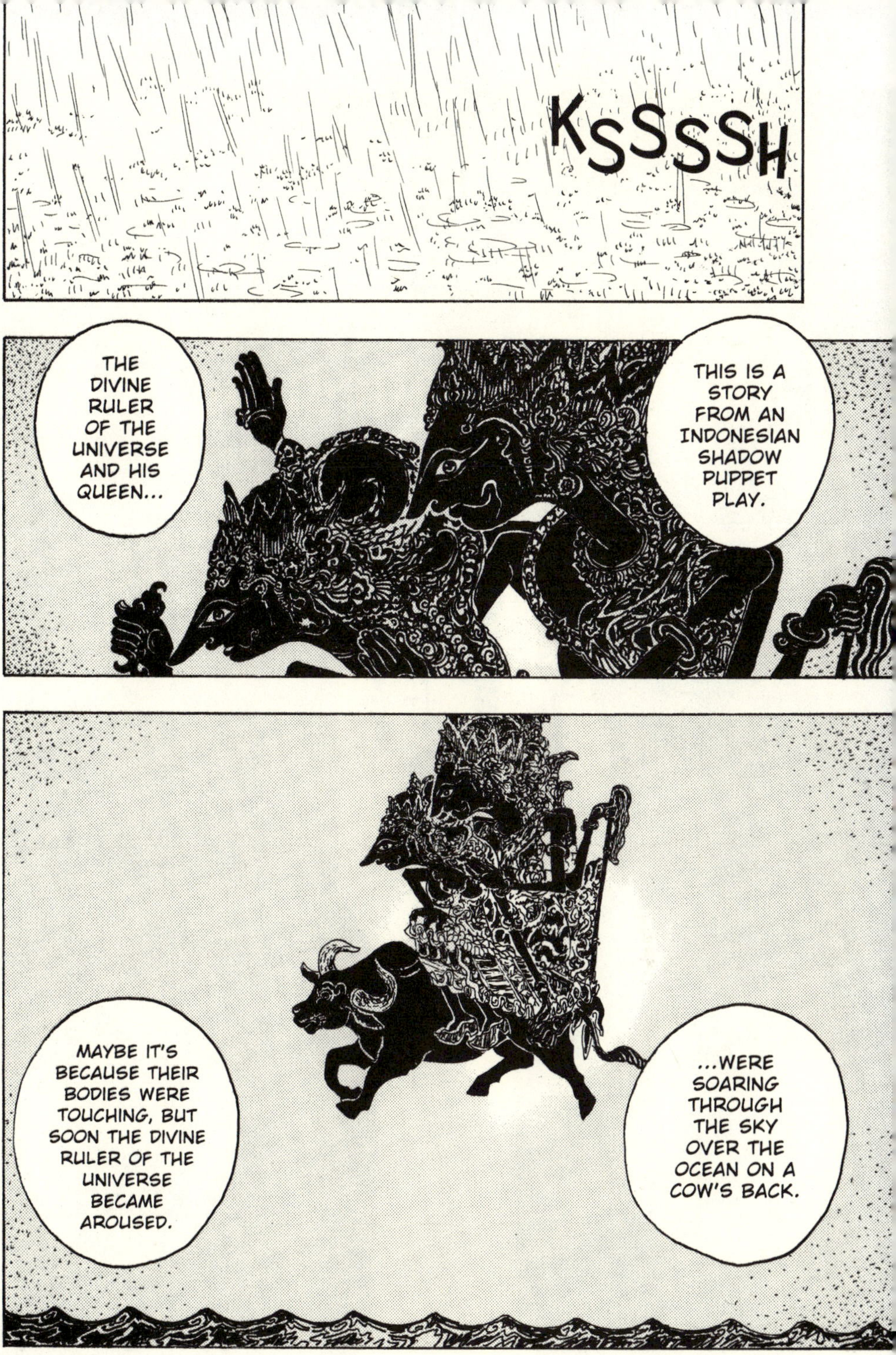
KSSSSH
THIS IS A STORY FROM AN INDONESIAN SHADOW PUPPET PLAY.
THE DIVINE RULER OF THE UNIVERSE AND HIS QUEEN...
...WERE SOARING THROUGH THE SKY OVER THE OCEAN ON A COW'S BACK.
MAYBE IT'S BECAUSE THEIR BODIES WERE TOUCHING, BUT SOON THE DIVINE RULER OF THE UNIVERSE BECAME AROUSED.

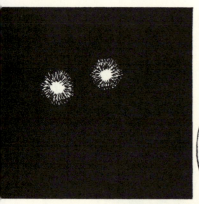

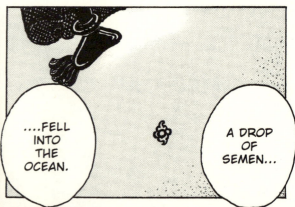

A DROP OF SEMEN...
....FELL INTO THE OCEAN.
IT BECAME A GIANT RAKSHASA AND ASCENDED INTO HEAVEN.
A RAKSHASA IS A TYPE OF EVIL SPIRIT THAT CAN LEAD PEOPLE ASTRAY OR EAT THEM.

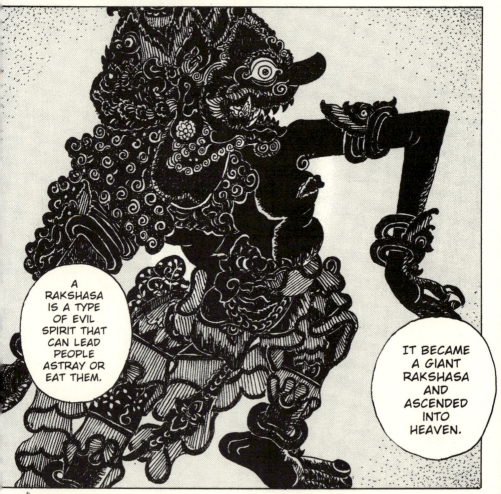

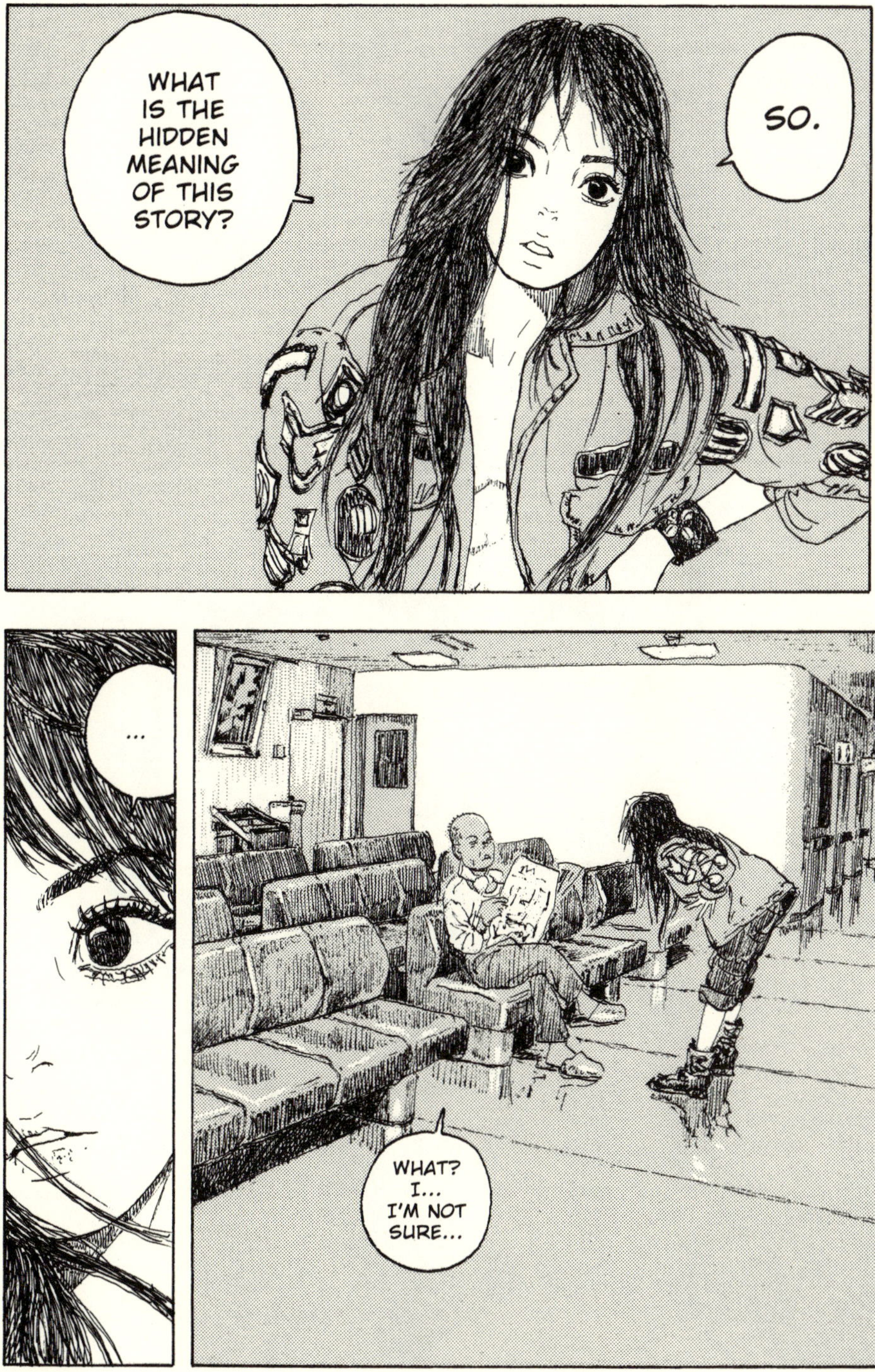
SO.
WHAT IS THE HIDDEN MEANING OF THIS STORY?
WHAT? I... I'M NOT SURE...
...

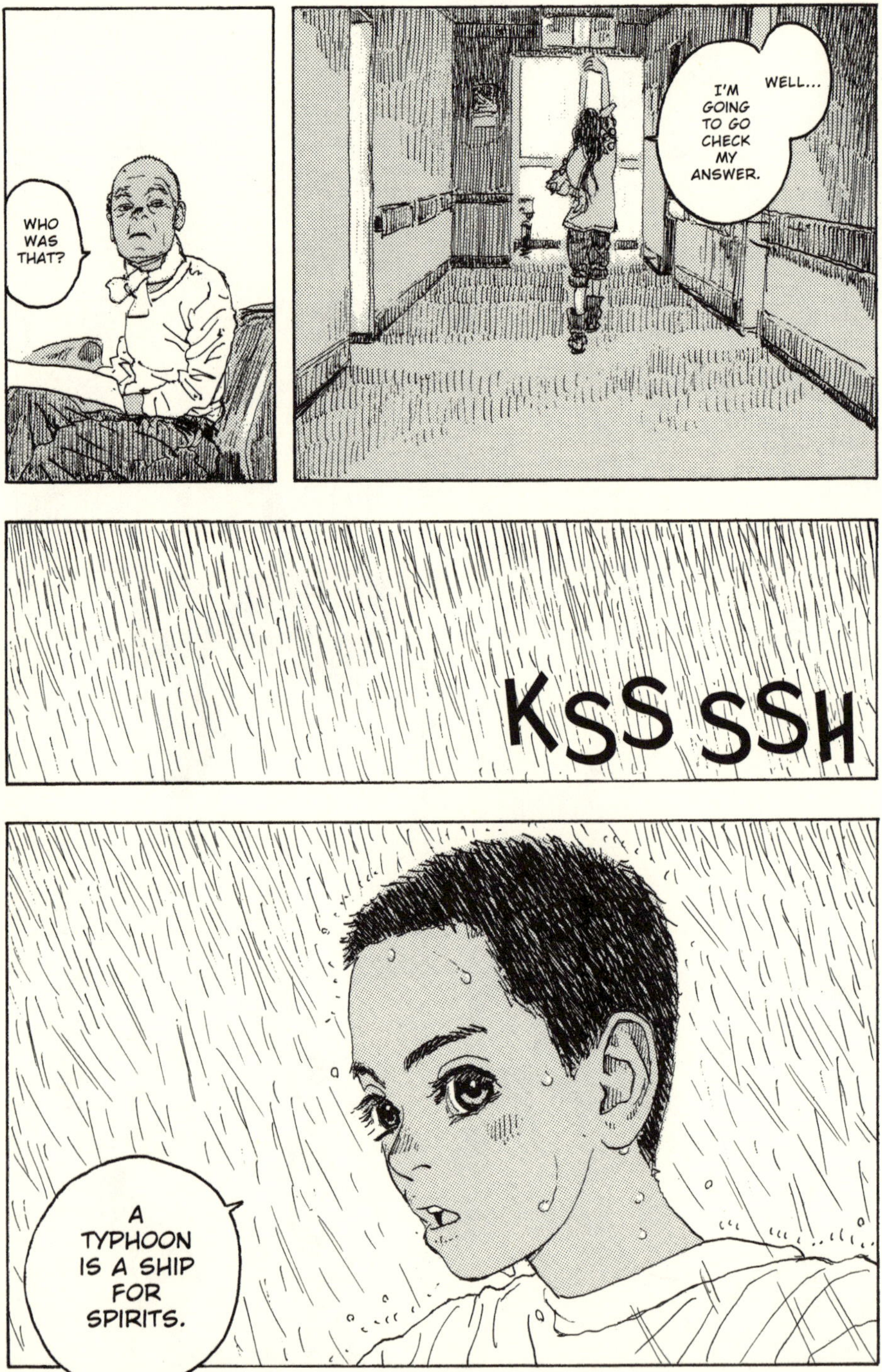
WELL...
I'M GOING TO GO CHECK MY ANSWER.
WHO WAS THAT?
KSSSSH
A TYPHOON IS A SHIP FOR SPIRITS.

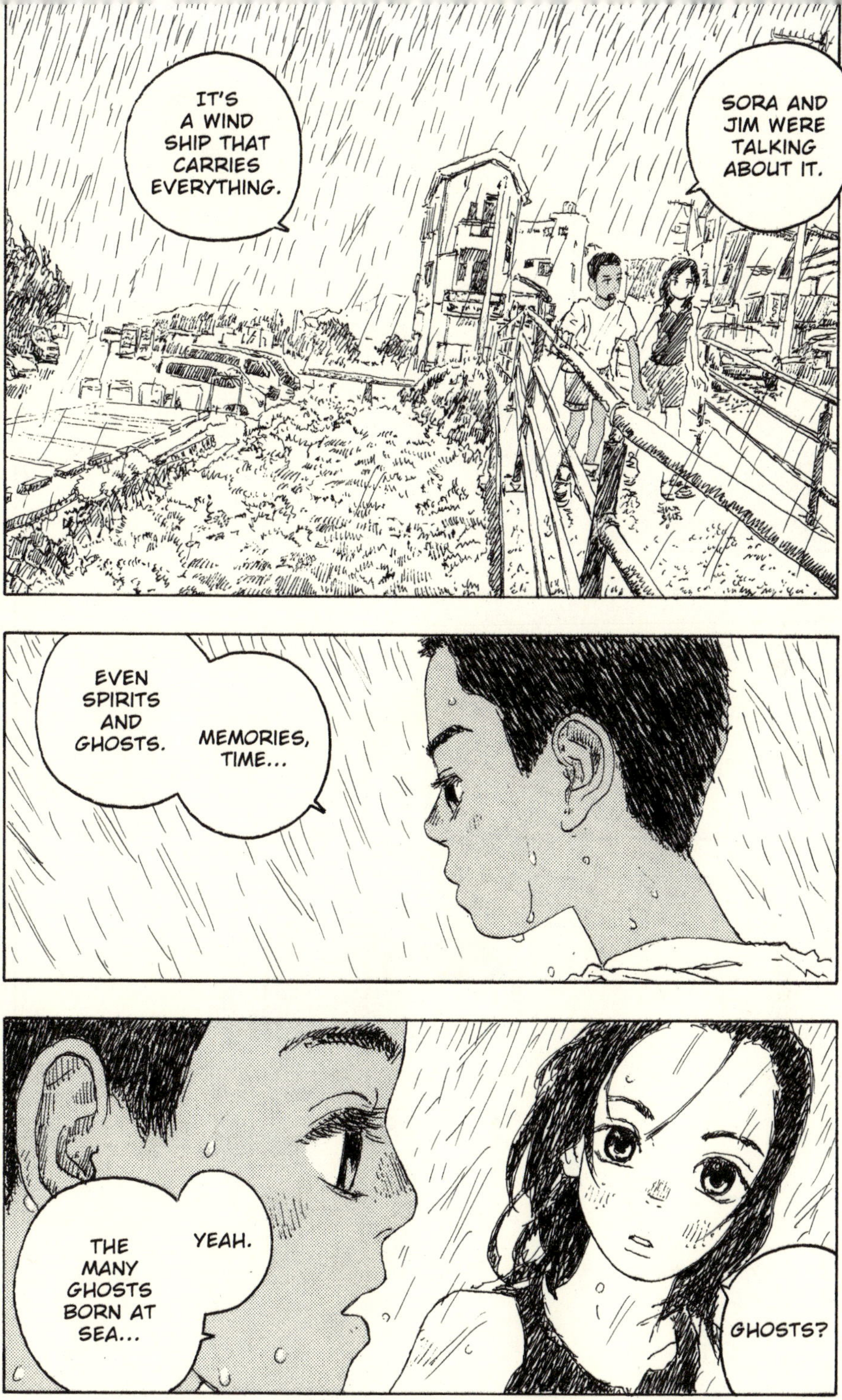
SORA AND JIM WERE TALKING ABOUT IT.
IT'S A WIND SHIP THAT CARRIES EVERYTHING.
MEMORIES, TIME...
EVEN SPIRITS AND GHOSTS.
GHOSTS?
YEAH.
THE MANY GHOSTS BORN AT SEA...

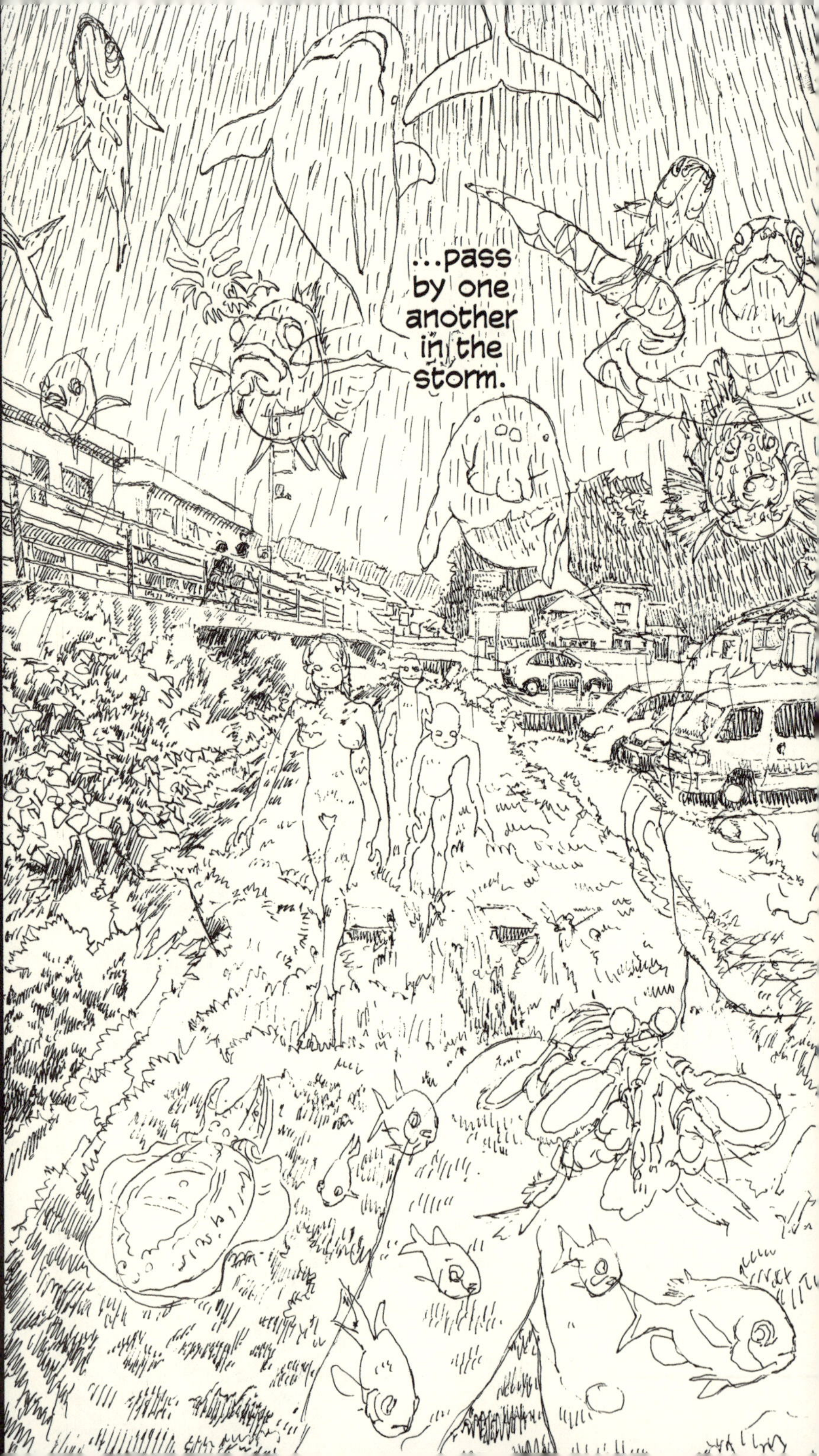
...pass by one another in the storm.

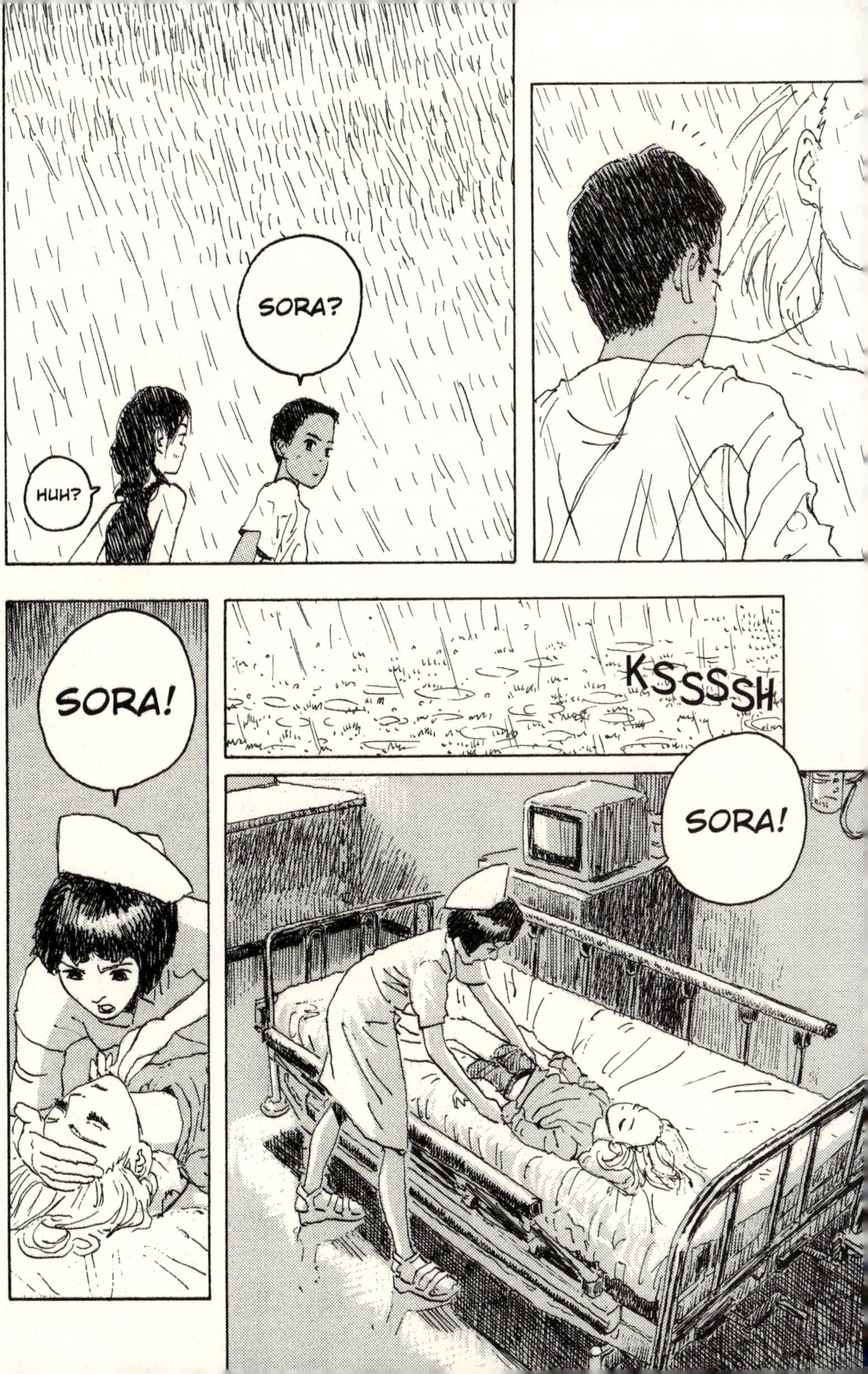
SORA?
HUH?
KSSSSH
SORA!
SORA!

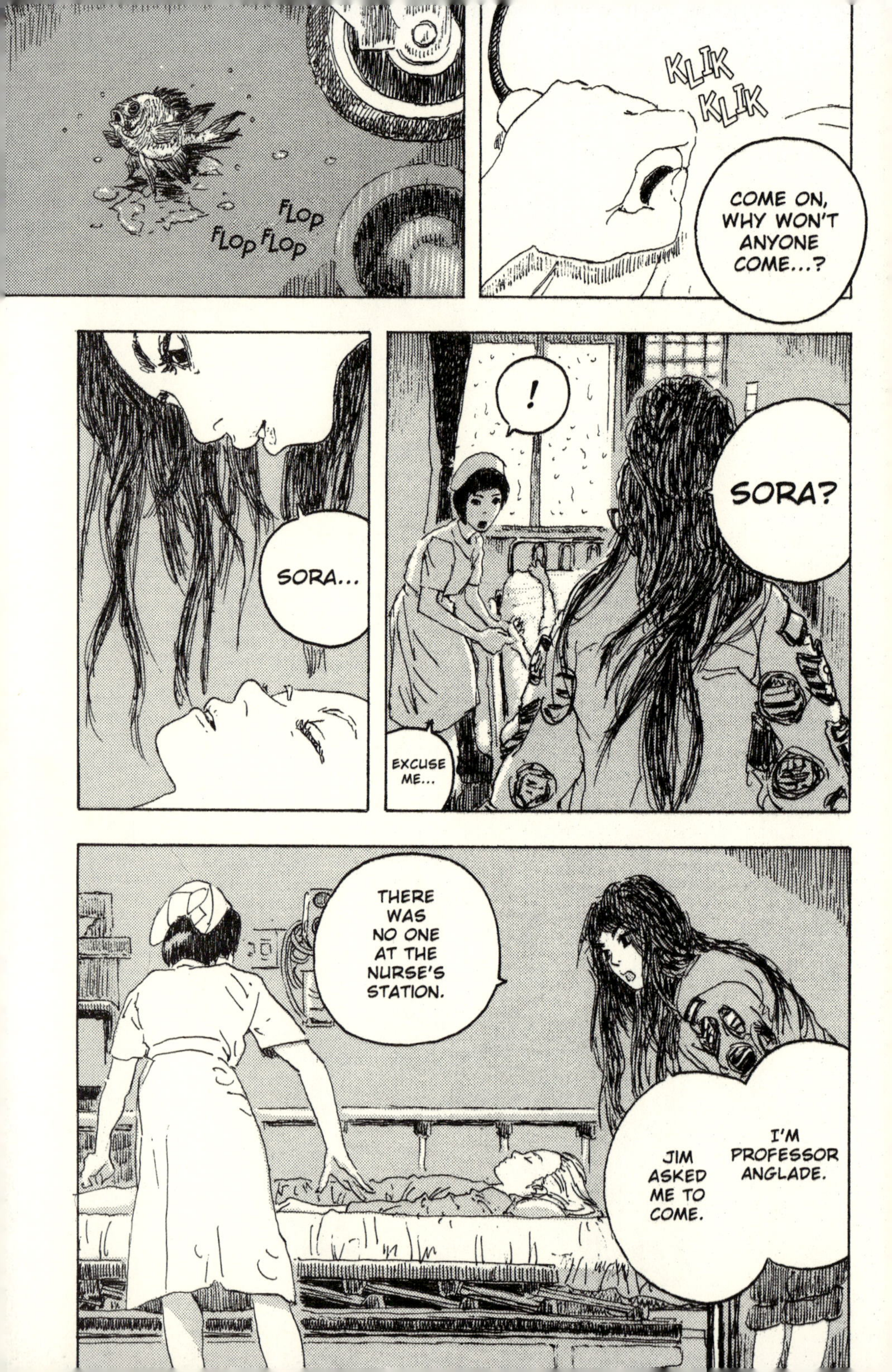
KLIK KLIK
COME ON, WHY WON'T ANYONE COME...?
FLOP FLOP FLOP
!
SORA?
EXCUSE ME...
SORA...
THERE WAS NO ONE AT THE NURSE'S STATION.
I'M PROFESSOR ANGLADE.
JIM ASKED ME TO COME.

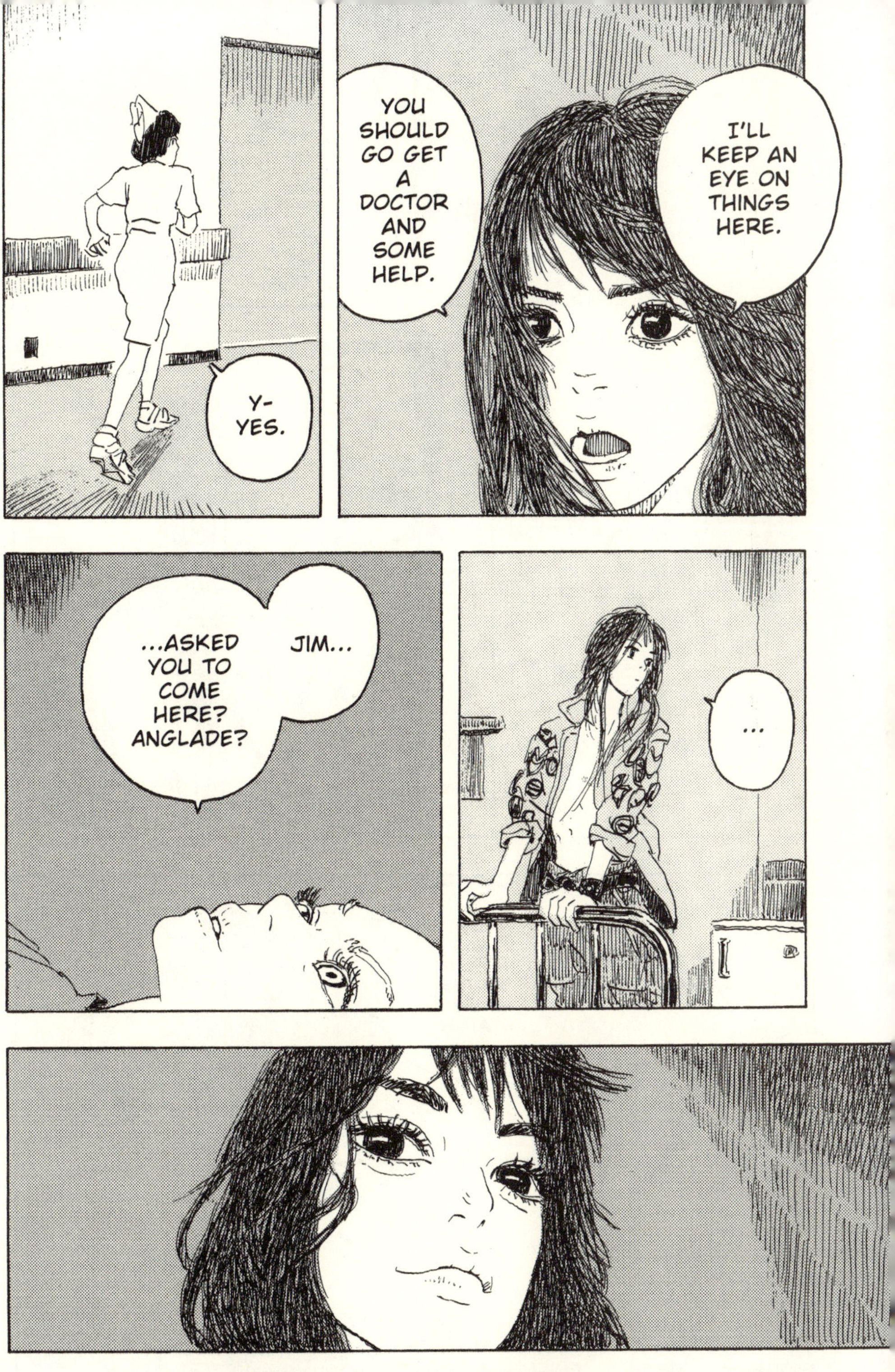
I'LL KEEP AN EYE ON THINGS HERE.
YOU SHOULD GO GET A DOCTOR AND SOME HELP.
Y- YES.
...
JIM...
...ASKED YOU TO COME HERE? ANGLADE?

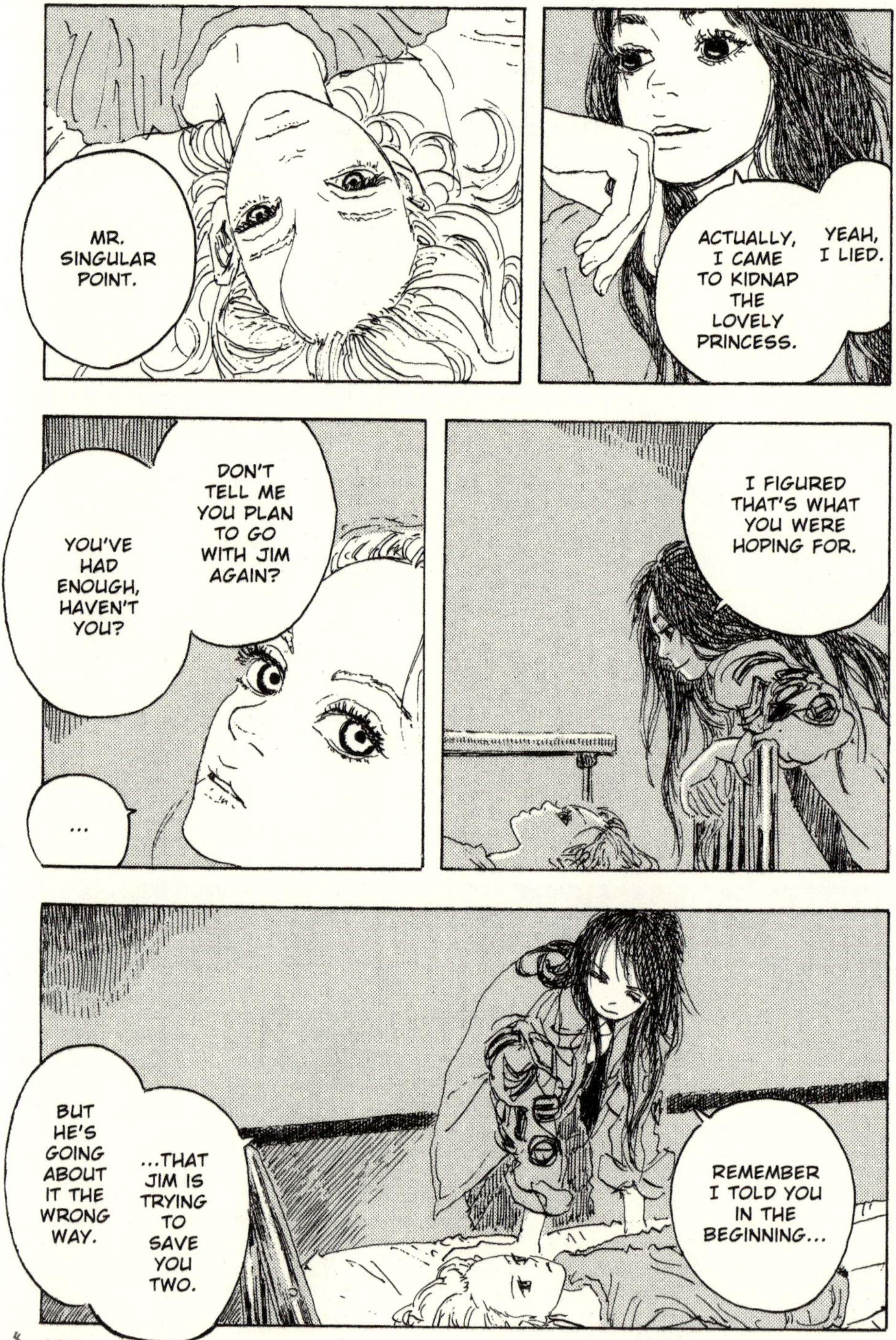
YEAH, I LIED.
ACTUALLY, I CAME TO KIDNAP THE LOVELY PRINCESS.
MR. SINGULAR POINT.
I FIGURED THAT'S WHAT YOU WERE HOPING FOR.
DON'T TELL ME YOU PLAN TO GO WITH JIM AGAIN?
YOU'VE HAD ENOUGH, HAVEN'T YOU?
...
REMEMBER I TOLD YOU IN THE BEGINNING...
...THAT JIM IS TRYING TO SAVE YOU TWO.
BUT HE'S GOING ABOUT IT THE WRONG WAY.

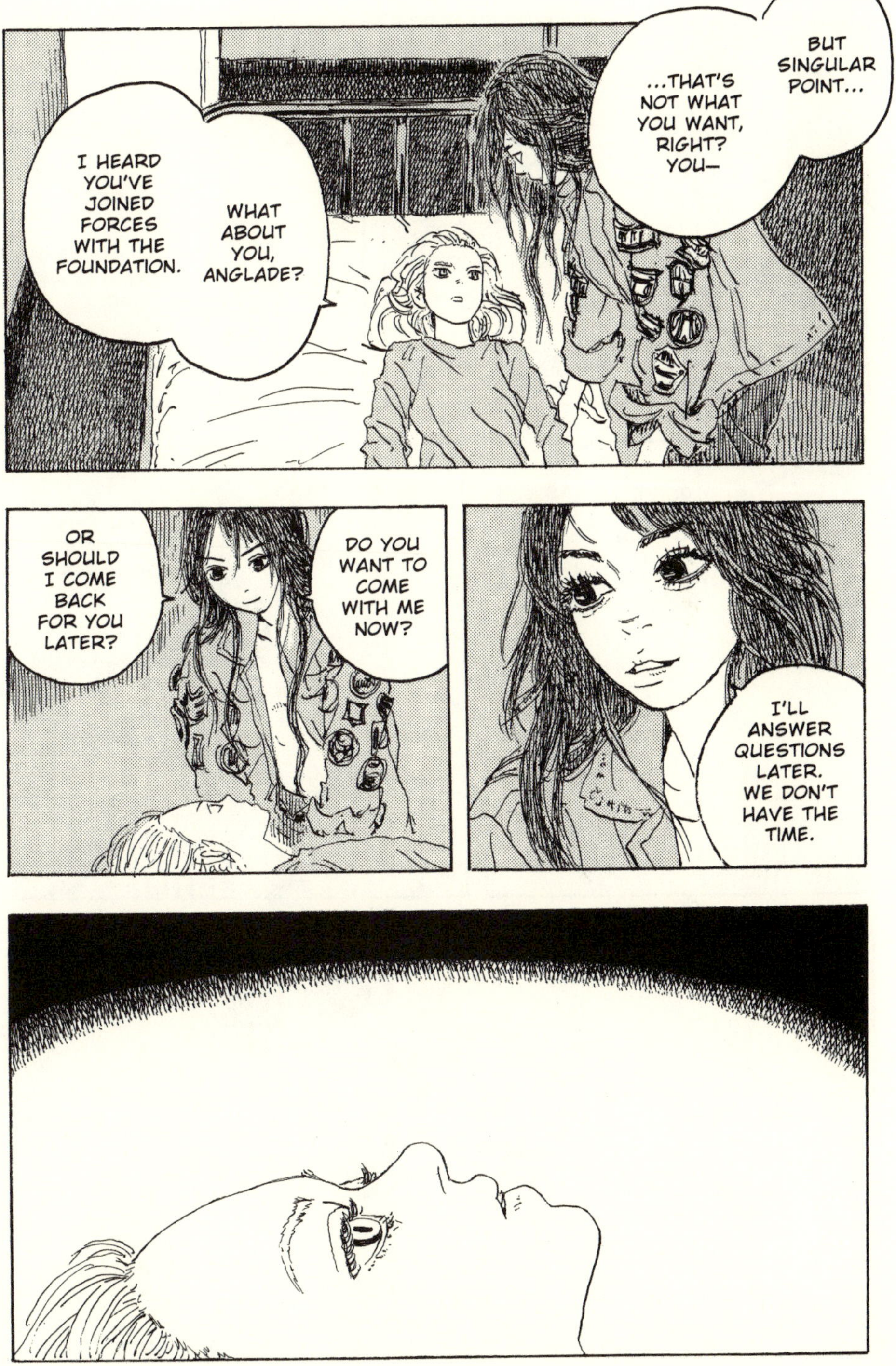
BUT SINGULAR POINT...
...THAT'S NOT WHAT YOU WANT, RIGHT? YOU—
WHAT ABOUT YOU, ANGLADE?
I HEARD YOU'VE JOINED FORCES WITH THE FOUNDATION.
I'LL ANSWER QUESTIONS LATER. WE DON'T HAVE THE TIME.
DO YOU WANT TO COME WITH ME NOW?
OR SHOULD I COME BACK FOR YOU LATER?

SORA!

DASH DASH DASH

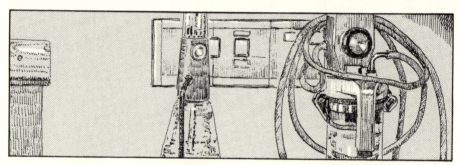

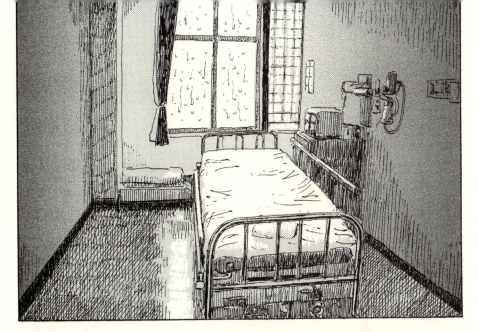

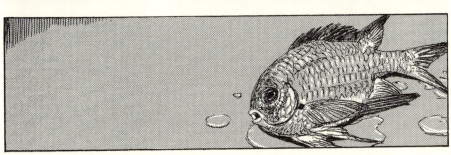

THE ROAD'S LIKE A RIVER...

KSSSSH

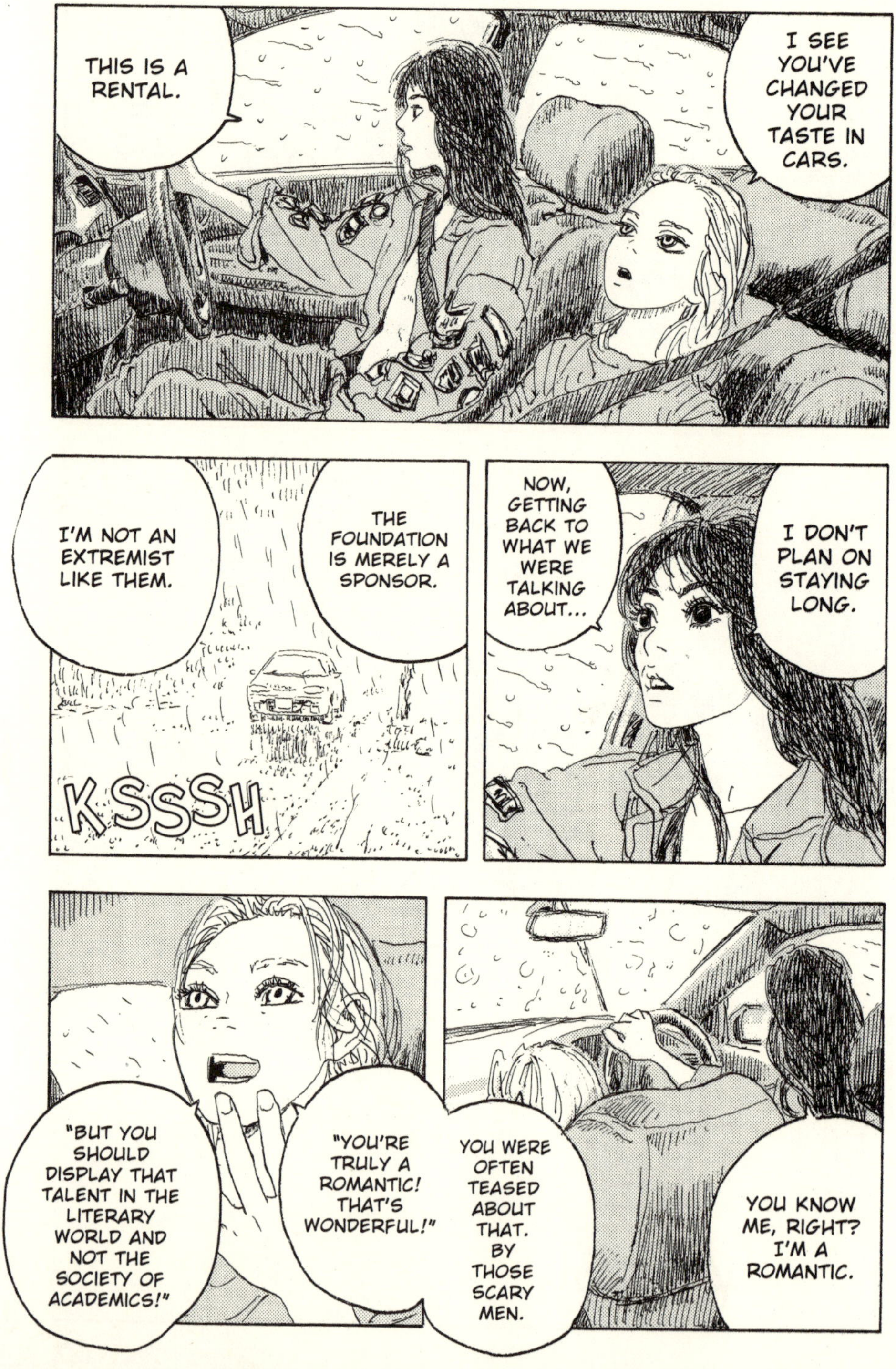
I SEE YOU'VE CHANGED YOUR TASTE IN CARS.
THIS IS A RENTAL.
I DON'T PLAN ON STAYING LONG.
NOW, GETTING BACK TO WHAT WE WERE TALKING ABOUT...
THE FOUNDATION IS MERELY A SPONSOR.
I'M NOT AN EXTREMIST LIKE THEM.
KSSSH
YOU KNOW ME, RIGHT? I'M A ROMANTIC.
YOU WERE OFTEN TEASED ABOUT THAT. BY THOSE SCARY MEN.
"YOU'RE TRULY A ROMANTIC! THAT'S WONDERFUL!"
"BUT YOU SHOULD DISPLAY THAT TALENT IN THE LITERARY WORLD AND NOT THE SOCIETY OF ACADEMICS!"

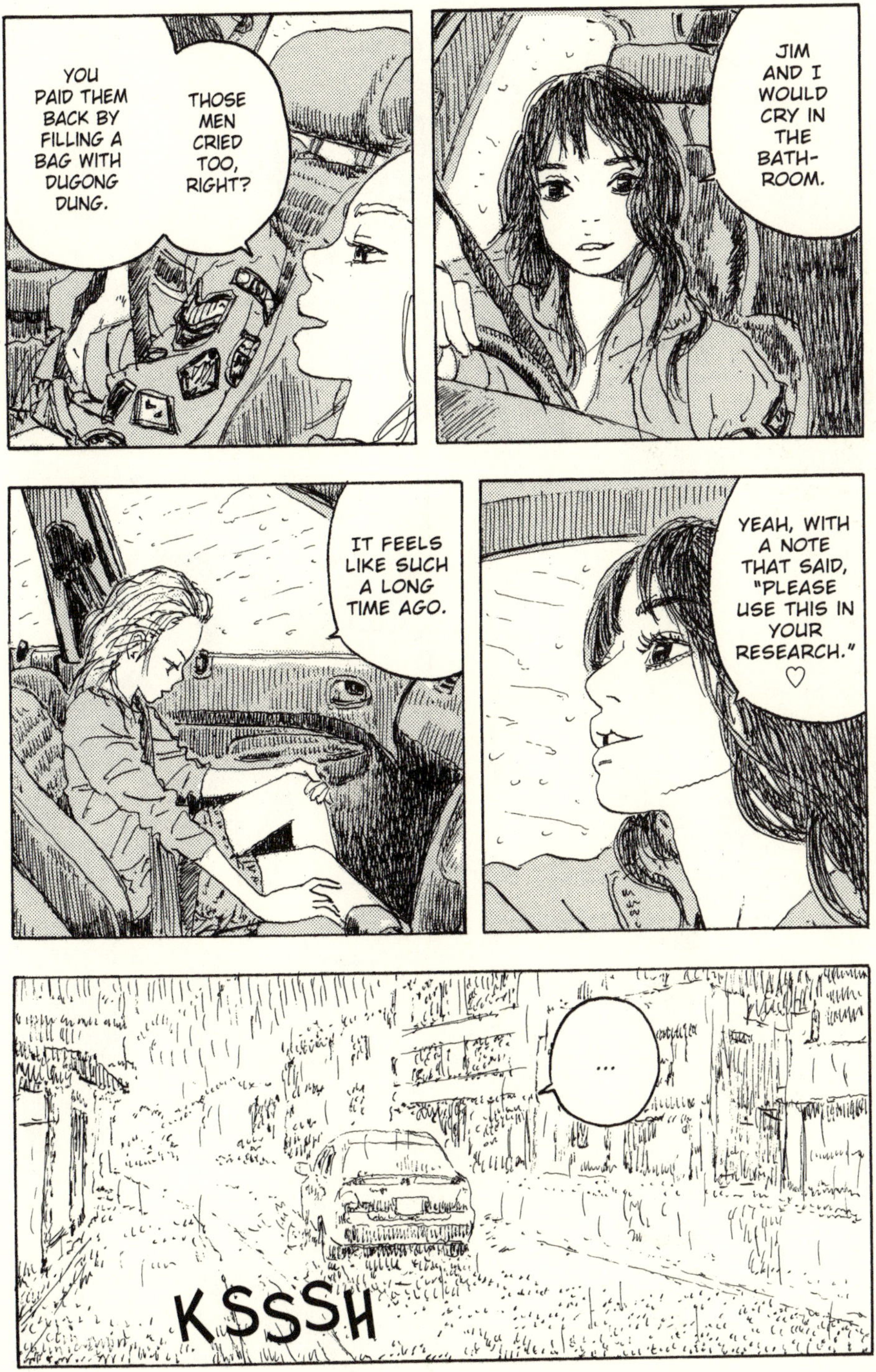
JIM AND I WOULD CRY IN THE BATH-ROOM.
THOSE MEN CRIED TOO, RIGHT?
YOU PAID THEM BACK BY FILLING A BAG WITH DUGONG DUNG.
YEAH, WITH A NOTE THAT SAID, "PLEASE USE THIS IN YOUR RESEARCH." ♡
IT FEELS LIKE SUCH A LONG TIME AGO.
...
KSSSH

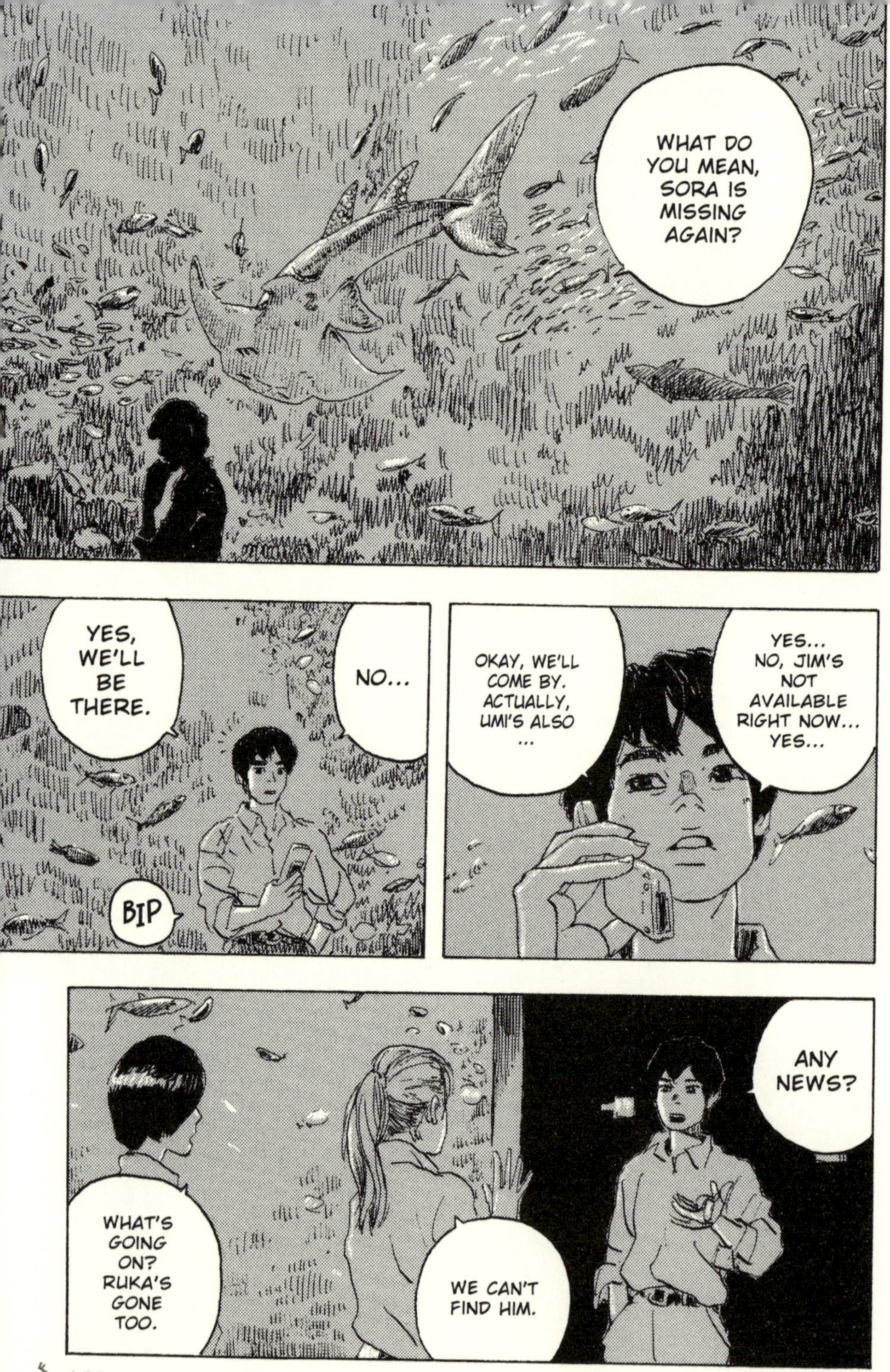
WHAT DO YOU MEAN, SORA IS MISSING AGAIN?
YES... NO, JIM'S NOT AVAILABLE RIGHT NOW... YES...
OKAY, WE'LL COME BY. ACTUALLY, UMI'S ALSO ...
NO...
YES, WE'LL BE THERE.
BIP
ANY NEWS?
WE CAN'T FIND HIM.
WHAT'S GOING ON? RUKA'S GONE TOO.

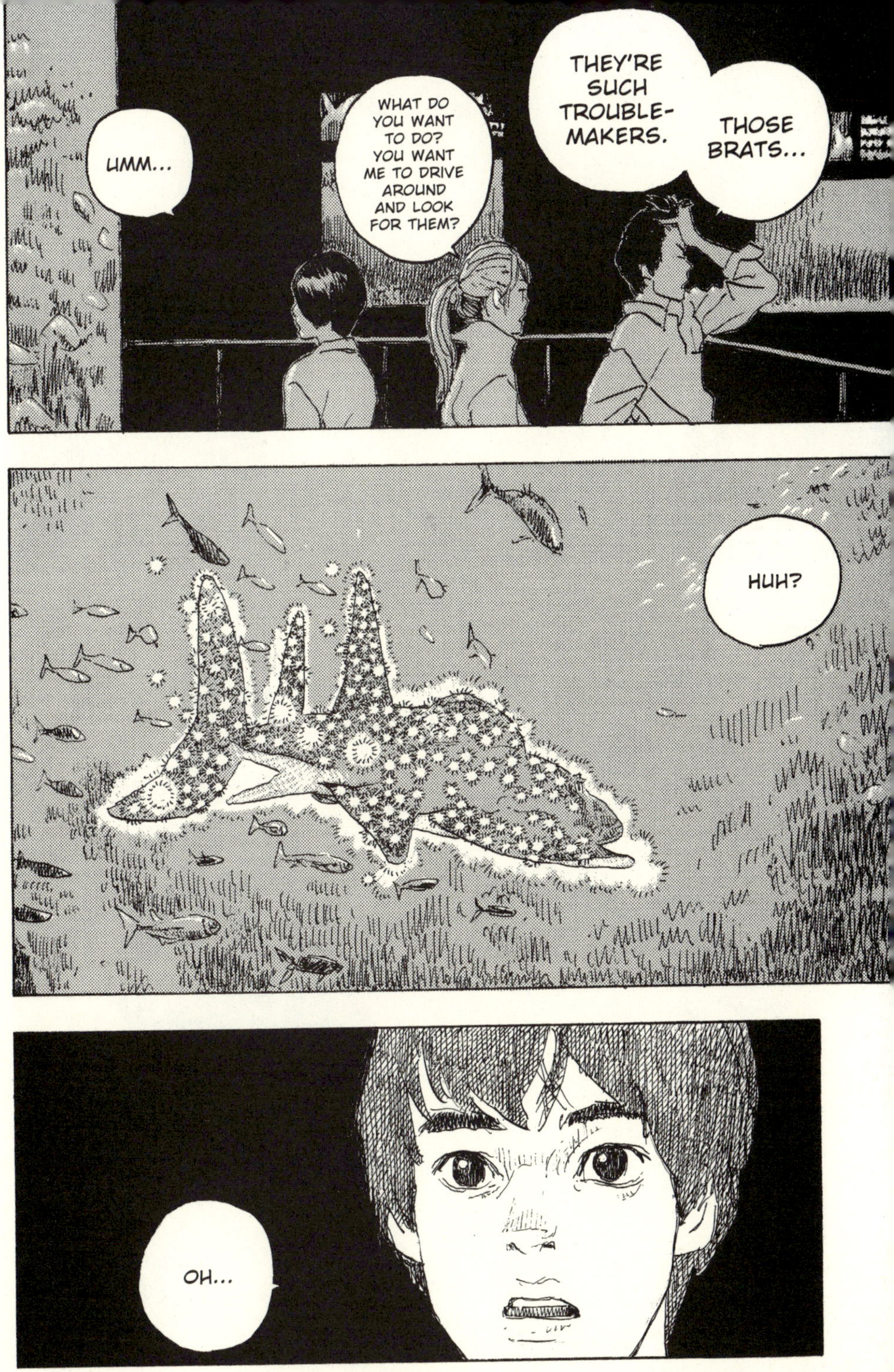
THOSE BRATS...
THEY'RE SUCH TROUBLE-MAKERS.
WHAT DO YOU WANT TO DO? YOU WANT ME TO DRIVE AROUND AND LOOK FOR THEM?
UMM...
HUH?
OH...

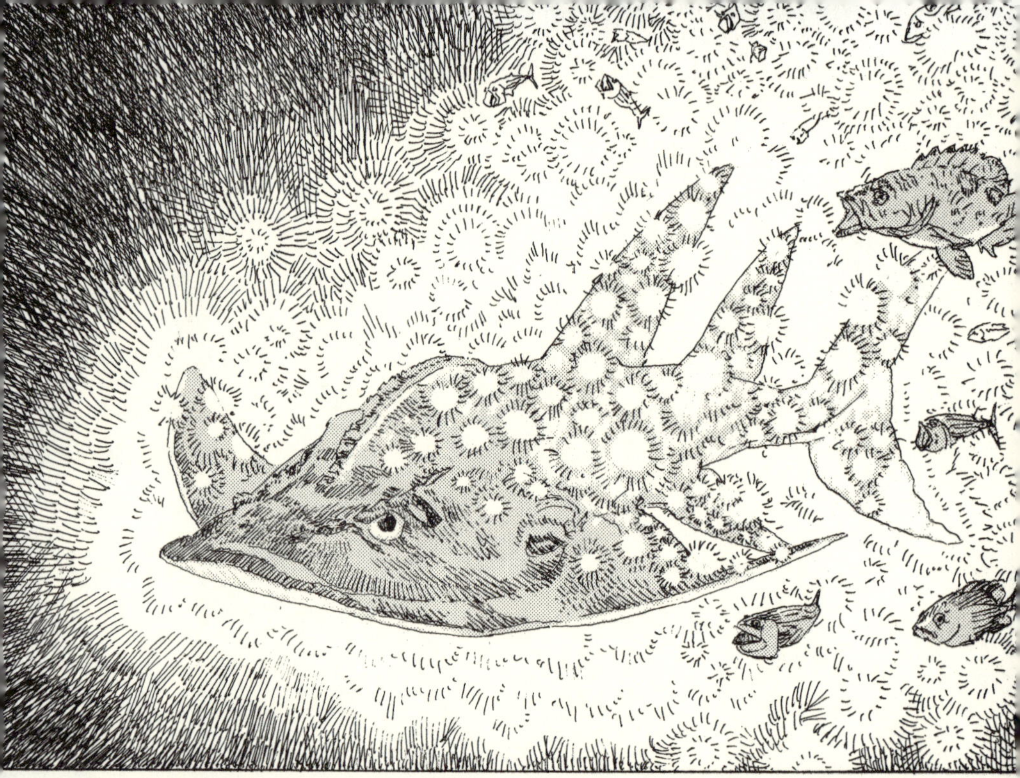
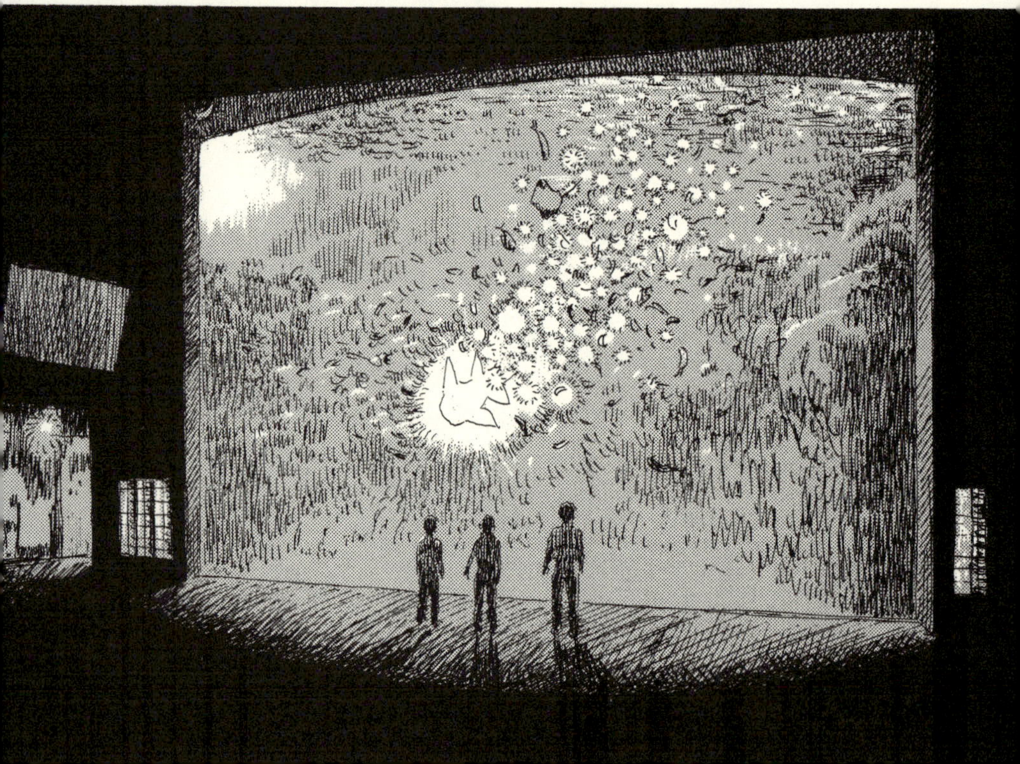

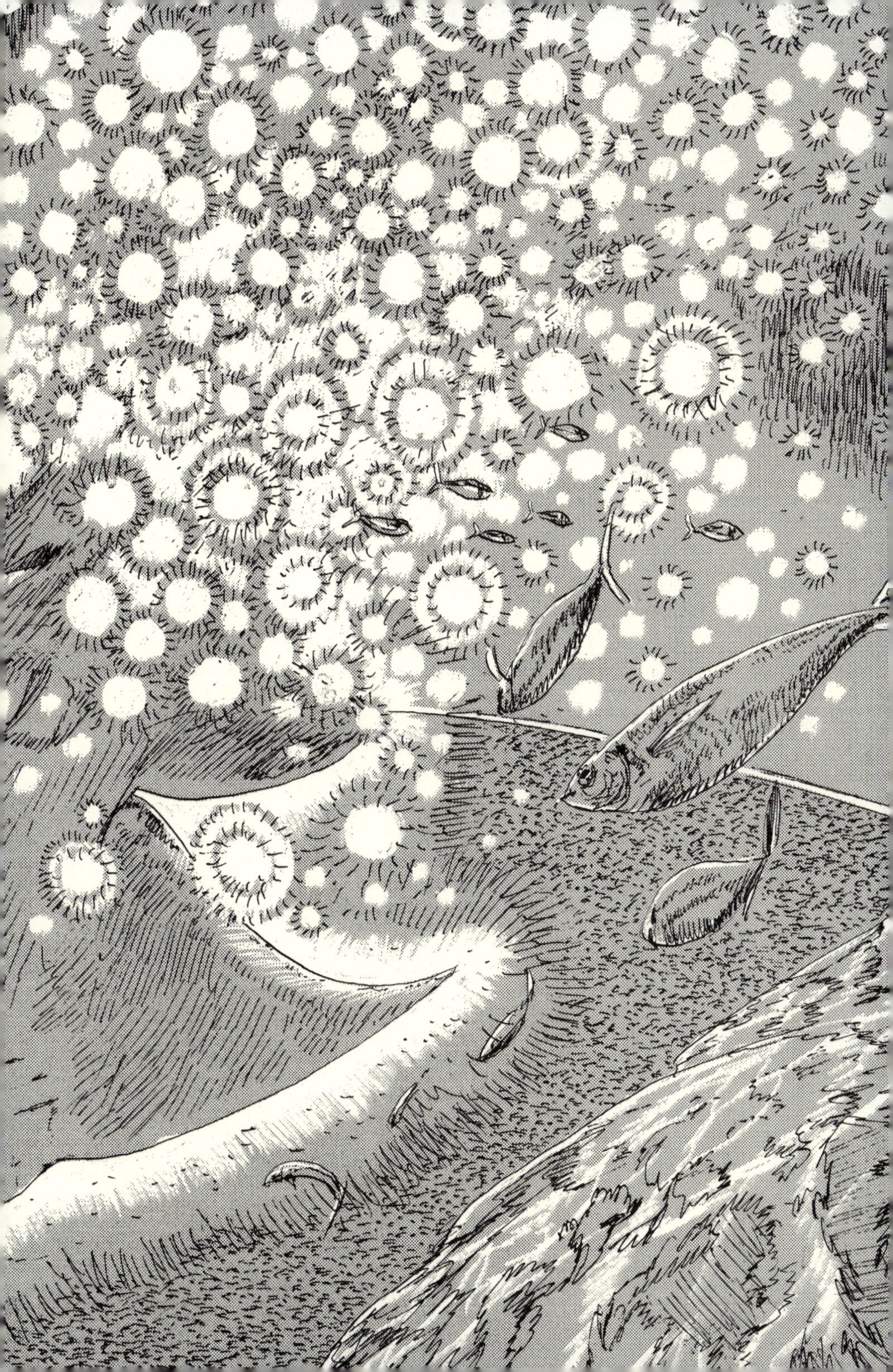

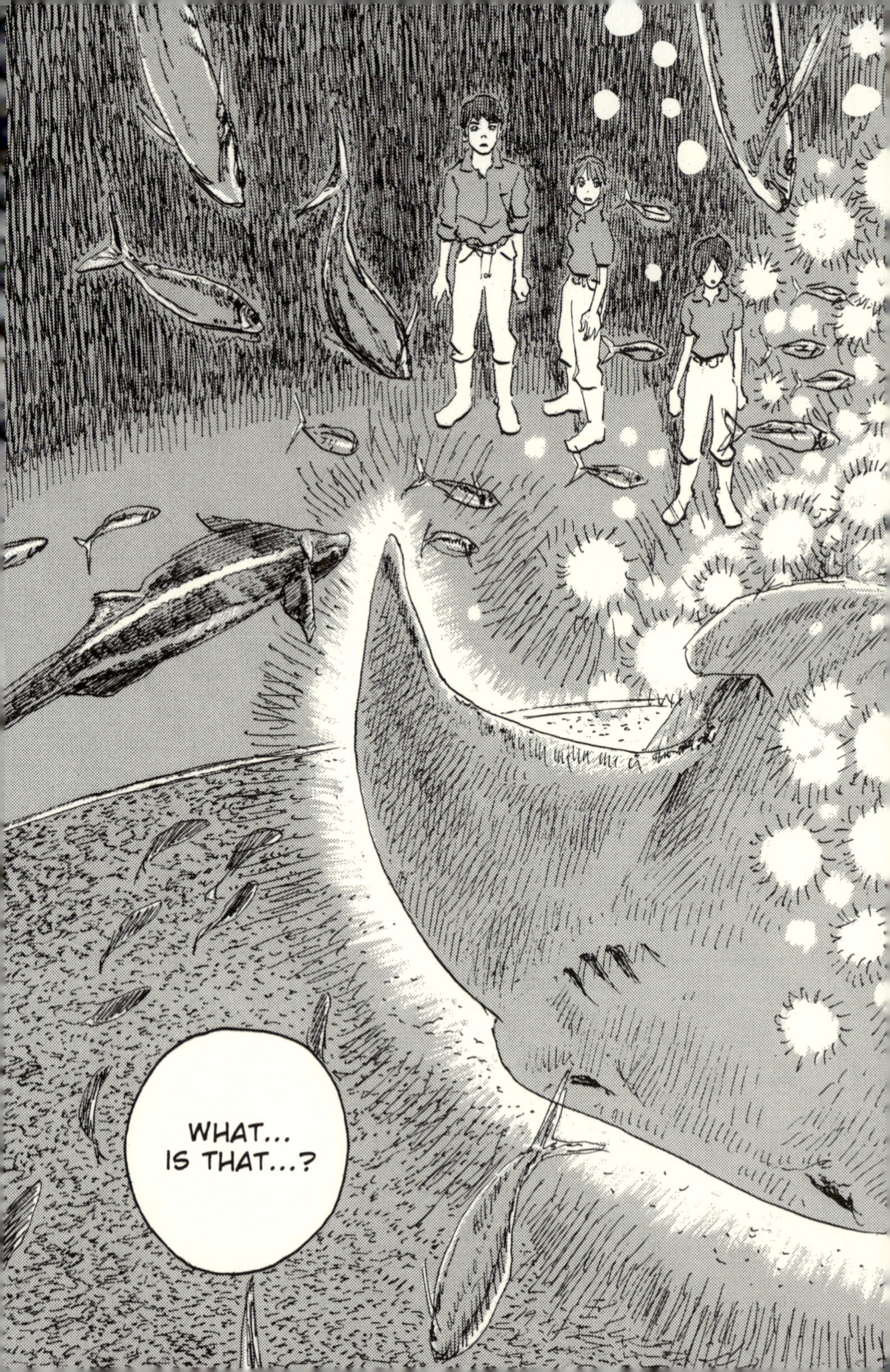
WHAT... IS THAT...?

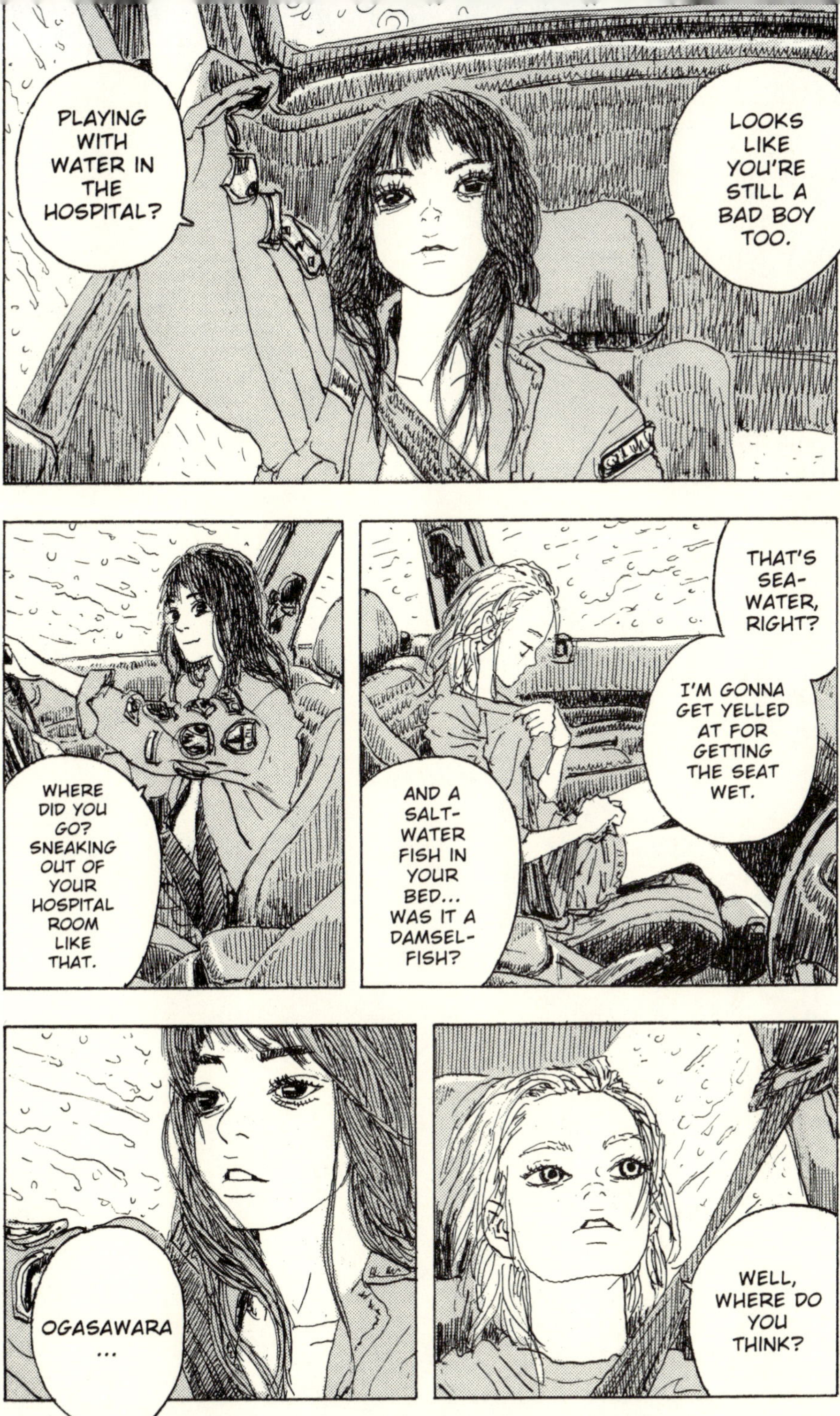

LOOKS LIKE YOU'RE STILL A BAD BOY TOO.
PLAYING WITH WATER IN THE HOSPITAL?
THAT'S SEA-WATER, RIGHT?
I'M GONNA GET YELLED AT FOR GETTING THE SEAT WET.
AND A SALT-WATER FISH IN YOUR BED... WAS IT A DAMSEL-FISH?
WHERE DID YOU GO? SNEAKING OUT OF YOUR HOSPITAL ROOM LIKE THAT.
WELL, WHERE DO YOU THINK?
OGASAWARA...

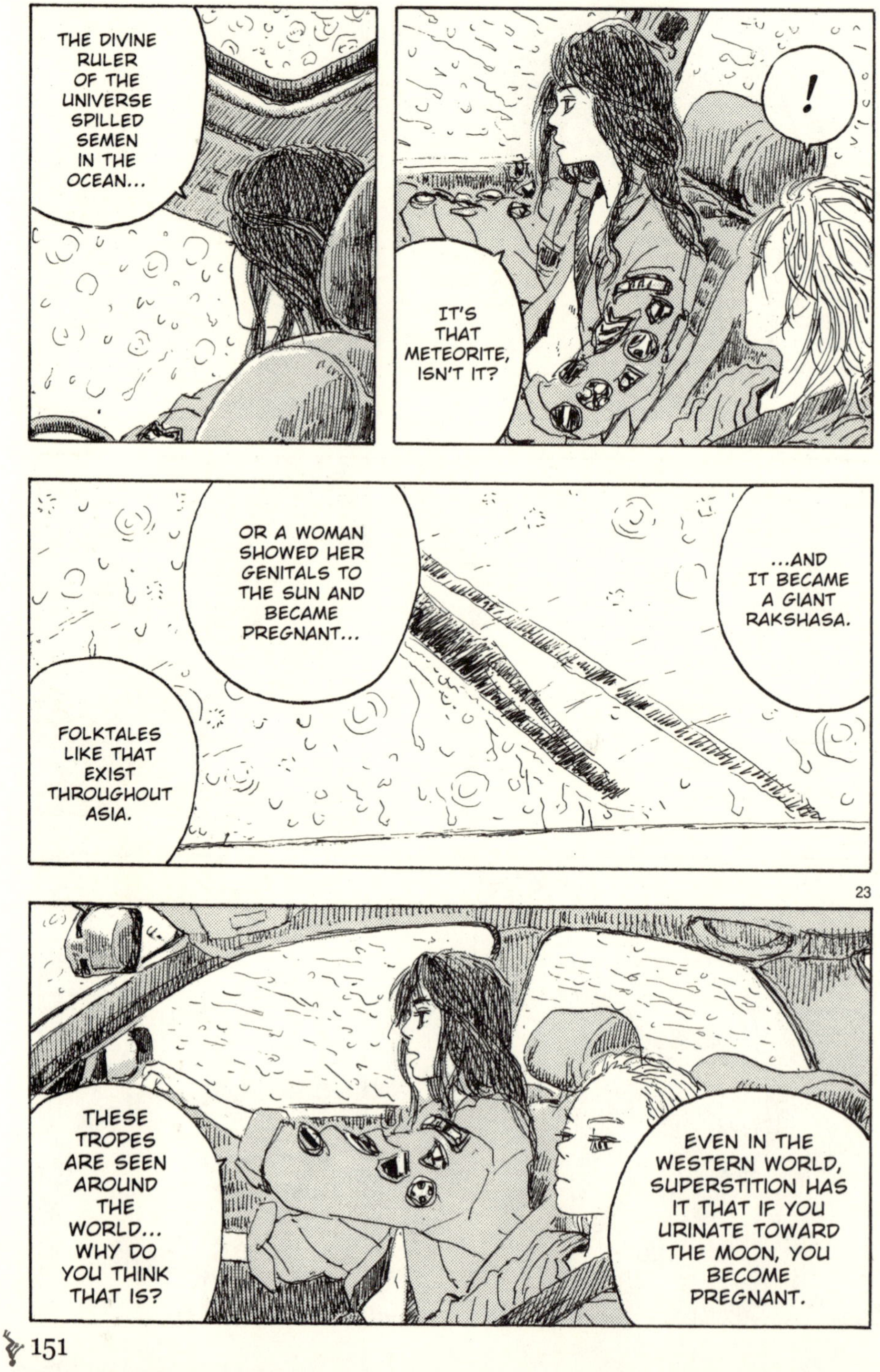
!
IT'S THAT METEORITE, ISN'T IT?
THE DIVINE RULER OF THE UNIVERSE SPILLED SEMEN IN THE OCEAN...
OR A WOMAN SHOWED HER GENITALS TO THE SUN AND BECAME PREGNANT...
...AND IT BECAME A GIANT RAKSHASA.
FOLKTALES LIKE THAT EXIST THROUGHOUT ASIA.
EVEN IN THE WESTERN WORLD, SUPERSTITION HAS IT THAT IF YOU URINATE TOWARD THE MOON, YOU BECOME PREGNANT.
THESE TROPES ARE SEEN AROUND THE WORLD... WHY DO YOU THINK THAT IS?

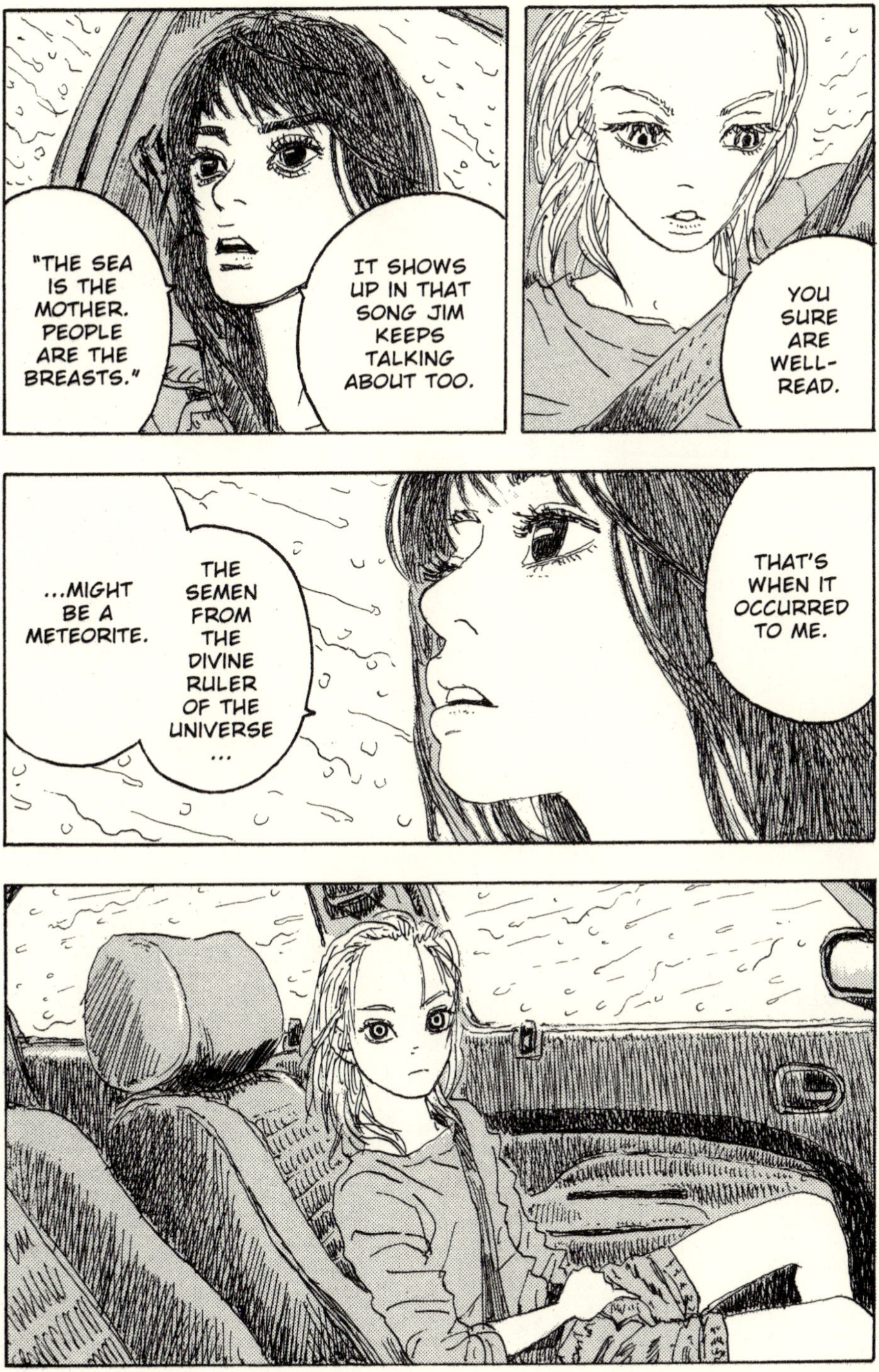
YOU SURE ARE WELL-READ.
IT SHOWS UP IN THAT SONG JIM KEEPS TALKING ABOUT TOO.
"THE SEA IS THE MOTHER. PEOPLE ARE THE BREASTS."
THAT'S WHEN IT OCCURRED TO ME.
THE SEMEN FROM THE DIVINE RULER OF THE UNIVERSE ...
...MIGHT BE A METEORITE.

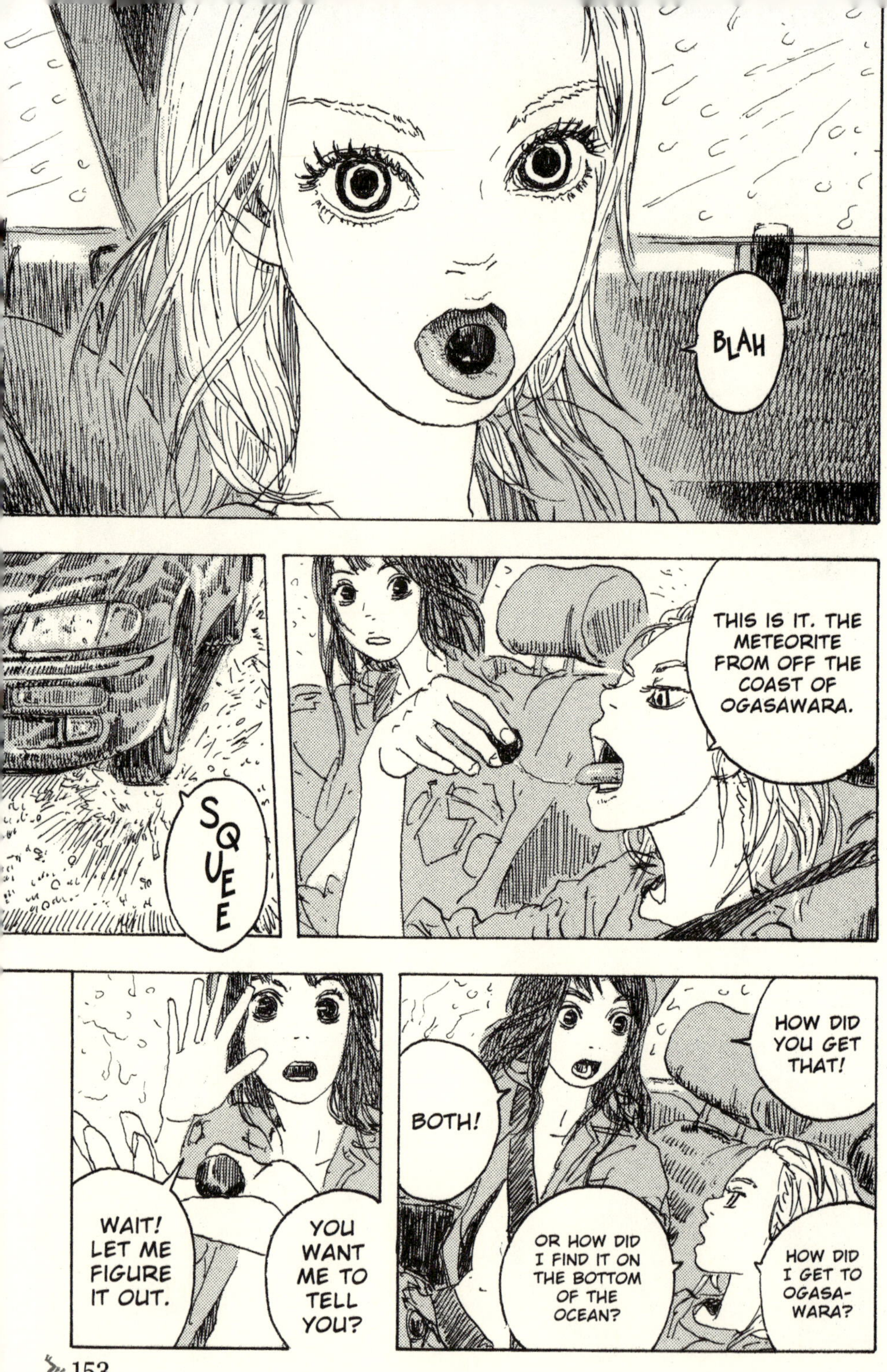
BLAH
THIS IS IT. THE METEORITE FROM OFF THE COAST OF OGASAWARA.
SQUEE
HOW DID YOU GET THAT!
HOW DID I GET TO OGASA-WARA?
OR HOW DID I FIND IT ON THE BOTTOM OF THE OCEAN?
BOTH!
YOU WANT ME TO TELL YOU?
WAIT! LET ME FIGURE IT OUT.

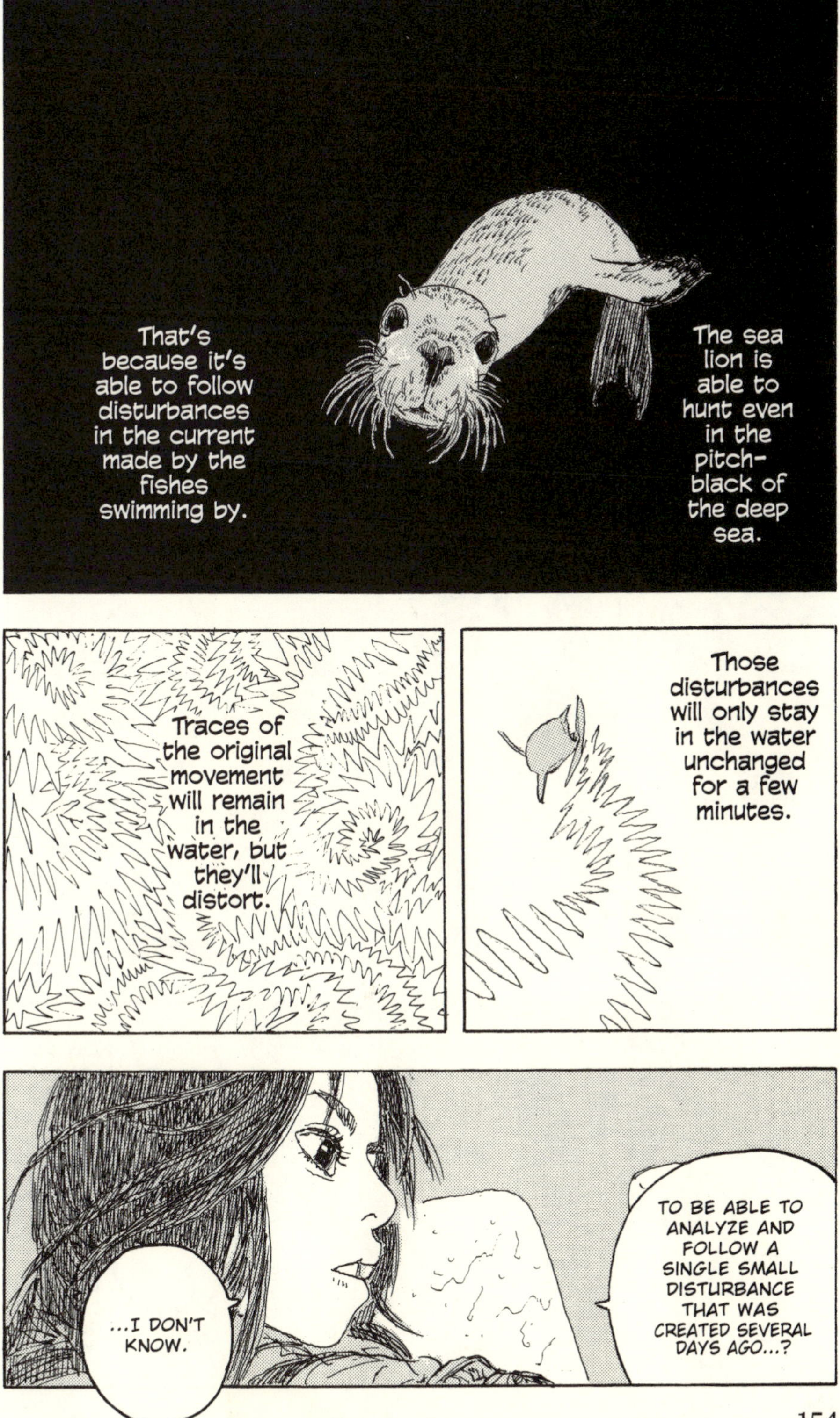
The sea lion is able to hunt even in the pitch-black of the deep sea.
That's because it's able to follow disturbances in the current made by the fishes swimming by.
Those disturbances will only stay in the water unchanged for a few minutes.
Traces of the original movement will remain in the water, but they'll distort.
TO BE ABLE TO ANALYZE AND FOLLOW A SINGLE SMALL DISTURBANCE THAT WAS CREATED SEVERAL DAYS AGO...?
...I DON'T KNOW.

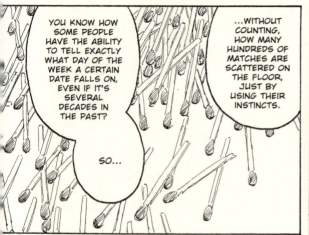

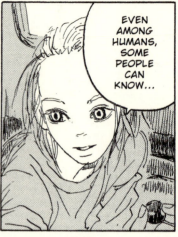

EVEN AMONG HUMANS, SOME PEOPLE CAN KNOW...
...WITHOUT COUNTING, HOW MANY HUNDREDS OF MATCHES ARE SCATTERED ON THE FLOOR, JUST BY USING THEIR INSTINCTS.
YOU KNOW HOW SOME PEOPLE HAVE THE ABILITY TO TELL EXACTLY WHAT DAY OF THE WEEK A CERTAIN DATE FALLS ON, EVEN IF IT'S SEVERAL DECADES IN THE PAST?
SO...
SO I GUESS IT'S NO MYSTERY THAT OTHER ANIMALS HAVE CAPABILITIES THAT GO BEYOND OUR HUMAN IMAGINATION.
SUCH AS THE ABILITY TO SEE LIGHT OR HEAR SOUNDS HUMANS CAN'T...
AND...
...YOU KNOW ...
...the ocean is a totally different world than what you think.
Information gets transmitted in many different forms.

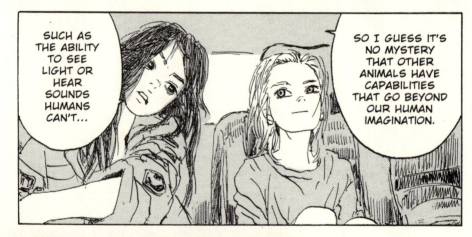

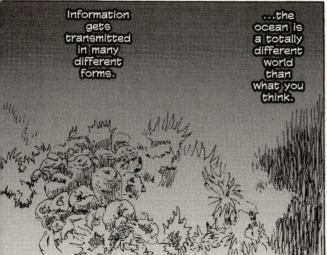

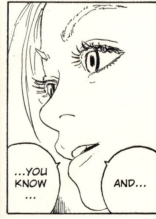

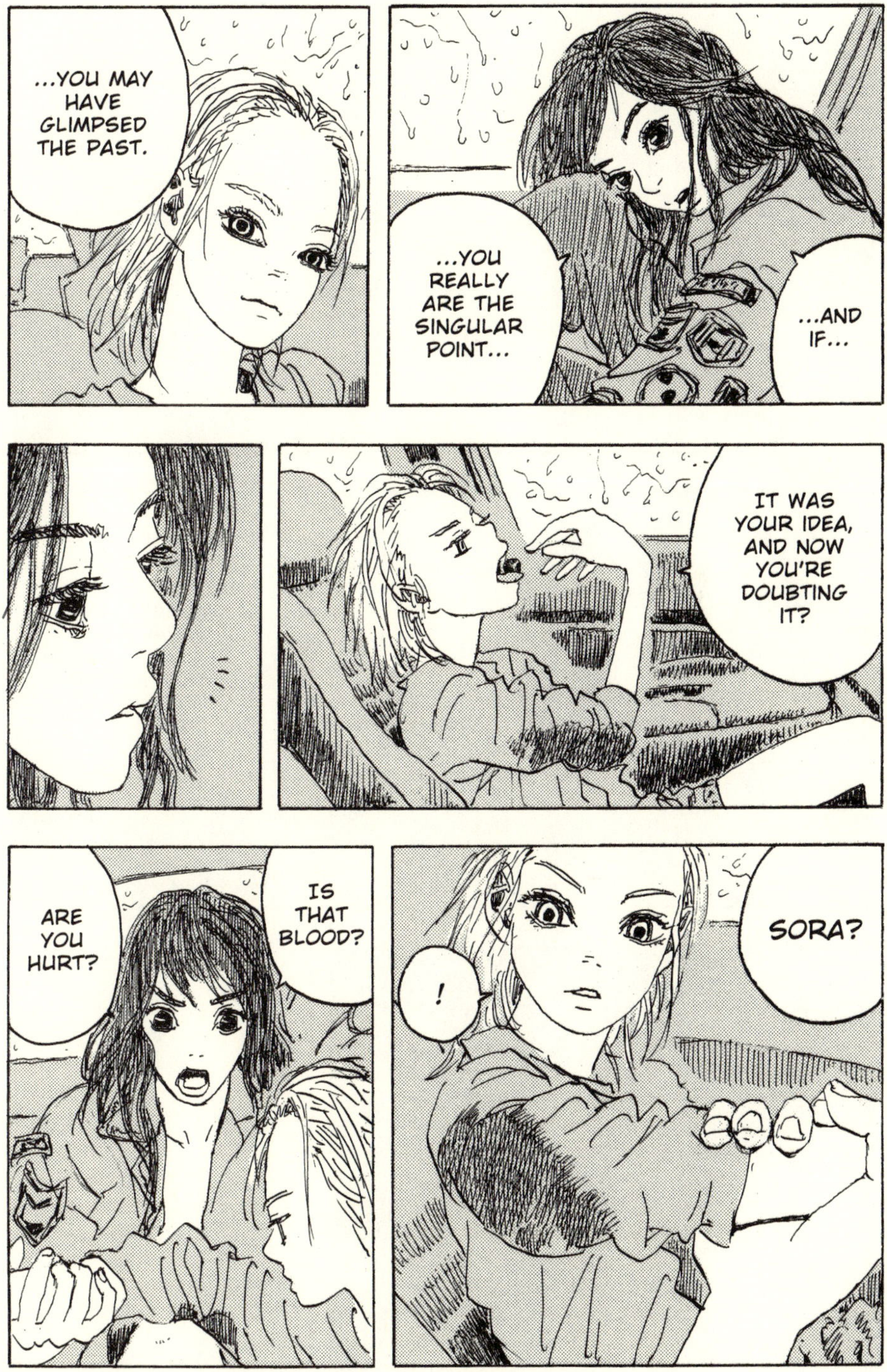
...AND IF...
...YOU REALLY ARE THE SINGULAR POINT...
...YOU MAY HAVE GLIMPSED THE PAST.
IT WAS YOUR IDEA, AND NOW YOU'RE DOUBTING IT?
SORA?
!
IS THAT BLOOD?
ARE YOU HURT?

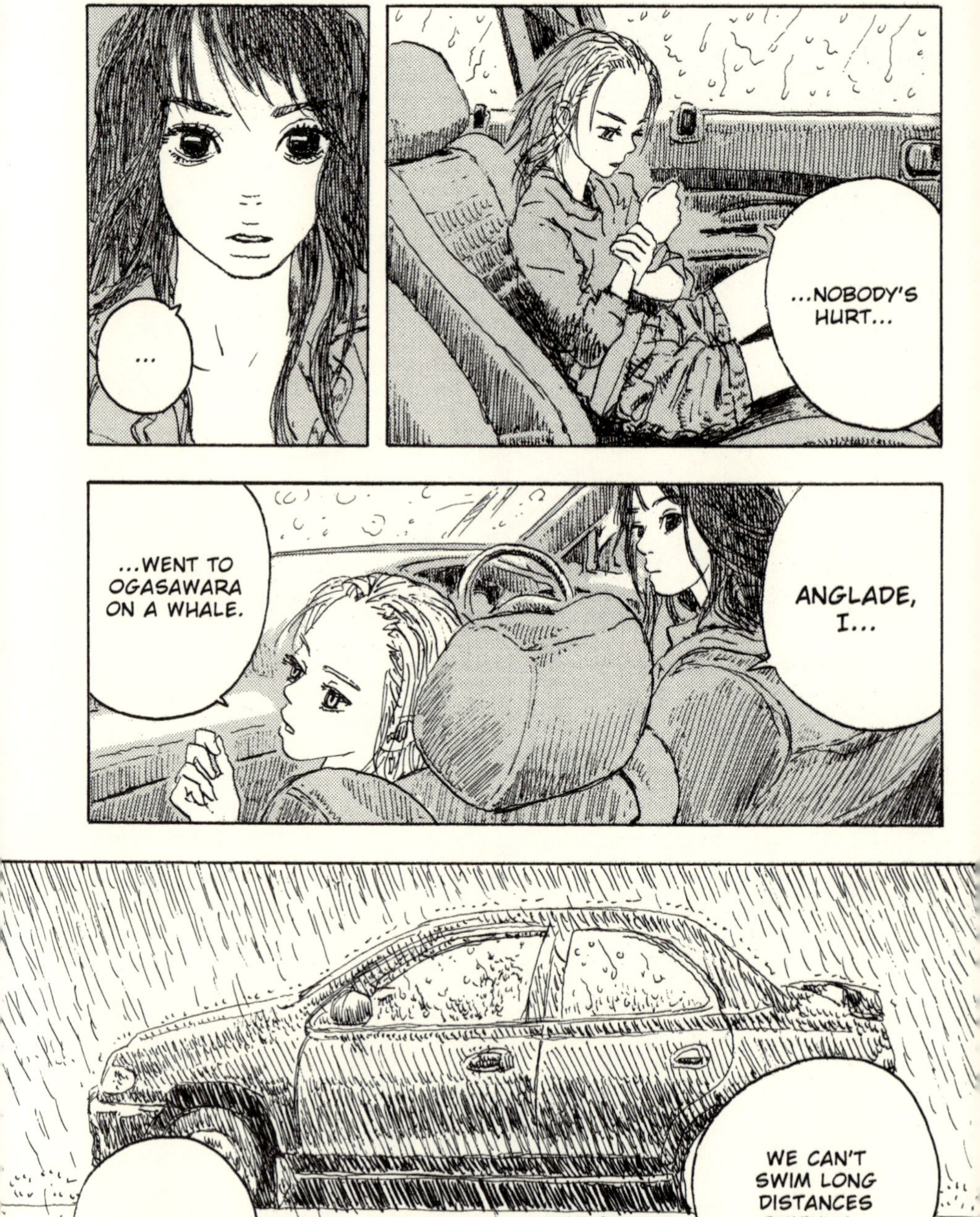
...NOBODY'S HURT...
...
ANGLADE, I...
...WENT TO OGASAWARA ON A WHALE.
WE CAN'T SWIM LONG DISTANCES QUICKLY...
KSSSH
THAT'S WHY THEY HELP US...

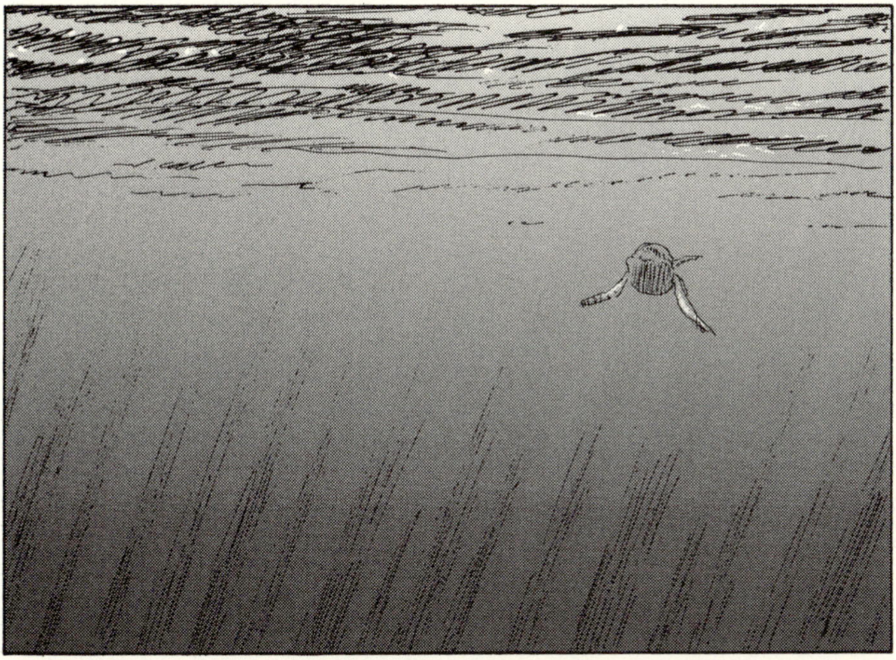
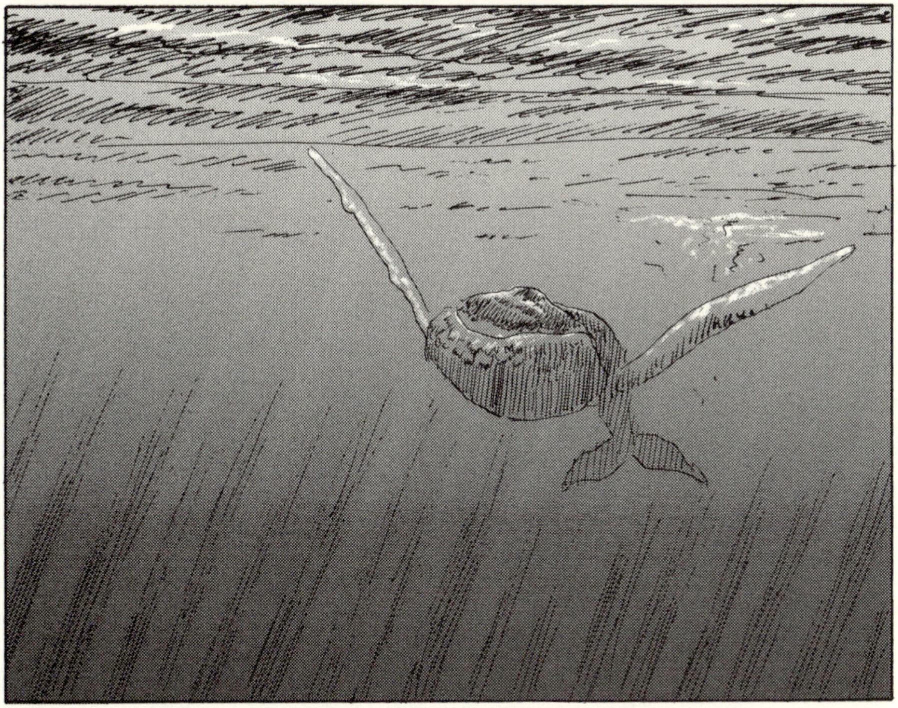

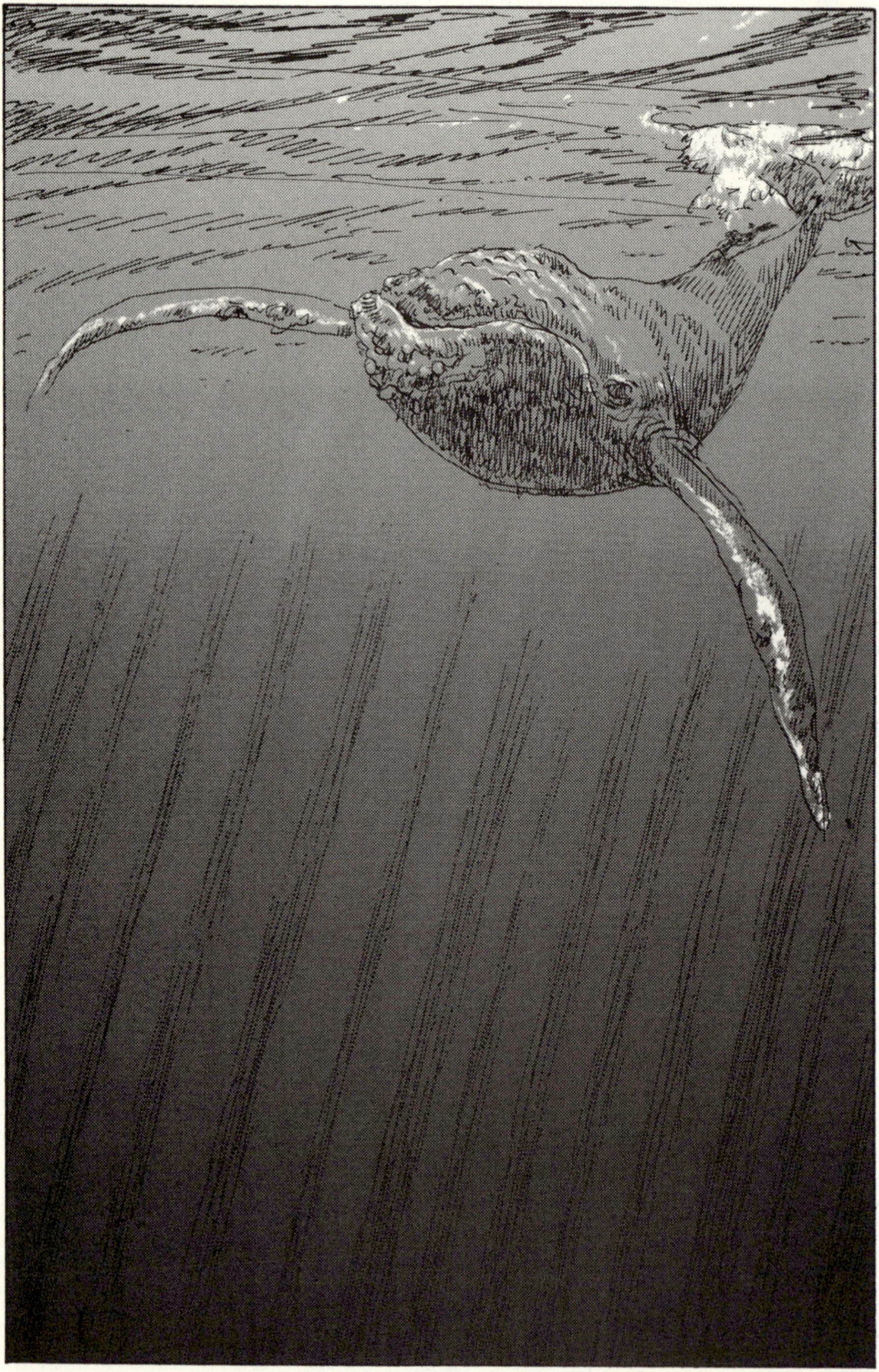

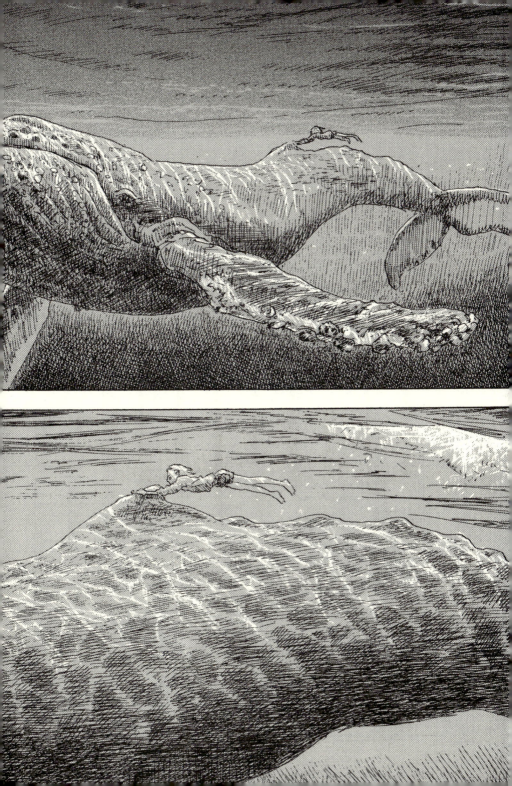

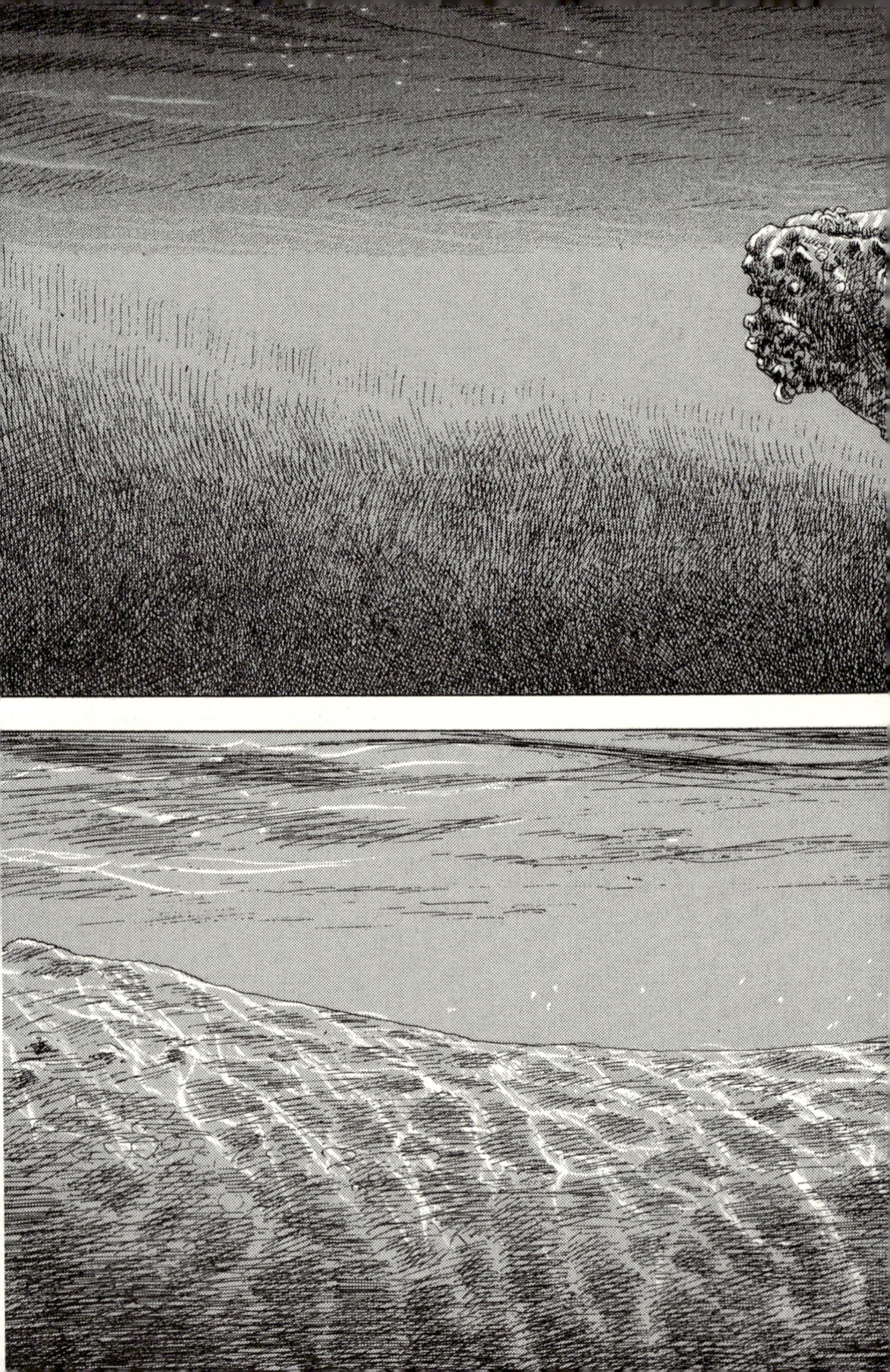

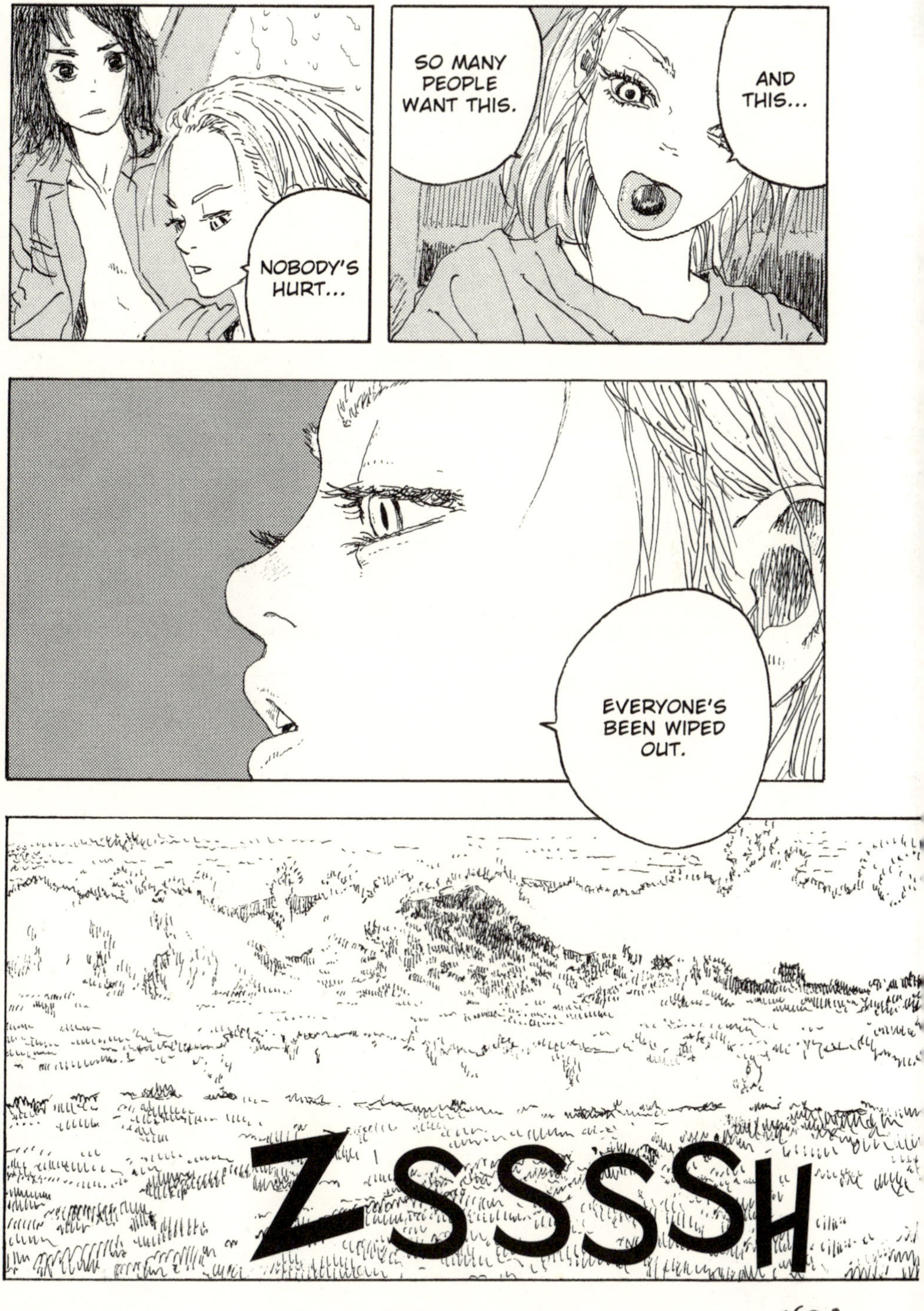
AND THIS...
SO MANY PEOPLE WANT THIS.
NOBODY'S HURT...
EVERYONE'S BEEN WIPED OUT.
ZSSSSH

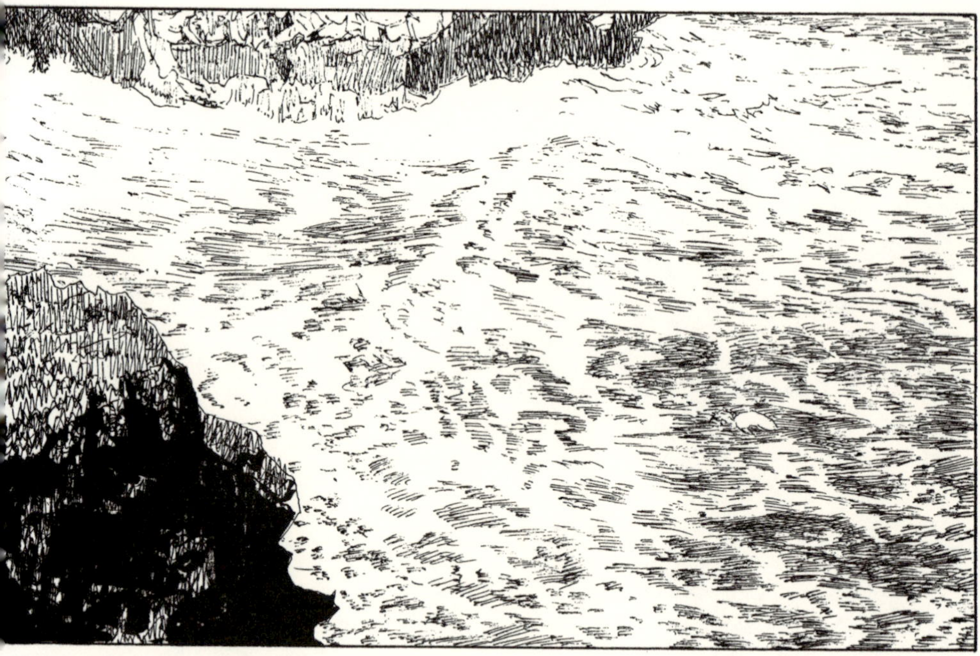

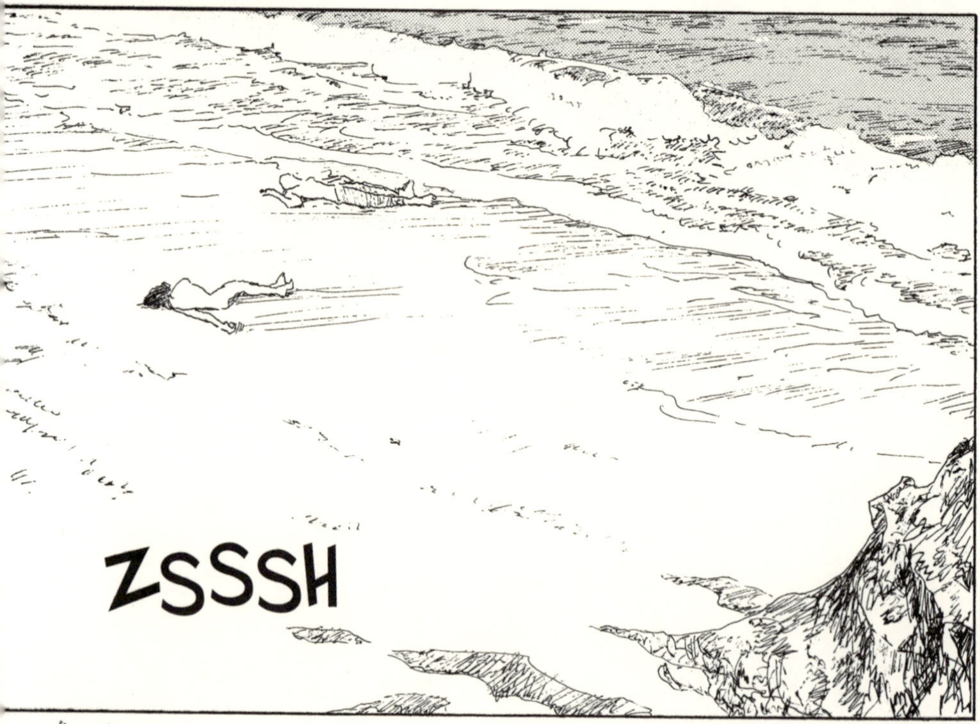
ZSSSH

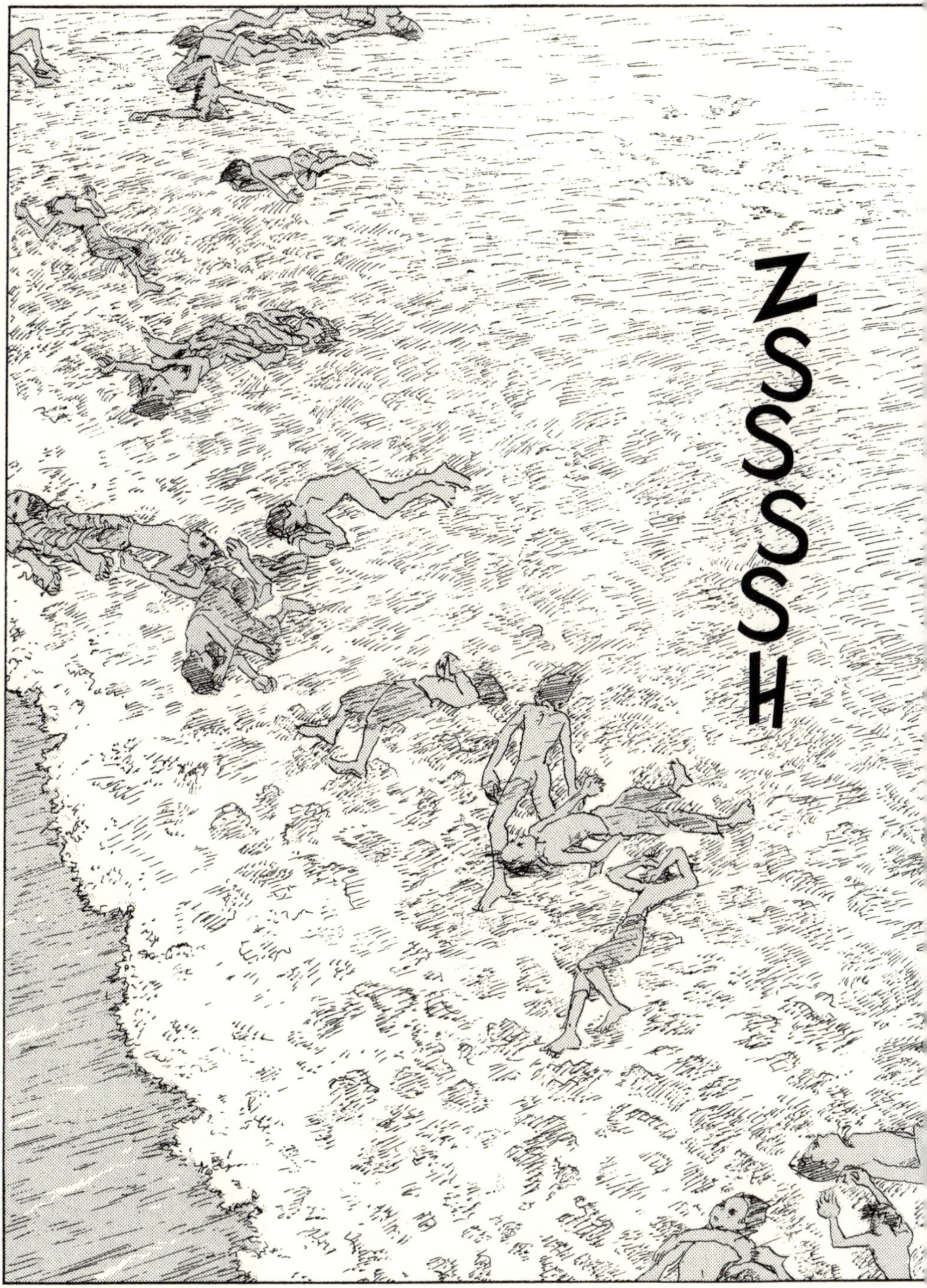
ZSSSSH

Chapter 13: Soaked Children

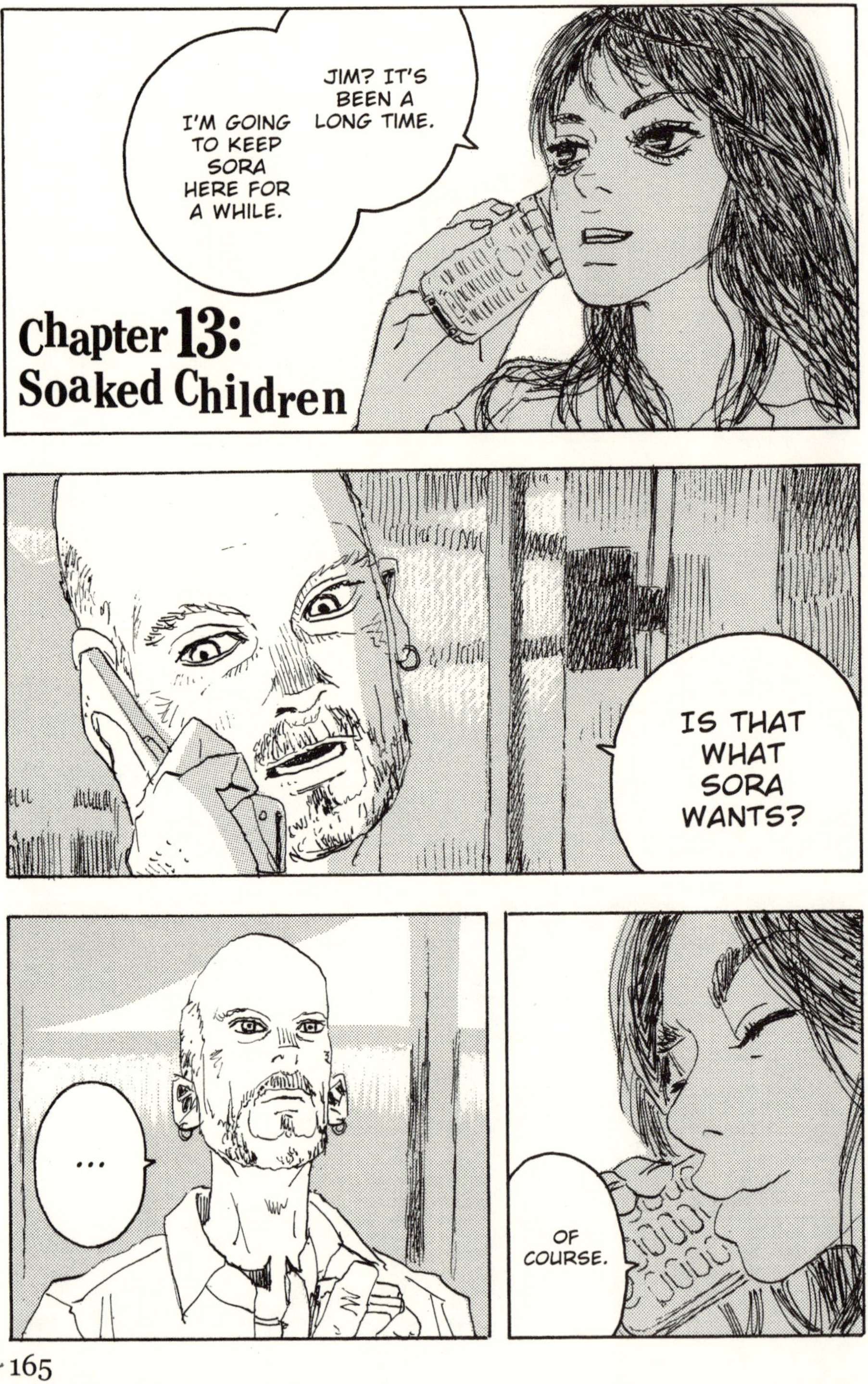
JIM? IT'S BEEN A LONG TIME.
I'M GOING TO KEEP SORA HERE FOR A WHILE.
IS THAT WHAT SORA WANTS?
OF COURSE.
...

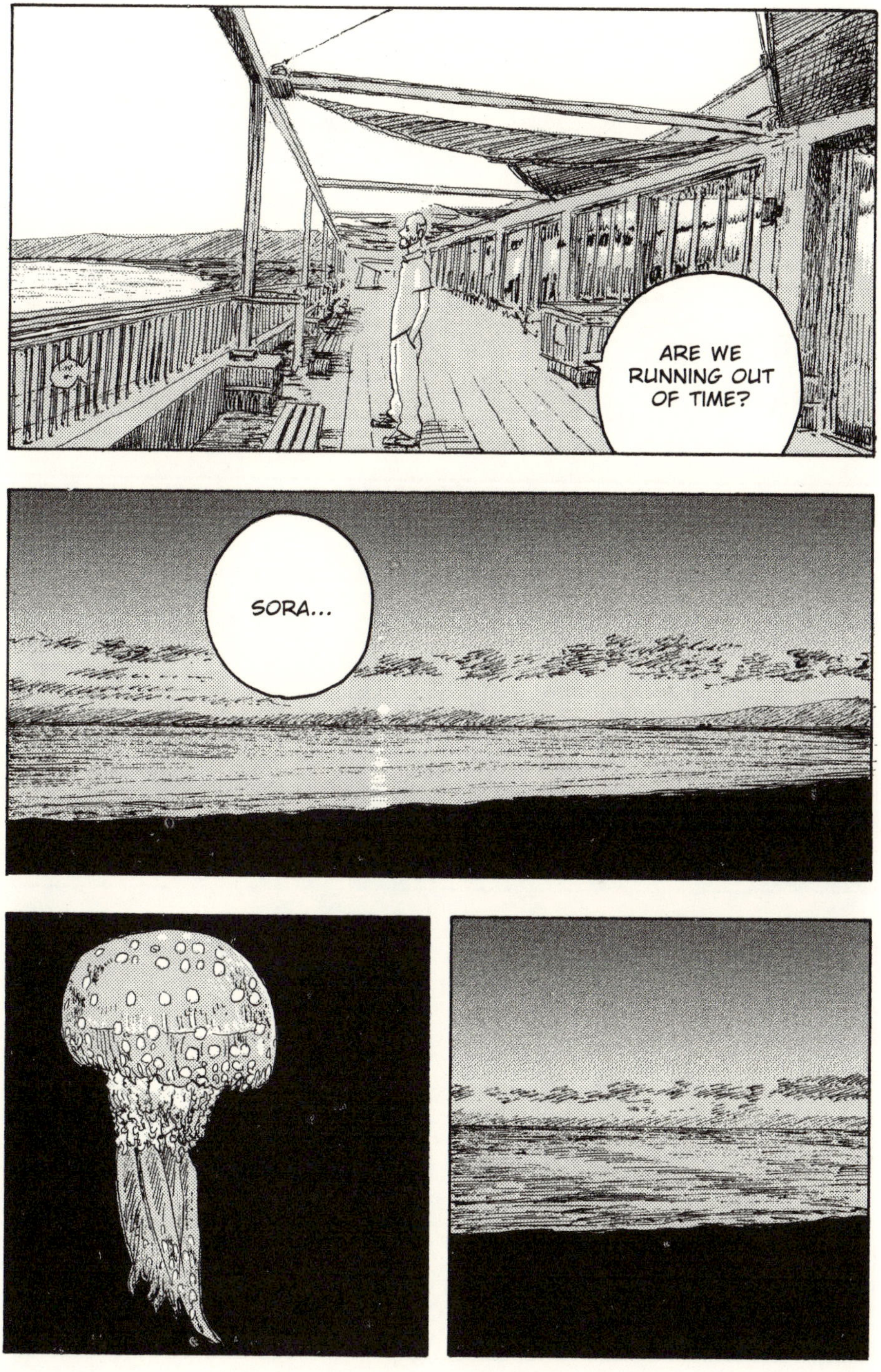
ARE WE RUNNING OUT OF TIME?
SORA...

Chapter 13: Soaked Children

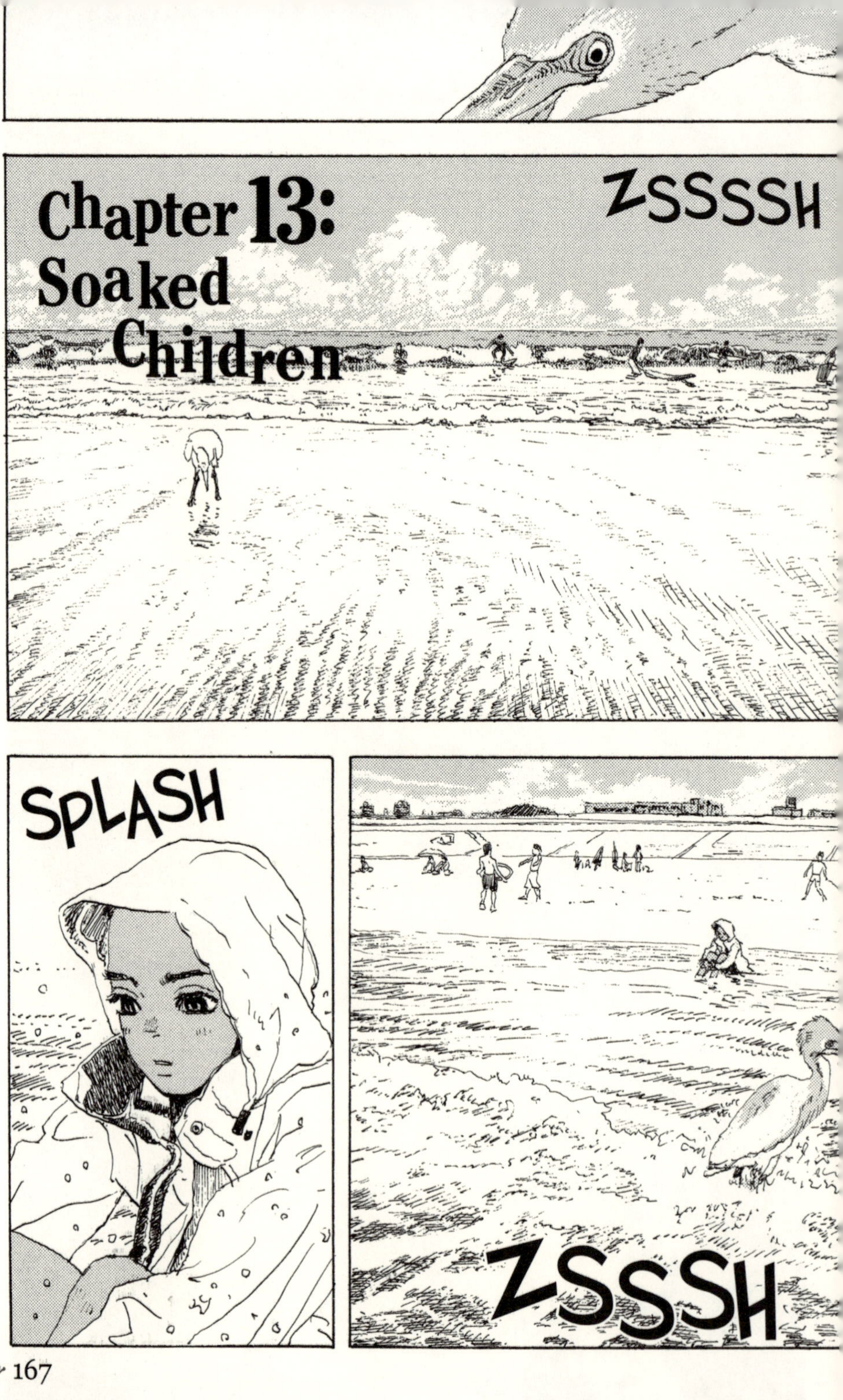
ZSSSSH
ZSSSH
SPLASH

There's a maelstrom deep down in my body.
Before the typhoon dissipated...
...it laid its baby in me...
It's steadily...

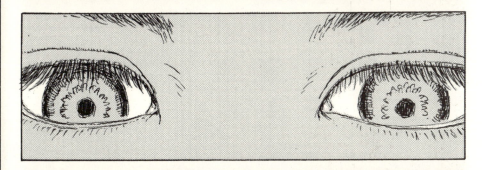

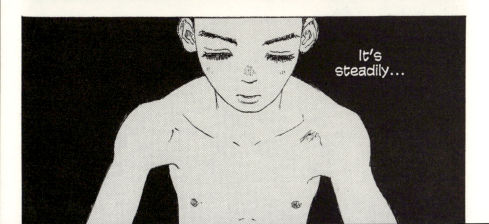

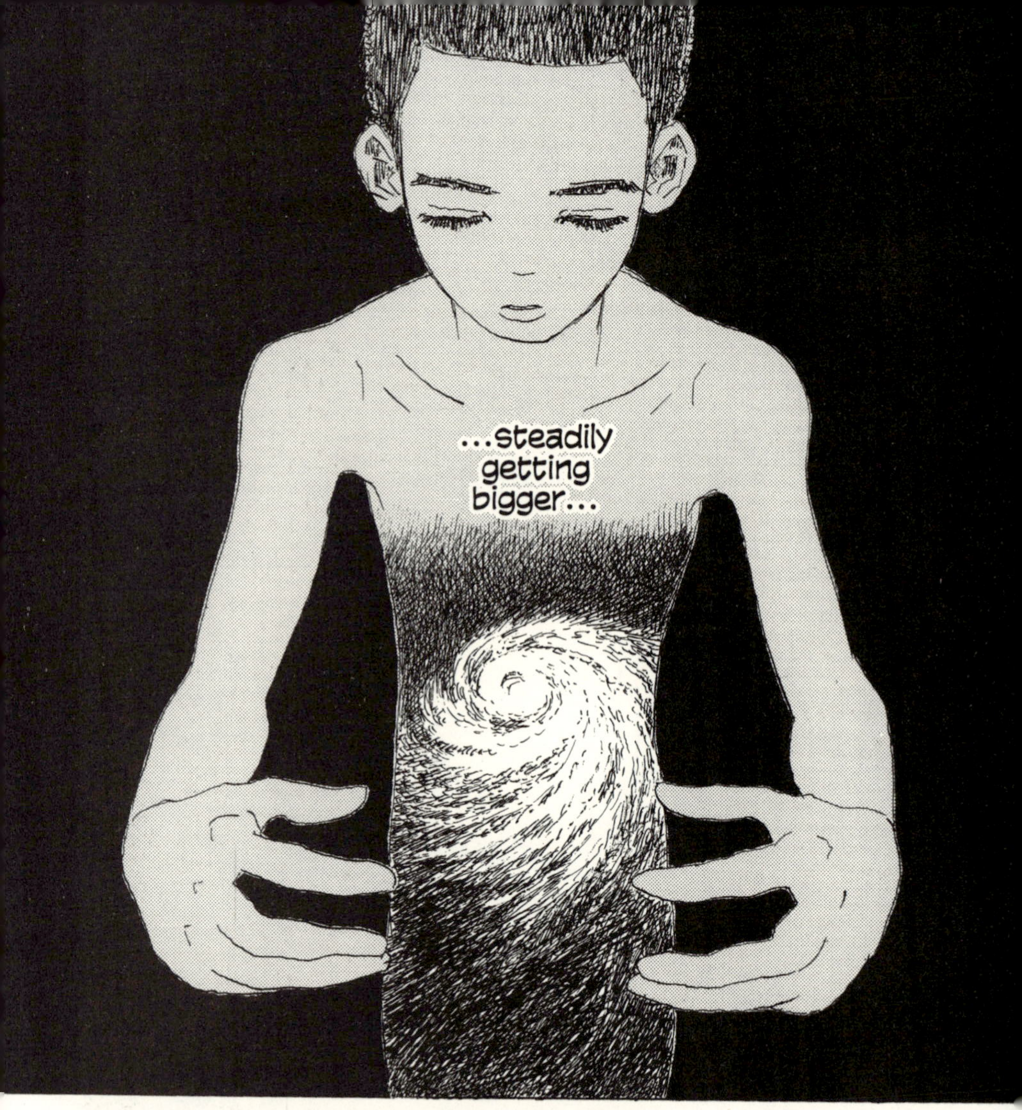
...steadily getting bigger...
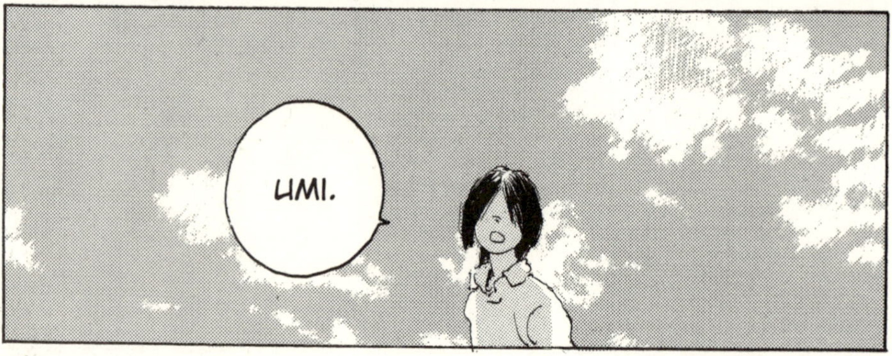
UMI.

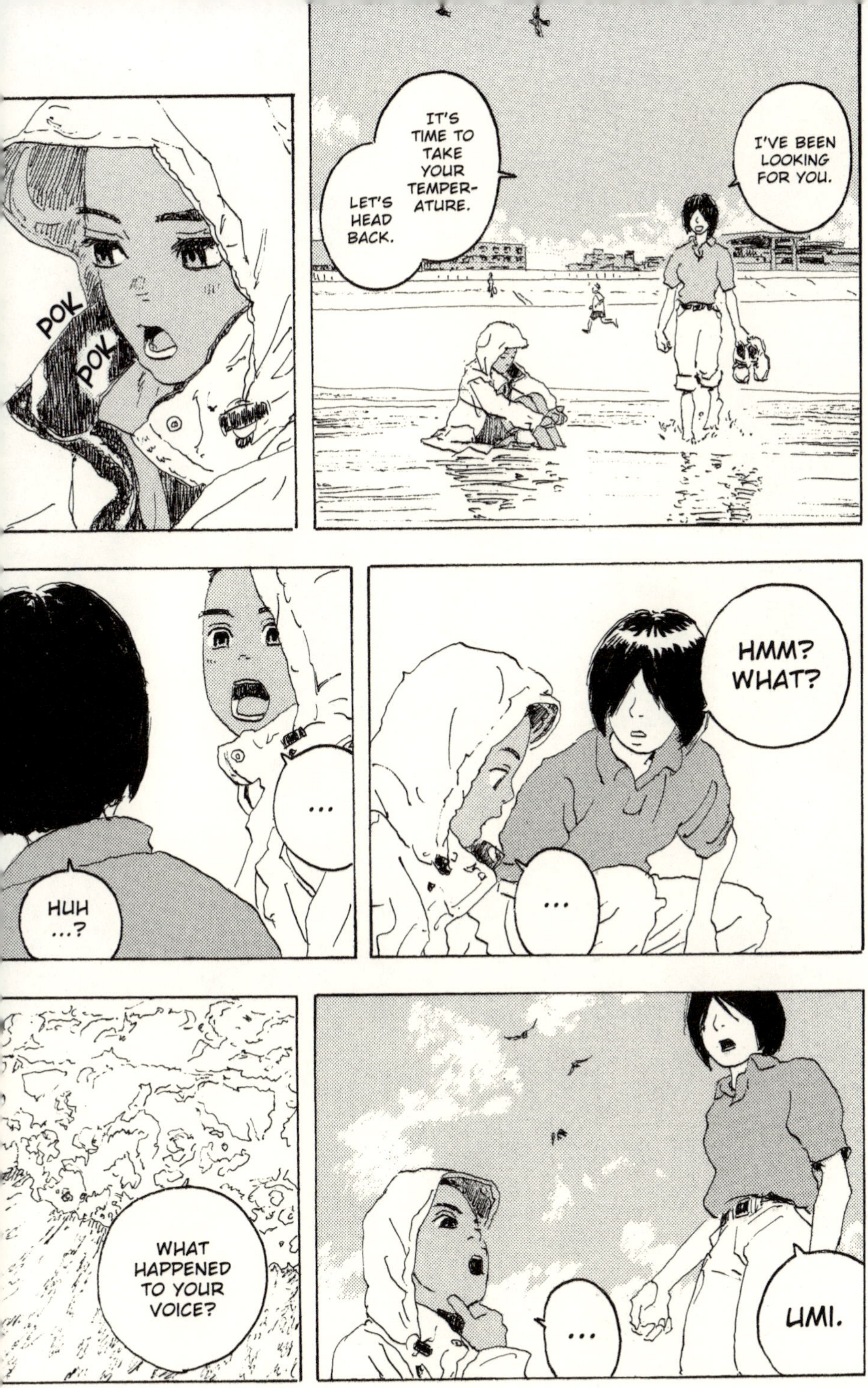
I'VE BEEN LOOKING FOR YOU.
IT'S TIME TO TAKE YOUR TEMPERATURE.
LET'S HEAD BACK.
POK
POK
HMM? WHAT?
...
...
HUH ...?
UMI.
...
WHAT HAPPENED TO YOUR VOICE?

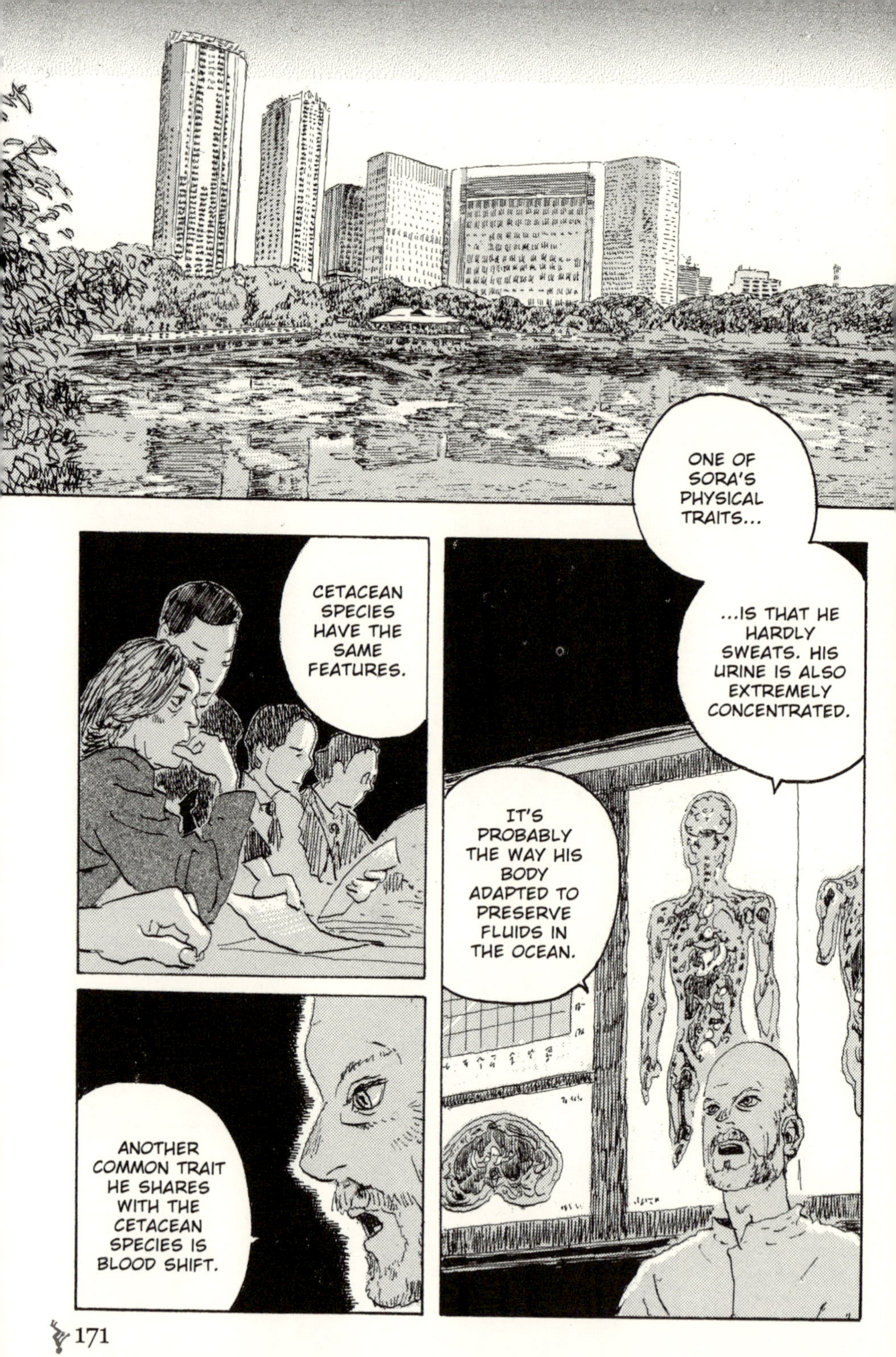
ONE OF SORA'S PHYSICAL TRAITS...
...IS THAT HE HARDLY SWEATS. HIS URINE IS ALSO EXTREMELY CONCENTRATED.
IT'S PROBABLY THE WAY HIS BODY ADAPTED TO PRESERVE FLUIDS IN THE OCEAN.
CETACEAN SPECIES HAVE THE SAME FEATURES.
ANOTHER COMMON TRAIT HE SHARES WITH THE CETACEAN SPECIES IS BLOOD SHIFT.

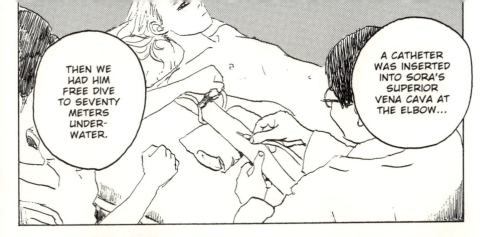

A CATHETER WAS INSERTED INTO SORA'S SUPERIOR VENA CAVA AT THE ELBOW...
THEN WE HAD HIM FREE DIVE TO SEVENTY METERS UNDER-WATER.
WE COLLECTED BLOOD AT THE THIRTY-, FIFTY- AND SEVENTY-METER MARKS, AND FOUND THAT...
...HIS BLOOD CONCENTRATED AROUND HIS CORE SO THAT HIS ORGANS WERE PROTECTED FROM THE INCREASING PRESSURE.
ISN'T THAT A DANGEROUS EXPERIMENT?
YES, IT IS.
AFTER THE EXPERIMENT, SORA CONTRACTED PHLEBITIS AND HAS BEEN SUFFERING FROM IT FOR 12 MONTHS.
ISN'T THAT ABUSE?
I UNDERSTAND THAT THE SUBJECT OF THIS EXPERIMENT HAS BEEN ABDUCTED.

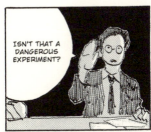

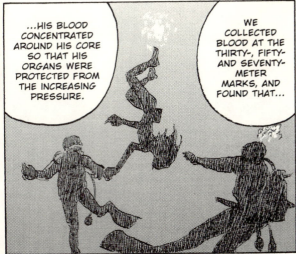

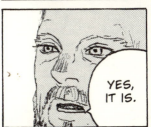

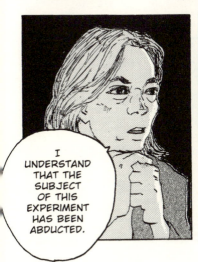

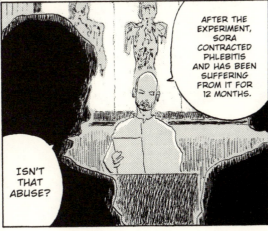

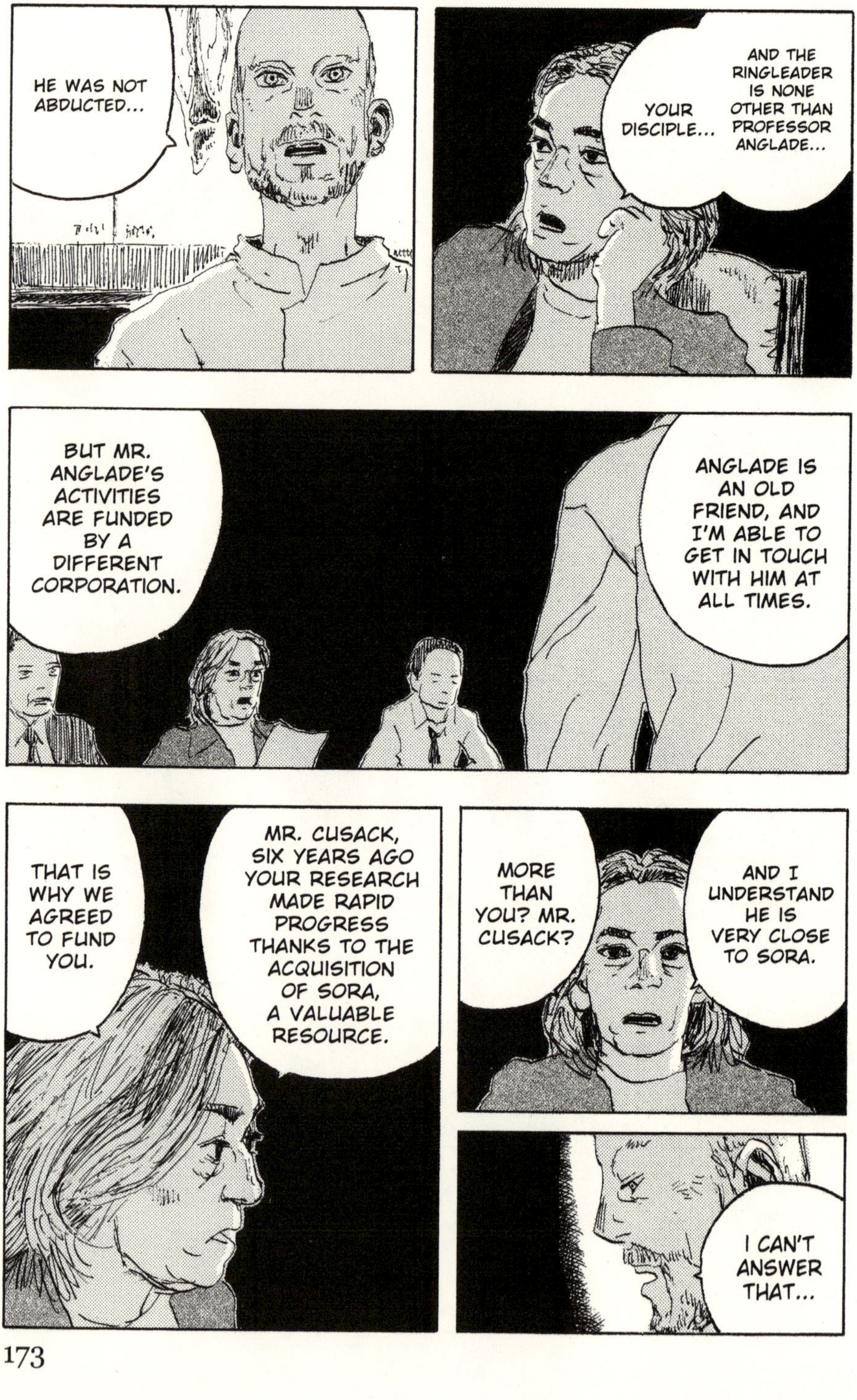
AND THE RINGLEADER IS NONE OTHER THAN PROFESSOR ANGLADE...
YOUR DISCIPLE...
HE WAS NOT ABDUCTED...
ANGLADE IS AN OLD FRIEND, AND I'M ABLE TO GET IN TOUCH WITH HIM AT ALL TIMES.
BUT MR. ANGLADE'S ACTIVITIES ARE FUNDED BY A DIFFERENT CORPORATION.
AND I UNDERSTAND HE IS VERY CLOSE TO SORA.
MORE THAN YOU? MR. CUSACK?
I CAN'T ANSWER THAT...
MR. CUSACK, SIX YEARS AGO YOUR RESEARCH MADE RAPID PROGRESS THANKS TO THE ACQUISITION OF SORA, A VALUABLE RESOURCE.
THAT IS WHY WE AGREED TO FUND YOU.

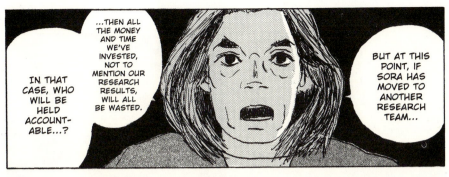

BUT AT THIS POINT, IF SORA HAS MOVED TO ANOTHER RESEARCH TEAM...
...THEN ALL THE MONEY AND TIME WE'VE INVESTED, NOT TO MENTION OUR RESEARCH RESULTS, WILL ALL BE WASTED.
IN THAT CASE, WHO WILL BE HELD ACCOUNTABLE...?
FURTHER-MORE...
...
...
...
...
PERHAPS WE'VE RUN OUT OF TIME AFTER ALL...
WHAT?
NO.
PROFESSOR ANGLADE'S RESEARCH IS FROM A TOTALLY DIFFERENT PERSPECTIVE THAN OURS.
WE ABSOLUTELY DO NOT NEED TO WORRY ABOUT HIM STEALING OUR RESULTS.

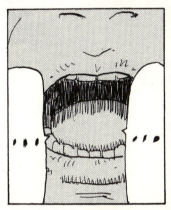

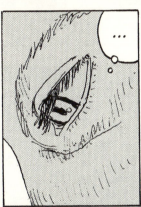

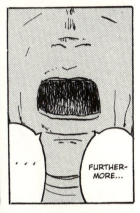

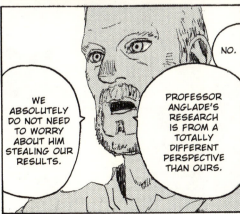

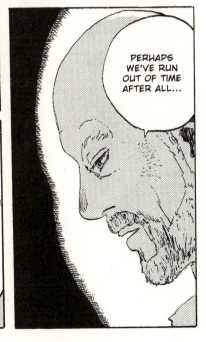

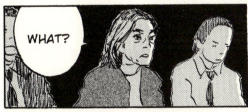

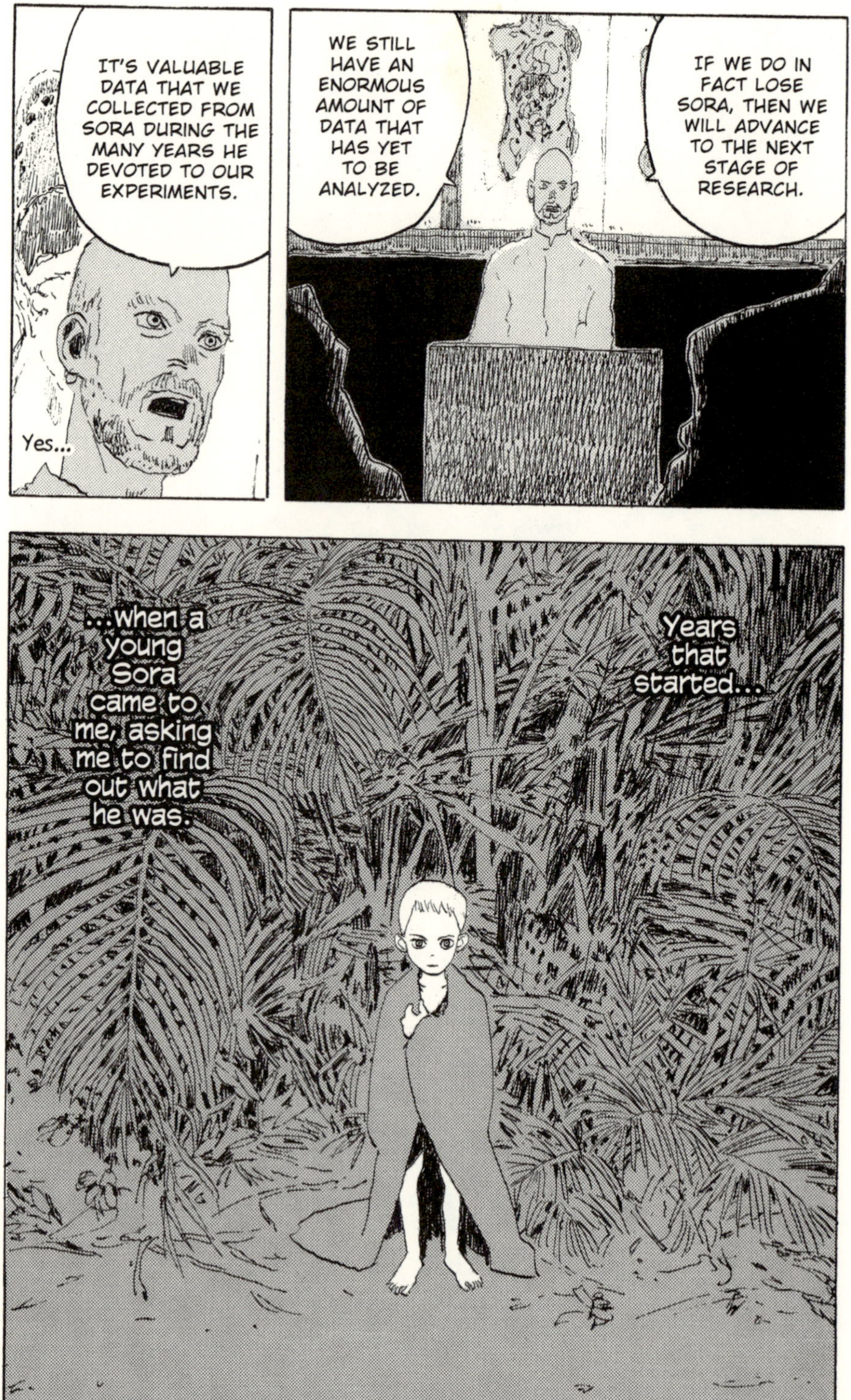
IF WE DO IN FACT LOSE SORA, THEN WE WILL ADVANCE TO THE NEXT STAGE OF RESEARCH.
WE STILL HAVE AN ENORMOUS AMOUNT OF DATA THAT HAS YET TO BE ANALYZED.
IT'S VALUABLE DATA THAT WE COLLECTED FROM SORA DURING THE MANY YEARS HE DEVOTED TO OUR EXPERIMENTS.
Yes...
Years that started...
...when a young Sora came to me, asking me to find out what he was.

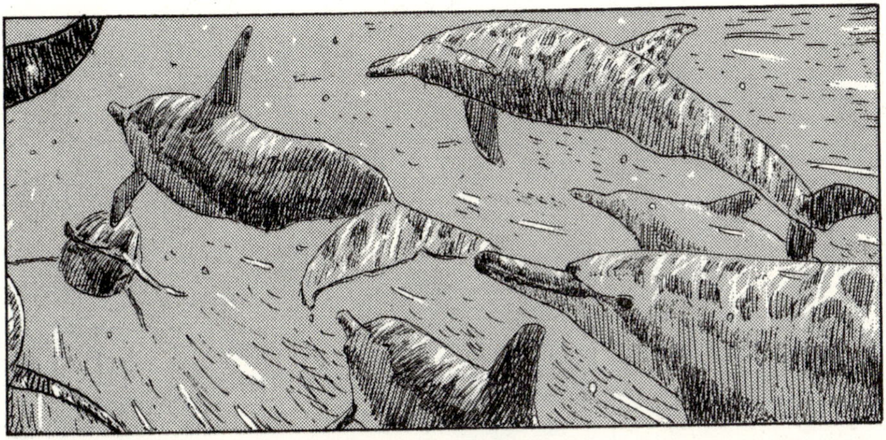

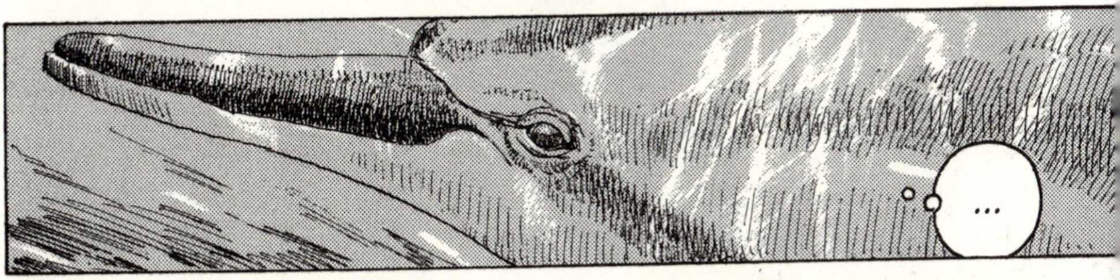
...

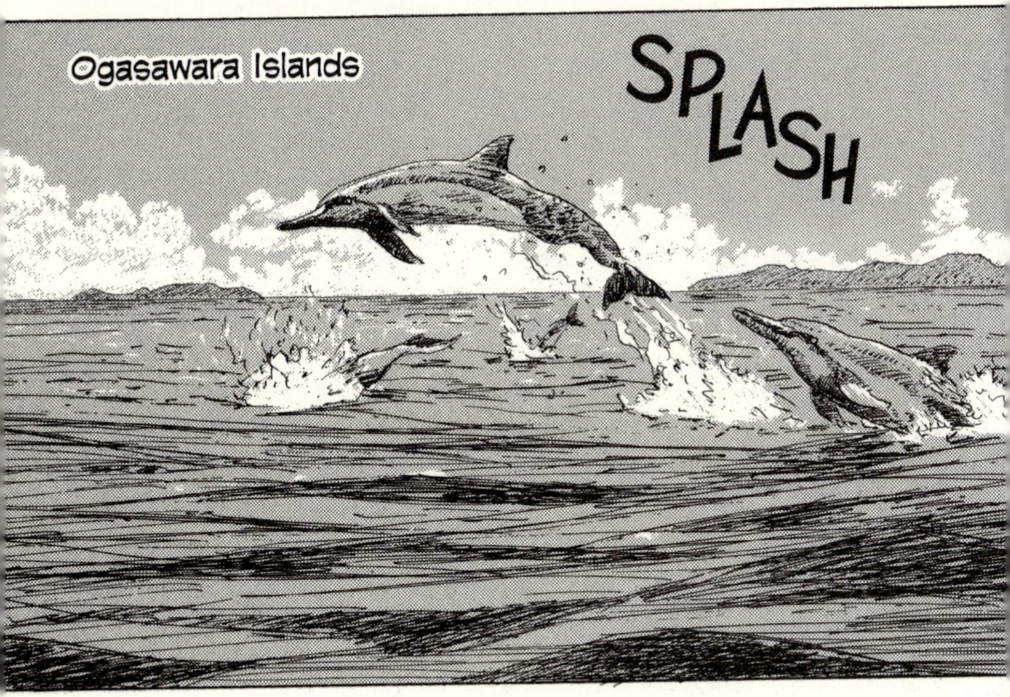
Ogasawara Islands
SPLASH

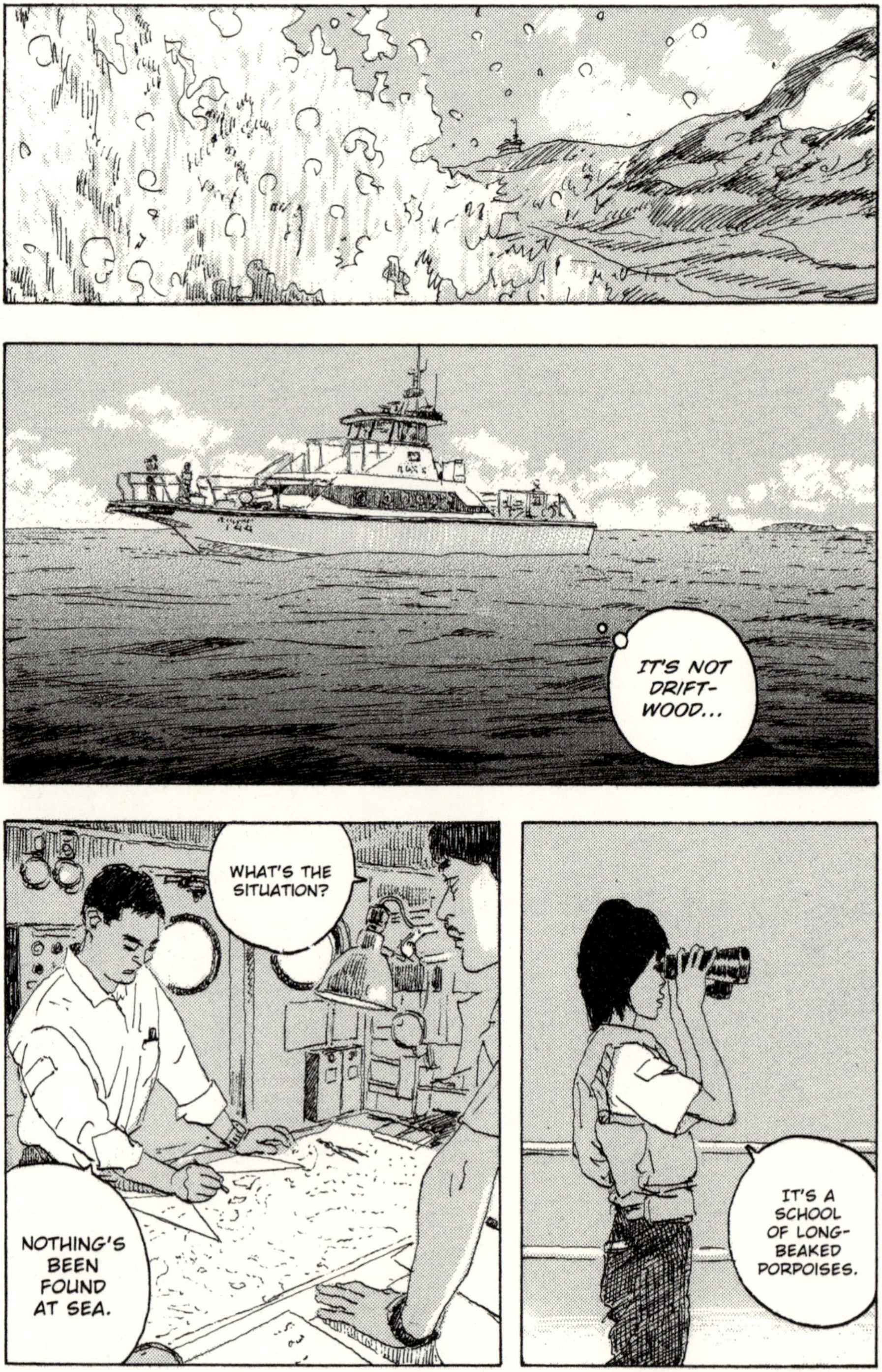
IT'S NOT DRIFT-WOOD...
IT'S A SCHOOL OF LONG-BEAKED PORPOISES.
WHAT'S THE SITUATION?
NOTHING'S BEEN FOUND AT SEA.

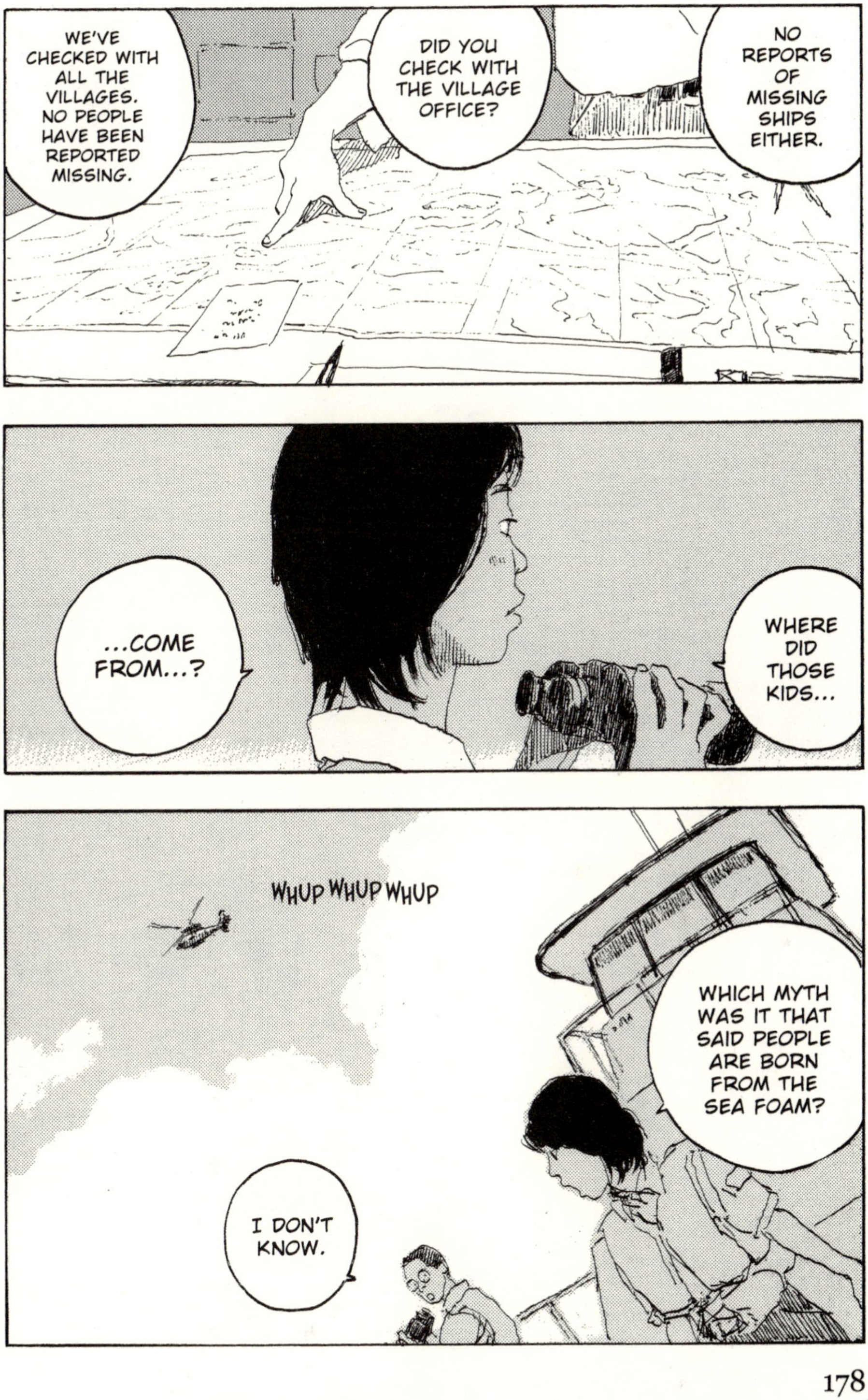
NO REPORTS OF MISSING SHIPS EITHER.
DID YOU CHECK WITH THE VILLAGE OFFICE?
WE'VE CHECKED WITH ALL THE VILLAGES. NO PEOPLE HAVE BEEN REPORTED MISSING.
WHERE DID THOSE KIDS...
...COME FROM...?
WHICH MYTH WAS IT THAT SAID PEOPLE ARE BORN FROM THE SEA FOAM?
WHUP WHUP WHUP
I DON'T KNOW.

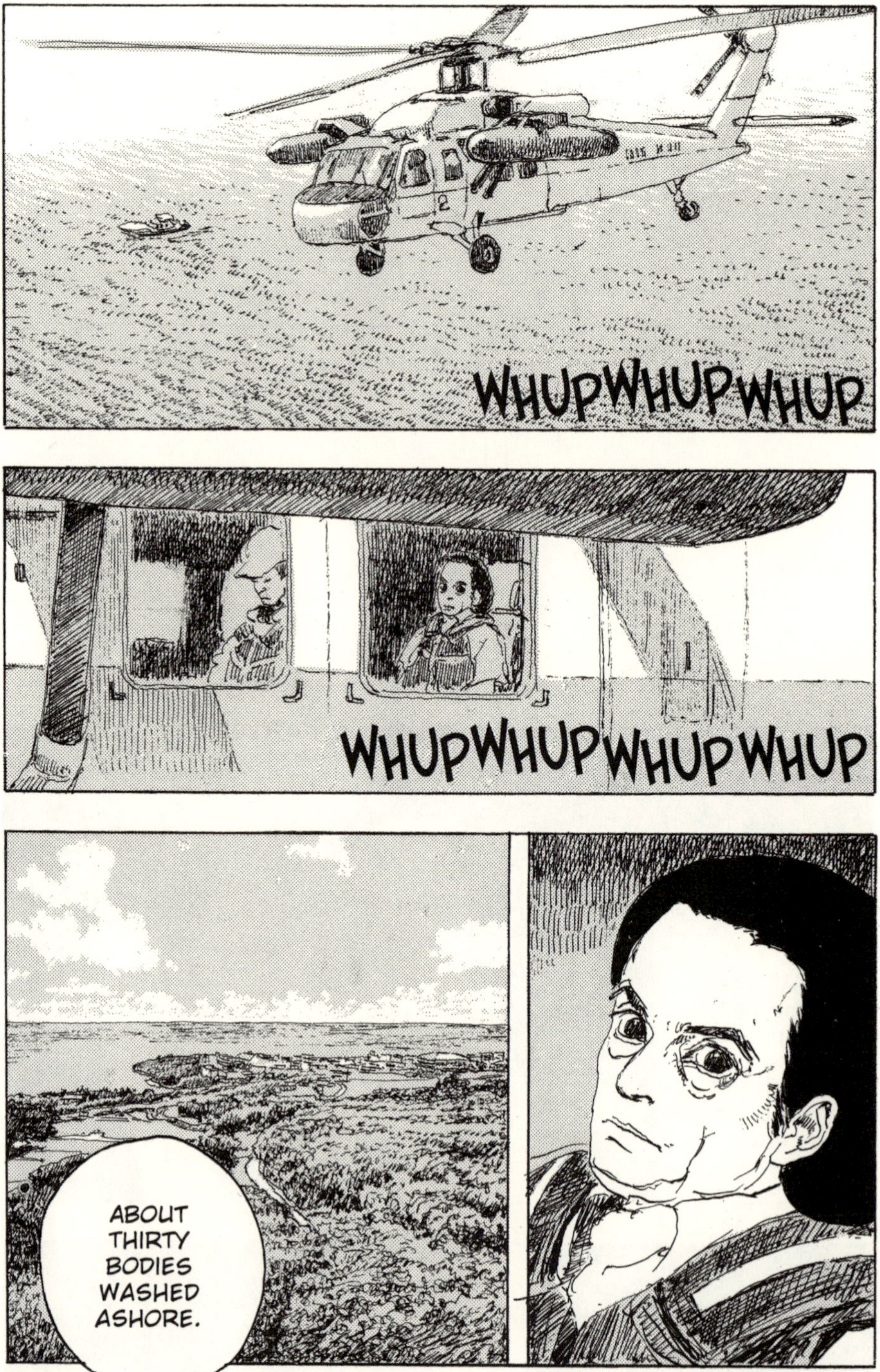
WHUPWHUPWHUP
WHUPWHUPWHUPWHUP
ABOUT THIRTY BODIES WASHED ASHORE.

SOME WERE ONLY PARTS, SO IT'S HARD TO GET AN ACCURATE COUNT...

THIS WAY.

OH, YOU SHOULD PUT A MASK ON, JUST IN CASE...

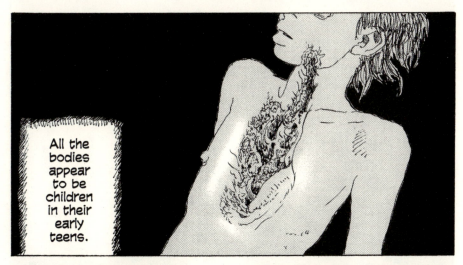

All the bodies appear to be children in their early teens.

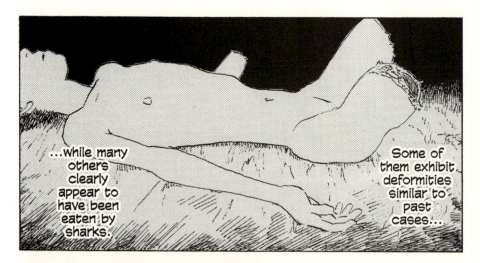

Some of them exhibit deformities similar to past cases...
...while many others clearly appear to have been eaten by sharks.
CLICK
Judging from the current and the condition of the bodies...
...there's a strong possibility that these bodies drifted from near where that meteorite struck.
...
KLAK KLAK KLAK KLAK
IF THESE BODIES ARE ALL THEM...

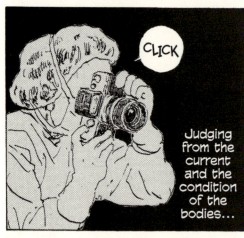

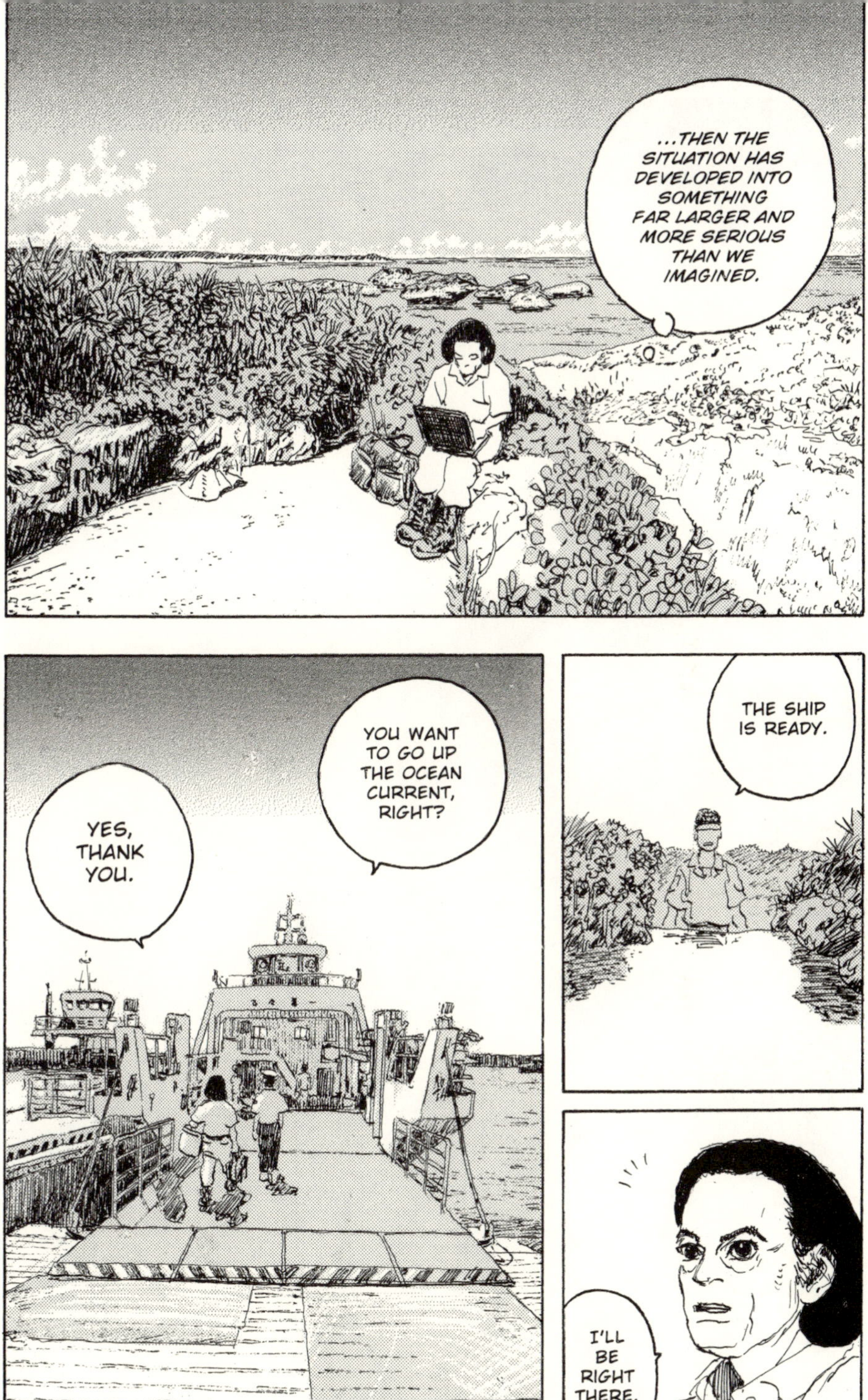
...THEN THE SITUATION HAS DEVELOPED INTO SOMETHING FAR LARGER AND MORE SERIOUS THAN WE IMAGINED.
THE SHIP IS READY.
I'LL BE RIGHT THERE.
YOU WANT TO GO UP THE OCEAN CURRENT, RIGHT?
YES, THANK YOU.

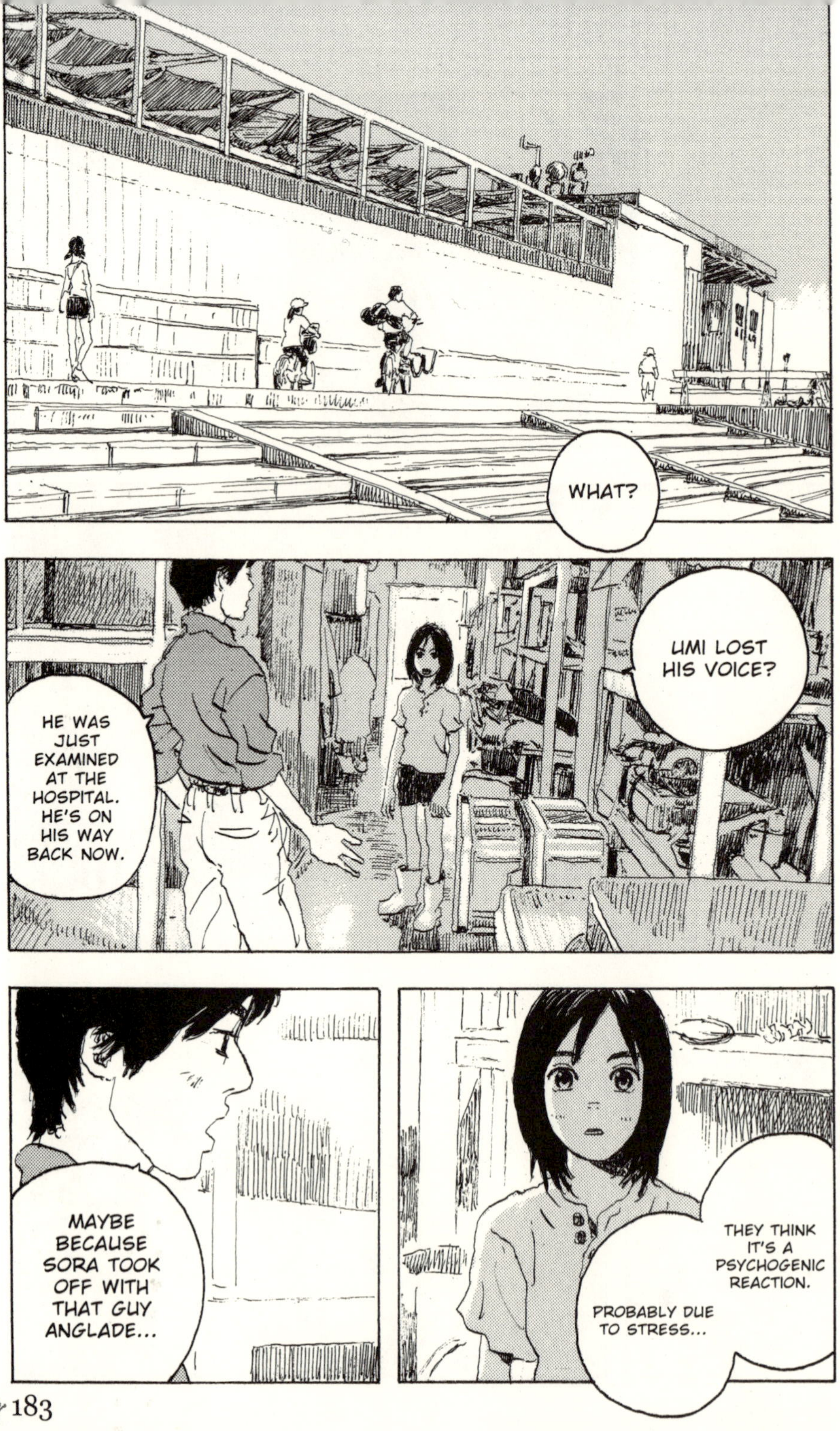
WHAT?
UMI LOST HIS VOICE?
HE WAS JUST EXAMINED AT THE HOSPITAL. HE'S ON HIS WAY BACK NOW.
THEY THINK IT'S A PSYCHOGENIC REACTION.
PROBABLY DUE TO STRESS...
MAYBE BECAUSE SORA TOOK OFF WITH THAT GUY ANGLADE...

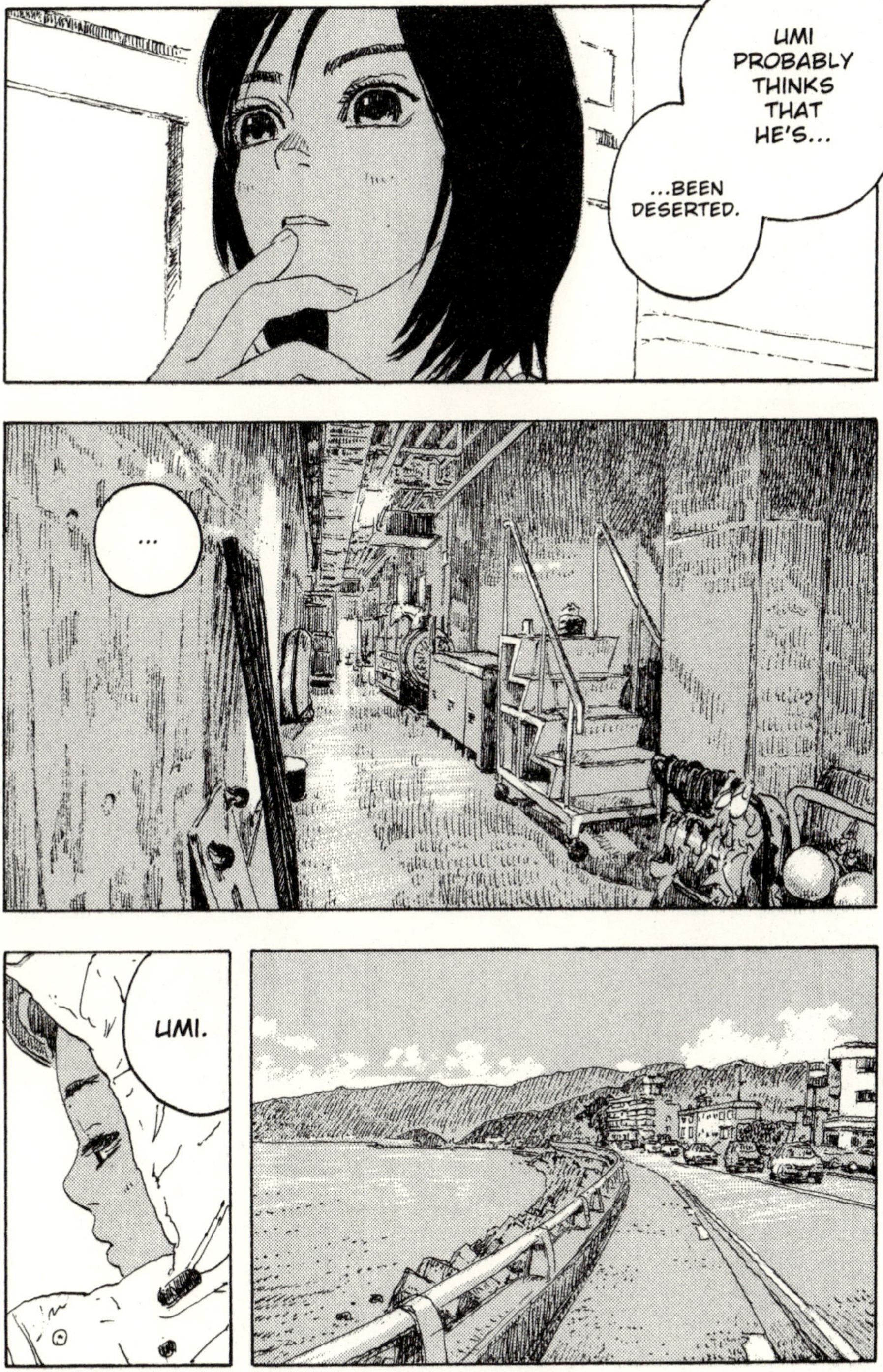
UMI PROBABLY THINKS THAT HE'S...
...BEEN DESERTED.
...
UMI.

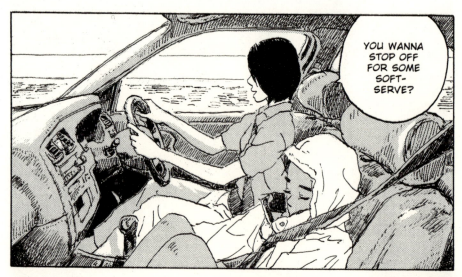

YOU WANNA STOP OFF FOR SOME SOFT-SERVE?

HE FELL ASLEEP?

TH-THU MP

TH-THU MP

TH-THU MP

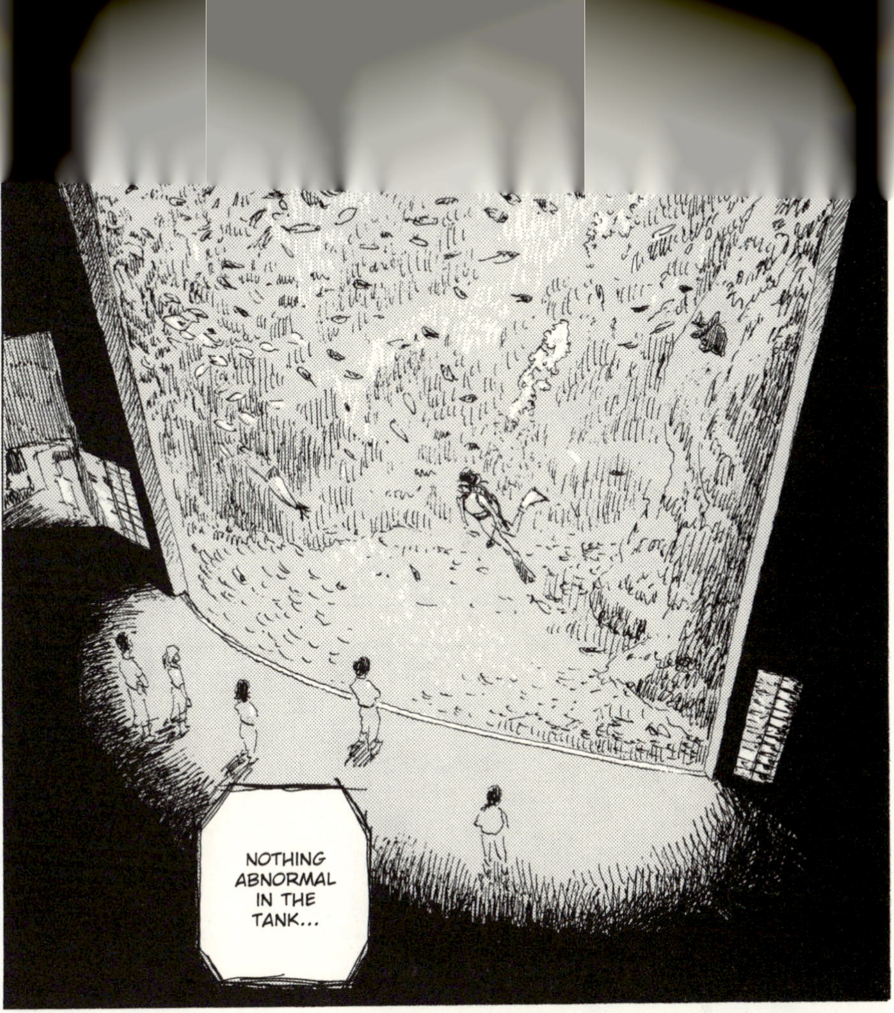
NOTHING ABNORMAL IN THE TANK...

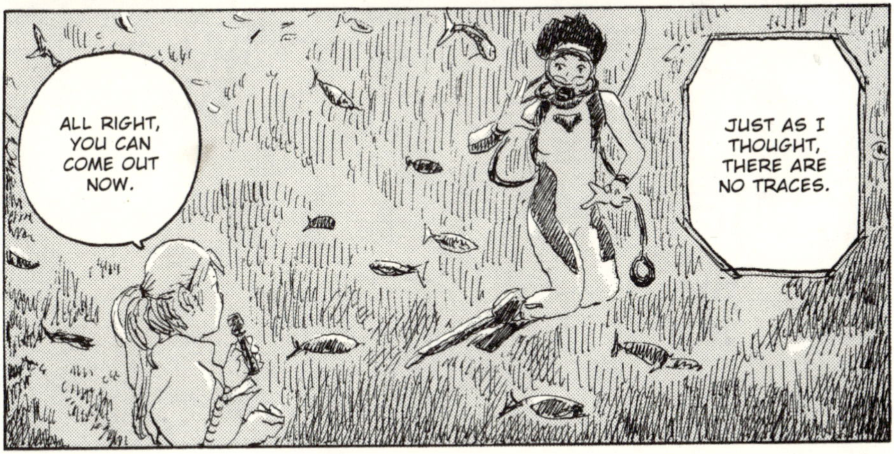
JUST AS I THOUGHT, THERE ARE NO TRACES.
ALL RIGHT, YOU CAN COME OUT NOW.

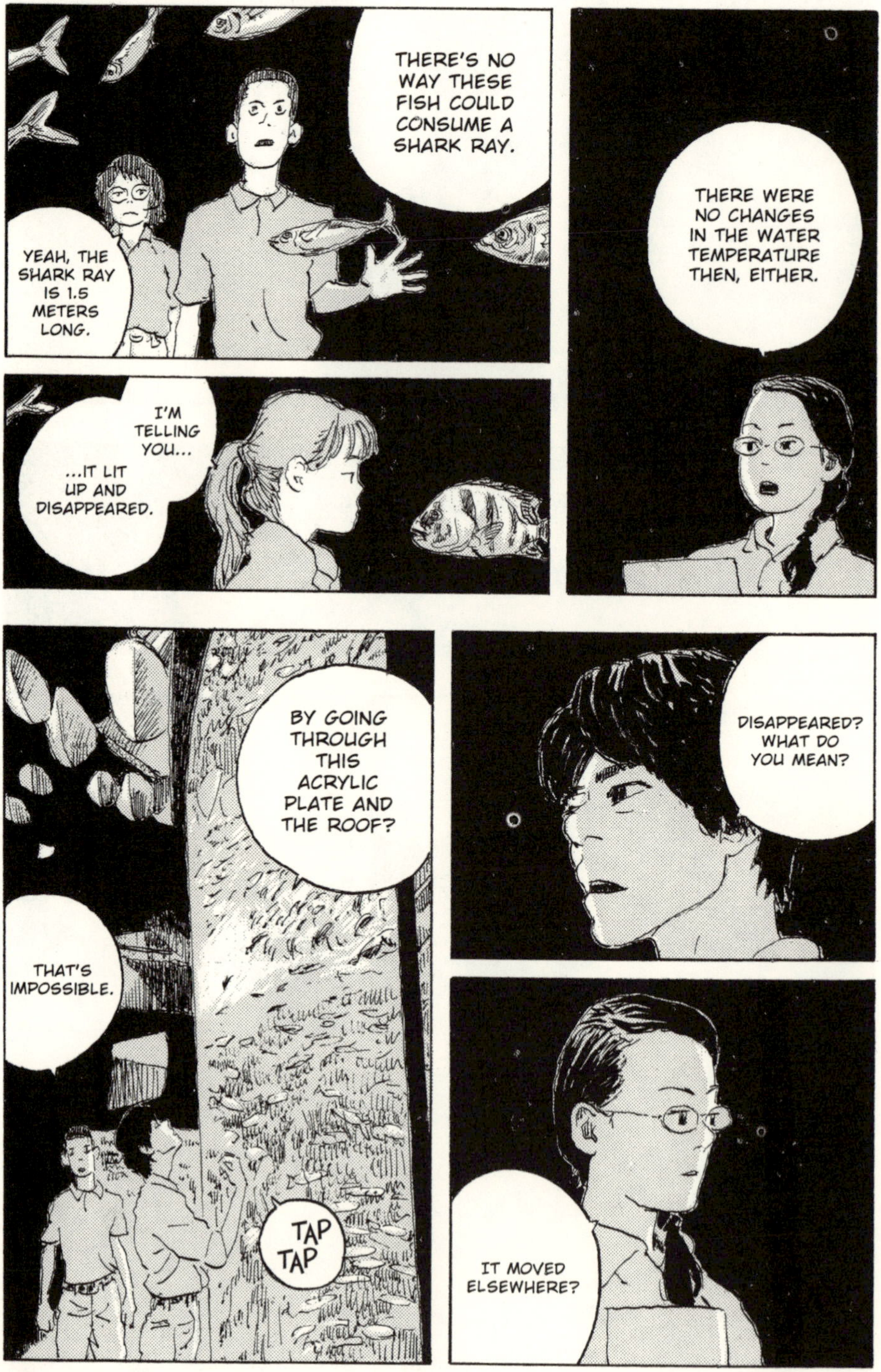
THERE WERE NO CHANGES IN THE WATER TEMPERATURE THEN, EITHER.
THERE'S NO WAY THESE FISH COULD CONSUME A SHARK RAY.
YEAH, THE SHARK RAY IS 1.5 METERS LONG.
I'M TELLING YOU...
...IT LIT UP AND DISAPPEARED.
DISAPPEARED? WHAT DO YOU MEAN?
IT MOVED ELSEWHERE?
BY GOING THROUGH THIS ACRYLIC PLATE AND THE ROOF?
THAT'S IMPOSSIBLE.
TAP TAP

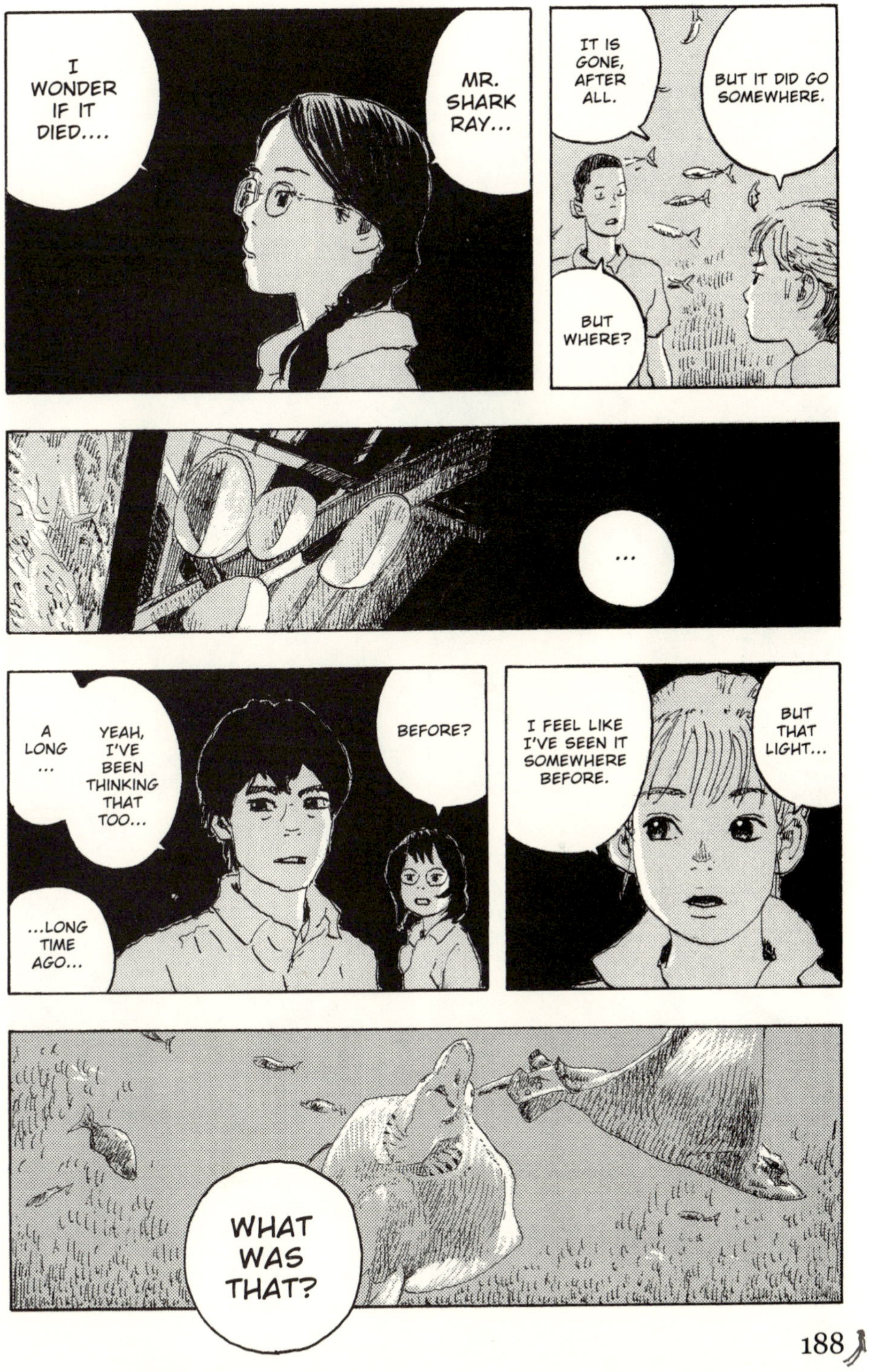
BUT IT DID GO SOMEWHERE.
IT IS GONE, AFTER ALL.
BUT WHERE?
MR. SHARK RAY...
I WONDER IF IT DIED....
...
BUT THAT LIGHT...
I FEEL LIKE I'VE SEEN IT SOMEWHERE BEFORE.
BEFORE?
YEAH, I'VE BEEN THINKING THAT TOO...
A LONG ...
...LONG TIME AGO...
WHAT WAS THAT?

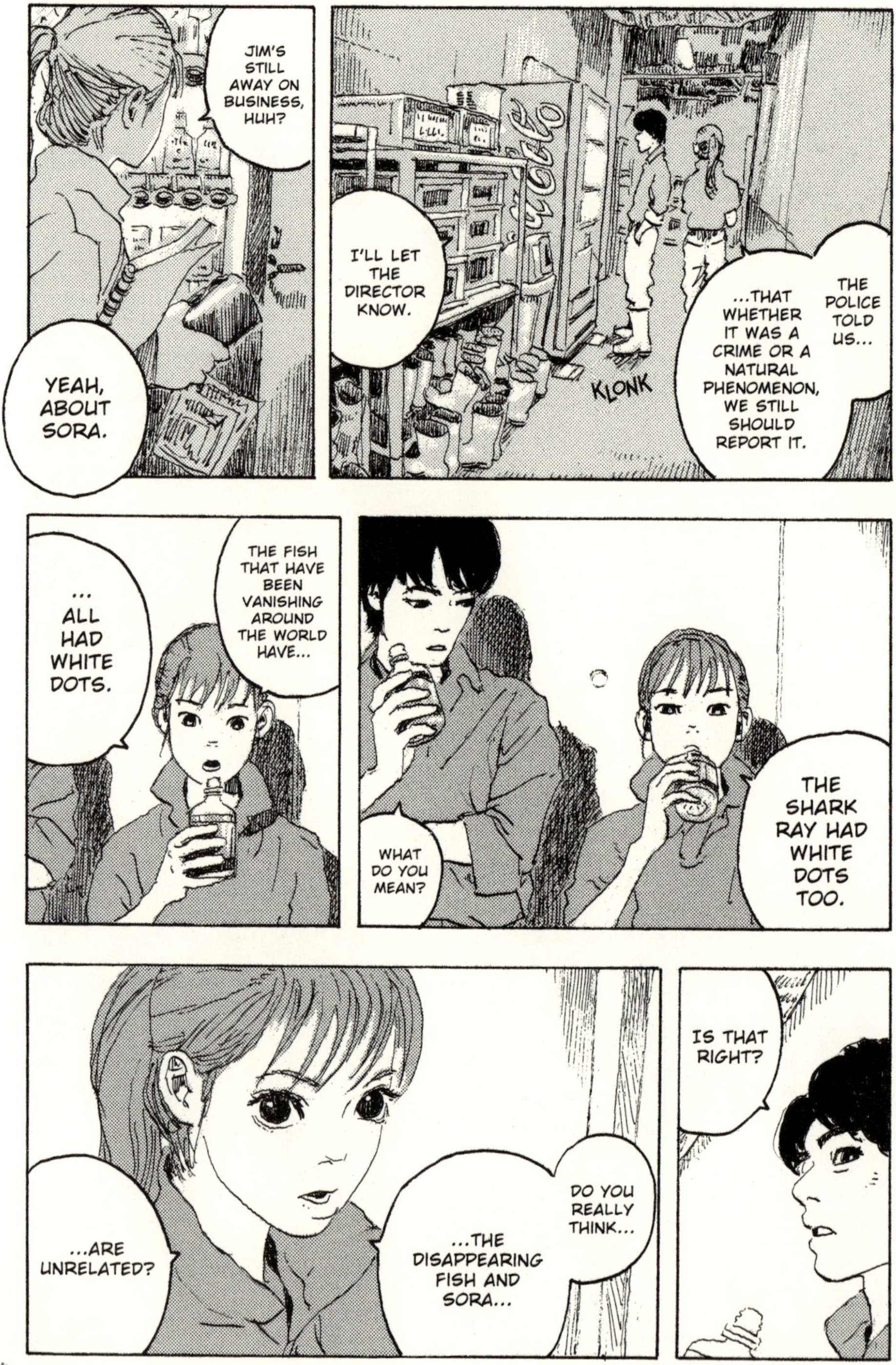
THE POLICE TOLD US...
...THAT WHETHER IT WAS A CRIME OR A NATURAL PHENOMENON, WE STILL SHOULD REPORT IT.
I'LL LET THE DIRECTOR KNOW.
KLONK
JIM'S STILL AWAY ON BUSINESS, HUH?
YEAH, ABOUT SORA.
THE SHARK RAY HAD WHITE DOTS TOO.
WHAT DO YOU MEAN?
THE FISH THAT HAVE BEEN VANISHING AROUND THE WORLD HAVE...
... ALL HAD WHITE DOTS.
IS THAT RIGHT?
DO YOU REALLY THINK...
...THE DISAPPEARING FISH AND SORA...
...ARE UNRELATED?

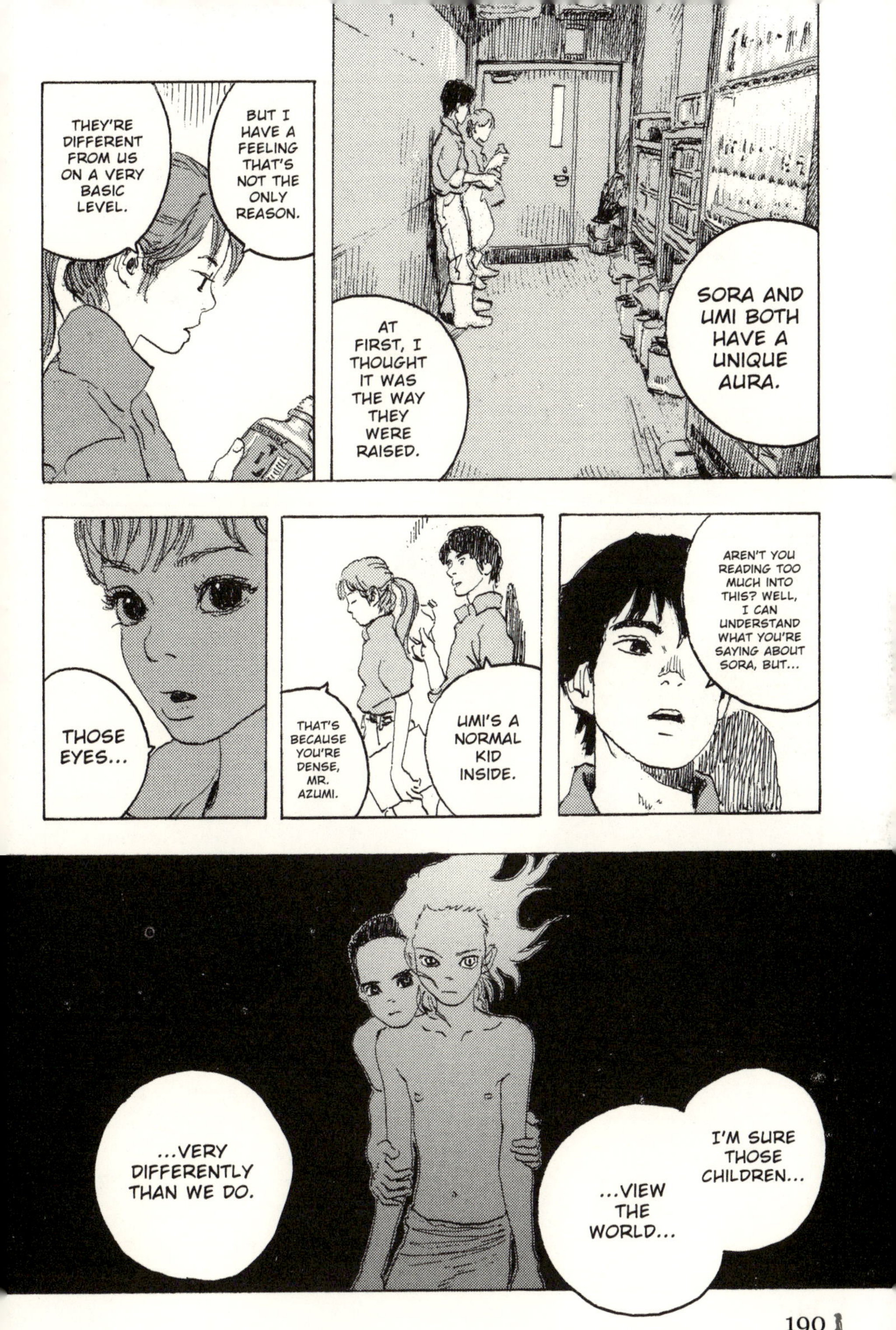
SORA AND UMI BOTH HAVE A UNIQUE AURA.
AT FIRST, I THOUGHT IT WAS THE WAY THEY WERE RAISED.
BUT I HAVE A FEELING THAT'S NOT THE ONLY REASON.
THEY'RE DIFFERENT FROM US ON A VERY BASIC LEVEL.
AREN'T YOU READING TOO MUCH INTO THIS? WELL, I CAN UNDERSTAND WHAT YOU'RE SAYING ABOUT SORA, BUT...
UMI'S A NORMAL KID INSIDE.
THAT'S BECAUSE YOU'RE DENSE, MR. AZUMI.
THOSE EYES...
I'M SURE THOSE CHILDREN...
...VIEW THE WORLD...
...VERY DIFFERENTLY THAN WE DO.

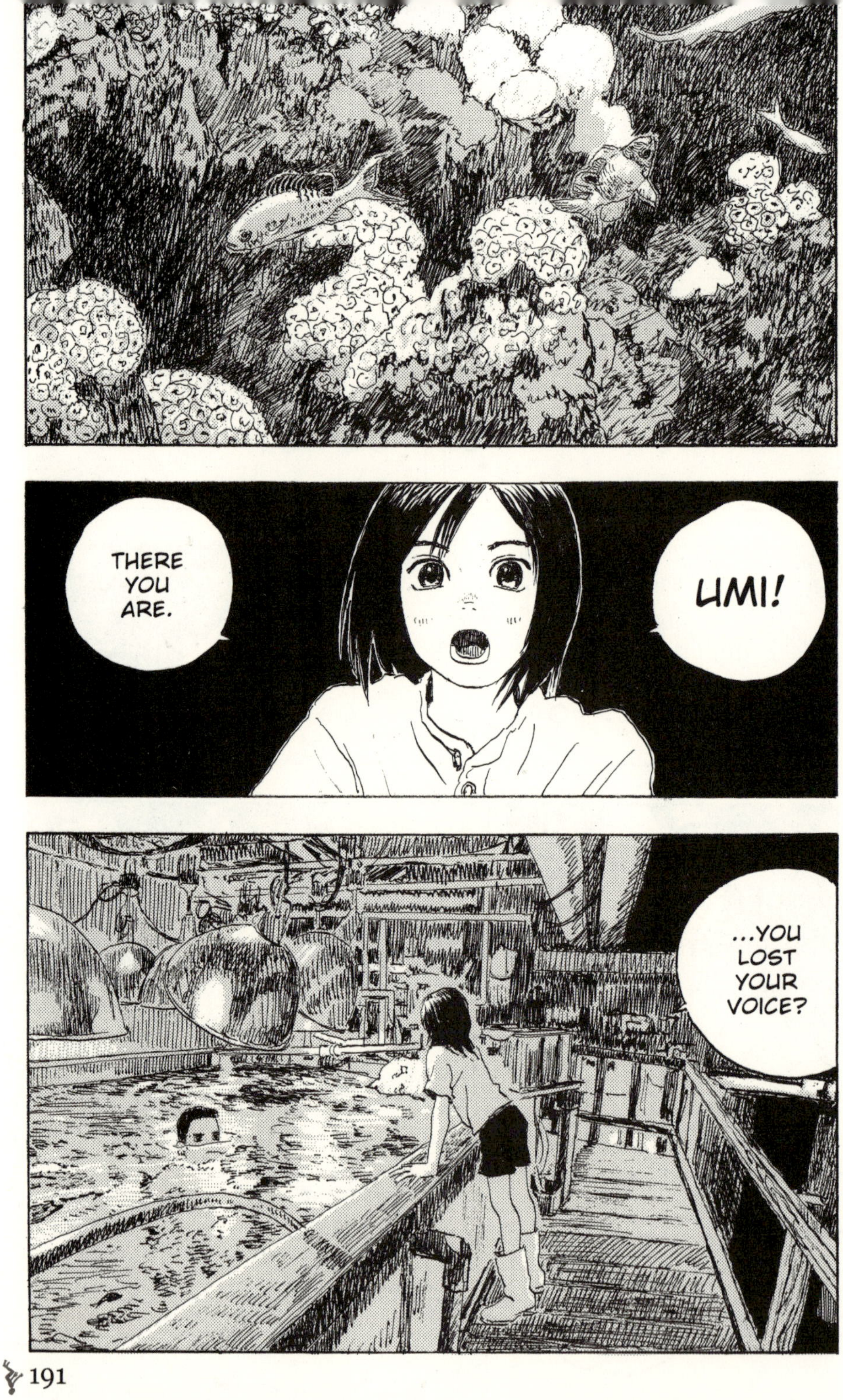
UMI!
THERE YOU ARE.
...YOU LOST YOUR VOICE?

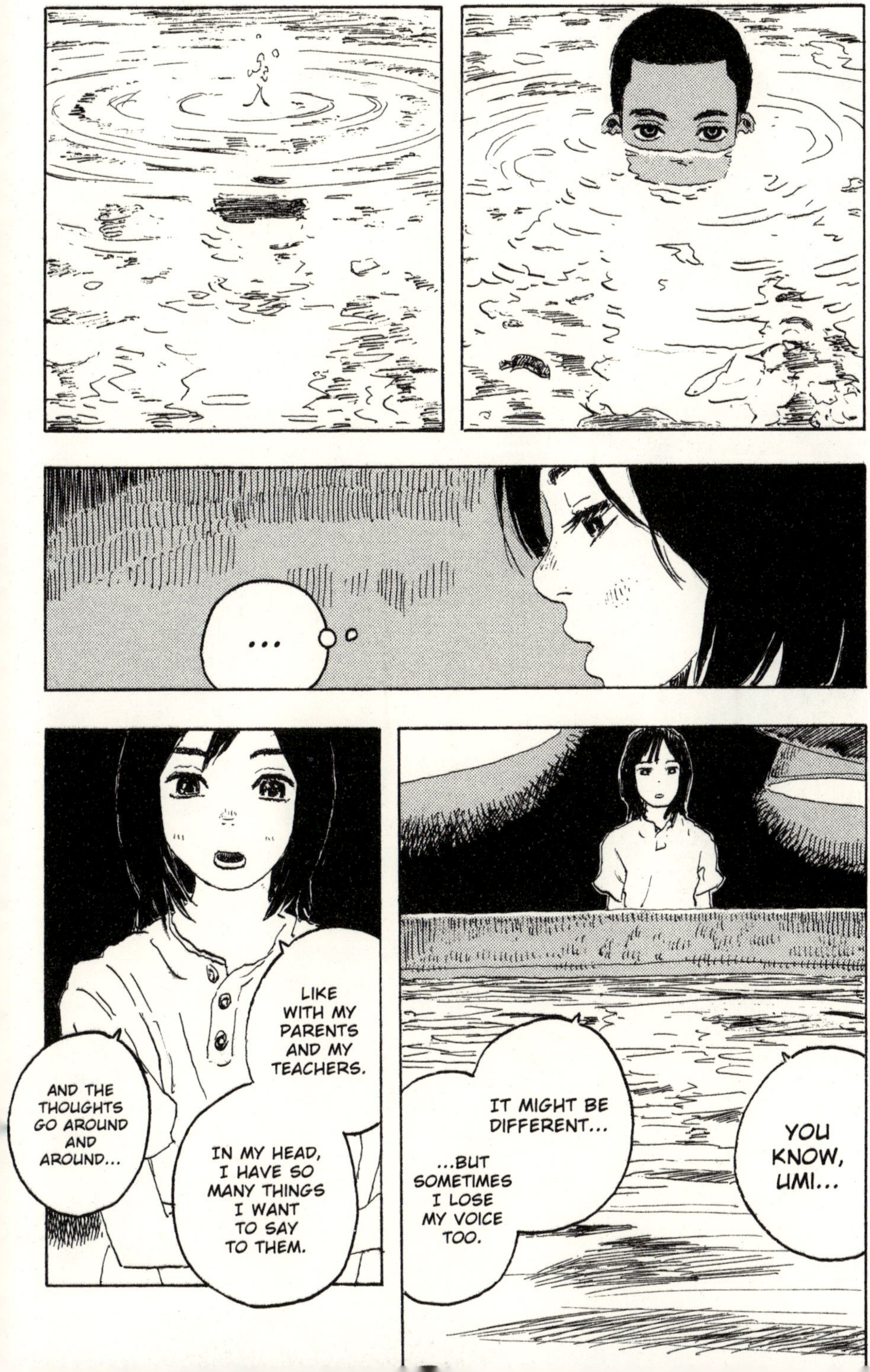
...
YOU KNOW, UMI...
IT MIGHT BE DIFFERENT...
...BUT SOMETIMES I LOSE MY VOICE TOO.
LIKE WITH MY PARENTS AND MY TEACHERS.
IN MY HEAD, I HAVE SO MANY THINGS I WANT TO SAY TO THEM.
AND THE THOUGHTS GO AROUND AND AROUND...

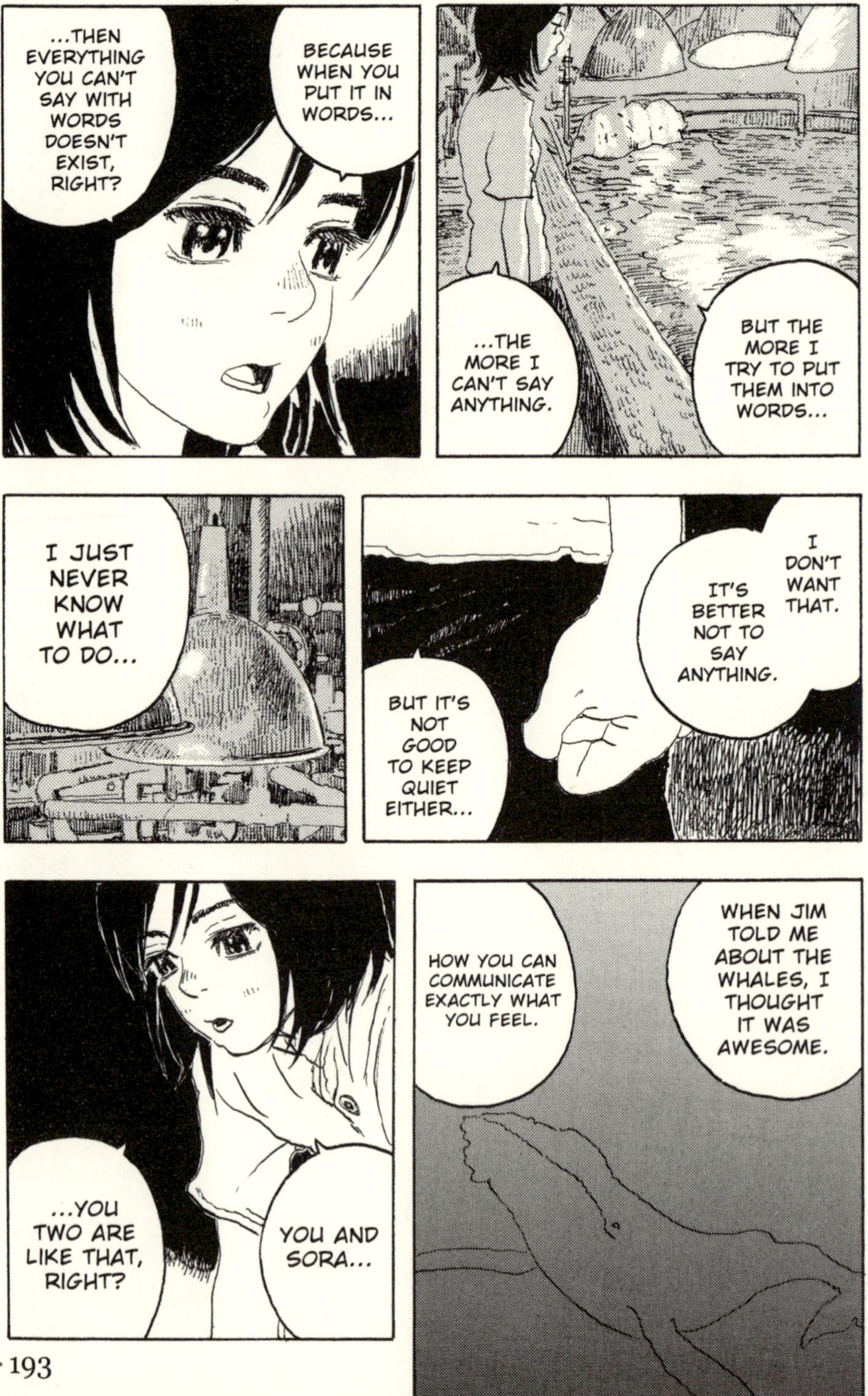
BUT THE MORE I TRY TO PUT THEM INTO WORDS...
...THE MORE I CAN'T SAY ANYTHING.
BECAUSE WHEN YOU PUT IT IN WORDS...
...THEN EVERYTHING YOU CAN'T SAY WITH WORDS DOESN'T EXIST, RIGHT?
I DON'T WANT THAT.
IT'S BETTER NOT TO SAY ANYTHING.
BUT IT'S NOT GOOD TO KEEP QUIET EITHER...
I JUST NEVER KNOW WHAT TO DO...
WHEN JIM TOLD ME ABOUT THE WHALES, I THOUGHT IT WAS AWESOME.
HOW YOU CAN COMMUNICATE EXACTLY WHAT YOU FEEL.
YOU AND SORA...
...YOU TWO ARE LIKE THAT, RIGHT?

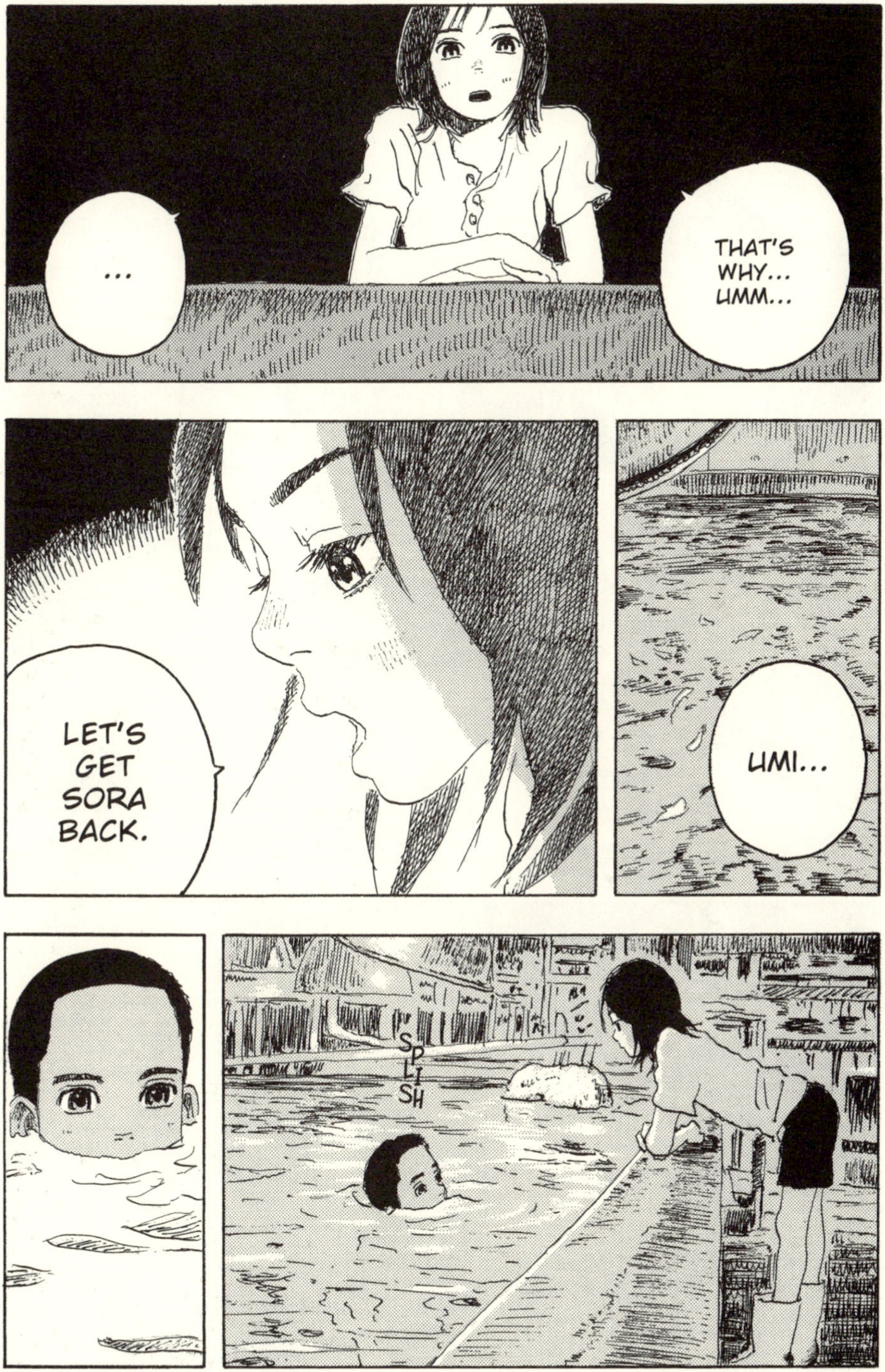
THAT'S WHY... UMM...
...
UMI...
LET'S GET SORA BACK.
SPLISH

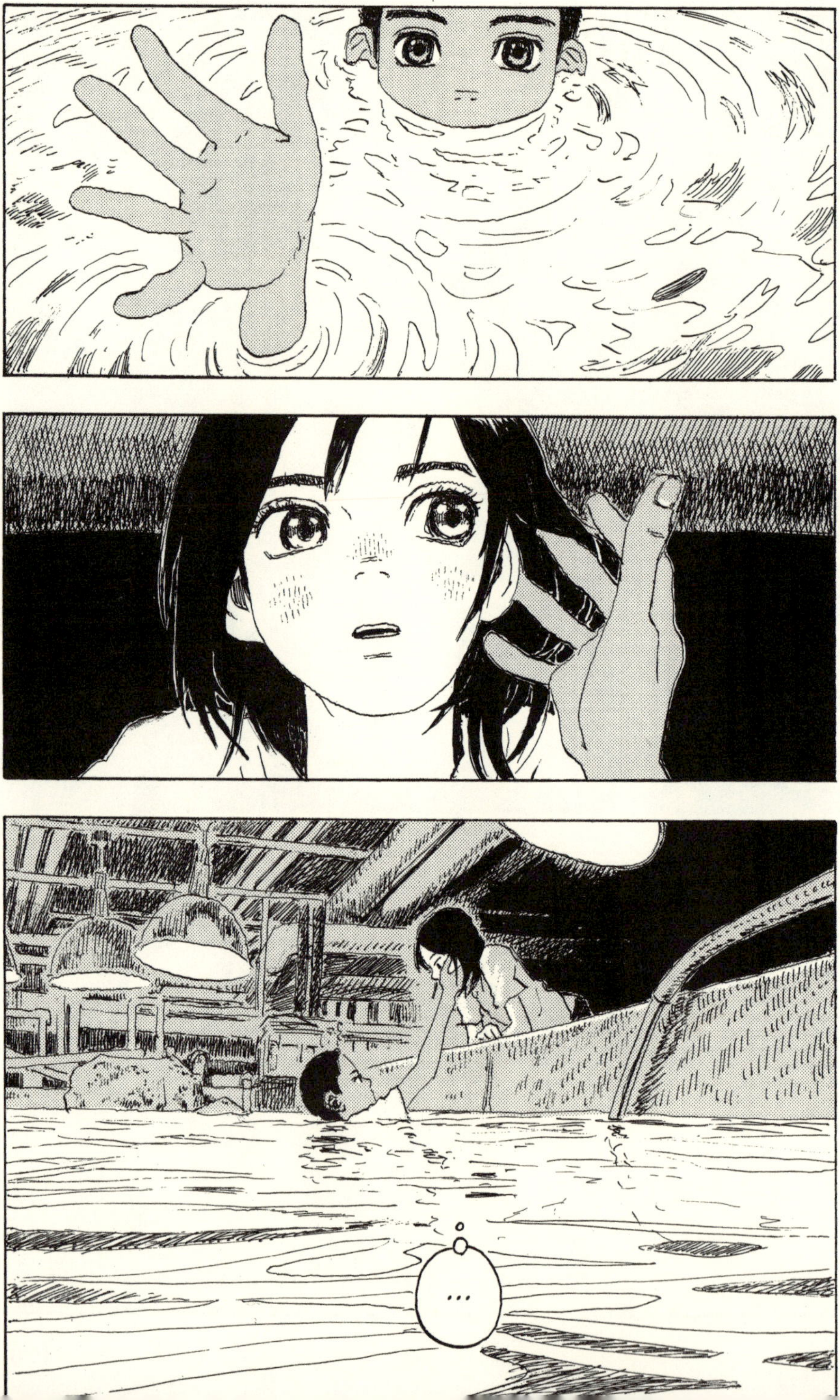
...

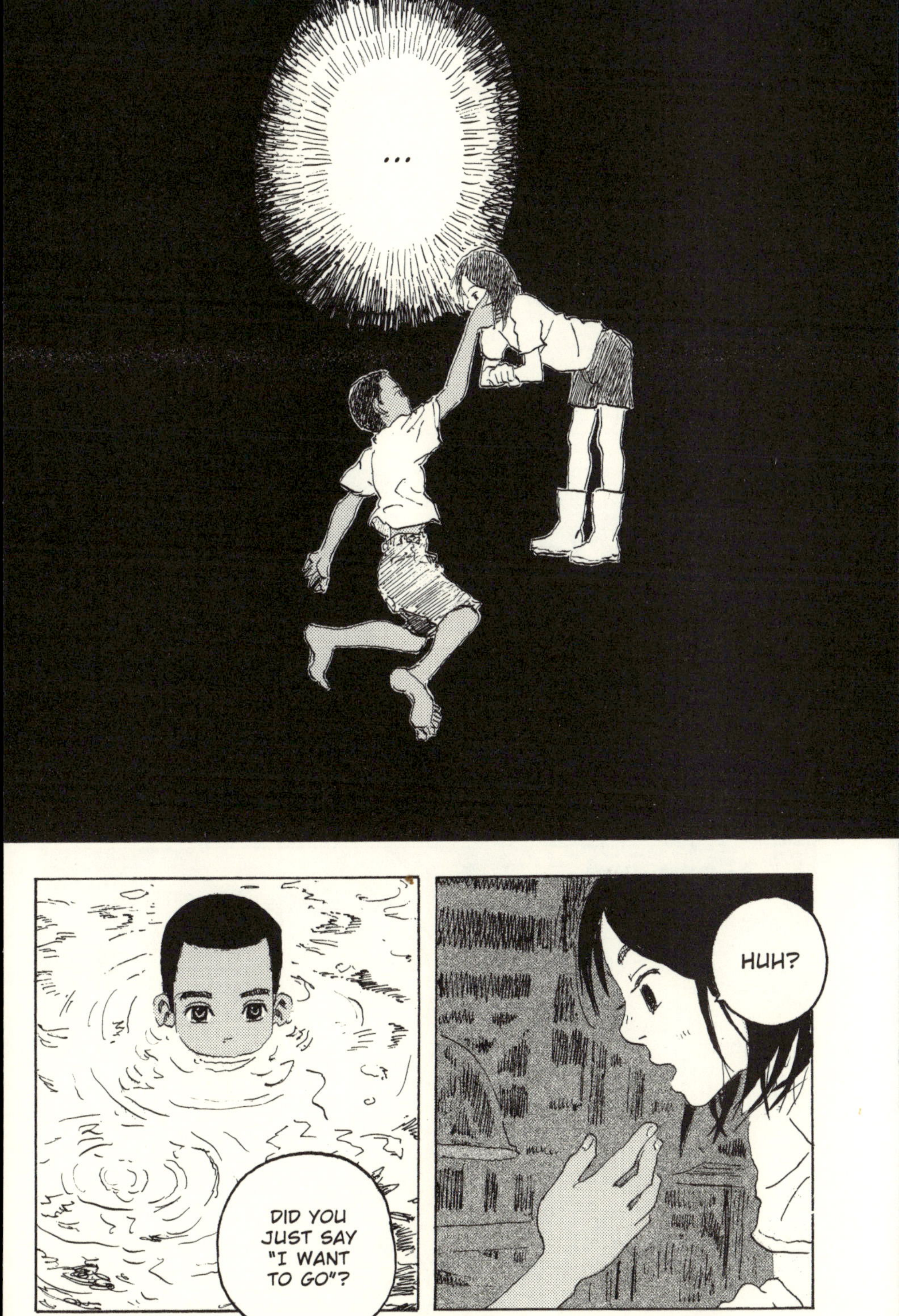
...
HUH?
DID YOU JUST SAY "I WANT TO GO"?

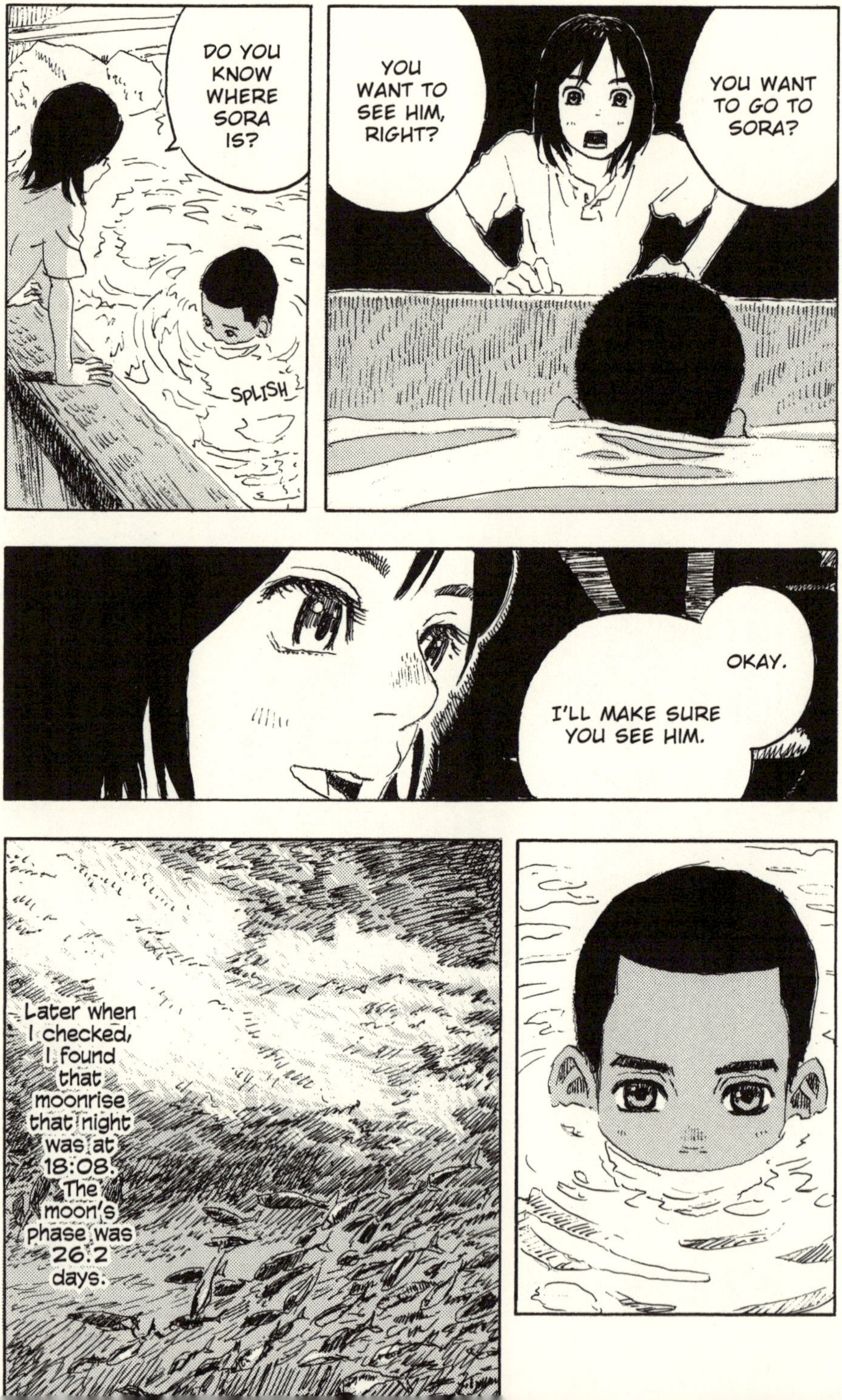
YOU WANT TO GO TO SORA?
YOU WANT TO SEE HIM, RIGHT?
DO YOU KNOW WHERE SORA IS?
SPLISH
OKAY.
I'LL MAKE SURE YOU SEE HIM.
Later when I checked, I found that moonrise that night was at 18:08. The moon's phase was 26.2 days.

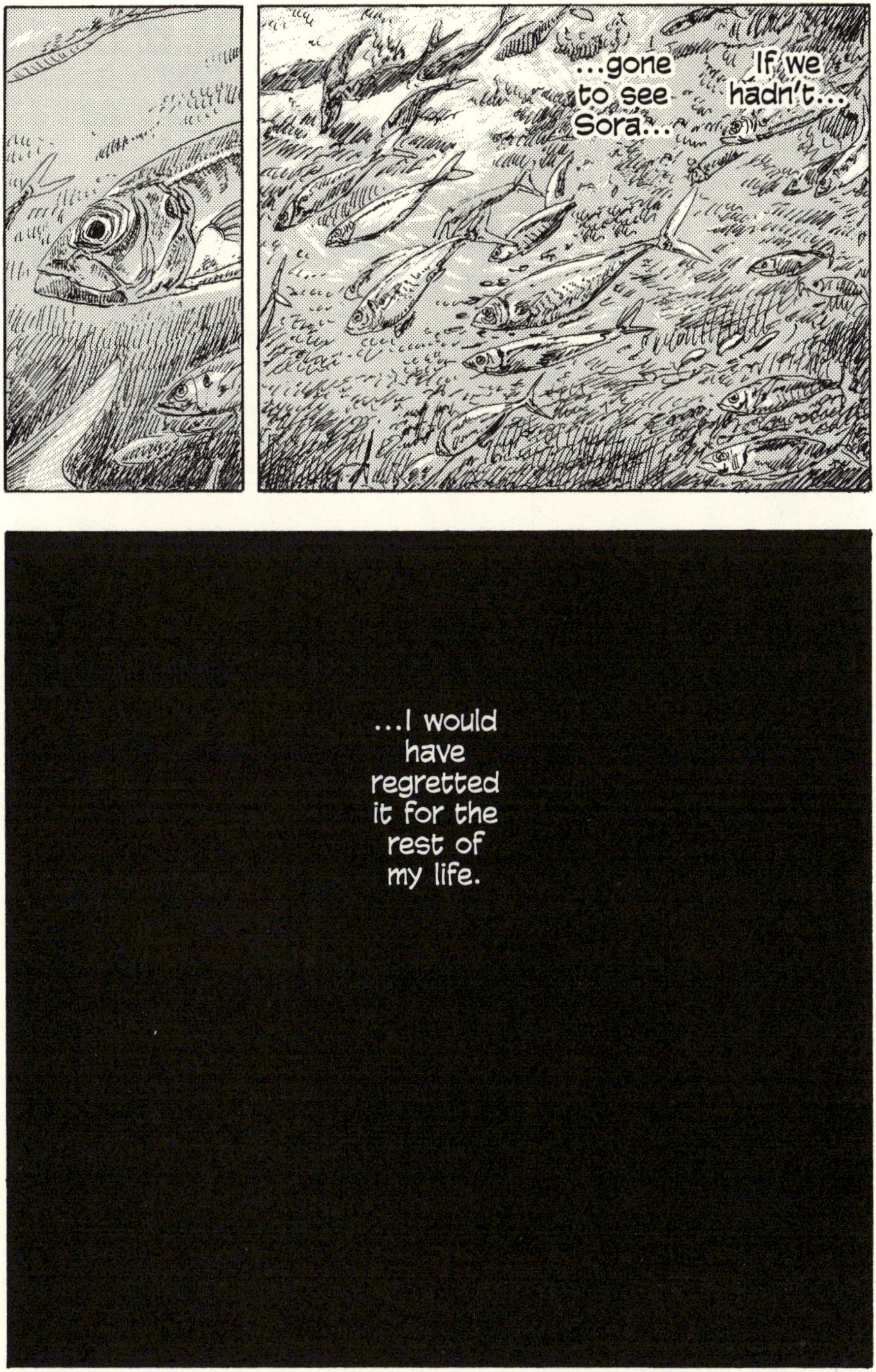
If we hadn't...
...gone to see Sora...
...I would have regretted it for the rest of my life.

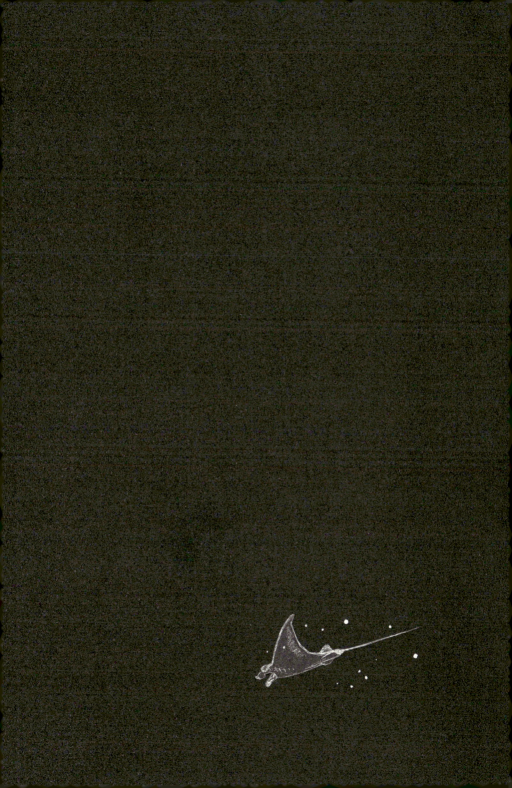

Chapter 14: Rakshasa

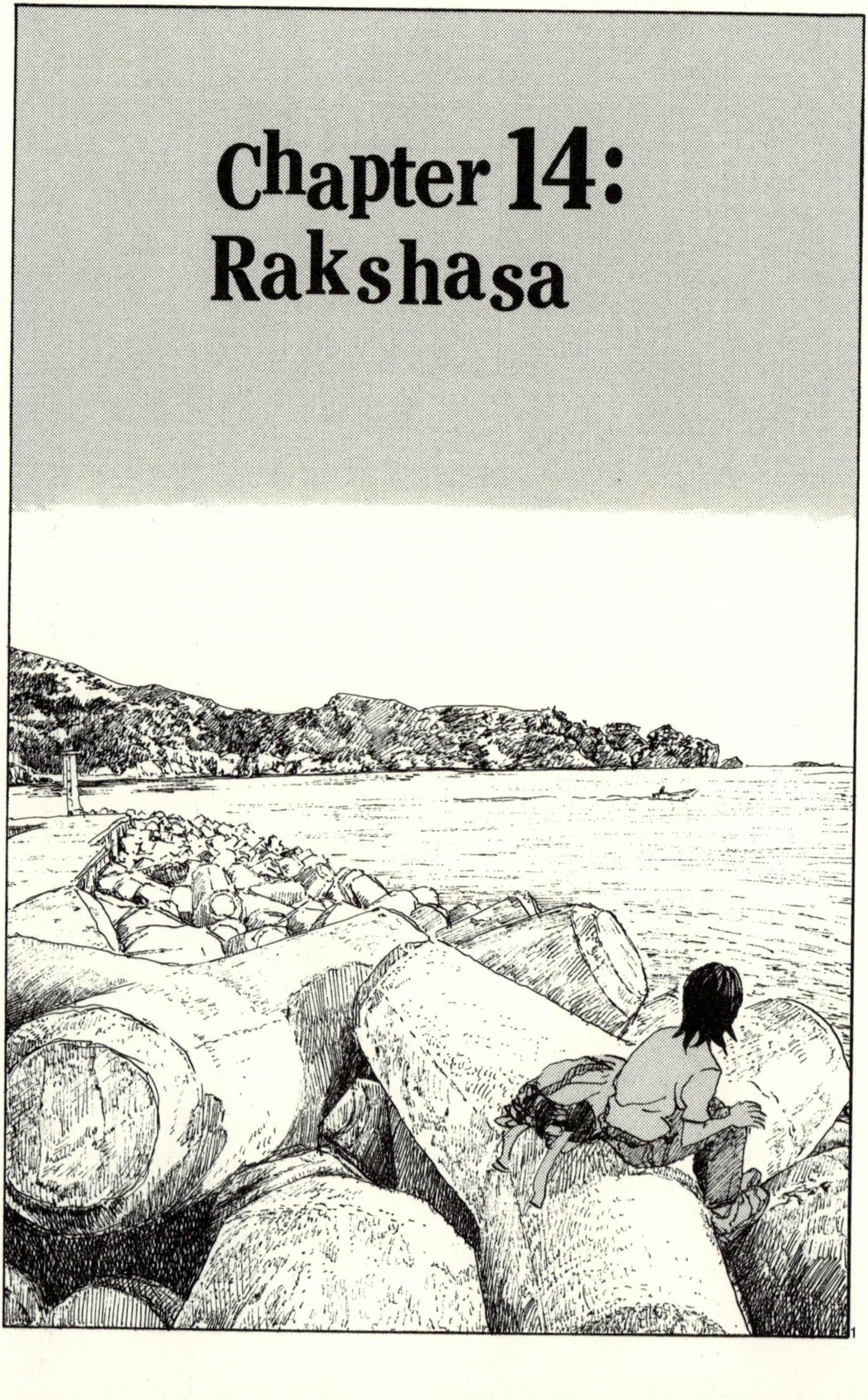

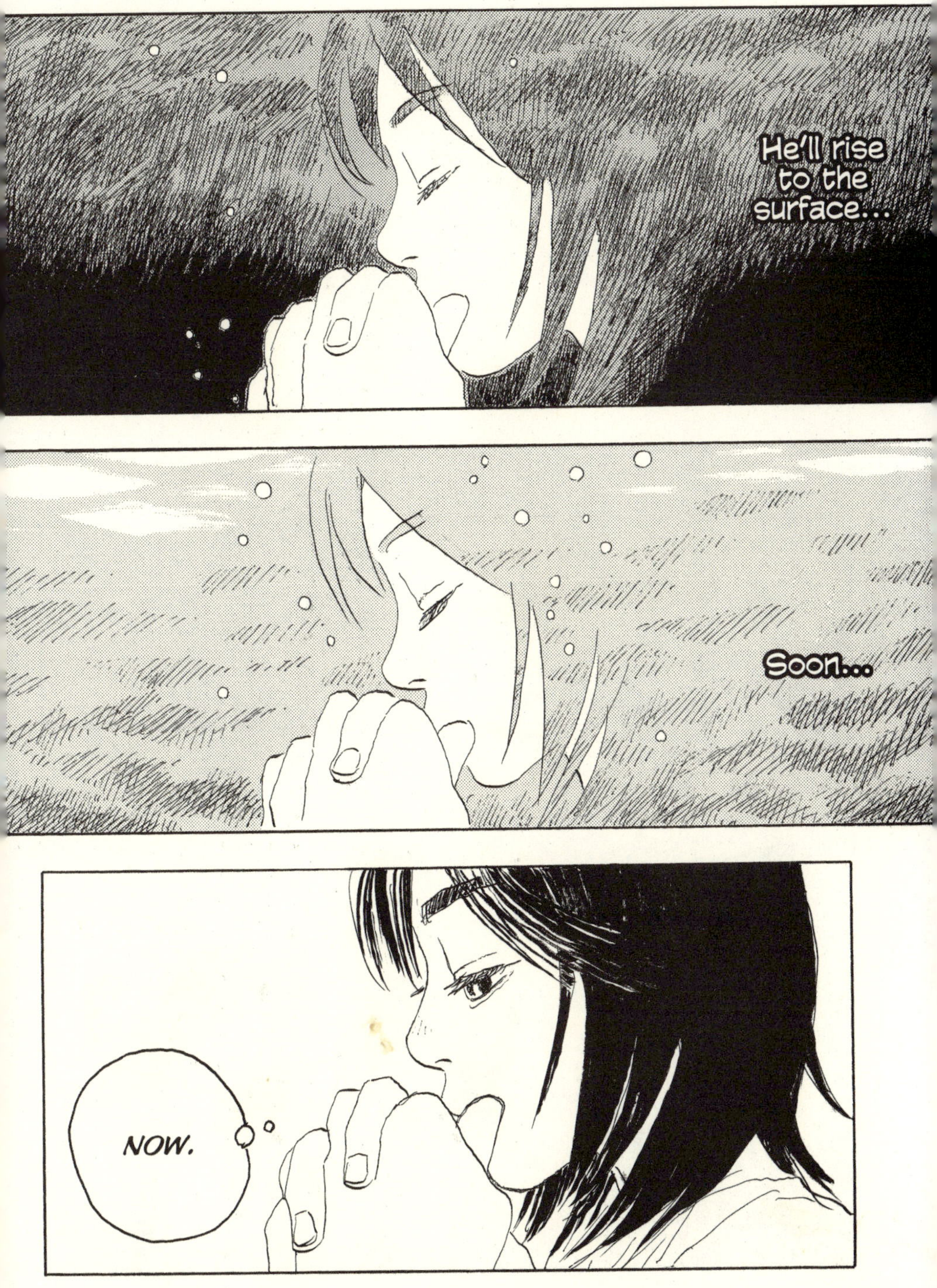
He'll rise to the surface...
Soon...
NOW.

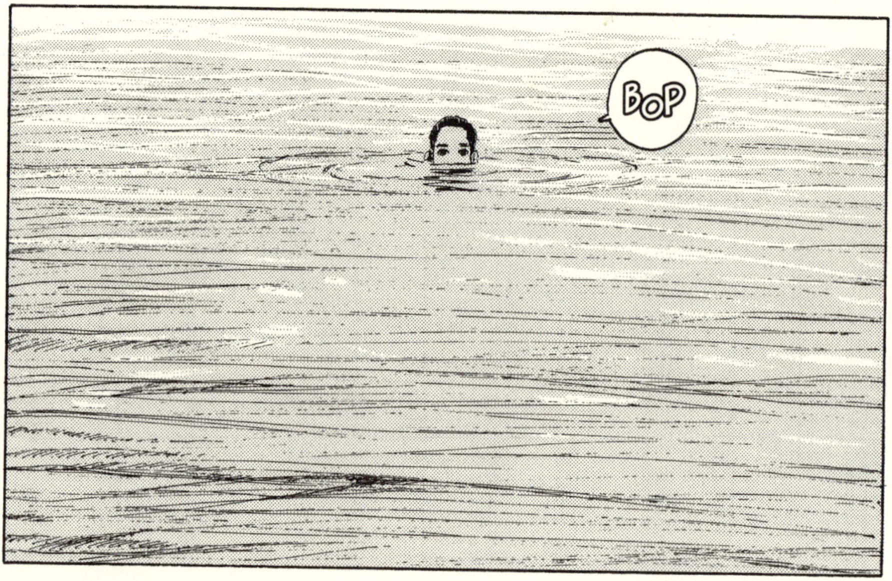
BOP

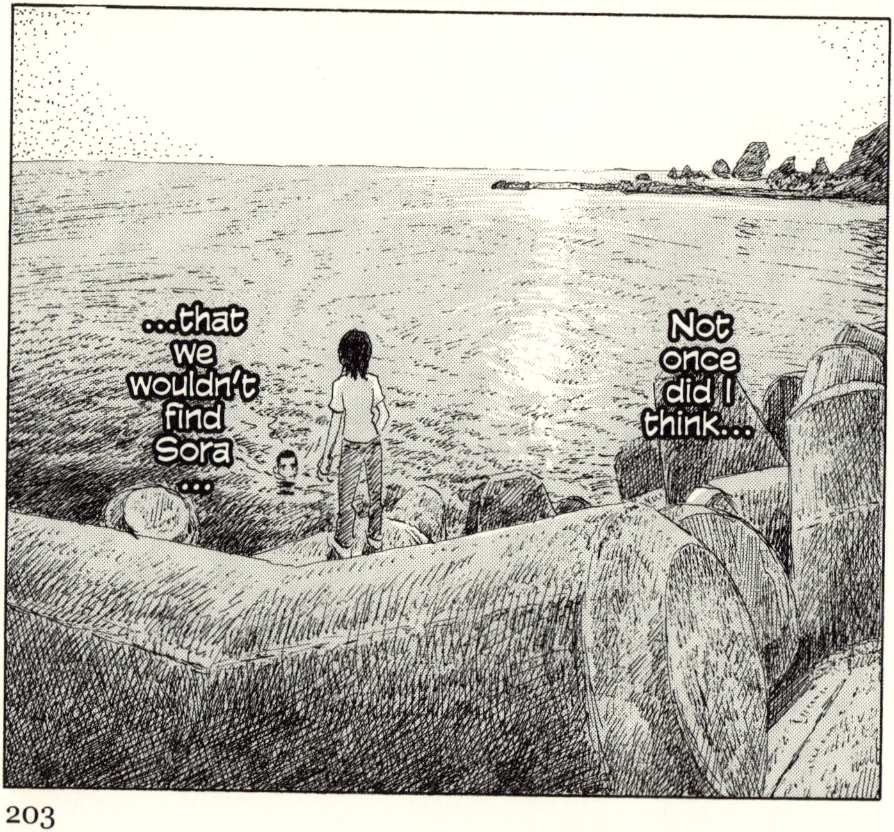
Not once did I think...
...that we wouldn't find Sora...

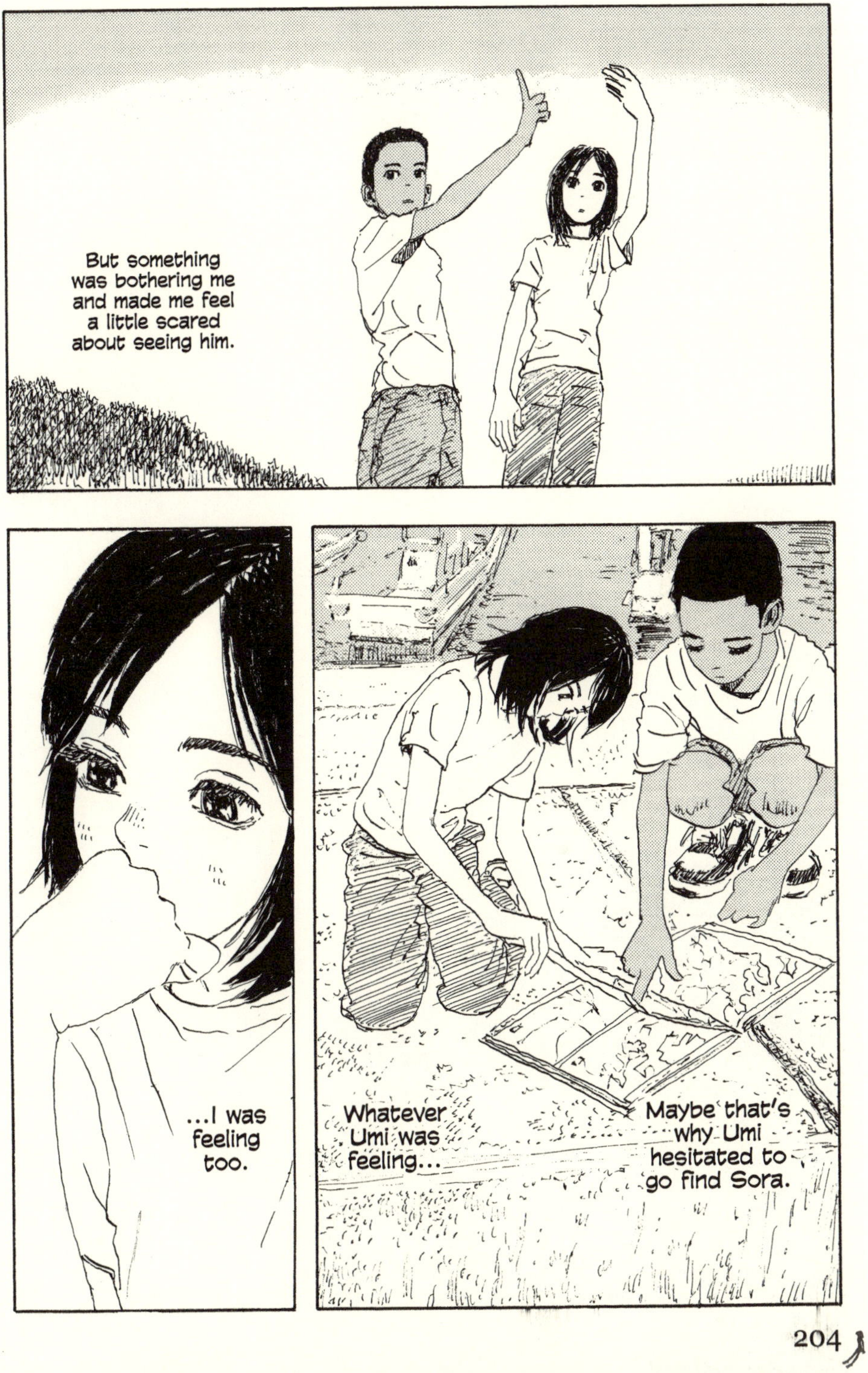
But something was bothering me and made me feel a little scared about seeing him.
Maybe that's why Umi hesitated to go find Sora.
Whatever Umi was feeling...
...I was feeling too.

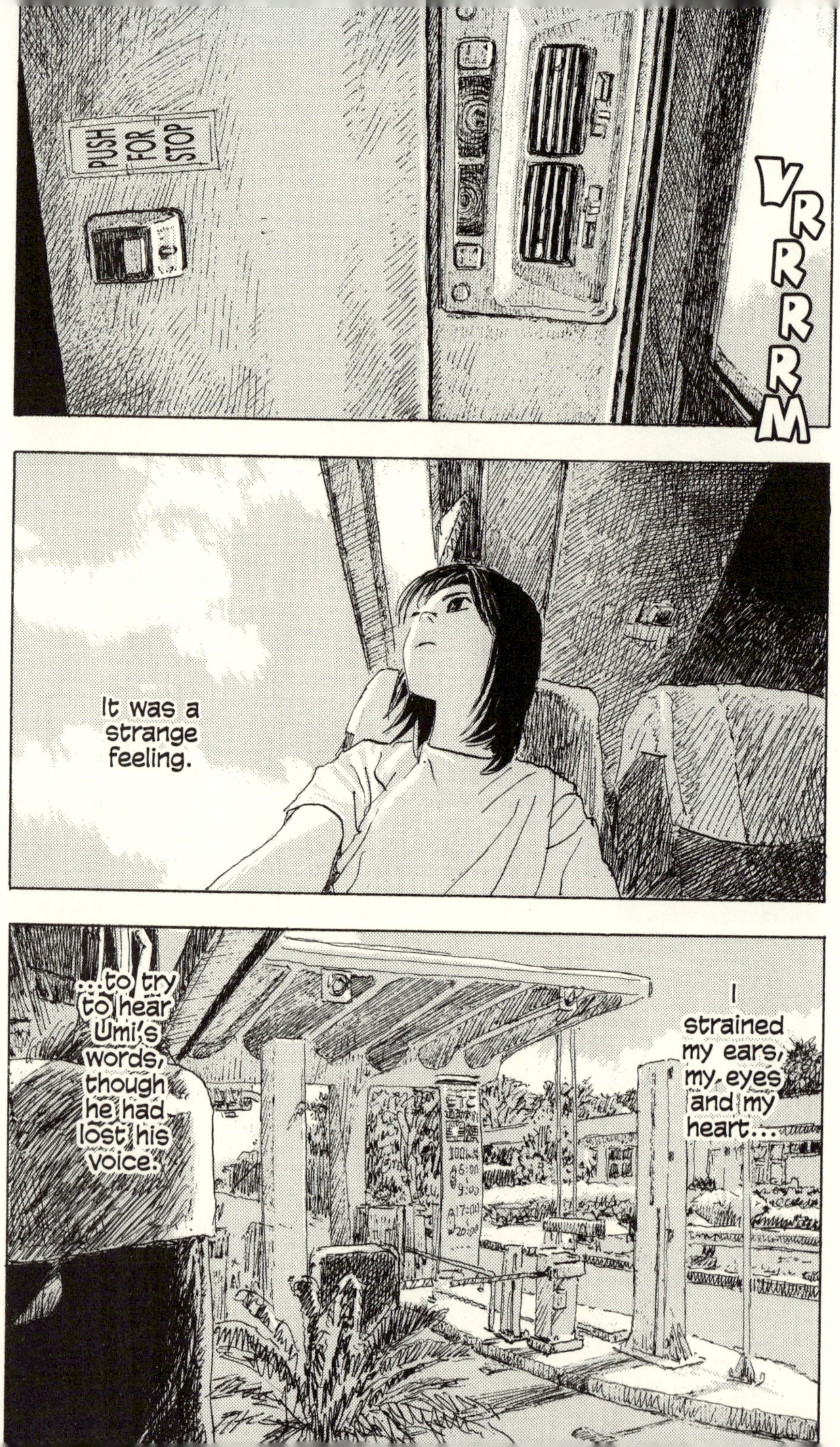
PUSH FOR STOP
VRRRRM
It was a strange feeling.
I strained my ears, my eyes and my heart...
...to try to hear Umi's words, though he had lost his voice.

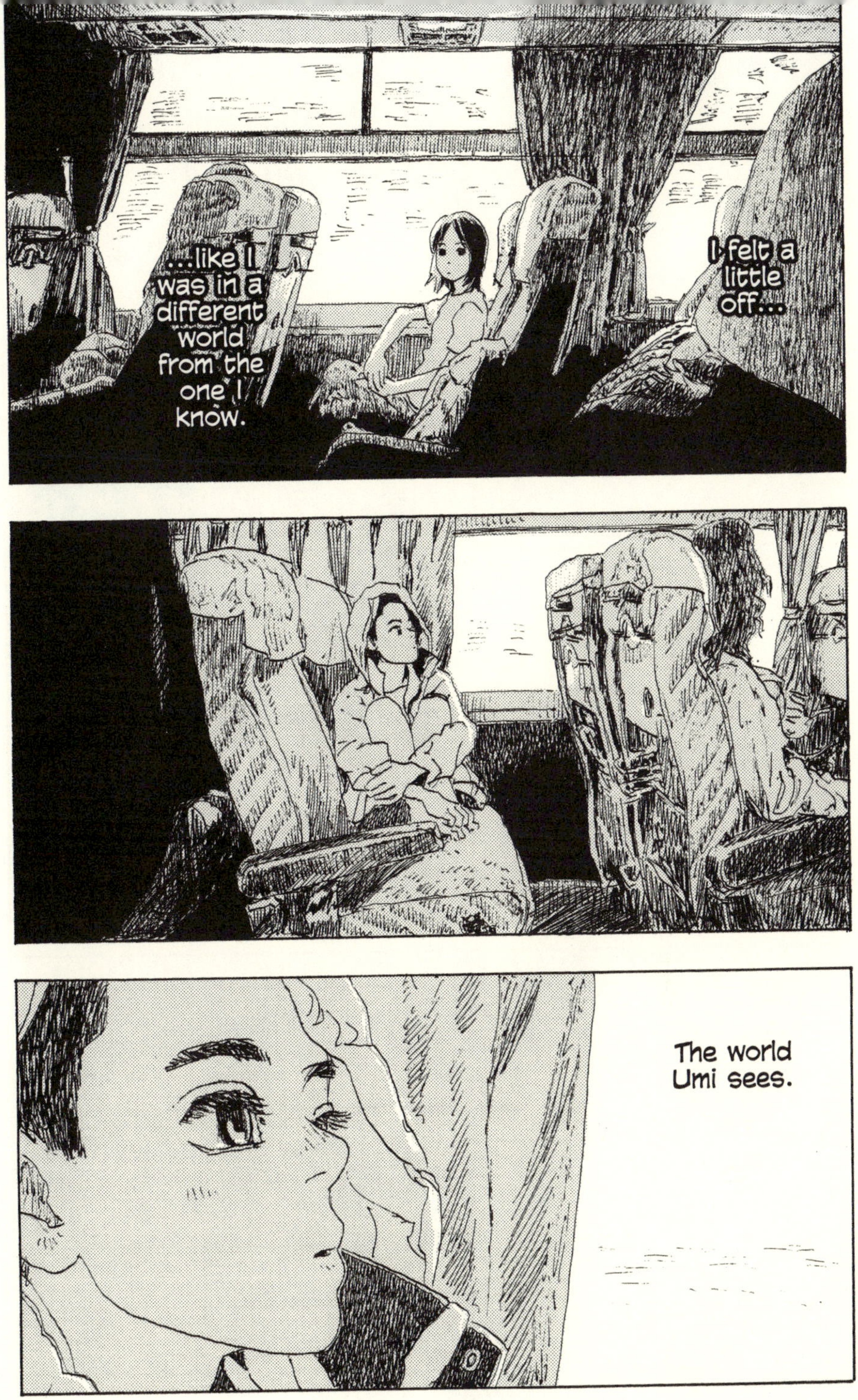
I felt a little off...
...like I was in a different world from the one I know.
The world Umi sees.

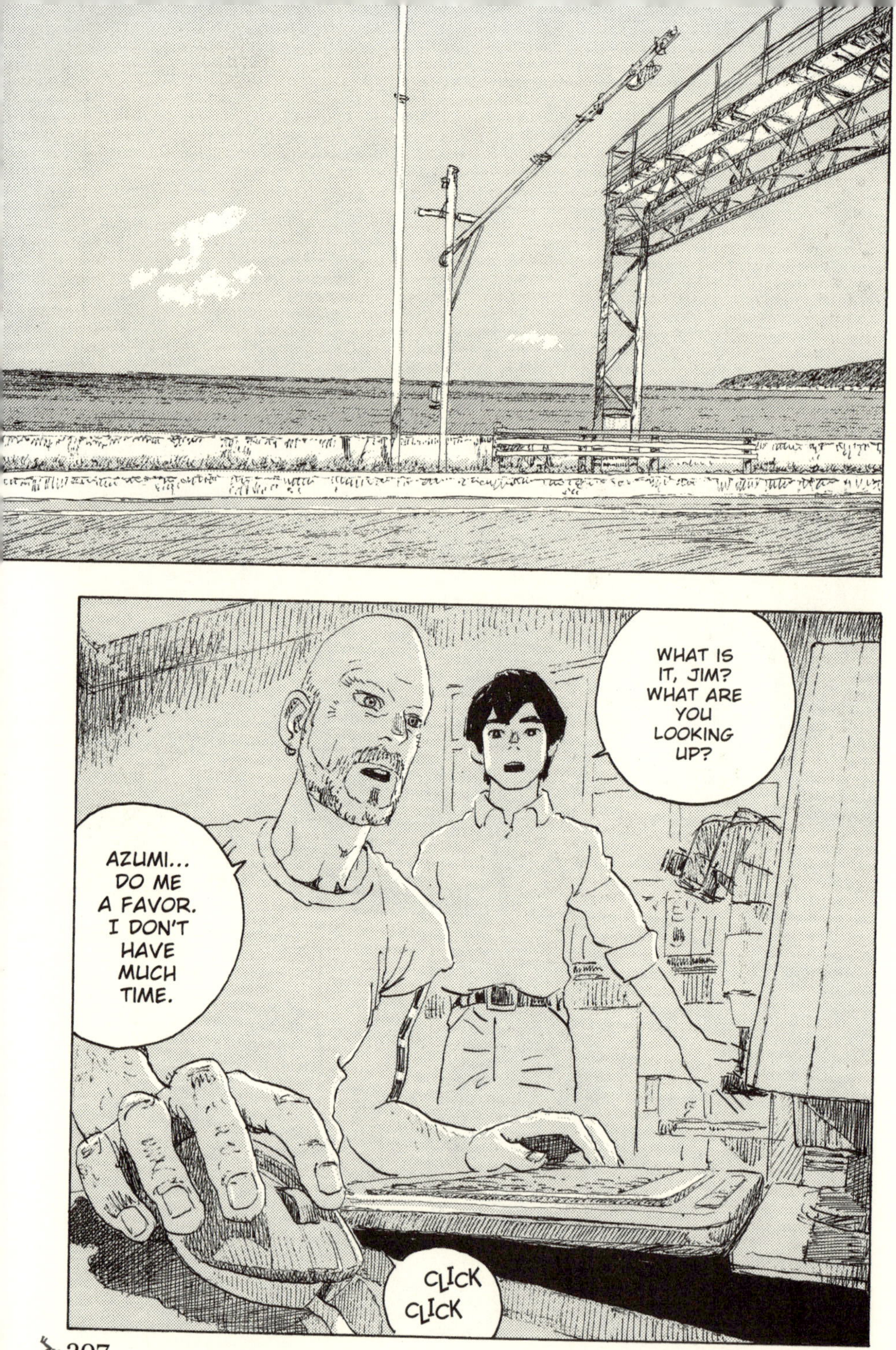
WHAT IS IT, JIM? WHAT ARE YOU LOOKING UP?
AZUMI... DO ME A FAVOR. I DON'T HAVE MUCH TIME.
CLICK CLICK

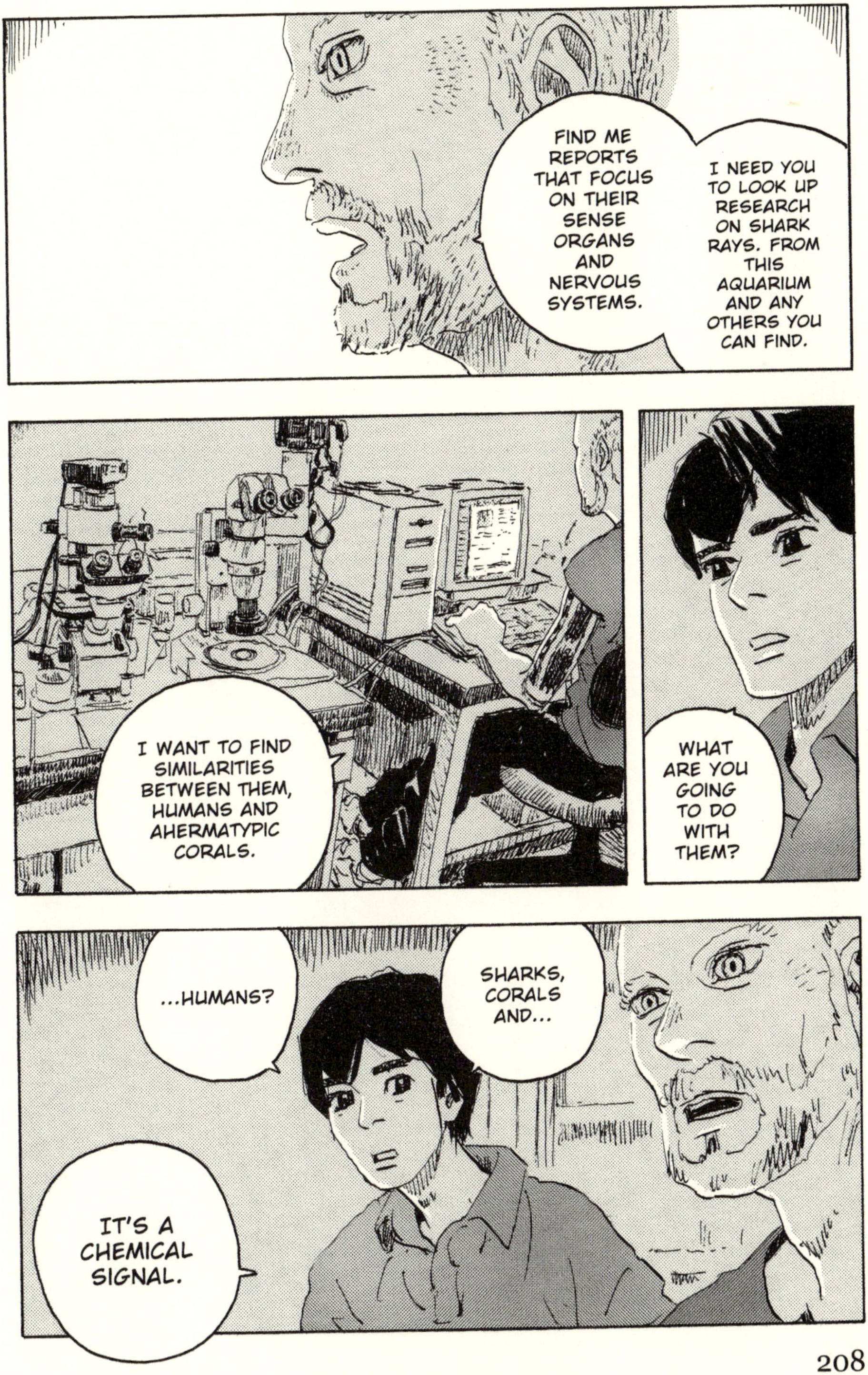
I NEED YOU TO LOOK UP RESEARCH ON SHARK RAYS. FROM THIS AQUARIUM AND ANY OTHERS YOU CAN FIND.
FIND ME REPORTS THAT FOCUS ON THEIR SENSE ORGANS AND NERVOUS SYSTEMS.
WHAT ARE YOU GOING TO DO WITH THEM?
I WANT TO FIND SIMILARITIES BETWEEN THEM, HUMANS AND AHERMATYPIC CORALS.
SHARKS, CORALS AND...
...HUMANS?
IT'S A CHEMICAL SIGNAL.

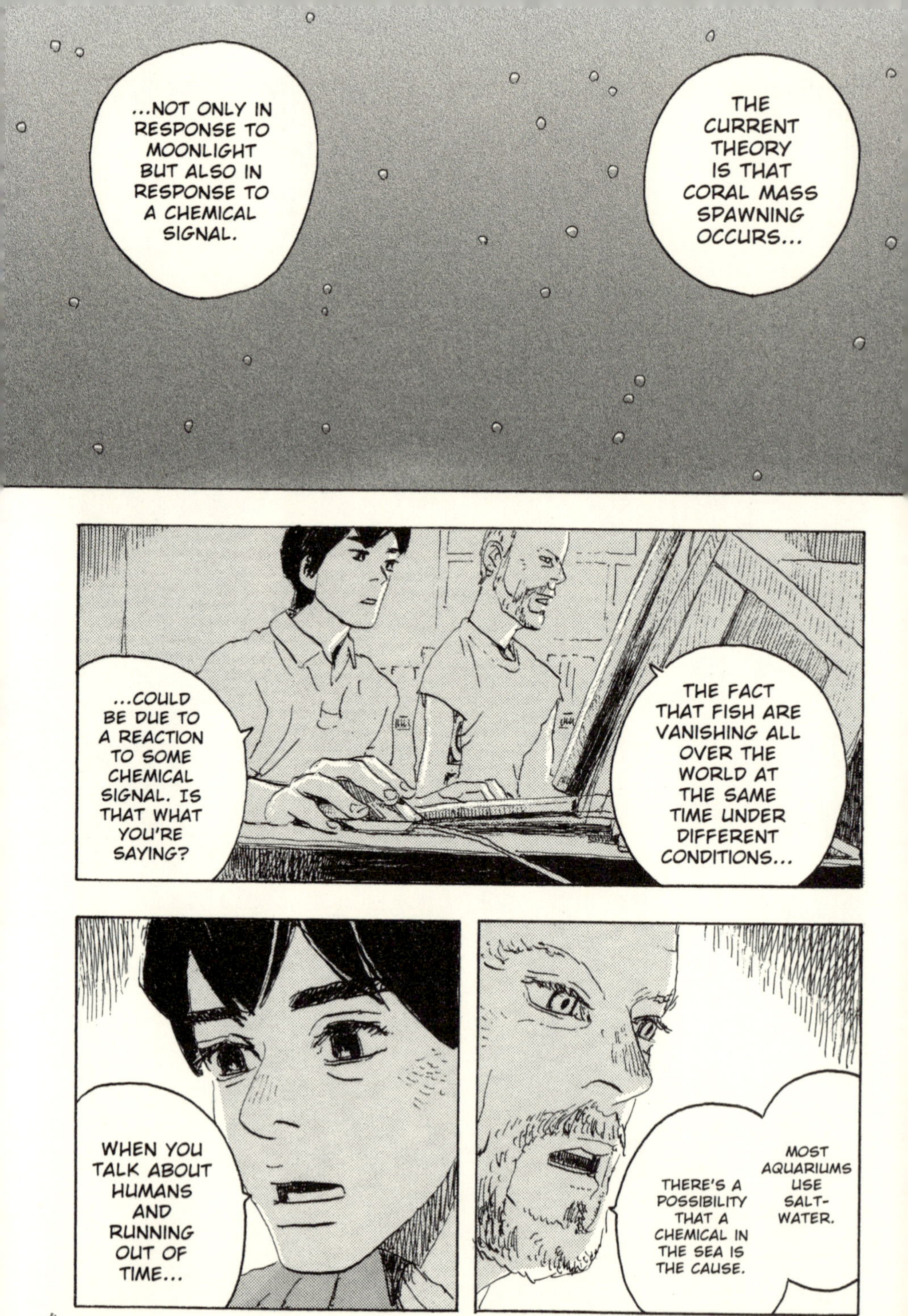
THE CURRENT THEORY IS THAT CORAL MASS SPAWNING OCCURS...
...NOT ONLY IN RESPONSE TO MOONLIGHT BUT ALSO IN RESPONSE TO A CHEMICAL SIGNAL.
THE FACT THAT FISH ARE VANISHING ALL OVER THE WORLD AT THE SAME TIME UNDER DIFFERENT CONDITIONS...
...COULD BE DUE TO A REACTION TO SOME CHEMICAL SIGNAL. IS THAT WHAT YOU'RE SAYING?
MOST AQUARIUMS USE SALT-WATER.
THERE'S A POSSIBILITY THAT A CHEMICAL IN THE SEA IS THE CAUSE.
WHEN YOU TALK ABOUT HUMANS AND RUNNING OUT OF TIME...

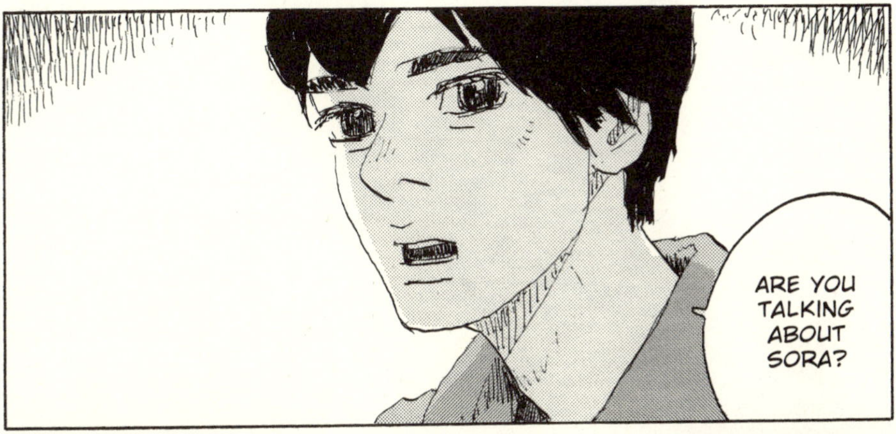
ARE YOU TALKING ABOUT SORA?
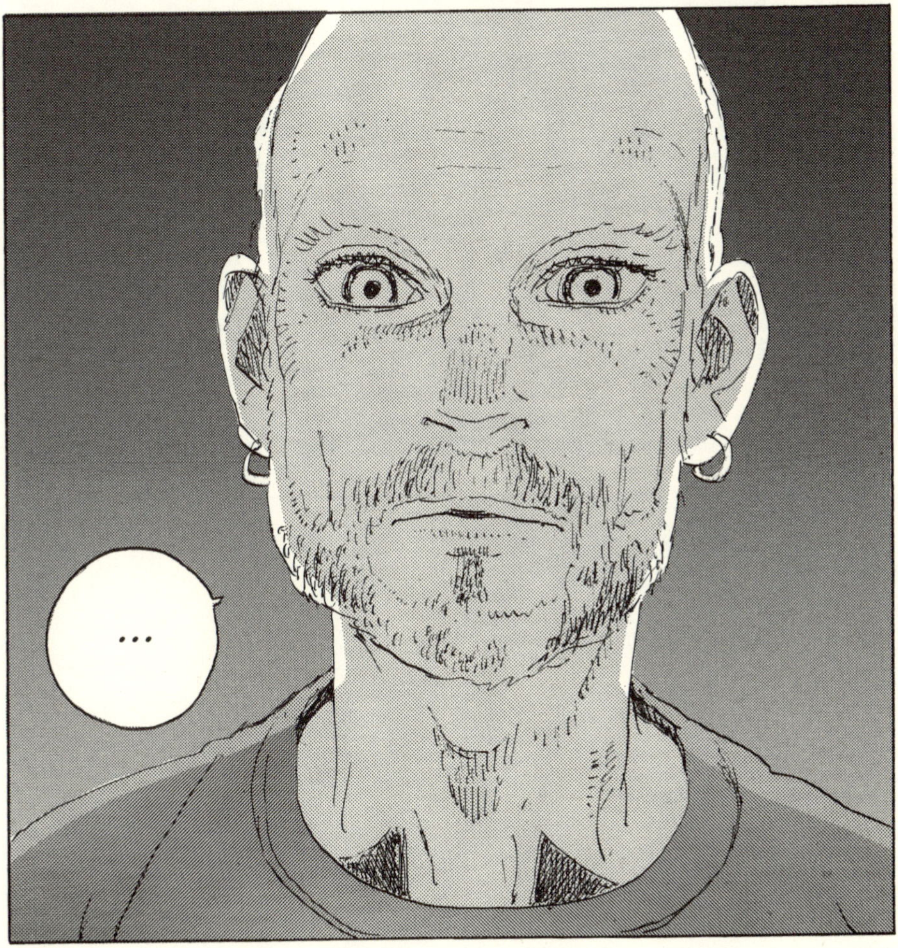
...

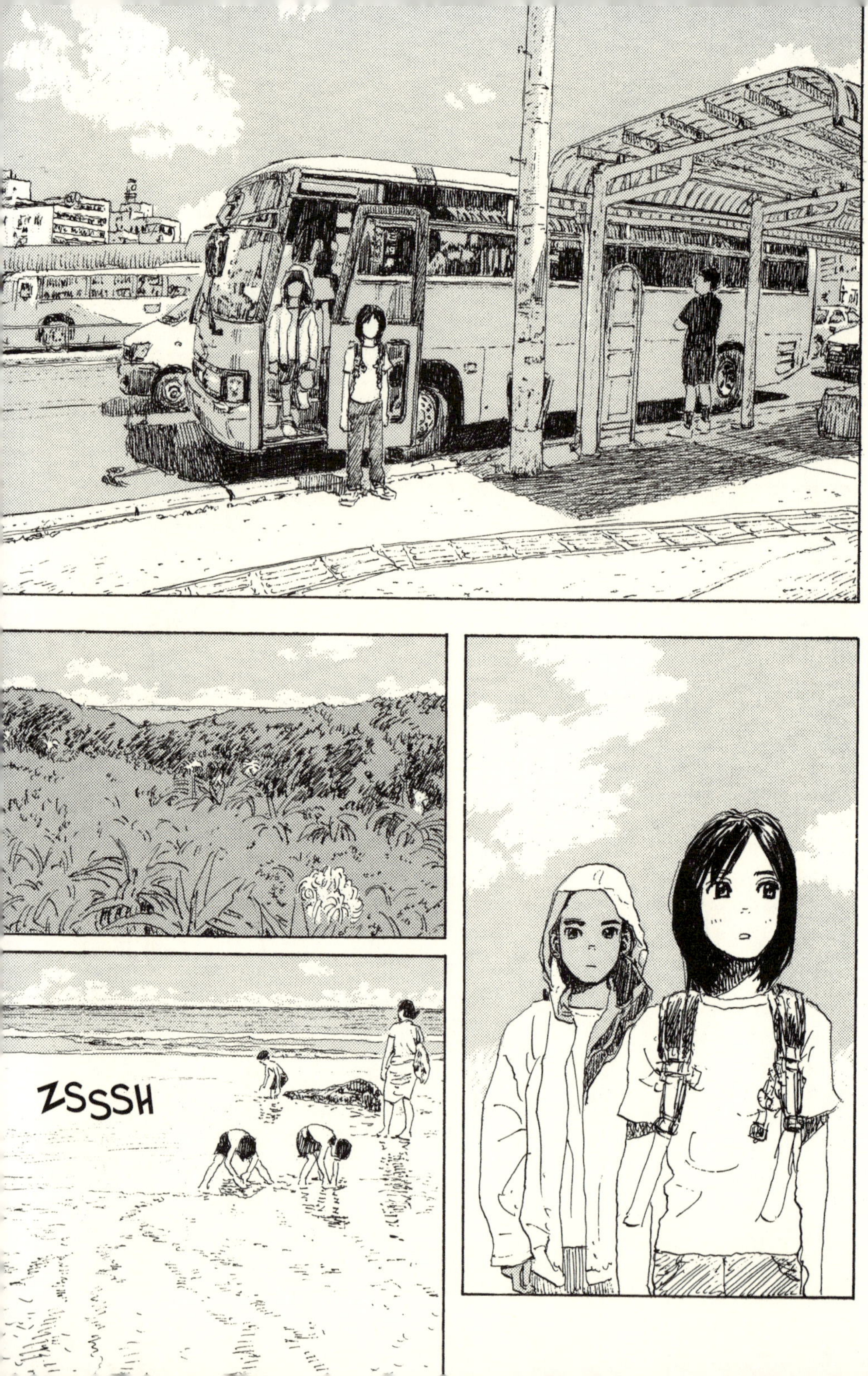
ZSSSH

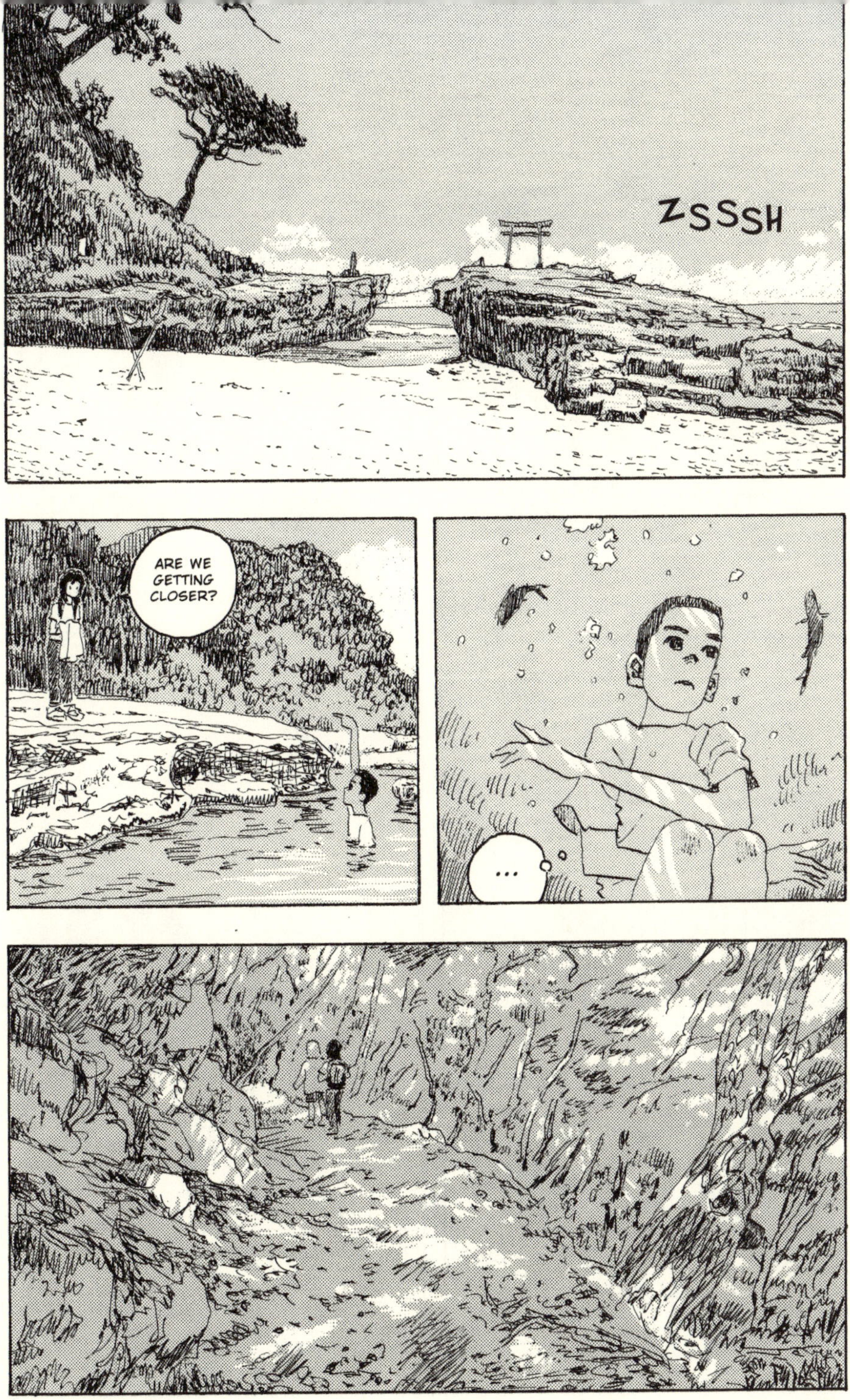
ZSSSH
...
ARE WE GETTING CLOSER?

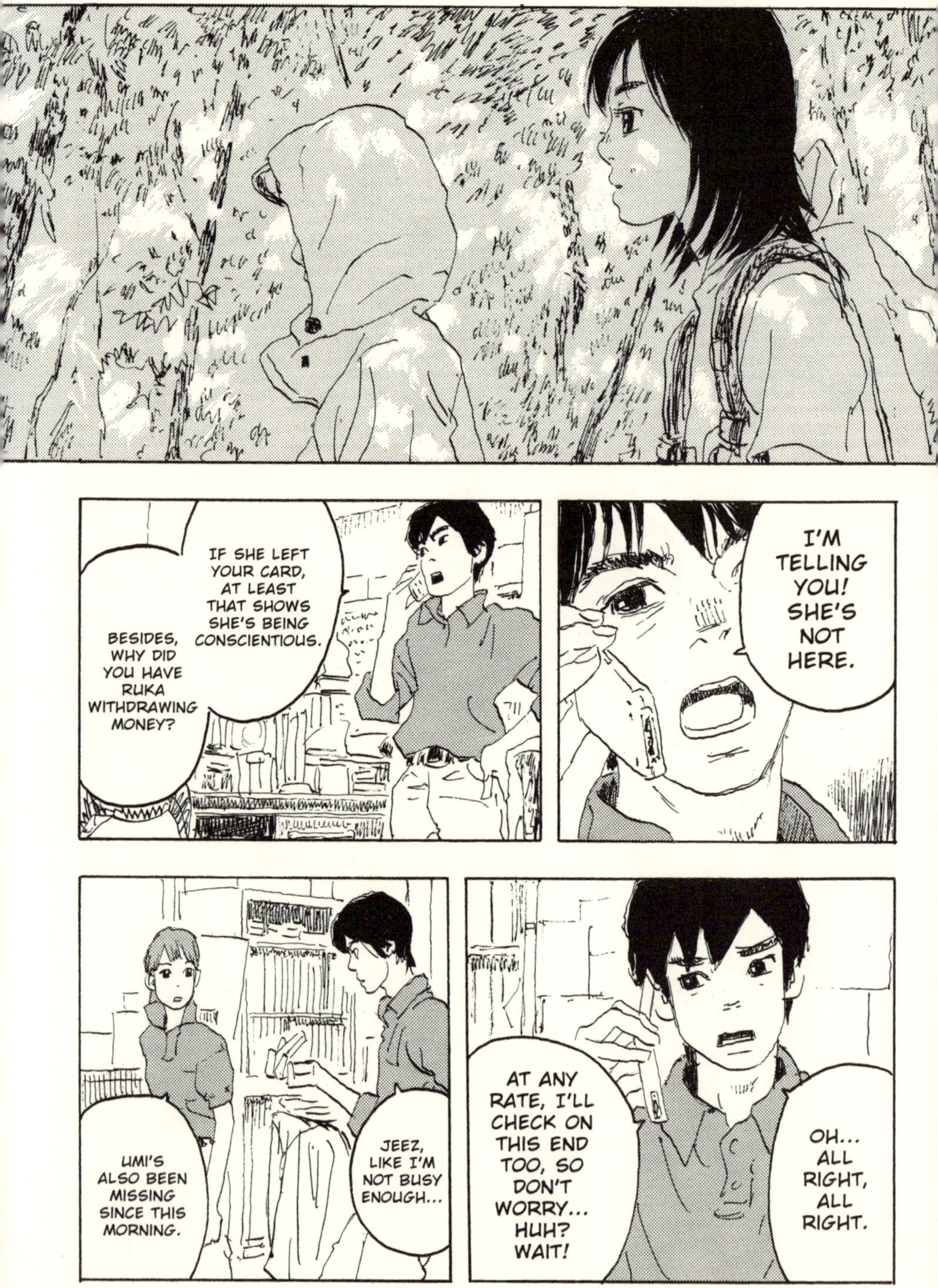
I'M TELLING YOU! SHE'S NOT HERE.
IF SHE LEFT YOUR CARD, AT LEAST THAT SHOWS SHE'S BEING CONSCIENTIOUS.
BESIDES, WHY DID YOU HAVE RUKA WITHDRAWING MONEY?
OH... ALL RIGHT, ALL RIGHT.
AT ANY RATE, I'LL CHECK ON THIS END TOO, SO DON'T WORRY... HUH? WAIT!
JEEZ, LIKE I'M NOT BUSY ENOUGH...
UMI'S ALSO BEEN MISSING SINCE THIS MORNING.

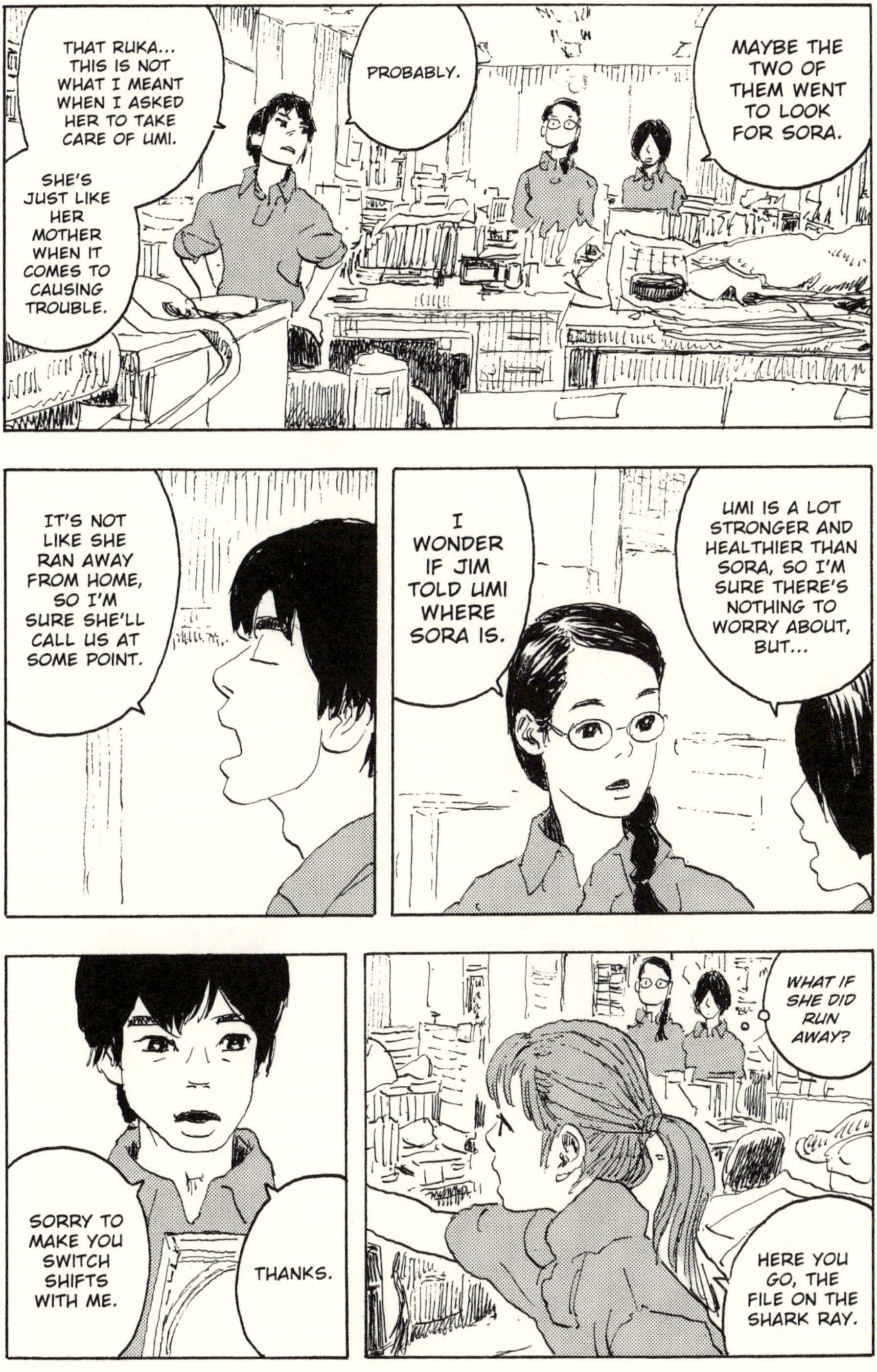
MAYBE THE TWO OF THEM WENT TO LOOK FOR SORA.
PROBABLY.
THAT RUKA... THIS IS NOT WHAT I MEANT WHEN I ASKED HER TO TAKE CARE OF UMI.
SHE'S JUST LIKE HER MOTHER WHEN IT COMES TO CAUSING TROUBLE.
UMI IS A LOT STRONGER AND HEALTHIER THAN SORA, SO I'M SURE THERE'S NOTHING TO WORRY ABOUT, BUT...
I WONDER IF JIM TOLD UMI WHERE SORA IS.
IT'S NOT LIKE SHE RAN AWAY FROM HOME, SO I'M SURE SHE'LL CALL US AT SOME POINT.
WHAT IF SHE DID RUN AWAY?
HERE YOU GO, THE FILE ON THE SHARK RAY.
THANKS.
SORRY TO MAKE YOU SWITCH SHIFTS WITH ME.

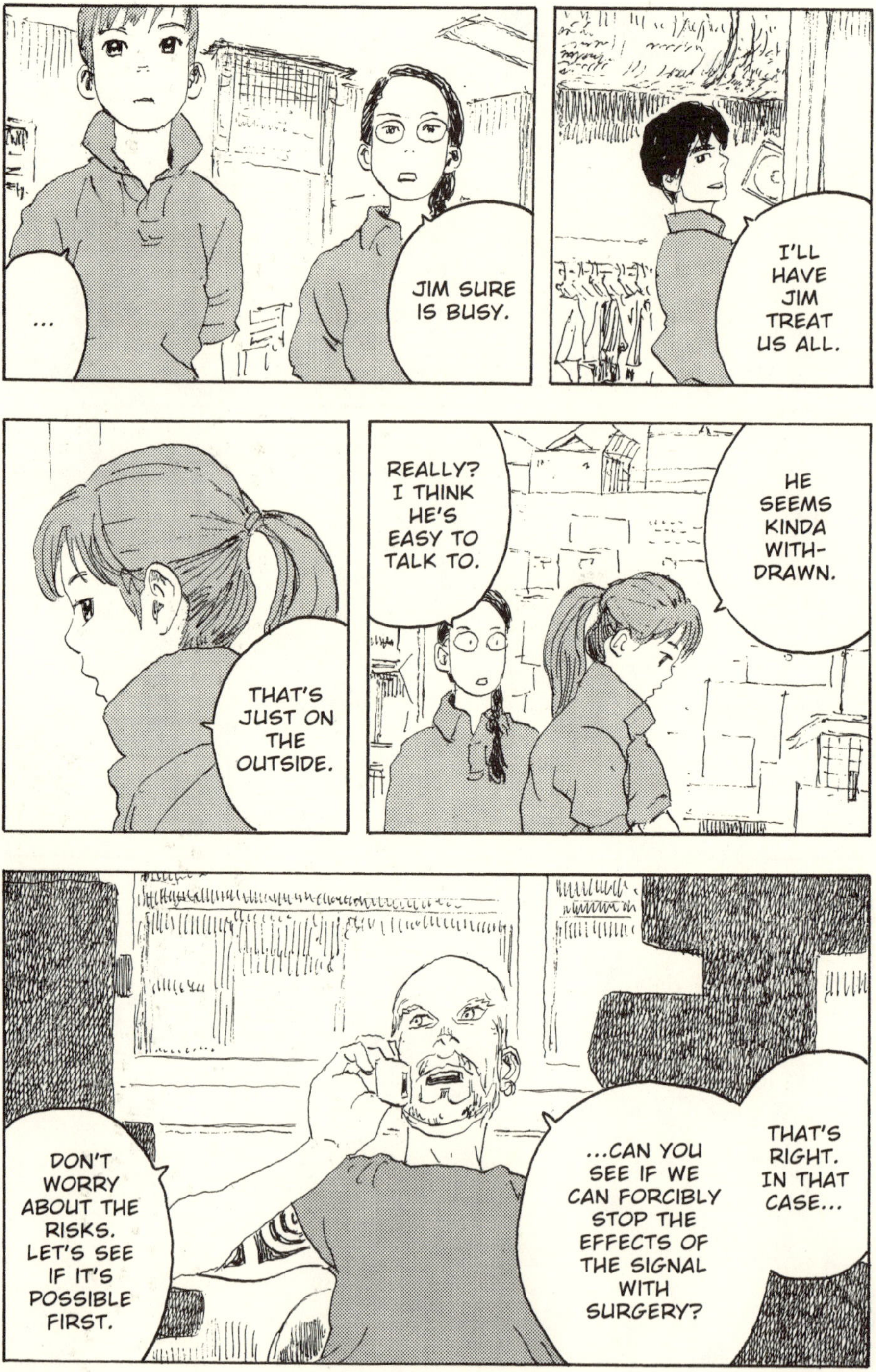
I'LL HAVE JIM TREAT US ALL.
JIM SURE IS BUSY.
...
HE SEEMS KINDA WITH-DRAWN.
REALLY? I THINK HE'S EASY TO TALK TO.
THAT'S JUST ON THE OUTSIDE.
THAT'S RIGHT. IN THAT CASE...
...CAN YOU SEE IF WE CAN FORCIBLY STOP THE EFFECTS OF THE SIGNAL WITH SURGERY?
DON'T WORRY ABOUT THE RISKS. LET'S SEE IF IT'S POSSIBLE FIRST.

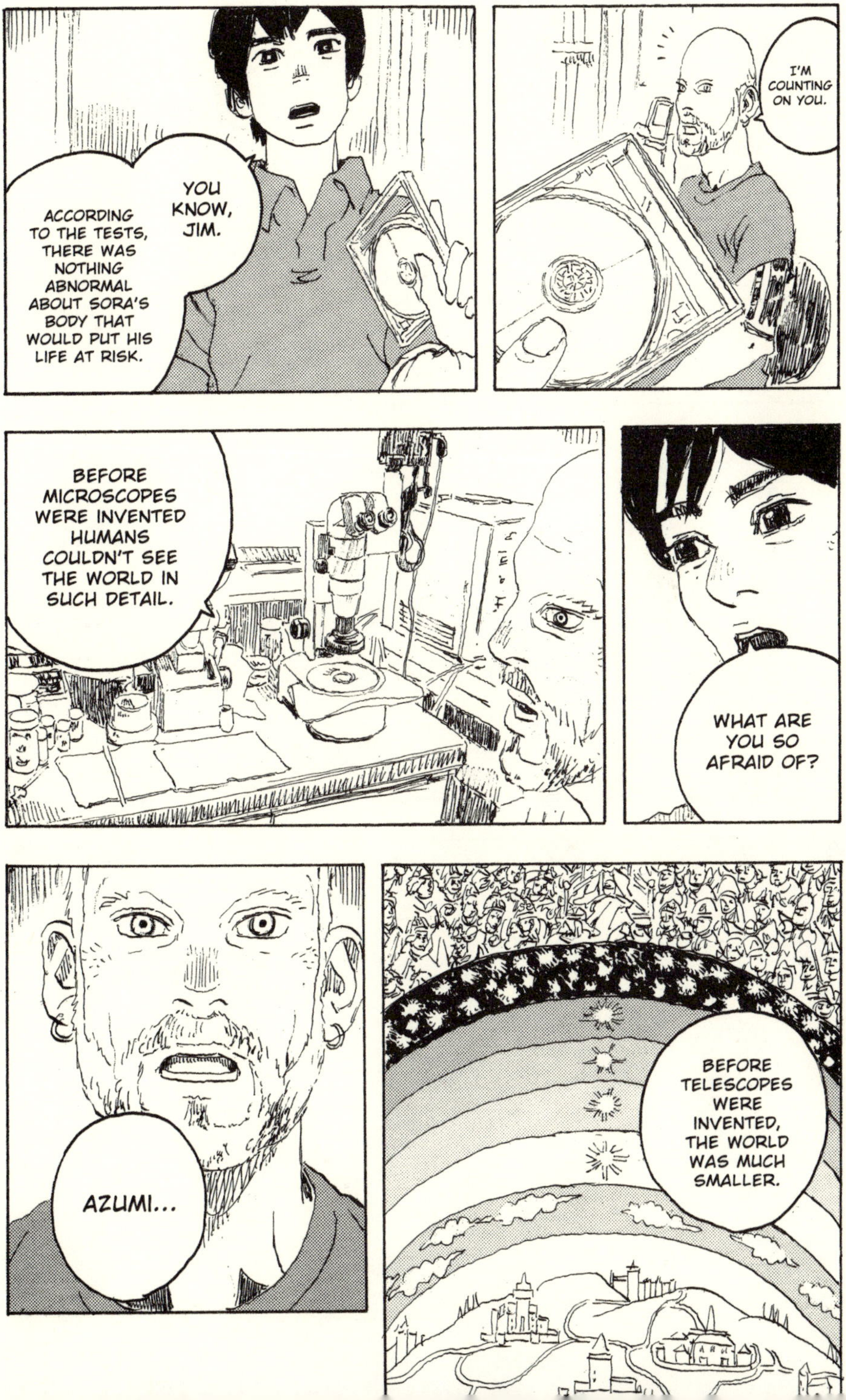
I'M COUNTING ON YOU.
YOU KNOW, JIM.
ACCORDING TO THE TESTS, THERE WAS NOTHING ABNORMAL ABOUT SORA'S BODY THAT WOULD PUT HIS LIFE AT RISK.
WHAT ARE YOU SO AFRAID OF?
BEFORE MICROSCOPES WERE INVENTED HUMANS COULDN'T SEE THE WORLD IN SUCH DETAIL.
BEFORE TELESCOPES WERE INVENTED, THE WORLD WAS MUCH SMALLER.
AZUMI...

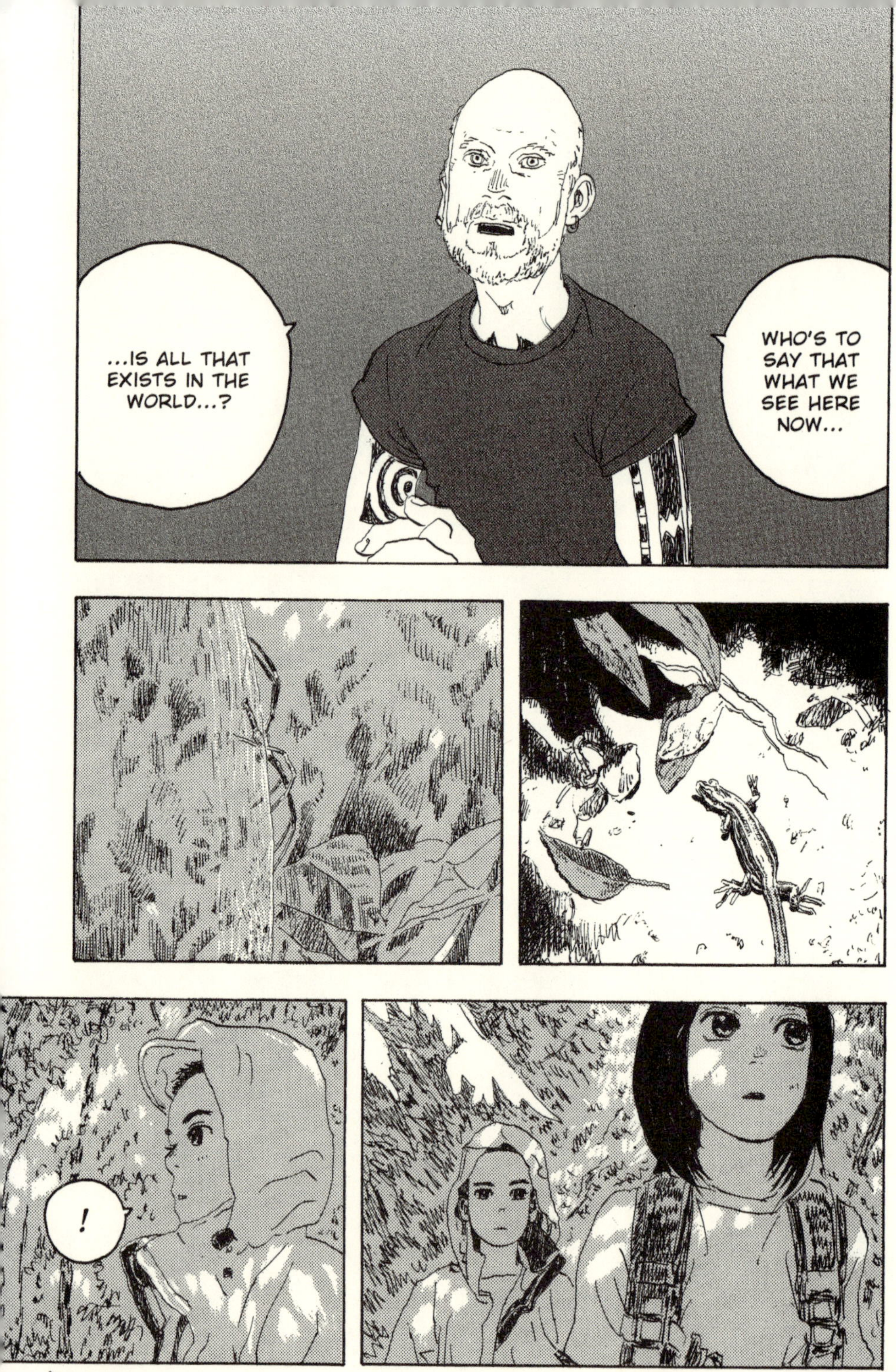
WHO'S TO SAY THAT WHAT WE SEE HERE NOW...
...IS ALL THAT EXISTS IN THE WORLD...?
!

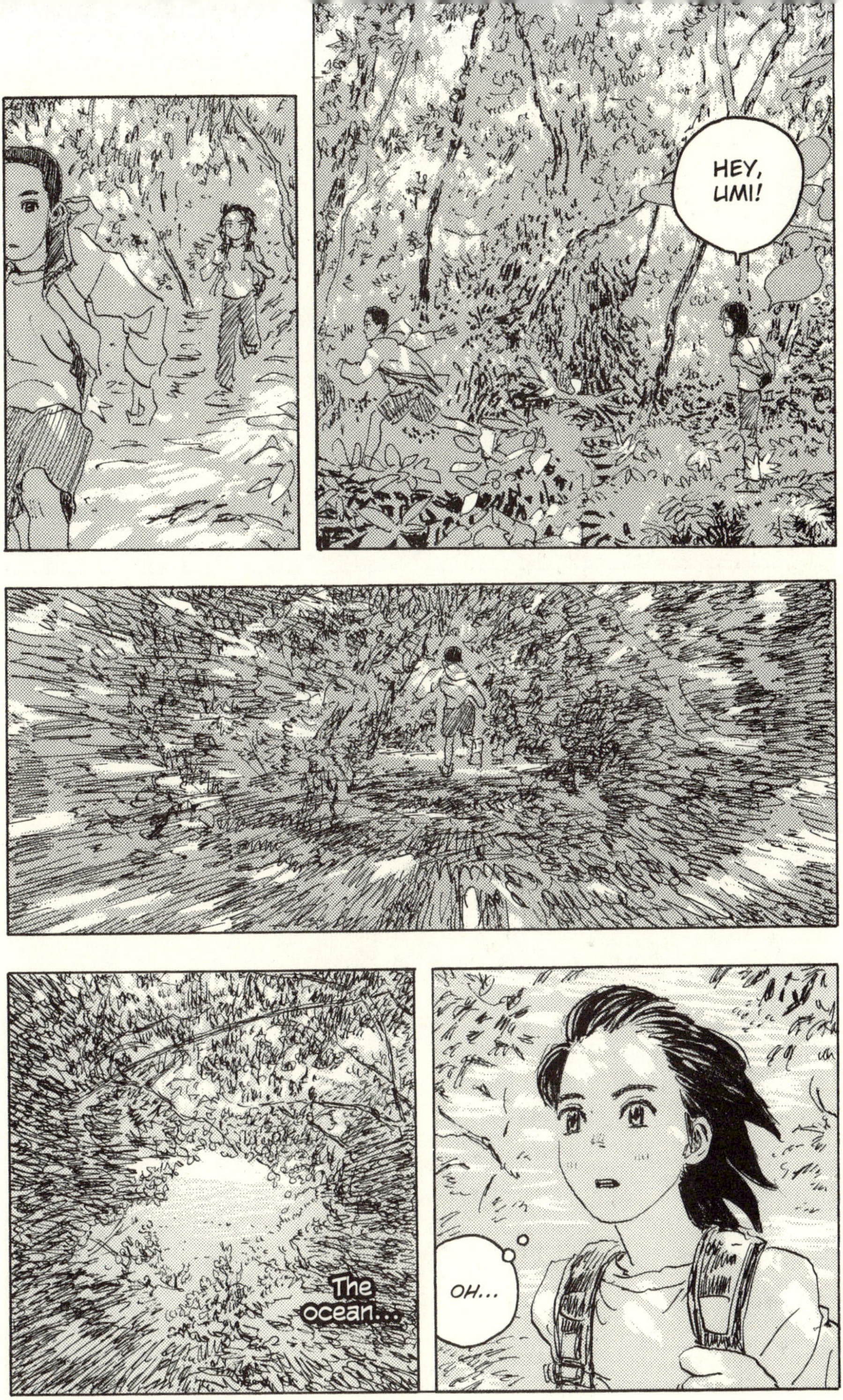
HEY, UMI!
OH...
The ocean...

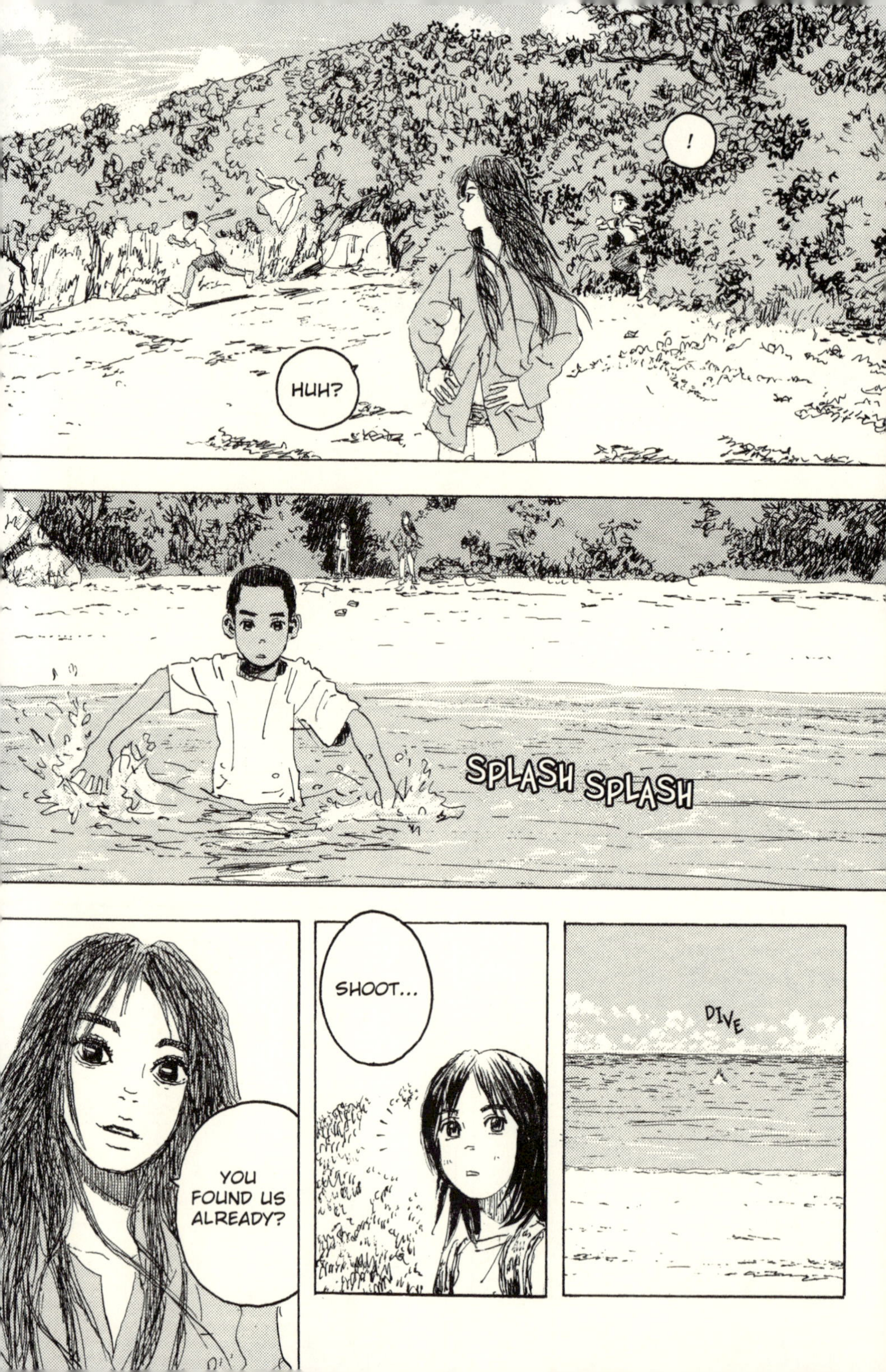
!
HUH?
SPLASH SPLASH
DIVE
SHOOT...
YOU FOUND US ALREADY?

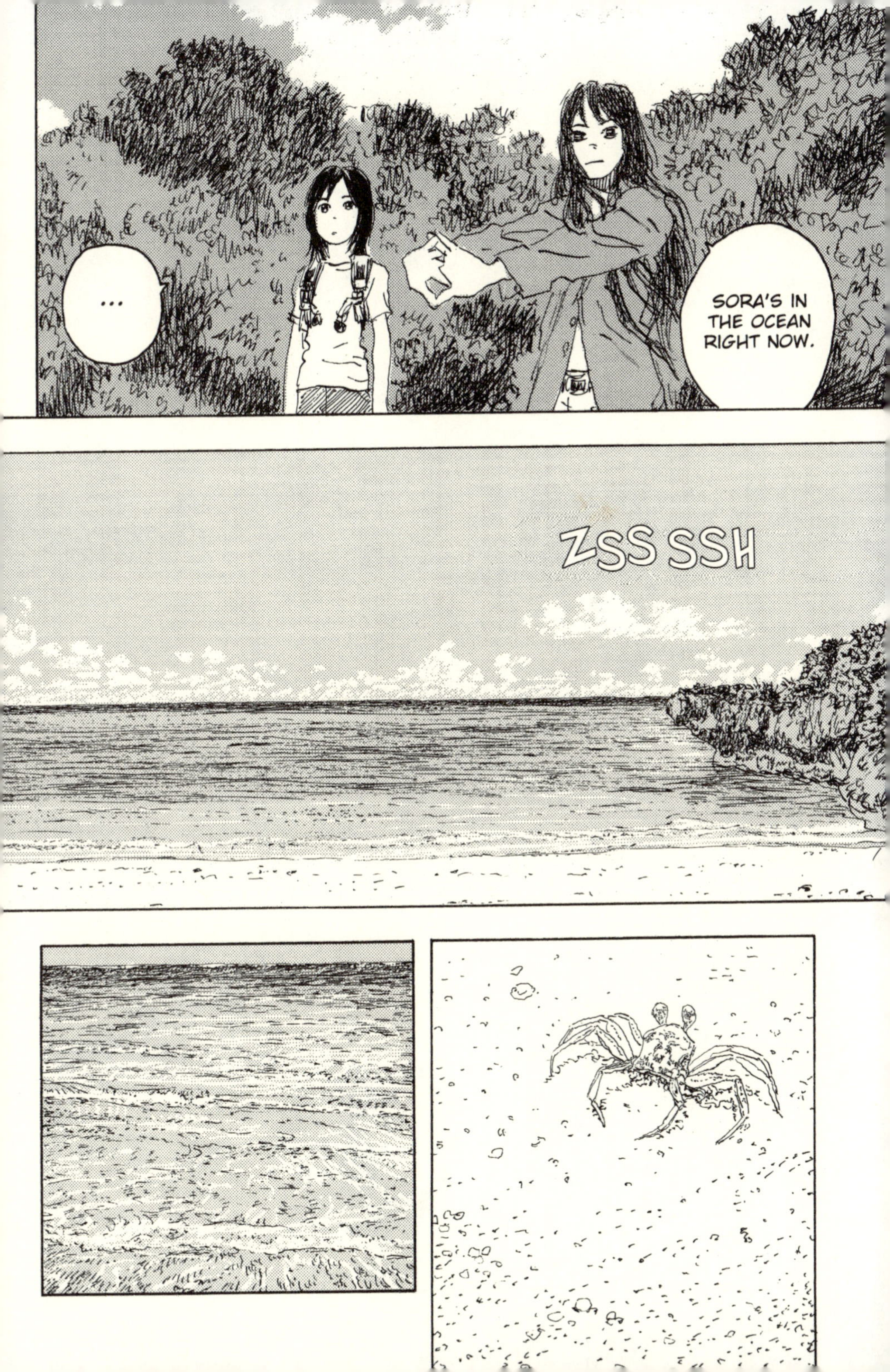
SORA'S IN THE OCEAN RIGHT NOW.
...
ZSS SSH

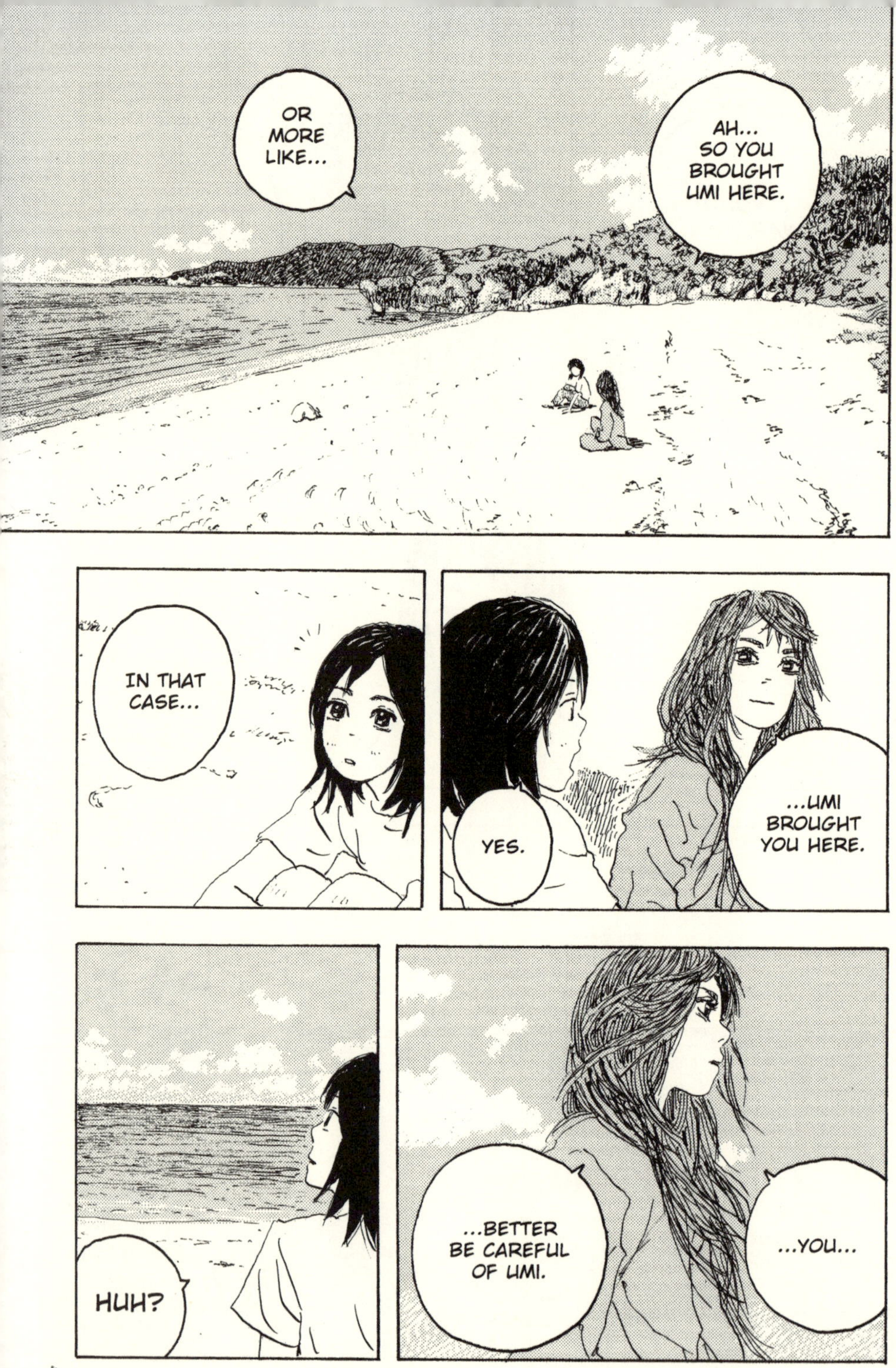
AH... SO YOU BROUGHT UMI HERE.
OR MORE LIKE...
...UMI BROUGHT YOU HERE.
YES.
IN THAT CASE...
...YOU...
...BETTER BE CAREFUL OF UMI.
HUH?

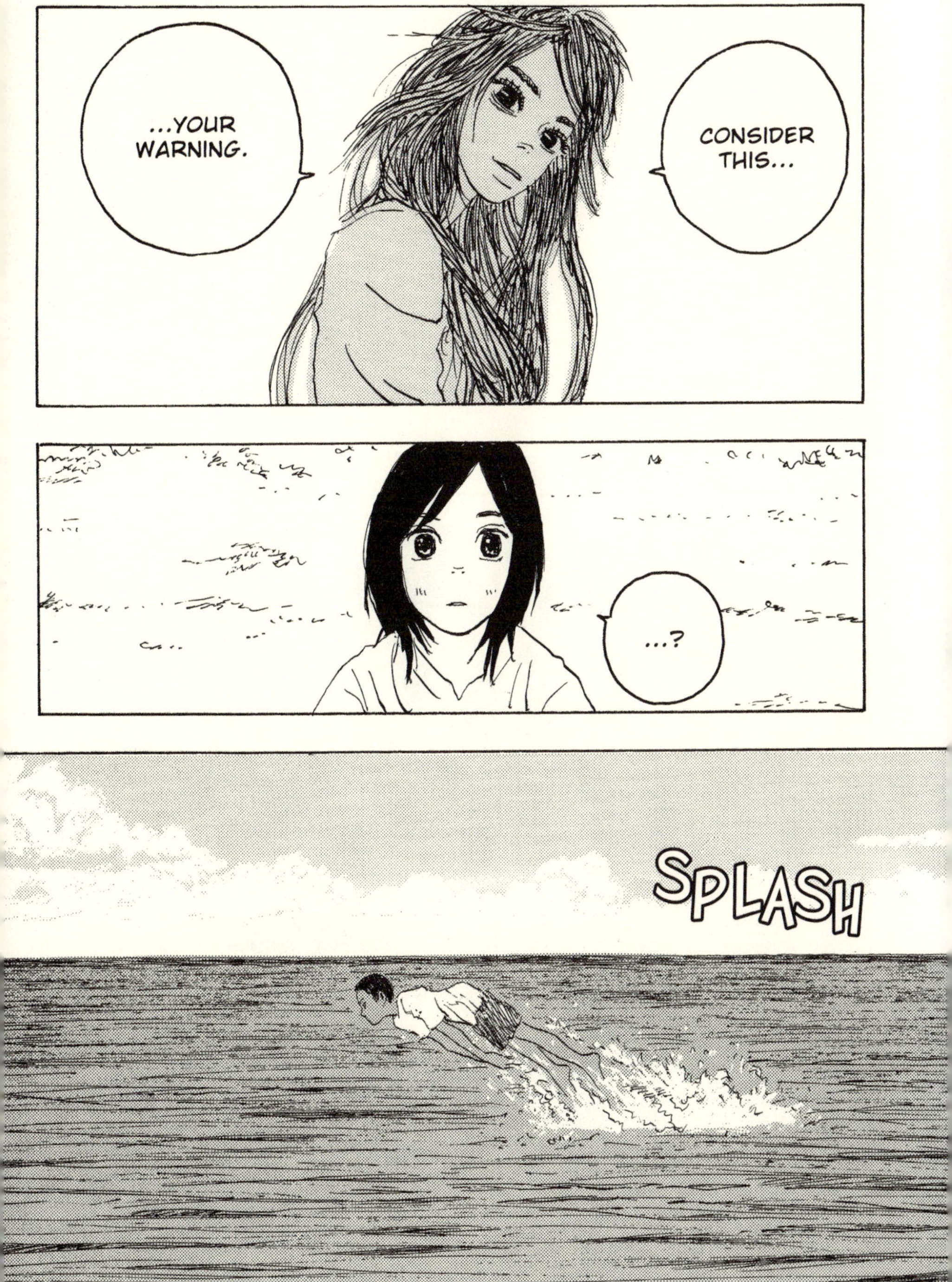
CONSIDER THIS...
...YOUR WARNING.
...?
SPLASH

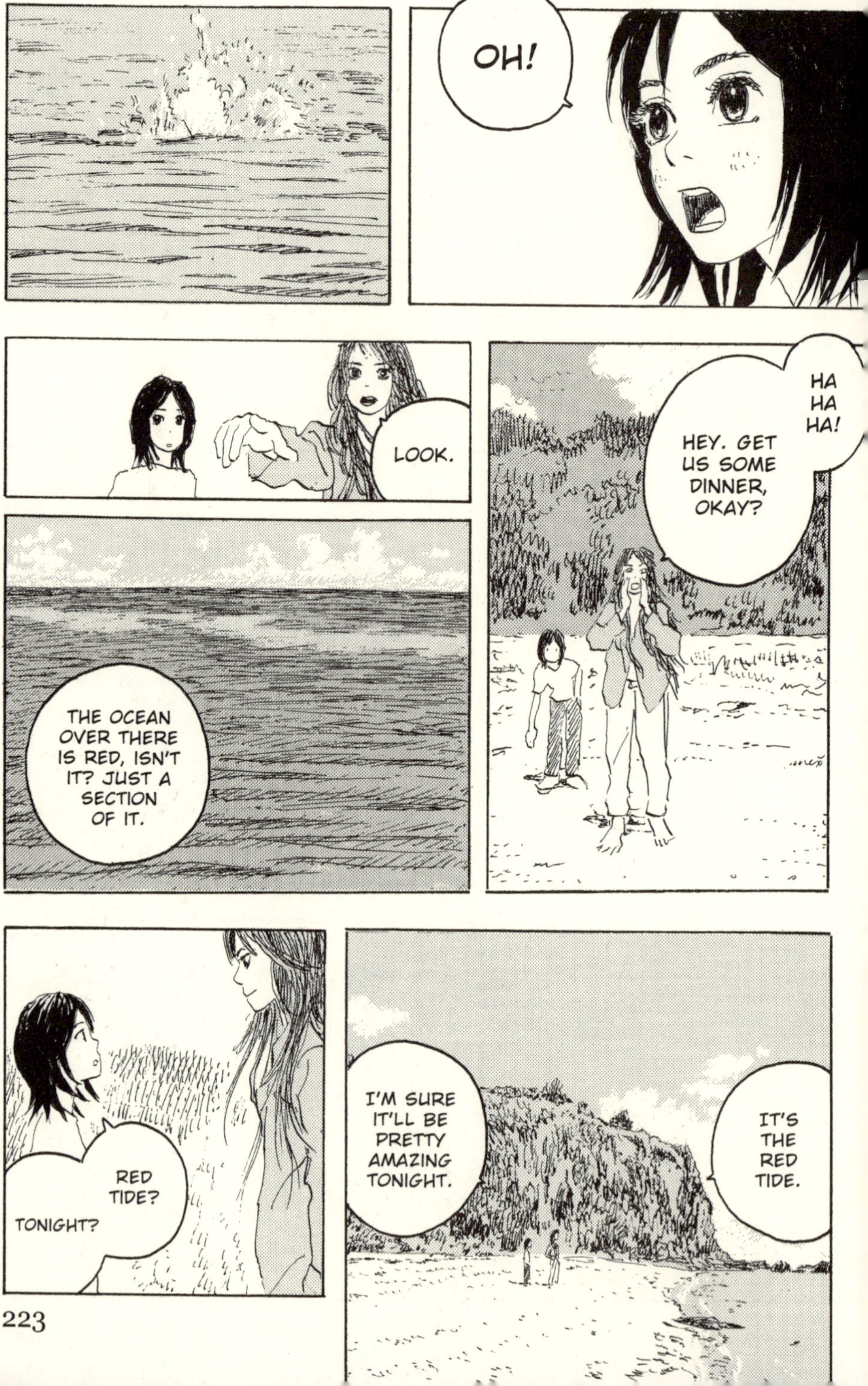

OH!
HA HA HA!
HEY. GET US SOME DINNER, OKAY?
LOOK.
THE OCEAN OVER THERE IS RED, ISN'T IT? JUST A SECTION OF IT.
IT'S THE RED TIDE.
I'M SURE IT'LL BE PRETTY AMAZING TONIGHT.
RED TIDE?
TONIGHT?

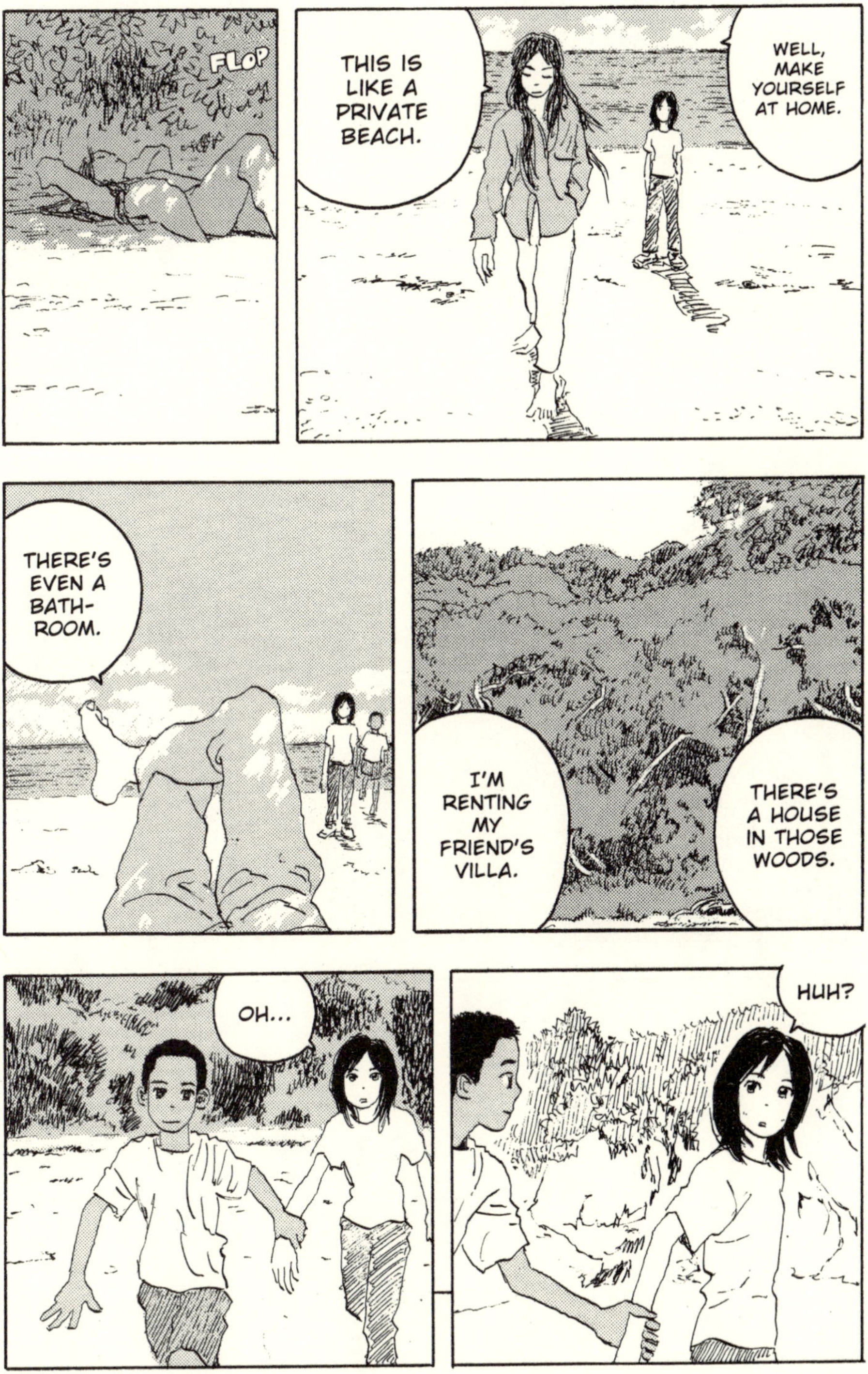
WELL, MAKE YOURSELF AT HOME.
THIS IS LIKE A PRIVATE BEACH.
FLOP
THERE'S A HOUSE IN THOSE WOODS.
I'M RENTING MY FRIEND'S VILLA.
THERE'S EVEN A BATH-ROOM.
HUH?
OH...

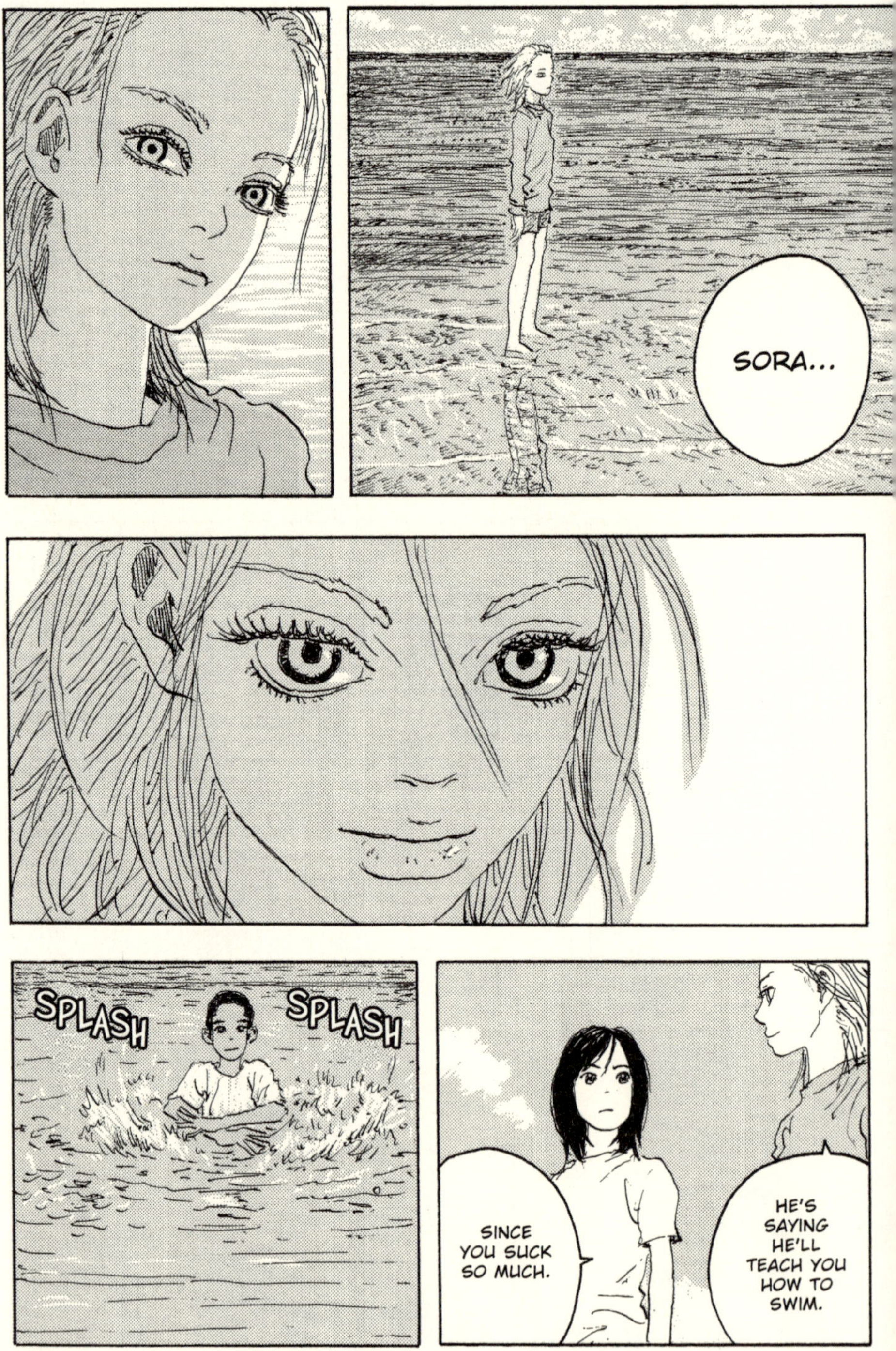
SORA...
HE'S SAYING HE'LL TEACH YOU HOW TO SWIM.
SINCE YOU SUCK SO MUCH.
SPLASH
SPLASH

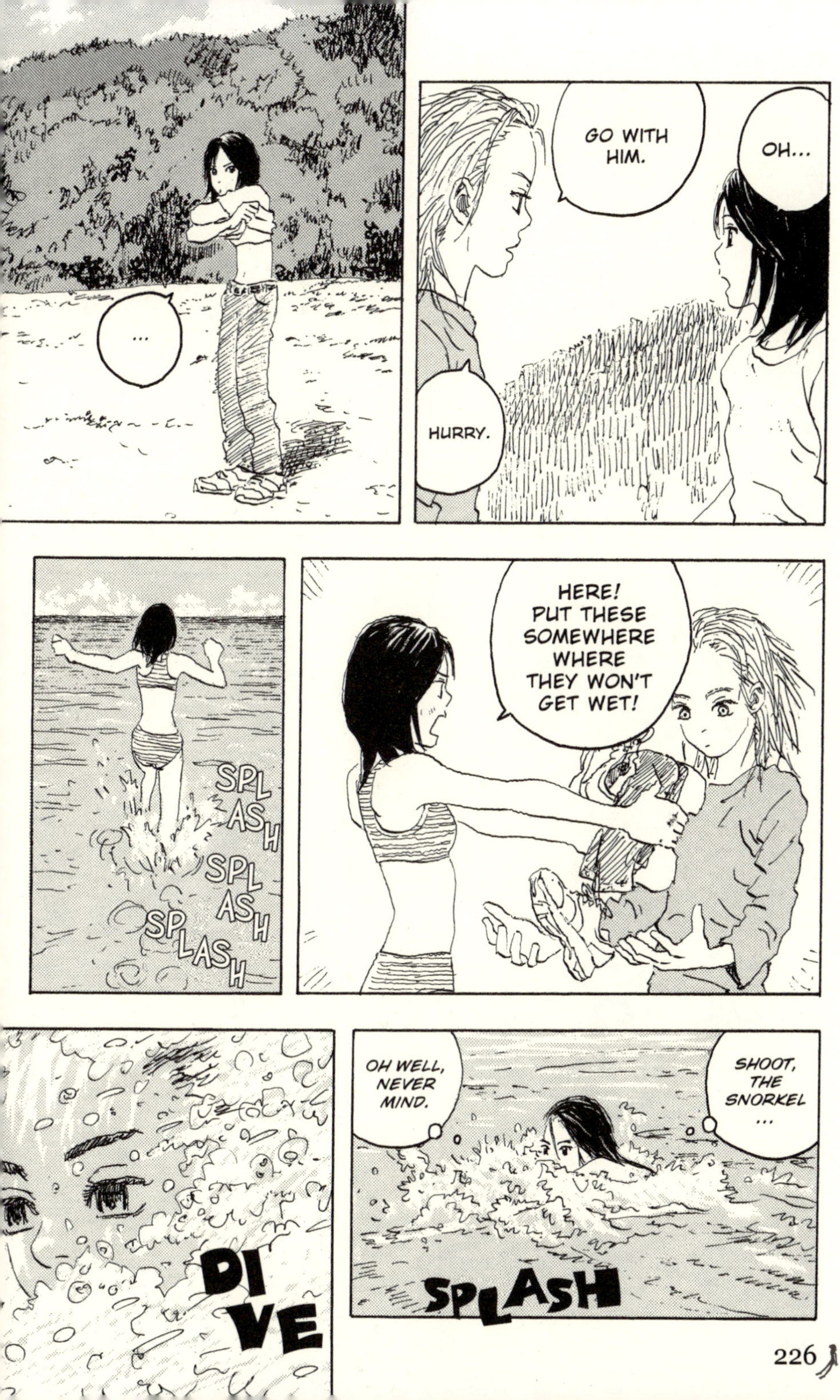
GO WITH HIM.
OH...
HURRY.
...
HERE! PUT THESE SOMEWHERE WHERE THEY WON'T GET WET!
SPLASH
SPLASH
SPLASH
SHOOT, THE SNORKEL ...
OH WELL, NEVER MIND.
SPLASH
DIVE

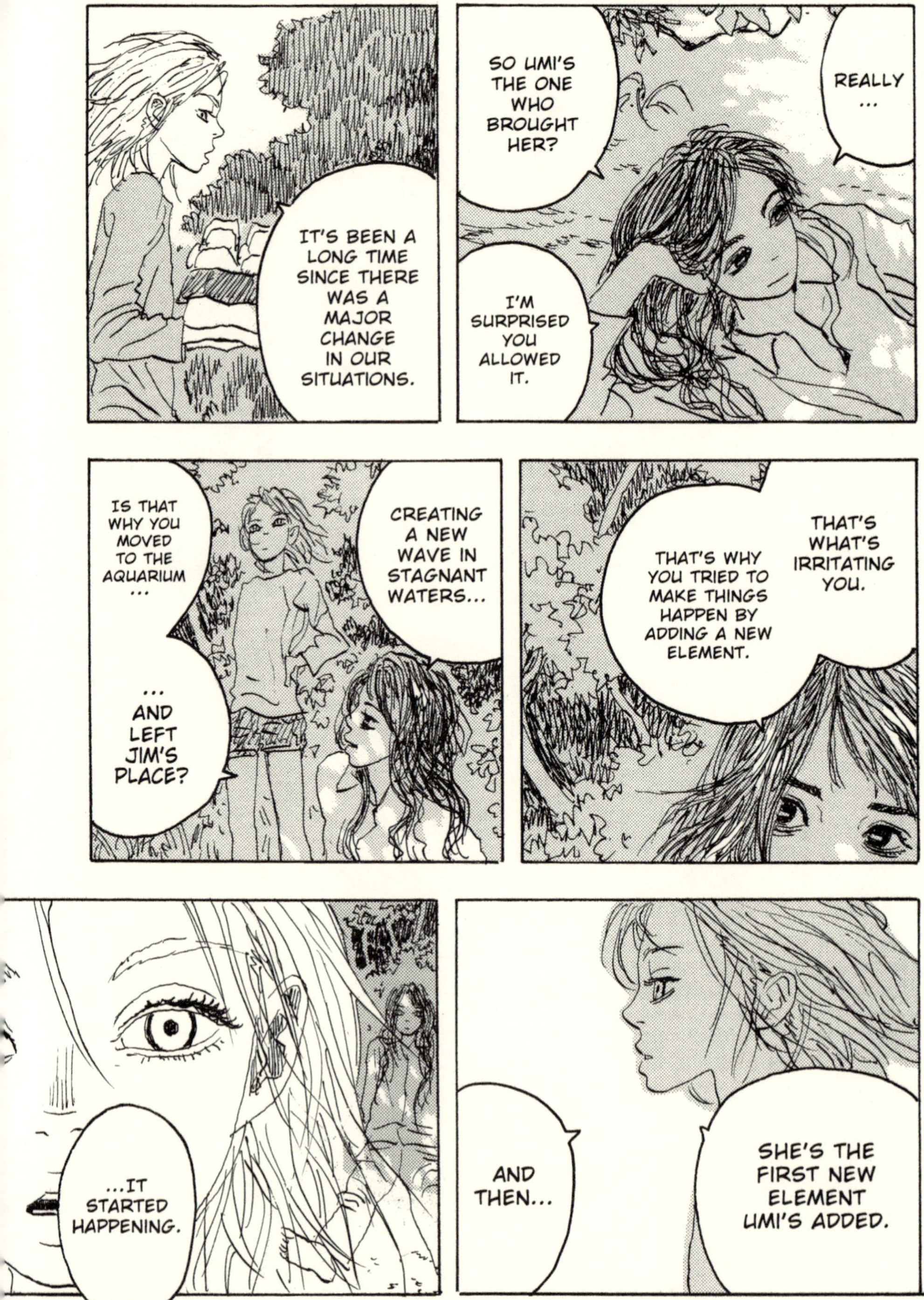
REALLY...
SO UMI'S THE ONE WHO BROUGHT HER?
I'M SURPRISED YOU ALLOWED IT.
IT'S BEEN A LONG TIME SINCE THERE WAS A MAJOR CHANGE IN OUR SITUATIONS.
THAT'S WHAT'S IRRITATING YOU.
THAT'S WHY YOU TRIED TO MAKE THINGS HAPPEN BY ADDING A NEW ELEMENT.
CREATING A NEW WAVE IN STAGNANT WATERS...
IS THAT WHY YOU MOVED TO THE AQUARIUM...
...AND LEFT JIM'S PLACE?
SHE'S THE FIRST NEW ELEMENT UMI'S ADDED.
AND THEN...
...IT STARTED HAPPENING.

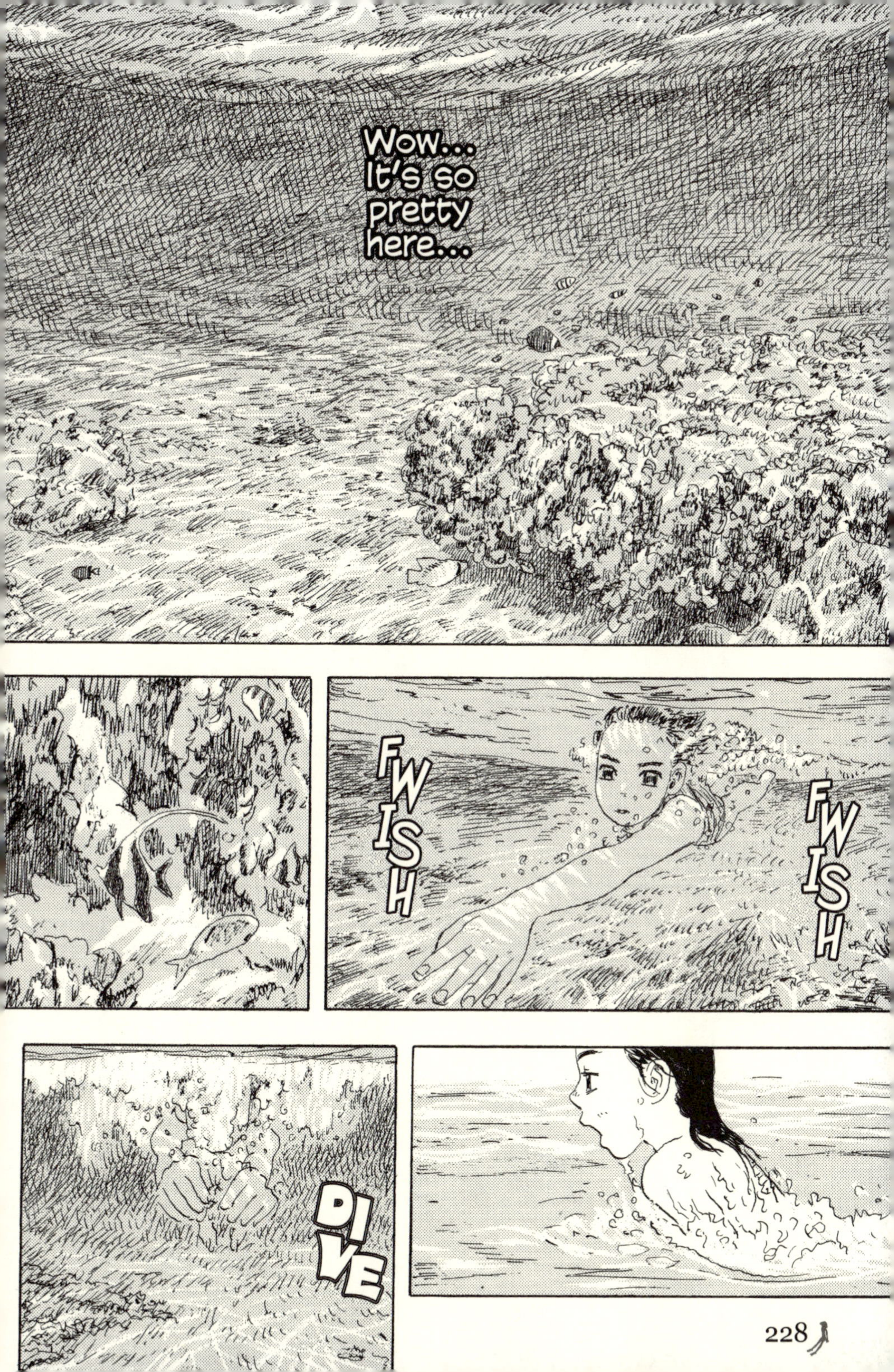
Wow... It's so pretty here...
FWISH
FWISH
DIVE

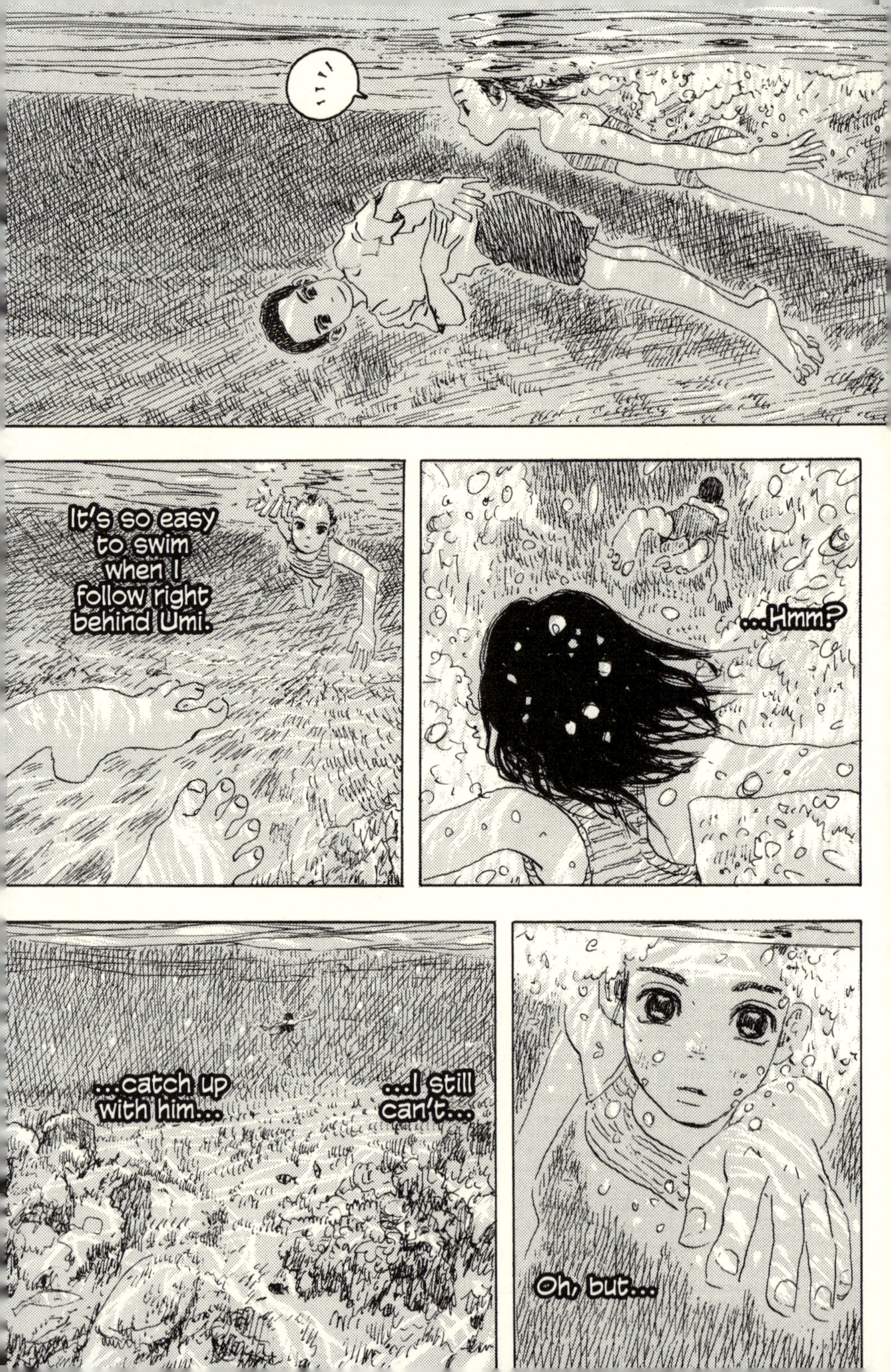
...Hmm?
It's so easy to swim when I follow right behind Umi.
Oh, but...
...I still can't...
...catch up with him...

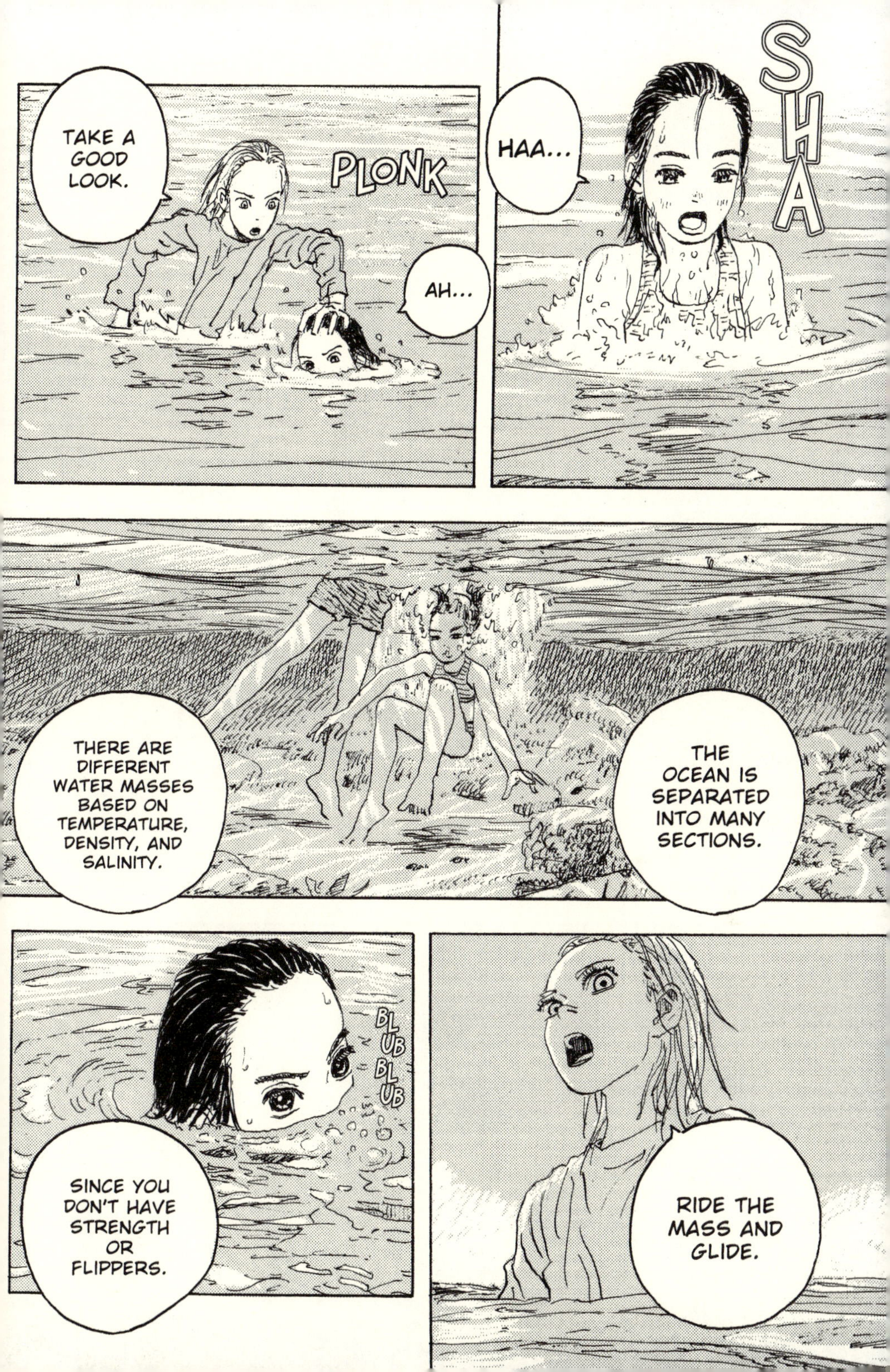
SHA
HAA...
AH...
PLONK
TAKE A GOOD LOOK.
THE OCEAN IS SEPARATED INTO MANY SECTIONS.
THERE ARE DIFFERENT WATER MASSES BASED ON TEMPERATURE, DENSITY, AND SALINITY.
RIDE THE MASS AND GLIDE.
BLUB BLUB
SINCE YOU DON'T HAVE STRENGTH OR FLIPPERS.

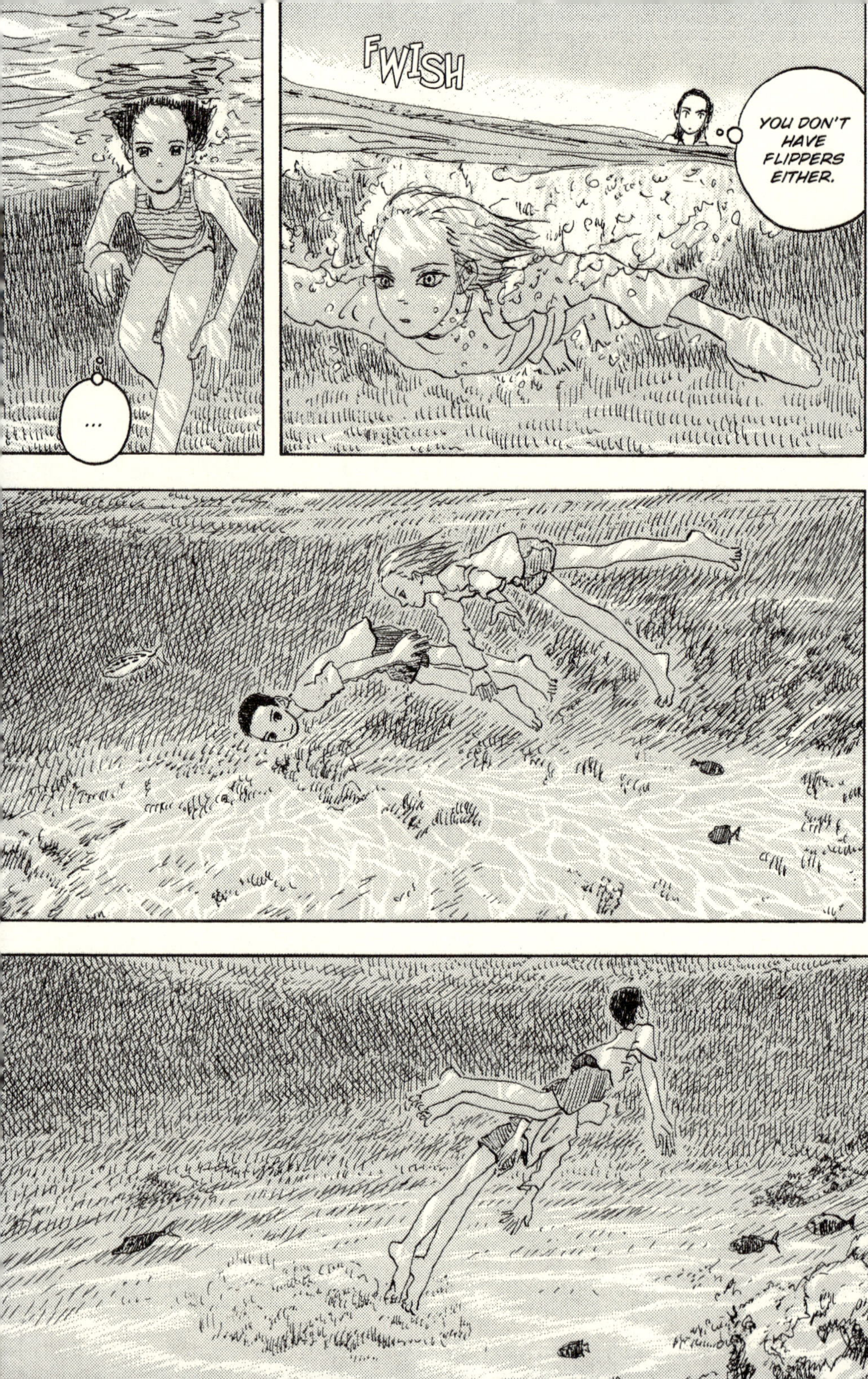
FWISH
YOU DON'T HAVE FLIPPERS EITHER.
...

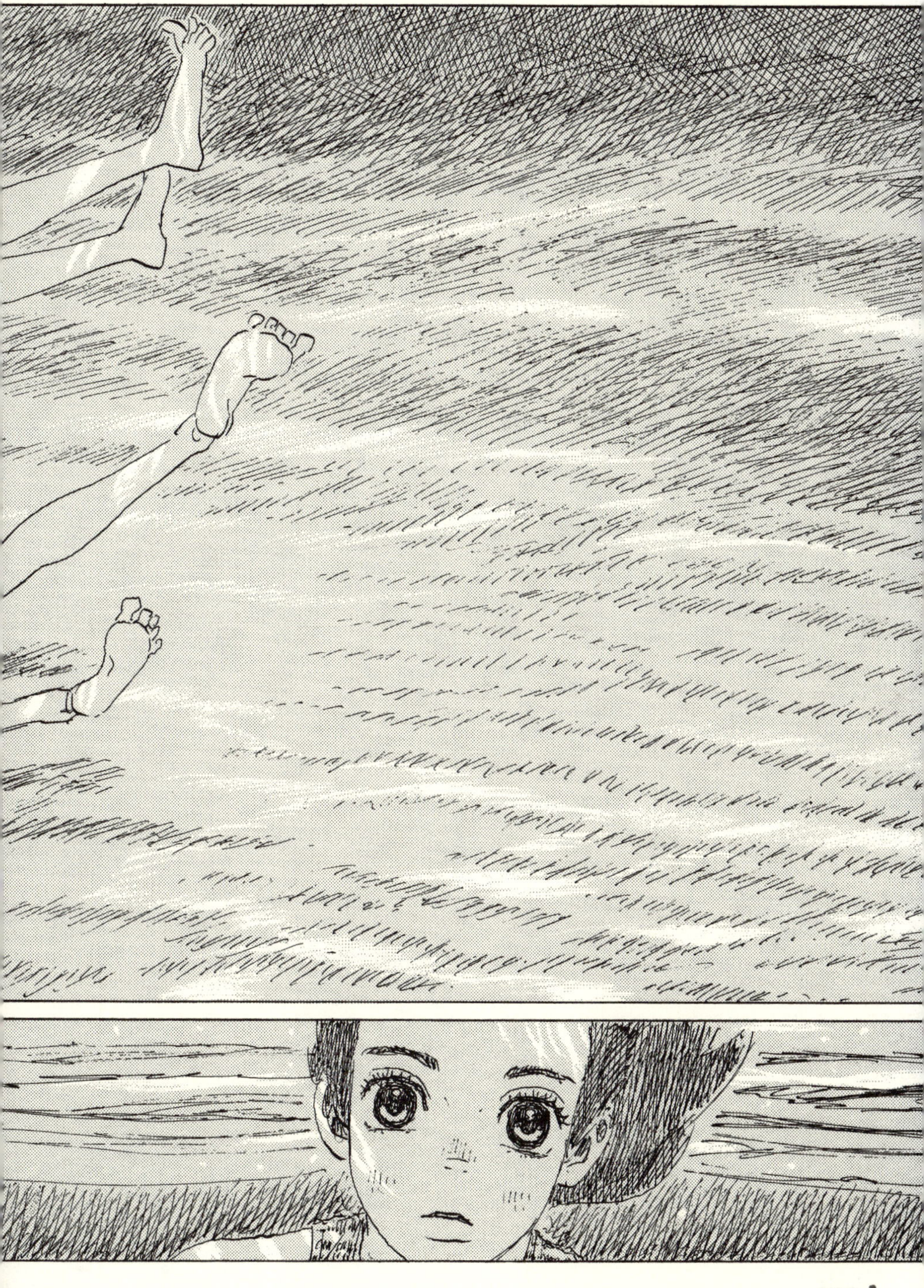

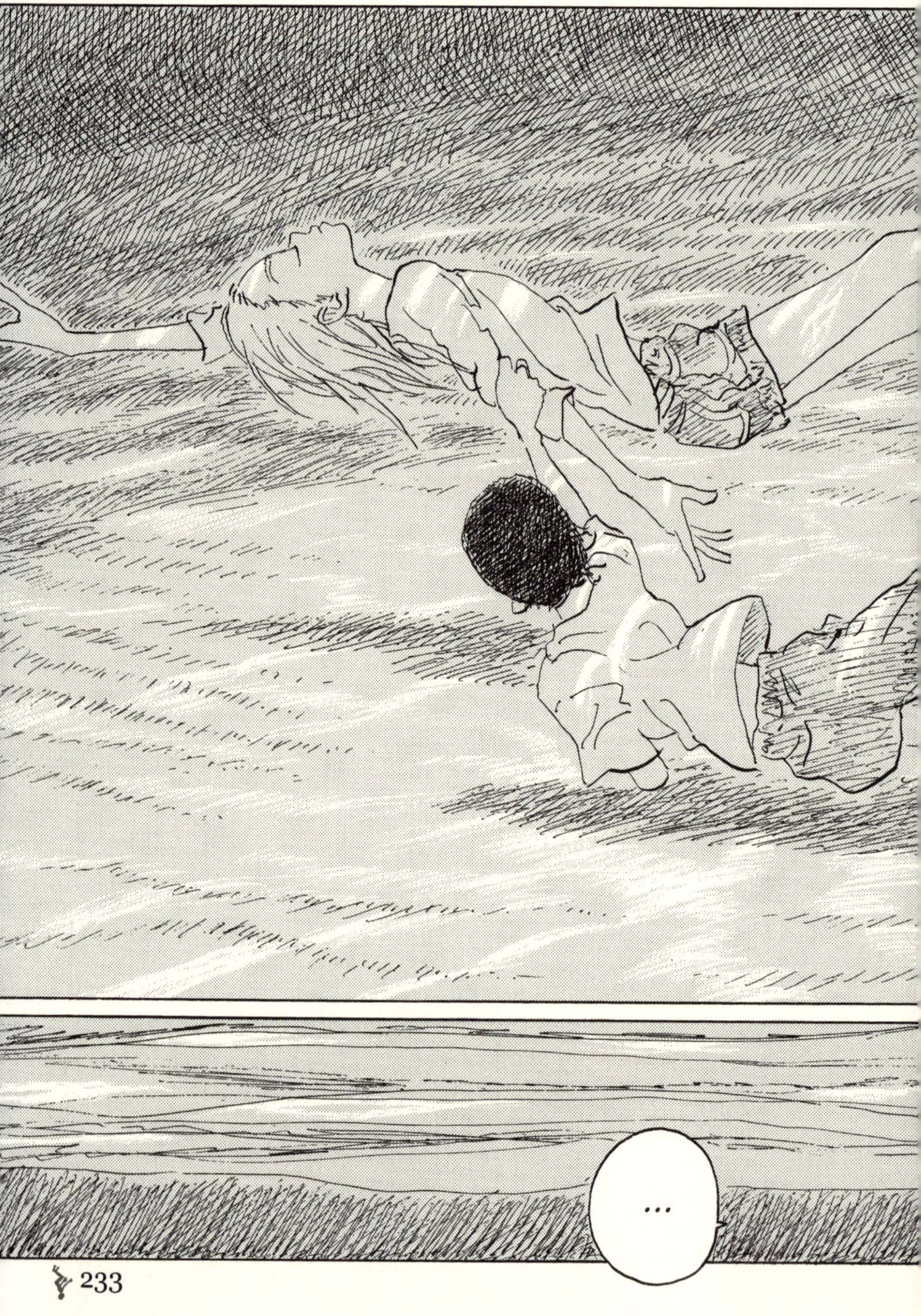
...

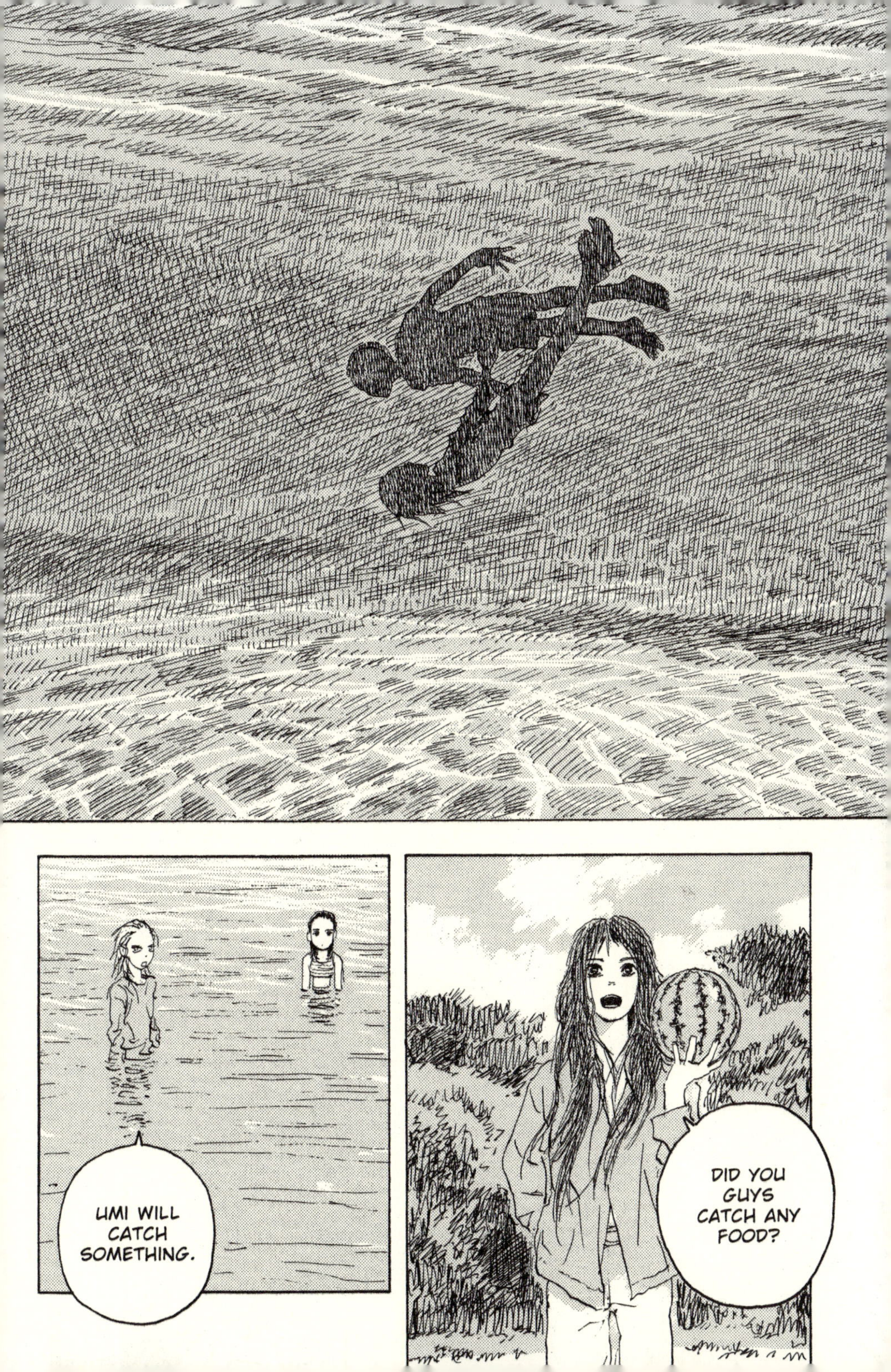
DID YOU GUYS CATCH ANY FOOD?
UMI WILL CATCH SOMETHING.

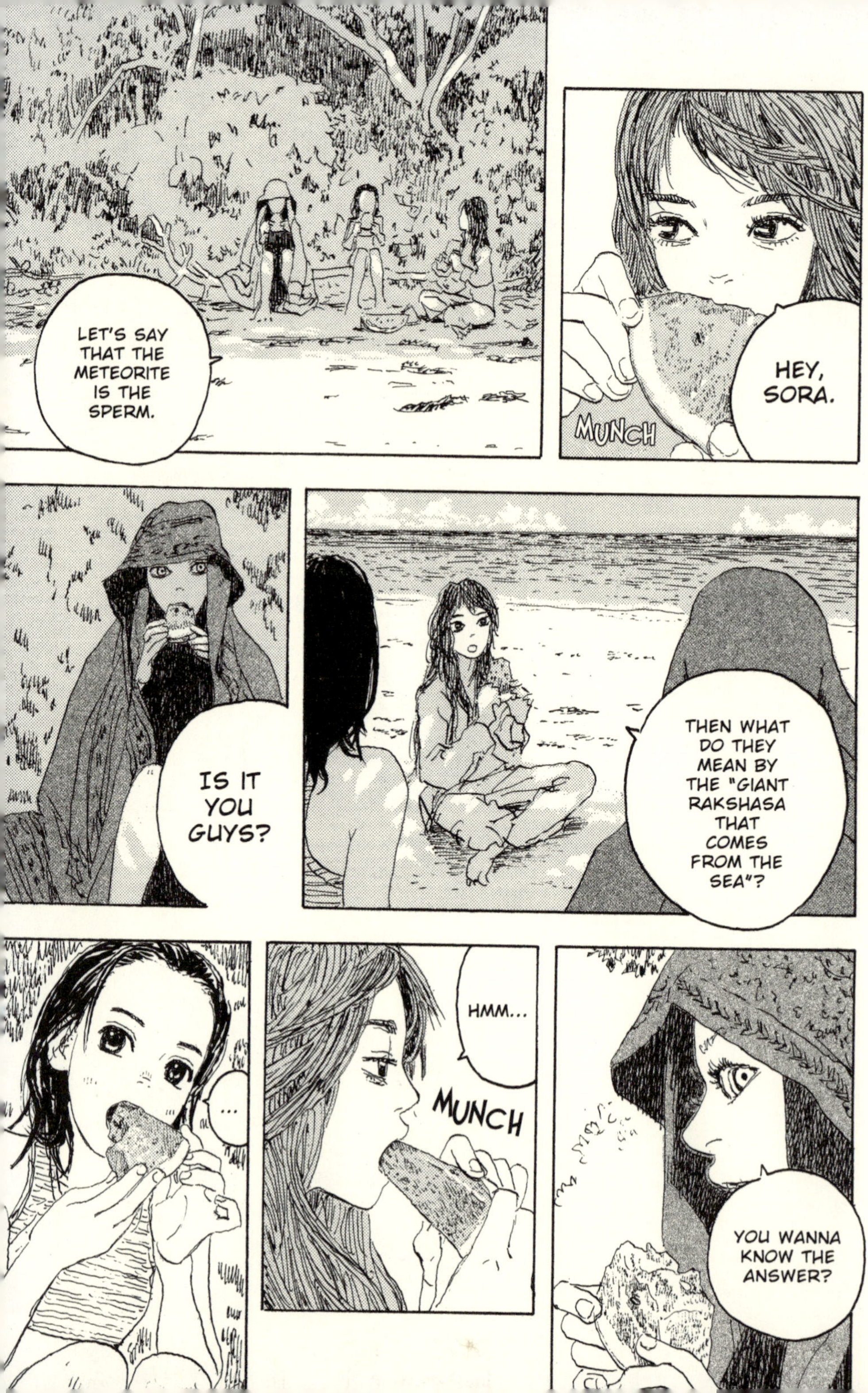
HEY, SORA.
MUNCH
LET'S SAY THAT THE METEORITE IS THE SPERM.
THEN WHAT DO THEY MEAN BY THE "GIANT RAKSHASA THAT COMES FROM THE SEA"?
IS IT YOU GUYS?
YOU WANNA KNOW THE ANSWER?
HMM...
MUNCH
...

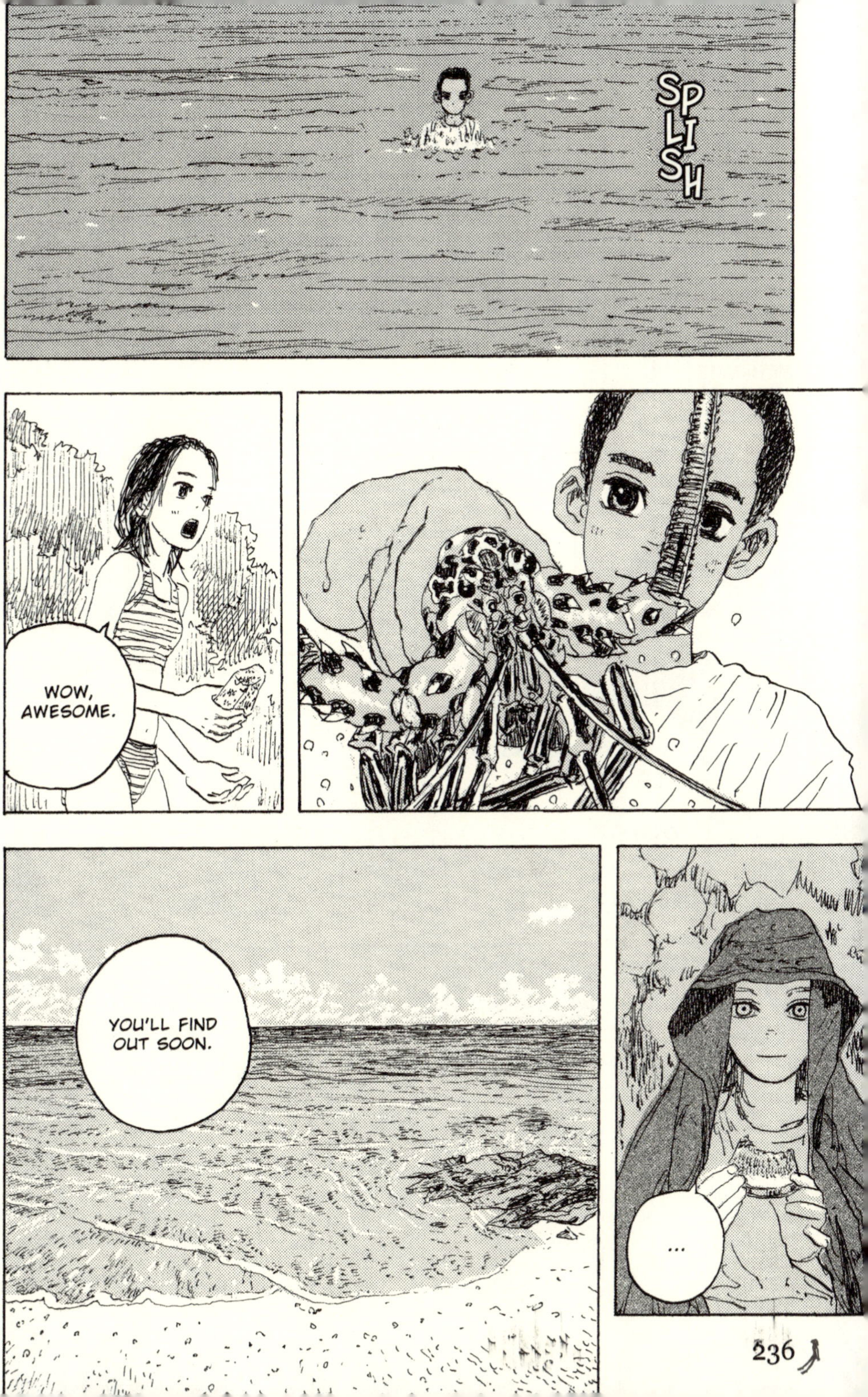
SPLISH
WOW, AWESOME.
...
YOU'LL FIND OUT SOON.

Chapter 15:
The Last Day of the Month

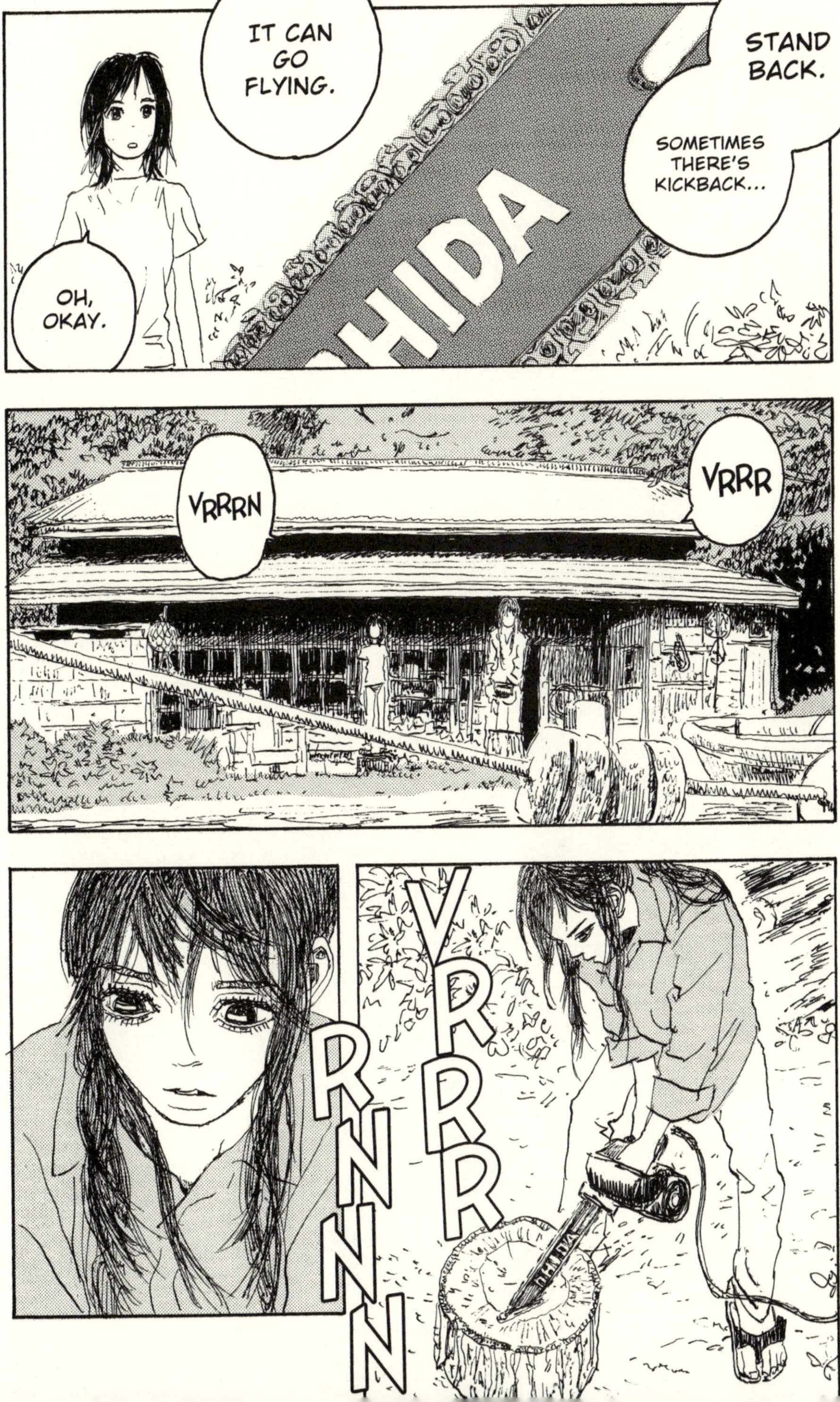
STAND BACK.
SOMETIMES THERE'S KICKBACK...
IT CAN GO FLYING.
OH, OKAY.
VRRR
VRRRN
VRRR
RNNNN

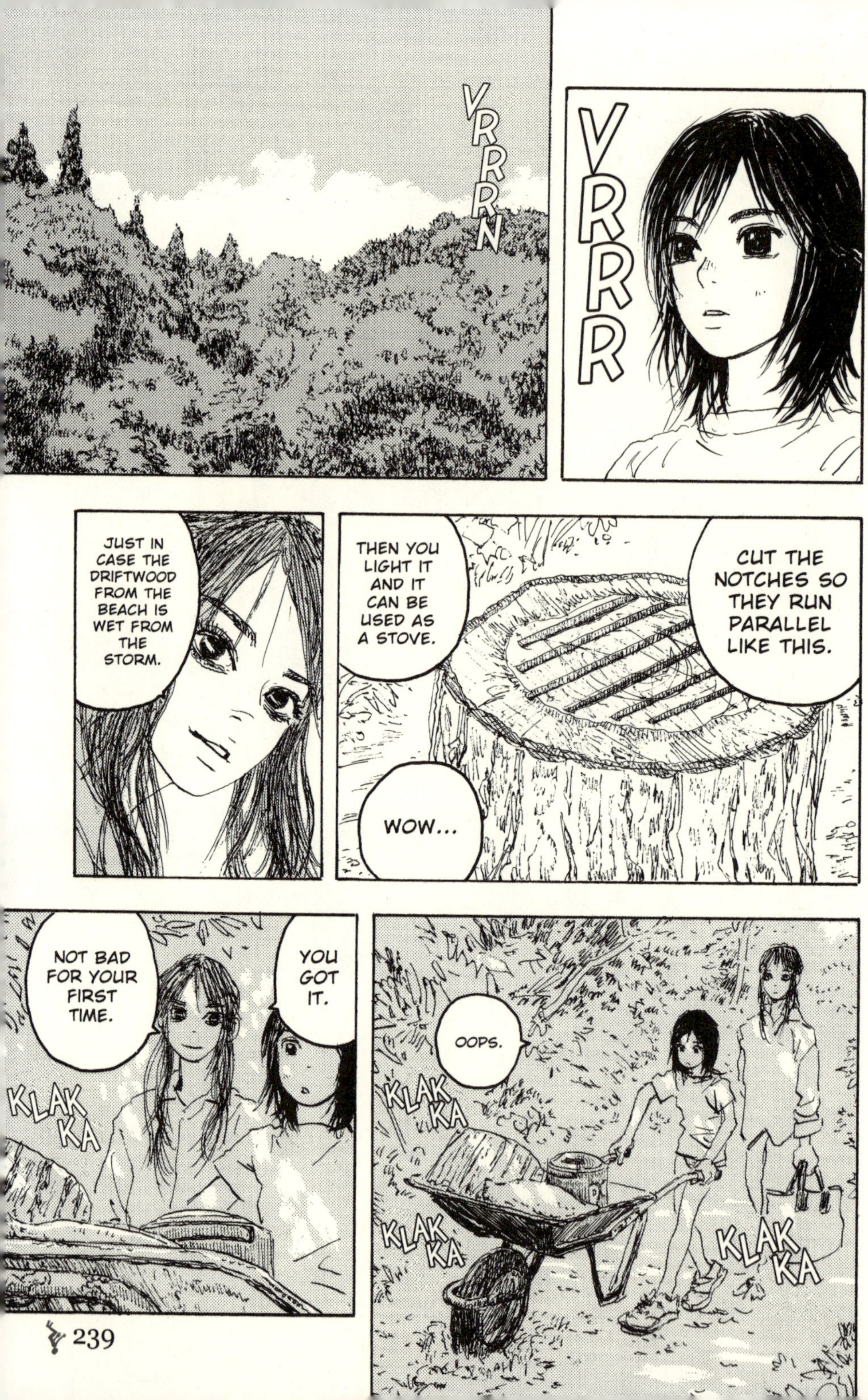
VRRR
VRRRN
CUT THE NOTCHES SO THEY RUN PARALLEL LIKE THIS.
THEN YOU LIGHT IT AND IT CAN BE USED AS A STOVE.
WOW...
JUST IN CASE THE DRIFTWOOD FROM THE BEACH IS WET FROM THE STORM.
OOPS.
KLAKKA
KLAKKA
KLAKKA
YOU GOT IT.
NOT BAD FOR YOUR FIRST TIME.
KLAKKA

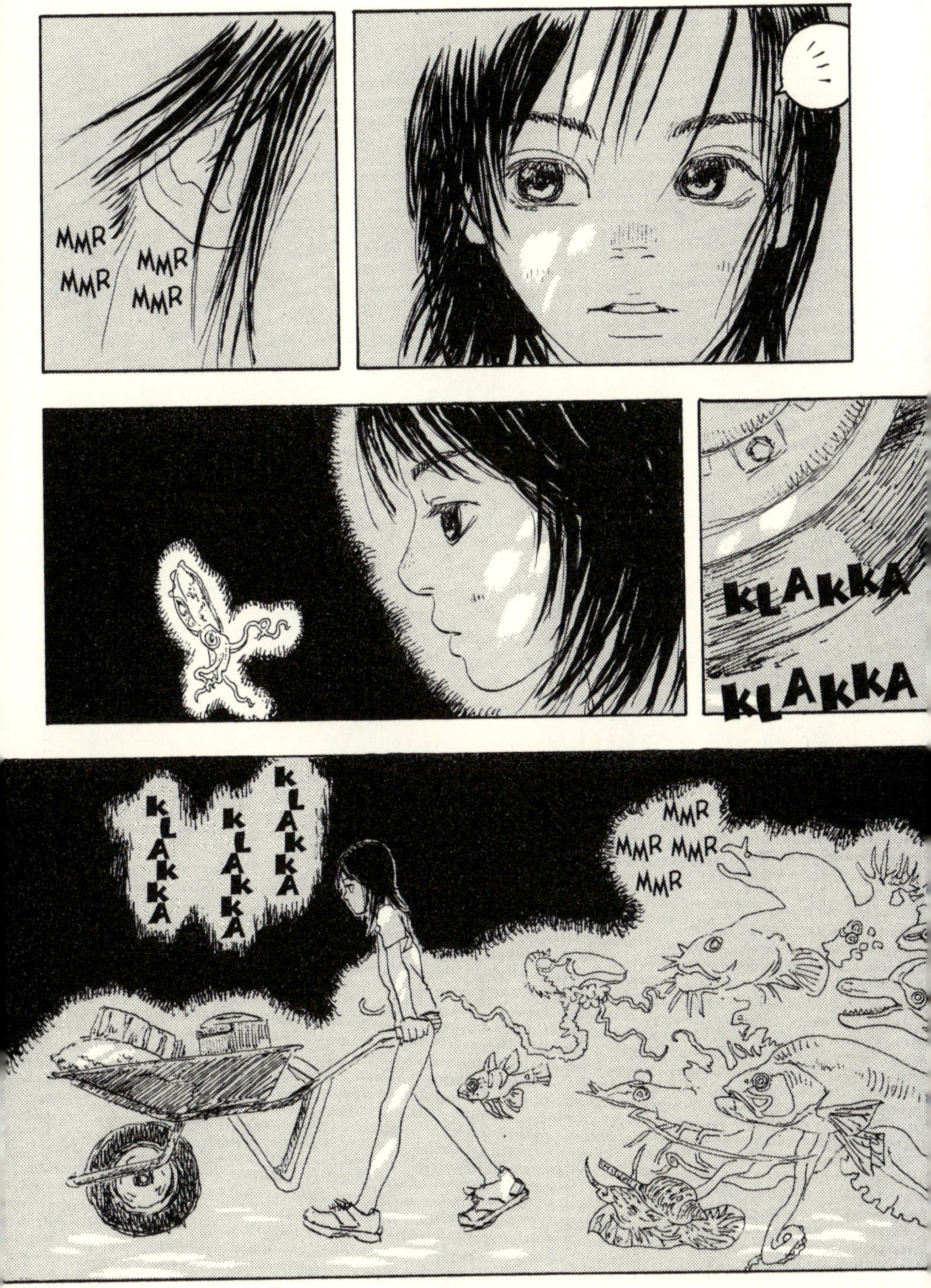
MMR
MMR
MMR
MMR
KLAKKA
KLAKKA
MMR
MMR MMR
MMR
KLAKKA
KLAKKA
KLAKKA

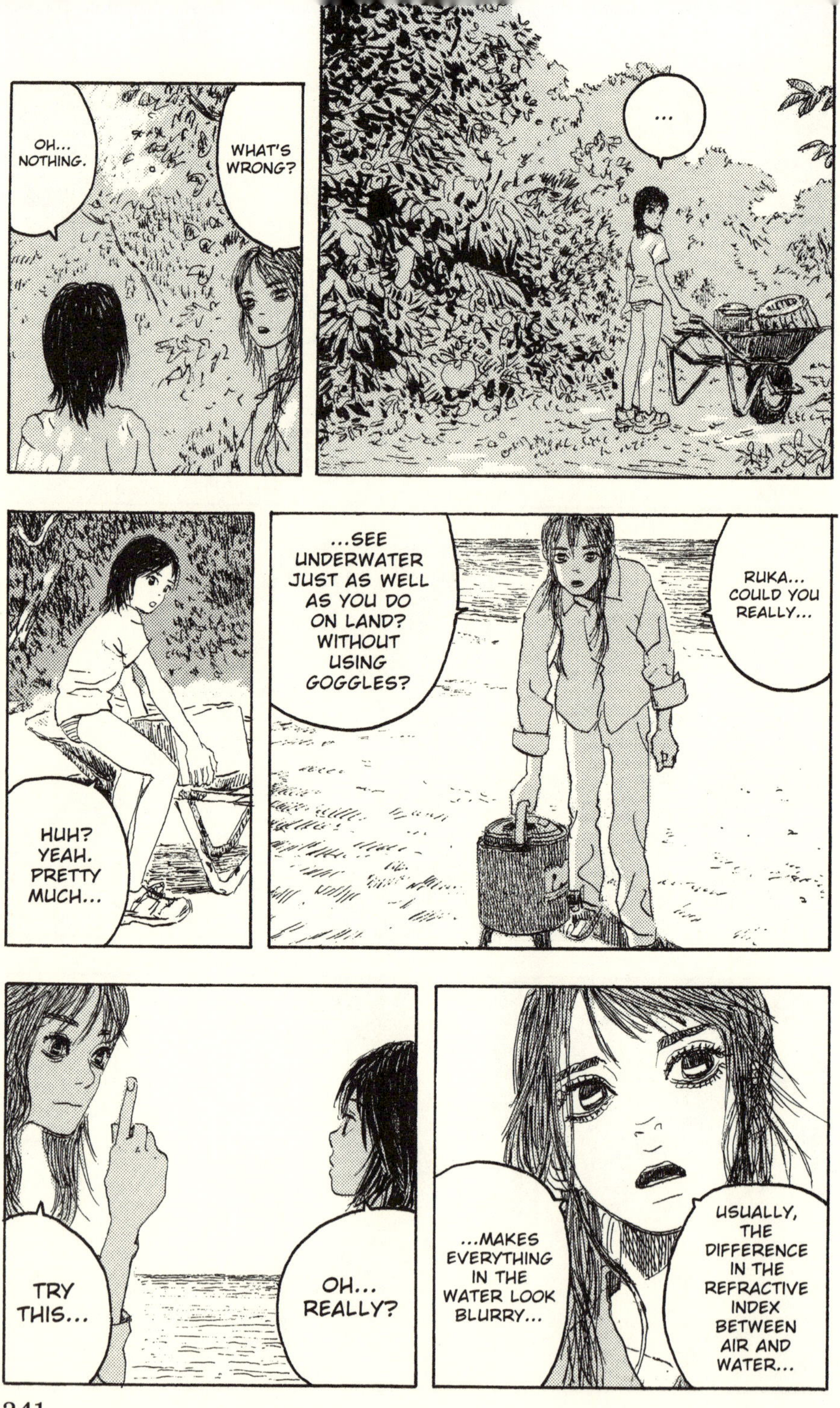
...
WHAT'S WRONG?
OH... NOTHING.
RUKA... COULD YOU REALLY...
...SEE UNDERWATER JUST AS WELL AS YOU DO ON LAND? WITHOUT USING GOGGLES?
HUH? YEAH. PRETTY MUCH...
USUALLY, THE DIFFERENCE IN THE REFRACTIVE INDEX BETWEEN AIR AND WATER...
...MAKES EVERYTHING IN THE WATER LOOK BLURRY...
OH... REALLY?
TRY THIS...

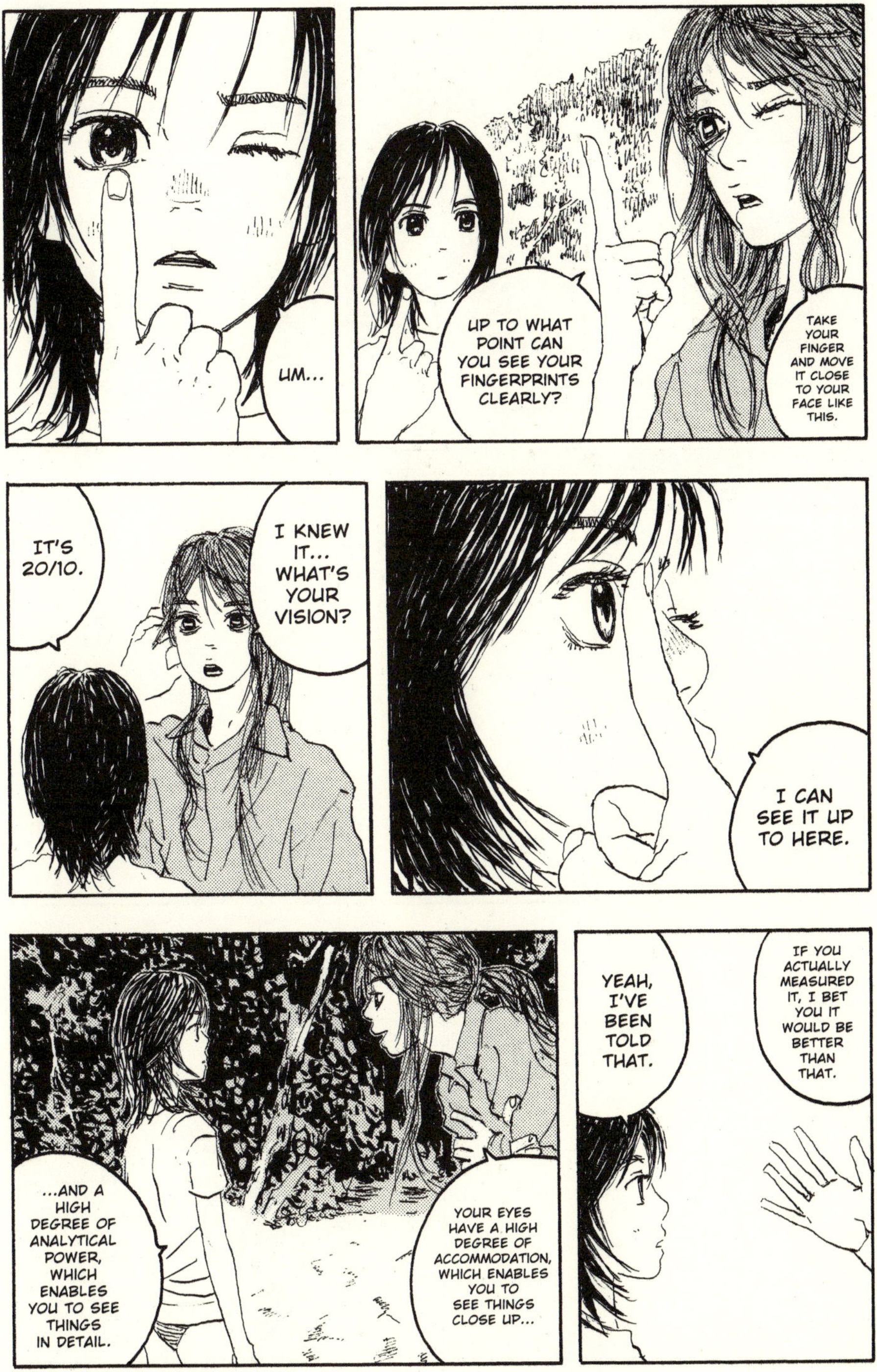
TAKE YOUR FINGER AND MOVE IT CLOSE TO YOUR FACE LIKE THIS.
UP TO WHAT POINT CAN YOU SEE YOUR FINGERPRINTS CLEARLY?
UM...
I CAN SEE IT UP TO HERE.
I KNEW IT... WHAT'S YOUR VISION?
IT'S 20/10.
IF YOU ACTUALLY MEASURED IT, I BET YOU IT WOULD BE BETTER THAN THAT.
YEAH, I'VE BEEN TOLD THAT.
YOUR EYES HAVE A HIGH DEGREE OF ACCOMMODATION, WHICH ENABLES YOU TO SEE THINGS CLOSE UP...
...AND A HIGH DEGREE OF ANALYTICAL POWER, WHICH ENABLES YOU TO SEE THINGS IN DETAIL.

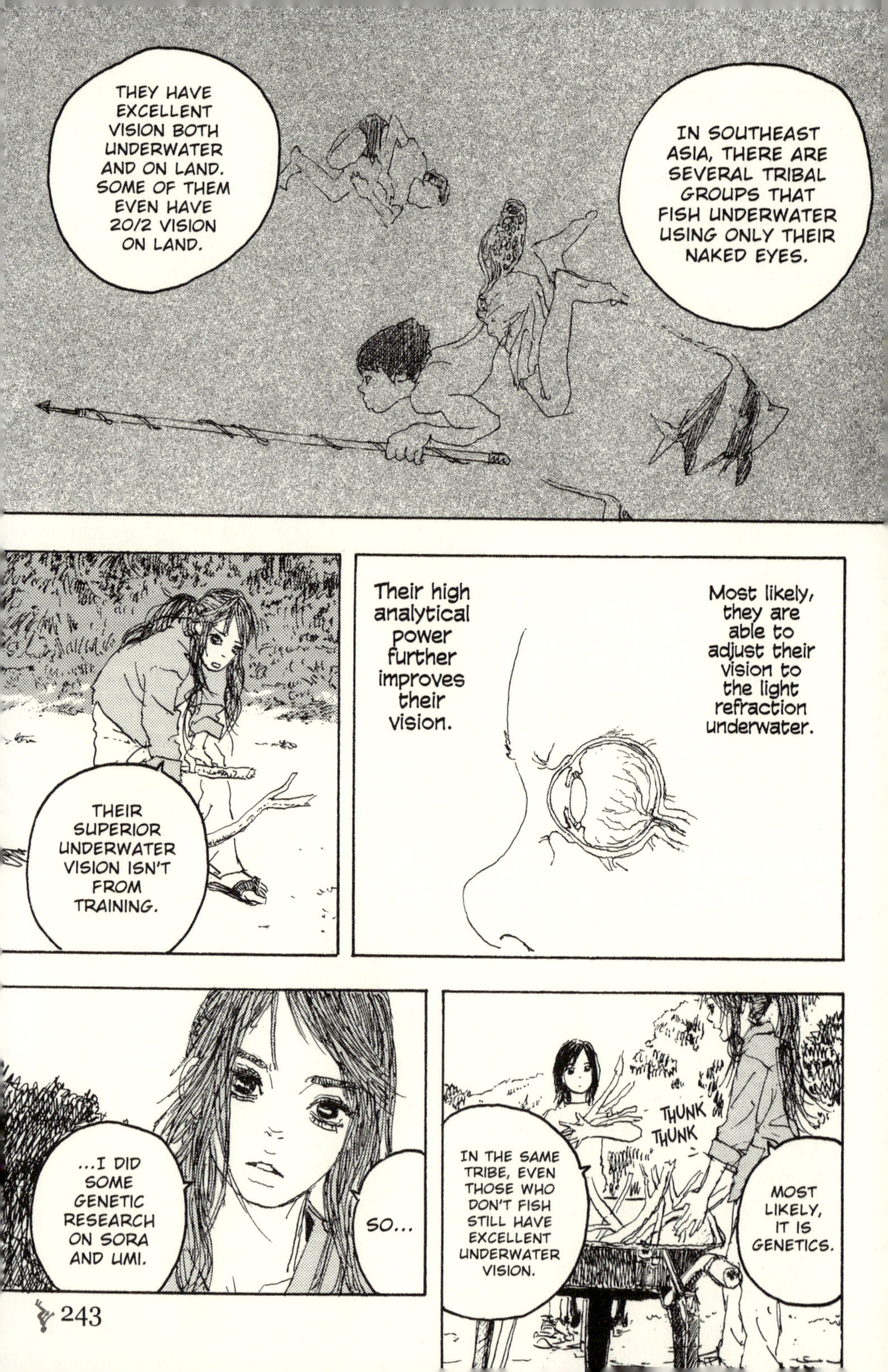
IN SOUTHEAST ASIA, THERE ARE SEVERAL TRIBAL GROUPS THAT FISH UNDERWATER USING ONLY THEIR NAKED EYES.
THEY HAVE EXCELLENT VISION BOTH UNDERWATER AND ON LAND. SOME OF THEM EVEN HAVE 20/2 VISION ON LAND.
Most likely, they are able to adjust their vision to the light refraction underwater.
Their high analytical power further improves their vision.
THEIR SUPERIOR UNDERWATER VISION ISN'T FROM TRAINING.
MOST LIKELY, IT IS GENETICS.
THUNK THUNK
IN THE SAME TRIBE, EVEN THOSE WHO DON'T FISH STILL HAVE EXCELLENT UNDERWATER VISION.
SO...
...I DID SOME GENETIC RESEARCH ON SORA AND UMI.

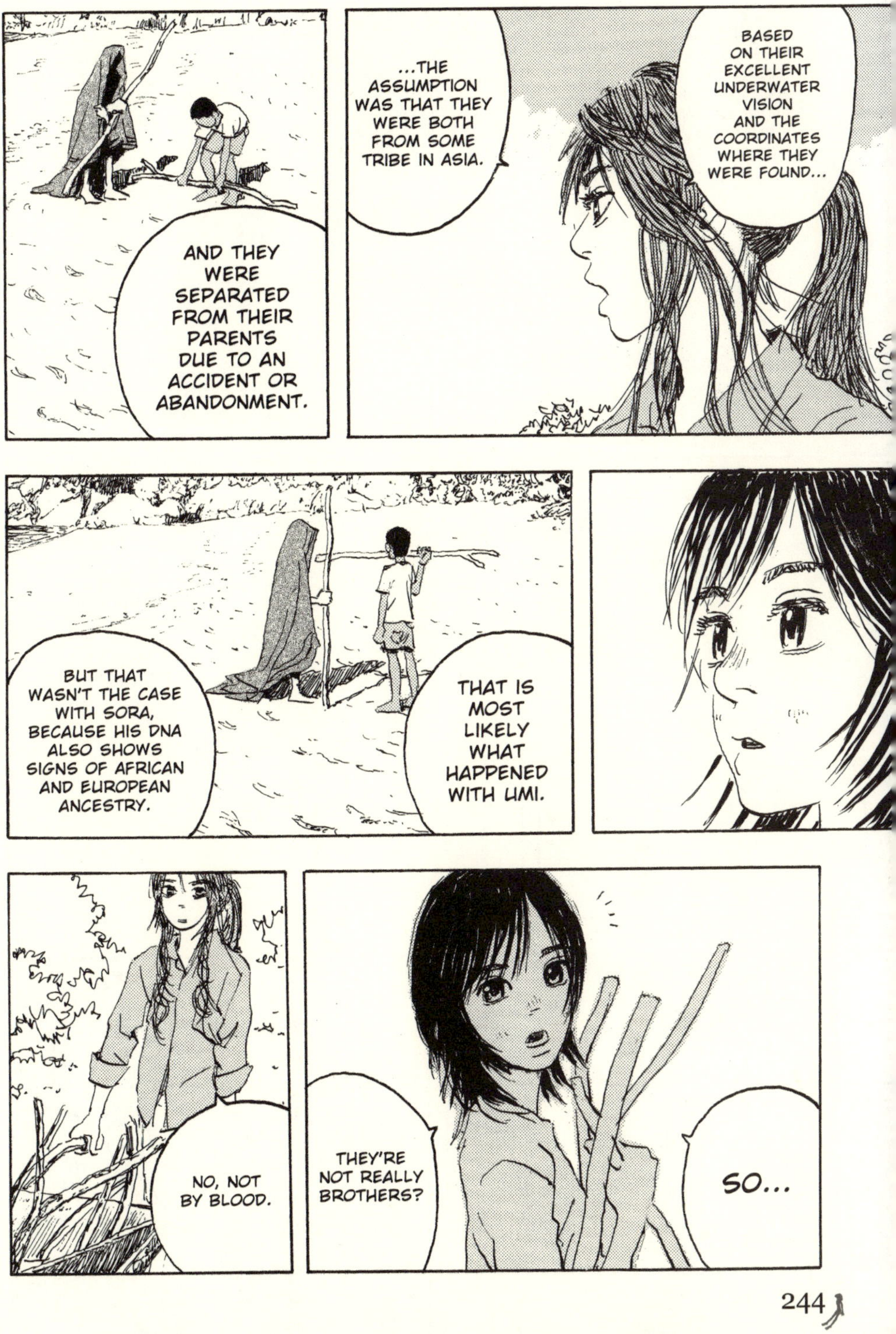
BASED ON THEIR EXCELLENT UNDERWATER VISION AND THE COORDINATES WHERE THEY WERE FOUND...
...THE ASSUMPTION WAS THAT THEY WERE BOTH FROM SOME TRIBE IN ASIA.
AND THEY WERE SEPARATED FROM THEIR PARENTS DUE TO AN ACCIDENT OR ABANDONMENT.
THAT IS MOST LIKELY WHAT HAPPENED WITH UMI.
BUT THAT WASN'T THE CASE WITH SORA, BECAUSE HIS DNA ALSO SHOWS SIGNS OF AFRICAN AND EUROPEAN ANCESTRY.
SO...
THEY'RE NOT REALLY BROTHERS?
NO, NOT BY BLOOD.

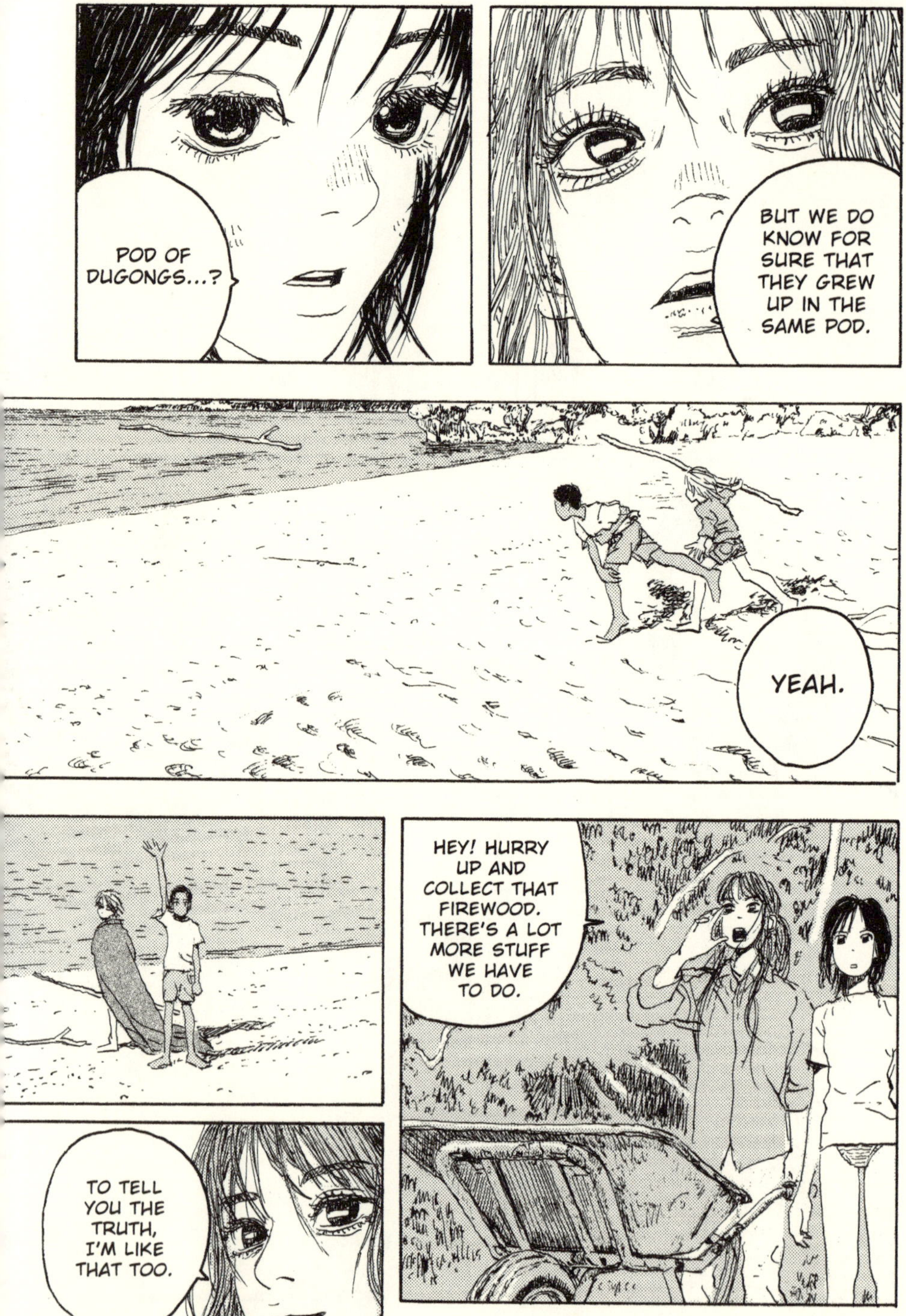
BUT WE DO KNOW FOR SURE THAT THEY GREW UP IN THE SAME POD.
POD OF DUGONGS...?
YEAH.
HEY! HURRY UP AND COLLECT THAT FIREWOOD. THERE'S A LOT MORE STUFF WE HAVE TO DO.
TO TELL YOU THE TRUTH, I'M LIKE THAT TOO.

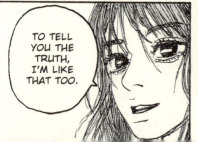

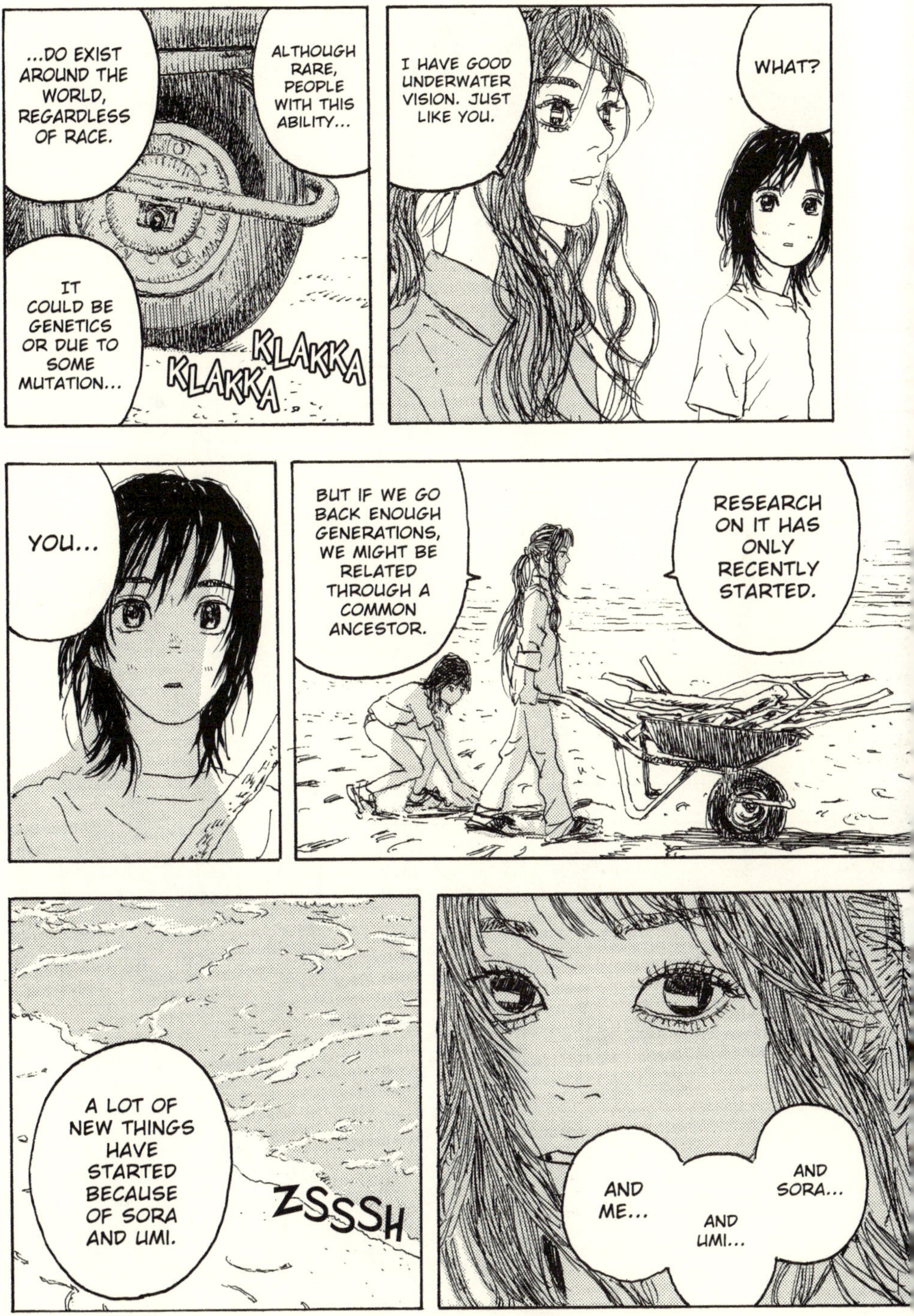
WHAT?
I HAVE GOOD UNDERWATER VISION. JUST LIKE YOU.
ALTHOUGH RARE, PEOPLE WITH THIS ABILITY...
...DO EXIST AROUND THE WORLD, REGARDLESS OF RACE.
IT COULD BE GENETICS OR DUE TO SOME MUTATION...
KLAKKA
KLAKKA
RESEARCH ON IT HAS ONLY RECENTLY STARTED.
BUT IF WE GO BACK ENOUGH GENERATIONS, WE MIGHT BE RELATED THROUGH A COMMON ANCESTOR.
YOU...
AND SORA...
AND UMI...
AND ME...
A LOT OF NEW THINGS HAVE STARTED BECAUSE OF SORA AND UMI.
ZSSSH

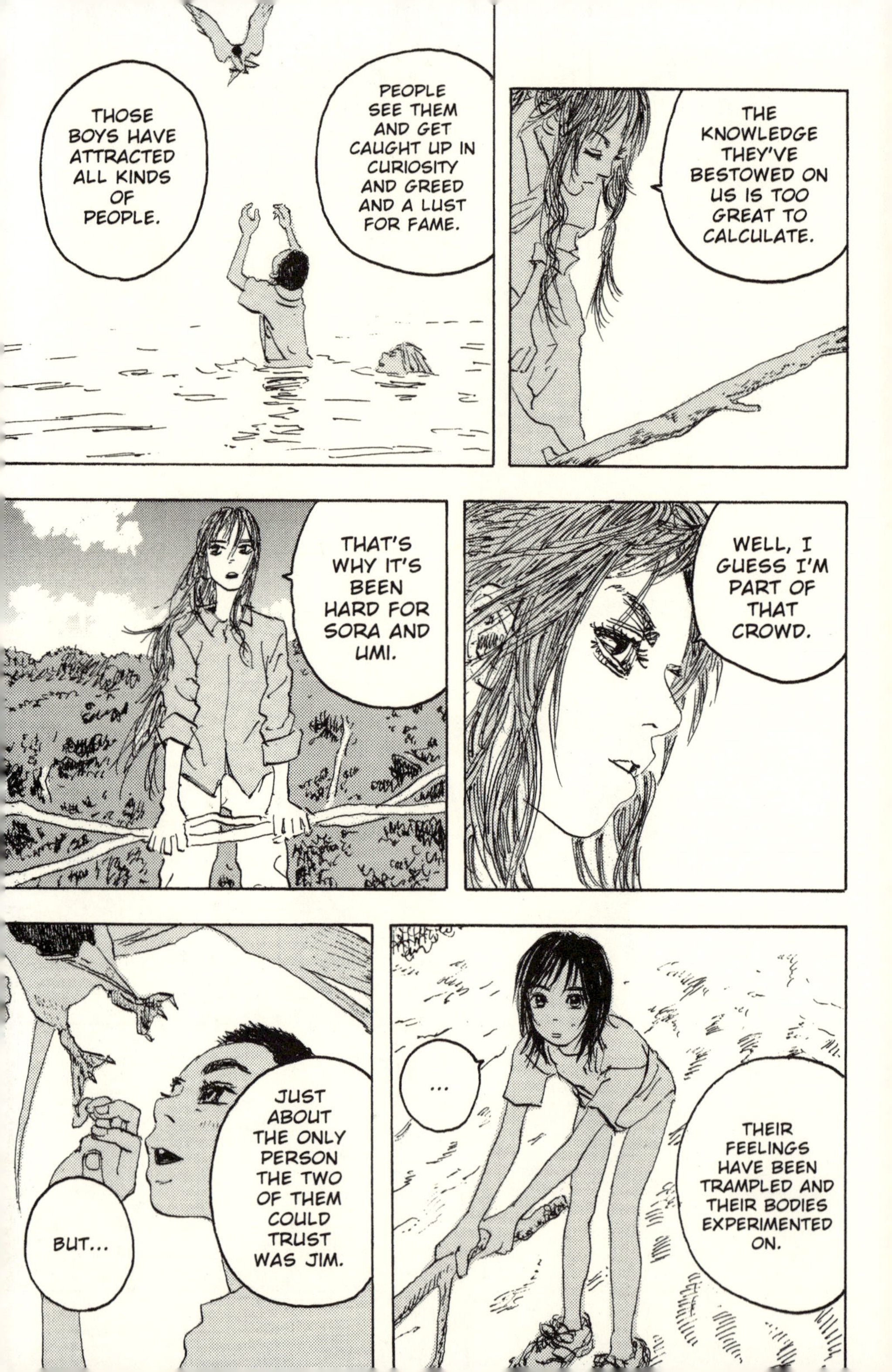
THOSE BOYS HAVE ATTRACTED ALL KINDS OF PEOPLE.
PEOPLE SEE THEM AND GET CAUGHT UP IN CURIOSITY AND GREED AND A LUST FOR FAME.
THE KNOWLEDGE THEY'VE BESTOWED ON US IS TOO GREAT TO CALCULATE.
THAT'S WHY IT'S BEEN HARD FOR SORA AND UMI.
WELL, I GUESS I'M PART OF THAT CROWD.
JUST ABOUT THE ONLY PERSON THE TWO OF THEM COULD TRUST WAS JIM.
BUT...
...
THEIR FEELINGS HAVE BEEN TRAMPLED AND THEIR BODIES EXPERIMENTED ON.

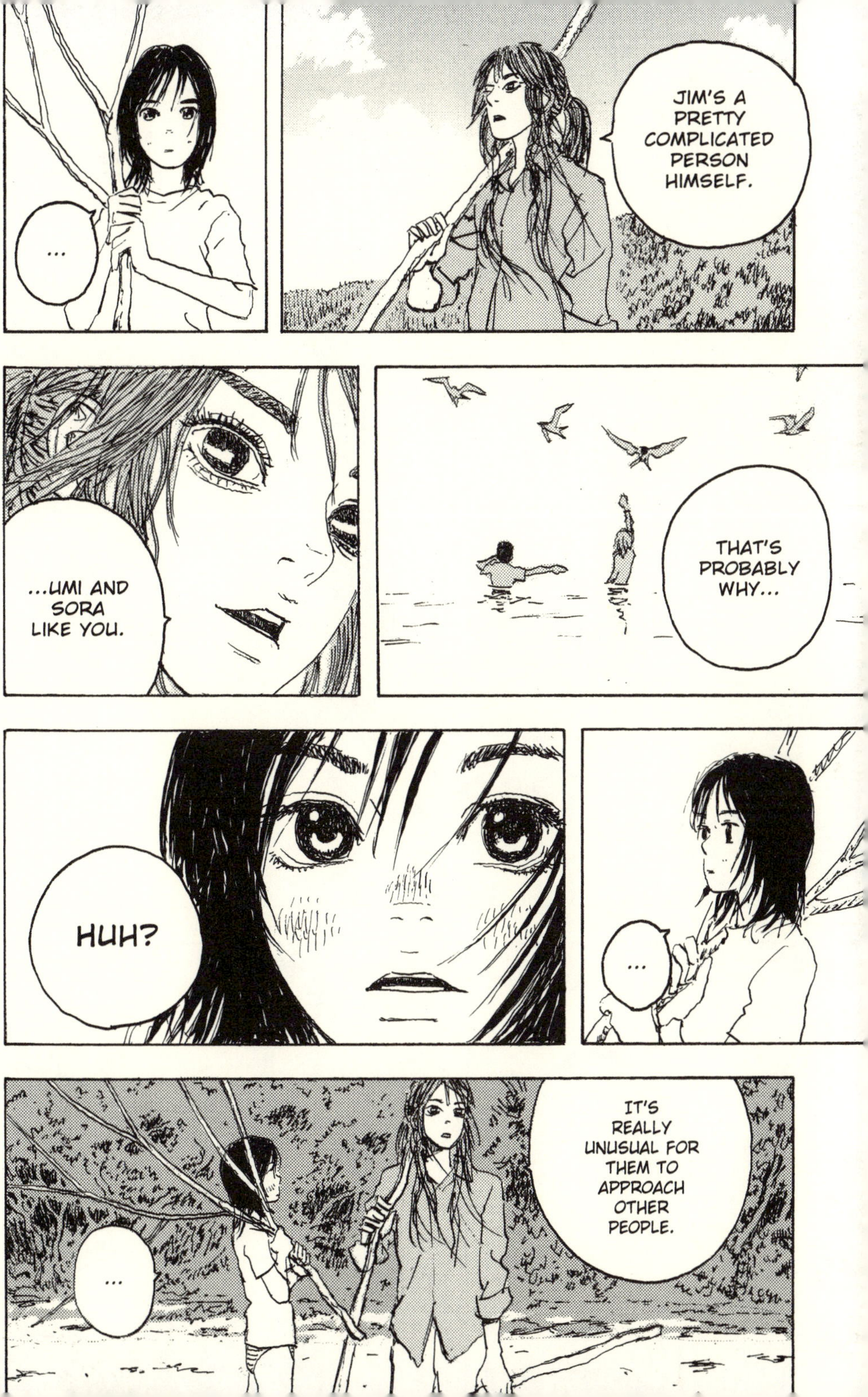
JIM'S A PRETTY COMPLICATED PERSON HIMSELF.
...
THAT'S PROBABLY WHY...
...UMI AND SORA LIKE YOU.
...
HUH?
IT'S REALLY UNUSUAL FOR THEM TO APPROACH OTHER PEOPLE.
...

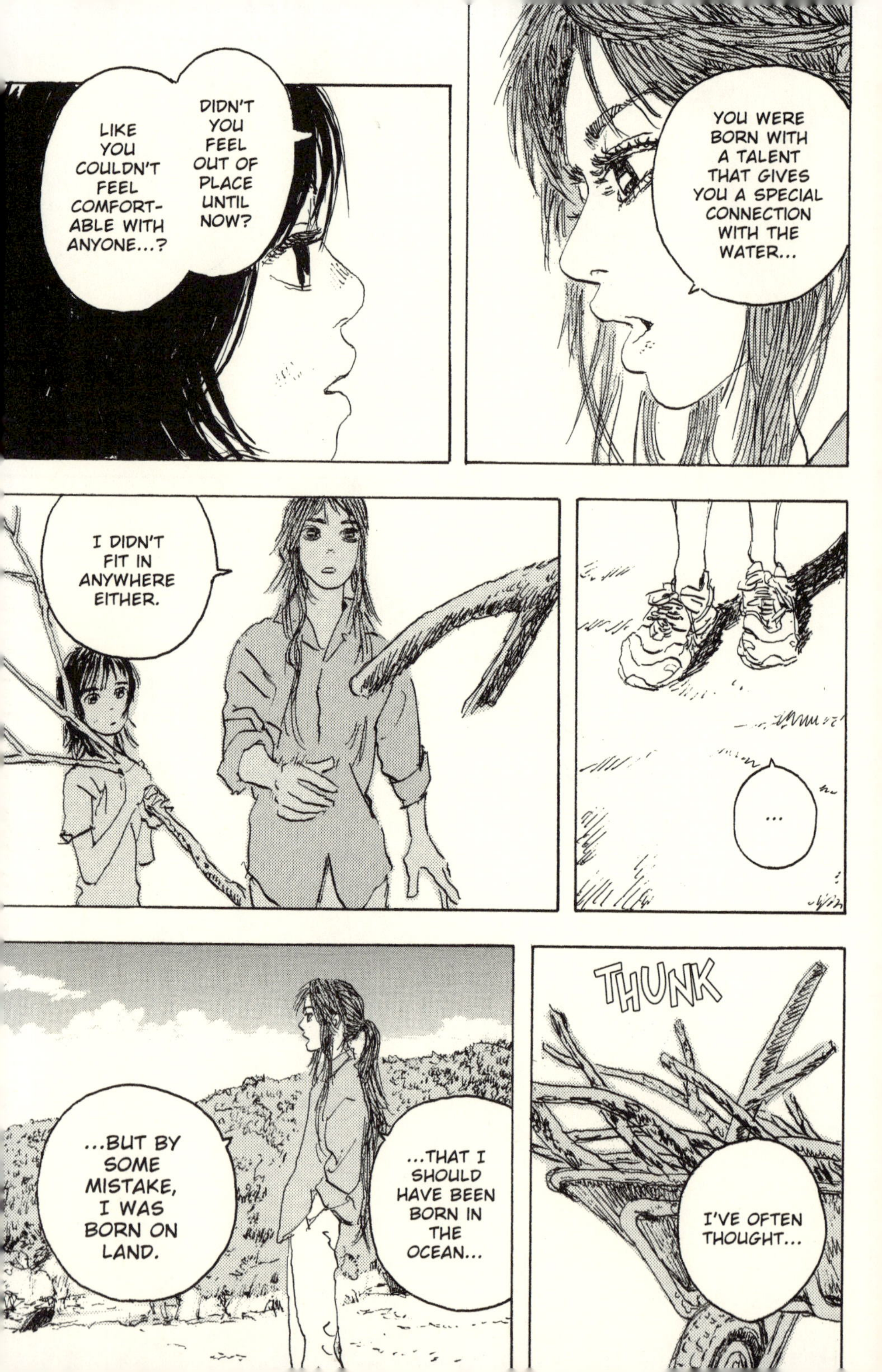
YOU WERE BORN WITH A TALENT THAT GIVES YOU A SPECIAL CONNECTION WITH THE WATER...
DIDN'T YOU FEEL OUT OF PLACE UNTIL NOW?
LIKE YOU COULDN'T FEEL COMFORT-ABLE WITH ANYONE...?
...
I DIDN'T FIT IN ANYWHERE EITHER.
THUNK
I'VE OFTEN THOUGHT...
...THAT I SHOULD HAVE BEEN BORN IN THE OCEAN...
...BUT BY SOME MISTAKE, I WAS BORN ON LAND.

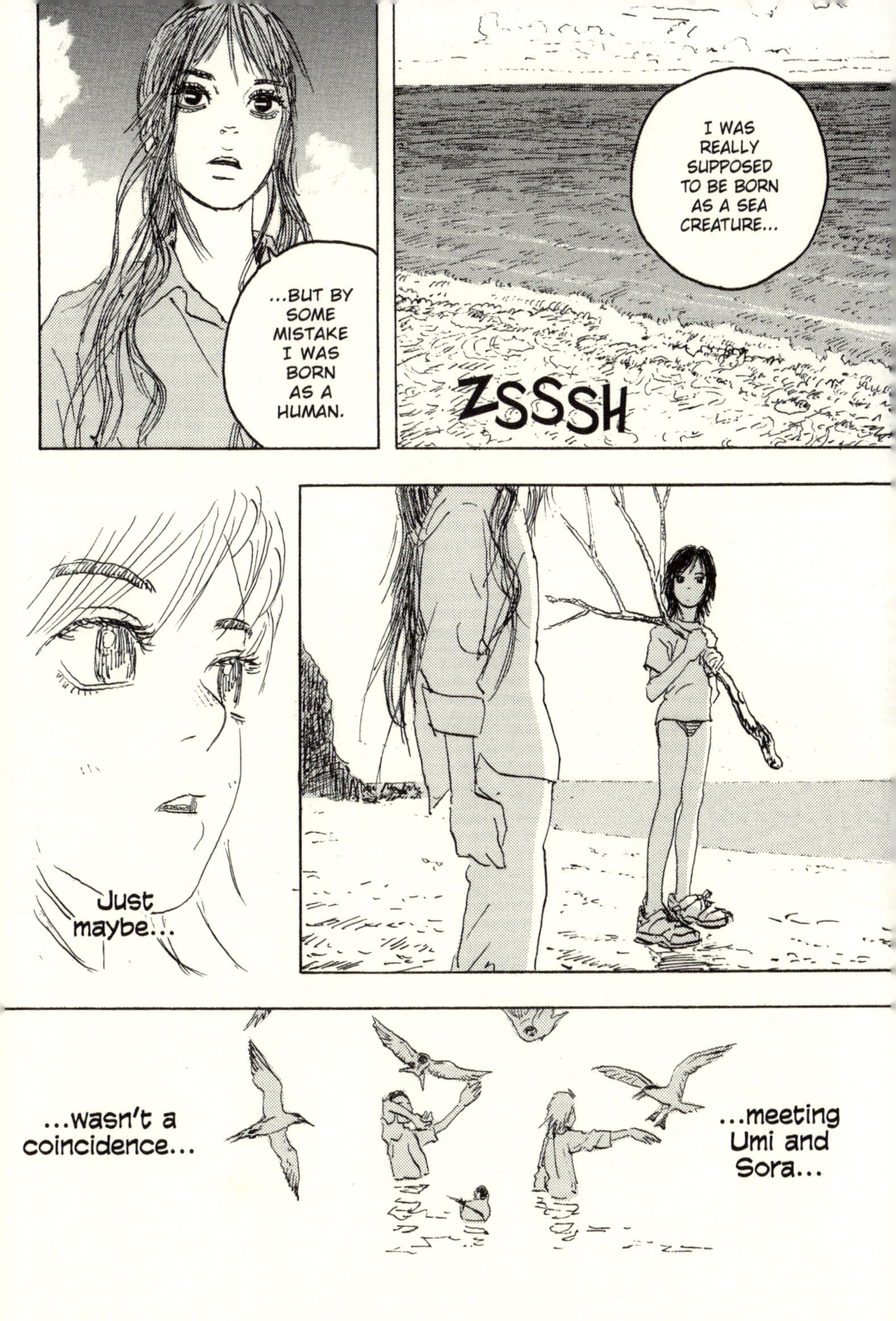
I WAS REALLY SUPPOSED TO BE BORN AS A SEA CREATURE...
ZSSSH
...BUT BY SOME MISTAKE I WAS BORN AS A HUMAN.
Just maybe...
...meeting Umi and Sora...
...wasn't a coincidence...

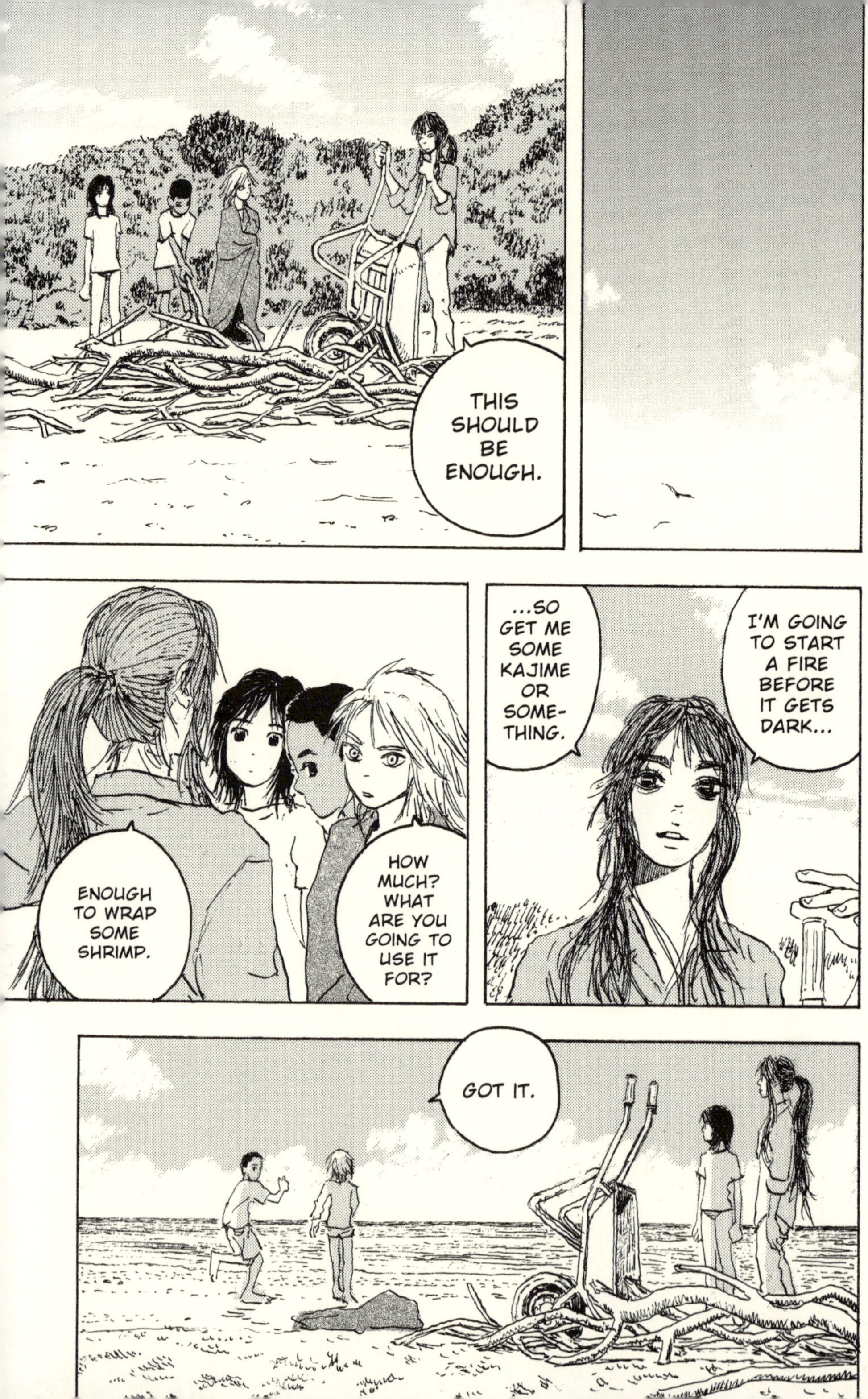
THIS SHOULD BE ENOUGH.
I'M GOING TO START A FIRE BEFORE IT GETS DARK...
...SO GET ME SOME KAJIME OR SOME-THING.
HOW MUCH? WHAT ARE YOU GOING TO USE IT FOR?
ENOUGH TO WRAP SOME SHRIMP.
GOT IT.

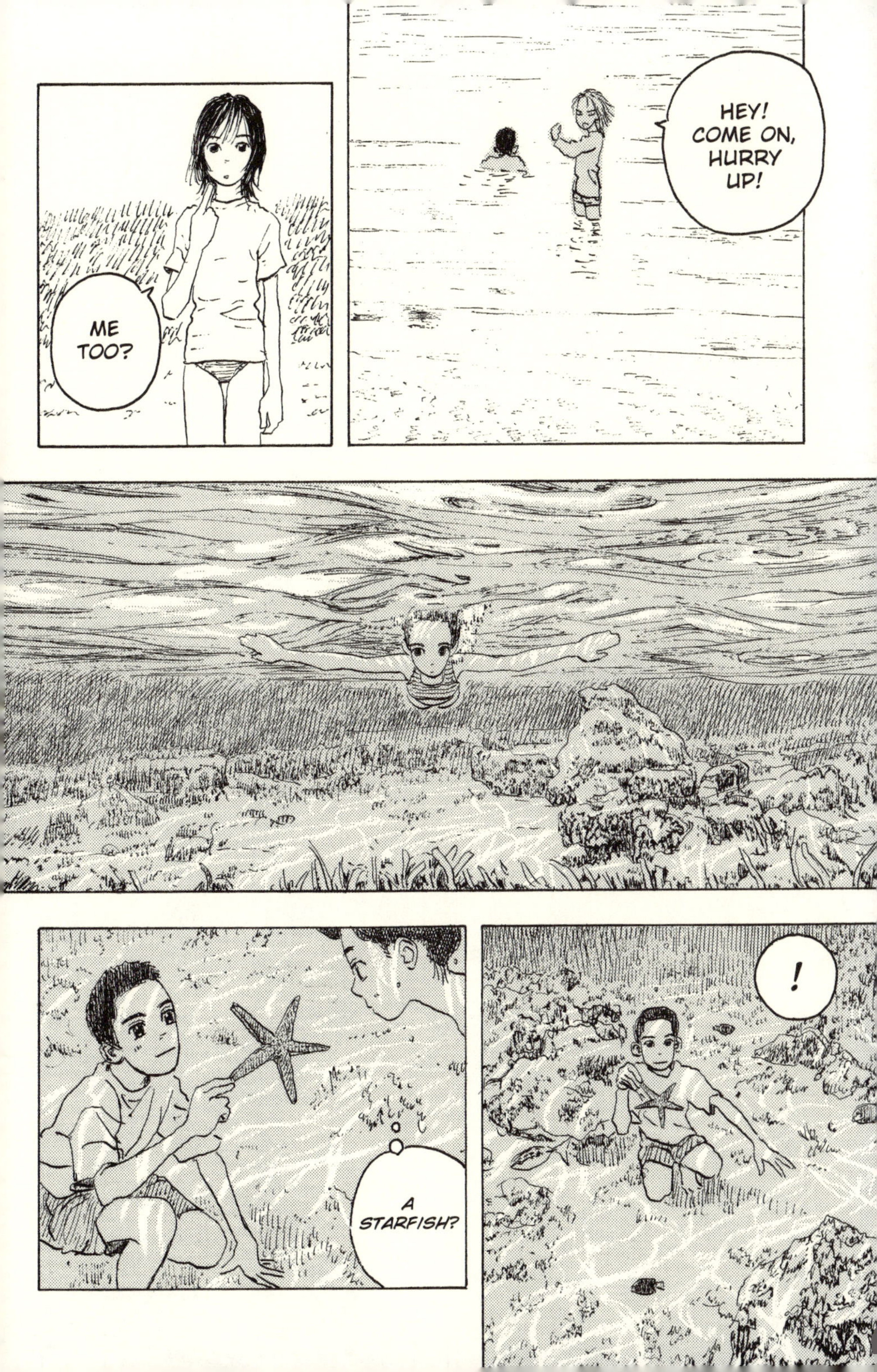
HEY! COME ON, HURRY UP!
ME TOO?
!
A STARFISH?

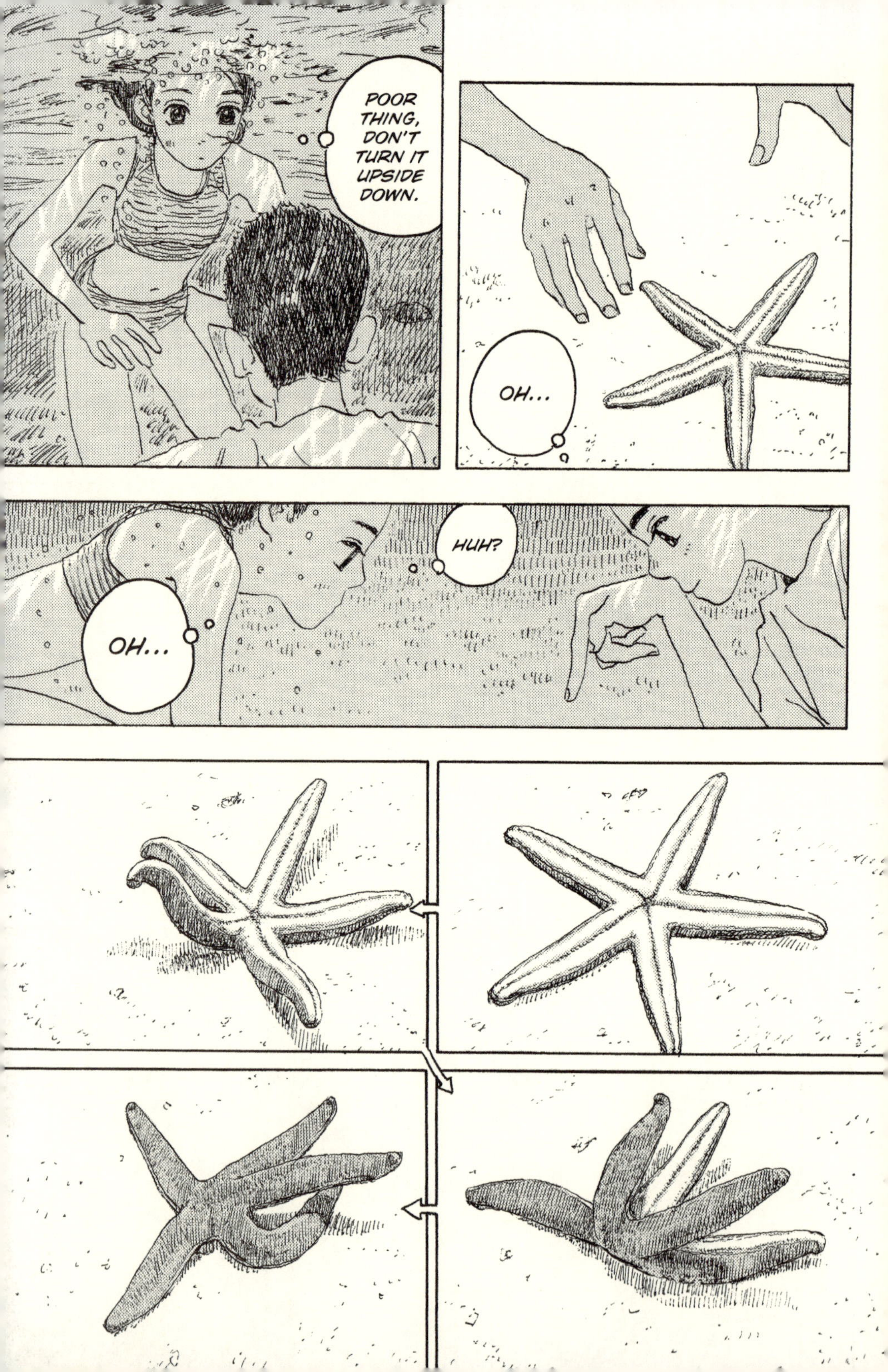
OH...
POOR THING, DON'T TURN IT UPSIDE DOWN.
HUH?
OH...

CLAP CLAP
YAY!
BLURB
OOPS, SORRY...
...

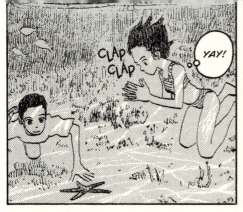

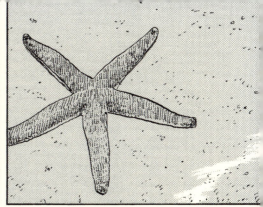

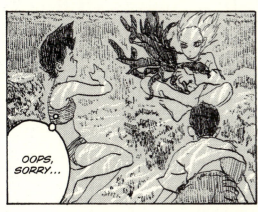

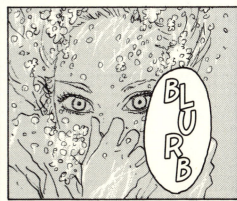

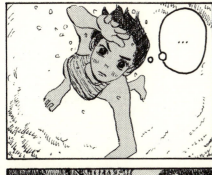

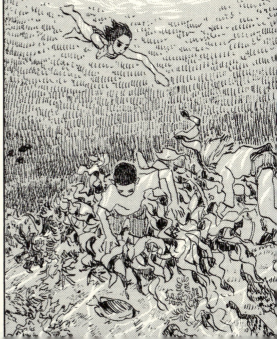

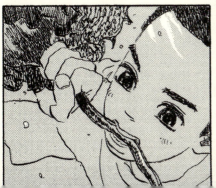

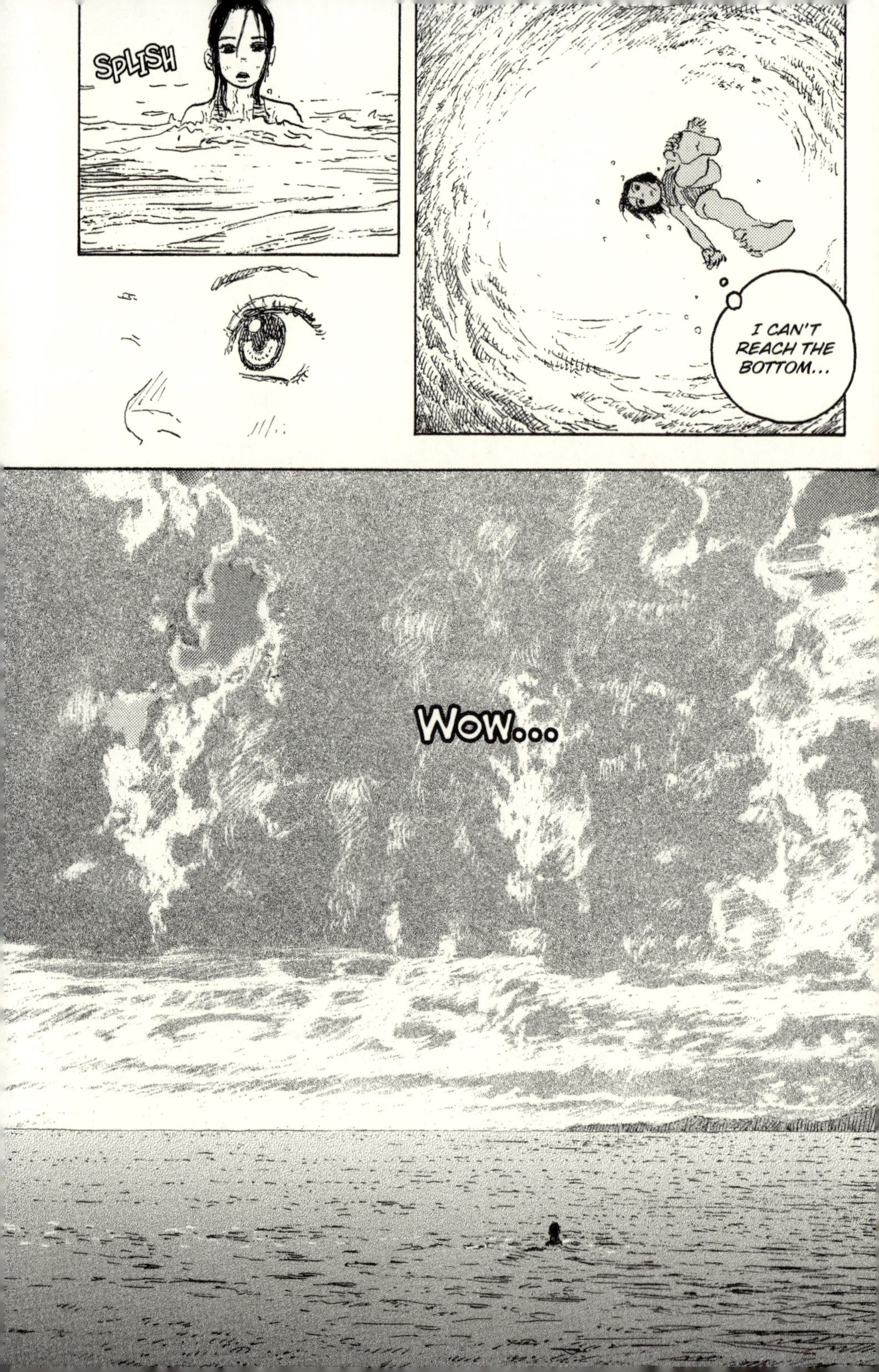
I CAN'T REACH THE BOTTOM...
SPLISH
Wow...

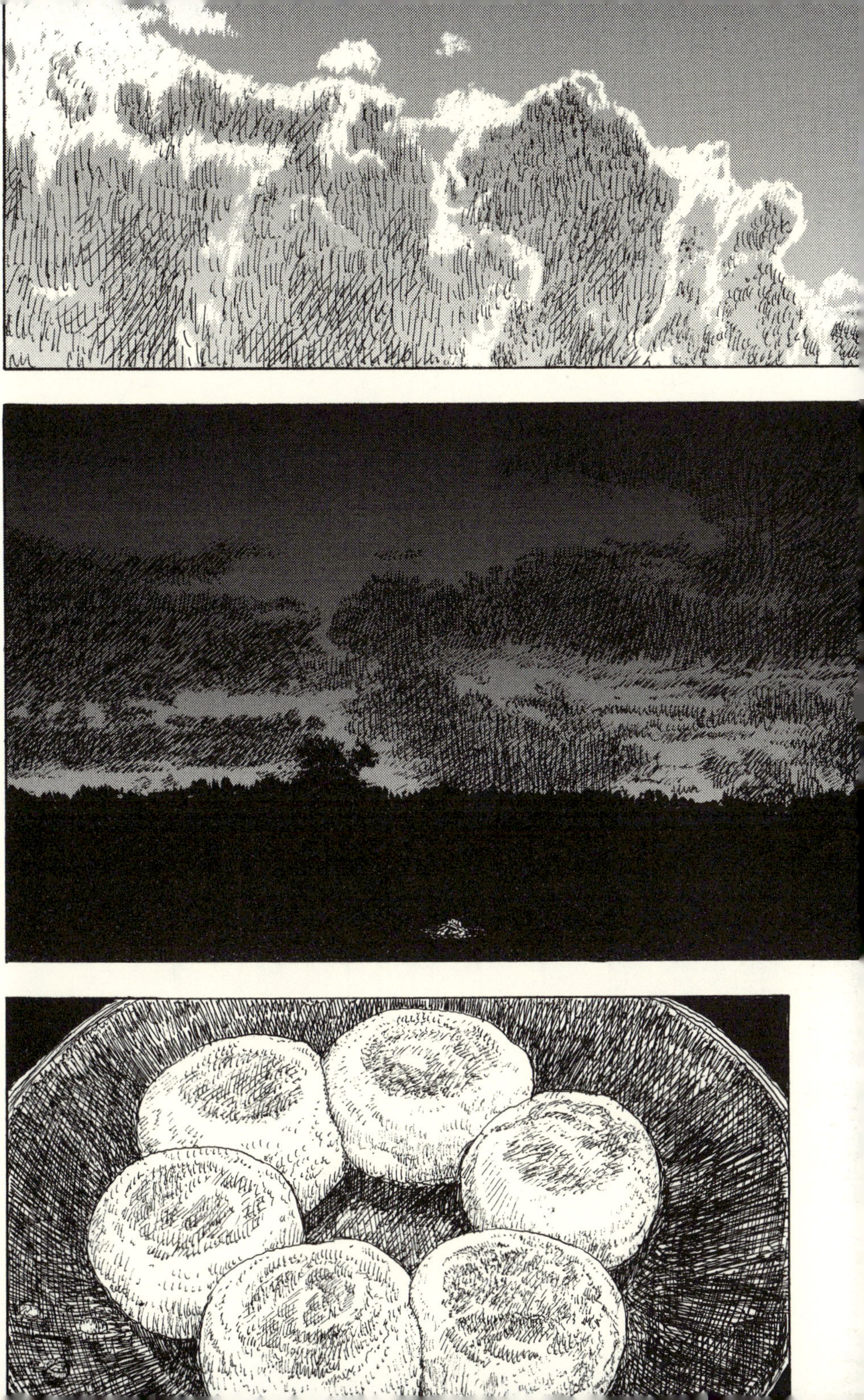

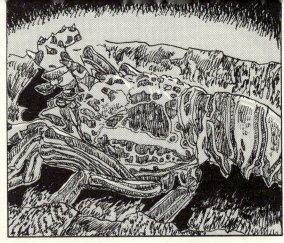
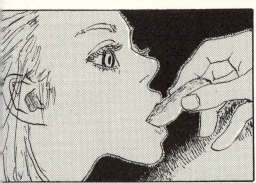

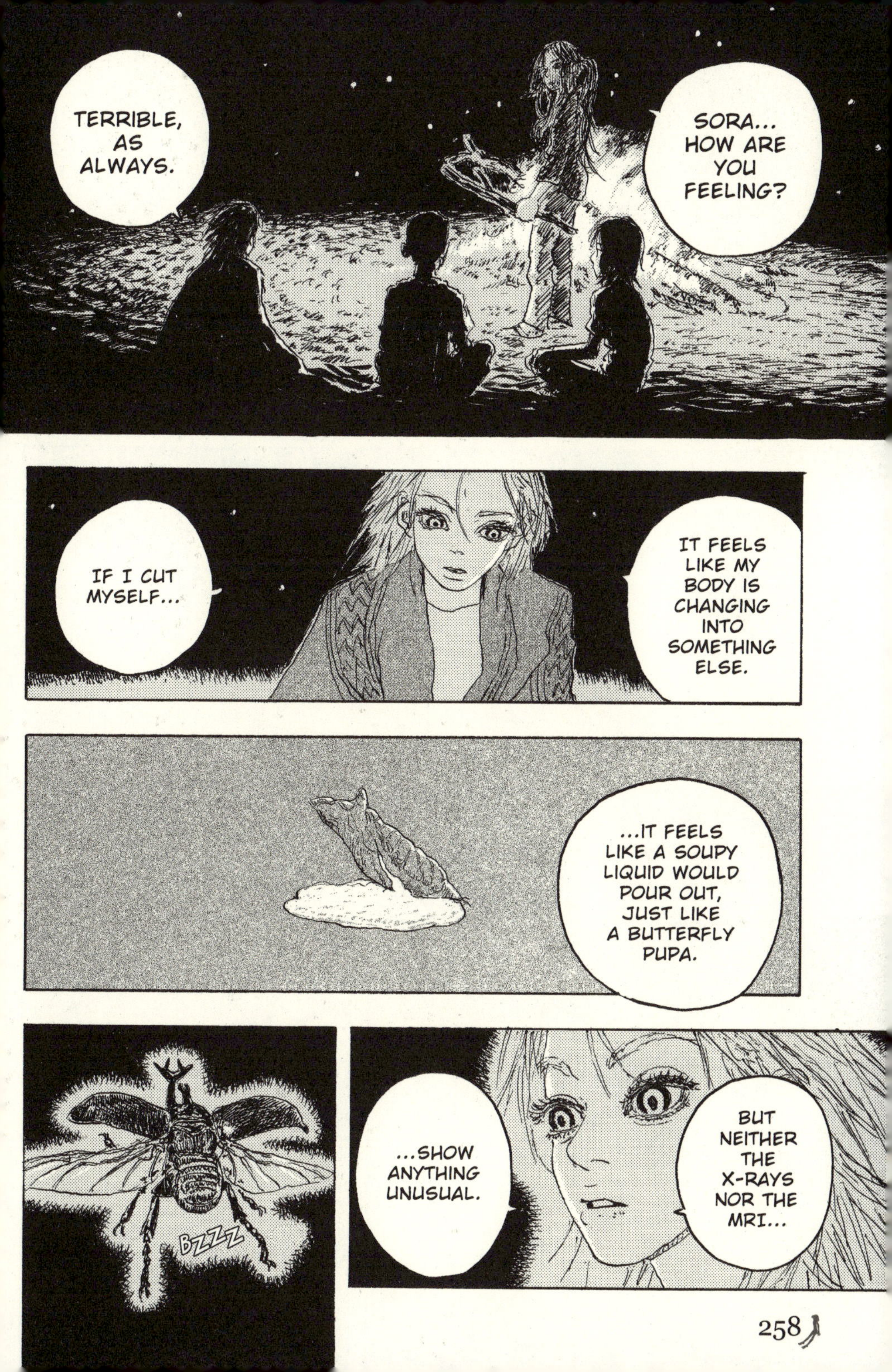
SORA... HOW ARE YOU FEELING?
TERRIBLE, AS ALWAYS.
IT FEELS LIKE MY BODY IS CHANGING INTO SOMETHING ELSE.
IF I CUT MYSELF...
...IT FEELS LIKE A SOUPY LIQUID WOULD POUR OUT, JUST LIKE A BUTTERFLY PUPA.
BUT NEITHER THE X-RAYS NOR THE MRI...
...SHOW ANYTHING UNUSUAL.
BZZZZ

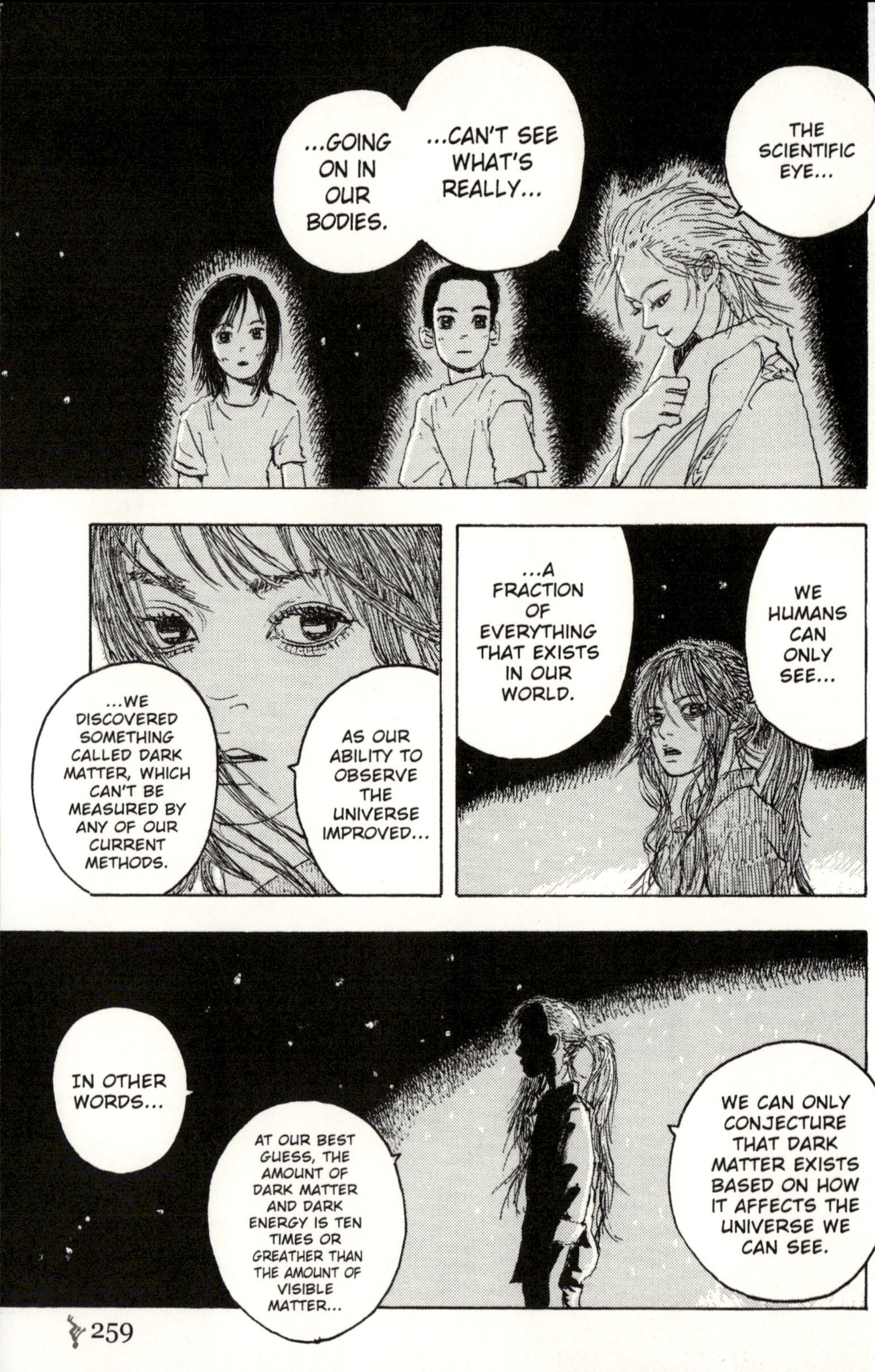
THE SCIENTIFIC EYE...
...CAN'T SEE WHAT'S REALLY...
...GOING ON IN OUR BODIES.
WE HUMANS CAN ONLY SEE...
...A FRACTION OF EVERYTHING THAT EXISTS IN OUR WORLD.
AS OUR ABILITY TO OBSERVE THE UNIVERSE IMPROVED...
...WE DISCOVERED SOMETHING CALLED DARK MATTER, WHICH CAN'T BE MEASURED BY ANY OF OUR CURRENT METHODS.
WE CAN ONLY CONJECTURE THAT DARK MATTER EXISTS BASED ON HOW IT AFFECTS THE UNIVERSE WE CAN SEE.
IN OTHER WORDS...
AT OUR BEST GUESS, THE AMOUNT OF DARK MATTER AND DARK ENERGY IS TEN TIMES OR GREATHER THAN THE AMOUNT OF VISIBLE MATTER...

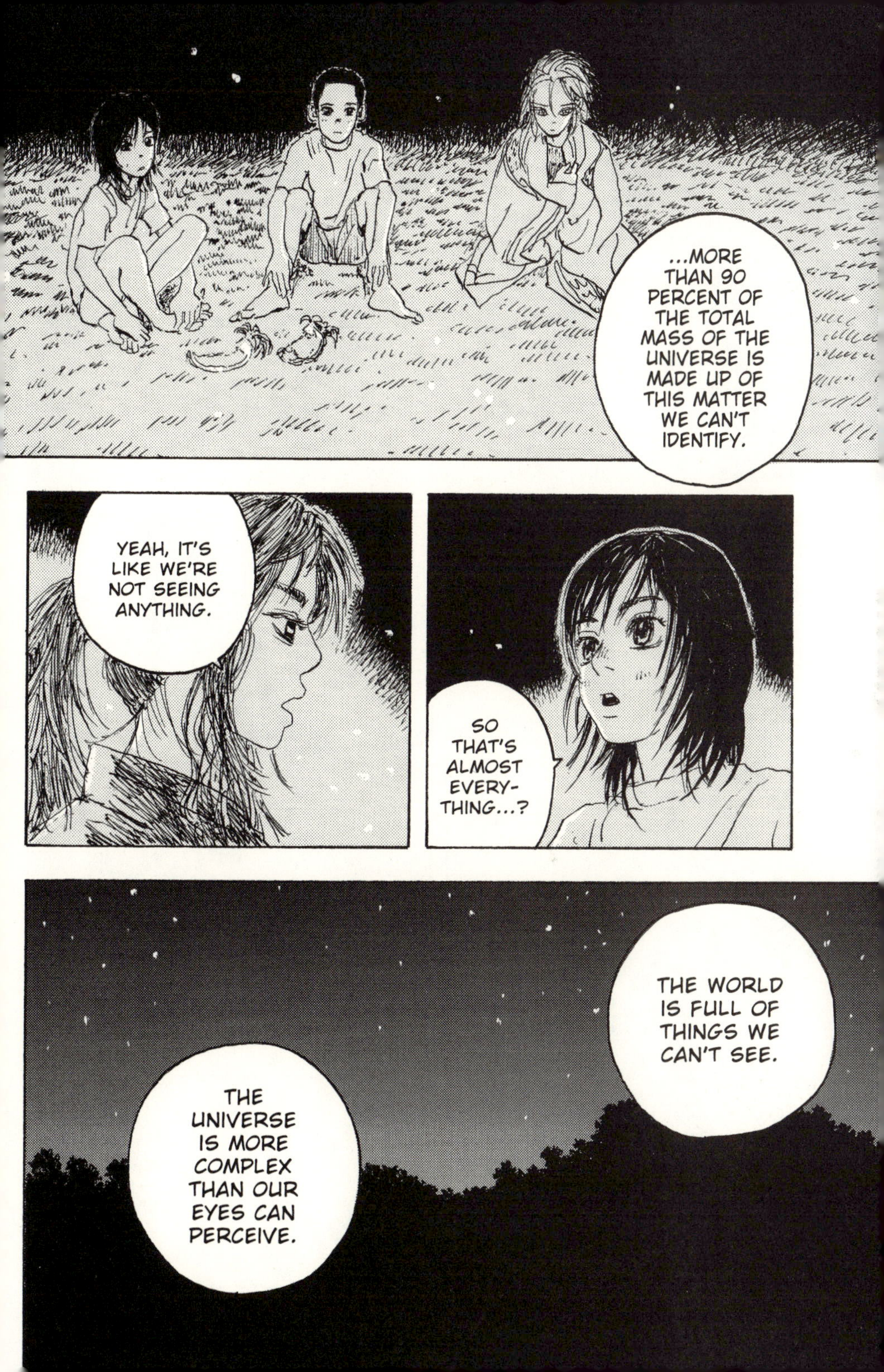
...MORE THAN 90 PERCENT OF THE TOTAL MASS OF THE UNIVERSE IS MADE UP OF THIS MATTER WE CAN'T IDENTIFY.
SO THAT'S ALMOST EVERY-THING...?
YEAH, IT'S LIKE WE'RE NOT SEEING ANYTHING.
THE WORLD IS FULL OF THINGS WE CAN'T SEE.
THE UNIVERSE IS MORE COMPLEX THAN OUR EYES CAN PERCEIVE.

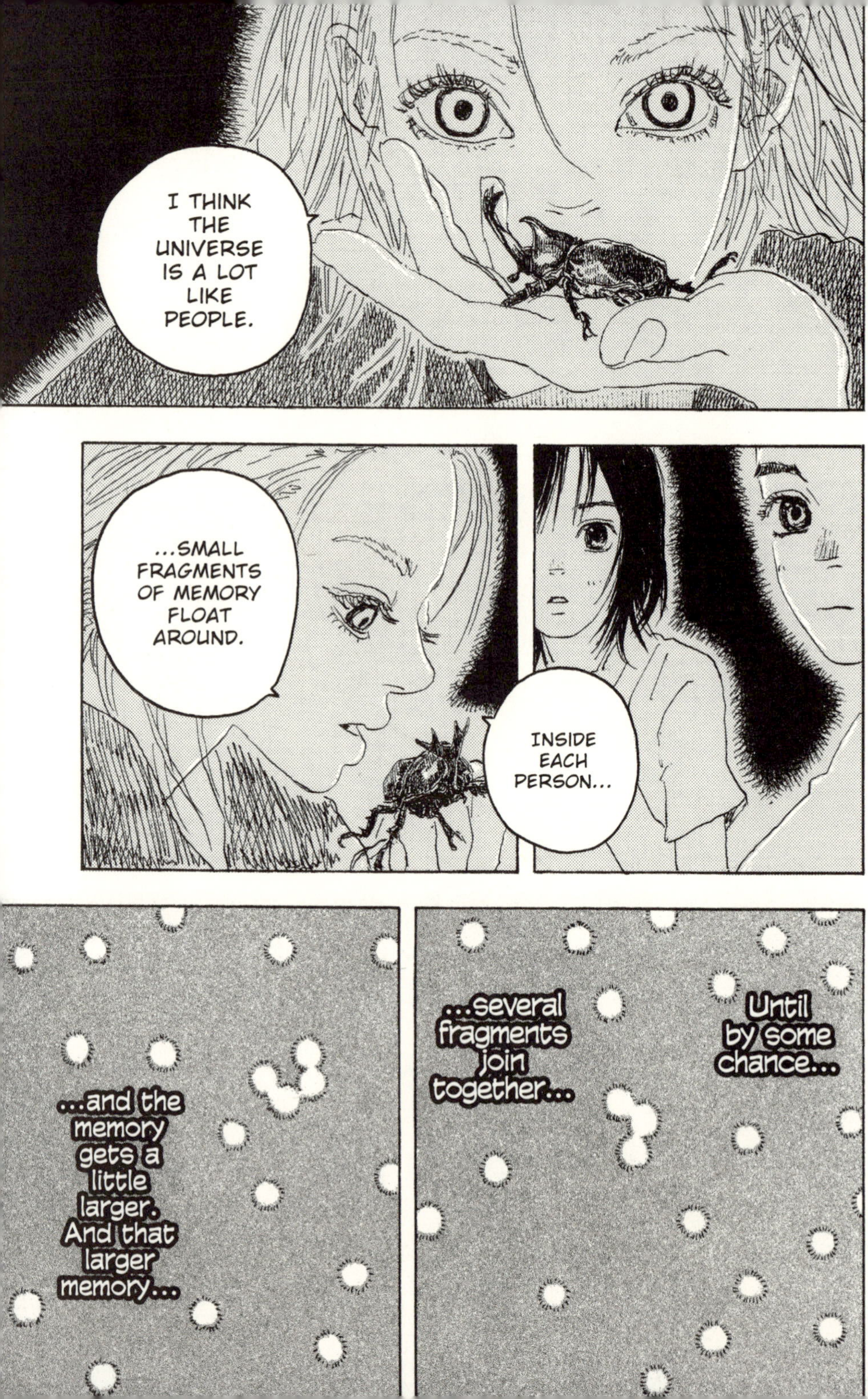
I THINK THE UNIVERSE IS A LOT LIKE PEOPLE.
INSIDE EACH PERSON...
...SMALL FRAGMENTS OF MEMORY FLOAT AROUND.
Until by some chance...
...several fragments join together...
...and the memory gets a little larger. And that larger memory...

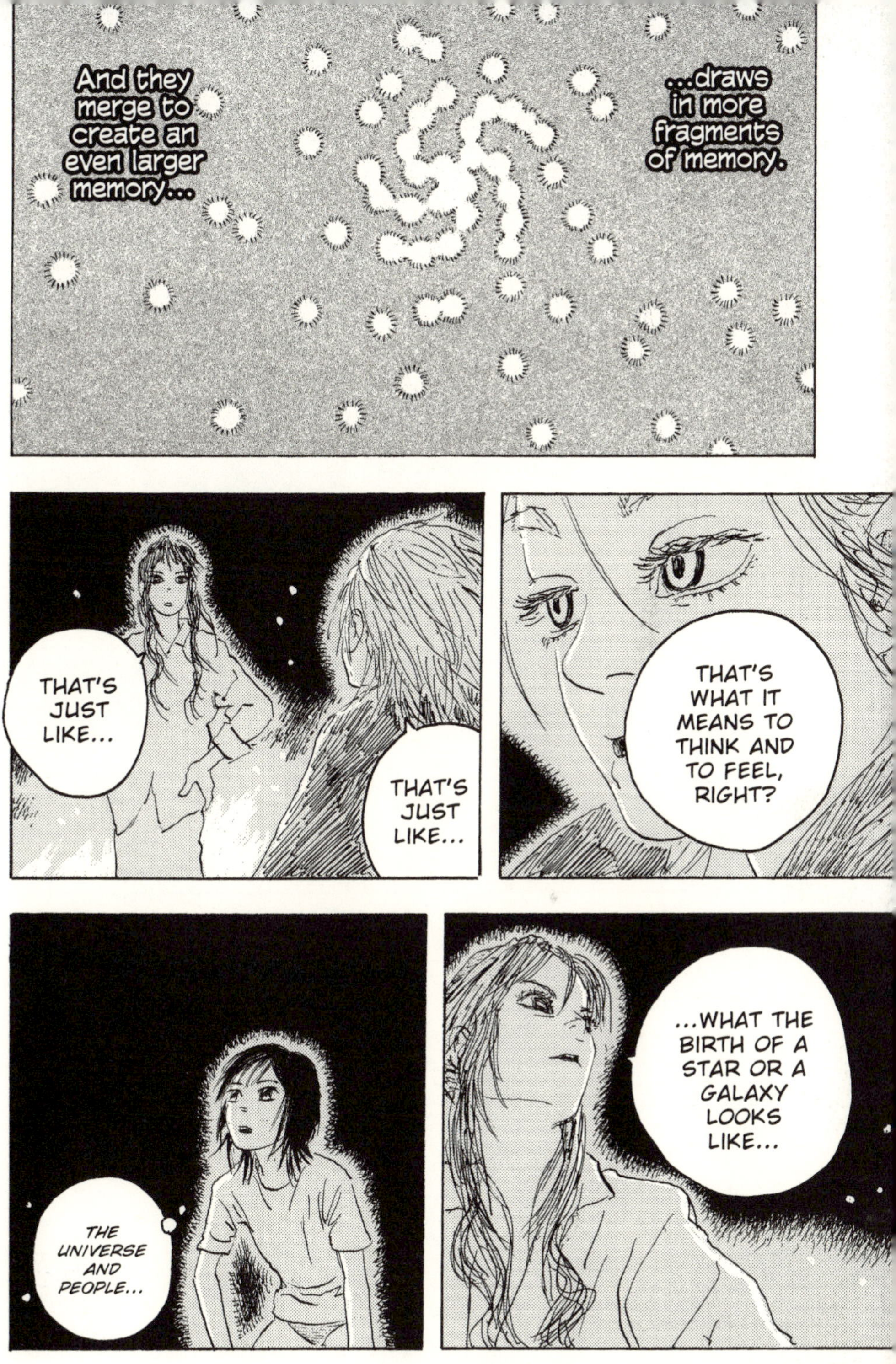
And they merge to create an even larger memory...
...draws in more fragments of memory.
THAT'S WHAT IT MEANS TO THINK AND TO FEEL, RIGHT?
THAT'S JUST LIKE...
THAT'S JUST LIKE...
...WHAT THE BIRTH OF A STAR OR A GALAXY LOOKS LIKE...
THE UNIVERSE AND PEOPLE...

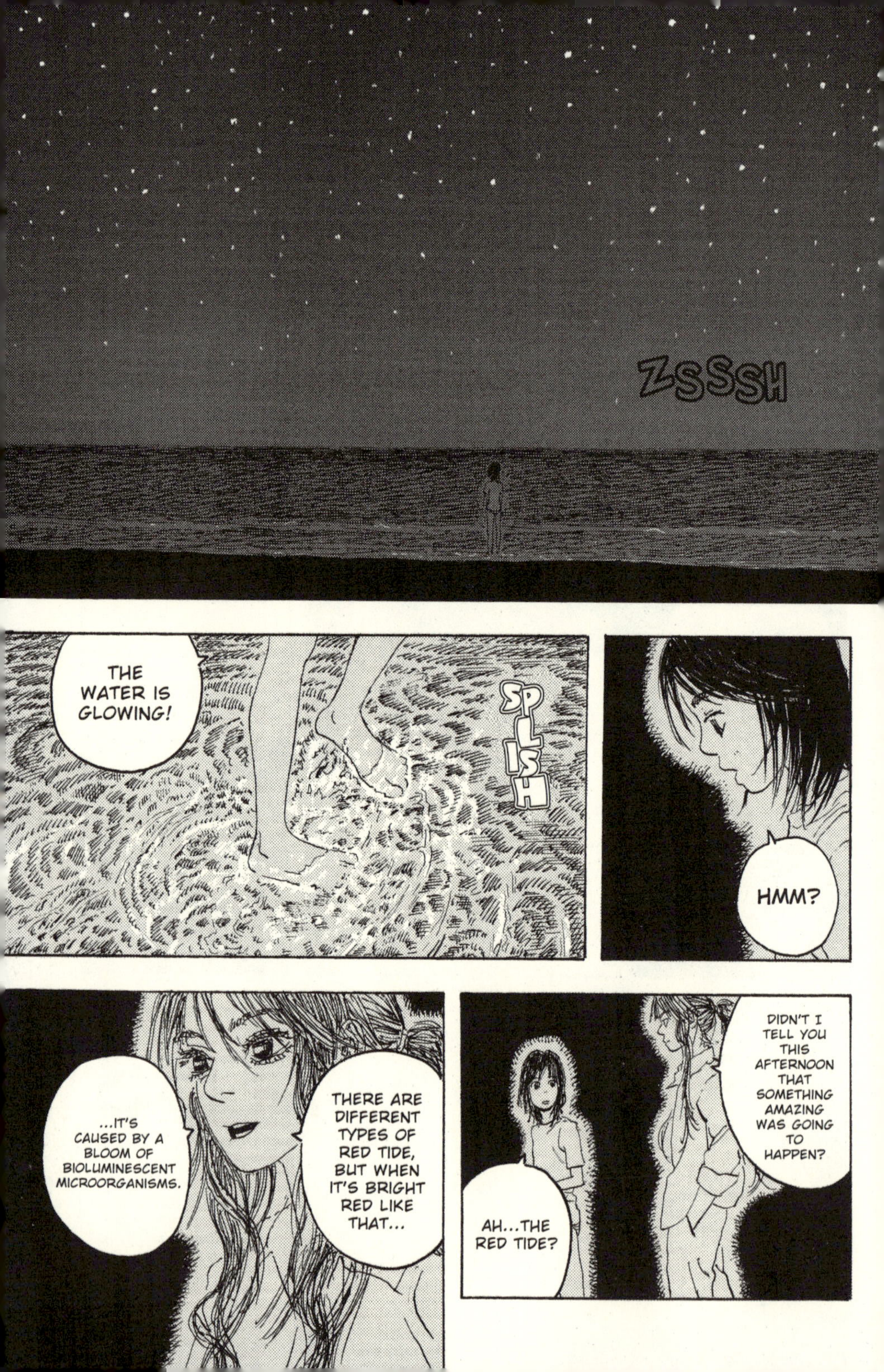
ZSSSH
HMM?
THE WATER IS GLOWING!
SPLISH
DIDN'T I TELL YOU THIS AFTERNOON THAT SOMETHING AMAZING WAS GOING TO HAPPEN?
AH...THE RED TIDE?
THERE ARE DIFFERENT TYPES OF RED TIDE, BUT WHEN IT'S BRIGHT RED LIKE THAT...
...IT'S CAUSED BY A BLOOM OF BIOLUMINESCENT MICROORGANISMS.

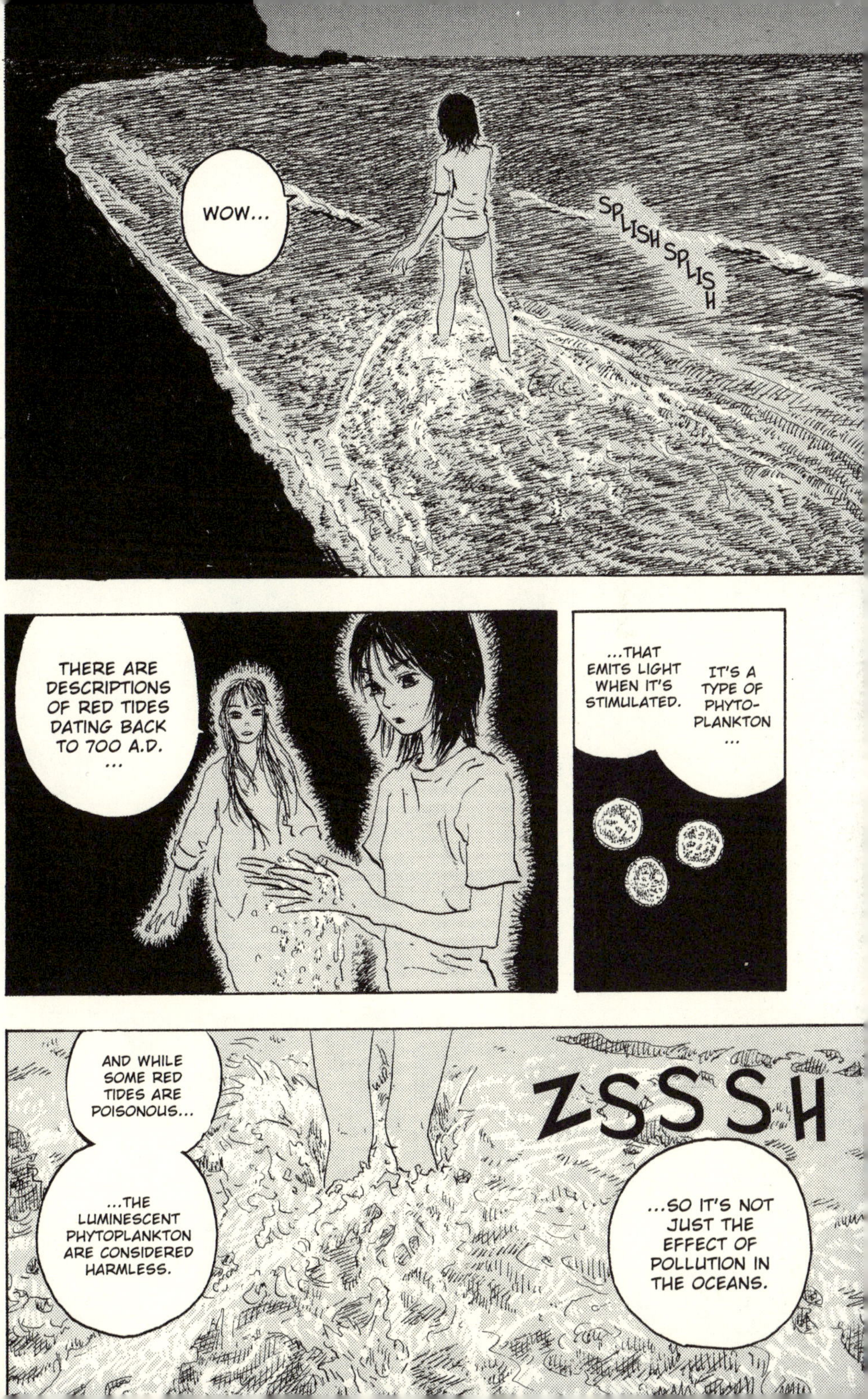
SPLISH SPLISH
WOW...
IT'S A TYPE OF PHYTO-PLANKTON ...
...THAT EMITS LIGHT WHEN IT'S STIMULATED.
THERE ARE DESCRIPTIONS OF RED TIDES DATING BACK TO 700 A.D. ...
ZSSSH
...SO IT'S NOT JUST THE EFFECT OF POLLUTION IN THE OCEANS.
AND WHILE SOME RED TIDES ARE POISONOUS...
...THE LUMINESCENT PHYTOPLANKTON ARE CONSIDERED HARMLESS.

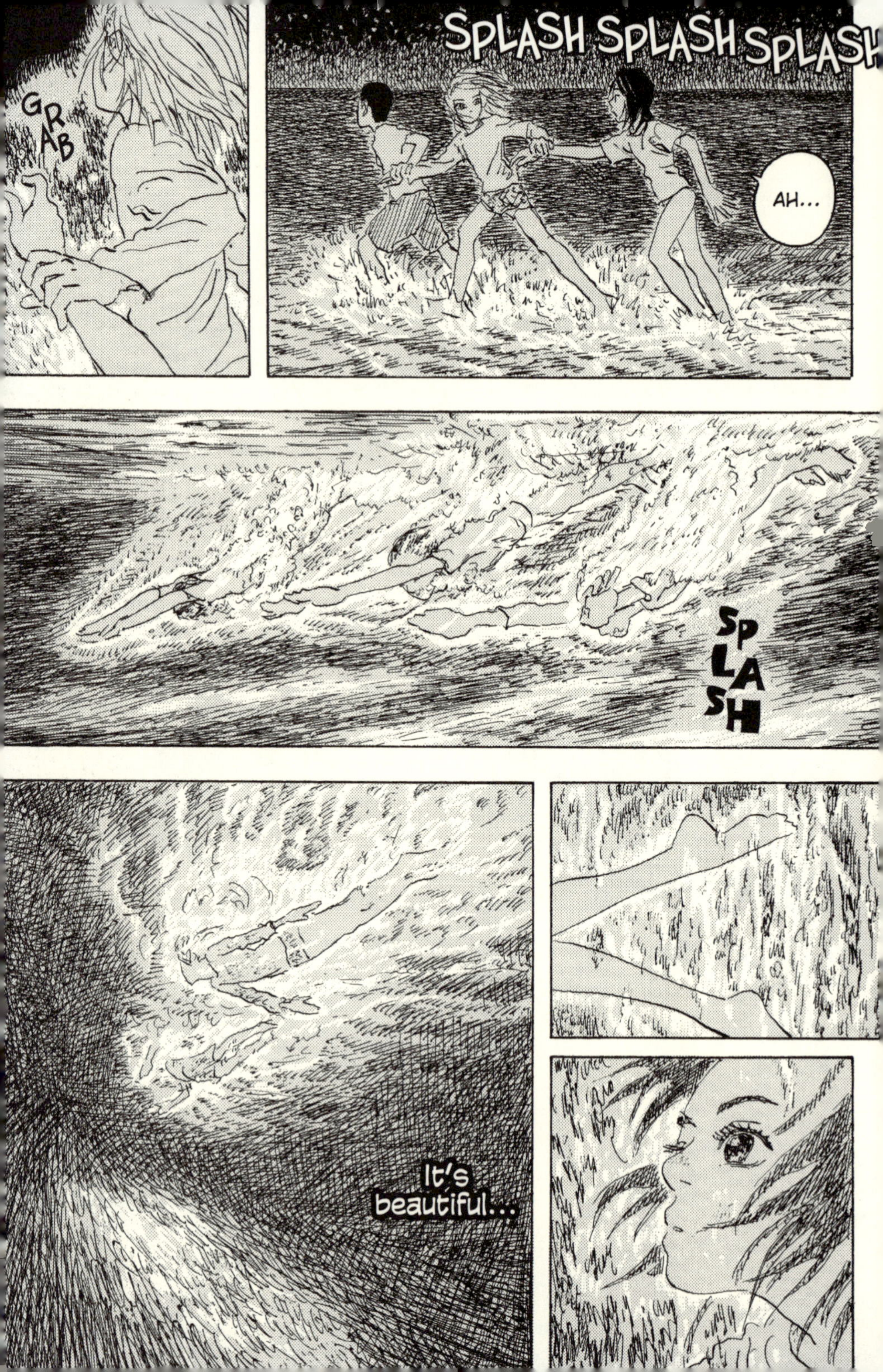
SPLASH SPLASH SPLASH
AH...
GRAB
SPLASH
It's beautiful...

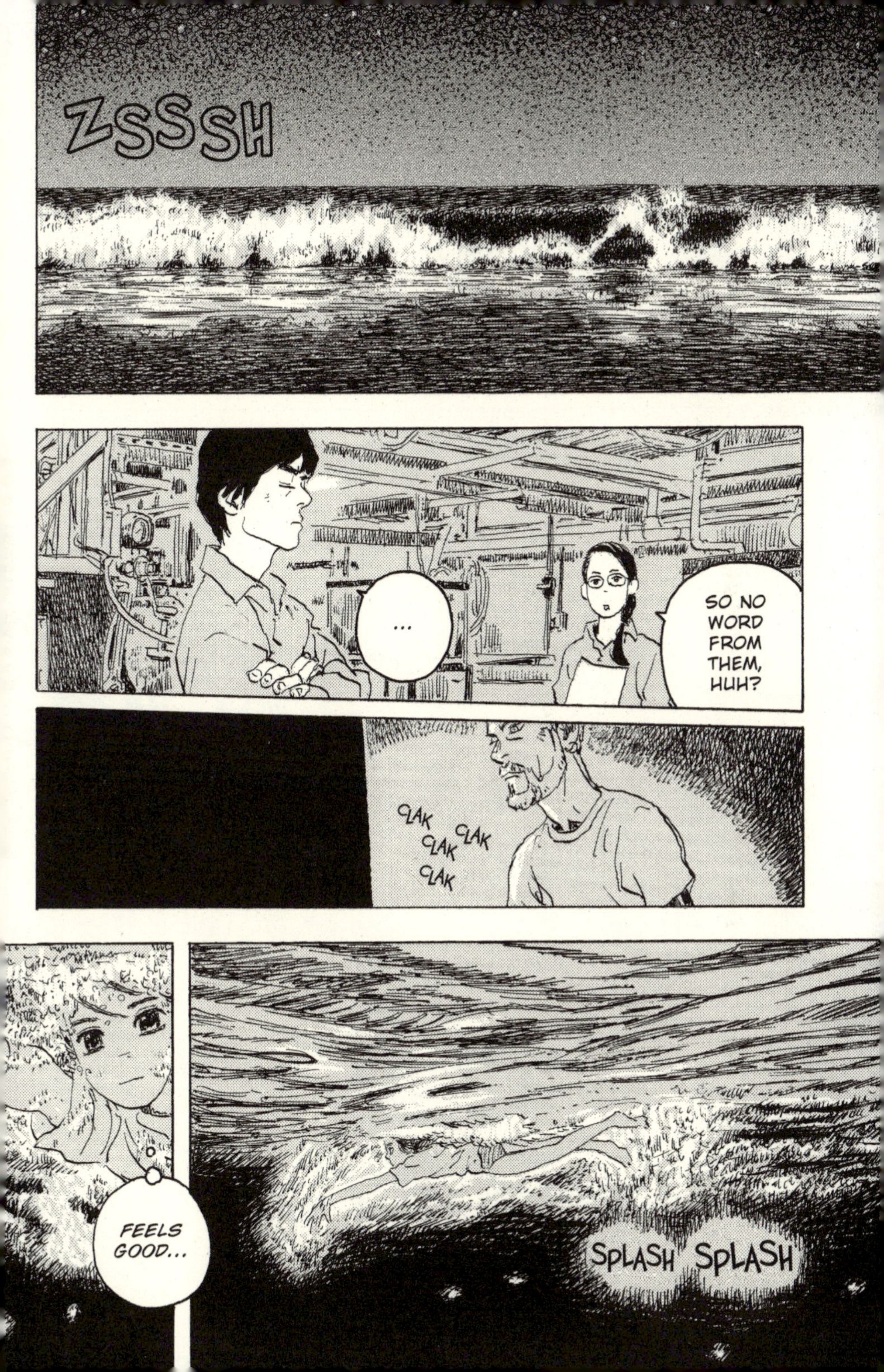
ZSSSH
SO NO WORD FROM THEM, HUH?
...
CLAK CLAK CLAK CLAK
SPLASH SPLASH
FEELS GOOD...

It was a very beautiful night.

!

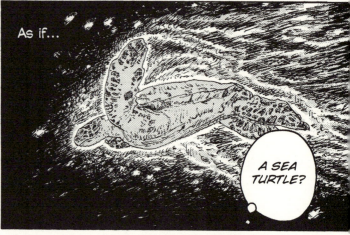

As if...

A SEA TURTLE?

As if it were a farewell gift to Sora.

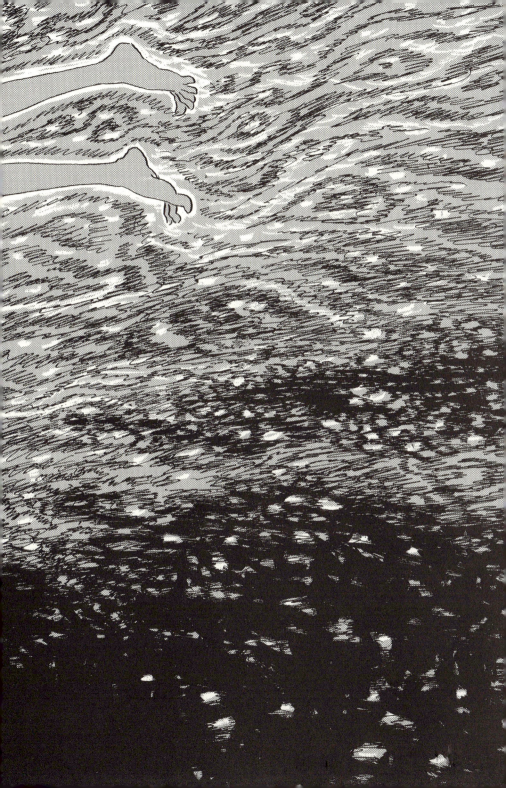

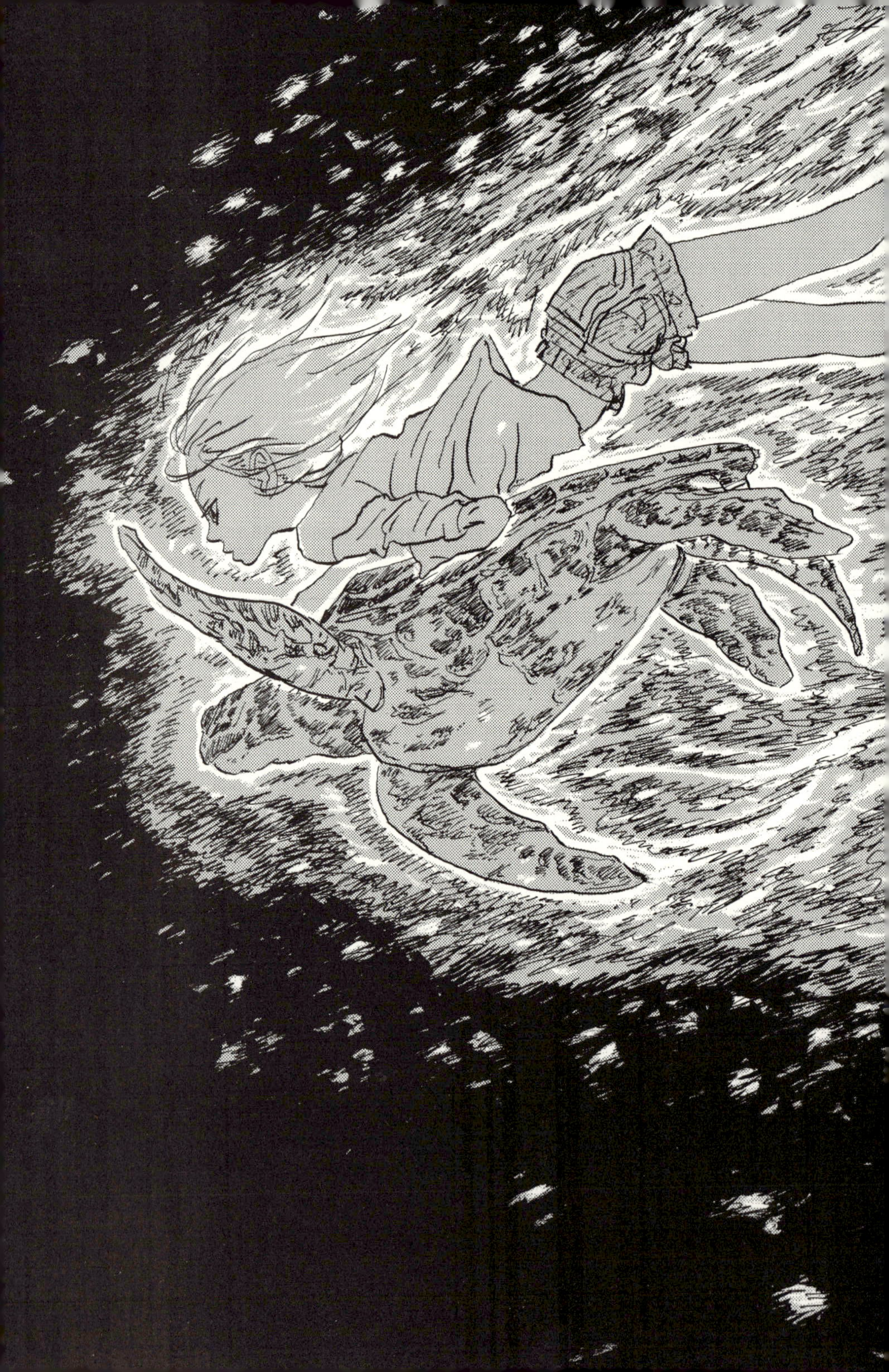

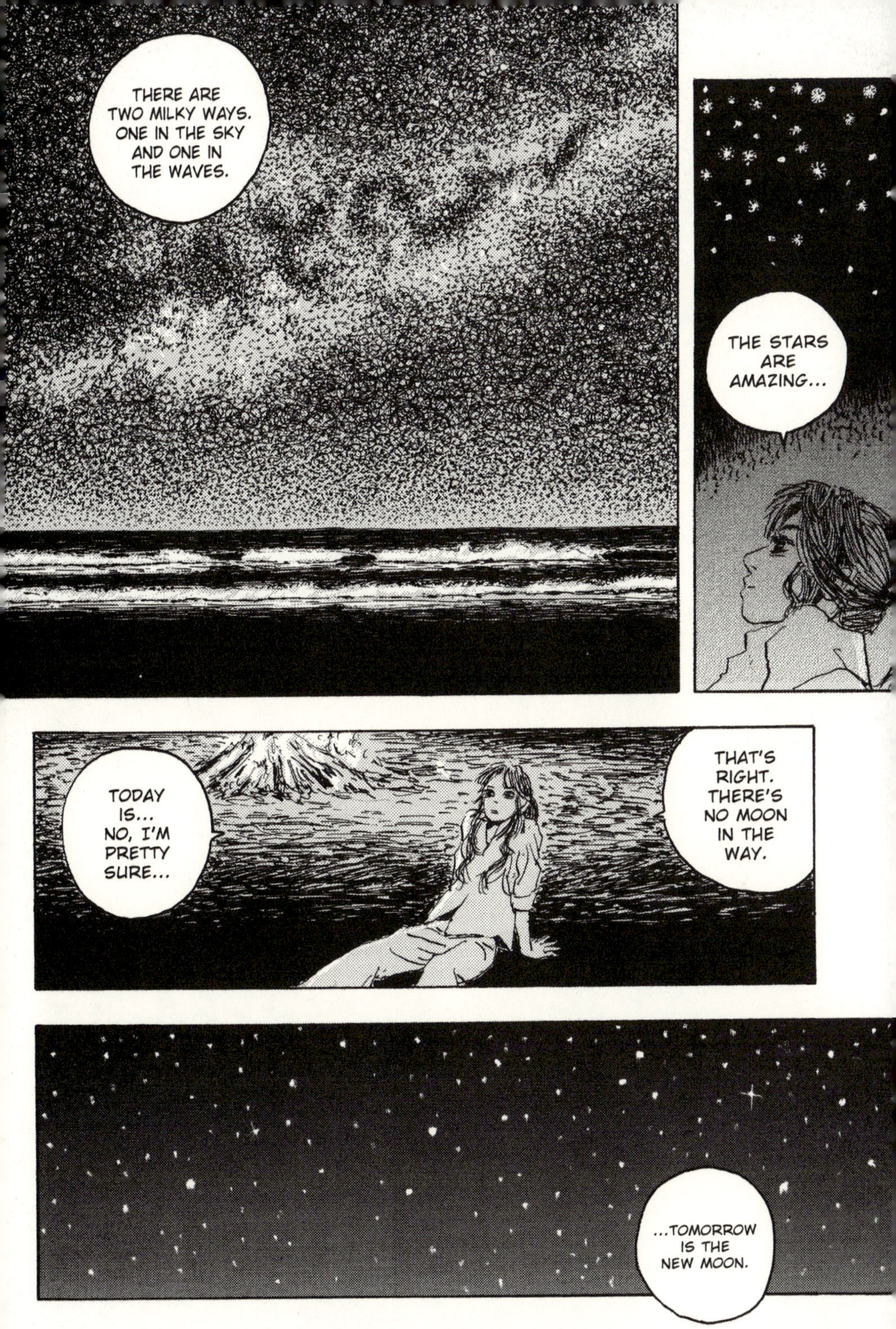
THE STARS ARE AMAZING...
THERE ARE TWO MILKY WAYS. ONE IN THE SKY AND ONE IN THE WAVES.
THAT'S RIGHT. THERE'S NO MOON IN THE WAY.
TODAY IS... NO, I'M PRETTY SURE...
...TOMORROW IS THE NEW MOON.

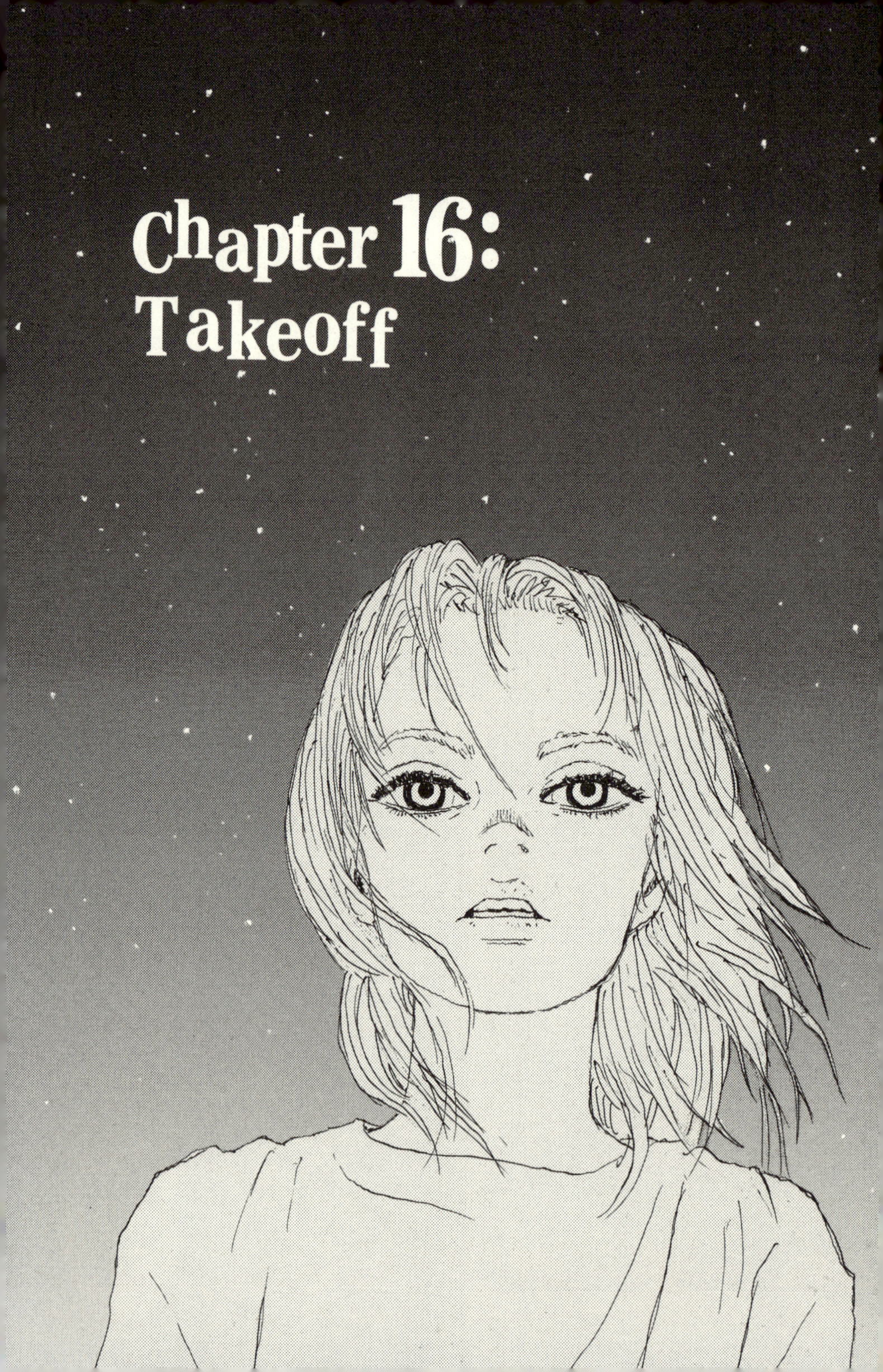
Chapter 16:
Takeoff

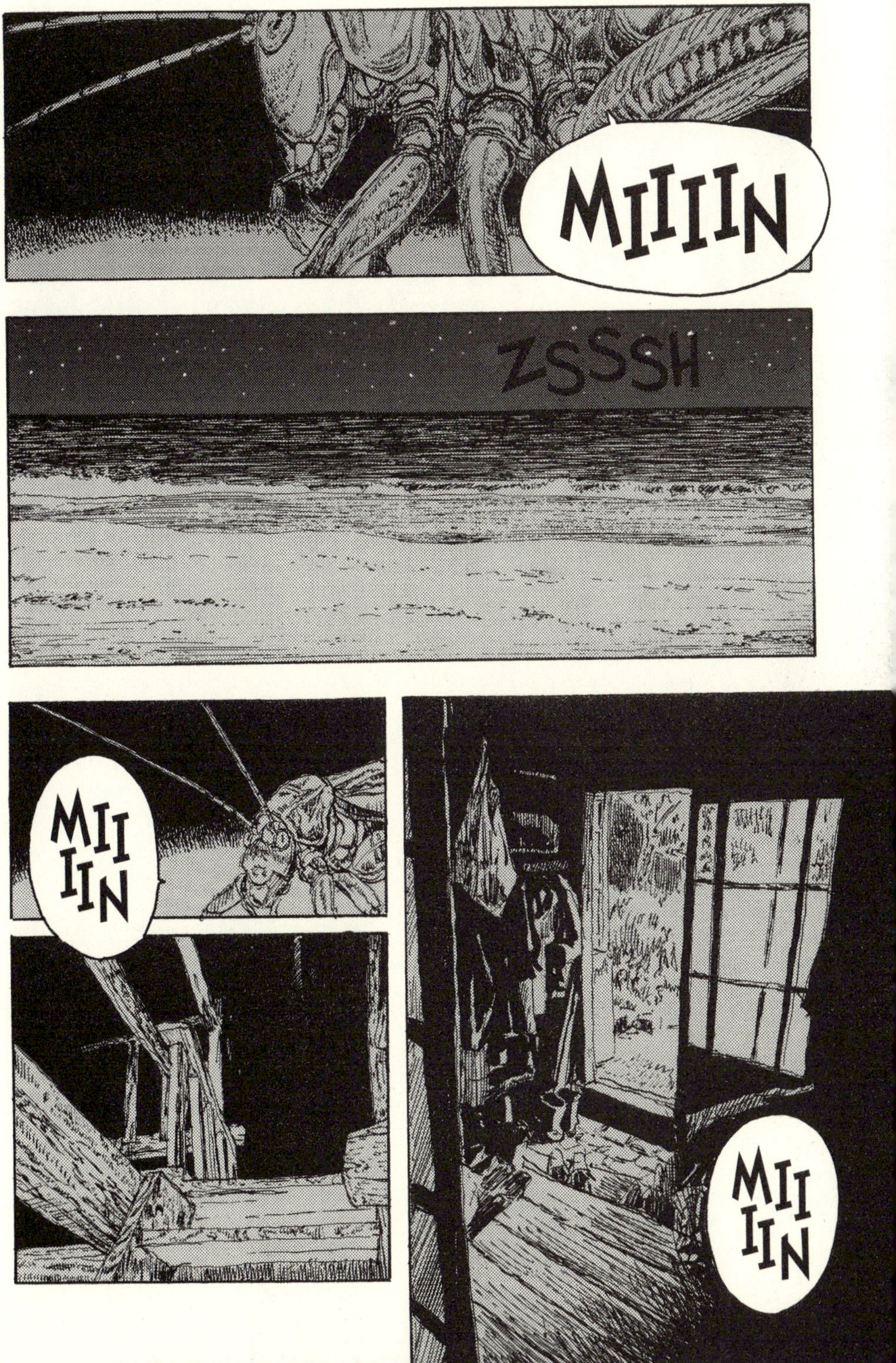
MIIIIN
ZSSSH
MIIIIN
MIIIIN

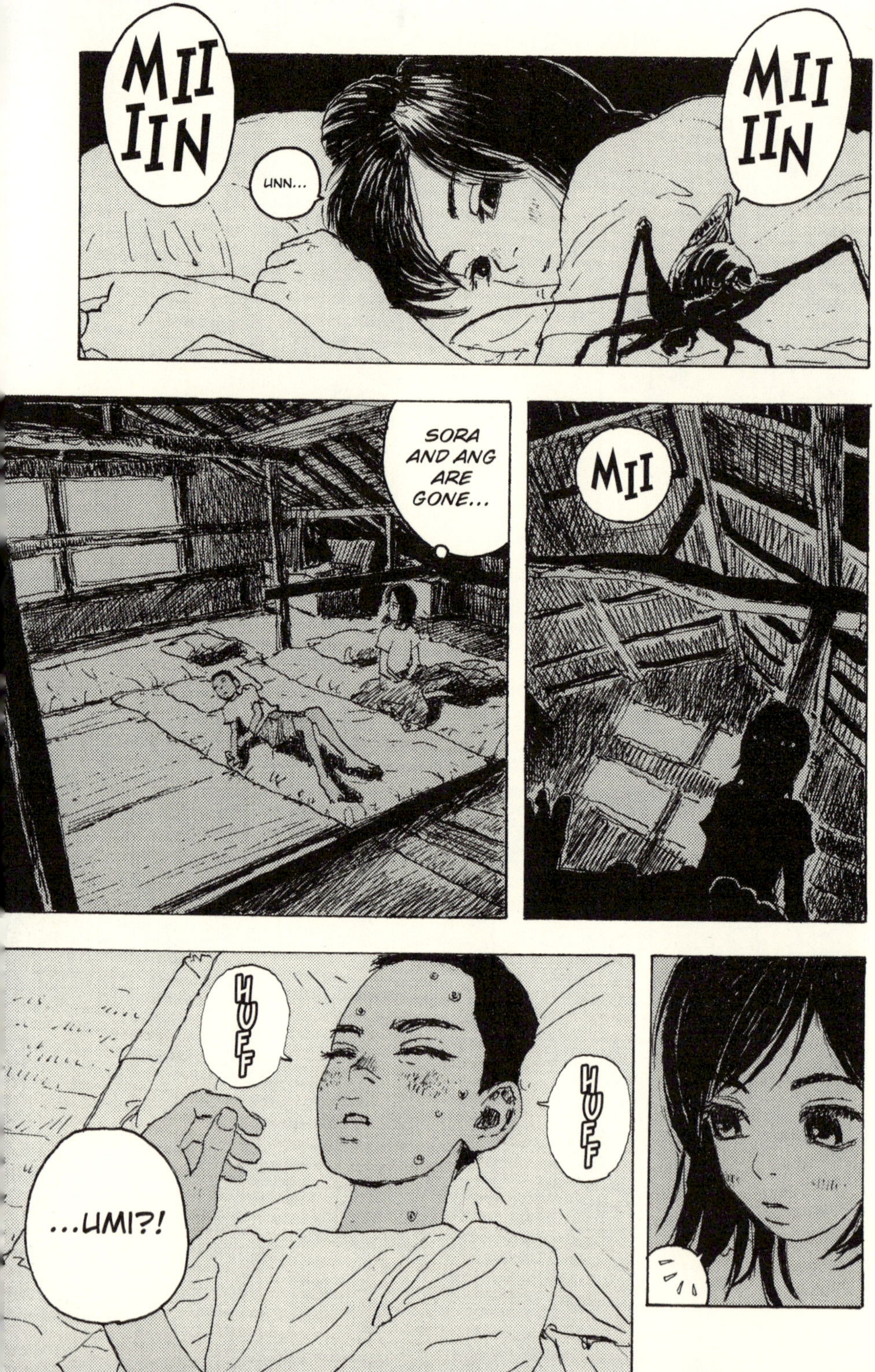
MII IIN
MII IIN
UNN...
MII
SORA AND ANG ARE GONE...
HUFF
HUFF
...UMI?!

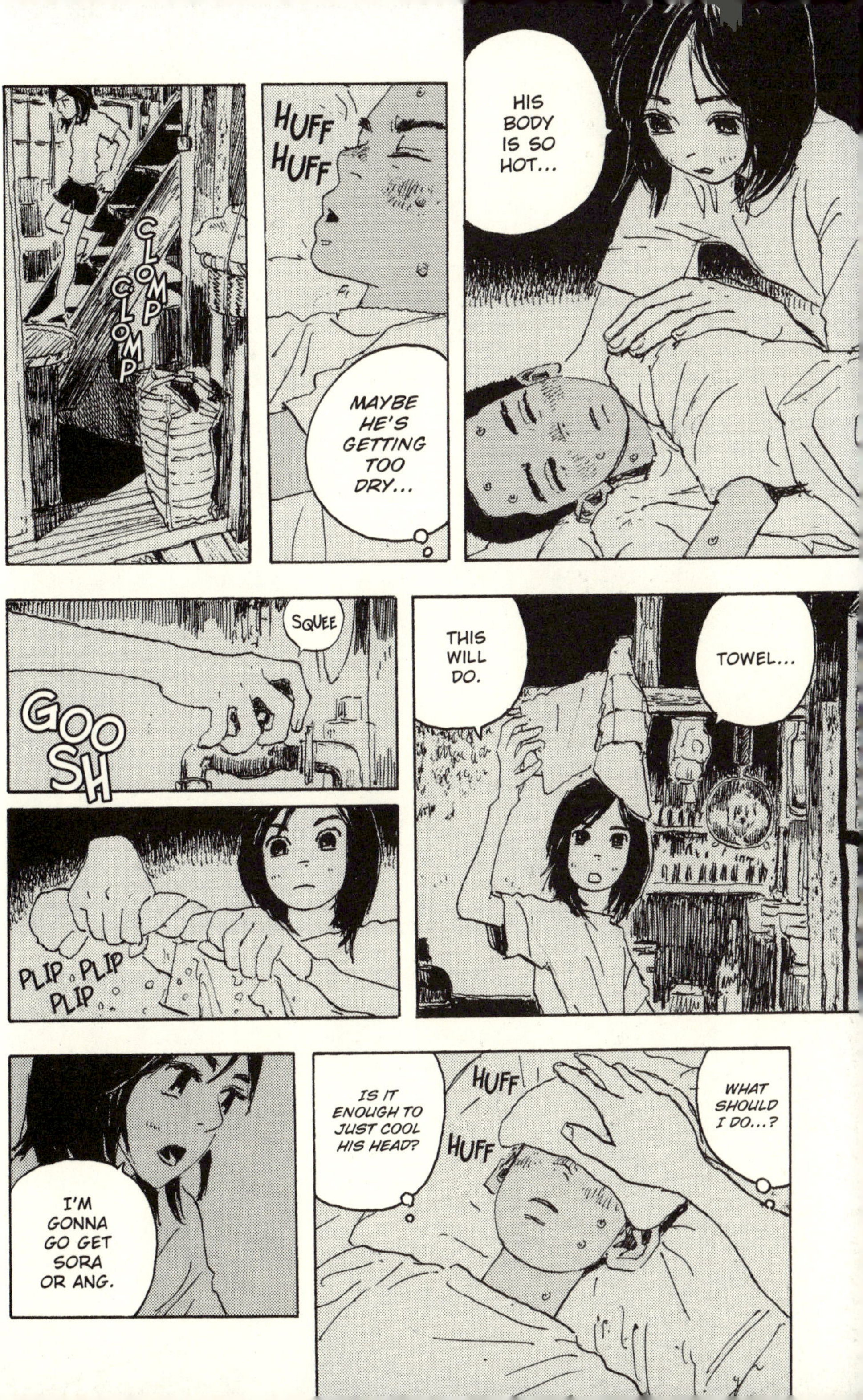
HIS BODY IS SO HOT...
HUFF HUFF
MAYBE HE'S GETTING TOO DRY...
CLOMP CLOMP CLOMP
TOWEL...
THIS WILL DO.
SQUEE
GOOSH
PLIP PLIP PLIP
WHAT SHOULD I DO...?
HUFF
HUFF
IS IT ENOUGH TO JUST COOL HIS HEAD?
I'M GONNA GO GET SORA OR ANG.

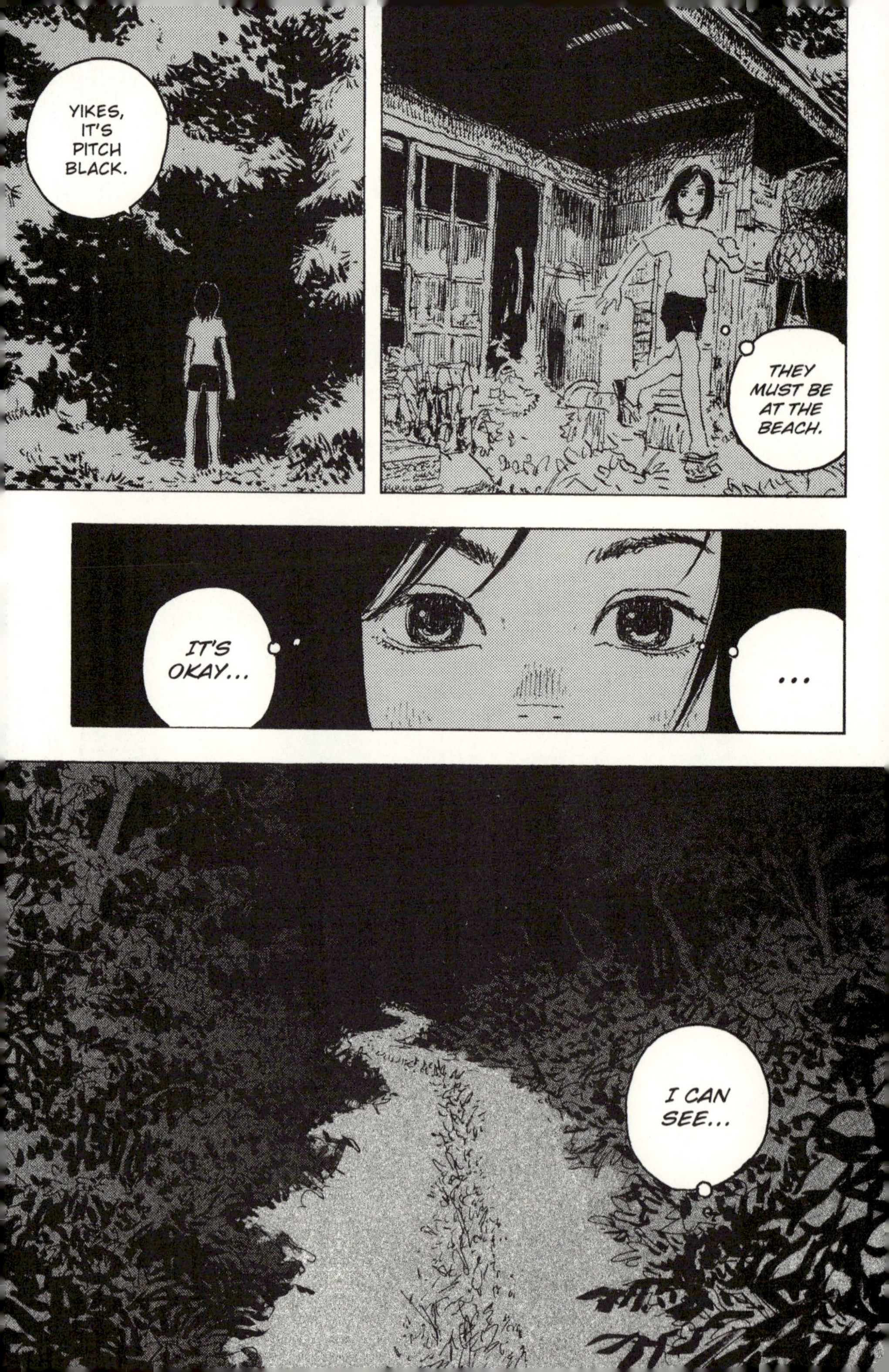
THEY MUST BE AT THE BEACH.
YIKES, IT'S PITCH BLACK.
...
IT'S OKAY...
I CAN SEE...

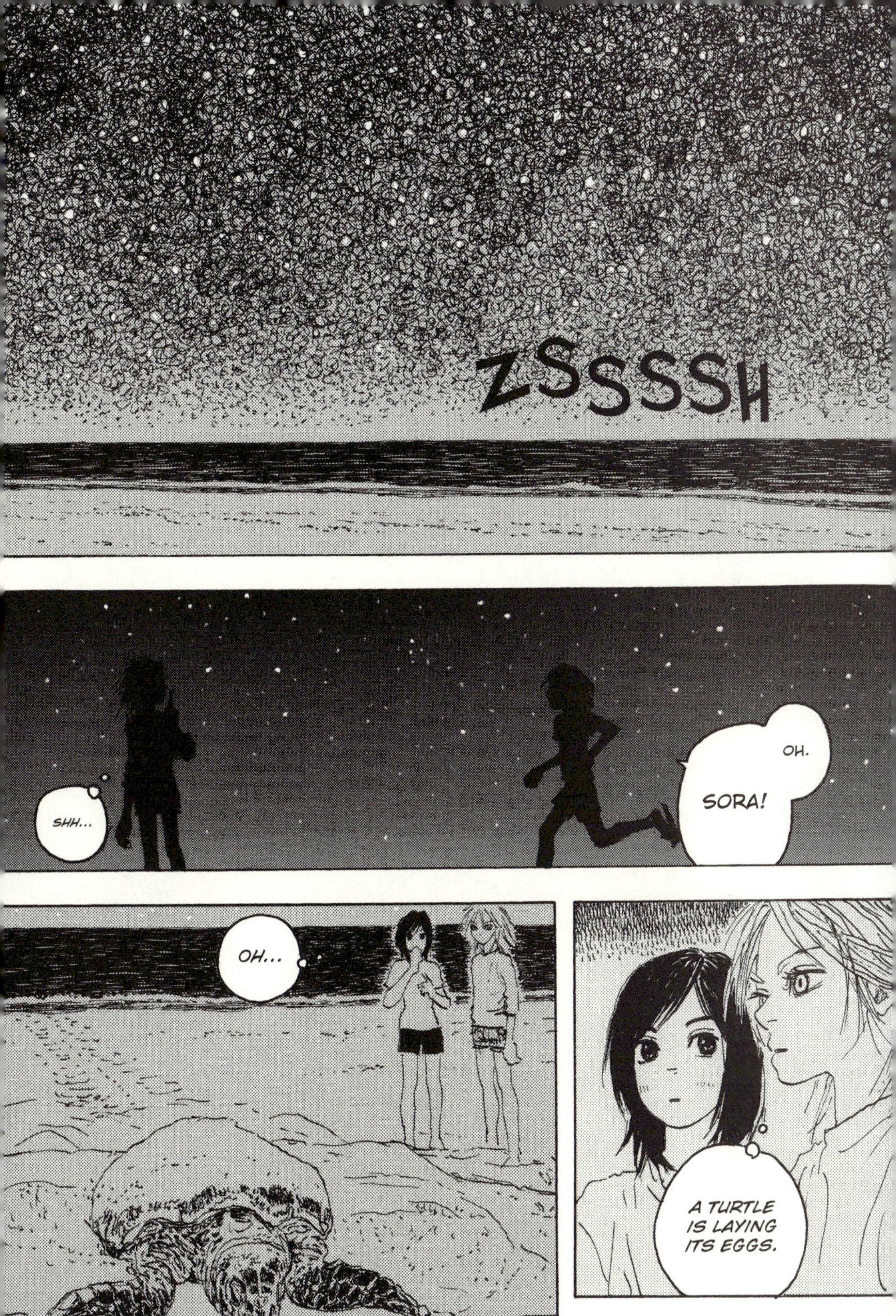
ZSSSSH
OH.
SORA!
SHH...
A TURTLE IS LAYING ITS EGGS.
OH...

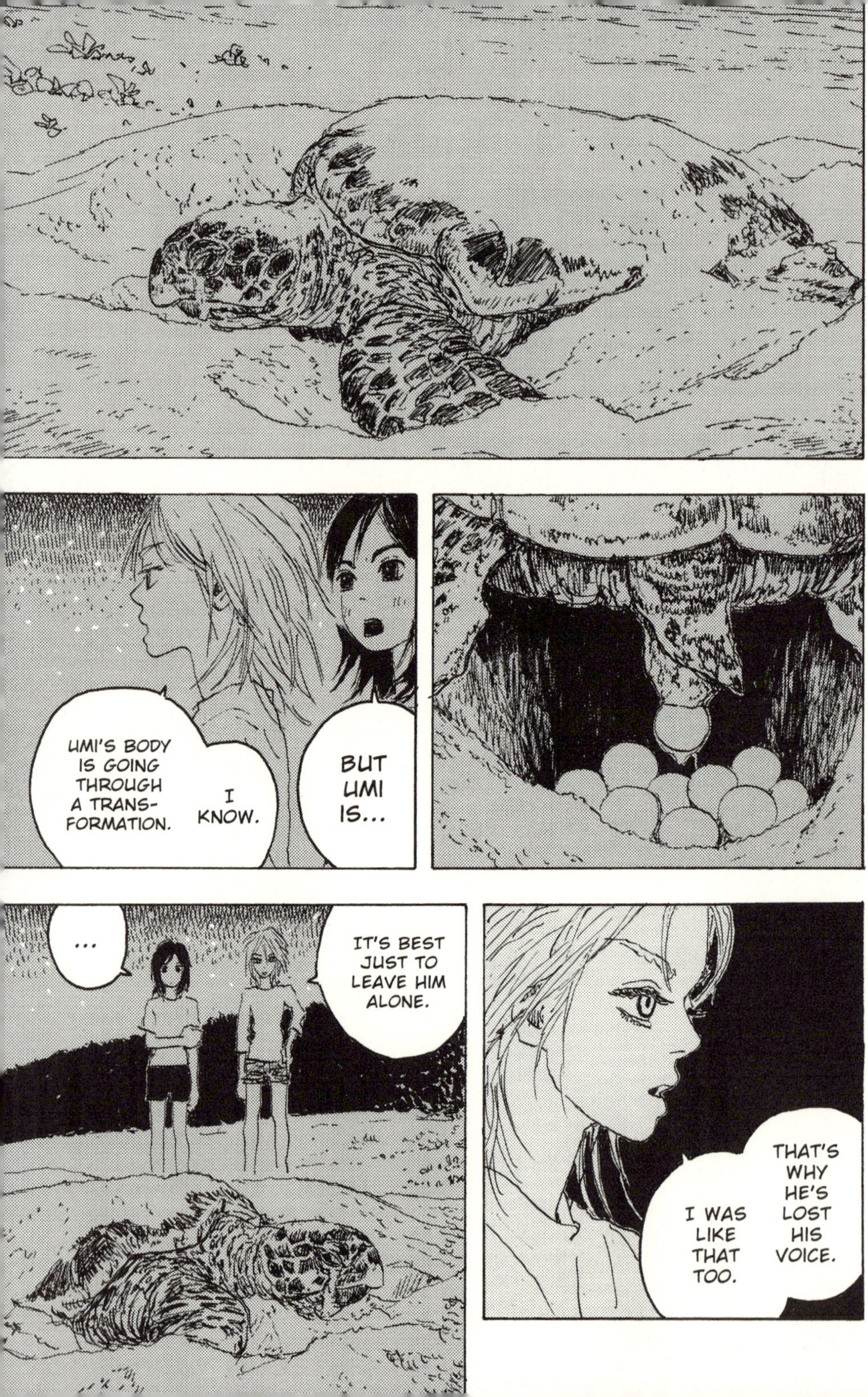
BUT UMI IS...
I KNOW.
UMI'S BODY IS GOING THROUGH A TRANS-FORMATION.
THAT'S WHY HE'S LOST HIS VOICE.
I WAS LIKE THAT TOO.
IT'S BEST JUST TO LEAVE HIM ALONE.
...

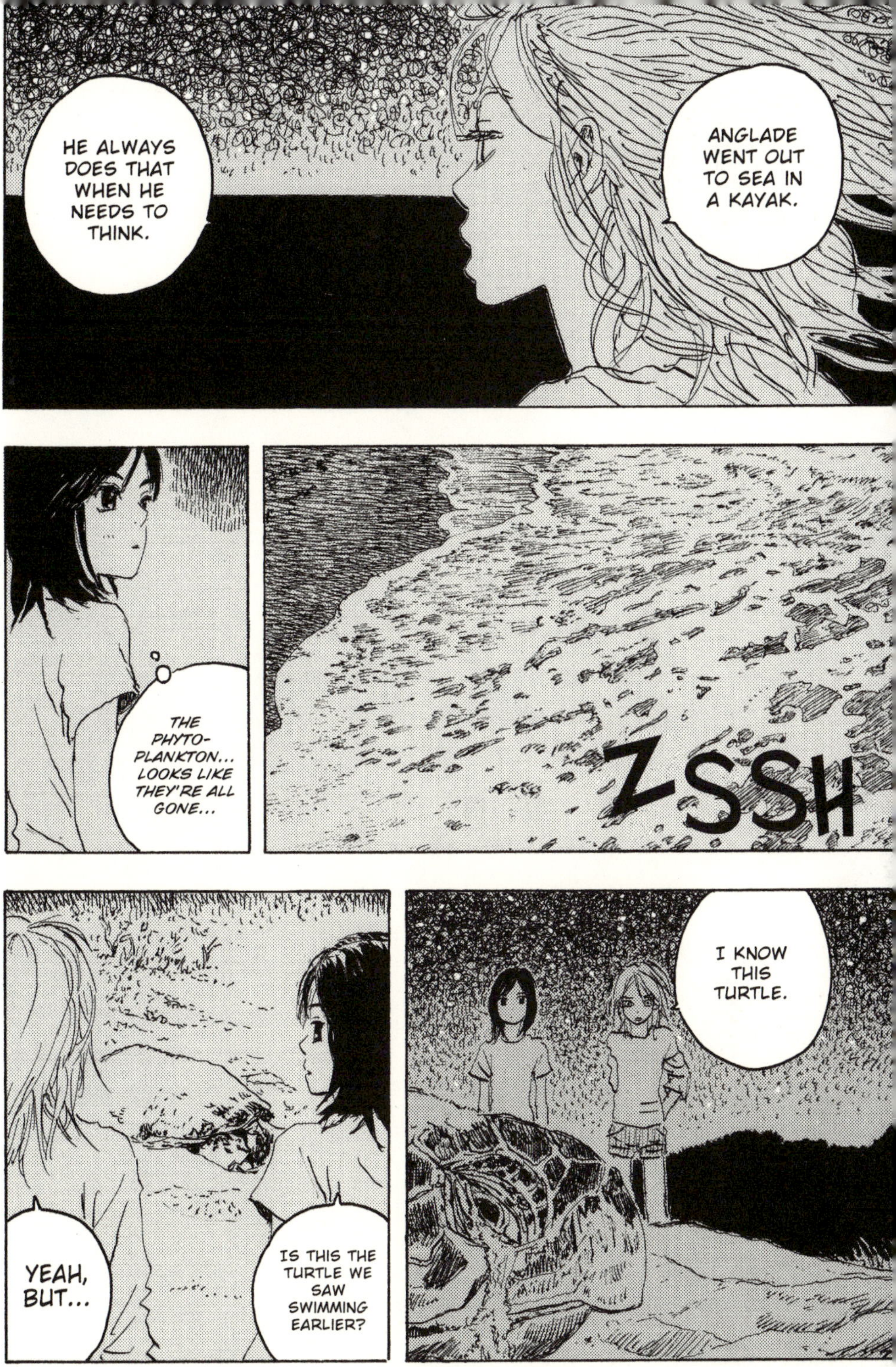
ANGLADE WENT OUT TO SEA IN A KAYAK.
HE ALWAYS DOES THAT WHEN HE NEEDS TO THINK.
ZSSH
THE PHYTO-PLANKTON... LOOKS LIKE THEY'RE ALL GONE...
I KNOW THIS TURTLE.
IS THIS THE TURTLE WE SAW SWIMMING EARLIER?
YEAH, BUT...

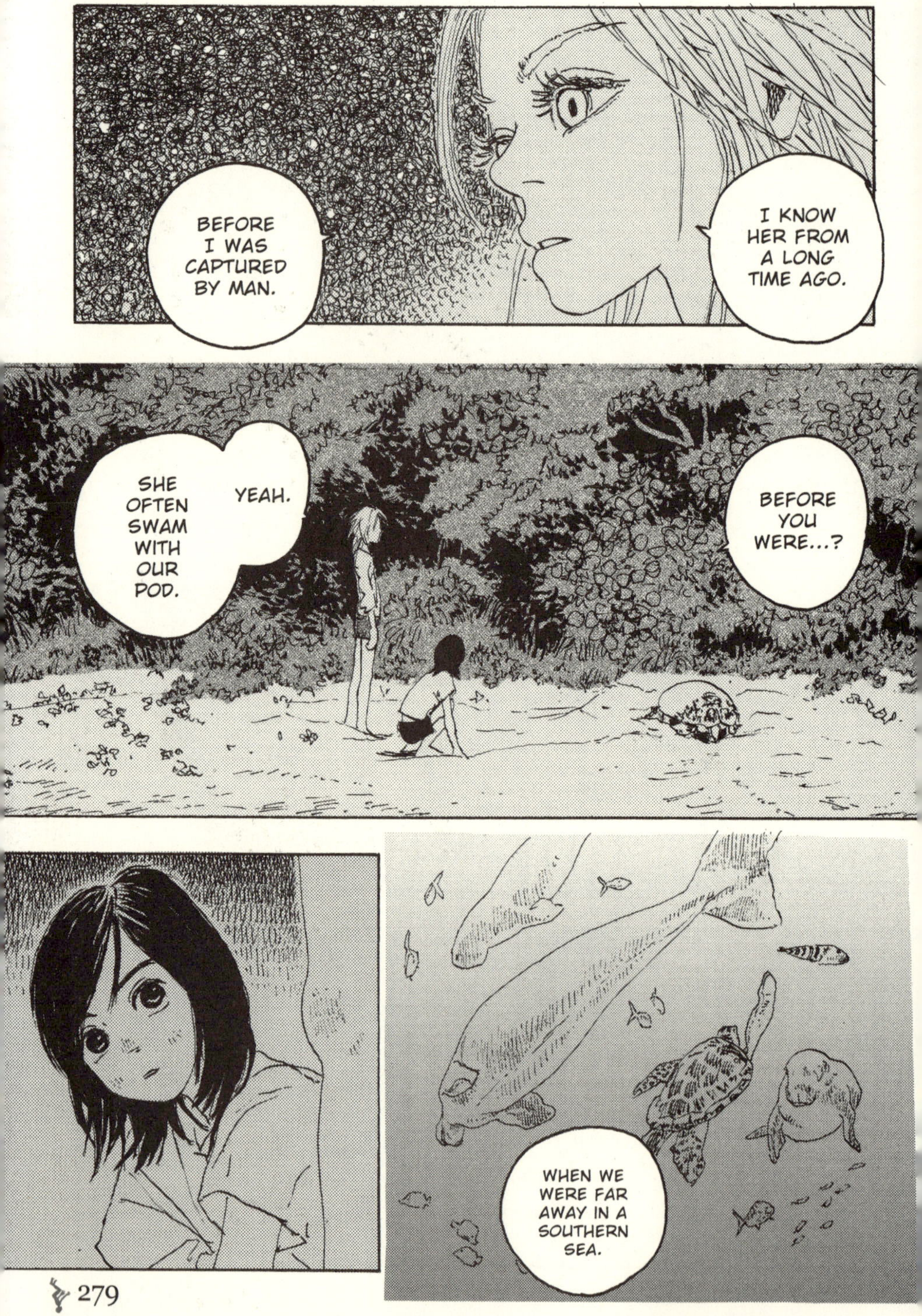
I KNOW HER FROM A LONG TIME AGO.
BEFORE I WAS CAPTURED BY MAN.
BEFORE YOU WERE...?
YEAH.
SHE OFTEN SWAM WITH OUR POD.
WHEN WE WERE FAR AWAY IN A SOUTHERN SEA.

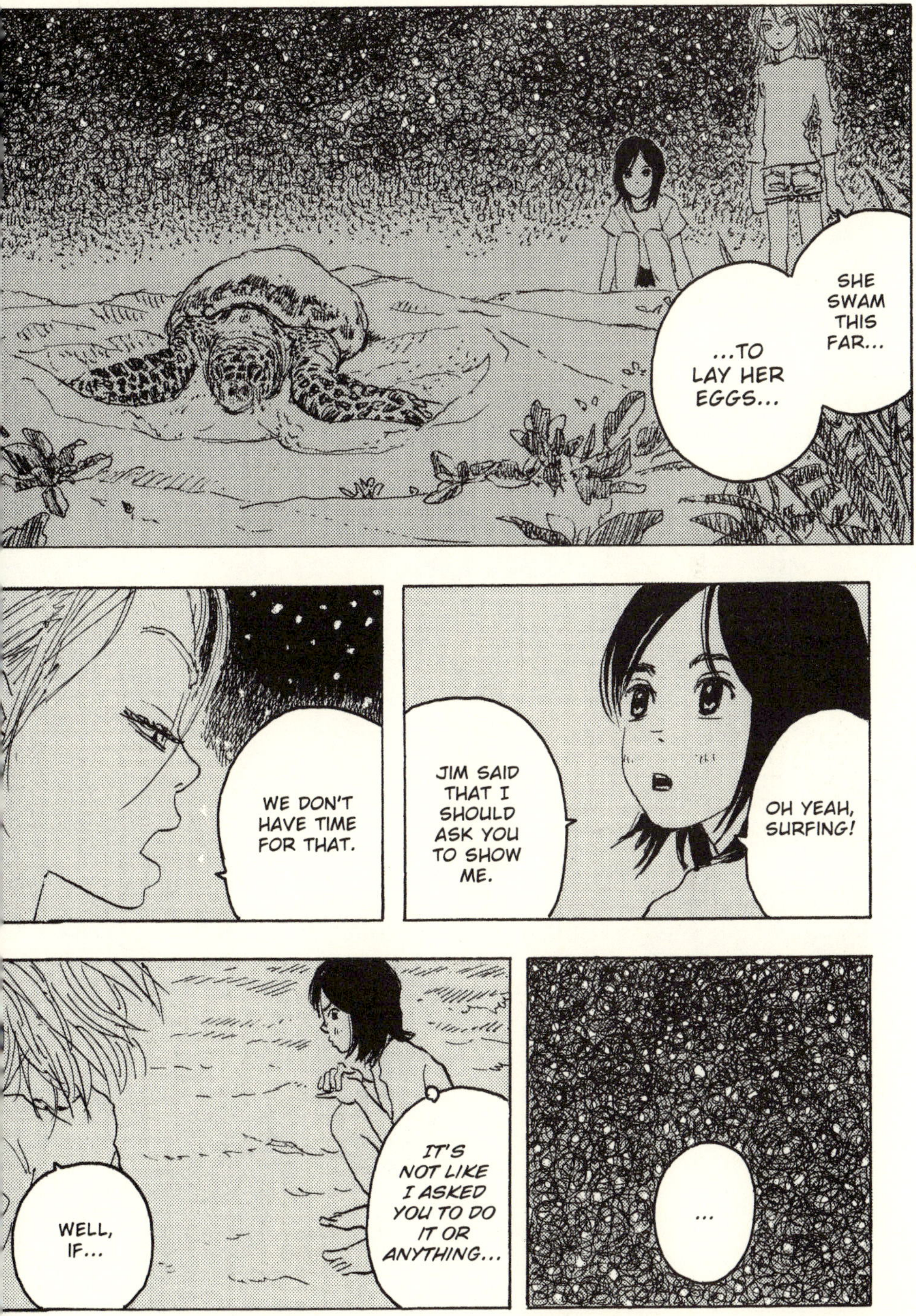
SHE SWAM THIS FAR...
...TO LAY HER EGGS...
OH YEAH, SURFING!
JIM SAID THAT I SHOULD ASK YOU TO SHOW ME.
WE DON'T HAVE TIME FOR THAT.
...
IT'S NOT LIKE I ASKED YOU TO DO IT OR ANYTHING...
WELL, IF...

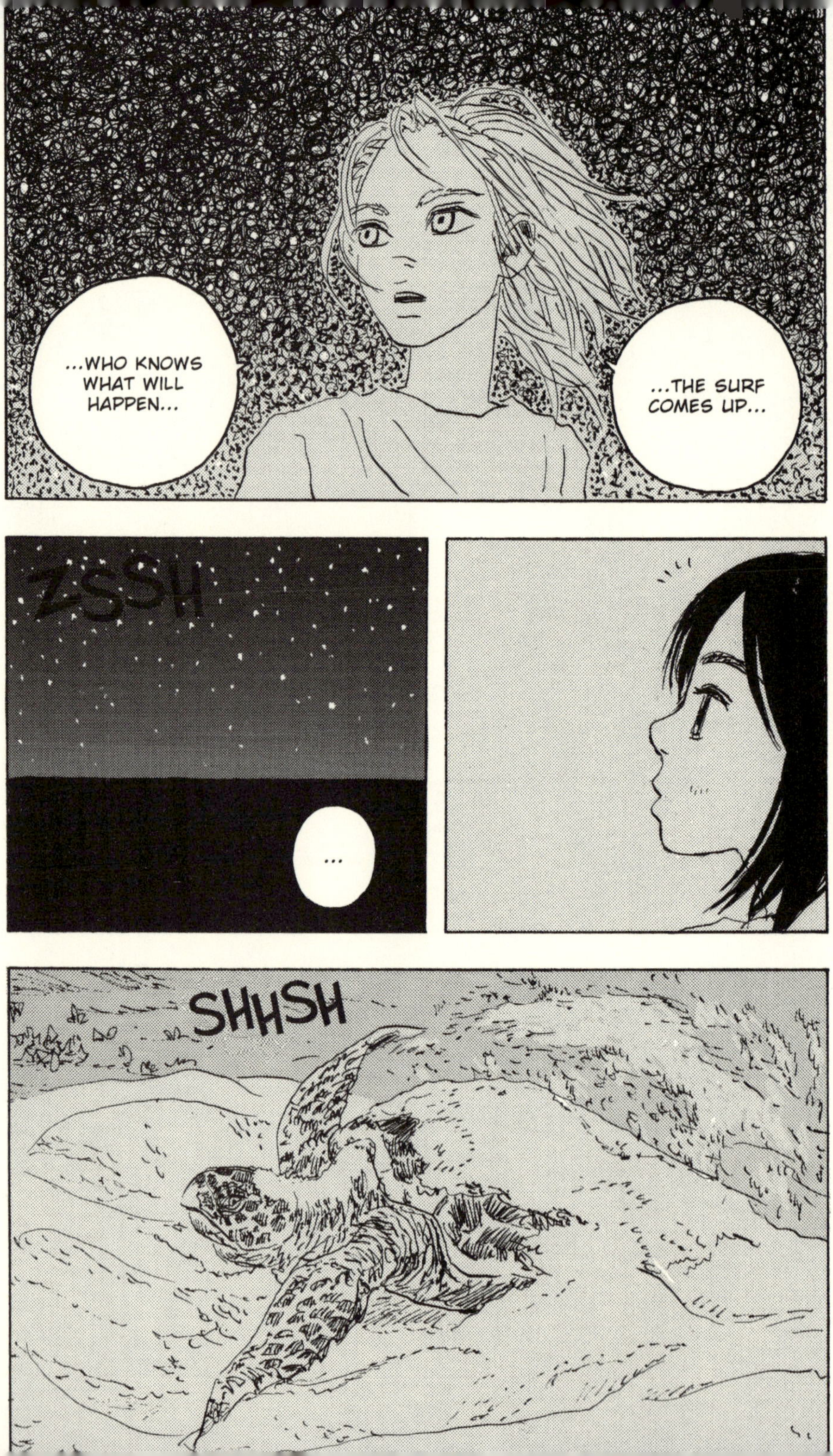
...THE SURF COMES UP...
...WHO KNOWS WHAT WILL HAPPEN...
ZSSH
...
SHHSH

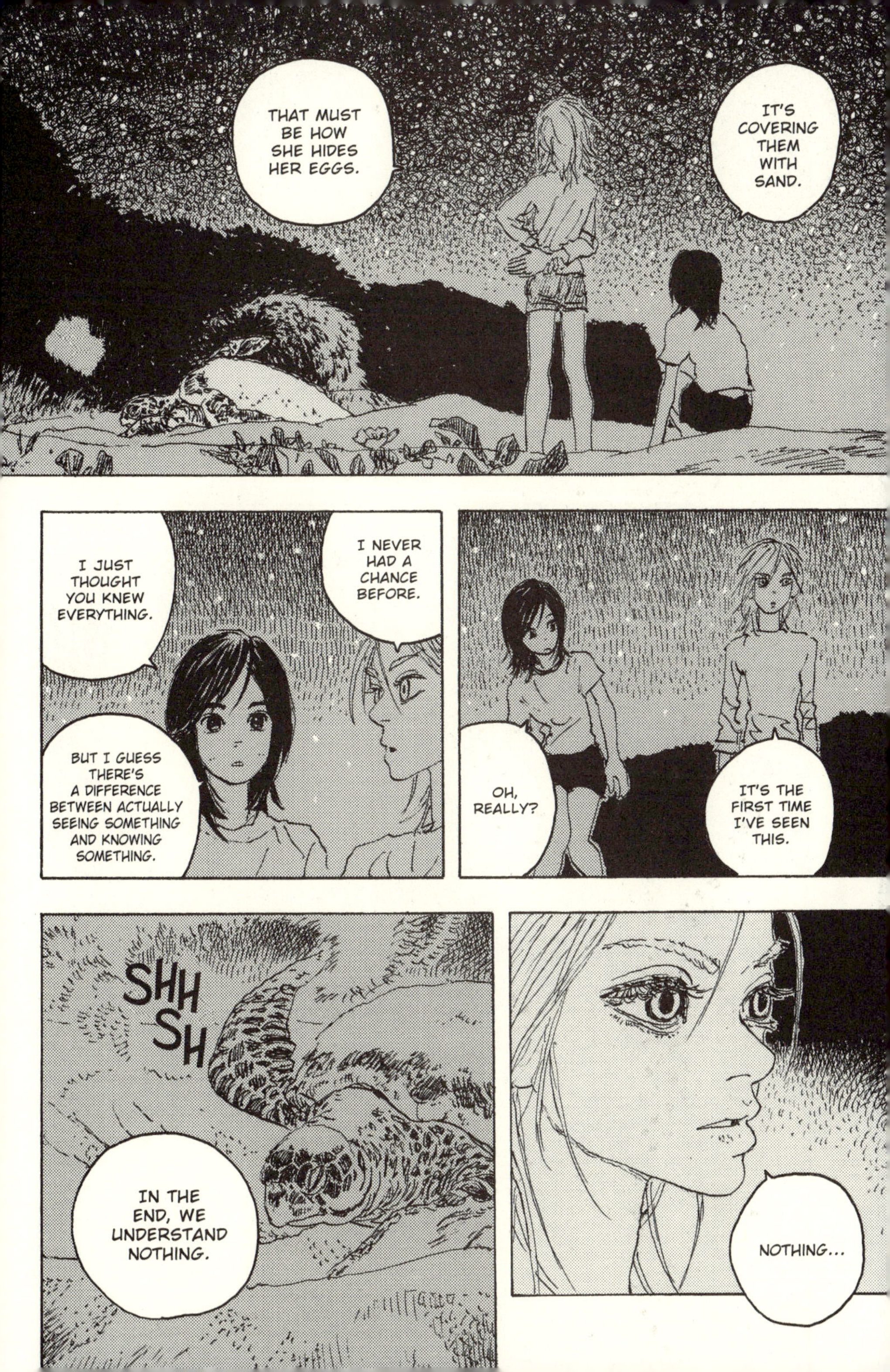
IT'S COVERING THEM WITH SAND.
THAT MUST BE HOW SHE HIDES HER EGGS.
IT'S THE FIRST TIME I'VE SEEN THIS.
OH, REALLY?
I NEVER HAD A CHANCE BEFORE.
I JUST THOUGHT YOU KNEW EVERYTHING.
BUT I GUESS THERE'S A DIFFERENCE BETWEEN ACTUALLY SEEING SOMETHING AND KNOWING SOMETHING.
NOTHING...
SHH SH
IN THE END, WE UNDERSTAND NOTHING.

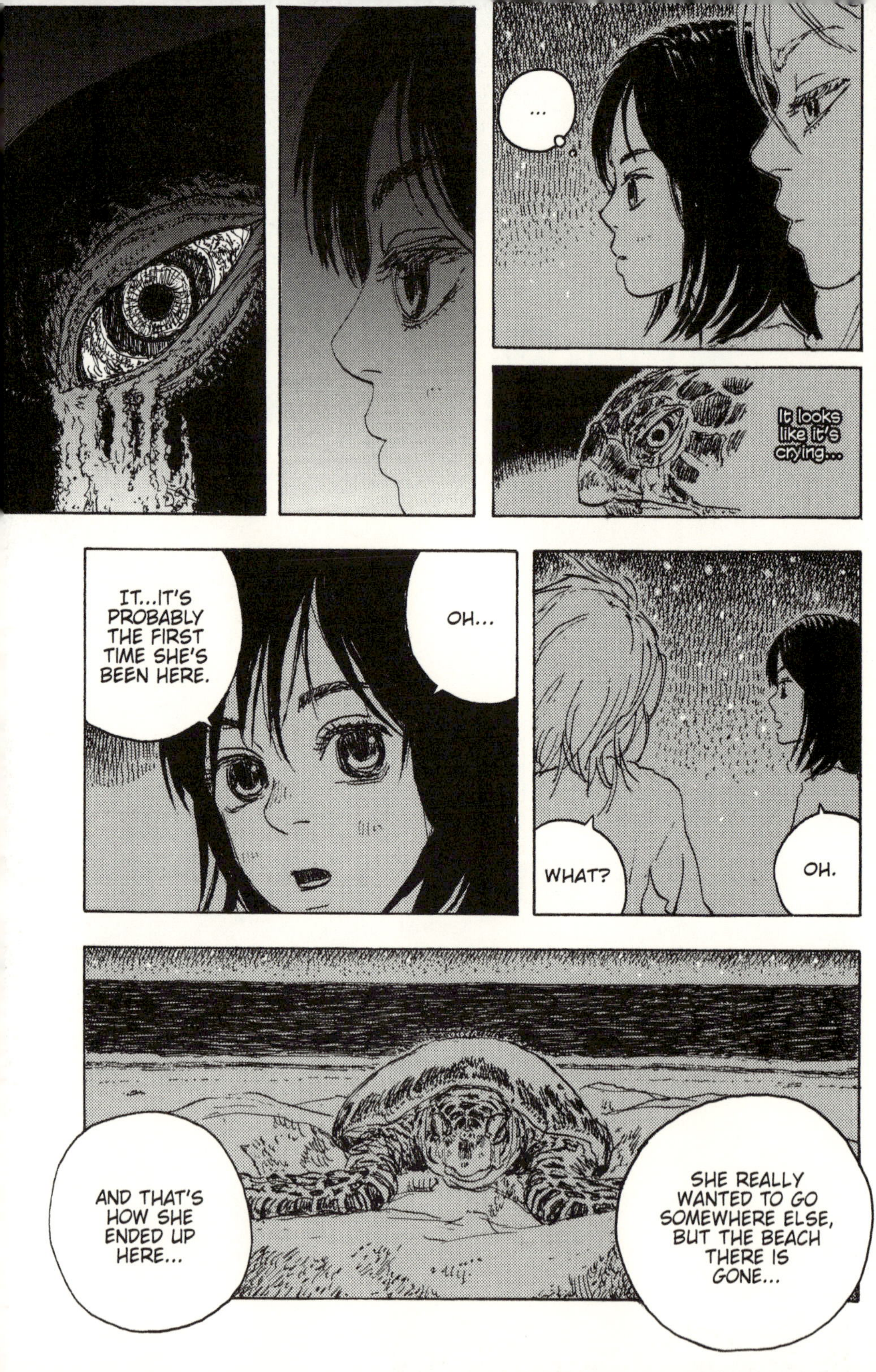
...
It looks like it's crying...
OH.
WHAT?
OH...
IT...IT'S PROBABLY THE FIRST TIME SHE'S BEEN HERE.
SHE REALLY WANTED TO GO SOMEWHERE ELSE, BUT THE BEACH THERE IS GONE...
AND THAT'S HOW SHE ENDED UP HERE...

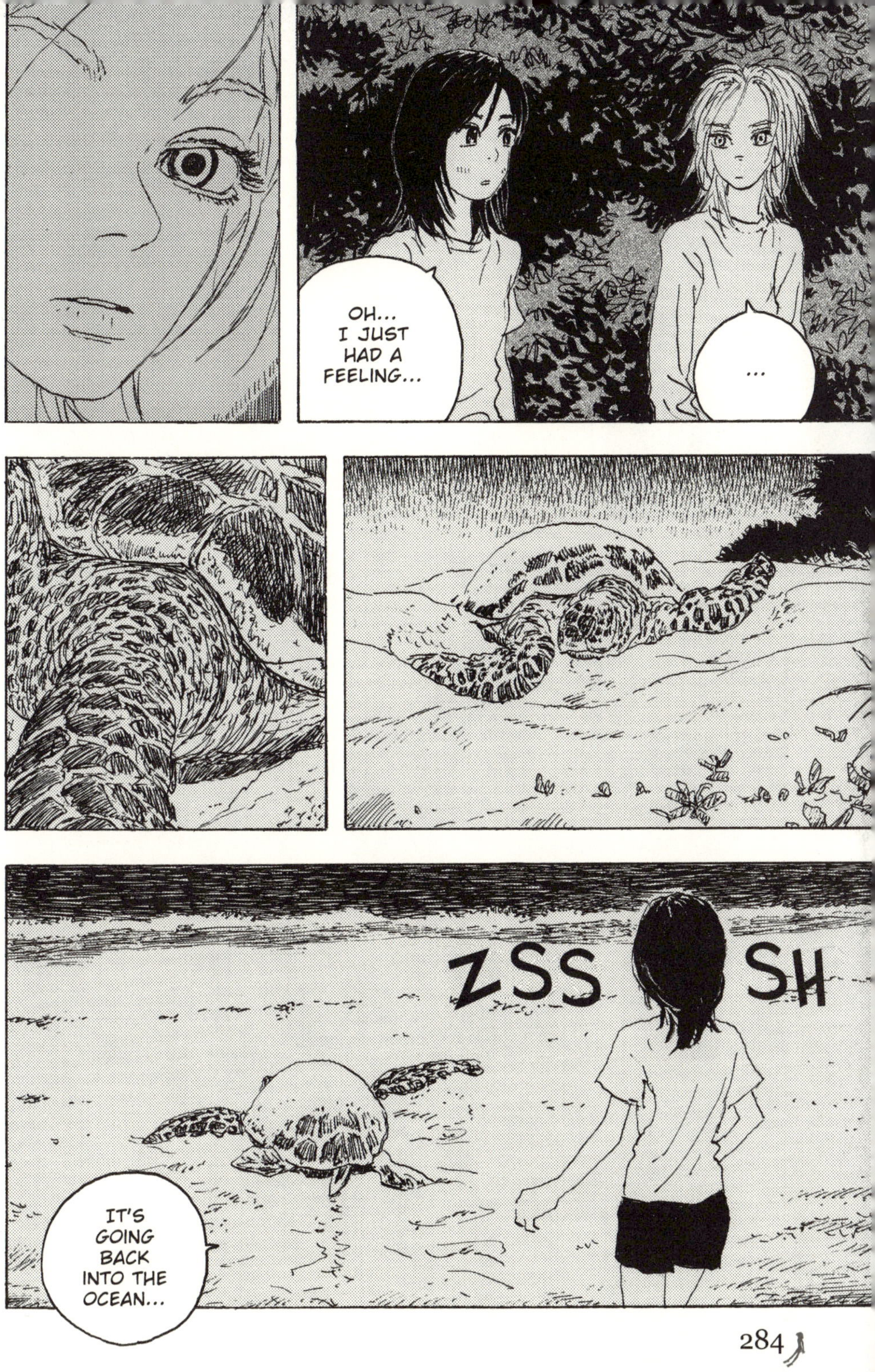
...
OH... I JUST HAD A FEELING...
ZSSSH
IT'S GOING BACK INTO THE OCEAN...

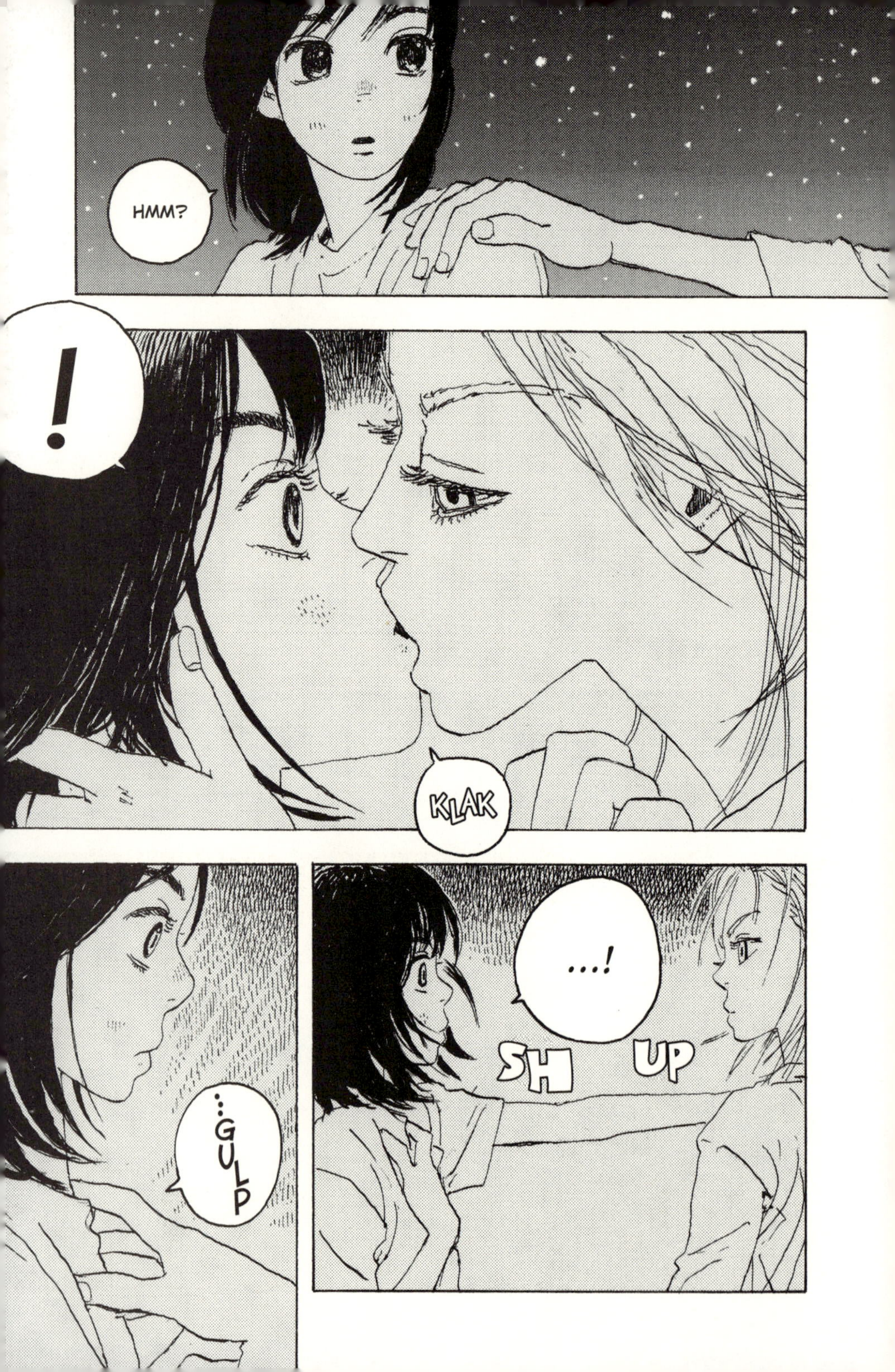
HMM?
!
KLAK
...!
SH UP
...GULP

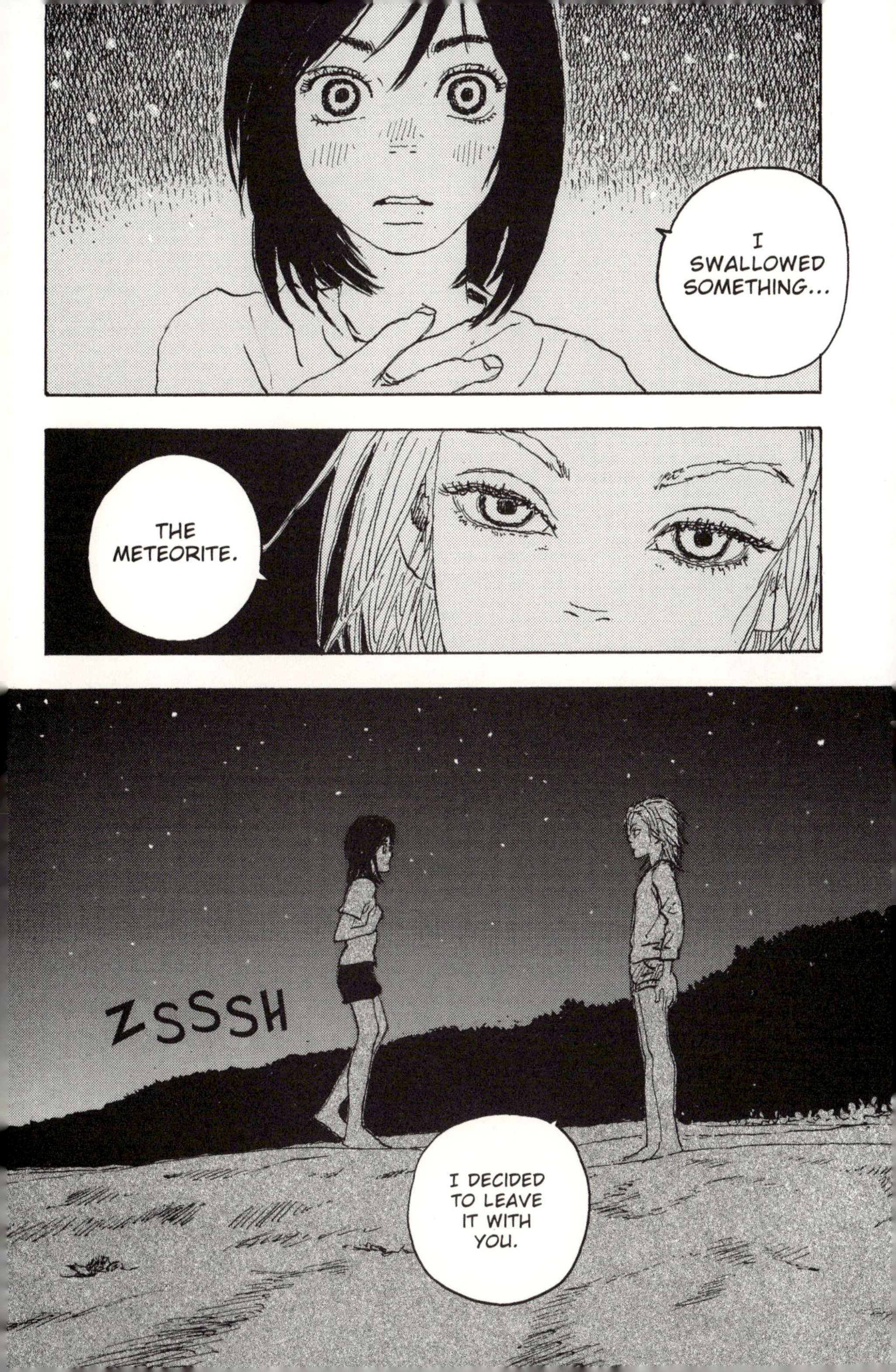
I SWALLOWED SOMETHING...
THE METEORITE.
ZSSSH
I DECIDED TO LEAVE IT WITH YOU.

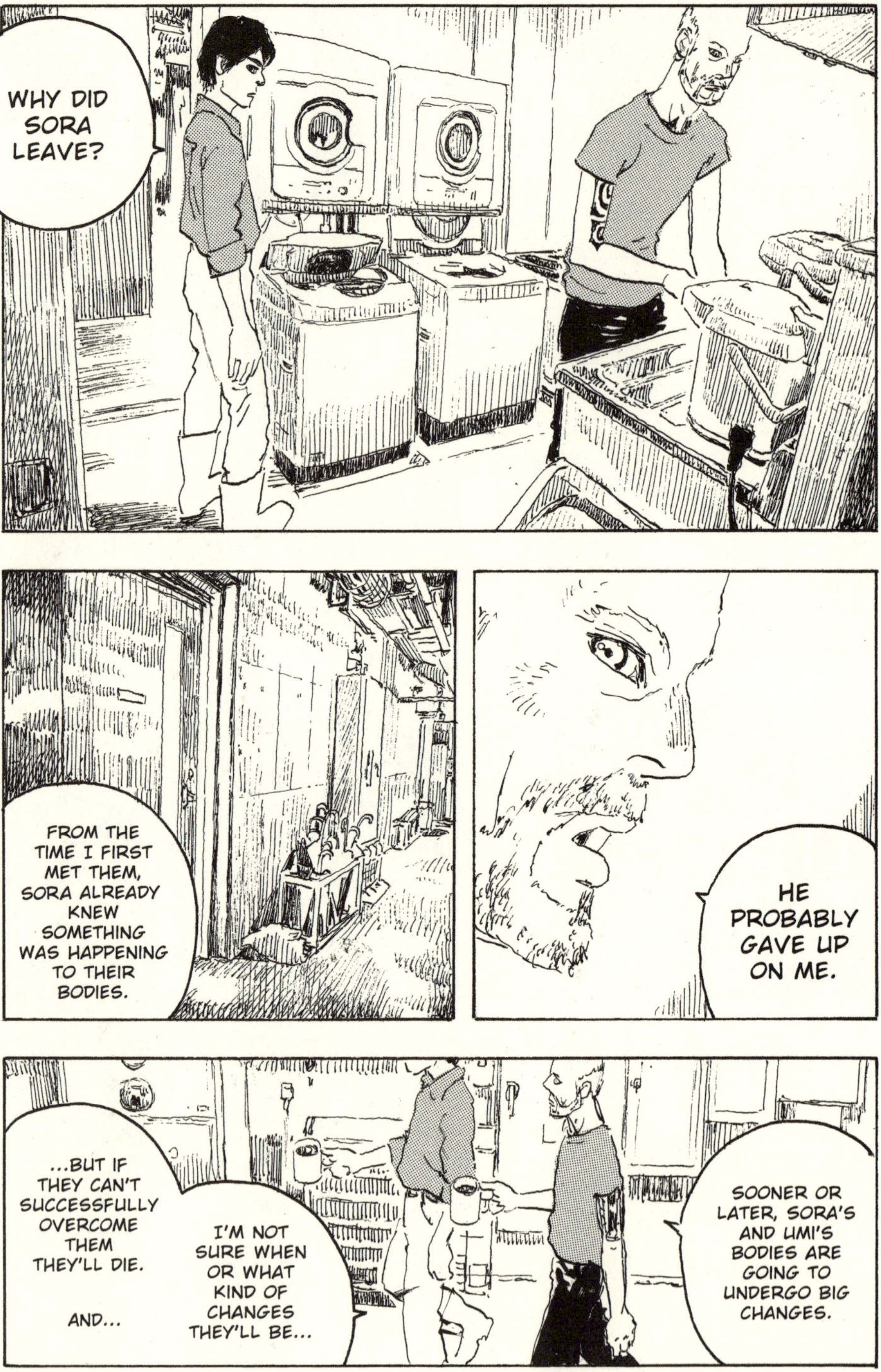
WHY DID SORA LEAVE?
HE PROBABLY GAVE UP ON ME.
FROM THE TIME I FIRST MET THEM, SORA ALREADY KNEW SOMETHING WAS HAPPENING TO THEIR BODIES.
SOONER OR LATER, SORA'S AND UMI'S BODIES ARE GOING TO UNDERGO BIG CHANGES.
I'M NOT SURE WHEN OR WHAT KIND OF CHANGES THEY'LL BE...
...BUT IF THEY CAN'T SUCCESSFULLY OVERCOME THEM THEY'LL DIE.
AND...

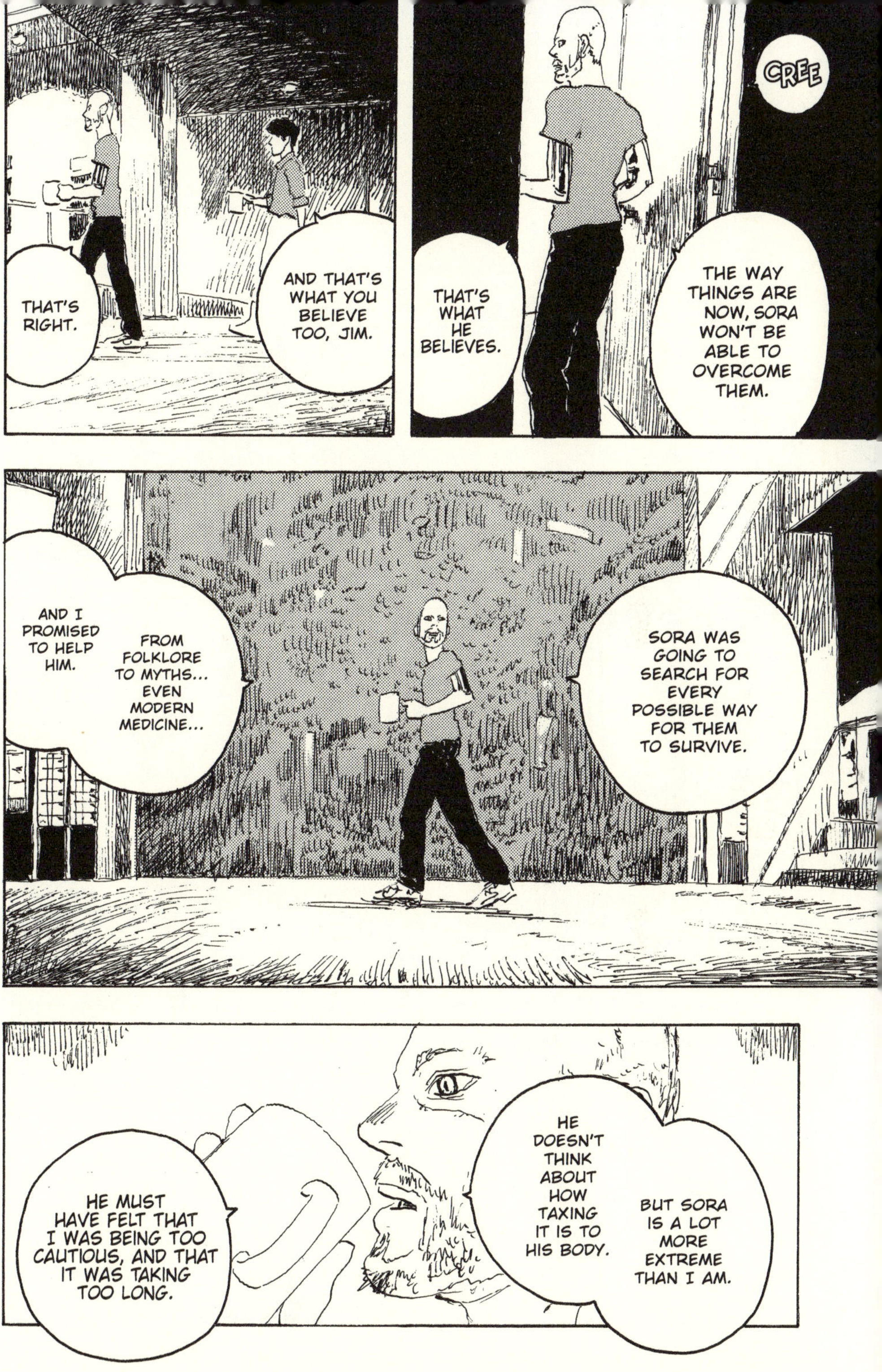
CREE
THE WAY THINGS ARE NOW, SORA WON'T BE ABLE TO OVERCOME THEM.
THAT'S WHAT HE BELIEVES.
AND THAT'S WHAT YOU BELIEVE TOO, JIM.
THAT'S RIGHT.
SORA WAS GOING TO SEARCH FOR EVERY POSSIBLE WAY FOR THEM TO SURVIVE.
FROM FOLKLORE TO MYTHS... EVEN MODERN MEDICINE...
AND I PROMISED TO HELP HIM.
BUT SORA IS A LOT MORE EXTREME THAN I AM.
HE DOESN'T THINK ABOUT HOW TAXING IT IS TO HIS BODY.
HE MUST HAVE FELT THAT I WAS BEING TOO CAUTIOUS, AND THAT IT WAS TAKING TOO LONG.

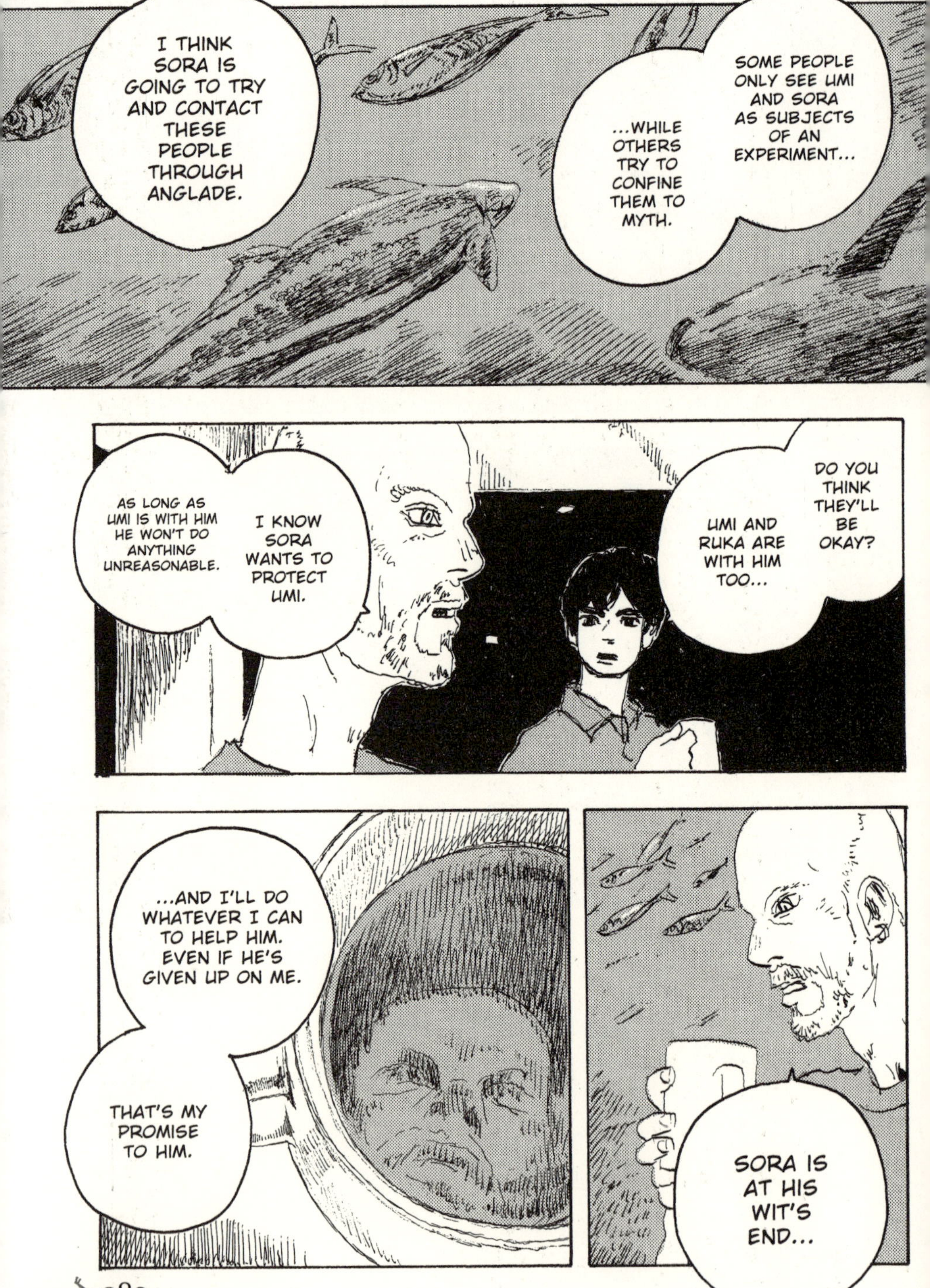
SOME PEOPLE ONLY SEE UMI AND SORA AS SUBJECTS OF AN EXPERIMENT...
...WHILE OTHERS TRY TO CONFINE THEM TO MYTH.
I THINK SORA IS GOING TO TRY AND CONTACT THESE PEOPLE THROUGH ANGLADE.
DO YOU THINK THEY'LL BE OKAY?
UMI AND RUKA ARE WITH HIM TOO...
I KNOW SORA WANTS TO PROTECT UMI.
AS LONG AS UMI IS WITH HIM HE WON'T DO ANYTHING UNREASONABLE.
SORA IS AT HIS WIT'S END...
...AND I'LL DO WHATEVER I CAN TO HELP HIM. EVEN IF HE'S GIVEN UP ON ME.
THAT'S MY PROMISE TO HIM.

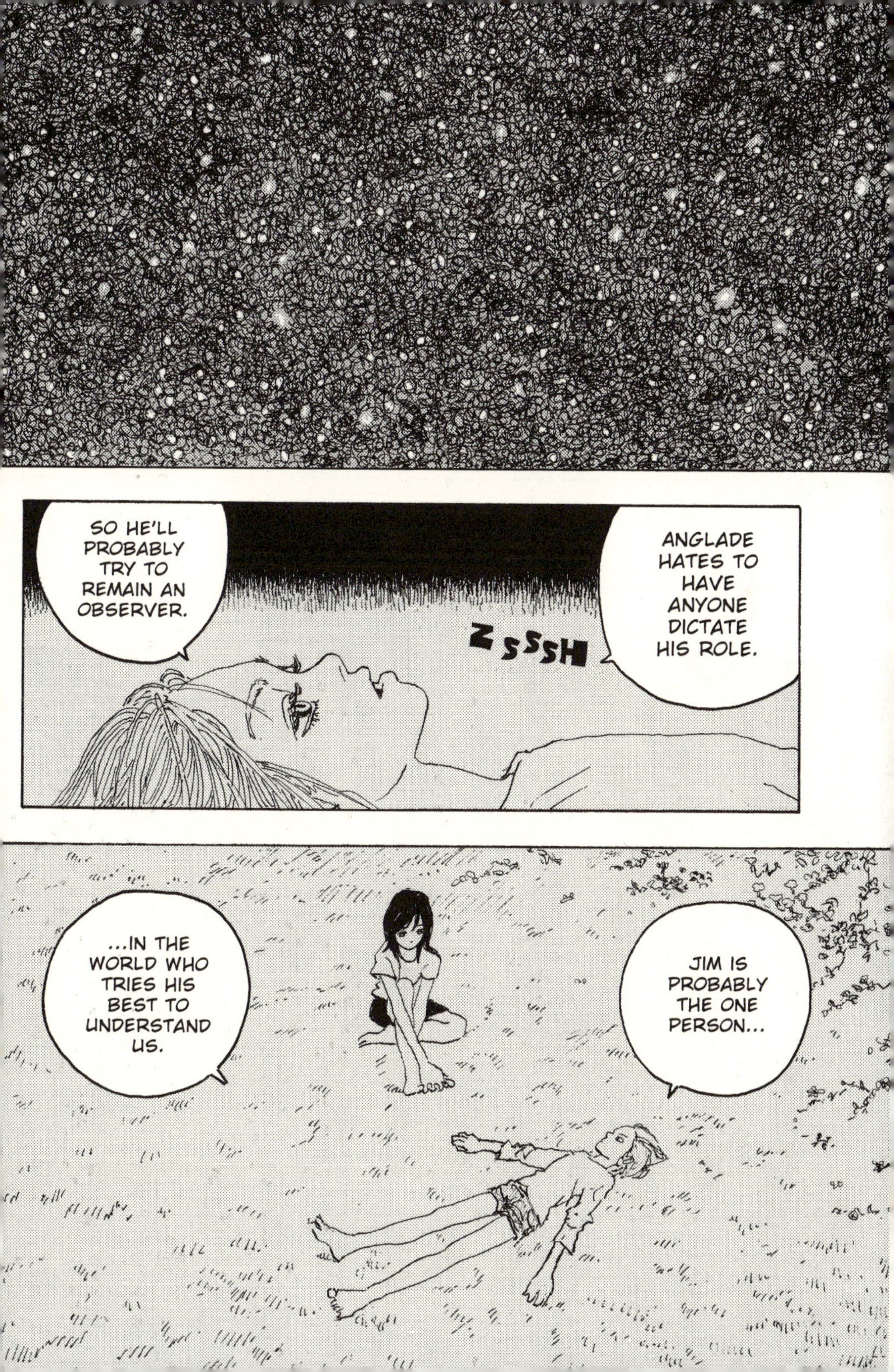
ANGLADE HATES TO HAVE ANYONE DICTATE HIS ROLE.
ZSSSH
SO HE'LL PROBABLY TRY TO REMAIN AN OBSERVER.
JIM IS PROBABLY THE ONE PERSON...
...IN THE WORLD WHO TRIES HIS BEST TO UNDERSTAND US.

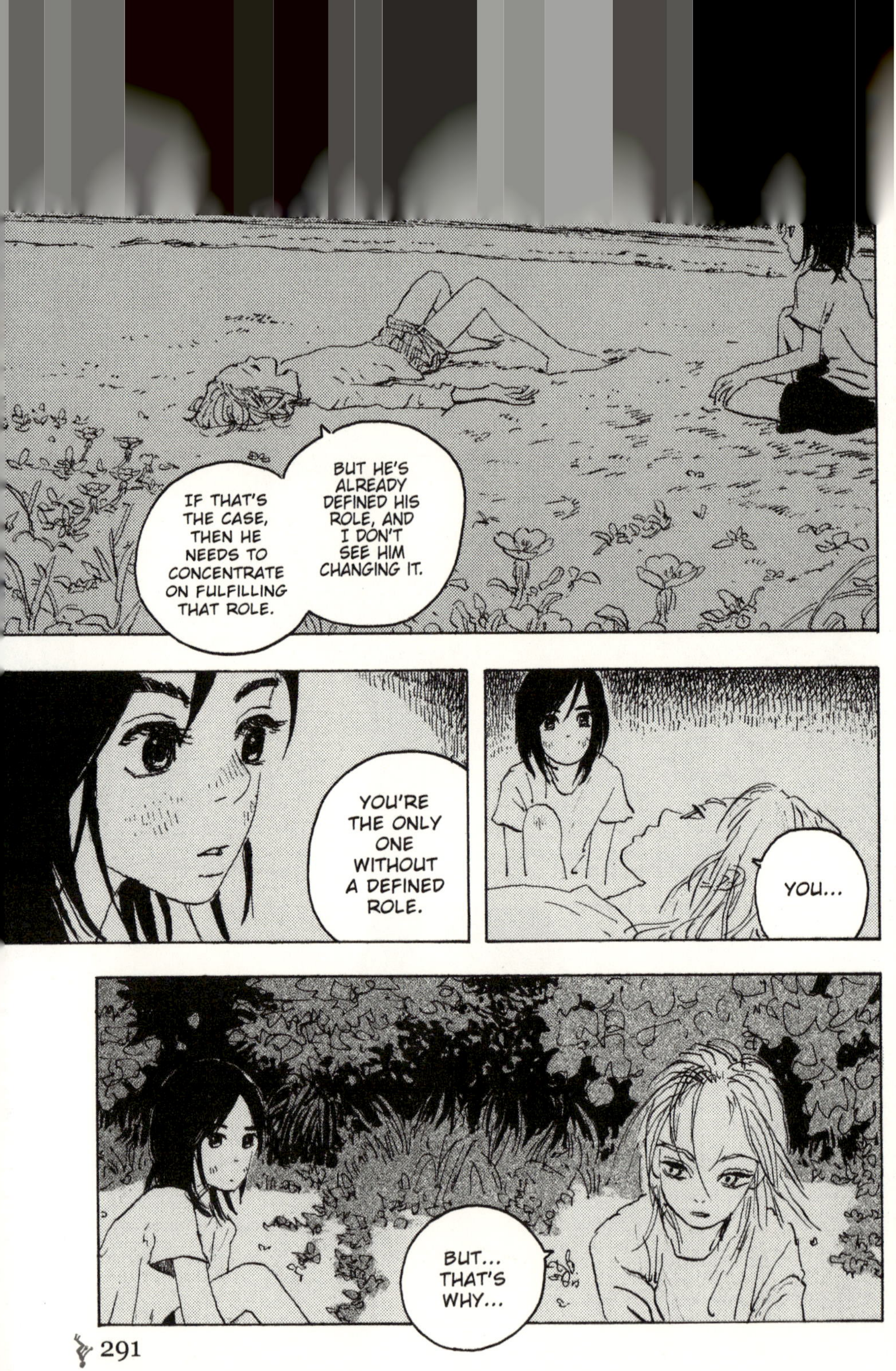
BUT HE'S ALREADY DEFINED HIS ROLE, AND I DON'T SEE HIM CHANGING IT.
IF THAT'S THE CASE, THEN HE NEEDS TO CONCENTRATE ON FULFILLING THAT ROLE.
YOU...
YOU'RE THE ONLY ONE WITHOUT A DEFINED ROLE.
BUT... THAT'S WHY...

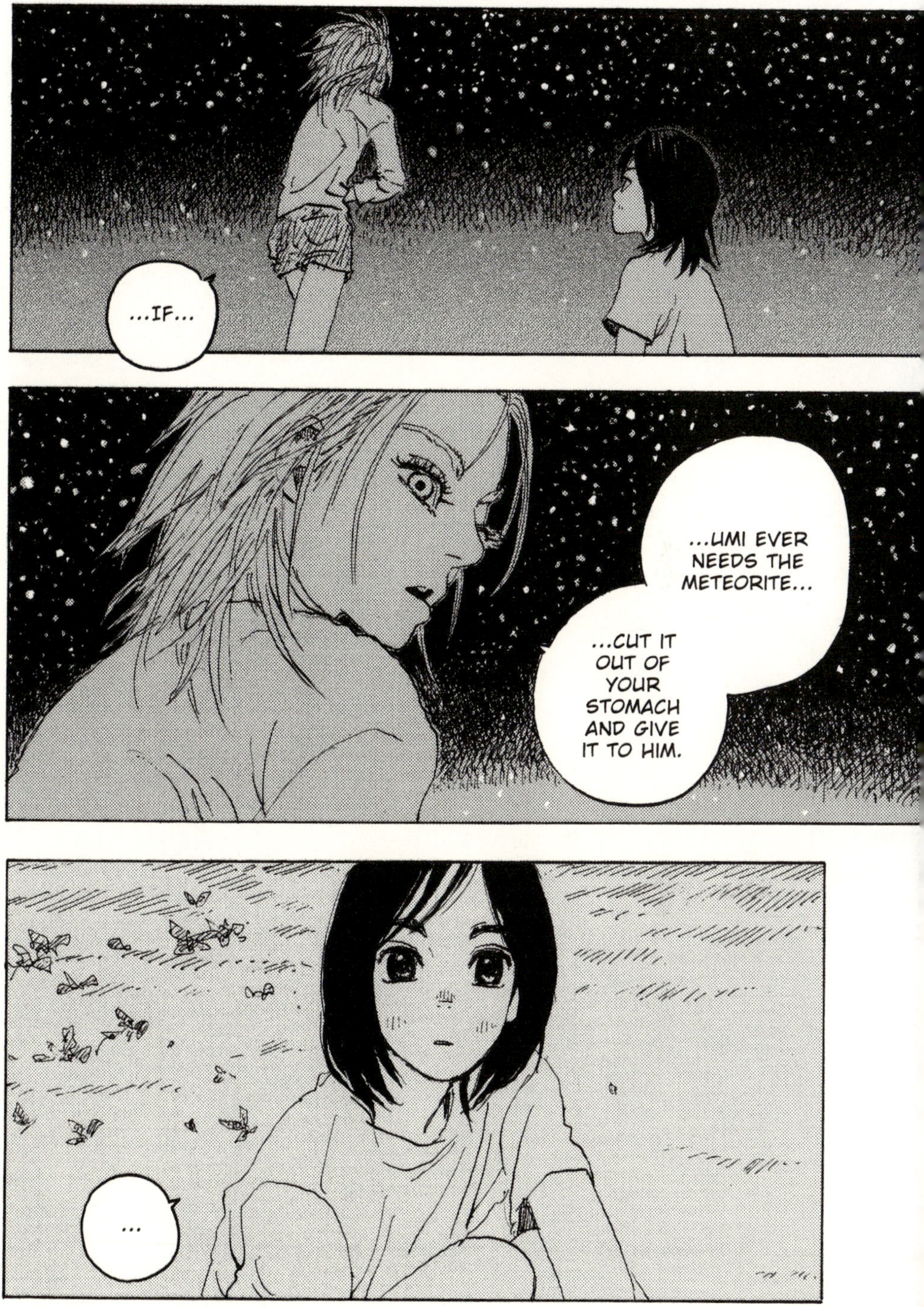
...IF...
...UMI EVER NEEDS THE METEORITE...
...CUT IT OUT OF YOUR STOMACH AND GIVE IT TO HIM.
...

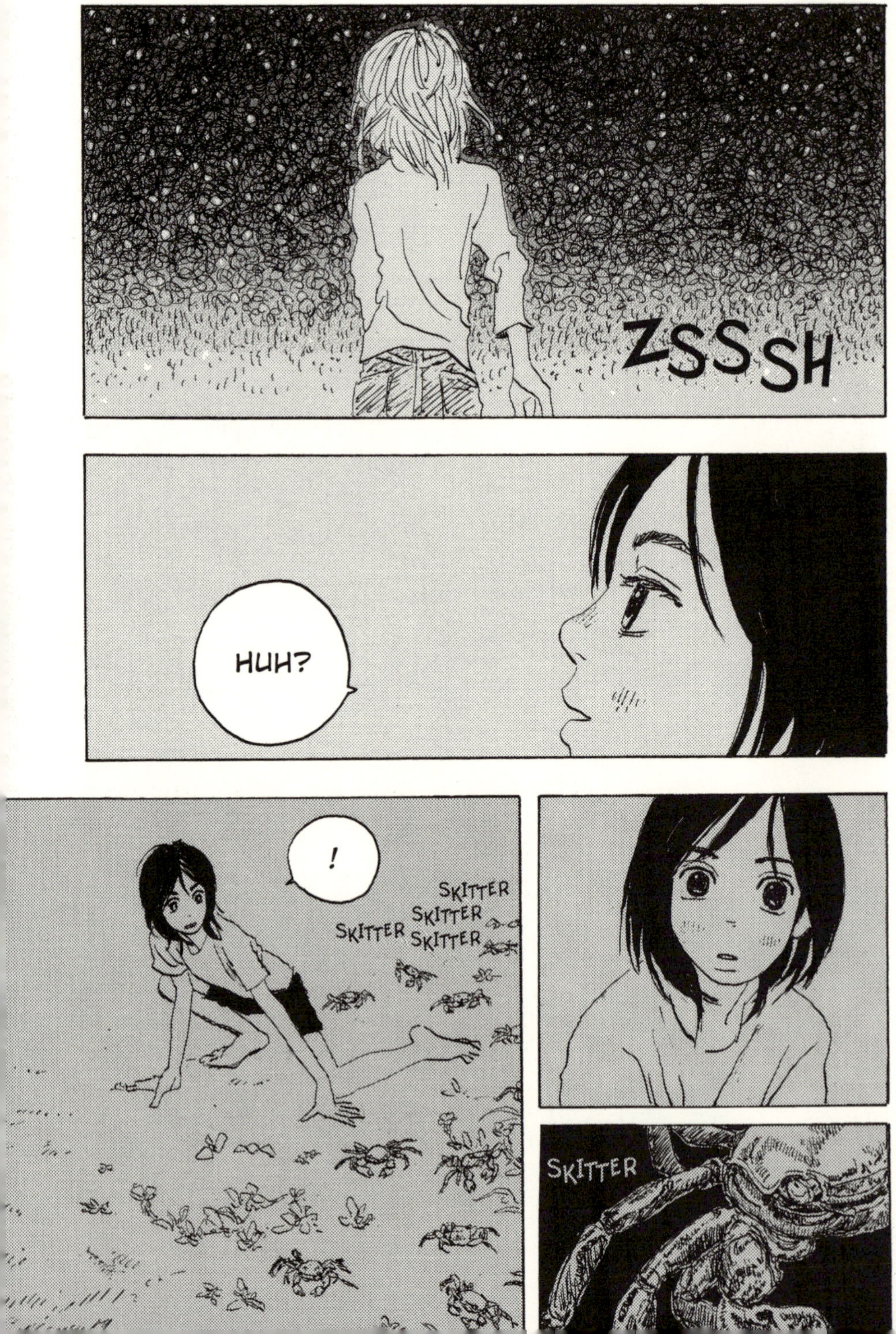
ZSSSH
HUH?
SKITTER
!
SKITTER
SKITTER
SKITTER
SKITTER

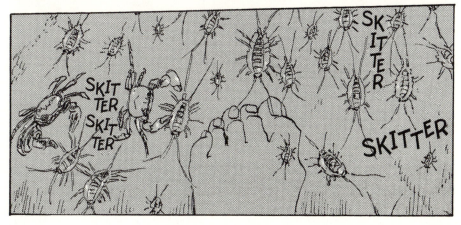

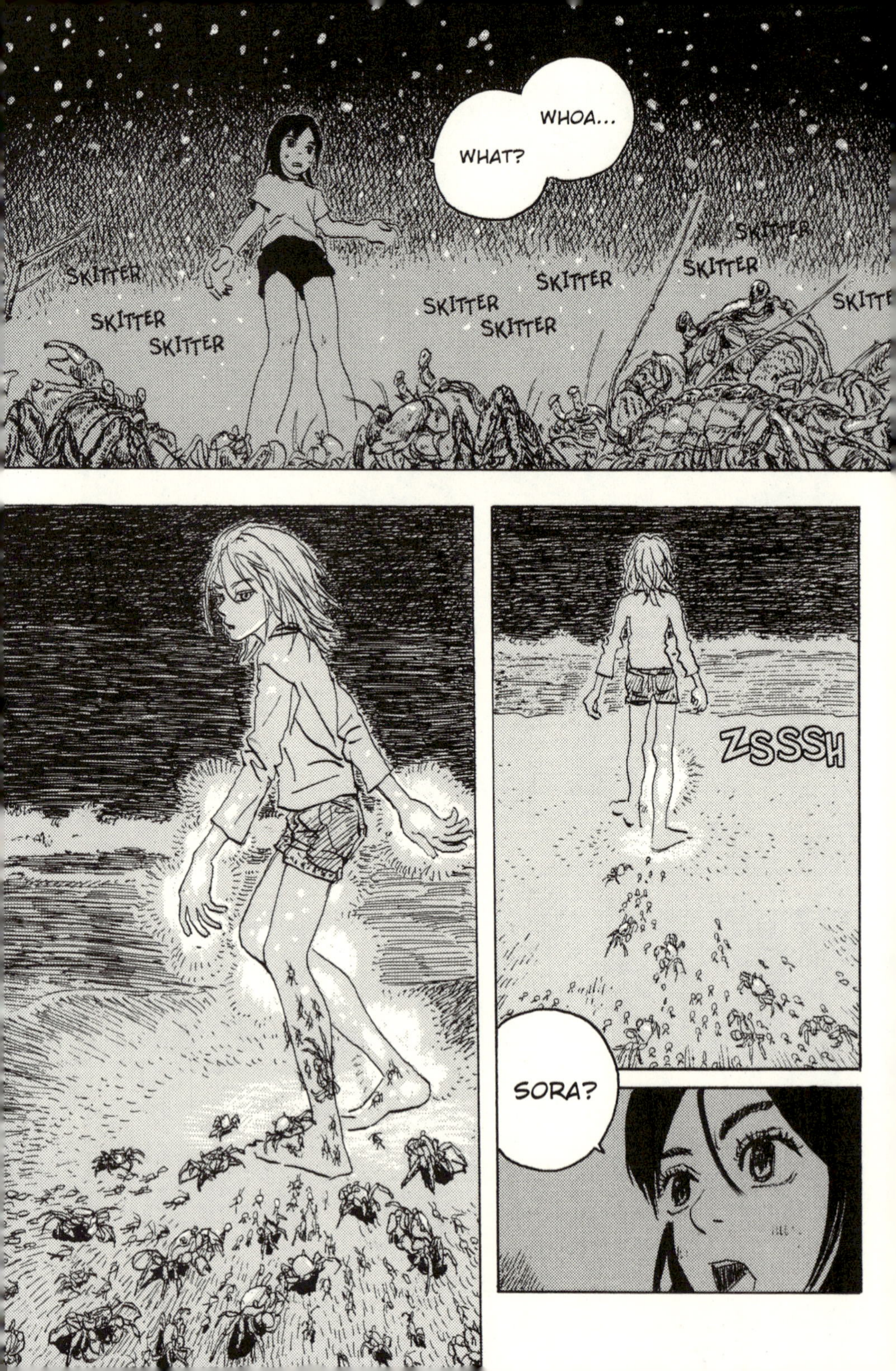
WHOA...
WHAT?
SKITTER
SKITTER
SKITTE
SKITTER
SKITTER
SKITTER
SKITTER
SKITTER
SKITTER
ZSSSH
SORA?

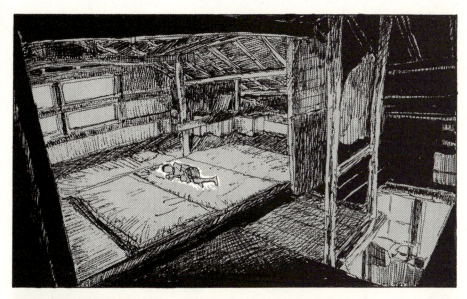

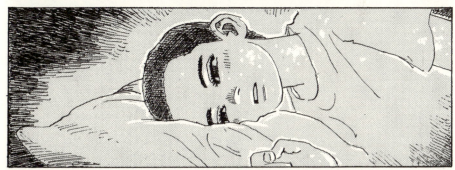

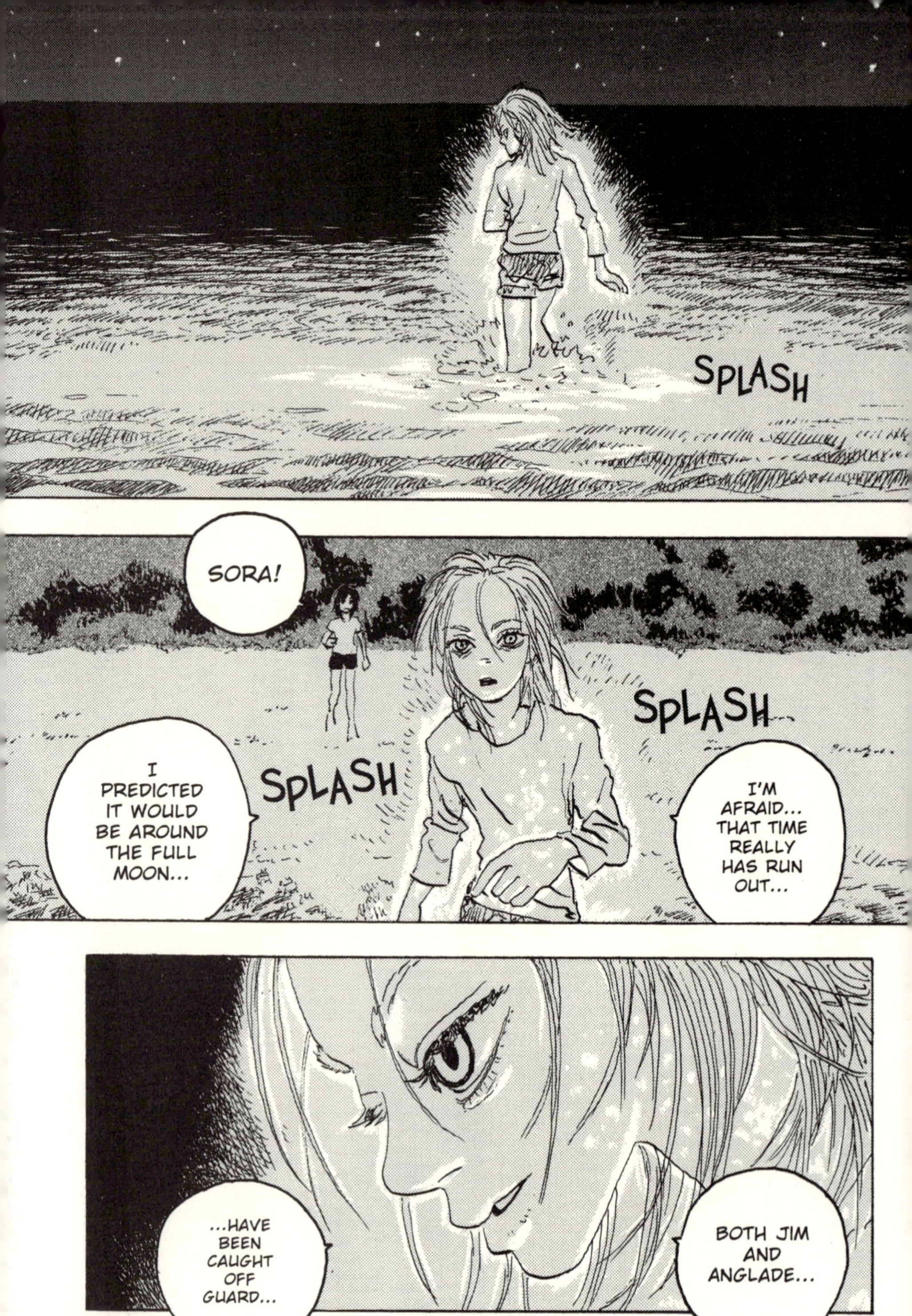
SPLASH
SORA!
SPLASH
I'M AFRAID... THAT TIME REALLY HAS RUN OUT...
SPLASH
I PREDICTED IT WOULD BE AROUND THE FULL MOON...
BOTH JIM AND ANGLADE...
...HAVE BEEN CAUGHT OFF GUARD...

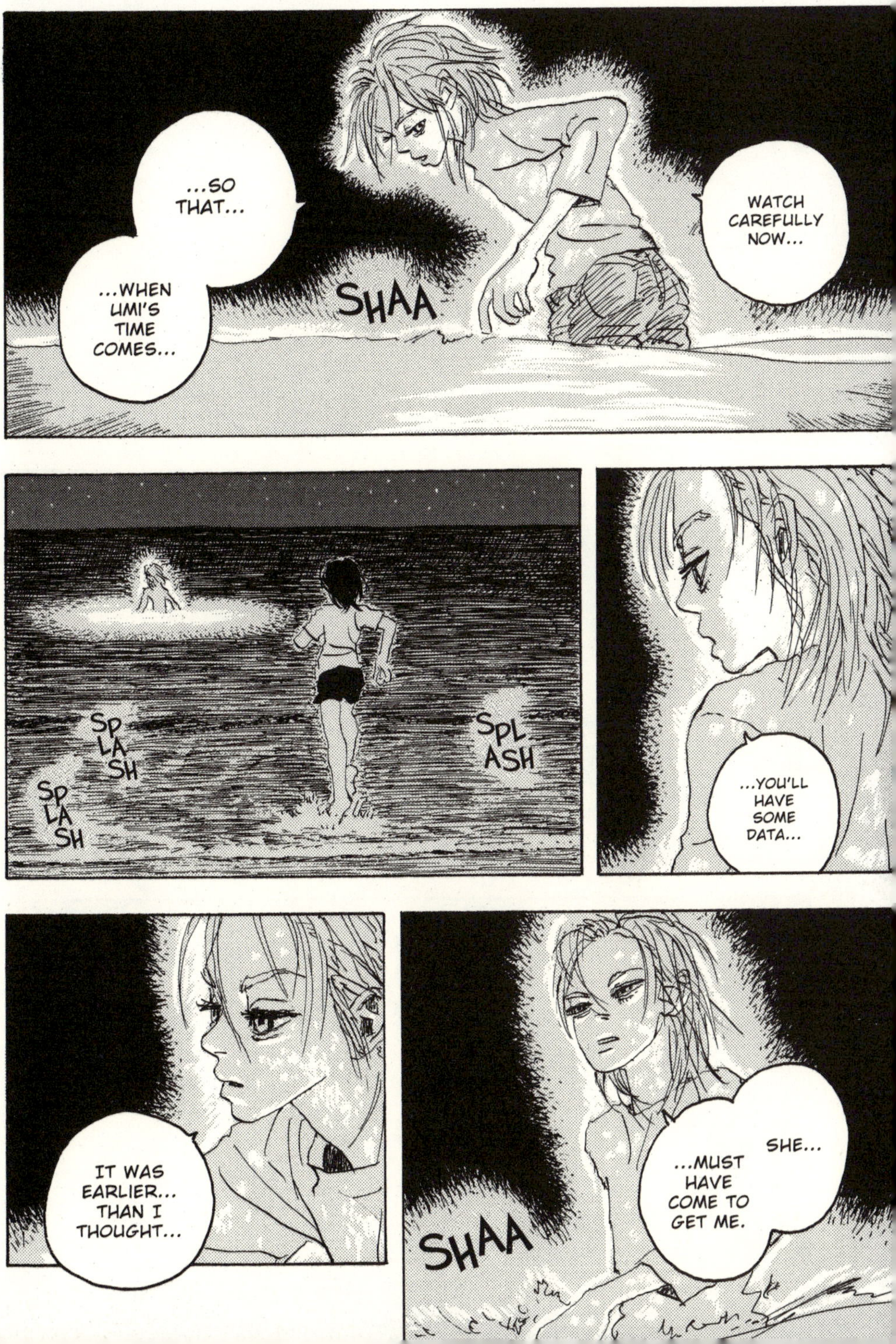
WATCH CAREFULLY NOW...
...SO THAT...
SHAA
...WHEN UMI'S TIME COMES...
...YOU'LL HAVE SOME DATA...
SPLASH
SPLASH
SPLASH
SHE...
...MUST HAVE COME TO GET ME.
SHAA
IT WAS EARLIER... THAN I THOUGHT...

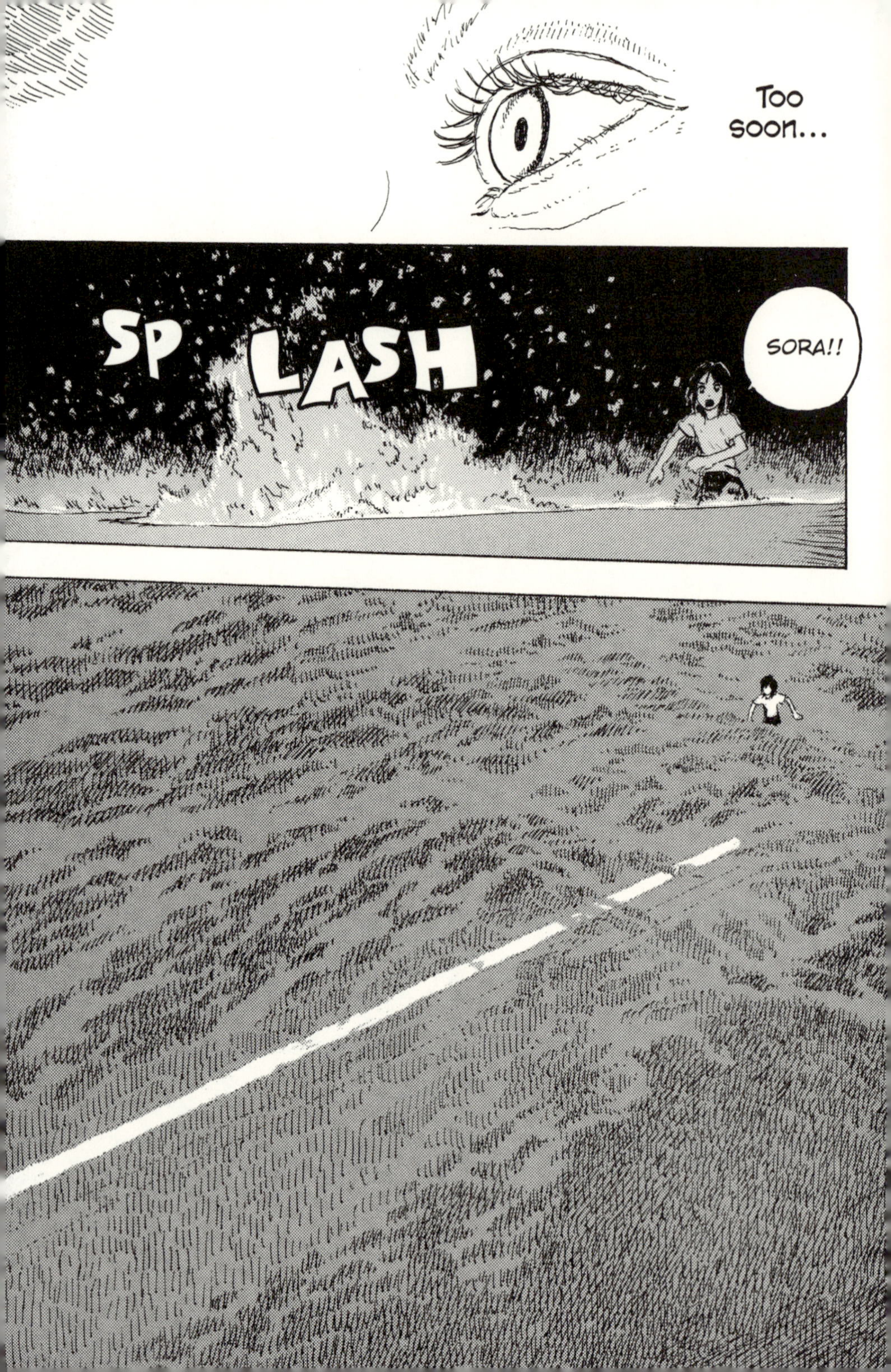
Too soon...
SORA!!
SPLASH

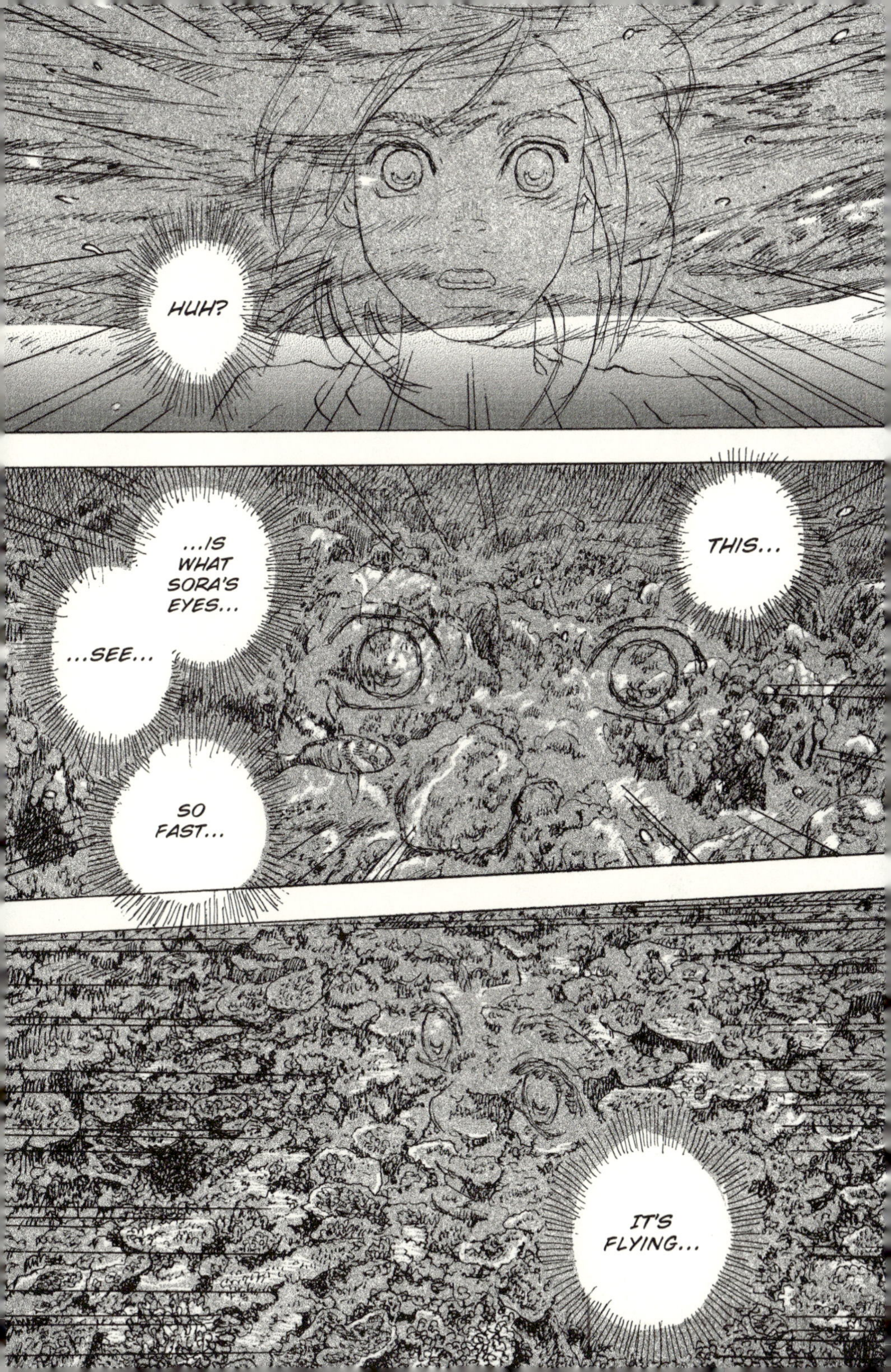
HUH?
THIS...
...IS WHAT SORA'S EYES...
...SEE...
SO FAST...
IT'S FLYING...

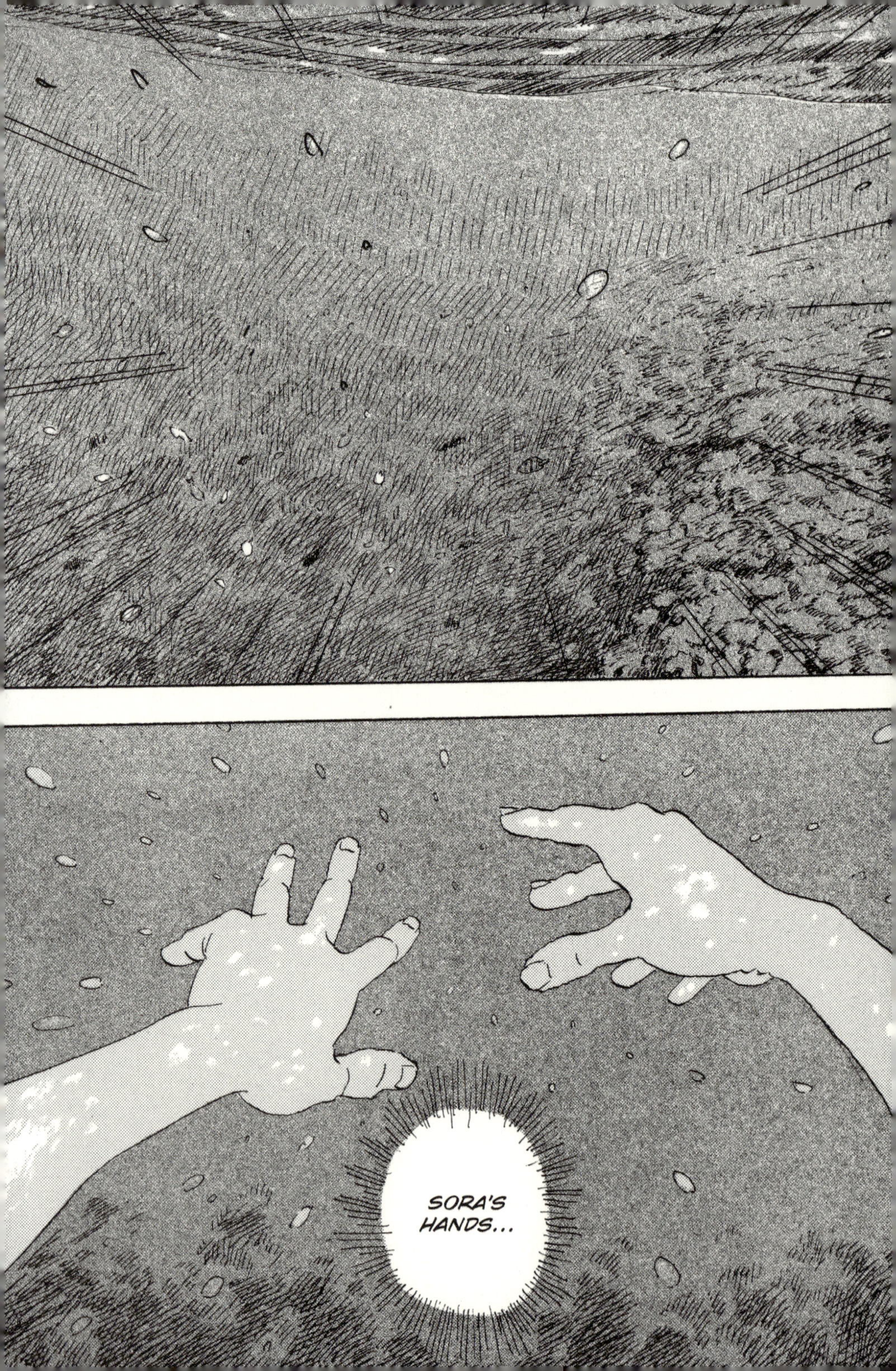
SORA'S HANDS...

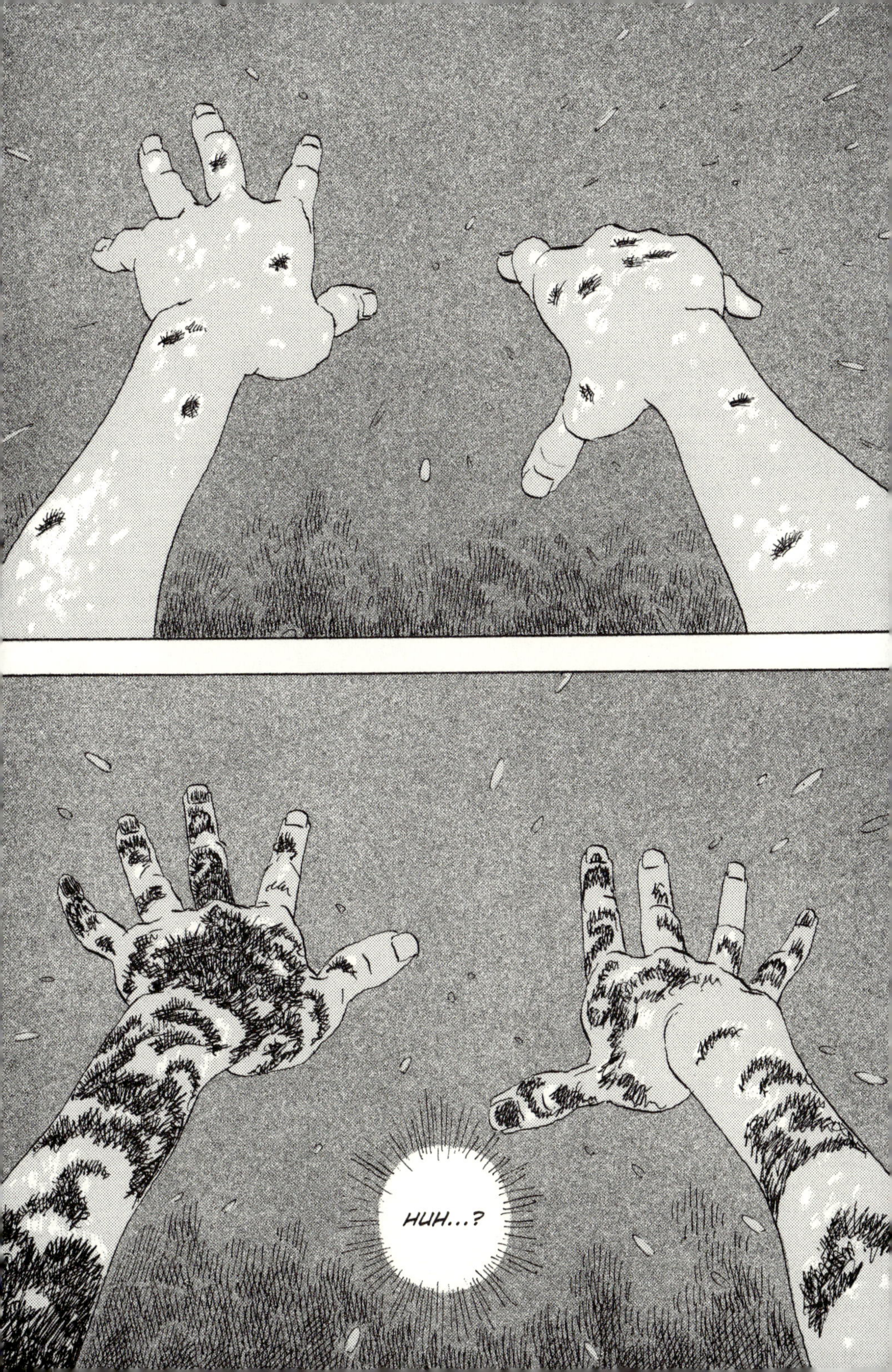
HUH...?

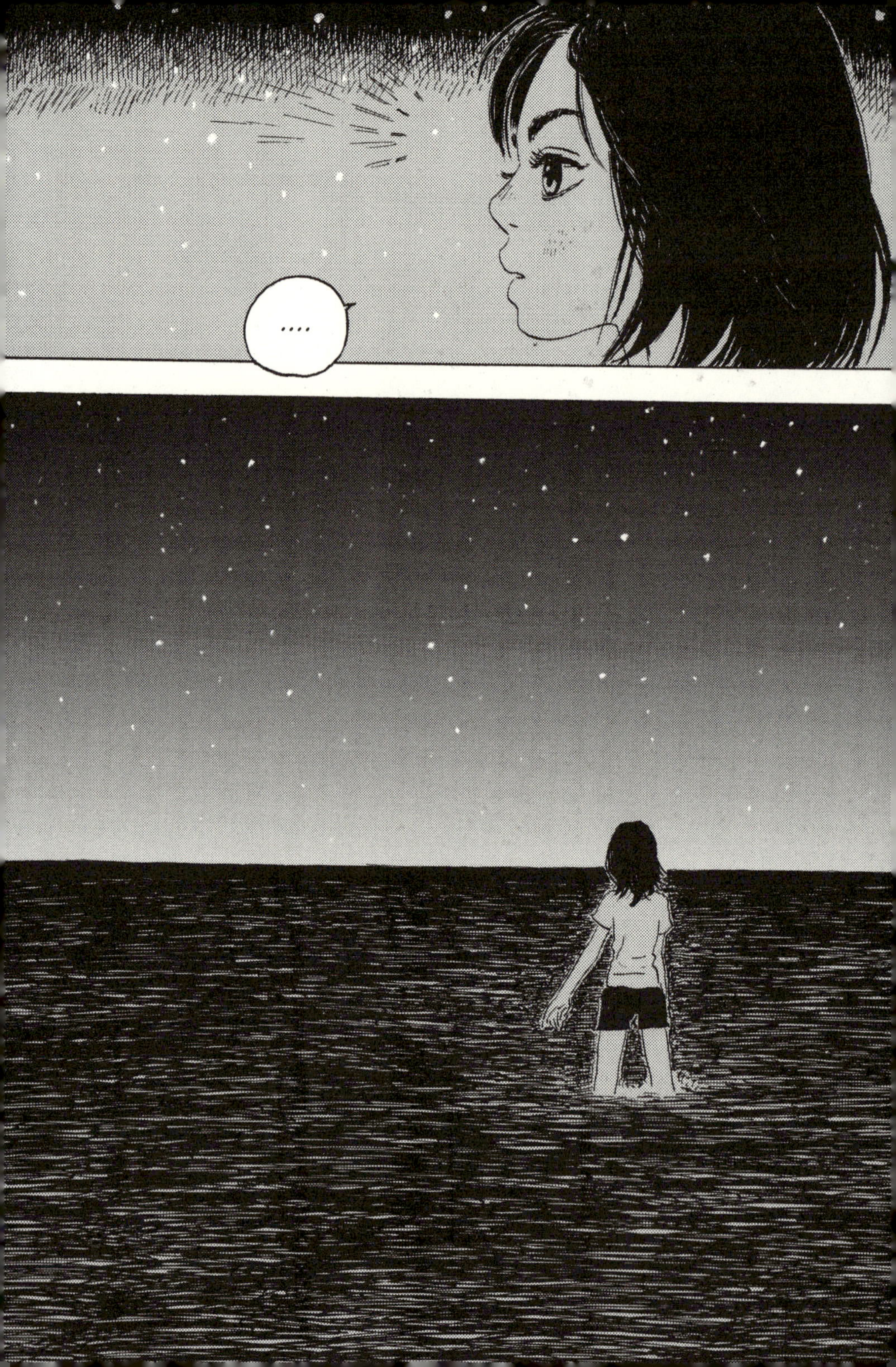
....

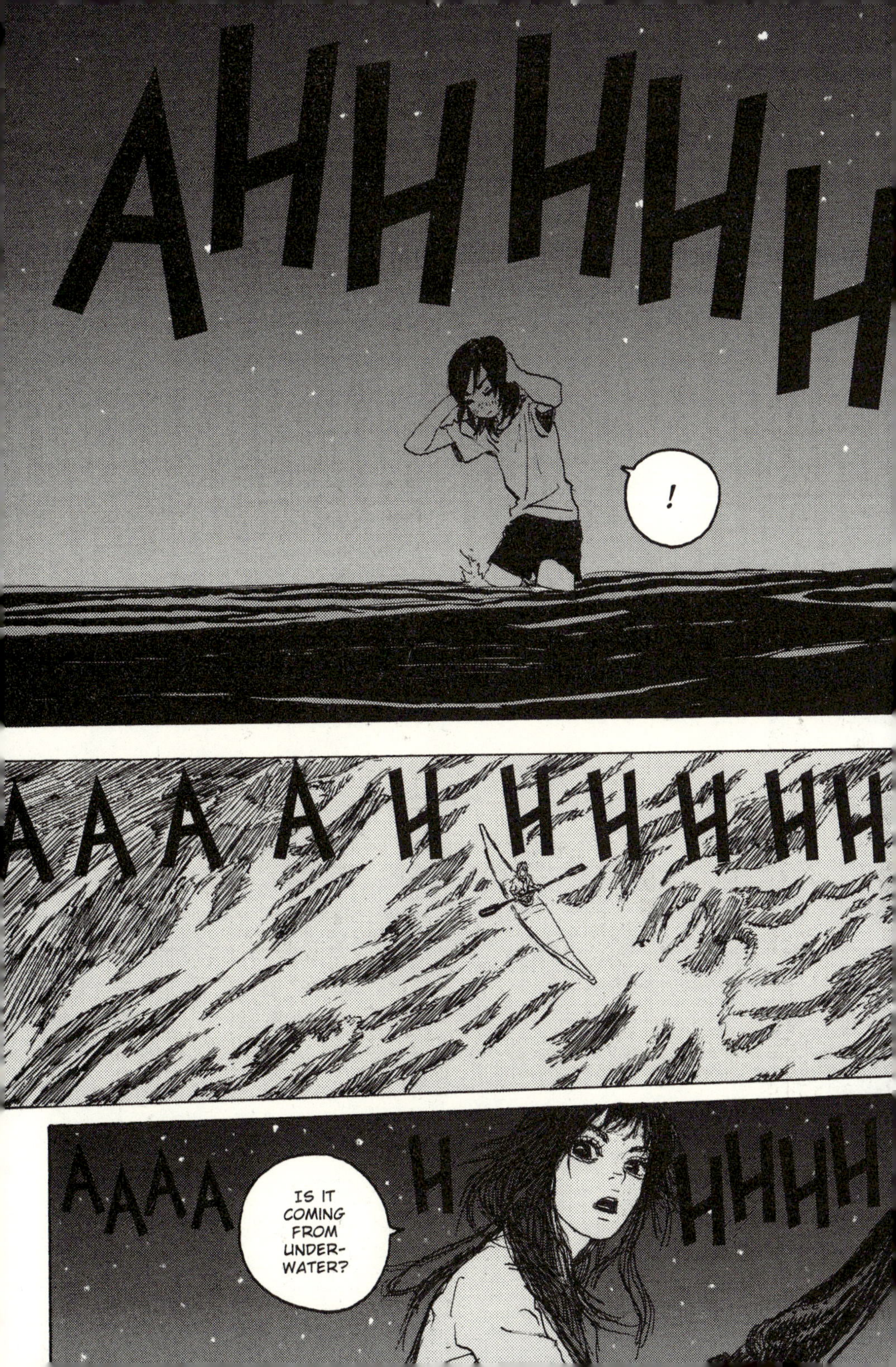
AHHHHHHHH
!
AAAAAHHHHHHH
AAAAHHHHH
IS IT COMING FROM UNDER-WATER?

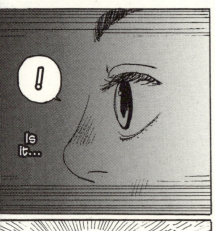

! Is it...

...Sora again...?

...WHAT IS THIS SOUND...?

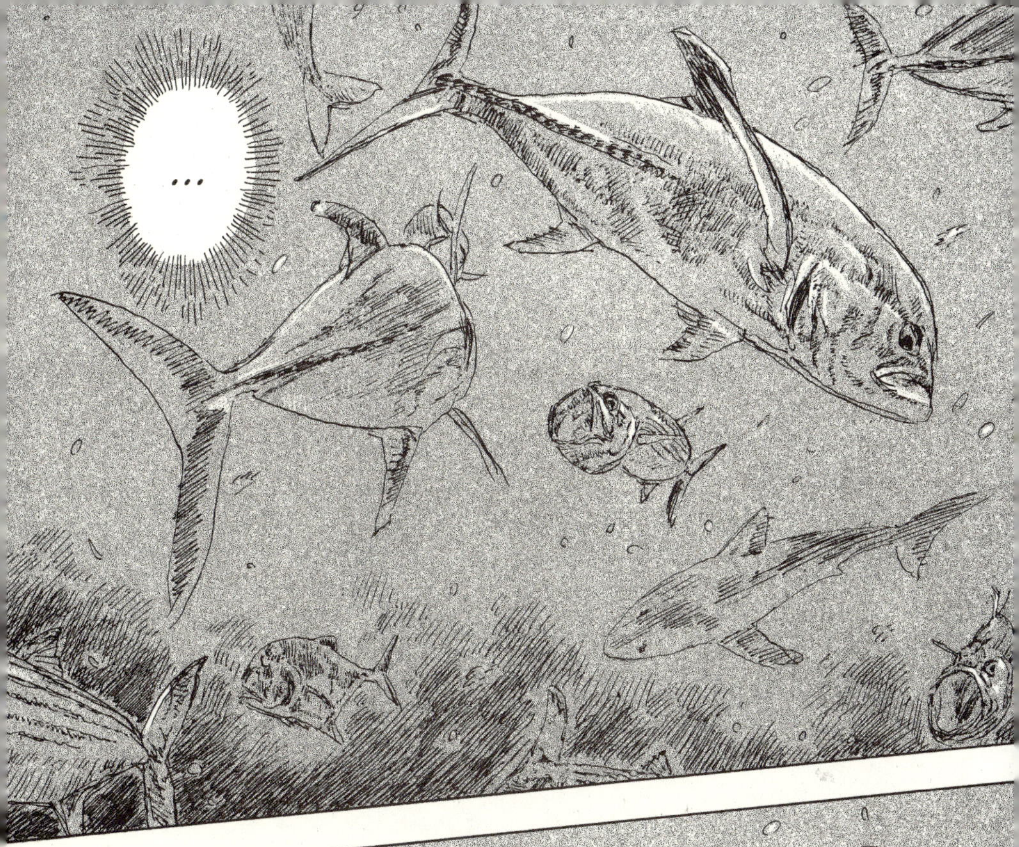
...
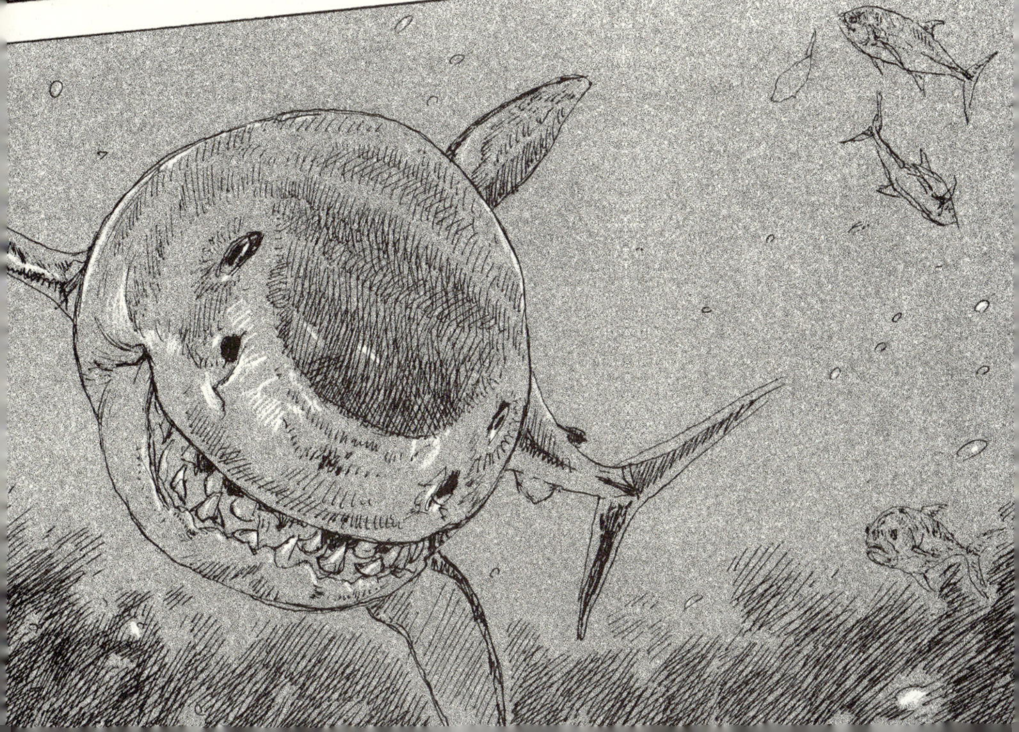

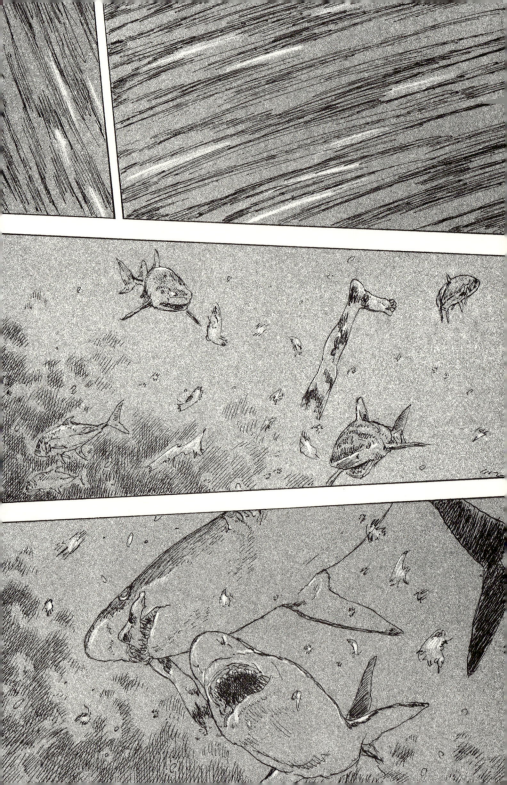

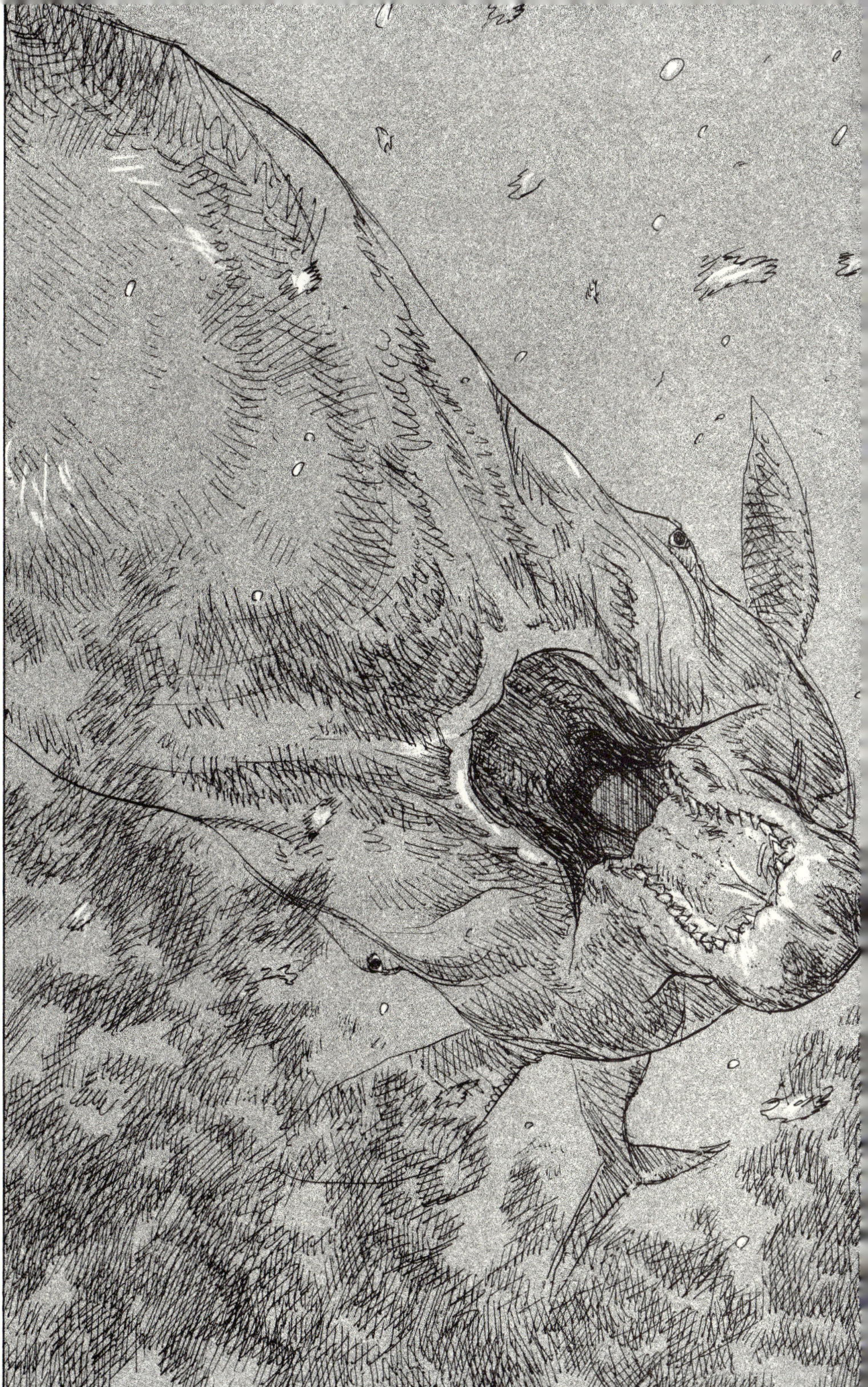

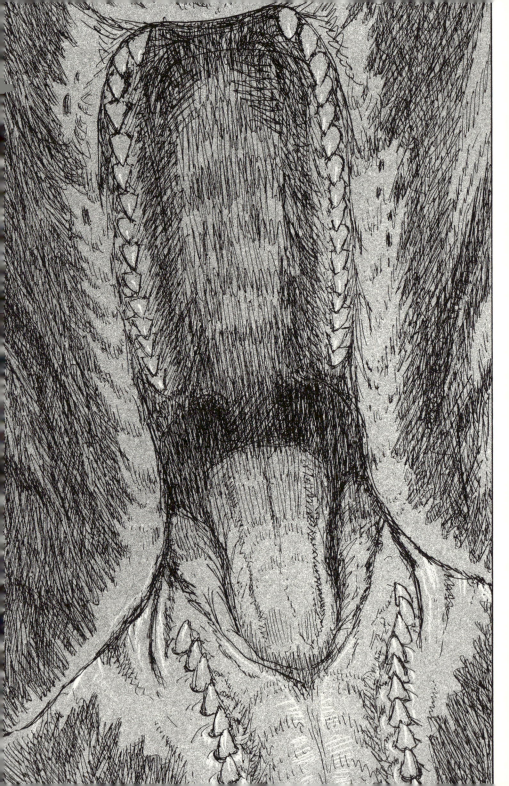

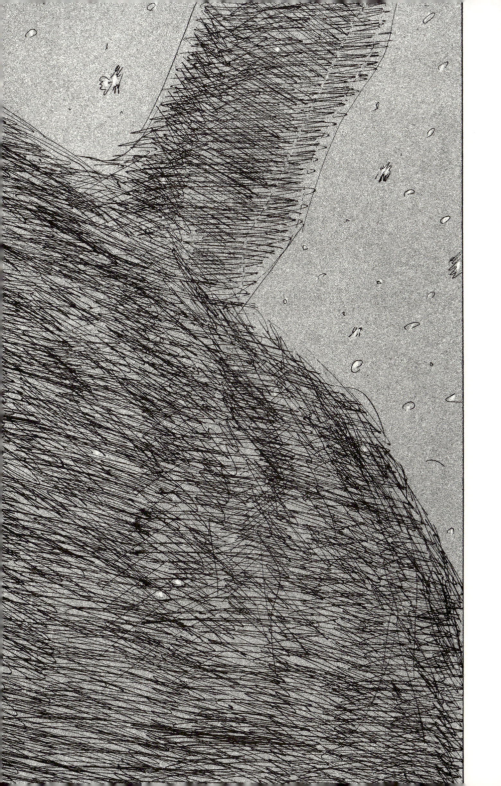

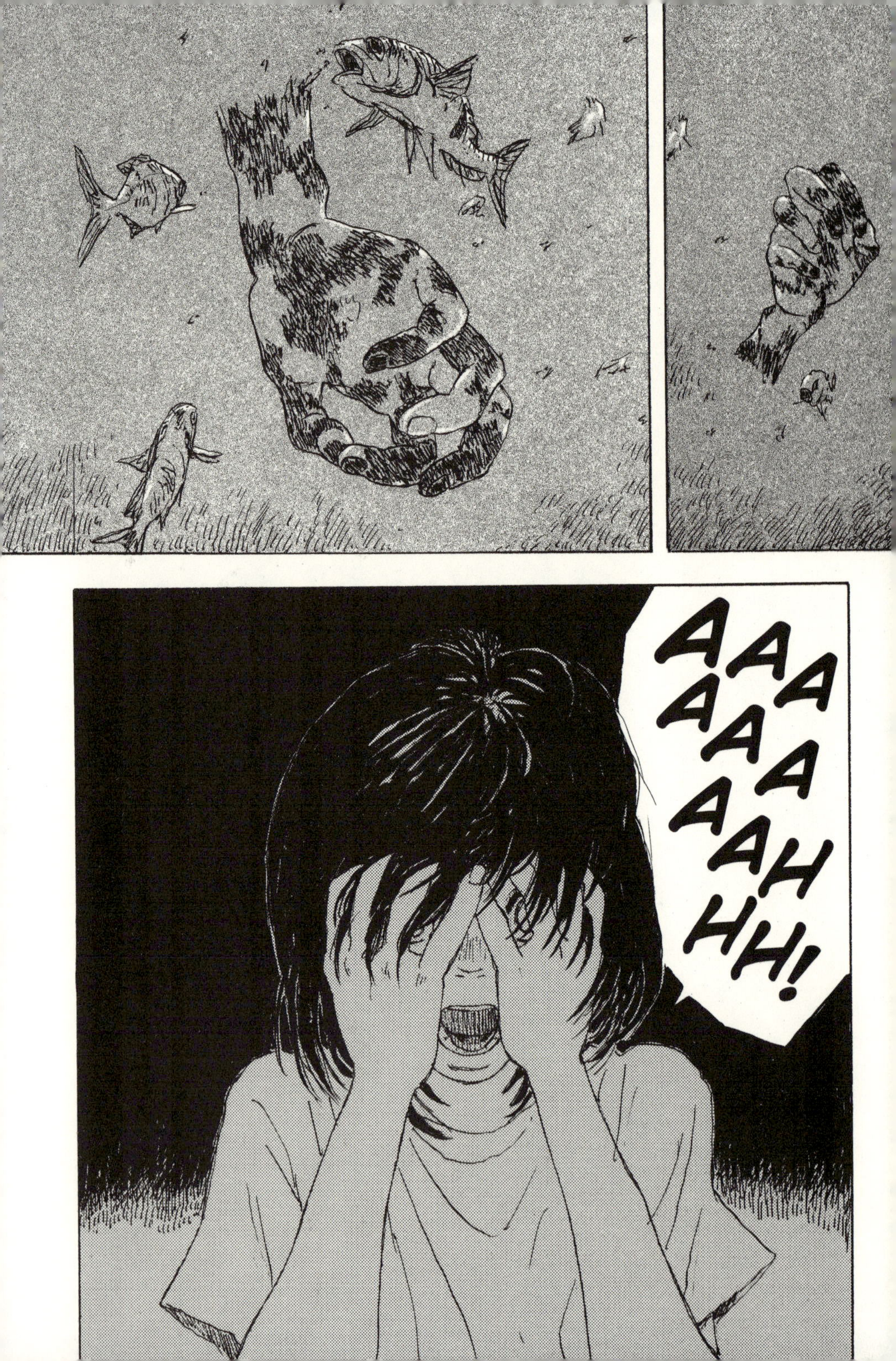
AAA
AAA
AAH
HH!

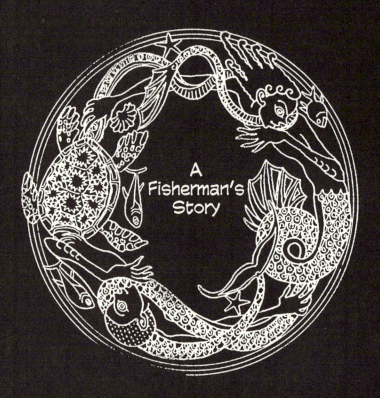

A
Fisherman's
Story

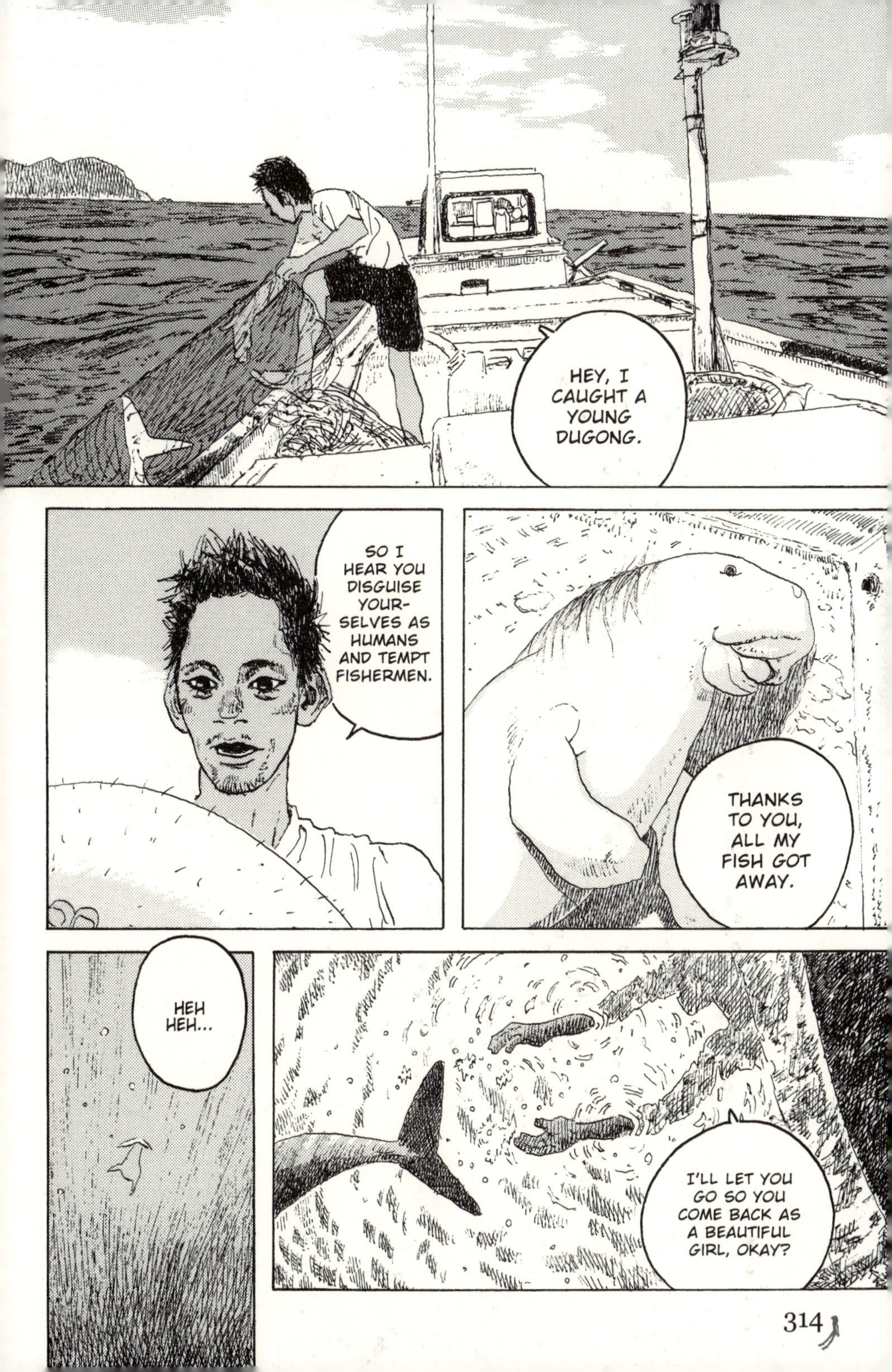
HEY, I CAUGHT A YOUNG DUGONG.
THANKS TO YOU, ALL MY FISH GOT AWAY.
SO I HEAR YOU DISGUISE YOUR-SELVES AS HUMANS AND TEMPT FISHERMEN.
I'LL LET YOU GO SO YOU COME BACK AS A BEAUTIFUL GIRL, OKAY?
HEH HEH...

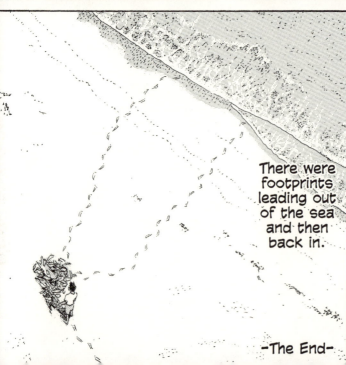

The next morning, on a deserted beach...

...there were piles of shrimp and fish.

There were footprints leading out of the sea and then back in.

FOOT-PRINTS ...

-The End-

Children of the Sea

VOLUME 2
END NOTES

Page 11: Isana
An ancient Japanese word for whale. 勇魚 literally means "brave fish."

Page 71, panel 4: Kuroshio Current
Also known as the Japan Current or the Black Current (the literal translation of the Japanese is "black tide"), it is the warm current that runs in the northwestern Pacific Ocean from Taiwan to Japan before joining the North Pacific Current.

Page 150, panel 5: Ogasawara
Also known as the Bonin Islands, it is an archipelago of over thirty islands about 620 miles south of Tokyo. Only two of the islands, Chichijima and Hahajima, are populated, although there is a manned air base on Iwojima.

Page 251, panel 3: Kajime
A type of brown seaweed that grows along the coasts of Japan and Korea. The scientific name is *Ecklonia cava*.

Children of the Sea 2

STORY AND ART BY Daisuke Igarashi
VIZ Signature Edition

TRANSLATION = JN Productions
TOUCH-UP ART & LETTERING = Jose Macasocol
DESIGN = Fawn Lau
EDITOR = Pancha Diaz

VP, PRODUCTION = Alvin Lu
VP, PUBLISHING LICENSING = Rika Inouye
VP, SALES & PRODUCT MARKETING = Gonzalo Ferreyra
VP, CREATIVE = Linda Espinosa
PUBLISHER = Hyoe Narita

Cooperation and assistance from Enoshima Aquarium

Printed in the U.S.A.

Published by VIZ Media, LLC
P.O. Box 77010
San Francisco, CA 94107

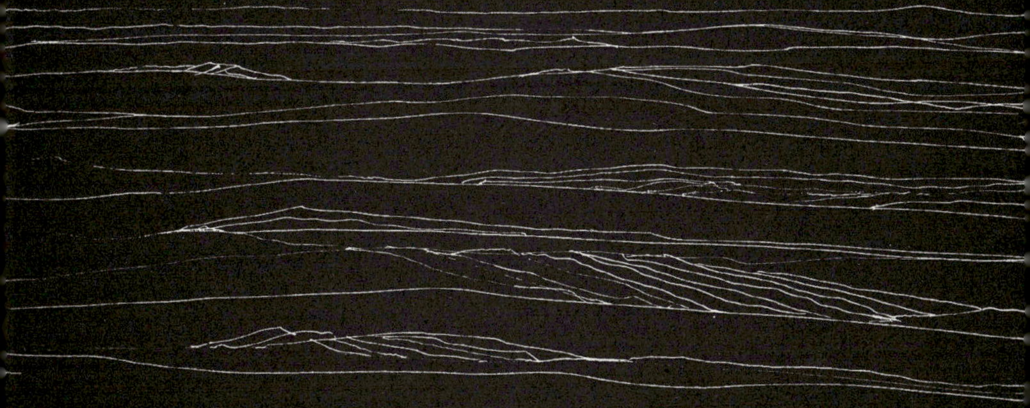

www.viz.com

PARENTAL ADVISORY
CHILDREN OF THE SEA is rated T+ for Older Teen and is recommended for ages 16 and up. Contains disturbing imagery.
ratings.viz.com

www.sigikki.com

10 9 8 7 6 5 4 3 2 1
First printing, December 2009

This is the **LAST PAGE** of this book.

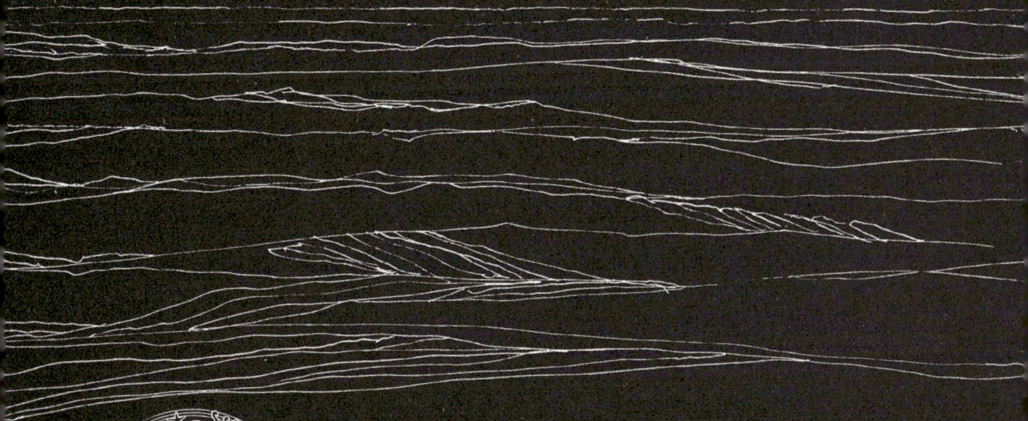

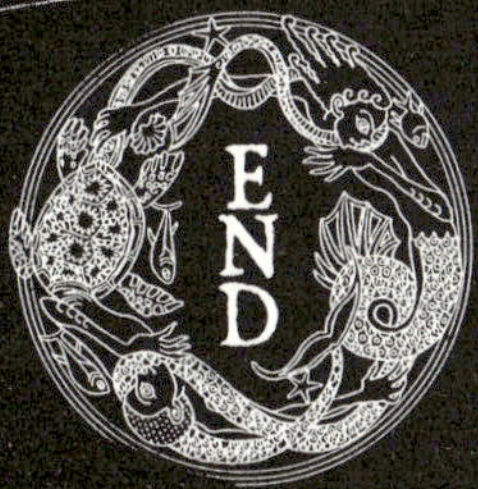
END

CHILDREN OF THE **SEA**
is printed from RIGHT TO LEFT in the original Japanese format in order to present **DAISUKE IGARASHI'S** stunning artwork the way it was meant to be seen.